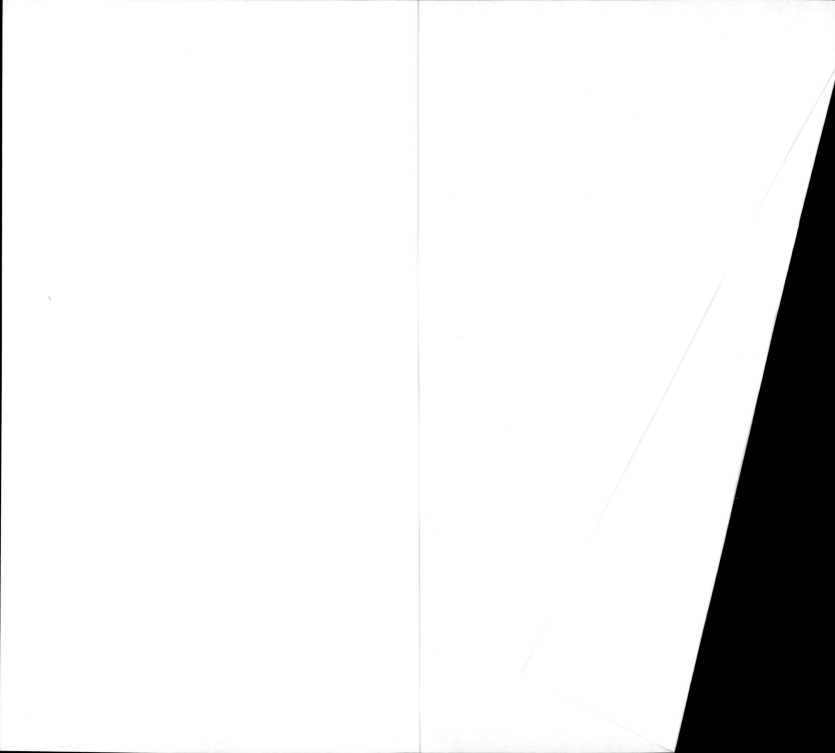

LAFCADIO HEARN

Lafcadio Hearn

AMERICAN WRITINGS
Some Chinese Ghosts
Chita
Two Years in the French West Indies
Youma
Selected Journalism & Letters

THE LIBRARY OF AMERICA

Distributed to the trade in the United States
by Penguin Putnam Inc.
and in Canada by Penguin Books Canada Ltd.

Library of Congress Control Number: 2008938732
ISBN 978-1-59853-039-1

———

First Printing
The Library of America—190

Manufactured in the United States of America

Contents

SOME CHINESE GHOSTS

If ye desire to witness prodigies and to behold marvels,
Be not concerned as to whether the mountains are distant
or the rivers far away.

KIN-KOU-KI-KOAN.

To my friend,

HENRY EDWARD KREHBIEL,

THE MUSICIAN,

WHO, SPEAKING THE SPEECH OF MELODY UNTO THE
CHILDREN OF TIEN-HIA,—

UNTO THE WANDERING TSING-JIN, WHOSE SKINS
HAVE THE COLOR OF GOLD,—

MOVED THEM TO MAKE STRANGE SOUNDS UPON THE
SERPENT-BELLIED SAN-HIEN;

PERSUADED THEM TO PLAY FOR ME UPON THE
SHRIEKING YA-HIEN;

PREVAILED ON THEM TO SING ME A SONG OF THEIR
NATIVE LAND,—

THE SONG OF MOHLÍ-HWA,

THE SONG OF THE JASMINE-FLOWER.

PREFACE

I THINK that my best apology for the insignificant size of this volume is the very character of the material composing it. In preparing the legends I sought especially for *weird beauty*; and I could not forget this striking observation in Sir Walter Scott's "Essay on Imitations of the Ancient Ballad:" "The supernatural, though appealing to certain powerful emotions very widely and deeply sown amongst the human race, is, nevertheless, *a spring which is peculiarly apt to lose its elasticity by being too much pressed upon.*"

Those desirous to familiarize themselves with Chinese literature as a whole have had the way made smooth for them by the labors of linguists like Julien, Pavie, Rémusat, De Rosny, Schlegel, Legge, Hervey-Saint-Denys, Williams, Biot, Giles, Wylie, Beal, and many other Sinologists. To such great explorers, indeed, the realm of Cathayan story belongs by right of discovery and conquest; yet the humbler traveller who follows wonderingly after them into the vast and mysterious pleasure-grounds of Chinese fancy may surely be permitted to cull a few of the marvellous flowers there growing,—a self-luminous *hwawang*, a black lily, a phosphoric rose or two,—as souvenirs of his curious voyage.

L. H.

New Orleans, March 15, 1886.

CONTENTS

She hath spoken, and her words still resound in his ears.

HAO-KHIEOU-TCHOUAN: c. ix.

The Soul of the Great Bell

THE water-clock marks the hour in the *Ta-chung sz'*,—in the Tower of the Great Bell: now the mallet is lifted to smite the lips of the metal monster,—the vast lips inscribed with Buddhist texts from the sacred *Fa-hwa-King*, from the chapters of the holy *Ling-yen-King*! Hear the great bell responding! —how mighty her voice, though tongueless!—*KO-NGAI*! All the little dragons on the high-tilted eaves of the green roofs shiver to the tips of their gilded tails under that deep wave of sound; all the porcelain gargoyles tremble on their carven perches; all the hundred little bells of the pagodas quiver with desire to speak. *KO-NGAI!*—all the green-and-gold tiles of the temple are vibrating; the wooden gold-fish above them are writhing against the sky; the uplifted finger of Fo shakes high over the heads of the worshippers through the blue fog of incense! *KO-NGAI!*—What a thunder tone was that! All the lacquered goblins on the palace cornices wriggle their fire-colored tongues! And after each huge shock, how wondrous the multiple echo and the great golden moan and, at last, the sudden sibilant sobbing in the ears when the immense tone faints away in broken whispers of silver,—as though a woman should whisper, "*Hiai!*" Even so the great bell hath sounded every day for wellnigh five hundred years,—*Ko-Ngai*: first with stupendous clang, then with immeasurable moan of gold, then with silver murmuring of "*Hiai!*" And there is not a child in all the many-colored ways of the old Chinese city who does not know the story of the great bell,—who cannot tell you why the great bell says *Ko-Ngai* and *Hiai!*

Now, this is the story of the great bell in the Ta-chung sz', as the same is related in the *Pe-Hiao-Tou-Choue*, written by the learned Yu-Pao-Tchen, of the City of Kwang-tchau-fu.

Nearly five hundred years ago the Celestially August, the Son of Heaven, Yong-Lo, of the "Illustrious," or Ming, dynasty, commanded the worthy official Kouan-Yu that he should have a bell made of such size that the sound thereof might be heard for one hundred *li*. And he further ordained

9

that the voice of the bell should be strengthened with brass, and deepened with gold, and sweetened with silver; and that the face and the great lips of it should be graven with blessed sayings from the sacred books, and that it should be suspended in the centre of the imperial capital, to sound through all the many colored ways of the City of Pe-king.

Therefore the worthy mandarin Kouan-Yu assembled the master-moulders and the renowned bellsmiths of the empire, and all men of great repute and cunning in foundry work; and they measured the materials for the alloy, and treated them skilfully, and prepared the moulds, the fires, the instruments, and the monstrous melting-pot for fusing the metal. And they labored exceedingly, like giants,—neglecting only rest and sleep and the comforts of life; toiling both night and day in obedience to Kouan-Yu, and striving in all things to do the behest of the Son of Heaven.

But when the metal had been cast, and the earthen mould separated from the glowing casting, it was discovered that, despite their great labor and ceaseless care, the result was void of worth; for the metals had rebelled one against the other,—the gold had scorned alliance with the brass, the silver would not mingle with the molten iron. Therefore the moulds had to be once more prepared, and the fires rekindled, and the metal remelted, and all the work tediously and toilsomely repeated. The Son of Heaven heard, and was angry, but spake nothing.

A second time the bell was cast, and the result was even worse. Still the metals obstinately refused to blend one with the other; and there was no uniformity in the bell, and the sides of it were cracked and fissured, and the lips of it were slagged and split asunder; so that all the labor had to be repeated even a third time, to the great dismay of Kouan-Yu. And when the Son of Heaven heard these things, he was angrier than before; and sent his messenger to Kouan-Yu with a letter, written upon lemon-colored silk, and sealed with the seal of the Dragon, containing these words:—

"*From the Mighty Yong-Lo, the Sublime Tait-Sung, the Celestial and August,—whose reign is called 'Ming,'—to Kouan-Yu the Fuh-yin: Twice thou hast betrayed the trust we have deigned graciously to place in thee; if thou fail a third time in fulfilling* our command, thy head shall be severed from thy neck. Tremble, and obey!"

Now, Kouan-Yu had a daughter of dazzling loveliness, whose name—Ko-Ngai—was ever in the mouths of poets, and whose heart was even more beautiful than her face. Ko-Ngai loved her father with such love that she had refused a hundred worthy suitors rather than make his home desolate by her absence; and when she had seen the awful yellow missive, sealed with the Dragon-Seal, she fainted away with fear for her father's sake. And when her senses and her strength returned to her, she could not rest or sleep for thinking of her parent's danger, until she had secretly sold some of her jewels, and with the money so obtained had hastened to an astrologer, and paid him a great price to advise her by what means her father might be saved from the peril impending over him. So the astrologer made observations of the heavens, and marked the aspect of the Silver Stream (which we call the Milky Way), and examined the signs of the Zodiac,—the *Hwang-tao*, or Yellow Road,—and consulted the table of the Five *Hin*, or Principles of the Universe, and the mystical books of the alchemists. And after a long silence, he made answer to her, saying: "Gold and brass will never meet in wedlock, silver and iron never will embrace, until the flesh of a maiden be melted in the crucible; until the blood of a virgin be mixed with the metals in their fusion." So Ko-Ngai returned home sorrowful at heart; but she kept secret all that she had heard, and told no one what she had done.

At last came the awful day when the third and last effort to cast the great bell was to be made; and Ko-Ngai, together with her waiting-woman, accompanied her father to the foundry, and they took their places upon a platform overlooking the toiling of the moulders and the lava of liquefied metal. All the workmen wrought their tasks in silence; there was no sound heard but the muttering of the fires. And the muttering deepened into a roar like the roar of typhoons approaching, and the blood-red lake of metal slowly brightened like the vermilion of a sunrise, and the vermilion was transmuted into a radiant glow of gold, and the gold whitened blindingly, like the silver face of a full moon. Then the workers ceased to feed the raving flame, and all fixed their eyes upon the eyes of Kouan-Yu; and Kouan-Yu prepared to give the signal to cast.

But ere ever he lifted his finger, a cry caused him to turn his head; and all heard the voice of Ko-Ngai sounding sharply sweet as a bird's song above the great thunder of the fires, —"*For thy sake, O my Father!*" And even as she cried, she leaped into the white flood of metal; and the lava of the furnace roared to receive her, and spattered monstrous flakes of flame to the roof, and burst over the verge of the earthen crater, and cast up a whirling fountain of many-colored fires, and subsided quakingly, with lightnings and with thunders and with mutterings.

Then the father of Ko-Ngai, wild with his grief, would have leaped in after her, but that strong men held him back and kept firm grasp upon him until he had fainted away and they could bear him like one dead to his home. And the serving-woman of Ko-Ngai, dizzy and speechless for pain, stood before the furnace, still holding in her hands a shoe, a tiny, dainty shoe, with embroidery of pearls and flowers,—the shoe of her beautiful mistress that was. For she had sought to grasp Ko-Ngai by the foot as she leaped, but had only been able to clutch the shoe, and the pretty shoe came off in her hand; and she continued to stare at it like one gone mad.

But in spite of all these things, the command of the Celestial and August had to be obeyed, and the work of the moulders to be finished, hopeless as the result might be. Yet the glow of the metal seemed purer and whiter than before; and there was no sign of the beautiful body that had been entombed therein. So the ponderous casting was made; and lo! when the metal had become cool, it was found that the bell was beautiful to look upon, and perfect in form, and wonderful in color above all other bells. Nor was there any trace found of the body of Ko-Ngai; for it had been totally absorbed by the precious alloy, and blended with the well-blended brass and gold, with the intermingling of the silver and the iron. And when they sounded the bell, its tones were found to be deeper and mellower and mightier than the tones of any other bell,—reaching even beyond the distance of one hundred *li*, like a pealing of summer thunder; and yet also like some vast voice uttering a name, a woman's name,—the name of Ko-Ngai!

And still, between each mighty stroke there is a long low moaning heard; and ever the moaning ends with a sound of sobbing and of complaining, as though a weeping woman should murmur, "*Hiai!*" And still, when the people hear that great golden moan they keep silence; but when the sharp, sweet shuddering comes in the air, and the sobbing of "*Hiai!*" then, indeed, do all the Chinese mothers in all the many-colored ways of Pe-king whisper to their little ones: "*Listen! that is Ko-Ngai crying for her shoe! That is Ko-Ngai calling for her shoe!*"

THE ANCIENT WORDS OF KOUEI,—MASTER OF MUSICIANS
IN THE COURTS OF THE EMPEROR YAO:—

*When ye make to resound the stone melodious, the
Ming-Khieou,—*

*When ye touch the lyre that is called Kin, or the guitar
that is called Ssé,—*

Accompanying their sound with song,—
Then do the grandfather and the father return;
Then do the ghosts of the ancestors come to hear.

The Story of Ming-Y

*Sang the Poet Tching-Kou: "Surely the Peach-
Flowers blossom over the tomb of Sië-Thao."*

Do you ask me who she was,—the beautiful Sië-Thao? For a thousand years and more the trees have been whispering above her bed of stone. And the syllables of her name come to the listener with the lisping of the leaves; with the quivering of many-fingered boughs; with the fluttering of lights and shadows; with the breath, sweet as a woman's presence of numberless savage flowers,—*Sië-Thao*. But, saving the whispering of her name, what the trees say cannot be understood; and they alone remember the years of Sië-Thao. Something about her you might, nevertheless, learn from any of those *Kiang-kou-jin*,—those famous Chinese story-tellers, who nightly narrate to listening crowds, in consideration of a few *tsien*, the legends of the past. Something concerning her you may also find in the book entitled "Kin-Kou-Ki-Koan," which signifies in our tongue: "The Marvellous Happenings of Ancient and of Recent Times." And perhaps of all things therein written, the most marvellous is this memory of Sië-Thao:—

Five hundred years ago, in the reign of the Emperor Houng-Wou, whose dynasty was *Ming*, there lived in the City of Genii, the city of Kwang-tchau-fu, a man celebrated for his learning and for his piety, named Tien-Pelou. This Tien-Pelou had one son, a beautiful boy, who for scholarship and for bodily grace and for polite accomplishments had no superior among the youths of his age. And his name was Ming-Y.

Now when the lad was in his eighteenth summer, it came to pass that Pelou, his father, was appointed Inspector of Public Instruction at the city of Tching-tou; and Ming-Y accompanied his parents thither. Near the city of Tching-tou lived a rich man of rank, a high commissioner of the government, whose name was Tchang, and who wanted to find a worthy teacher for his children. On hearing of the arrival of the new Inspector of Public Instruction, the noble Tchang visited him to obtain advice in this matter; and happening to meet and

15

converse with Pelou's accomplished son, immediately engaged Ming-Y as a private tutor for his family.

Now as the house of this Lord Tchang was situated several miles from town, it was deemed best that Ming-Y should abide in the house of his employer. Accordingly the youth made ready all things necessary for his new sojourn; and his parents, bidding him farewell, counselled him wisely, and cited to him the words of Lao-tseu and of the ancient sages: "*By a beautiful face the world is filled with love; but Heaven may never be deceived thereby. Shouldst thou behold a woman coming from the East, look thou to the West; shouldst thou perceive a maiden approaching from the West, turn thine eyes to the East.*" If Ming-Y did not heed this counsel in after days, it was only because of his youth and the thoughtlessness of a naturally joyous heart.

And he departed to abide in the house of Lord Tchang, while the autumn passed, and the winter also.

When the time of the second moon of spring was drawing near, and that happy day which the Chinese call *Hoa-tchao*, or, "The Birthday of a Hundred Flowers," a longing came upon Ming-Y to see his parents; and he opened his heart to the good Tchang, who not only gave him the permission he desired, but also pressed into his hand a silver gift of two ounces, thinking that the lad might wish to bring some little memento to his father and mother. For it is the Chinese custom, on the feast of Hoa-tchao, to make presents to friends and relations.

That day all the air was drowsy with blossom perfume, and vibrant with the droning of bees. It seemed to Ming-Y that the path he followed had not been trodden by any other for many long years: the grass was tall upon it; vast trees on either side interlocked their mighty and moss-grown arms above him, beshadowing the way; but the leafy obscurities quivered with bird-song, and the deep vistas of the wood were glorified by vapors of gold, and odorous with flower-breathings as a temple with incense. The dreamy joy of the day entered into the heart of Ming-Y; and he sat him down among the young blossoms, under the branches swaying against the violet sky, to drink in the perfume and the light, and to enjoy the great sweet silence. Even while thus reposing, a sound caused him to turn his eyes toward a shady place where wild peach-trees were in bloom; and he beheld a young woman, beautiful as the pinkening blossoms themselves, trying to hide among them. Though he looked for a moment only, Ming-Y could not avoid discerning the loveliness of her face, the golden purity of her complexion, and the brightness of her long eyes, that sparkled under a pair of brows as daintily curved as the wings of the silkworm butterfly outspread. Ming-Y at once turned his gaze away, and, rising quickly, proceeded on his journey. But so much embarrassed did he feel at the idea of those charming eyes peeping at him through the leaves, that he suffered the money he had been carrying in his sleeve to fall, without being aware of it. A few moments later he heard the patter of light feet running behind him, and a woman's voice calling him by name. Turning his face in great surprise, he saw a comely servant-maid, who said to him, "Sir, my mistress bade me pick up and return you this silver which you dropped upon the road." Ming-Y thanked the girl gracefully, and requested her to convey his compliments to her mistress. Then he proceeded on his way through the perfumed silence, athwart the shadows that dreamed along the forgotten path, dreaming himself also, and feeling his heart beating with strange quickness at the thought of the beautiful being that he had seen.

It was just such another day when Ming-Y, returning by the same path, paused once more at the spot where the gracious figure had momentarily appeared before him. But this time he was surprised to perceive, through a long vista of immense trees, a dwelling that had previously escaped his notice,—a country residence, not large, yet elegant to an unusual degree. The bright blue tiles of its curved and serrated double roof, rising above the foliage, seemed to blend their color with the luminous azure of the day; the green-and-gold designs of its carven porticos were exquisite artistic mockeries of leaves and flowers bathed in sunshine. And at the summit of terrace-steps before it, guarded by great porcelain tortoises, Ming-Y saw standing the mistress of the mansion,—the idol of his passionate fancy,—accompanied by the same waiting-maid who had borne to her his message of gratitude. While Ming-Y looked, he perceived that their eyes were upon him; they smiled and conversed together as if speaking about him; and, shy though he was, the youth found courage to salute the fair one from a distance. To his astonishment, the young servant beckoned him to approach; and opening a rustic gate half veiled by trailing plants bearing crimson flowers, Ming-Y advanced along the verdant alley leading to the terrace, with mingled feelings of surprise and timid joy. As he drew near, the beautiful lady withdrew from sight; but the maid waited at the broad steps to receive him, and said as he ascended:

"Sir, my mistress understands you wish to thank her for the trifling service she recently bade me do you, and requests that you will enter the house, as she knows you already by repute, and desires to have the pleasure of bidding you good-day."

Ming-Y entered bashfully, his feet making no sound upon a matting elastically soft as forest moss, and found himself in a reception-chamber vast, cool, and fragrant with scent of blossoms freshly gathered. A delicious quiet pervaded the mansion; shadows of flying birds passed over the bands of light that fell through the half-blinds of bamboo; great butterflies, with pinions of fiery color, found their way in, to hover a moment about the painted vases, and pass out again into the mysterious woods. And noiselessly as they, the young mistress of the mansion entered by another door, and kindly greeted the boy, who lifted his hands to his breast and bowed low in salutation. She was taller than he had deemed her, and supplely-slender as a beauteous lily; her black hair was interwoven with the creamy blossoms of the *chu-sha-kih*; her robes of pale silk took shifting tints when she moved, as vapors change hue with the changing of the light.

"If I be not mistaken," she said, when both had seated themselves after having exchanged the customary formalities of politeness, "my honored visitor is none other than Tien-chou, surnamed Ming-Y, educator of the children of my respected relative, the High Commissioner Tchang. As the family of Lord Tchang is my family also, I cannot but consider the teacher of his children as one of my own kin."

"Lady," replied Ming-Y, not a little astonished, "may I dare to inquire the name of your honored family, and to ask the relation which you hold to my noble patron?"

"The name of my poor family," responded the comely lady,

"is *Ping*,—an ancient family of the city of Tching-tou. I am the daughter of a certain Sië of Moun-hao; Sië is my name, likewise; and I was married to a young man of the Ping family, whose name was Khang. By this marriage I became related to your excellent patron; but my husband died soon after our wedding, and I have chosen this solitary place to reside in during the period of my widowhood."

There was a drowsy music in her voice, as of the melody of brooks, the murmurings of spring; and such a strange grace in the manner of her speech as Ming-Y had never heard before. Yet, on learning that she was a widow, the youth would not have presumed to remain long in her presence without a formal invitation; and after having sipped the cup of rich tea presented to him, he arose to depart. Sië would not suffer him to go so quickly.

"Nay, friend," she said; "stay yet a little while in my house, I pray you; for, should your honored patron ever learn that you had been here, and that I had not treated you as a respected guest, and regaled you even as I would him, I know that he would be greatly angered. Remain at least to supper."

So Ming-Y remained, rejoicing secretly in his heart, for Sië seemed to him the fairest and sweetest being he had ever known, and he felt that he loved her even more than his father and his mother. And while they talked the long shadows of the evening slowly blended into one violet darkness; the great citron-light of the sunset faded out; and those starry beings that are called the Three Councillors, who preside over life and death and the destinies of men, opened their cold bright eyes in the northern sky. Within the mansion of Sië the painted lanterns were lighted; the table was laid for the evening repast; and Ming-Y took his place at it, feeling little inclination to eat, and thinking only of the charming face before him. Observing that he scarcely tasted the dainties laid upon his plate, Sië pressed her young guest to partake of wine; and they drank several cups together. It was a purple wine, so cool that the cup into which it was poured became covered with vapory dew; yet it seemed to warm the veins with strange fire. To Ming-Y, as he drank, all things became more luminous as by enchantment; the walls of the chamber appeared to recede, and the roof to heighten; the lamps glowed like stars in their chains, and the voice of Sië floated to the boy's ears like some far melody heard through the spaces of a drowsy night. His heart swelled; his tongue loosened; and words flitted from his lips that he had fancied he could never dare to utter. Yet Sië sought not to restrain him; her lips gave no smile; but her long bright eyes seemed to laugh with pleasure at his words of praise, and to return his gaze of passionate admiration with affectionate interest.

"I have heard," she said, "of your rare talent, and of your many elegant accomplishments. I know how to sing a little, although I cannot claim to possess any musical learning; and now that I have the honor of finding myself in the society of a musical professor, I will venture to lay modesty aside, and beg you to sing a few songs with me. I should deem it no small gratification if you would condescend to examine my musical compositions."

"The honor and the gratification, dear lady," replied Ming-Y, "will be mine; and I feel helpless to express the gratitude which the offer of so rare a favor deserves."

The serving-maid, obedient to the summons of a little silver gong, brought in the music and retired. Ming-Y took the manuscripts, and began to examine them with eager delight. The paper upon which they were written had a pale yellow tint, and was light as a fabric of gossamer; but the characters were antiquely beautiful, as though they had been traced by the brush of Heï-song Ché-Tchoo himself,—that divine Genius of Ink, who is no bigger than a fly; and the signatures attached to the compositions were the signatures of Youen-tchin, Kao-pien, and Thou-mou,—mighty poets and musicians of the dynasty of Thang! Ming-Y could not repress a scream of delight at the sight of treasures so inestimable and so unique; scarcely could he summon resolution enough to permit them to leave his hands even for a moment.

"O Lady!" he cried, "these are veritably priceless things, surpassing in worth the treasures of all kings. This indeed is the handwriting of those great masters who sang five hundred years before our birth. How marvellously it has been preserved! Is not this the wondrous ink of which it was written: *Po-nien-jou-chi, i-tien-jou-ki,*—'After centuries I remain firm as stone, and the letters that I make like lacquer'? And how divine the charm of this composition!—the song of Kao-pien, prince of poets, and Governor of Sze-tchouen five hundred years ago!"

"Kao-pien! darling Kao-pien!" murmured Sië, with a singular light in her eyes. "Kao-pien is also my favorite. Dear Ming-Y, let us chant his verses together, to the melody of old,—the music of those grand years when men were nobler and wiser than today."

And their voices rose through the perfumed night like the voices of the wonder-birds,—of the Fung-hoang,—blending together in liquid sweetness. Yet a moment, and Ming-Y, overcome by the witchery of his companion's voice, could only listen in speechless ecstasy, while the lights of the chamber swam dim before his sight, and tears of pleasure trickled down his cheeks.

So the ninth hour passed; and they continued to converse, and to drink the cool purple wine, and to sing the songs of the years of Thang, until far into the night. More than once Ming-Y thought of departing; but each time Sië would begin, in that silver-sweet voice of hers, so wondrous a story of the great poets of the past, and of the women whom they loved, that he became as one entranced; or she would sing for him a song so strange that all his senses seemed to die except that of hearing. And at last, as she paused to pledge him in a cup of wine, Ming-Y could not restrain himself from putting his arm about her round neck and drawing her dainty head closer to him, and kissing the lips that were so much ruddier and sweeter than the wine. Then their lips separated no more;—the night grew old, and they knew it not.

The birds awakened, the flowers opened their eyes to the rising sun, and Ming-Y found himself at last compelled to bid his lovely enchantress farewell. Sië, accompanying him to the terrace, kissed him fondly and said, "Dear boy, come hither as often as you are able,—as often as your heart whispers you to come. I know that you are not of those without faith and truth, who betray secrets; yet, being so young, you might also be sometimes thoughtless; and I pray you never to forget that only the stars have been the witnesses of our love. Speak of it to no living person, dearest; and take with you this little souvenir of our happy night."

And she presented him with an exquisite and curious little thing,—a paper-weight in likeness of a couchant lion, wrought from a jade-stone yellow as that created by a rainbow in honor of Kong-fu-tze. Tenderly the boy kissed the gift and the beautiful hand that gave it. "May the Spirits punish me," he vowed, "if ever I knowingly give you cause to reproach me, sweetheart!" And they separated with mutual vows.

That morning, on returning to the house of Lord Tchang, Ming-Y told the first falsehood which had ever passed his lips. He averred that his mother had requested him thenceforward to pass his nights at home, now that the weather had become so pleasant; for, though the way was somewhat long, he was strong and active, and needed both air and healthy exercise. Tchang believed all Ming-Y said, and offered no objection. Accordingly the lad found himself enabled to pass all his evenings at the house of the beautiful Sië. Each night they devoted to the same pleasures which had made their first acquaintance so charming: they sang and conversed by turns; they played at chess,—the learned game invented by Wu-Wang, which is an imitation of war; they composed pieces of eighty rhymes upon the flowers, the trees, the clouds, the streams, the birds, the bees. But in all accomplishments Sië far excelled her young sweetheart. Whenever they played at chess, it was always Ming-Y's general, Ming-Y's *tsiang*, who was surrounded and vanquished; when they composed verses, Sië's poems were ever superior to his in harmony of word-coloring, in elegance of form, in classic loftiness of thought. And the themes they selected were always the most difficult,—those of the poets of the Thang dynasty; the songs they sang were also the songs of five hundred years before,—the songs of Youen-tchin, of Thou-mou, of Kao-pien above all, high poet and ruler of the province of Sze-tchouen.

So the summer waxed and waned upon their love, and the luminous autumn came, with its vapors of phantom gold, its shadows of magical purple.

Then it unexpectedly happened that the father of Ming-Y, meeting his son's employer at Tching-tou, was asked by him: "Why must your boy continue to travel every evening to the city, now that the winter is approaching? The way is long, and when he returns in the morning he looks fordone with weariness. Why not permit him to slumber in my house during the season of snow?" And the father of Ming-Y, greatly astonished, responded: "Sir, my son has not visited the city, nor has he been to our house all this summer. I fear that he must have acquired wicked habits, and that he passes his nights in evil company,—perhaps in gaming, or in drinking with the women of the flower-boats." But the High Commissioner returned: "Nay! that is not to be thought of. I have never found any evil in the boy, and there are no taverns nor flower-boats nor any places of dissipation in our neighborhood. No doubt Ming-Y has found some amiable youth of his own age with whom to spend his evenings, and only told me an untruth for fear that I would not otherwise permit him to leave my residence. I beg that you will say nothing to him until I shall have sought to discover this mystery; and this very evening I shall send my servant to follow after him, and to watch whither he goes."

Pelou readily assented to this proposal, and promising to visit Tchang the following morning, returned to his home. In the evening, when Ming-Y left the house of Tchang, a servant followed him unobserved at a distance. But on reaching the most obscure portion of the road, the boy disappeared from sight as suddenly as though the earth had swallowed him. After having long sought after him in vain, the domestic returned in great bewilderment to the house, and related what had taken place. Tchang immediately sent a messenger to Pelou.

In the mean time Ming-Y, entering the chamber of his beloved, was surprised and deeply pained to find her in tears. "Sweetheart," she sobbed, wreathing her arms around his neck, "we are about to be separated forever, because of reasons which I cannot tell you. From the very first I knew this must come to pass; and nevertheless it seemed to me for the moment so cruelly sudden a loss, so unexpected a misfortune, that I could not prevent myself from weeping! After this night we shall never see each other again, beloved, and I know that you will not be able to forget me while you live; but I know also that you will become a great scholar, and that honors and riches will be showered upon you, and that some beautiful and loving woman will console you for my loss. And now let us speak no more of grief; but let us pass this last evening joyously, so that your recollection of me may not be a painful one, and that you may remember my laughter rather than my tears."

She brushed the bright drops away, and brought wine and music and the melodious *kin* of seven silken strings, and would not suffer Ming-Y to speak for one moment of the coming separation. And she sang him an ancient song about the calmness of summer lakes reflecting the blue of heaven only, and the calmness of the heart also, before the clouds of care and of grief and of weariness darken its little world. Soon they forgot their sorrow in the joy of song and wine; and those last hours seemed to Ming-Y more celestial than even the hours of their first bliss.

But when the yellow beauty of morning came their sadness returned, and they wept. Once more Sië accompanied her lover to the terrace-steps; and as she kissed him farewell, she pressed into his hand a parting gift,—a little brush-case of agate, wonderfully chiselled, and worthy the table of a great poet. And they separated forever, shedding many tears.

Still Ming-Y could not believe it was an eternal parting. "No!" he thought, "I shall visit her to-morrow; for I cannot now live without her, and I feel assured that she cannot refuse to receive me." Such were the thoughts that filled his mind as he reached the house of Tchang, to find his father and his patron standing on the porch awaiting him. Ere he could speak a word, Pelou demanded: "Son, in what place have you been passing your nights?"

Seeing that his falsehood had been discovered, Ming-Y dared not make any reply, and remained abashed and silent, with bowed head, in the presence of his father. Then Pelou, striking the boy violently with his staff, commanded him to divulge the secret; and at last, partly through fear of his parent, and partly through fear of the law which ordains that "*the son refusing to obey his father shall be punished with one hundred blows of the bamboo*," Ming-Y faltered out the history of his love.

Tchang changed color at the boy's tale. "Child," exclaimed the High Commissioner, "I have no relative of the name of Ping; I have never heard of the woman you describe; I have never heard even of the house which you speak of. But I know also that you cannot dare to lie to Pelou, your honored father; there is some strange delusion in all this affair."

Then Ming-Y produced the gifts that Sië had given him,—the lion of yellow jade, the brush-case of carven agate, also some original compositions made by the beautiful lady herself. The astonishment of Tchang was now shared by Pelou. Both observed that the brush-case of agate and the lion of jade bore the appearance of objects that had lain buried in the earth for centuries, and were of a workmanship beyond the power of living man to imitate; while the compositions proved to be veritable master-pieces of poetry, written in the style of the poets of the dynasty of Thang.

"Friend Pelou," cried the High Commissioner, "let us immediately accompany the boy to the place where he obtained these miraculous things, and apply the testimony of our senses to this mystery. The boy is no doubt telling the truth; yet his story passes my understanding." And all three proceeded toward the place of the habitation of Sië.

But when they had arrived at the shadiest part of the road, where the perfumes were most sweet and the mosses were greenest, and the fruits of the wild peach flushed most pinkly, Ming-Y, gazing through the groves, uttered a cry of dismay. Where the azure-tiled roof had risen against the sky, there was now only the blue emptiness of air; where the green-and-gold façade had been, there was visible only the flickering of leaves under the aureate autumn light; and where the broad terrace had extended, could be discerned only a ruin,—a tomb so ancient, so deeply gnawed by moss, that the name graven upon it was no longer decipherable. The home of Sië had disappeared!

All suddenly the High Commissioner smote his forehead with his hand, and turning to Pelou, recited the well-known verse of the ancient poet Tching-Kou:—

"*Surely the peach-flowers blossom over the tomb of SIË-THAO.*"

"Friend Pelou," continued Tchang, "the beauty who bewitched your son was no other than she whose tomb stands there in ruin before us! Did she not say she was wedded to Ping-Khang? There is no family of that name, but Ping-Khang is indeed the name of a broad alley in the city near. There was

a dark riddle in all that she said. She called herself Sië of
Moun-Hiao: there is no person of that name; there is no street
of that name; but the Chinese characters *Moun* and *hiao*,
placed together, form the character 'Kiao.' Listen! The alley
Ping-Khang, situated in the street Kiao, was the place where
dwelt the great courtesans of the dynasty of Thang! Did she
not sing the songs of Kao-pien? And upon the brush-case and
the paperweight she gave your son, are there not characters
which read, '*Pure object of art belonging to Kao, of the city of
Pho-hai*'? That city no longer exists; but the memory of Kao-
pien remains, for he was governor of the province of Sze-
tchouen, and a mighty poet. And when he dwelt in the land of
Chou, was not his favorite the beautiful wanton Sië,—Sië-
Thao, unmatched for grace among all the women of her day?
It was he who made her a gift of those manuscripts of song; it
was he who gave her those objects of rare art. Sië-Thao died
not as other women die. Her limbs may have crumbled to
dust; yet something of her still lives in this deep wood,—her
Shadow still haunts this shadowy place."

Tchang ceased to speak. A vague fear fell upon the three.
The thin mists of the morning made dim the distances of
green, and deepened the ghostly beauty of the woods. A faint
breeze passed by, leaving a trail of blossom-scent,—a last odor
of dying flowers,—thin as that which clings to the silk of a forgotten robe; and, as it passed, the trees seemed to whisper
across the silence, "*Sië-Thao.*"

Fearing greatly for his son, Pelou sent the lad away at once
to the city of Kwang-tchau-fu. And there, in after years, Ming-
Y obtained high dignities and honors by reason of his talents
and his learning; and he married the daughter of an illustrious
house, by whom he became the father of sons and daughters
famous for their virtues and their accomplishments. Never
could he forget Sië-Thao; and yet it is said that he never spoke
of her,—not even when his children begged him to tell them
the story of two beautiful objects that always lay upon his
writing-table: a lion of yellow jade, and a brush-case of carven
agate.

黑松使者

A SOUND OF GONGS, A SOUND OF SONG,—THE SONG OF THE
BUILDERS BUILDING THE DWELLINGS OF THE DEAD:—

Khiû tchî yîng-yîng.
Toû tchî hoûng-hoûng.
Tchŏ tchî tông-tông.
Siŏ liú pîng-pîng.

The Legend of Tchi-Niu

IN the quaint commentary accompanying the text of that holy book of Lao-tseu called *Kan-ing-p'ien* may be found a little story so old that the name of the one who first told it has been forgotten for a thousand years, yet so beautiful that it lives still in the memory of four hundred millions of people, like a prayer that, once learned, is forever remembered. The Chinese writer makes no mention of any city nor of any province, although even in the relation of the most ancient traditions such an omission is rare: we are only told that the name of the hero of the legend was Tong-yong, and that he lived in the years of the great dynasty of Han, some twenty centuries ago.

Tong-yong's mother had died while he was yet an infant; and when he became a youth of nineteen years his father also passed away, leaving him utterly alone in the world, and without resources of any sort; for, being a very poor man, Tong's father had put himself to great straits to educate the lad, and had not been able to lay by even one copper coin of his earnings. And Tong lamented greatly to find himself so destitute that he could not honor the memory of that good father by having the customary rites of burial performed, and a carven tomb erected upon a propitious site. The poor only are friends of the poor; and among all those whom Tong knew, there was no one able to assist him in defraying the expenses of the funeral. In one way only could the youth obtain money,—by selling himself as a slave to some rich cultivator; and this he at last decided to do. In vain his friends did their utmost to dissuade him; and to no purpose did they attempt to delay the accomplishment of his sacrifice by beguiling promises of future aid. Tong only replied that he would sell his freedom a hundred times, if it were possible, rather than suffer his father's memory to remain unhonored even for a brief season. And furthermore, confiding in his youth and strength, he determined to put a high price upon his servitude,—a price which would enable him to build a handsome tomb, but which it would be well-nigh impossible for him ever to repay.

Accordingly he repaired to the broad public place where slaves and debtors were exposed for sale, and seated himself upon a bench of stone, having affixed to his shoulders a placard inscribed with the terms of his servitude and the list of his qualifications as a laborer. Many who read the characters upon the placard smiled disdainfully at the price asked, and passed on without a word; others lingered only to question him out of simple curiosity; some commended him with hollow praise; some openly mocked his unselfishness, and laughed at his childish piety. Thus many hours wearily passed, and Tong had almost despaired of finding a master, when there rode up a high official of the province,—a grave and handsome man, lord of a thousand slaves, and owner of vast estates. Reining in his Tartar horse, the official halted to read the placard and to consider the value of the slave. He did not smile, or advise, or ask any questions; but having observed the price asked, and the fine strong limbs of the youth, purchased him without further ado, merely ordering his attendant to pay the sum and to see that the necessary papers were made out.

Thus Tong found himself enabled to fulfil the wish of his heart, and to have a monument built which, although of small size, was destined to delight the eyes of all who beheld it, being designed by cunning artists and executed by skilful sculptors. And while it was yet designed only, the pious rites were performed, the silver coin was placed in the mouth of the dead, the white lanterns were hung at the door, the holy prayers were recited, and paper shapes of all things the departed might need in the land of the Genii were consumed in consecrated fire. And after the geomancers and the necromancers had chosen a burial-spot which no unlucky star could shine upon, a place of rest which no demon or dragon might ever disturb, the beautiful *chih* was built. Then was the phantom money strewn along the way; the funeral procession departed from the dwelling of the dead, and with prayers and lamentation the mortal remains of Tong's good father were borne to the tomb.

Then Tong entered as a slave into the service of his purchaser, who allotted him a little hut to dwell in; and thither
Tong carried with him those wooden tablets, bearing the
ancestral names, before which filial piety must daily burn the
incense of prayer, and perform the tender duties of family
worship.

Thrice had spring perfumed the breast of the land with
flowers, and thrice had been celebrated that festival of the dead
which is called *Siu-fan-ti*, and thrice had Tong swept and gar-
nished his father's tomb and presented his fivefold offering of
fruits and meats. The period of mourning had passed, yet he
had not ceased to mourn for his parent. The years revolved
with their moons, bringing him no hour of joy, no day of
happy rest; yet he never lamented his servitude, or failed to
perform the rites of ancestral worship,—until at last the fever
of the rice-fields laid strong hold upon him, and he could not
arise from his couch; and his fellow-laborers thought him destined to die. There was no one to wait upon him, no one to
care for his needs, inasmuch as slaves and servants were wholly
busied with the duties of the household or the labor of the
fields,—all departing to toil at sunrise and returning weary
only after the sundown.

Now, while the sick youth slumbered the fitful slumber of
exhaustion one sultry noon, he dreamed that a strange and
beautiful woman stood by him, and bent above him and
touched his forehead with the long, fine fingers of her shapely
hand. And at her cool touch a weird sweet shock passed
through him, and all his veins tingled as if thrilled by new life.
Opening his eyes in wonder, he saw verily bending over him
the charming being of whom he had dreamed, and he knew
that her lithe hand really caressed his throbbing forehead.
But the flame of the fever was gone, a delicious coolness now
penetrated every fibre of his body, and the thrill of which he
had dreamed still tingled in his blood like a great joy. Even at
the same moment the eyes of the gentle visitor met his own,
and he saw they were singularly beautiful, and shone like
splendid black jewels under brows curved like the wings of the
swallow. Yet their calm gaze seemed to pass through him as light
through crystal; and a vague awe came upon him, so that the

question which had risen to his lips found no utterance. Then she, still caressing him, smiled and said: "I have come to restore thy strength and to be thy wife. Arise and worship with me."

Her clear voice had tones melodious as a bird's song; but in her gaze there was an imperious power which Tong felt he dare not resist. Rising from his couch, he was astounded to find his strength wholly restored; but the cool, slender hand which held his own led him away so swiftly that he had little time for amazement. He would have given years of existence for courage to speak of his misery, to declare his utter inability to maintain a wife; but something irresistible in the long dark eyes of his companion forbade him to speak; and as though his inmost thought had been discerned by that wondrous gaze, she said to him, in the same clear voice, "*I will provide.*" Then shame made him blush at the thought of his wretched aspect and tattered apparel; but he observed that she also was poorly attired, like a woman of the people,—wearing no ornament of any sort, nor even shoes upon her feet. And before he had yet spoken to her, they came before the ancestral tablets; and there she knelt with him and prayed, and pledged him in a cup of wine,—brought he knew not from whence,—and together they worshipped Heaven and Earth. Thus she became his wife.

A mysterious marriage it seemed; for neither on that day nor at any future time could Tong venture to ask his wife the name of her family, or of the place whence she came, and he could not answer any of the curious questions which his fellow-laborers put to him concerning her; and she, moreover, never uttered a word about herself, except to say that her name was Tchi. But although Tong had such awe of her that while her eyes were upon him he was as one having no will of his own, he loved her unspeakably; and the thought of his serfdom ceased to weigh upon him from the hour of his marriage. As through magic the little dwelling had become transformed: its misery was masked with charming paper devices,—with dainty decorations created out of nothing by that pretty jugglery of which woman only knows the secret.

Each morning at dawn the young husband found a well-prepared and ample repast awaiting him, and each evening also upon his return; but the wife all day sat at her loom, weaving silk after a fashion unlike anything which had ever been seen before in that province. For as she wove, the silk flowed from the loom like a slow current of glossy gold, bearing upon its undulations strange forms of violet and crimson and jewel-green: shapes of ghostly horsemen riding upon horses, and of phantom chariots dragon-drawn, and of standards of trailing cloud. In every dragon's beard glimmered the mystic pearl; in every rider's helmet sparkled the gem of rank. And each day Tchi would weave a great piece of such figured silk; and the fame of her weaving spread abroad. From far and near people thronged to see the marvellous work; and the silk-merchants of great cities heard of it, and they sent messengers to Tchi, asking her that she should weave for them and teach them her secret. Then she wove for them, as they desired, in return for the silver cubes which they brought her; but when they prayed her to teach them, she laughed and said, "Assuredly I could never teach you, for no one among you has fingers like mine." And indeed no man could discern her fingers when she wove, any more than he might behold the wings of a bee vibrating in swift flight.

The seasons passed, and Tong never knew want, so well did his beautiful wife fulfil her promise,—"*I will provide*;" and the cubes of bright silver brought by the silk-merchants were piled up higher and higher in the great carven chest which Tchi had bought for the storage of the household goods.

One morning, at last, when Tong, having finished his repast, was about to depart to the fields, Tchi unexpectedly bade him remain; and opening the great chest, she took out of it and gave him a document written in the official characters called *li-shu*. And Tong, looking at it, cried out and leaped in his joy, for it was the certificate of his manumission. Tchi had secretly purchased her husband's freedom with the price of her wondrous silks!

"Thou shalt labor no more for any master," she said, "but for thy own sake only. And I have also bought this dwelling, with all which is therein, and the tea-fields to the south, and the mulberry groves hard by,—all of which are thine."

Then Tong, beside himself for gratefulness, would have prostrated himself in worship before her, but that she would not suffer it.

Thus he was made free; and prosperity came to him with his freedom; and whatsoever he gave to the sacred earth was returned to him centupled; and his servants loved him and blessed the beautiful Tchi, so silent and yet so kindly to all about her. But the silk-loom soon remained untouched, for Tchi gave birth to a son,—a boy so beautiful that Tong wept with delight when he looked upon him. And thereafter the wife devoted herself wholly to the care of the child.

Now it soon became manifest that the boy was not less wonderful than his wonderful mother. In the third month of his age he could speak; in the seventh month he could repeat by heart the proverbs of the sages, and recite the holy prayers; before the eleventh month he could use the writing-brush with skill, and copy in shapely characters the precepts of Lao-tseu. And the priests of the temples came to behold him and to converse with him, and they marvelled at the charm of the child and the wisdom of what he said; and they blessed Tong, saying: "Surely this son of thine is a gift from the Master of Heaven, a sign that the immortals love thee. May thine eyes behold a hundred happy summers!"

It was in the Period of the Eleventh Moon: the flowers had passed away, the perfume of the summer had flown, the winds were growing chill, and in Tong's home the evening fires were lighted. Long the husband and wife sat in the mellow glow,— he speaking much of his hopes and joys, and of his son that was to be so grand a man, and of many paternal projects; while she, speaking little, listened to his words, and often turned her wonderful eyes upon him with an answering smile. Never had she seemed so beautiful before; and Tong, watching her face, marked not how the night waned, nor how the fire sank low, nor how the wind sang in the leafless trees without.

All suddenly Tchi arose without speaking, and took his hand in hers and led him, gently as on that strange wedding-morning, to the cradle where their boy slumbered, faintly smiling in his dreams. And in that moment there came upon

Tong the same strange fear that he knew when Tchi's eyes had first met his own,—the vague fear that love and trust had calmed, but never wholly cast out, like unto the fear of the gods. And all unknowingly, like one yielding to the pressure of mighty invisible hands, he bowed himself low before her, kneeling as to a divinity. Now, when he lifted his eyes again to her face, he closed them forthwith in awe; for she towered before him taller than any mortal woman, and there was a glow about her as of sunbeams, and the light of her limbs shone through her garments. But her sweet voice came to him with all the tenderness of other hours, saying: *"Lo! my beloved, the moment has come in which I must forsake thee; for I was never of mortal born, and the Invisible may incarnate themselves for a time only. Yet I leave with thee the pledge of our love,—this fair son, who shall ever be to thee as faithful and as fond as thou thyself hast been. Know, my beloved, that I was sent to thee even by the Master of Heaven, in reward of thy filial piety, and that I must now return to the glory of His house:* I AM THE GODDESS TCHI-NIU."

Even as she ceased to speak, the great glow faded; and Tong, re-opening his eyes, knew that she had passed away forever,—mysteriously as pass the winds of heaven, irrevocably as the light of a flame blown out. Yet all the doors were barred, all the windows unopened. Still the child slept, smiling in his sleep. Outside, the darkness was breaking; the sky was brightening swiftly; the night was past. With splendid majesty the East threw open high gates of gold for the coming of the sun; and, illuminated by the glory of his coming, the vapors of morning wrought themselves into marvellous shapes of shifting color,—into forms weirdly beautiful as the silken dreams woven in the loom of Tchi-Niu.

籥應感上太

Before me ran, as a herald runneth, the Leader of the Moon;
And the Spirit of the Wind followed after me,—quickening his flight.

LI-SAO.

The Return of Yen-Tchin-King

IN the thirty-eighth chapter of the holy book, *Kan-ing-p'ien*, wherein the Recompense of Immortality is considered, may be found the legend of Yen-Tchin-King. A thousand years have passed since the passing of the good Tchin-King; for it was in the period of the greatness of Thang that he lived and died.

Now, in those days when Yen-Tchin-King was Supreme Judge of one of the Six August Tribunals, one Li-hi-lié, a soldier mighty for evil, lifted the black banner of revolt, and drew after him, as a tide of destruction, the millions of the northern provinces. And learning of these things, and knowing also that Hi-lié was the most ferocious of men, who respected nothing on earth save fearlessness, the Son of Heaven commanded Tchin-King that he should visit Hi-lié and strive to recall the rebel to duty, and read unto the people who followed after him in revolt the Emperor's letter of reproof and warning. For Tchin-King was famed throughout the provinces for his wisdom, his rectitude, and his fearlessness; and the Son of Heaven believed that if Hi-lié would listen to the words of any living man steadfast in loyalty and virtue, he would listen to the words of Tchin-King. So Tchin-King arrayed himself in his robes of office, and set his house in order; and, having embraced his wife and his children, mounted his horse and rode away alone to the roaring camp of the rebels, bearing the Emperor's letter in his bosom. "I shall return; fear not!" were his last words to the gray servant who watched him from the terrace as he rode.

And Tchin-King at last descended from his horse, and entered into the rebel camp, and, passing through that huge gathering of war, stood in the presence of Hi-lié. High sat the rebel among his chiefs, encircled by the wave-lightning of swords and the thunders of ten thousand gongs: above him undulated the silken folds of the Black Dragon, while a vast fire rose bickering before him. Also Tchin-King saw that the tongues of that fire were licking human bones, and that skulls

of men lay blackening among the ashes. Yet he was not afraid
to look upon the fire, nor into the eyes of Hi-lié; but drawing
from his bosom the roll of perfumed yellow silk upon which
the words of the Emperor were written, and kissing it, he
made ready to read, while the multitude became silent. Then,
in a strong, clear voice he began:—

*"The words of the Celestial and August, the Son of Heaven, the
Divine Ko-Tsu-Tchin-Yao-ti, unto the rebel Li-Hi-lié and those
that follow him."*

And a roar went up like the roar of the sea,—a roar of rage,
and the hideous battle-moan, like the moan of a forest in
storm,—*"Hoo! hoo-oo-oo-oo!"*—and the sword-lightnings brake
loose, and the thunder of the gongs moved the ground beneath
the messenger's feet. But Hi-lié waved his gilded wand, and
again there was silence. "Nay!" spake the rebel chief; "let the
dog bark!" So Tchin-King spake on:—

*"Knowest thou not, O most rash and foolish of men, that thou
leadest the people only into the mouth of the Dragon of Destruction? Knowest thou not, also, that the people of my kingdom are
the first-born of the Master of Heaven? So it hath been written
that he who doth needlessly subject the people to wounds and death
shall not be suffered by Heaven to live! Thou who wouldst subvert
those laws founded by the wise,—those laws in obedience to which
may happiness and prosperity alone be found,—thou art committing the greatest of all crimes,—the crime that is never forgiven!*

*"O my people, think not that I your Emperor, I your Father,
seek your destruction. I desire only your happiness, your prosperity,
your greatness; let not your folly provoke the severity of your Celestial Parent. Follow not after madness and blind rage; hearken
rather to the wise words of my messenger."*

"Hoo! hoo-oo-oo-oo-oo!" roared the people, gathering fury.
"Hoo! hoo-oo-oo-oo!"—till the mountains rolled back the cry
like the rolling of a typhoon; and once more the pealing of the
gongs paralyzed voice and hearing. Then Tchin-King, looking
at Hi-lié, saw that he laughed, and that the words of the letter
would not again be listened to. Therefore he read on to the
end without looking about him, resolved to perform his mission in so far as lay in his power. And having read all, he would
have given the letter to Hi-lié; but Hi-lié would not extend his
hand to take it. Therefore Tchin-King replaced it in his bosom,

and folding his arms, looked Hi-lié calmly in the face, and waited. Again Hi-lié waved his gilded wand; and the roaring ceased, and the booming of the gongs, until nothing save the fluttering of the Dragon-banner could be heard. Then spake Hi-lié, with an evil smile,—

"Tchin-King, O son of a dog! if thou dost not now take the oath of fealty, and bow thyself before me, and salute me with the salutation of Emperors,—even with the *luh-kao*, the triple prostration,—into that fire thou shalt be thrown."

But Tchin-King, turning his back upon the usurper, bowed himself a moment in worship to Heaven and Earth; and then rising suddenly, ere any man could lay hand upon him, he leaped into the towering flame, and stood there, with folded arms, like a God.

Then Hi-lié leaped to his feet in amazement, and shouted to his men; and they snatched Tchin-King from the fire, and wrung the flames from his robes with their naked hands, and extolled him, and praised him to his face. And even Hi-lié himself descended from his seat, and spoke fair words to him, saying: "O Tchin-King, I see thou art indeed a brave man and true, and worthy of all honor; be seated among us, I pray thee, and partake of whatever it is in our power to bestow!"

But Tchin-King, looking upon him unswervingly, replied in a voice clear as the voice of a great bell,—

"Never, O Hi-lié, shall I accept aught from thy hand, save death, so long as thou shalt continue in the path of wrath and folly. And never shall it be said that Tchin-King sat him down among rebels and traitors, among murderers and robbers."

Then Hi-lié, in sudden fury, smote him with his sword; and Tchin-King fell to the earth and died, striving even in his death to bow his head toward the south,—toward the place of the Emperor's palace,—toward the presence of his beloved Master.

Even at the same hour the Son of Heaven, alone in the inner chamber of his palace became aware of a Shape prostrate before his feet; and when he spake, the Shape arose and stood before him, and he saw that it was Tchin-King. And the Emperor would have questioned him; yet ere he could question, the familiar voice spake, saying:

"Son of Heaven, the mission confided to me I have

performed; and thy command hath been accomplished to the extent of thy humble servant's feeble power. But even now must I depart, that I may enter the service of another Master."

And looking, the Emperor perceived that the Golden Tigers upon the wall were visible through the form of Tchin-King; and a strange coldness, like a winter wind, passed through the chamber; and the figure faded out. Then the Emperor knew that the Master of whom his faithful servant had spoken was none other than the Master of Heaven.

Also at the same hour the gray servant of Tchin-King's house beheld him passing through the apartments, smiling as he was wont to smile when he saw that all things were as he desired. "Is it well with thee, my lord?" questioned the aged man. And a voice answered him: "It is well;" but the presence of Tchin-King had passed away before the answer came.

So the armies of the Son of Heaven strove with the rebels. But the land was soaked with blood and blackened with fire; and the corpses of whole populations were carried by the rivers to feed the fishes of the sea; and still the war prevailed through many a long red year. Then came to aid the Son of Heaven the hordes that dwell in the desolations of the west and north,— horsemen born, a nation of wild archers, each mighty to bend a two-hundred-pound bow, until the ears should meet. And as a whirlwind they came against rebellion, raining raven-feathered arrows in a storm of death; and they prevailed against Hi-lié and his people. Then those that survived destruction and defeat submitted, and promised allegiance; and once more was the law of righteousness restored. But Tchin-King had been dead for many summers.

And the Son of Heaven sent word to his victorious generals that they should bring back with them the bones of his faithful servant, to be laid with honor in a mausoleum erected by imperial decree. So the generals of the Celestial and August sought after the nameless grave and found it, and had the earth taken up, and made ready to remove the coffin.

But the coffin crumbled into dust before their eyes; for the worms had gnawed it, and the hungry earth had devoured its substance, leaving only a phantom shell that vanished at touch of the light. And lo! as it vanished, all beheld lying there the perfect form and features of the good Tchin-King. Corruption had not touched him, nor had the worms disturbed his rest, nor had the bloom of life departed from his face. And he seemed to dream only,—comely to see as upon the morning of his bridal, and smiling as the holy images smile, with eyelids closed, in the twilight of the great pagodas.

Then spoke a priest, standing by the grave: "O my children, this is indeed a Sign from the Master of Heaven; in such wise do the Powers Celestial preserve them that are chosen to be numbered with the Immortals. Death may not prevail over them, neither may corruption come nigh them. Verily the blessed Tchin-King hath taken his place among the divinities of Heaven!"

Then they bore Tchin-King back to his native place, and laid him with highest honors in the mausoleum which the Emperor had commanded; and there he sleeps, incorruptible forever, arrayed in his robes of state. Upon his tomb are sculptured the emblems of his greatness and his wisdom and his virtue, and the signs of his office, and the Four Precious Things: and the monsters which are holy symbols mount giant guard in stone about it; and the weird Dogs of Fo keep watch before it, as before the temples of the gods.

SANG A CHINESE HEART, FOURTEEN HUNDRED YEARS AGO:—

There is Somebody of whom I am thinking.
Far away there is Somebody of whom I am thinking.
A hundred leagues of mountains lie between us;—
Yet the same Moon shines upon us, and the passing
Wind breathes upon us both.

The Tradition of the Tea-Plant

"Good is the continence of the eye;
Good is the continence of the ear;
Good is the continence of the nostrils;
Good is the continence of the tongue;
Good is the continence of the body;
Good is the continence of speech;
Good is all. . . ."

AGAIN the Vulture of Temptation soared to the highest heaven of his contemplation, bringing his soul down, down, reeling and fluttering back to the World of Illusion. Again the memory made dizzy his thought, like the perfume of some venomous flower. Yet he had seen the bayadere for an instant only, when passing through Kasí upon his way to China,—to the vast empire of souls that thirsted after the refreshment of Buddha's law, as sun-parched fields thirst for the life-giving rain. When she called him, and dropped her little gift into his mendicant's bowl, he had indeed lifted his fan before his face, yet not quickly enough; and the penalty of that fault had followed him a thousand leagues,—pursued after him even into the strange land to which he had come to bear the words of the Universal Teacher. Accursed beauty! surely framed by the Tempter of tempters, by Mara himself, for the perdition of the just! Wisely had Bhagavat warned his disciples: "O ye Çramanas, women are not to be looked upon! And if ye chance to meet women, ye must not suffer your eyes to dwell upon them; but, maintaining holy reserve, speak not to them at all. Then fail not to whisper unto your own hearts, 'Lo, we are Çramanas, whose duty it is to remain uncontaminated by the corruptions of this world, even as the Lotos, which suffereth no vileness to cling unto its leaves, though it blossom amid the refuse of the wayside ditch.'" Then also came to his memory, but with a new and terrible meaning, the words of the Twenti-eth-and-Third of the Admonitions:—

"Of all attachments unto objects of desire, the strongest indeed is the attachment to Form. Happily, this passion is unique; for were there any other like unto it, then to enter the Perfect Way were impossible."

How, indeed, thus haunted by the illusion of form, was he to fulfil the vow that he had made to pass a night and a day in perfect and unbroken meditation? Already the night was beginning! Assuredly, for sickness of the soul, for fever of the spirit, there was no physic save prayer. The sunset was swiftly fading out. He strove to pray:—

"*O the Jewel in the Lotos!*

"Even as the tortoise withdraweth its extremities into its shell, let me, O Blessed One, withdraw my senses wholly into meditation!

"*O the Jewel in the Lotos!*

"For even as rain penetrateth the broken roof of a dwelling long uninhabited, so may passion enter the soul uninhabited by meditation.

"*O the Jewel in the Lotos!*

"Even as still water that hath deposited all its slime, so let my soul, O Tathâgata, be made pure! Give me strong power to rise above the world, O Master, even as the wild bird rises from its marsh to follow the pathway of the Sun!

"*O the Jewel in the Lotos!*

"By day shineth the sun, by night shineth the moon; shineth also the warrior in harness of war; shineth likewise in meditations the Çramana. But the Buddha at all times, by night or by day, shineth ever the same, illuminating the world.

"*O the Jewel in the Lotos!*

"Let me cease, O thou Perfectly Awakened, to remain as an Ape in the World-forest, forever ascending and descending in search of the fruits of folly. Swift as the twining of serpents, vast as the growth of lianas in a forest, are the all-encircling growths of the Plant of Desire.

"*O the Jewel in the Lotos!*"

Vain his prayer, alas! vain also his invocation! The mystic meaning of the holy text—the sense of the Lotos, the sense of the Jewel—had evaporated from the words, and their monotonous utterance now served only to lend more dangerous definition to the memory that tempted and tortured him. *O the jewel in her ear!* What lotos-bud more dainty than the folded flower of flesh, with its dripping of diamond-fire! Again he saw it, and the curve of the cheek beyond, luscious to look upon as beautiful brown fruit. How true the Two Hundred and Eighty-Fourth verse of the Admonitions!—"So long as a man shall not have torn from his heart even the smallest rootlet of that liana of desire which draweth his thought toward women, even so long shall his soul remain fettered." And there came to his mind also the Three Hundred and Forty-Fifth verse of the same blessed book, regarding fetters:

"In bonds of rope, wise teachers have said, there is no strength; nor in fetters of wood, nor yet in fetters of iron. Much stronger than any of these is the fetter of *concern for the jewelled earrings of women.*"

"Omniscient Gotama!" he cried,—"all-seeing Tathâgata! How multiform the consolation of Thy Word! how marvellous Thy understanding of the human heart! Was this also one of Thy temptations?—one of the myriad illusions marshalled before Thee by Mara in that night when the earth rocked as a chariot, and the sacred trembling passed from sun to sun, from system to system, from universe to universe, from eternity to eternity?"

O the jewel in her ear! The vision would not go! Nay, each time it hovered before his thought it seemed to take a warmer life, a fonder look, a fairer form; to develop with his weakness; to gain force from his enervation. He saw the eyes, large, limpid, soft, and black as a deer's; the pearls in the dark hair, and the pearls in the pink mouth; the lips curling to a kiss, a flower-kiss; and a fragrance seemed to float to his senses, sweet, strange, soporific,—a perfume of youth, an odor of woman. Rising to his feet, with strong resolve he pronounced again the sacred invocation; and he recited the holy words of the *Chapter of Impermanency*:

"Gazing upon the heavens and upon the earth ye must say, *These are not permanent.* Gazing upon the mountains and the rivers, ye must say, *These are not permanent.* Gazing upon the forms and upon the faces of exterior beings, and beholding their growth and their development, ye must say, *These are not permanent.*"

And nevertheless! how sweet illusion! The illusion of the great sun; the illusion of the shadow-casting hills; the illusion of waters, formless and multiform; the illusion of— Nay, nay!

what impious fancy! Accursed girl! yet, yet! why should he curse her? Had she ever done ought to merit the malediction of an ascetic? Never, never! Only her form, the memory of her, the beautiful phantom of her, the accursed phantom of her! What was she? An illusion creating illusions, a mockery, a dream, a shadow, a vanity, a vexation of spirit! The fault, the sin, was in himself, in his rebellious thought, in his untamed memory. Though mobile as water, intangible as vapor, Thought, nevertheless, may be tamed by the Will, may be harnessed to the chariot of Wisdom—must be!—that happiness be found. And he recited the blessed verses of the "Book of the Way of the Law:"—

"*All forms are only temporary.*" When this great truth is fully comprehended by any one, then is he delivered from all pain. This is the Way of Purification.

"*All forms are subject unto pain.*" When this great truth is fully comprehended by any one, then is he delivered from all pain. This is the Way of Purification.

"*All forms are without substantial reality.*" When this great truth is fully comprehended by any one, then is he delivered from all pain. This is the way of . . .

Her form, too, unsubstantial, unreal, an illusion only, though comeliest of illusions? She had given him alms! Was the merit of the giver illusive also,—illusive like the grace of the supple fingers that gave? Assuredly there were mysteries in the Abhidharma impenetrable, incomprehensible! . . . It was a golden coin, stamped with the symbol of an elephant,—not more of an illusion, indeed, than the gifts of Kings to the Buddha! Gold upon her bosom also, less fine than the gold of her skin. Naked between the silken sash and the narrow breast-corslet, her young waist curved glossy and pliant as a bow. Richer the silver in her voice than in the hollow *pagals* that made a moonlight about her ankles! But her smile!—the little teeth like flower-stamens in the perfumed blossom of her mouth!

O weakness! O shame! How had the strong Charioteer of Resolve thus lost his control over the wild team of fancy! Was this languor of the Will a signal of coming peril, the peril of slumber? So strangely vivid those fancies were, so brightly definite, as about to take visible form, to move with factitious life, to play some unholy drama upon the stage of dreams! "O Thou Fully Awakened!" he cried aloud, "help now thy humble disciple to obtain the blessed wakefulness of perfect contemplation! let him find force to fulfil his vow! suffer not Mara to prevail against him!" And he recited the eternal verses of the Chapter of Wakefulness:—

"*Completely and eternally awake are the disciples of Gotama!* Unceasingly, by day and night, their thoughts are fixed upon the Law.

"*Completely and eternally awake are the disciples of Gotama!* Unceasingly, by day and night, their thoughts are fixed upon the Community.

"*Completely and eternally awake are the disciples of Gotama!* Unceasingly, by day and night, their thoughts are fixed upon the Body.

"*Completely and eternally awake are the disciples of Gotama!* Unceasingly, by day and night, their minds know the sweetness of perfect peace.

"*Completely and eternally awake are the disciples of Gotama!* Unceasingly, by day and night, their minds enjoy the deep peace of meditation."

There came a murmur to his ears; a murmuring of many voices, smothering the utterances of his own, like a tumult of waters. The stars went out before his sight; the heavens darkened their infinities: all things became viewless, became blackness; and the great murmur deepened, like the murmur of a rising tide; and the earth seemed to sink from beneath him. His feet no longer touched the ground; a sense of supernatural buoyancy pervaded every fibre of his body: he felt himself floating in obscurity; then sinking softly, slowly, like a feather dropped from the pinnacle of a temple. Was this death? Nay, for all suddenly, as transported by the Sixth Supernatural Power, he stood again in light,—a perfumed, sleepy light, vapory, beautiful,—that bathed the marvellous streets of some Indian city. Now the nature of the murmur became manifest to him; for he moved with a mighty throng, a people of pilgrims, a nation of worshippers. But these were not of his faith; they bore upon their foreheads the smeared symbols of obscene gods! Still, he could not escape from their midst; the mile-broad human torrent bore him irresistibly with it, as a leaf is swept by the waters of the Ganges. Rajahs were there with their trains, and princes riding upon elephants, and Brahmins robed in their vestments, and swarms of voluptuous dancing-girls, moving to chant of *kabit* and *damâri*. But whither, whither? Out of the city into the sun they passed, between avenues of banyan, down colonnades of palm. But whither, whither?

Blue-distant, a mountain of carven stone appeared before them,—the Temple, lifting to heaven its wilderness of chiselled pinnacles, flinging to the sky the golden spray of its decoration. Higher it grew with approach, the blue tones changed to gray, the outlines sharpened in the light. Then each detail became visible: the elephants of the pedestals standing upon tortoises of rock; the great grim faces of the capitals; the serpents and monsters writhing among the friezes; the many-headed gods of basalt in their galleries of fretted niches, tier above tier; the pictured foulnesses, the painted lusts, the divinities of abomination. And, yawning in the sloping precipice of sculpture, beneath a frenzied swarming of gods and Gopia, —a beetling pyramid of limbs and bodies interlocked,—the Gate, cavernous and shadowy as the mouth of Siva, devoured the living multitude.

The eddy of the throng whirled him with it to the vastness of the interior. None seemed to note his yellow robe, none even to observe his presence. Giant aisles intercrossed their heights above him; myriads of mighty pillars, fantastically carven, filed away to invisibility behind the yellow illumination of torch-fires. Strange images, weirdly sensuous, loomed up through haze of incense. Colossal figures, that at a distance assumed the form of elephants or garuda-birds, changed aspect when approached, and revealed as the secret of their design an interplaiting of the bodies of women; while one divinity rode all the monstrous allegories,—one divinity or demon, eternally the same in the repetition of the sculptor, universally visible as though self-multiplied. The huge pillars themselves were symbols, figures, carnalities; the orgiastic spirit of that worship lived and writhed in the contorted bronze of the lamps, the twisted gold of the cups, the chiselled marble of the tanks. . . .

How far had he proceeded? He knew not; the journey among those countless columns, past those armies of petrified gods, down lanes of flickering lights, seemed longer than the voyage of a caravan, longer than his pilgrimage to China! But suddenly, inexplicably, there came a silence as of cemeteries; the living ocean seemed to have ebbed away from about him, to have been engulfed within abysses of subterranean architecture! He found himself alone in some strange crypt before a basin, shell-shaped and shallow, bearing in its centre a rounded column of less than human height, whose smooth and spherical summit was wreathed with flowers. Lamps similarly formed, and fed with oil of palm, hung above it. There was no other graven image, no visible divinity. Flowers of countless varieties lay heaped upon the pavement; they covered its surface like a carpet, thick, soft; they exhaled their ghosts beneath his feet. The perfume seemed to penetrate his brain,—a perfume sensuous, intoxicating, unholy; an unconquerable languor mastered his will, and he sank to rest upon the floral offerings.

The sound of a tread, light as a whisper, approached through the heavy stillness, with a drowsy tinkling of *pagals*, a tintinnabulation of anklets. All suddenly he felt glide about his neck the tepid smoothness of a woman's arm. *She, she!* his Illusion, his Temptation; but how transformed, transfigured!—preternatural in her loveliness, incomprehensible in her charm! Delicate as a jasmine-petal the cheek that touched his own; deep as night, sweet as summer, the eyes that watched him. "*Heart's-thief*," her flower-lips whispered,—"*heart's-thief, how have I sought for thee! How have I found thee! Sweets I bring thee, my beloved; lips and bosom; fruit and blossom. Hast thirst? Drink from the well of mine eyes! Wouldst sacrifice? I am thine altar! Wouldst pray? I am thy God!*"

Their lips touched; her kiss seemed to change the cells of his blood to flame. For a moment Illusion triumphed; Mara prevailed! . . . With a shock of resolve the dreamer awoke in the night,—under the stars of the Chinese sky.

Only a mockery of sleep! But the vow had been violated, the sacred purpose unfulfilled! Humiliated, penitent, but resolved, the ascetic drew from his girdle a keen knife, and with unfaltering hands severed his eyelids from his eyes, and flung them from him. "O Thou Perfectly Awakened!" he prayed, "thy disciple hath not been overcome save through the feebleness of the body; and his vow hath been renewed. Here shall he linger, without food or drink, until the moment of its fulfilment." And having assumed the hieratic posture,—seated himself with his lower limbs folded beneath him, and the palms of his hands upward, the right upon the left, the left resting upon the sole of his upturned foot,—he resumed his meditation.

Dawn blushed; day brightened. The sun shortened all the shadows of the land, and lengthened them again, and sank at last upon his funeral pyre of crimson-burning cloud. Night came and glittered and passed. But Mara had tempted in vain. This time the vow had been fulfilled, the holy purpose accomplished.

And again the sun arose to fill the world with laughter of light; flowers opened their hearts to him; birds sang their morning hymn of fire worship; the deep forest trembled with delight; and far upon the plain, the eaves of many-storied temples and the peaked caps of the city-towers caught aureate glory. Strong in the holiness of his accomplished vow, the Indian pilgrim arose in the morning glow. He started for amazement as he lifted his hands to his eyes. What! was everything a dream? Impossible! Yet now his eyes felt no pain; neither were they lidless; not even so much as one of their lashes was lacking. What marvel had been wrought? In vain he looked for the severed lids that he had flung upon the ground; they had mysteriously vanished. But lo! there where he had cast them two wondrous shrubs were growing, with dainty leaflets eyelid-shaped, and snowy buds just opening to the east.

Then, by virtue of the supernatural power acquired in that mighty meditation, it was given the holy missionary to know the secret of that newly created plant,—the subtle virtue of its leaves. And he named it, in the language of the nation to whom he brought the Lotos of the Good Law, "*TE*;" and he spake to it, saying:—

"Blessed be thou, sweet plant, beneficent, life-giving, formed by the spirit of virtuous resolve! Lo! the fame of thee shall yet spread unto the ends of the earth; and the perfume of thy life be borne unto the uttermost parts by all the winds of heaven! Verily, for all time to come men who drink of thy sap shall find such refreshment that weariness may not overcome them nor languor seize upon them;—neither shall they know the confusion of drowsiness, nor any desire for slumber in the hour of duty or of prayer. Blessed be thou!"

And still, as a mist of incense, as a smoke of universal sacrifice, perpetually ascends to heaven from all the lands of earth the pleasant vapor of TE, created for the refreshment of mankind by the power of a holy vow, the virtue of a pious atonement.

It is written in the FONG-HO-CHIN-TCH'OUEN, *that whenever the artist Thsang-kong was in doubt, he would look into the fire of the great oven in which his vases were baking, and question the Guardian-Spirit dwelling in the flame. And the Spirit of the Oven-fires so aided him with his counsels, that the porcelains made by Thsang-Kong were indeed finer and lovelier to look upon than all other porcelains. And they were baked in the years of Khang-hi,—sacredly called Jin Houang-ti.*

The Tale of the Porcelain-God

WHO first of men discovered the secret of the *Kao-ling*, of the *Pe-tun-tse,*—the bones and the flesh, the skeleton and the skin, of the beauteous Vase? Who first discovered the virtue of the curd-white clay? Who first prepared the ice-pure bricks of *tun*: the gathered-hoariness of mountains that have died for age; blanched dust of the rocky bones and the stony flesh of sun-seeking Giants that have ceased to be? Unto whom was it first given to discover the divine art of porcelain?

Unto Pu, once a man, now a god, before whose snowy statues bow the myriad populations enrolled in the guilds of the potteries. But the place of his birth we know not; perhaps the tradition of it may have been effaced from remembrance by that awful war which in our own day consumed the lives of twenty millions of the Black-haired Race, and obliterated from the face of the world even the wonderful City of Porcelain itself,—the City of King-te-chin, that of old shone like a jewel of fire in the blue mountain-girdle of Feou-liang.

Before his time indeed the Spirit of the Furnace had being; had issued from the Infinite Vitality; had become manifest as an emanation of the Supreme Tao. For Hoang-ti, nearly five thousand years ago, taught men to make good vessels of baked clay; and in his time all potters had learned to know the God of Oven-fires, and turned their wheels to the murmuring of prayer. But Hoang-ti had been gathered unto his fathers for thrice ten hundred years before that man was born destined by the Master of Heaven to become the Porcelain-God.

And his divine ghost, ever hovering above the smoking and the toiling of the potteries, still gives power to the thought of the shaper, grace to the genius of the designer, luminosity to the touch of the enamellist. For by his heaven-taught wisdom was the art of porcelain created; by his inspiration were accomplished all the miracles of Thao-yu, maker of the *Kia-yu-ki*, and all the marvels made by those who followed after him;—

All the azure porcelains called *You-kouo-thien-tsing*; brilliant as a mirror, thin as paper of rice, sonorous as the melodious stone *Khing*, and colored, in obedience to the mandate of the

Emperor Chi-tsong, "blue as the sky is after rain, when viewed through the rifts of the clouds." These were, indeed, the first of all porcelains, likewise called *Tchai-yao*, which no man, howsoever wicked, could find courage to break, for they charmed the eye like jewels of price;—

And the *Jou-yao*, second in rank among all porcelains, sometimes mocking the aspect and the sonority of bronze, sometimes blue as summer waters, and deluding the sight with mucid appearance of thickly floating spawn of fish;—

And the *Kouan-yao*, which are the Porcelains of Magistrates, and third in rank of merit among all wondrous porcelains, colored with colors of the morning,—skyey blueness, with the rose of a great dawn blushing and bursting through it, and long-limbed marshbirds flying against the glow;

Also the *Ko-yao*,—fourth in rank among perfect porcelains, —of fair, faint, changing colors, like the body of a living fish, or made in the likeness of opal substance, milk mixed with fire; the work of Sing-I, elder of the immortal brothers Tchang;

Also the *Ting-yao*,—fifth in rank among all perfect porcelains, —white as the mourning garments of a spouse bereaved, and beautiful with a trickling as of tears,—the porcelains sung of by the poet Son-tong-po;

Also the porcelains called *Pi-se-yao*, whose colors are called "hidden," being alternately invisible and visible, like the tints of ice beneath the sun,—the porcelains celebrated by the far-famed singer Sin-in;

Also the wondrous *Chu-yao*,—the pallid porcelains that utter a mournful cry when smitten,—the porcelains chanted of by the mighty chanter, Thou-chao-ling;

Also the porcelains called *Thsin-yao*, white or blue, surface-wrinkled as the face of water by the fluttering of many fins. . . . And ye can see the fish!

Also the vases called *Tsi-hong-khi*, red as sunset after a rain; and the *T'o-t'ai-khi*, fragile as the wings of the silkworm moth, lighter than the shell of an egg;

Also the *Kia-tsing*,—fair cups pearl-white when empty, yet, by some incomprehensible witchcraft of construction, seeming to swarm with purple fish the moment they are filled with water;

Also the porcelains called *Yao-pien*, whose tints are transmuted by the alchemy of fire; for they enter blood-crimson

into the heat, and change there to lizard-green, and at last
come forth azure as the cheek of the sky;

Also the *Ki-tcheou-yao*, which are all violet as a summer's
night; and the *Hing-yao* that sparkle with the sparklings of
mingled silver and snow;

Also the *Sieouen-yao*,—some ruddy as iron in the furnace,
some diaphanous and ruby-red, some granulated and yellow as
the rind of an orange, some softly flushed as the skin of a
peach;

Also the *Tsoui khi-yao*, crackled and green as ancient ice is;
and the *Tchou-fou-yao*, which are the Porcelains of Emperors,
with dragons wriggling and snarling in gold; and those *yao*
that are pink-ribbed and have their angles serrated as the claws
of crabs are;

Also the *Ou-ni-yao*, black as the pupil of the eye and as lustrous; and the *Hou-tien-yao*, darkly yellow as the faces of men
of India and the *Ou-kong-yao*, whose color is the dead-gold of
autumn-leaves;

Also the *Long-kang-yao*, green as the seedling of a pea, but
bearing also paintings of sun-silvered cloud, and of the Dragons of Heaven;

Also the *Tching-hoa-yao*,—pictured with the amber bloom
of grapes and the verdure of vine-leaves and the blossoming of
poppies, or decorated in relief with figures of fighting crickets;

Also the *Khang-hi-nien-ts'ang-yao*, celestial azure sown with
star-dust of gold; and the *Khien-long-nien-thang-yao*, splendid
in sable and silver as a fervid night that is flashed with lightnings.

Not indeed the *Long-Ouang-yao*,—painted with the lascivi-
ous *Pi-hi*, with the obscene *Nan-niu-ssé-sie*, with the shameful
Tchun-hoa, or "Pictures of Spring:" abominations created by
command of the wicked Emperor Mou-tsong, though the
Spirit of the Furnace hid his face and fled away;

But all other vases of startling form and substance, magically
articulated, and ornamented with figures in relief, in cameo, in
transparency,—the vases with orifices belled like the cups of
flowers, or cleft like the bills of birds, or fanged like the jaws of
serpents, or pink-lipped as the mouth of a girl; the vases flesh-
colored and purple-veined and dimpled, with ears and with
earrings; the vases in likeness of mushrooms, of lotos-flowers,
of lizards, of horse-footed dragons woman-faced; the vases

strangely translucid, that simulate the white glimmering of grains of prepared rice, that counterfeit the vapory lace-work of frost, that imitate the efflorescences of coral;—

Also the statues in porcelain of divinities: the Genius of the Hearth; the Long-pinn who are the Twelve Deities of Ink; the blessed Lao-tseu, born with silver hair; Kong-fu-tse, grasping the scroll of written wisdom; Kouan-in, sweetest Goddess of Mercy, standing snowy-footed upon the heart of her golden lily; Chi-nong, the god who taught men how to cook; Fo, with long eyes closed in meditation, and lips smiling the mysterious smile of Supreme Beatitude; Cheou-lao, god of Longevity, bestriding his aerial steed, the white-winged stork; Pou-t'ai, Lord of Contentment and of Wealth, obese and dreamy; and that fairest Goddess of Talent, from whose beneficent hands eternally streams the iridescent rain of pearls.

And though many a secret of that matchless art that Pu bequeathed unto men may indeed have been forgotten and lost forever, the story of the Porcelain-God is remembered; and I doubt not that any of the aged *Jeou-yen-liao-kong*, any one of the old blind men of the great potteries, who sit all day grinding colors in the sun, could tell you Pu was once a humble Chinese workman, who grew to be a great artist by dint of tireless study and patience and by the inspiration of Heaven. So famed he became that some deemed him an alchemist, who possessed the secret called *White-and-Yellow*, by which stones might be turned into gold; and others thought him a magician, having the ghastly power of murdering men with horror of nightmare, by hiding charmed effigies of them under the tiles of their own roofs; and others, again, averred that he was an astrologer who had discovered the mystery of those Five Hing which influence all things,—those Powers that move even in the currents of the star-drift, in the milky *Tien-ho*, or River of the Sky. Thus, at least, the ignorant spoke of him; but even those who stood about the Son of Heaven, those whose hearts had been strengthened by the acquisition of wisdom, wildly praised the marvels of his handicraft, and asked each other if there might be any imaginable form of beauty which Pu could not evoke from that beauteous substance so docile to the touch of his cunning hand.

And one day it came to pass that Pu sent a priceless gift to the Celestial and August: a vase imitating the substance of ore-rock, all aflame with pyritic scintillation,—a shape of glittering splendor with chameleons sprawling over it; chameleons of porcelain that shifted color as often as the beholder changed his position. And the Emperor, wondering exceedingly at the splendor of the work, questioned the princes and the mandarins concerning him that made it. And the princes and the mandarins answered that he was a workman named Pu, and that he was without equal among potters, knowing secrets that seemed to have been inspired either by gods or by demons. Whereupon the Son of Heaven sent his officers to Pu with a noble gift, and summoned him unto his presence.

So the humble artisan entered before the Emperor, and having performed the supreme prostration,—thrice kneeling, and thrice nine times touching the ground with his forehead, —awaited the command of the August.

And the Emperor spake to him, saying: "Son, thy gracious gift hath found high favor in our sight; and for the charm of that offering we have bestowed upon thee a reward of five thousand silver *liang*. But thrice that sum shall be awarded thee so soon as thou shalt have fulfilled our behest. Hearken, therefore, O matchless artificer! it is now our will that thou make for us a vase having the tint and the aspect of living flesh, but— mark well our desire!—*of flesh made to creep by the utterance of such words as poets utter,—flesh moved by an Idea, flesh horripilated by a Thought!* Obey, and answer not! We have spoken."

Now Pu was the most cunning of all the *P'ei-se-kong*,—the men who marry colors together; of all the *Hoa-yang-kong*, who draw the shapes of vase-decoration; of all the *Hoei-sse-kong*, who paint in enamel; of all the *T'ien-thsai-kong*, who brighten color; of all the *Chao-lou-kong*, who watch the furnace-fires and the porcelain-ovens. But he went away sorrowing from the Palace of the Son of Heaven, notwithstanding the gift of five thousand silver *liang* which had been given to him. For he thought to himself: "Surely the mystery of the comeliness of flesh, and the mystery of that by which it is moved, are the secrets of the Supreme Tao. How shall man lend the aspect of sentient life to dead clay? Who save the Infinite can give soul?"

Now Pu had discovered those witchcrafts of color, those surprises of grace, that make the art of the ceramist. He had found the secret of the *feng-hong*, the wizard flush of the Rose; of the *hoa-hong*, the delicious incarnadine; of the mountain-green called *chan-lou*; of the pale soft yellow termed *hiao-hoang-yeou*; and of the *hoang-kin*, which is the blazing beauty of gold. He had found those eel-tints, those serpent-greens, those pansy-violets, those furnace-crimsons, those carminates and lilacs, subtle as spirit-flame, which our enamellists of the Occident long sought without success to reproduce. But he trembled at the task assigned him, as he returned to the toil of his studio, saying: "How shall any miserable man render in clay the quivering of flesh to an Idea,—the inexplicable horrip-ilation of a Thought? Shall a man venture to mock the magic of that Eternal Moulder by whose infinite power a million suns are shapen more readily than one small jar might be rounded upon my wheel?"

Yet the command of the Celestial and August might never be disobeyed; and the patient workman strove with all his power to fulfil the Son of Heaven's desire. But vainly for days, for weeks, for months, for season after season, did he strive; vainly also he prayed unto the gods to aid him; vainly he be-sought the Spirit of the Furnace, crying: "O thou Spirit of Fire, hear me, heed me, help me! how shall I,—a miserable man, unable to breathe into clay a living soul,—how shall I render in this inanimate substance the aspect of flesh made to creep by the utterance of a Word, sentient to the horripilation of a Thought?"

For the Spirit of the Furnace made strange answer to him with whispering of fire: "*Vast thy faith, weird thy prayer! Has Thought feet, that man may perceive the trace of its passing? Canst thou measure me the blast of the Wind?*"

Nevertheless, with purpose unmoved, nine-and-forty times did Pu seek to fulfil the Emperor's command; nine-and-forty times he strove to obey the behest of the Son of Heaven. Vainly, alas! did he consume his substance; vainly did he ex-pend his strength; vainly did he exhaust his knowledge: success smiled not upon him; and Evil visited his home, and Poverty sat in his dwelling, and Misery shivered at his hearth.

Sometimes, when the hour of trial came, it was found that the colors had become strangely transmuted in the firing, or had faded into ashen pallor, or had darkened into the fuliginous hue of forest-mould. And Pu, beholding these misfortunes, made wail to the Spirit of the Furnace, praying: "O thou Spirit of Fire, how shall I render the likeness of lustrous flesh, the warm glow of living color, unless thou aid me?"

And the Spirit of the Furnace mysteriously answered him with murmuring of fire: "*Canst thou learn the art of that Infinite Enameller who hath made beautiful the Arch of Heaven,— whose brush is Light; whose paints are the colors of the Evening?*"

Sometimes, again, even when the tints had not changed, after the pricked and labored surface had seemed about to quicken in the heat, to assume the vibratility of living skin,— even at the last hour all the labor of the workers proved to have been wasted; for the fickle substance rebelled against their efforts, producing only crinklings grotesque as those upon the rind of a withered fruit, or granulations like those upon the skin of a dead bird from which the feathers have been rudely plucked. And Pu wept, and cried out unto the Spirit of the Furnace: "O thou Spirit of Flame, how shall I be able to imitate the thrill of flesh touched by a Thought, unless thou wilt vouchsafe to lend me thine aid?"

And the Spirit of the Furnace mysteriously answered him with muttering of fire: "*Canst thou give ghost unto a stone? Canst thou thrill with a Thought the entrails of the granite hills?*"

Sometimes it was found that all the work indeed had not failed; for the color seemed good, and all faultless the matter of the vase appeared to be, having neither crack nor wrinkling nor crankling; but the pliant softness of warm skin did not meet the eye; the flesh-tinted surface offered only the harsh aspect and hard glimmer of metal. All their exquisite toil to mock the pulpiness of sentient substance had left no trace; had been brought to nought by the breath of the furnace. And Pu, in his despair, shrieked to the Spirit of the Furnace: "O thou merciless divinity! O thou most pitiless god!—thou whom I have worshipped with ten thousand sacrifices!—for what fault hast thou abandoned me? for what error hast thou forsaken me? How may I, most wretched of men! ever render the aspect of flesh made to creep with the utterance of a Word, sentient to the titillation of a Thought, if thou wilt not aid me?"

And the Spirit of the Furnace made answer unto him with roaring of fire: "*Canst thou divide a Soul? Nay!* . . . *Thy life for the life of thy work!—thy soul for the soul of thy Vase!*"

And hearing these words Pu arose with a terrible resolve swelling at his heart, and made ready for the last and fiftieth time to fashion his work for the oven.

One hundred times did he sift the clay and the quartz, the *kao-ling* and the *tun*; one hundred times did he purify them in clearest water; one hundred times with tireless hands did he knead the creamy paste, mingling it at last with colors known only to himself. Then was the vase shapen and reshapen, and touched and retouched by the hands of Pu, until its blandness seemed to live, until it appeared to quiver and to palpitate, as with vitality from within, as with the quiver of rounded muscle undulating beneath the integument. For the hues of life were upon it and infiltrated throughout its innermost substance, imitating the carnation of blood-bright tissue, and the reticulated purple of the veins; and over all was laid the envelope of sun-colored *Pe-kia-ho*, the lucid and glossy enamel, half diaphanous, even like the substance that it counterfeited,—the polished skin of a woman. Never since the making of the world had any work comparable to this been wrought by the skill of man.

Then Pu bade those who aided him that they should feed the furnace well with wood of *tcha*; but he told his resolve unto none. Yet after the oven began to glow, and he saw the work of his hands blossoming and blushing in the heat, he bowed himself before the Spirit of Flame, and murmured: "O thou Spirit and Master of Fire, I know the truth of thy words! I know that a Soul may never be divided! Therefore my life for the life of my work!—my soul for the soul of my Vase!"

And for nine days and for eight nights the furnaces were fed unceasingly with wood of *tcha*; for nine days and for eight nights men watched the wondrous vase crystallizing into being, rose-lighted by the breath of the flame. Now upon the coming of the ninth night, Pu bade all his weary comrades retire to rest, for that the work was wellnigh done, and the success assured. "If you find me not here at sunrise," he said, "fear not to take forth the vase; for I know that the task will have been accomplished according to the command of the August." So they departed.

But in that same ninth night Pu entered the flame, and yielded up his ghost in the embrace of the Spirit of the Furnace, giving his life for the life of his work,—his soul for the soul of his Vase.

And when the workmen came upon the tenth morning to take forth the porcelain marvel, even the bones of Pu had ceased to be; but lo! the Vase lived as they looked upon it: seeming to be flesh moved by the utterance of a Word, creeping to the titillation of a Thought. And whenever tapped by the finger it uttered a voice and a name,—the voice of its maker, the name of its creator: PU.

And the Son of Heaven, hearing of these things, and viewing the miracle of the vase, said unto those about him: "Verily, the Impossible hath been wrought by the strength of faith, by the force of obedience! Yet never was it our desire that so cruel a sacrifice should have been; we sought only to know whether the skill of the matchless artificer came from the Divinities or from the Demons,—from heaven or from hell. Now, indeed, we discern that Pu hath taken his place among the gods." And the Emperor mourned exceedingly for his faithful servant. But he ordained that godlike honors should be paid unto the spirit of the marvellous artist, and that his memory should be revered forevermore, and that fair statues of him should be set up in all the cities of the Celestial Empire, and above all the toiling of the potteries, that the multitude of workers might unceasingly call upon his name and invoke his benediction upon their labors.

NOTES

"*The Soul of the Great Bell.*"—The story of Ko-Ngai is one of the collection entitled *Te-Hiao-Tou-Choué*, or "A Hundred Examples of Filial Piety." It is very simply told by the Chinese narrator. The scholarly French consul, P. Dabry de Thiersant, translated and published in 1877 a portion of the book, including the legend of the Bell. His translation is enriched with a number of Chinese drawings; and there is a quaint little picture of Ko-Ngai leaping into the molten metal.

"*The Story of Ming-Y.*"—The singular phantom-tale upon which my work is based forms the thirty-fourth story of the famous collection *Kin-Kou-Ki-Koan*, and was first translated under the title, "La Bachelière du Pays de Chu," by the learned Gustave Schlegel, as an introduction to his publication (accompanied by a French version) of the curious and obscene *Mai-yu-lang-toú-tchen-hoa-koueï* (Leyden, 1877), which itself forms the seventh recital of the same work. Schlegel, Julien, Gardner, Birch, D'Entrecolles, Rémusat, Pavie, Olyphant, Grisebach, Hervey-Saint-Denys, and others, have given the Occidental world translations of eighteen stories from the *Kin-Kou-Ki-Koan*; namely, Nos. 2, 3, 5, 6, 7, 8, 10, 14, 19, 20, 26, 27, 29, 30, 31, 34, 35, and 39. The Chinese work itself dates back to the thirteenth century; but as it forms only a collection of the most popular tales of that epoch, many of the stories selected by the Chinese editor may have had a much more ancient origin. There are forty tales in the *Kin-Kou-Ki-Koan*.

"*The Legend of Tchi-Niu.*"—My authority for this tale is the following legend from the thirty-fourth chapter of the *Kan-ing-p'ien*, or "Book of Rewards and Punishments,"—a work attributed to Lao-tseu, which contains some four hundred anecdotes and traditions of the most curious kind:—

Tong-yong, who lived under the Han dynasty, was reduced to a state of extreme poverty. Having lost his father, he sold himself in order to obtain . . . the wherewithal to bury him and to build him a tomb. The Master of Heaven took pity on him, and sent the Goddess Tchi-Niu to him to become his wife. She wove a piece of silk for him every day until she was able to buy his freedom, after which she gave him a son, and went back to heaven.—*Julien's French Translation*, p. 119.

Lest the reader should suppose, however, that I have drawn wholly upon my own imagination for the details of the apparition, the cure, the marriage ceremony, etc., I refer him to No. XCVI. of Giles's "Strange Stories from a Chinese Studio," entitled, "A Supernatural Wife," in which he will find that my narrative is at least conformable to Chinese ideas. (This story first appeared in "Harper's Bazar," and is republished here by permission.)

"*The Return of Yen-Tchin-King.*"—There may be an involuntary anachronism in my version of this legend, which is very pithily narrated in the *Kan-ing-p'ien*. No emperor's name is cited by the homilist; and the date of the revolt seems to have been left wholly to conjecture.—Baber, in his "Memoirs," mentions one of his Mongol archers as able to bend a two-hundred-pound bow until the ears met.

"*The Tradition of the Tea-Plant.*"—My authority for this bit of folklore is the brief statement published by Bretschneider in the "Chinese Recorder" for 1871:—

> "A Japanese legend says that about A.D. 519, a Buddhist priest came to China, and, in order to dedicate his soul entirely to God, he made a vow to pass the day and night in an uninterrupted and unbroken meditation. After many years of this continual watching, he was at length so tired that he fell asleep. On awaking the following morning, he was so sorry he had broken his vow that he cut off both his eyelids and threw them upon the ground. Returning to the same place the following day he observed that each eyelid had become a shrub. This was the *tea-shrub*, unknown until that time."

Bretschneider adds that the legend in question seems not to be known to the Chinese; yet in view of the fact that Buddhism itself, with all its marvellous legends, was received by the Japanese from China, it is certainly probable this legend had a Chinese origin,—subsequently disguised by Japanese chronology. My Buddhist texts were drawn from Fernand Hû's translation of the Dhammapada, and from Leon Feer's translation from the Thibetan of the "Sutra in Forty-two Articles." An Orientalist who should condescend in a rare leisure-moment to glance at my work might also discover that I had borrowed an idea or two from the Sanscrit poet, Bhâminî-Vilâsa.

"*The Tale of the Porcelain-God*."—The good Père d'Entrecolles, who first gave to Europe the secrets of Chinese porcelain-manufacture, wrote one hundred and sixty years ago:—

> "The Emperors of China are, during their lifetime, the most redoubted of divinities; and they believe that nothing should ever stand in the way of their desires. . . .
>
> "It is related that once upon a time a certain Emperor insisted that some porcelains should be made for him according to a model which he gave. It was answered that the thing was simply impossible; but all such remonstrances only served to excite his desire more and more. . . . The officers charged by the demigod to supervise and hasten the work treated the workmen with great harshness. The poor wretches spent all their money, took exceeding pains, and received only blows in return. One of them, in a fit of despair, leaped into the blazing furnace, and was instantly burnt to ashes. But the porcelain that was being baked there at the time came out, they say, perfectly beautiful and to the satisfaction of the Emperor. . . . From that time, the unfortunate workman was regarded as a hero; and his image was made the idol which presides over the manufacture of porcelain."

It appears that D'Entrecolles mistook the statue of Pou't'ai, God of Comfort, for that of the real porcelain-deity, as Jacquemart and others observe. This error does not, however, destroy the beauty of the myth; and there is no good reason to doubt that D'Entrecolles related it as it had been told him by some of his Chinese friends at King-te-chin. The researches of Stanislas Julien and others have only tended to confirm the trustworthiness of the Catholic missionary's statements in other respects; and both Julien and Salvétat, in their admirable French rendering of the *King-te-chin-thao-lou*, "History of the Porcelains of King-te-chin" (a work which has been of the greatest service to me in the preparation of my little story), quote from his letters at considerable length, and award him the highest praise as a conscientious investigator. So far as I have been able to learn, D'Entrecolles remains the sole authority for the myth; but his affirmations in regard to other matters have withstood the severe tests of time astonishingly well; and since the Tai-ping rebellion destroyed King-te-chin and paralyzed its noble industry, the value of the French missionary's documents and testimony has become widely recognized. In lieu of any other name for the hero of the legend, I have been obliged to retain that of Pou, or Pu,—only using it without the affix "t'ai,"—so as to distinguish it from the deity of comfort and repose.

GLOSSARY

ABHIDHARMA.—The metaphysics of Buddhism. Buddhist literature is classed into three great divisions, or "baskets;" the highest of these is the Abhidharma. . . . According to a passage in Spence Hardy's "Manual of Buddhism," the full comprehension of the Abhidharma is possible only for a Buddha to acquire.

CHIH.—"House;" but especially the house of the dead,—a tomb.

CHU-SHA-KIH.—The mandarin-orange.

ÇRAMANA.—An ascetic; one who has subdued his senses. For an interesting history of this term, see Burnouf,—"Introduction à l'histoire du Buddhisme Indien."

DAMÂRI.—A peculiar chant, of somewhat licentious character, most commonly sung during the period of the Indian carnival. For an account, at once brief and entertaining, of Hindoo popular songs and hymns, see Garcin de Tassy,—"Chants populaires de l'Inde."

DOGS OF FO.—The *Dog of Fo* is one of those fabulous monsters in the sculptural representation of which Chinese art has found its most grotesque expression. It is really an exaggerated lion; and the symbolical relation of the lion to Buddhism is well known. Statues of these mythical animals—sometimes of a grandiose and colossal execution—are placed in pairs before the entrances of temples, palaces, and tombs, as tokens of honor, and as emblems of divine protection.

FO.—Buddha is called *Fo, Fuh, Fuh-tu, Hwut, Făt*, in various Chinese dialects. The name is thought to be a corruption of the Hindoo *Bodh*, or "Truth," due to the imperfect articulation of the Chinese. . . . It is a curious fact that the Chinese Buddhist liturgy is Sanscrit transliterated into Chinese characters, and that the priests have lost all recollection of the antique tongue,—repeating the texts without the least comprehension of their meaning.

FUH-YIN.—An official holding in Chinese cities a position corresponding to that of mayor in the Occident.

FUNG-HOANG.—This allegorical bird, corresponding to the Arabian phœnix in some respects, is described as being five cubits high, having feathers of five different colors, and singing in five modulations. . . . The female is said to sing in imperfect tones; the male in perfect tones. The *fung-hoang* figures largely in Chinese musical myths and legends.

GOPIA (*or* GOPÌS).—Daughters and wives of the cowherds of Vrindavana, among whom Krishna was brought up after his incarnation as the eighth avatar of Vishnu. Krishna's amours with the shepherdesses, or Gopia, form the subject of various celebrated mystical writings, especially the *Prem-Ságar*, or "Ocean of Love"(translated by Eastwick and by others); and the sensuous *Gita-Govinda* of the Bengalese lyric poet Jayadeva (translated into French prose by Hippolyte Fauche, and chastely rendered into English verse by Edwin Arnold in the "Indian Song of Songs"). See also Burnouf's partial translation of the *Bhagavata Purana*, and Théodore Pavie's "Kriçhna et sa doctrine." . . . The same theme has inspired some of the strangest productions of Hindoo art: for examples, see plates 65 and 66 of Moor's "Hindoo Pantheon"(edition of 1861). For accounts of the erotic mysticism connected with the worship of Krishna and the Gopia, the reader may also be referred to authorities cited in Barth's "Religions of India;" De Tassy's "Chants populaires de l'Inde;" and Lamairesse's "Poésies populaires du Sud de l'Inde."

HAO-KHIEOU-TCHOUAN.—This celebrated Chinese novel was translated into French by M. Guillard d'Arcy in 1842, and appeared under the title, "Hao-Khieou-Tchouan; ou, La Femme Accomplie." The first translation of the romance into any European tongue was a Portuguese rendering; and the English version of Percy is based upon the Portuguese text. The work is rich in poetical quotations.

HEÏ-SONG-CHÉ-TCHOO.—"One day when the Emperor Hiuan-tsong of the Thang dynasty," says the *Tao-kia-ping-yu-che*, "was at work in his study, a tiny Taoist priest, no bigger than a fly, rose out of the inkstand lying upon his table, and said to him: 'I am the Genius of Ink; my name is Heï-song-ché-tchoo [*Envoy of the Black Fir*]; and I have come to tell you that whenever a true sage shall sit down to write, the Twelve Divinities of Ink [*Long-pinn*] will appear upon the surface of the ink he uses.'" See "L'Encre de Chine," by Maurice Jametel. Paris, 1882.

HOA-TCHAO. The "Birthday of a Hundred Flowers" falls upon the fifteenth of the second spring-moon.

JADE.—Jade, or nephrite, a variety of jasper,—called by the Chinese *yuh*,—has always been highly valued by them as artistic material. . . . In the "Book of Rewards and Punishments," there is a curious legend to the effect that Confucius, after the completion of his *Hiao-King* ("Book of Filial Piety"), having addressed himself to Heaven, a crimson rainbow fell from the sky, and changed itself at his feet into a piece of yellow jade. See Stanislas Julien's translation, p. 495.

KABIT.—A poetical form much in favor with composers of Hindoo religious chants: the *kabit* always consists of four verses.

KAO-LING.—Literally, "the High Ridge," and originally the name of a hilly range which furnished the best quality of clay to the porcelain-makers. Subsequently the term applied by long custom to designate the material itself became corrupted into the word now familiar in all countries,—kaolin. In the language of the Chinese potters, the *kaolin*, or clay, was poetically termed the "bones," and the *tun*, or quartz, the "flesh" of the porcelain; while the prepared bricks of the combined substances were known as *pe-tun-tse*. Both substances, the infusible and the fusible, are productions of the same geological formation,—decomposed feldspathic rock.

KASÍ (*or* VARANASI).—Ancient name of Benares, the "Sacred City," believed to have been founded by the gods. It is also called "The Lotos of the World." Barth terms it "the Jerusalem of all the sects both of ancient and modern India." It still boasts two thousand shrines, and half a million images of divinities. See also Sherring's "Sacred City of the Hindoos."

KIANG-KOU-JIN.—Literally, the "tell-old-story-men." For a brief account of Chinese professional storytellers, the reader may consult Schlegel's entertaining introduction to the *Mai-yu-lang-toú-tchen-hoa-koueï*.

KIN.—The most perfect of Chinese musical instruments, also called "the Scholar's Lute." The word *kin* also means "to prohibit;" and this name is said to have been given to the instrument because music, according to Chinese belief, "*restrains evil passions, and corrects the human heart.*" See Williams's "Middle Kingdom."

KOUEI.—Kouei, musician to the Emperor Yao, must have held his office between 2357 and 2277 B.C. The extract selected from one of his songs, which I have given at the beginning of the "Story of Ming-Y," is therefore more than four thousand years old. The same chant contains another remarkable fancy, evidencing Chinese faith in musical magic:—

> "When I smite my [*musical*] stone,—
>   Be it gently, be it strongly,—
>   Then do the fiercest beasts of prey leap high for joy,
>   And the chiefs among the public officials do agree among
>   themselves."

KWANG-CHAU-FU.—Literally, "The Broad City,"—the name of Canton. It is also called "The City of Genii."

LÍ.—A measure of distance. The length of the *lí* has varied considerably in ancient and in modern times. The present is given by Williams as ten *lí* to a league.

LI-SAO.—"The Dissipation of Grief," one of the most celebrated Chinese poems of the classic period. It is said to have been written about 314 B.C., by Kiu-ping-youen, minister to the King of Tsou. Finding himself the victim of a base court-intrigue, Kin-ping wrote the *Li-Sao* as a vindication of his character, and as a rebuke to the malice of his enemies, after which he committed suicide by drowning. . . . A fine French translation of the *Li-Sao* has been made by the Marquis Hervey de Saint-Denys (Paris, 1870).

LI-SHU.—The second of the six styles of Chinese writing, for an account of which see Williams's "Middle Kingdom." . . . According to various Taoist legends, the decrees of Heaven are recorded in the "Seal-character," the oldest of all; and marks upon the bodies of persons killed by lightning have been interpreted as judgments written in it. The following extraordinary tale from the *Kan-ing-p'ien* affords a good example of the superstition in question:—

Tchang-tchun was Minister of State under the reign of Hoeï-tsong, of the Song dynasty. He occupied himself wholly in weaving perfidious plots. He died in exile at Mo-tcheou. Some time after, while the Emperor was hunting, there fell a heavy rain, which obliged him to seek shelter in a poor man's hut. The thunder rolled with violence; and the lightning killed a man, a woman, and a little boy. On the backs of the man and woman were found red characters, which could not be deciphered; but on the back of the little boy the following six words could be read, written in Tchouen (*antique*) characters: TSÉ-TCH'IN-TCHANG-TCHUN-HEOU-CHIN,—which mean: "Child of the issue of Tchang-tchun, who was a rebellious subject."—*Le Livre des Récompenses et des Peines, traduit par Stanislas Julien*, p. 446.

PAGAL.—The ankle-ring commonly worn by Hindoo women; it is also called *nupur*. It is hollow, and contains loose bits of metal, which tinkle when the foot is moved.

SAN-HIEN.—A three-stringed Chinese guitar. Its belly is usually covered with snake-skin.

SIU-FAN-TI.—Literally, "the Sweeping of the Tombs."—the day of the general worship of ancestors; the Chinese "All-Souls'." It falls in the early part of April, the period called *tsing-ming*.

TA-CHUNG SZ'.—Literally, "Temple of the Bell." The building at Pekin so named covers probably the largest suspended bell in the world, cast in the reign of Yong-lo, about 1406 A.D., and weighing upwards of 120,000 pounds.

TAO.—The infinite being, or Universal Life, whence all forms proceed: Literally, "the Way," in the sense of the First Cause. Lao-tseu uses the term in other ways; but that primal and most important philosophical sense which he gave to it is well explained in the celebrated Chapter XXV. of the *Tao-te-king*. . . . The difference between the great Chinese thinker's conception of the First Cause, —the Unknowable,—and the theories of other famous metaphysicians, Oriental and Occidental, is set forth with some definiteness in Stanislas Julien's introduction to the *Tao-te-king*, pp. x–xv. ("Le Livre de la Voie et de la Vertu." Paris, 1842.)

THANG.—The Dynasty of Thang, which flourished between 620 and 907 A.D., encouraged literature and art, and gave to China its most brilliant period. The three poets of the Thang dynasty mentioned in the second story flourished between 779 and 852 A.D.

"THREE COUNCILLORS."—Six stars of the Great-Bear constellation (ικ—λμ—νξ), as apparently arranged in pairs, are thus called by the Chinese astrologers and mythologists. The three couples are further distinguished as the Superior Councillor, Middle Councillor, and Inferior Councillor; and, together with the Genius of the Northern Heaven, form a celestial tribunal, presiding over the duration of human life, and deciding the course of mortal destiny. (Note by Stanislas Julien in "Le Livre des Récompenses et des Peines.")

TIEN-HIA.—Literally, "Under-Heaven," or "Beneath-the-Sky,"— one of the most ancient of those many names given by the Chinese to China. The name "China" itself is never applied by the Black-haired Race to their own country, and is supposed to have had its origin in the fame of the first *Tsin* dynasty, whose founder Tsin Chí-Houang-tí, built the Great, or "Myriad-Mile," Wall, twenty-two and a half degrees of latitude in length. . . . See Williams regarding occurrence of the name "China" in Sanscrit literature.

TSIEN.—The well-known Chinese copper coin, with a square hole in the middle for stringing, is thus named. According to quality of metal it takes from 900 to 1,800 *tsien* to make one silver dollar.

TSING-JIN.—"Men of Tsing." From very ancient times the Chinese have been wont to call themselves by the names of their famous dynasties,—*Han-jin*, "the men of Han;" *Thang-jin*, "the men of Thang," etc. *Ta Tsing Kwoh* ("Great Pure Kingdom") is the name given by the present dynasty to China,—according to which the people might call themselves *Tsing-jin*, or "men of Tsing." Williams, however, remarks that they will not yet accept the appellation.

VERSES (CHINESE).—The verses preceding "The Legend of Tchi-Niu" afford some remarkable examples of Chinese onomatopœia. They occur in the sixth strophe of *Miên-miên*, which is the third chant of the first section of *Ta-ya*, the Third Book of the *Chi-King*.

(See G. Pauthier's French version.) Dr. Legge translates the strophe thus:—

> . . . Crowds brought the earth in baskets; they threw it with shouts into the frames; they beat it with responsive blows; they pared the walls repeatedly till they sounded strong.—*Sacred Books of the East;* Vol. III., *The She-King*, p. 384.

Pauthier translates the verses somewhat differently; preserving the onomatopœia in three of the lines. *Hoúng-hoúng* are the sounds heard in the timber-yards where the wood is being measured; from the workshops of the builders respond the sounds of *tông-tông*; and the solid walls, when fully finished off, give out the sound of *píng-píng*.

YAO.—"Porcelain." The reader who desires detailed information respecting the technology, history, or legends of Chinese porcelain-manufacture, should consult Stanislas Julien's admirable "Histoire de la Porcelaine Chinoise" (Paris, 1856). With some trifling exceptions, the names of the various porcelains cited in my "Tale of the Porcelain-God" were selected from Julien's work. Though oddly musical and otherwise attractive in Chinese, these names lose interest by translation. The majority of them merely refer to centres of manufacture or famous potteries: *Chou-yao*, "porcelains of Chou;" *Hong-tcheou-yao*, "porcelains of Hong-tcheou;" *Jou-yao*, "porcelains of Jou-tcheou;" *Ting-yao*, "porcelains of Ting-tcheou;" *Ko-yao*, "porcelains of the Elder Brother [Thsang];" *Khang-hi-nien-t'sang-yao*, "porcelains of Thsang made in the reign of Khang-hi." Some porcelains were distinguished by the names of dynasties, or the titles of civic office holders; such as the celebrated *Tch'aï-yoa*, "the porcelains of Tch'aï" (which was the name of the family of the Emperor Chi-tsong); and the *Kouan-yao*, or "Porcelains of Magistrates." Much more rarely the names refer directly to the material or artistic peculiarity of porcelains,—as *Ou-ni-yao*, the "black-paste porcelains," or *Pi-se-yao*, the "porcelains of hidden color." The word *khi*, sometimes substituted for *yao* in these compound names, means "vases;" as *Jou-khi*, "vases of Jou-tcheou;" *Kouan-khi*, "vases for Magistrates."

CHITA:

A MEMORY OF LAST ISLAND

"But Nature whistled with all her winds,
Did as she pleased, and went her way."
—EMERSON

To my friend

DR. RODOLFO MATAS

OF

NEW ORLEANS

CONTENTS

Je suis la vaste mêlée,—
Reptile, étant l'onde; ailée,
Étant le vent,—
Force et fuite, haine et vie,
Houle immense, poursuivie
Et poursuivant.
—Victor Hugo

PART I

The Legend of L'Île Dernière

TRAVELLING south from New Orleans to the Islands, you pass through a strange land into a strange sea, by various winding waterways. You can journey to the Gulf by lugger if you please; but the trip may be made much more rapidly and agreeably on some one of those light, narrow steamers, built especially for bayou-travel, which usually receive passengers at a point not far from the foot of old Saint-Louis Street, hard by the sugar-landing, where there is ever a pushing and flocking of steam-craft—all striving for place to rest their white breasts against the levée, side by side,—like great weary swans. But the miniature steamboat on which you engage passage to the Gulf never lingers long in the Mississippi: she crosses the river, slips into some canal-mouth, labors along the artificial channel awhile, and then leaves it with a scream of joy, to puff her free way down many a league of heavily shadowed bayou. Perhaps thereafter she may bear you through the immense silence of drenched rice-fields, where the yellow-green level is broken at long intervals by the black silhouette of some irrigating machine;—but, whichever of the five different routes be pursued, you will find yourself more than once floating through sombre mazes of swamp-forest,—past assemblages of cypresses all hoary with the parasitic tillandsia, and grotesque as gatherings of fetich-gods. Ever from river or from lakelet the steamer glides again into canal or bayou,—from bayou or canal once more into lake or bay; and sometimes the swamp-forest visibly thins away from these shores into wastes of reedy morass where, even of breathless nights, the quaggy soil trembles to a sound like thunder of breakers on a coast: the storm-roar of billions of reptile voices chanting in cadence,—rhythmically surging in stupendous *crescendo* and *diminuendo*,—a monstrous and appalling chorus of frogs! . . . .

Panting, screaming, scraping her bottom over the sand-bars, —all day the little steamer strives to reach the grand blaze of blue open water below the marsh-lands; and perhaps she may be fortunate enough to enter the Gulf about the time of sunset. For the sake of passengers, she travels by day only; but there are other vessels which make the journey also by night—threading the bayou-labyrinths winter and summer: sometimes steering by the North Star,—sometimes feeling the way with poles in the white season of fogs,—sometimes, again, steering by that Star of Evening which in our sky glows like another moon, and drops over the silent lakes as she passes a quivering trail of silver fire.

Shadows lengthen; and at last the woods dwindle away behind you into thin bluish lines;—land and water alike take more luminous color;—bayous open into broad passes;—lakes link themselves with sea-bays;—and the ocean-wind bursts upon you,—keen, cool, and full of light. For the first time the vessel begins to swing,—rocking to the great living pulse of the tides. And gazing from the deck around you, with no forest walls to break the view, it will seem to you that the low land must have once been rent asunder by the sea, and strewn about the Gulf in fantastic tatters. . . .

Sometimes above a waste of wind-blown prairie-cane you see an oasis emerging,—a ridge or hillock heavily umbraged with the rounded foliage of evergreen oaks:—a *chénière*. And from the shining flood also kindred green knolls arise,—pretty islets, each with its beach-girdle of dazzling sand and shells, yellow-white,—and all radiant with semi-tropical foliage, myrtle and palmetto, orange and magnolia. Under their emerald shadows curious little villages of palmetto huts are drowsing, where dwell a swarthy population of Orientals,—Malay fishermen, who speak the Spanish-Creole of the Philippines as well as their own Tagal, and perpetuate in Louisiana the Catholic traditions of the Indies. There are girls in those unfamiliar villages worthy to inspire any statuary,—beautiful with the beauty of ruddy bronze,—gracile as the palmettoes that sway above them. . . . Further seaward you may also pass a Chinese settlement: some queer camp of wooden dwellings clustering around a vast platform that stands above the water upon a thousand piles;—over the miniature wharf you can scarcely fail to observe a white sign-board painted with crimson ideographs. The great platform is used for drying fish in the sun;

and the fantastic characters of the sign, literally translated, mean: "*Heap—Shrimp—Plenty.*" . . . And finally all the land melts down into desolations of sea-marsh, whose stillness is seldom broken, except by the melancholy cry of long-legged birds, and in wild seasons by that sound which shakes all shores when the weird Musician of the Sea touches the bass keys of his mighty organ. . . .

II.

Beyond the sea-marshes a curious archipelago lies. If you travel by steamer to the sea-islands to-day, you are tolerably certain to enter the Gulf by Grande Pass—skirting Grande Terre, the most familiar island of all, not so much because of its proximity as because of its great crumbling fort and its graceful pharos: the stationary White-Light of Barataria. Otherwise the place is bleakly uninteresting: a wilderness of wind-swept grasses and sinewy weeds waving away from a thin beach ever speckled with drift and decaying things,—worm-riddled timbers, dead porpoises. Eastward the russet level is broken by the columnar silhouette of the light-house, and again, beyond it, by some puny scrub timber, above which rises the angular ruddy mass of the old brick fort, whose ditches swarm with crabs, and whose sluiceways are half choked by obsolete cannon-shot, now thickly covered with incrustation of oyster shells. . . . Around all the gray circling of a shark-haunted sea. . . .

Sometimes of autumn evenings there, when the hollow of heaven flames like the interior of a chalice, and waves and clouds are flying in one wild rout of broken gold,—you may see the tawny grasses all covered with something like husks,—wheat-colored husks,—large, flat, and disposed evenly along the lee-side of each swaying stalk, so as to present only their edges to the wind. But, if you approach, those pale husks all break open to display strange splendors of scarlet and seal-brown, with arabesque mottlings in white and black: they change into wondrous living blossoms, which detach themselves before your eyes and rise in air, and flutter away by thousands to settle down farther off, and turn into wheat-colored husks once more . . . a whirling flower-drift of sleepy butterflies!

*

Southwest, across the pass, gleams beautiful Grande Isle: primitively a wilderness of palmetto (*latanier*);—then drained, diked, and cultivated by Spanish sugar-planters; and now familiar chiefly as a bathing-resort. Since the war the ocean reclaimed its own;—the cane-fields have degenerated into sandy plains, over which tramways wind to the smooth beach;—the plantation-residences have been converted into rustic hotels, and the negro-quarters remodelled into villages of cozy cottages for the reception of guests. But with its imposing groves of oak, its golden wealth of orange-trees, its odorous lanes of oleander, its broad grazing-meadows yellow-starred with wild camomile, Grande Isle remains the prettiest island of the Gulf; and its loveliness is exceptional. For the bleakness of Grand Terre is reiterated by most of the other islands,—Caillou, Cassetête, Calumet, Wine Island, the twin Timbaliers, Gull Island, and the many islets haunted by the gray pelican,—all of which are little more than sand-bars covered with wiry grasses, prairie-cane, and scrub-timber. Last Island (*L'Île Dernière*),— well worthy a long visit in other years, in spite of its remoteness, is now a ghastly desolation twenty-five miles long. Lying nearly forty miles west of Grande Isle, it was nevertheless far more populated a generation ago: it was not only the most celebrated island of the group, but also the most fashionable watering-place of the aristocratic South;—to-day it is visited by fishermen only, at long intervals. Its admirable beach in many respects resembled that of Grande Isle to-day; the accommodations also were much similar, although finer: a charming village of cottages facing the Gulf near the western end. The hotel itself was a massive two-story construction of timber, containing many apartments, together with a large dining-room and dancing-hall. In rear of the hotel was a bayou, where passengers landed—"Village Bayou" it is still called by seamen;—but the deep channel which now cuts the island in two a little eastwardly did not exist while the village remained. The sea tore it out in one night—the same night when trees, fields, dwellings, all vanished into the Gulf, leaving no vestige of former human habitation except a few of those strong brick props and foundations upon which the frame houses and cisterns had been raised. One living creature was found there after the cataclysm—a cow! But how that solitary cow survived the fury of a storm-flood that actually rent the island in twain has ever remained a mystery. . . .

III.

On the Gulf side of these islands you may observe that the trees—when there are any trees—all bend away from the sea; and, even of bright, hot days when the wind sleeps, there is something grotesquely pathetic in their look of agonized terror. A group of oaks at Grande Isle I remember as especially suggestive: five stooping silhouettes in line against the horizon, like fleeing women with streaming garments and wind-blown hair,—bowing grievously and thrusting out arms desperately northward as to save themselves from falling. And they are being pursued indeed;—for the sea is devouring the land. Many and many a mile of ground has yielded to the tireless charging of Ocean's cavalry: far out you can see, through a good glass, the porpoises at play where of old the sugar-cane shook out its million bannerets; and shark-fins now seam deep water above a site where pigeons used to coo. Men build dikes; but the besieging tides bring up their battering-rams— whole forests of drift—huge trunks of water-oak and weighty cypress. Forever the yellow Mississippi strives to build; forever the sea struggles to destroy;—and amid their eternal strife the islands and the promontories change shape, more slowly, but not less fantastically, than the clouds of heaven.

And worthy of study are those wan battle-grounds where the woods made their last brave stand against the irresistible invasion,—usually at some long point of sea-marsh, widely fringed with billowing sand. Just where the waves curl beyond such a point you may discern a multitude of blackened, snaggy shapes protruding above the water,—some high enough to resemble ruined chimneys, others bearing a startling likeness to enormous skeleton-feet and skeleton-hands,—with crustaceous white growths clinging to them here and there like remnants of integument. These are bodies and limbs of drowned oaks,—so long drowned that the shell-scurf is inch-thick upon parts of them. Farther in upon the beach immense trunks lie overthrown. Some look like vast broken columns; some suggest colossal torsos imbedded, and seem to reach out mutilated stumps in despair from their deepening graves;—and beside these are others which have kept their feet with astounding obstinacy, although the barbarian tides have been charging them for twenty years, and gradually torn away the soil above and beneath their roots. The sand around,—soft beneath and thinly crusted upon the surface,—is everywhere pierced with holes made by a beautifully mottled and semi-diaphanous crab, with hairy legs, big staring eyes, and milk-white claws;— while in the green sedges beyond there is a perpetual rustling, as of some strong wind beating among reeds: a marvellous creeping of "fiddlers," which the inexperienced visitor might at first mistake for so many peculiar beetles, as they run about sideways, each with his huge single claw folded upon his body like a wing-case. Year by year that rustling strip of green land grows narrower; the sand spreads and sinks, shuddering and wrinkling like a living brown skin; and the last standing corpses of the oaks, ever clinging with naked, dead feet to the sliding beach, lean more and more out of the perpendicular. As the sands subside, the stumps appear to creep; their inter-twisted masses of snakish roots seem to crawl, to writhe,—like the reaching arms of cephalopods. . . .

    . . . Grande Terre is going: the sea mines her fort, and will before many years carry the ramparts by storm. Grande Isle is going,—slowly but surely: the Gulf has eaten three miles into her meadowed land. Last Island has gone! How it went I first heard from the lips of a veteran pilot, while we sat one evening together on the trunk of a drifted cypress which some high tide had pressed deeply into the Grande Isle beach. The day had been tropically warm; we had sought the shore for a breath of living air. Sunset came, and with it the ponderous heat lifted,—a sudden breeze blew,—lightnings flickered in the darkening horizon,—wind and water began to strive together, —and soon all the low coast boomed. Then my companion began his story; perhaps the coming of the storm inspired him to speak! And as I listened to him, listening also to the clamoring of the coast, there flashed back to me recollection of a singular Breton fancy: that the Voice of the Sea is never one voice, but a tumult of many voices—voices of drowned men,—the mut-tering of multitudinous dead,—the moaning of innumerable ghosts, all rising, to rage against the living, at the great Witch-call of storms. . . .

IV.

The charm of a single summer day on these island shores is something impossible to express, never to be forgotten. Rarely, in the paler zones, do earth and heaven take such luminosity: those will best understand me who have seen the splendor of a West Indian sky. And yet there is a tenderness of tint, a caress of color, in these Gulf-days which is not of the Antilles,—a spirituality, as of eternal tropical spring. It must have been to even such a sky that Xenophanes lifted up his eyes of old when he vowed the Infinite Blue was God;—it was indeed under such a sky that De Soto named the vastest and grandest of Southern havens Espiritu Santo,—the Bay of the Holy Ghost. There is a something unutterable in this bright Gulf-air that compels awe,—something vital, something holy, something pantheistic: and reverentially the mind asks itself if what the eye beholds is not the Πνεῦμα indeed, the Infinite Breath, the Divine Ghost, the great Blue Soul of the Unknown. All, all is blue in the calm,—save the low land under your feet, which you almost forget, since it seems only as a tiny green flake afloat in the liquid eternity of day. Then slowly, caressingly, irresistibly, the witchery of the Infinite grows upon you: out of Time and Space you begin to dream with open eyes,—to drift into delicious oblivion of facts,—to forget the past, the present, the substantial,—to comprehend nothing but the existence of that infinite Blue Ghost as something into which you would wish to melt utterly away forever. . . .

And this day-magic of azure endures sometimes for months together. Cloudlessly the dawn reddens up through a violet east: there is no speck upon the blossoming of its Mystical Rose, —unless it be the silhouette of some passing gull, whirling his sickle-wings against the crimsoning. Ever, as the sun floats higher, the flood shifts its color. Sometimes smooth and gray, yet flickering with the morning gold, it is the vision of John,— the apocalyptic Sea of Glass mixed with fire;—again, with the growing breeze, it takes that incredible purple tint familiar mostly to painters of West Indian scenery;—once more, under the blaze of noon, it changes to a waste of broken emerald. With evening, the horizon assumes tints of inexpressible sweetness,—pearl-lights, opaline colors of milk and fire; and in the west are topaz-glowings and wondrous flushings as of nacre. Then, if the sea sleeps, it dreams of all these,—faintly, weirdly,—shadowing them even to the verge of heaven.

Beautiful, too, are those white phantasmagoria which, at the approach of equinoctial days, mark the coming of the winds. Over the rim of the sea a bright cloud gently pushes up its head. It rises; and others rise with it, to right and left—slowly at first; then more swiftly. All are brilliantly white and flocculent, like loose new cotton. Gradually they mount in enormous line high above the Gulf, rolling and wreathing into an arch that expands and advances,—bending from horizon to horizon. A clear, cold breath accompanies its coming. Reaching the zenith, it seems there to hang poised awhile,—a ghostly bridge arching the empyrean,—upreaching its measureless span from either underside of the world. Then the colossal phantom begins to turn, as on a pivot of air,—always preserving its curvilinear symmetry, but moving its unseen ends beyond and below the sky-circle. And at last it floats away unbroken beyond the blue sweep of the world, with a wind following after. Day after day, almost at the same hour, the white arc rises, wheels, and passes. . . .

. . . Never a glimpse of rock on these low shores;—only long sloping beaches and bars of smooth tawny sand. Sand and sea teem with vitality;—over all the dunes there is a constant susurration, a blattering and swarming of crustacea;—through all the sea there is a ceaseless play of silver lightning,—flashing of myriad fish. Sometimes the shallows are thickened with minute, transparent, crab-like organisms,—all colorless as gelatine. There are days also when countless medusæ drift in —beautiful veined creatures that throb like hearts, with perpetual systole and diastole of their diaphanous envelops: some, of translucent azure or rose, seem in the flood the shadows or ghosts of huge campanulate flowers;—others have the semblance of strange living vegetables,—great milky tubers, just beginning to sprout. But woe to the human skin grazed by those shadowy sproutings and spectral stamens!—the touch of glowing iron is not more painful. . . . Within an hour or two after their appearance all these tremulous jellies vanish mysteriously as they came.

Perhaps, if a bold swimmer, you may venture out alone a long way—once! Not twice!—even in company. As the water deepens beneath you, and you feel those ascending wave-currents of coldness arising which bespeak profundity, you will also begin to feel innumerable touches, as of groping fingers—touches of the bodies of fish, innumerable fish, fleeing towards shore. The farther you advance, the more thickly you will feel them come; and above you and around you, to right and left, others will leap and fall so swiftly as to daze the sight, like intercrossing fountain-jets of fluid silver. The gulls fly lower about you, circling with sinister squeaking cries;—perhaps for an instant your feet touch in the deep something heavy, swift, lithe, that rushes past with a swirling shock. Then the fear of the Abyss, the vast and voiceless Nightmare of the Sea, will come upon you; the silent panic of all those opaline millions that flee glimmering by will enter into you also. . . .

From what do they flee thus perpetually? Is it from the giant sawfish or the ravening shark?—from the herds of the porpoises, or from the *grande-écaille*,—that splendid monster whom no net may hold,—all helmed and armored in argent plate-mail?—or from the hideous devil-fish of the Gulf,—gigantic, flat-bodied, black, with immense side-fins ever outspread like the pinions of a bat,—the terror of luggermen, the uprooter of anchors? From all these, perhaps, and from other monsters likewise—goblin shapes evolved by Nature as destroyers, as equilibrists, as counterchecks to that prodigious fecundity, which, unhindered, would thicken the deep into one measureless and waveless ferment of being. . . . But when there are many bathers these perils are forgotten,—numbers give courage,—one can abandon one's self, without fear of the invisible, to the long, quivering, electrical caresses of the sea. . . .

V.

Thirty years ago, Last Island lay steeped in the enormous light of even such magical days. July was dying;—for weeks no fleck of cloud had broken the heaven's blue dream of eternity;

winds held their breath; slow wavelets caressed the bland brown beach with a sound as of kisses and whispers. To one who found himself alone, beyond the limits of the village and beyond the hearing of its voices,—the vast silence, the vast light, seemed full of weirdness. And these hushes, these transparencies, do not always inspire a causeless apprehension: they are omens sometimes—omens of coming tempest. Nature,—incomprehensible Sphinx!—before her mightiest bursts of rage, ever puts forth her divinest witchery, makes more manifest her awful beauty. . . .

But in that forgotten summer the witchery lasted many long days,—days born in rose-light, buried in gold. It was the height of the season. The long myrtle-shadowed village was thronged with its summer population;—the big hotel could hardly accommodate all its guests;—the bathing-houses were too few for the crowds who flocked to the water morning and evening. There were diversions for all,—hunting and fishing parties, yachting excursions, rides, music, games, promenades. Carriage wheels whirled flickering along the beach, seaming its smoothness noiselessly, as if muffled. Love wrote its dreams upon the sand. . . .

. . . Then one great noon, when the blue abyss of day seemed to yawn over the world more deeply than ever before, a sudden change touched the quicksilver smoothness of the waters—the swaying shadow of a vast motion. First the whole sea-circle appeared to rise up bodily at the sky; the horizon-curve lifted to a straight line; the line darkened and approached,—a monstrous wrinkle, an immeasurable fold of green water, moving swift as a cloud-shadow pursued by sunlight. But it had looked formidable only by startling contrast with the previous placidity of the open: it was scarcely two feet high;—it curled slowly as it neared the beach, and combed itself out in sheets of woolly foam with a low, rich roll of whispered thunder. Swift in pursuit another followed—a third—a feebler fourth; then the sea only swayed a little, and stilled again. Minutes passed, and the immeasurable heaving recommenced—one, two, three, four . . . seven long swells this time;—and the Gulf smoothed itself once more. Irregularly the phenomenon continued to repeat itself, each time with heavier billowing and briefer intervals of quiet—until at last the whole sea grew restless and shifted color and flickered green;—the swells became shorter and changed form. Then from horizon to shore ran one uninterrupted heaving—one vast green swarming of snaky shapes, rolling in to hiss and flatten upon the sand. Yet no single cirrus-speck revealed itself through all the violet heights: there was no wind!—you might have fancied the sea had been upheaved from beneath. . . .

And indeed the fancy of a seismic origin for a windless surge would not appear in these latitudes to be utterly without foundation. On the fairest days a southeast breeze may bear you an odor singular enough to startle you from sleep,—a strong, sharp smell as of fish-oil; and gazing at the sea you might be still more startled at the sudden apparition of great oleaginous patches spreading over the water, sheeting over the swells. That is, if you had never heard of the mysterious submarine oil-wells, the volcanic fountains, unexplored, that well up with the eternal pulsing of the Gulf-Stream. . . .

But the pleasure-seekers of Last Island knew there must have been a "great blow" somewhere that day. Still the sea swelled; and a splendid surf made the evening bath delightful. Then, just at sundown, a beautiful cloud-bridge grew up and arched the sky with a single span of cottony pink vapor, that changed and deepened color with the dying of the iridescent day. And the cloud-bridge approached, stretched, strained, and swung round at last to make way for the coming of the gale,— even as the light bridges that traverse the dreamy Têche swing open when luggermen sound through their conch-shells the long, bellowing signal of approach.

Then the wind began to blow, with the passing of July. It blew from the northeast, clear, cool. It blew in enormous sighs, dying away at regular intervals, as if pausing to draw breath. All night it blew; and in each pause could be heard the answering moan of the rising surf,—as if the rhythm of the sea moulded itself after the rhythm of the air,—as if the waving of the water responded precisely to the waving of the wind,—a billow for every puff, a surge for every sigh.

The August morning broke in a bright sky;—the breeze still came cool and clear from the northeast. The waves were running now at a sharp angle to the shore: they began to carry fleeces, an innumerable flock of vague green shapes, wind-driven to be despoiled of their ghostly wool. Far as the eye could follow the line of the beach, all the slope was white with the great shearing of them. Clouds came, flew as in a panic against the face of the sun, and passed. All that day and through the night and into the morning again the breeze continued from the northeast, blowing like an equinoctial gale. . . .

Then day by day the vast breath freshened steadily, and the waters heightened. A week later sea-bathing had become perilous: colossal breakers were herding in, like moving leviathan-backs, twice the height of a man. Still the gale grew, and the billowing waxed mightier, and faster and faster overhead flew the tatters of torn cloud. The gray morning of the 9th wanly lighted a surf that appalled the best swimmers: the sea was one wild agony of foam, the gale was rending off the heads of the waves and veiling the horizon with a fog of salt spray. Shadowless and gray the day remained; there were mad bursts of lashing rain. Evening brought with it a sinister apparition, looming through a cloud-rent in the west—a scarlet sun in a green sky. His sanguine disk, enormously magnified, seemed barred like the body of a belted planet. A moment, and the crimson spectre vanished; and the moonless night came.

Then the Wind grew weird. It ceased being a breath; it became a Voice moaning across the world,—hooting,—uttering nightmare sounds,—*Whoo!—whoo!—whoo!*—and with each stupendous owl-cry the mooing of the waters seemed to deepen, more and more abysmally, through all the hours of darkness. From the northwest the breakers of the bay began to roll high over the sandy slope, into the salines;—the village bayou broadened to a bellowing flood. . . . So the tumult swelled and the turmoil heightened until morning,—a morning of gray gloom and whistling rain. Rain of bursting clouds and rain of wind-blown brine from the great spuming agony of the sea.

The steamer *Star* was due from St. Mary's that fearful morning. Could she come? No one really believed it,—no one. And nevertheless men struggled to the roaring beach to look for her, because hope is stronger than reason. . . .

Even to-day, in these Creole islands, the advent of the steamer is the great event of the week. There are no telegraph lines, no telephones: the mail-packet is the only trustworthy medium of communication with the outer world, bringing

friends, news, letters. The magic of steam has placed New
Orleans nearer to New York than to the Timbaliers, nearer to
Washington than to Wine Island, nearer to Chicago than to
Barataria Bay. And even during the deepest sleep of waves and
winds there will come betimes to sojourners in this unfamiliar
archipelago a feeling of lonesomeness that is a fear, a feeling of
isolation from the world of men,—totally unlike that sense of
solitude which haunts one in the silence of mountain-heights,
or amid the eternal tumult of lofty granitic coasts: a sense of
helpless insecurity. The land seems but an undulation of the
sea-bed: its highest ridges do not rise more than the height of
a man above the salines on either side;—the salines themselves
lie almost level with the level of the flood-tides;—the tides are
variable, treacherous, mysterious. But when all around and
above these ever-changing shores the twin vastnesses of heaven
and sea begin to utter the tremendous revelation of themselves
as infinite forces in contention, then indeed this sense of separation from humanity appals. . . . Perhaps it was such a feeling
which forced men, on the tenth day of August, eighteen hundred and fifty-six, to hope against hope for the coming of
the *Star*, and to strain their eyes towards far-off Terrebonne.
"It was a wind you could lie down on," said my friend the
pilot.
    . . . "Great God!" shrieked a voice above the shouting of
the storm,—"*she is coming!*" . . . It was true. Down the
Atchafalaya, and thence through strange mazes of bayou,
lakelet, and pass, by a rear route familiar only to the best of
pilots, the frail river-craft had toiled into Caillou Bay, running
close to the main shore;—and now she was heading right for
the island, with the wind aft, over the monstrous sea. On she
came swaying, rocking, plunging,—with a great whiteness wrapping her about like a cloud, and moving with her moving,—a
tempest-whirl of spray;—ghost-white and like a ghost she
came, for her smoke-stacks exhaled no visible smoke—the wind
devoured it! The excitement on shore became wild;—men
shouted themselves hoarse; women laughed and cried. Every
telescope and opera-glass was directed upon the coming apparition; all wondered how the pilot kept his feet; all marvelled
at the madness of the captain.
But Captain Abraham Smith was not mad. A veteran

American sailor, he had learned to know the great Gulf as scholars know deep books by heart: he knew the birthplace of its tempests, the mystery of its tides, the omens of its hurricanes. While lying at Brashear City he felt the storm had not yet reached its highest, vaguely foresaw a mighty peril, and resolved to wait no longer for a lull. "Boys," he said, "we've got to take her out in spite of Hell!" And they "took her out." Through all the peril, his men stayed by him and obeyed him. By midmorning the wind had deepened to a roar,—lowering sometimes to a rumble, sometimes bursting upon the ears like a measureless and deafening crash. Then the captain knew the *Star* was running a race with Death. "She'll win it," he muttered;—"she'll stand it. . . . Perhaps they'll have need of me to-night."

She won! With a sonorous steam-chant of triumph the brave little vessel rode at last into the bayou, and anchored hard by her accustomed resting-place, in full view of the hotel, though not near enough to shore to lower her gang-plank. . . . But she had sung her swan-song. Gathering in from the northeast, the waters of the bay were already marbling over the salines and half across the island; and still the wind increased its paroxysmal power.

Cottages began to rock. Some slid away from the solid props upon which they rested. A chimney tumbled. Shutters were wrenched off; verandas demolished. Light roofs lifted, dropped again, and flapped into ruin. Trees bent their heads to the earth. And still the storm grew louder and blacker with every passing hour.

The *Star* rose with the rising of the waters, dragging her anchor. Two more anchors were put out, and still she dragged— dragged in with the flood,—twisting, shuddering, careening in her agony. Evening fell; the sand began to move with the wind, stinging faces like a continuous fire of fine shot; and frenzied blasts came to buffet the steamer forward, sideward. Then one of her hog-chains parted with a clang like the boom of a big bell. Then another! . . . Then the captain bade his men to cut away all her upper works, clean to the deck. Overboard into the seething went her stacks, her pilot-house, her cabins,—and whirled away. And the naked hull of the *Star*, still dragging her three anchors, labored on through the darkness, nearer and nearer to the immense silhouette of the hotel, whose hundred windows were now all aflame. The vast timber building seemed to defy the storm. The wind, roaring round its broad verandas,—hissing through every crevice with the sound and force of steam,—appeared to waste its rage. And in the half-lull between two terrible gusts there came to the captain's ears a sound that seemed strange in that night of multitudinous terrors . . . a sound of music!

VI.

. . . Almost every evening throughout the season there had been dancing in the great hall;—there was dancing that night also. The population of the hotel had been augmented by the advent of families from other parts of the island, who found their summer cottages insecure places of shelter: there were nearly four hundred guests assembled. Perhaps it was for this reason that the entertainment had been prepared upon a grander plan than usual, that it assumed the form of a fashionable ball. And all those pleasure-seekers,—representing the wealth and beauty of the Creole parishes,—whether from Ascension or Assumption, St. Mary's or St. Landry's, Iberville or Terrebonne, whether inhabitants of the multi-colored and many-balconied Creole quarter of the quaint metropolis, or dwellers in the dreamy paradises of the Têche,—mingled joyously, knowing each other, feeling in some sort akin—whether affiliated by blood, connaturalized by caste, or simply interassociated by traditional sympathies of class sentiment and class interest. Perhaps in the more than ordinary merriment of that evening something of nervous exaltation might have been discerned,—something like a feverish resolve to oppose apprehension with gayety, to combat uneasiness by diversion. But the hours passed in mirthfulness; the first general feeling of depression began to weigh less and less upon the guests; they had found reason to confide in the solidity of the massive building; there were no positive terrors, no outspoken fears; and the new conviction of all had found expression in the words of the host himself,—"*Il n'y a rien de mieux à faire que de s'amuser!*" Of what avail to lament the prospective devastation of cane-fields,—to discuss the possible ruin of crops? Better to seek solace in choregraphic harmonies, in the rhythm of gracious motion and of perfect melody, than hearken to the discords of the wild orchestra of storms;—wiser to admire the grace of Parisian toilets, the eddy of trailing robes with its fairy-foam of lace, the ivorine loveliness of glossy shoulders and jewelled throats, the glimmering of satin-slippered feet,—than to watch the raging of the flood without, or the flying of the wrack. . . .

So the music and the mirth went on: they made joy for themselves—those elegant guests;—they jested and sipped rich wines;—they pledged, and hoped, and loved, and promised, with never a thought of the morrow, on the night of the tenth of August, eighteen hundred and fifty-six. Observant parents were there, planning for the future bliss of their nearest and dearest;—mothers and fathers of handsome lads, lithe and elegant as young pines, and fresh from the polish of foreign university training;—mothers and fathers of splendid girls whose simplest attitudes were witcheries. Young cheeks flushed, young hearts fluttered with an emotion more puissant than the excitement of the dance;—young eyes betrayed the happy secret discreeter lips would have preserved. Slave-servants circled through the aristocratic press, bearing dainties and wines, praying permission to pass in terms at once humble and officious,—always in the excellent French which well-trained house-servants were taught to use on such occasions.

. . . Night wore on: still the shining floor palpitated to the feet of the dancers; still the piano-forte pealed, and still the violins sang,—and the sound of their singing shrilled through the darkness, in gasps of the gale, to the ears of Captain Smith, as he strove to keep his footing on the spray-drenched deck of the *Star*.

—"Christ!" he muttered,—"a dance! If that wind whips round south, there'll be another dance! . . . But I guess the *Star* will stay." . . .

Half an hour might have passed; still the lights flamed calmly, and the violins trilled, and the perfumed whirl went on. . . . And suddenly the wind veered!

Again the *Star* reeled, and shuddered, and turned, and began to drag all her anchors. But she now dragged away from the great

building and its lights,—away from the voluptuous thunder of
the grand piano,—even at that moment outpouring the great
joy of Weber's melody orchestrated by Berlioz: *l'Invitation à
la Valse,*—with its marvellous musical swing!

—"Waltzing!" cried the captain. "God help them!—God
help us all now! . . . *The Wind waltzes to-night, with the Sea
for his partner!*" . . .

O the stupendous Valse-Tourbillon! O the mighty Dancer!
One—two—three! From northeast to east, from east to south-
east, from southeast to south: then from the south he came,
whirling the Sea in his arms. . . .

. . . Some one shrieked in the midst of the revels;—some
girl who found her pretty slippers wet. What could it be? Thin
streams of water were spreading over the level planking,—
curling about the feet of the dancers. . . . What could it be?
All the land had begun to quake, even as, but a moment
before, the polished floor was trembling to the pressure of circling steps;—all the building shook now; every beam uttered
its groan. What could it be? . . .

There was a clamor, a panic, a rush to the windy night. Infinite darkness above and beyond; but the lantern-beams
danced far out over an unbroken circle of heaving and swirling
black water. Stealthily, swiftly, the measureless sea-flood was
rising.

—"*Messieurs—mesdames, ce n'est rien.* Nothing serious,
ladies, I assure you. . . . *Mais nous en avons vu bien souvent,
les inondations comme celle-ci; ça passe vite!* The water will go
down in a few hours, ladies;—it never rises higher than this; *il
n'y a pas le moindre danger, je vous dis! Allons! il n'y a—* My
God! what is that?" . . .

For a moment there was a ghastly hush of voices. And
through that hush there burst upon the ears of all a fearful and
unfamiliar sound, as of a colossal cannonade—rolling up from
the south, with volleying lightnings. Vastly and swiftly, nearer
and nearer it came,—a ponderous and unbroken thunder-roll,
terrible as the long muttering of an earthquake.

The nearest mainland,—across mad Caillou Bay to the sea-
marshes,—lay twelve miles north; west, by the Gulf, the nearest

solid ground was twenty miles distant. There were boats, yes!—but the stoutest swimmer might never reach them now! . . .

Then rose a frightful cry,—the hoarse, hideous, indescribable cry of hopeless fear,—the despairing animal-cry man utters when suddenly brought face to face with Nothingness, without preparation, without consolation, without possibility of respite. . . . *Sauve qui peut!* Some wrenched down the doors; some clung to the heavy banquet-tables, to the sofas, to the billiard-tables:—during one terrible instant,—against fruitless heroisms, against futile generosities,—raged all the frenzy of selfishness, all the brutalities of panic. And then—then came, thundering through the blackness, the giant swells, boom on boom! . . . One crash!—the huge frame building rocks like a cradle, seesaws, crackles. What are human shrieks now?—the tornado is shrieking! Another!—chandeliers splinter; lights are dashed out; a sweeping cataract hurls in: the immense hall rises, —oscillates,—twirls as upon a pivot,—crepitates,—crumbles into ruin. Crash again!—the swirling wreck dissolves into the wallowing of another monster billow; and a hundred cottages overturn, spin in sudden eddies, quiver, disjoint, and melt into the seething.

. . . So the hurricane passed,—tearing off the heads of the prodigious waves, to hurl them a hundred feet in air,—heaping up the ocean against the land,—upturning the woods. Bays and passes were swollen to abysses; rivers regorged; the sea-marshes were changed to raging wastes of water. Before New Orleans the flood of the mile-broad Mississippi rose six feet above highest water-mark. One hundred and ten miles away, Donaldsonville trembled at the towering tide of the Lafourche. Lakes strove to burst their boundaries. Far-off river steamers tugged wildly at their cables,—shivering like tethered creatures that hear by night the approaching howl of destroyers. Smokestacks were hurled overboard, pilot-houses torn away, cabins blown to fragments.

And over roaring Kaimbuck Pass,—over the agony of Caillou Bay,—the billowing tide rushed unresisted from the Gulf, —tearing and swallowing the land in its course,—ploughing out deep-sea channels where sleek herds had been grazing but a few hours before,—rending islands in twain,—and ever bearing with it, through the night, enormous vortex of wreck and vast wan drift of corpses. . . .

But the *Star* remained. And Captain Abraham Smith, with a long, good rope about his waist, dashed again and again into that awful surging to snatch victims from death,—clutching at passing hands, heads, garments, in the cataract-sweep of the seas,—saving, aiding, cheering, though blinded by spray and battered by drifting wreck, until his strength failed in the unequal struggle at last, and his men drew him aboard senseless, with some beautiful half-drowned girl safe in his arms. But well-nigh twoscore souls had been rescued by him; and the *Star* stayed on through it all.

Long years after, the weed-grown ribs of her graceful skeleton could still be seen, curving up from the sand-dunes of Last Island, in valiant witness of how well she stayed.

VII.

Day breaks through the flying wrack, over the infinite heaving of the sea, over the low land made vast with desolation. It is a spectral dawn: a wan light, like the light of a dying sun.

The wind has waned and veered; the flood sinks slowly back to its abysses—abandoning its plunder,—scattering its piteous waifs over bar and dune, over shoal and marsh, among the silences of the mango-swamps, over the long low reaches of sand-grasses and drowned weeds, for more than a hundred miles. From the shell-reefs of Pointe-au-Fer to the shallows of Pelto Bay the dead lie mingled with the high-heaped drift;— from their cypress groves the vultures rise to dispute a share of the feast with the shrieking frigate-birds and squeaking gulls. And as the tremendous tide withdraws its plunging waters, all the pirates of air follow the great white-gleaming retreat: a storm of billowing wings and screaming throats.

And swift in the wake of gull and frigate-bird the Wreckers come, the Spoilers of the dead,—savage skimmers of the sea,— hurricane-riders wont to spread their canvas-pinions in the face of storms; Sicilian and Corsican outlaws, Manila-men from the marshes, deserters from many navies, Lascars, marooners, refugees of a hundred nationalities,—fishers and shrimpers by name, smugglers by opportunity,—wild channel-finders from obscure bayous and unfamiliar *chénières*, all skilled in the mysteries of these mysterious waters beyond the comprehension of the oldest licensed pilot. . . .

There is plunder for all—birds and men. There are drowned sheep in multitude, heaped carcasses of kine. There are casks of claret and kegs of brandy and legions of bottles bobbing in the surf. There are billiard-tables overturned upon the sand;— there are sofas, pianos, footstools and music-stools, luxurious chairs, lounges of bamboo. There are chests of cedar, and toilet-tables of rosewood, and trunks of fine stamped leather stored with precious apparel. There are *objets de luxe* innumerable. There are children's playthings: French dolls in marvellous toilets, and toy carts, and wooden horses, and wooden spades, and brave little wooden ships that rode out the gale in which the great *Nautilus* went down. There is money in notes and in coin—in purses, in pocketbooks, and in pockets: plenty of it! There are silks, satins, laces, and fine linen to be stripped from the bodies of the drowned,—and necklaces, bracelets, watches, finger-rings and fine chains, brooches and trinkets. . . . "*Chi bidizza!—Oh! chi bedda mughieri! Eccu, la bidizza!*" That ball-dress was made in Paris by— But you never heard of him, Sicilian Vicenzu. . . . "*Che bella sposina!*" Her betrothal ring will not come off, Giuseppe; but the delicate bone snaps easily: your oyster-knife can sever the tendon. . . . "*Guardate! chi bedda picciota!*" Over her heart you will find it, Valentino—the locket held by that fine Swiss chain of woven hair—"*Caya manan!*" And it is not your quadroon bondsmaid, sweet lady, who now disrobes you so roughly; those Malay hands are less deft than hers,—but she slumbers very far away from you, and may not be aroused from her sleep. "*Na quita mo! dalaga!— na quita maganda!*" . . . Juan, the fastenings of those diamond ear-drops are much too complicated for your peon fingers: tear them out!—"*Dispense, chulita!*" . . .

. . . Suddenly a long, mighty silver trilling fills the ears of all: there is a wild hurrying and scurrying; swiftly, one after another, the overburdened luggers spread wings and flutter away.

Thrice the great cry rings rippling through the gray air, and over the green sea, and over the far-flooded shell-reefs, where the huge white flashes are,—sheet-lightning of breakers,—and over the weird wash of corpses coming in.

It is the steam-call of the relief-boat, hastening to rescue the living, to gather in the dead.

The tremendous tragedy is over!

PART II

Out of the Sea's Strength

THERE are regions of Louisiana coast whose aspect seems not of the present, but of the immemorial past—of that epoch when low flat reaches of primordial continent first rose into form above a Silurian Sea. To indulge this geologic dream, any fervid and breezeless day there, it is only necessary to ignore the evolutional protests of a few blue asters or a few composite flowers of the *coryopsis* sort, which contrive to display their rare flashes of color through the general waving of cat-heads, blood-weeds, wild cane, and marsh grasses. For, at a hasty glance, the general appearance of this marsh verdure is vague enough, as it ranges away towards the sand, to convey the idea of amphibious vegetation,—a primitive flora as yet undecided whether to retain marine habits and forms, or to assume terrestrial ones;—and the occasional inspection of surprising shapes might strengthen this fancy. Queer flat-lying and many-branching things, which resemble sea-weeds in juiciness and color and consistency, crackle under your feet from time to time; the moist and weighty air seems heated rather from below than from above,—less by the sun than by the radiation of a cooling world; and the mists of morning or evening appear to simulate the vapory exhalation of volcanic forces,— latent, but only dozing, and uncomfortably close to the surface. And indeed geologists have actually averred that those rare elevations of the soil,—which, with their heavy coronets of evergreen foliage, not only look like islands, but are so called in the French nomenclature of the coast,—have been prominences created by ancient mud volcanoes.

The family of a Spanish fisherman, Feliu Viosca, once occupied and gave its name to such an islet, quite close to the Gulf-shore,—the loftiest bit of land along fourteen miles of just such marshy coast as I have spoken of. Landward, it dominated a desolation that wearied the eye to look at, a wilderness of reedy sloughs, patched at intervals with ranges of bitterweed, tufts of elbow-bushes, and broad reaches of saw-grass, stretching away to a bluish-green line of woods that closed the horizon, and imperfectly drained in the driest season by a slimy little bayou that continually vomited foul water into the sea. The point had been much discussed by geologists; it proved a godsend to United States surveyors weary of attempting to take observations among quagmires, moccasins, and arborescent weeds from fifteen to twenty feet high. Savage fishermen, at some unrecorded time, had heaped upon the eminence a hill of clam-shells,—refuse of a million feasts; earth again had been formed over these, perhaps by the blind agency of worms working through centuries unnumbered; and the new soil had given birth to a luxuriant vegetation. Millennial oaks interknotted their roots below its surface, and vouchsafed protection to many a frailer growth of shrub or tree,—wild orange, water-willow, palmetto, locust, pomegranate, and many trailing tendrilled things, both green and gray. Then,—perhaps about half a century ago,—a few white fishermen cleared a place for themselves in this grove, and built a few palmetto cottages, with boat-houses and a wharf, facing the bayou. Later on this temporary fishing station became a permanent settlement: homes constructed of heavy timber and plaster mixed with the trailing moss of the oaks and cypresses took the places of the frail and fragrant huts of palmetto. Still the population itself retained a floating character: it ebbed and came, according to season and circumstances, according to luck or loss in the tilling of the sea. Viosca, the founder of the settlement, always remained; he always managed to do well. He owned several luggers and sloops, which were hired out upon excellent terms; he could make large and profitable contracts with New Orleans fish-dealers; and he was vaguely suspected of possessing more occult resources. There were some confused stories current about his having once been a daring smuggler, and having only been reformed by the pleadings of his wife Carmen,—a little brown woman who had followed him from Barcelona to share his fortunes in the western world.

On hot days, when the shade was full of thin sweet scents, the place had a tropical charm, a drowsy peace. Nothing except the peculiar appearance of the line of oaks facing the Gulf could have conveyed to the visitor any suggestion of days in which the trilling of crickets and the fluting of birds had ceased, of nights when the voices of the marsh had been hushed for fear. In one enormous rank the veteran trees stood shoulder to shoulder, but in the attitude of giants overmastered,—forced backward towards the marsh,—made to recoil by the might of the ghostly enemy with whom they had striven a thousand years,—the Shrieker, the Sky-Sweeper, the awful Sea-Wind!

Never had he given them so terrible a wrestle as on the night of the tenth of August, eighteen hundred and fifty-six. All the waves of the excited Gulf thronged in as if to see, and lifted up their voices, and pushed, and roared, until the *chénière* was islanded by such a billowing as no white man's eyes had ever looked upon before. Grandly the oaks bore themselves, but every fibre of their knotted thews was strained in the unequal contest, and two of the giants were overthrown, upturning, as they fell, roots coiled and huge as the serpent-limbs of Titans. Moved to its entrails, all the islet trembled, while the sea magnified its menace, and reached out whitely to the prostrate trees; but the rest of the oaks stood on, and strove in line, and saved the habitations defended by them. . . .

II.

Before a little waxen image of the Mother and Child,—an odd little Virgin with an Indian face, brought home by Feliu as a gift after one of his Mexican voyages,—Carmen Viosca had burned candles and prayed; sometimes telling her beads; sometimes murmuring the litanies she knew by heart; sometimes also reading from a prayer-book worn and greasy as a long-used pack of cards. It was particularly stained at one page, a page on which her tears had fallen many a lonely night—a page with a clumsy wood-cut representing a celestial lamp, a symbolic radiance, shining through darkness, and on either side a kneeling angel with folded wings. And beneath this rudely wrought symbol of the Perpetual Calm appeared in big, coarse type the title of a prayer that has been offered up through many a century, doubtless, by wives of Spanish mariners,— *Contra las Tempestades.*

Once she became very much frightened. After a partial lull the storm had suddenly redoubled its force: the ground shook;

the house quivered and creaked; the wind brayed and screamed and pushed and scuffled at the door; and the water, which had been whipping in through every crevice, all at once rose over the threshold and flooded the dwelling. Carmen dipped her finger in the water and tasted it. It was salt!

And none of Feliu's boats had yet come in;—doubtless they had been driven into some far-away bayous by the storm. The only boat at the settlement, the *Carmencita*, had been almost wrecked by running upon a snag three days before;—there was at least a fortnight's work for the ship-carpenter of Dead Cypress Point. And Feliu was sleeping as if nothing unusual had happened—the heavy sleep of a sailor, heedless of commotions and voices. And his men, Miguel and Mateo, were at the other end of the *chénière*.

With a scream Carmen aroused Feliu. He raised himself upon his elbow, rubbed his eyes, and asked her, with exasperating calmness, "*Que tienes? que tienes?*" (What ails thee?)

—"Oh, Feliu! the sea is coming upon us!" she answered, in the same tongue. But she screamed out a word inspired by her fear: she did not cry, "*Se nos viene el mar encima!*" but "*Se nos viene* LA ALTURA!"—the name that conveys the terrible thought of depth swallowed up in height,—the height of the *high sea*.

"*No lo creo!*" muttered Feliu, looking at the floor; then in a quiet, deep voice he said, pointing to an oar in the corner of the room, "*Echame ese remo.*"

She gave it to him. Still reclining upon one elbow, Feliu measured the depth of the water with his thumb-nail upon the blade of the oar, and then bade Carmen light his pipe for him. His calmness reassured her. For half an hour more, undismayed by the clamoring of the wind or the calling of the sea, Feliu silently smoked his pipe and watched his oar. The water rose a little higher, and he made another mark;—then it climbed a little more, but not so rapidly; and he smiled at Carmen as he made a third mark. "*Como creia!*" he exclaimed, "*no hay porque asustarse: el agua baja!*" And as Carmen would have continued to pray, he rebuked her fears, and bade her try to obtain some rest: "*Basta ya de plegarios, querida!—vete y duerme.*" His tone, though kindly, was imperative; and Carmen, accustomed to obey him, laid herself down by his side, and soon, for very weariness, slept.

It was a feverish sleep, nevertheless, shattered at brief intervals by terrible sounds,—sounds magnified by her nervous condition—a sleep visited by dreams that mingled in a strange way with the impressions of the storm, and more than once made her heart stop, and start again at its own stopping. One of these fancies she never could forget—a dream about little Concha,—Conchita, her first-born, who now slept far away in the old churchyard at Barcelona. She had tried to become resigned,—not to think. But the child would come back night after night, though the earth lay heavy upon her—night after night, through long distances of Time and Space. Oh! the fancied clinging of infant-lips!—the thrilling touch of little ghostly hands!—those phantom-caresses that torture mothers' hearts! . . . Night after night, through many a month of pain. Then for a time the gentle presence ceased to haunt her,— seemed to have lain down to sleep forever under the high bright grass and yellow flowers. Why did it return, that night of all nights, to kiss her, to cling to her, to nestle in her arms? . . .

For in her dream she thought herself still kneeling before the waxen Image, while the terrors of the tempest were ever deepening about her,—raving of winds and booming of waters and a shaking of the land. And before her, even as she prayed her dream-prayer, the waxen Virgin became tall as a woman, and taller,—rising to the roof and smiling as she grew. Then Carmen would have cried out for fear, but that something smothered her voice,—paralyzed her tongue. And the Virgin silently stooped above her, and placed in her arms the Child,— the brown Child with the Indian face. And the Child whitened in her hands and changed,—seeming as it changed to send a sharp pain through her heart: an old pain linked somehow with memories of bright windy Spanish hills, and summer-scent of olive groves, and all the luminous Past;—it looked into her face with the soft dark gaze, with the unforgotten smile of . . . dead Conchita!

And Carmen wished to thank the smiling Virgin for that priceless bliss, and lifted up her eyes; but the sickness of ghostly fear returned upon her when she looked; for now the Mother seemed as a woman long dead, and the smile was the smile of fleshlessness, and the places of the eyes were voids and darknesses. . . . And the sea sent up so vast a roar that the dwelling rocked.

Carmen started from sleep to find her heart throbbing so that the couch shook with it. Night was growing gray; the door had just been opened and slammed again. Through the rain-whipped panes she discerned the passing shape of Feliu, making for the beach—a broad and bearded silhouette, bending against the wind. Still the waxen Virgin smiled her Mexican smile,—but now she was only seven inches high; and her bead-glass eyes seemed to twinkle with kindliness while the flame of the last expiring taper struggled for life in the earthen socket at her feet.

III.

Rain and a blind sky and a bursting sea. Feliu and his men, Miguel and Mateo, looked out upon the thundering and flashing of the monstrous tide. The wind had fallen, and the gray air was full of gulls. Behind the *chénière*, back to the cloudy line of low woods many miles away, stretched a wash of lead-colored water, with a green point piercing it here and there—elbow-bushes or wild cane tall enough to keep their heads above the flood. But the inundation was visibly decreasing;—with the passing of each hour more and more green patches and points had been showing themselves: by degrees the course of the bayou had become defined—two parallel winding lines of dwarf-timber and bushy shrubs traversing the water toward the distant cypress-swamps. Before the *chénière* all the shell-beach slope was piled with wreck—uptorn trees with the foliage still fresh upon them, splintered timbers of mysterious origin, and logs in multitude, scarred with gashes of the axe. Feliu and his comrades had saved wood enough to build a little town,—working up to their waists in the surf, with ropes, poles, and boat-hooks. The whole sea was full of flotsam. *Voto á Cristo!*—what a wrecking there must have been! And to think the *Carmencita* could not be taken out!

They had seen other luggers making eastward during the morning—could recognize some by their sails, others by their gait,—exaggerated in their struggle with the pitching of the sea: the *San Pablo*, the *Gasparina*, the *Enriqueta*, the *Agueda*, the *Constanza*. Ugly water, yes!—but what a chance for wreckers! . . . Some great ship must have gone to pieces;—scores of casks were rolling in the trough,—casks of wine. Perhaps it was the *Manila*,—perhaps the *Nautilus*!

A dead cow floated near enough for Mateo to throw his rope over one horn; and they all helped to get it out. It was a milch cow of some expensive breed; and the owner's brand had been burned upon the horns:—a monographic combination of the letters A and P. Feliu said he knew that brand: Old-man Preaulx, of Belle-Isle, who kept a sort of dairy at Last Island during the summer season, used to mark all his cows that way. Strange!

But, as they worked on, they began to see stranger things—white dead faces and dead hands, which did not look like the hands or the faces of drowned sailors: the ebb was beginning to run strongly, and these were passing out with it on the other side of the mouth of the bayou;—perhaps they had been washed into the marsh during the night, when the great rush of the sea came. Then the three men left the water, and retired to higher ground to scan the furrowed Gulf;—their practised eyes began to search the courses of the sea-currents,—keen as the gaze of birds that watch the wake of the plough. And soon the casks and the drift were forgotten; for it seemed to them that the tide was heavy with human dead—passing out, processionally, to the great open. Very far, where the huge pitching of the swells was diminished by distance into a mere fluttering of ripples, the water appeared as if sprinkled with them;—they vanished and became visible again at irregular intervals, here and there—floating most thickly eastward,—tossing, swaying patches of white or pink or blue or black, each with its tiny speck of flesh-color showing as the sea lifted or lowered the body. Nearer to shore there were few; but of these two were close enough to be almost recognizable: Miguel first discerned them. They were rising and falling where the water was deepest —well out in front of the mouth of the bayou, beyond the flooded sand-bars, and moving toward the shell-reef westward. They were drifting almost side by side. One was that of a negro, apparently well attired, and wearing a white apron;—the other seemed to be a young colored girl, clad in a blue dress; she was floating upon her face; they could observe that she had nearly straight hair, braided and tied with a red ribbon. These were evidently house-servants,—slaves. But from whence? Nothing could be learned until the luggers should return; and none of them was yet in sight. Still Feliu was not anxious as to the fate of his boats, manned by the best sailors of the coast. Rarely are these Louisiana fishermen lost in sudden storms; even when to other eyes the appearances are most pacific and the skies most splendidly blue, they divine some far-off danger, like the gulls; and like the gulls also, you see their light vessels fleeing land-ward. These men seem living barometers, exquisitely sensitive to all the invisible changes of atmospheric expansion and com-pression; they are not easily caught in those awful dead calms which suddenly paralyze the wings of a bark, and hold her help-less in their charmed circle, as in a nightmare, until the black-ness overtakes her, and the long-sleeping sea leaps up foaming to devour her.

—"*Carajo!*"

The word all at once bursts from Feliu's mouth, with that peculiar guttural snarl of the "r" betokening strong excitement, —while he points to something rocking in the ebb, beyond the foaming of the shell-reef, under a circling of gulls. More dead? Yes—but something too that lives and moves, like a quivering speck of gold; and Mateo also perceives it, a gleam of bright hair,—and Miguel likewise, after a moment's gazing. A living child;—a lifeless mother. *Pobrecíta!* No boat within reach, and only a mighty surf-wrestler could hope to swim thither and return!

But already, without a word, brown Feliu has stripped for the struggle;—another second, and he is shooting through the surf, head and hands tunnelling the foam-hills. . . . One—two—three lines passed!—four!—that is where they first begin to crumble white from the summit,—five!—that he can ride fearlessly! . . . Then swiftly, easily, he advances, with a long, powerful breast-stroke,—keeping his bearded head well up to watch for drift,—seeming to slide with a swing from swell to swell,—ascending, sinking,—alternately presenting breast or shoulder to the wave; always diminishing more and more to the eyes of Mateo and Miguel,—till he becomes a moving speck, occasionally hard to follow through the confusion of heaping waters. . . . You are not afraid of the sharks, Feliu!—no: they are afraid of you; right and left they slunk away from your coming that morning you swam for life in West-Indian waters, with your knife in your teeth, while the balls of the Cuban coast-guard were purring all around you. That day the swarming sea was warm,—warm like soup—and clear, with an emerald flash in every ripple,—not opaque and clamorous like the Gulf to-day. . . . Miguel and his comrade are anxious. Ropes are un-rolled and interknotted into a line. Miguel remains on the beach; but Mateo, bearing the end of the line, fights his way out,—swimming and wading by turns, to the further sand-bar, where the water is shallow enough to stand in,—if you know how to jump when the breaker comes.

But Feliu, nearing the flooded shell-bank, watches the white flashings,—knows when the time comes to keep flat and take a long, long breath. One heavy volleying of foam,—darkness and hissing as of a steam-burst; a vibrant lifting up; a rush into light, —and again the volleying and the seething darkness. Once more,—and the fight is won! He feels the upcoming chill of deeper water,—sees before him the green quaking of unbro-ken swells,—and far beyond him Mateo leaping on the bar,— and beside him, almost within arm's-reach, a great billiard-table swaying, and a dead woman clinging there, and . . . the child.

A moment more, and Feliu has lifted himself beside the waifs. . . . How fast the dead woman clings, as if with the one power which is strong as death,—the desperate force of love! Not in vain; for the frail creature bound to the mother's corpse with a silken scarf has still the strength to cry out:— "*Maman! maman!*" But time is life now; and the tiny hands must be pulled away from the fair dead neck, and the scarf taken to bind the infant firmly to Feliu's broad shoulders,— quickly, roughly; for the ebb will not wait. . . .

And now Feliu has a burden; but his style of swimming has totally changed;—he rises from the water like a Triton, and his powerful arms seem to spin in circles, like the spokes of a flying wheel. For now is the wrestle indeed!—after each passing swell comes a prodigious pulling from beneath,—the sea clutching for its prey. But the reef is gained, is passed;—the wild horses of the deep seem to know the swimmer who has learned to ride them so well. And still the brown arms spin in an ever-nearing mist of spray; and the outer sand-bar is not far off,—and there is shouting Mateo, leaping in the surf, swinging something about his head, as a vaquero swings his noose! . . . Sough! splash!—it struggles in the trough beside Feliu, and the sinewy hand descends upon it. *Tiene!—tira, Miguel!* And their feet touch land again! . . .

She is very cold, the child, and very still, with eyes closed.

—"*Esta muerta, Feliu?*" asks Mateo.

—"*No!*" the panting swimmer makes answer, emerging, while the waves reach whitely up the sand as in pursuit,—"*no; vive!—respira todavía!*"

Behind him the deep lifts up its million hands, and thunders as in acclaim.

IV.

—"*Madre de Dios!—mi sueno!*" screamed Carmen, abandoning her preparations for the morning meal, as Feliu, nude, like a marine god, rushed in and held out to her a dripping and gasping baby-girl,—"Mother of God! my dream!" But there was no time then to tell of dreams; the child might die. In one instant Carmen's quick, deft hands had stripped the slender little body; and while Mateo and Feliu were finding dry clothing and stimulants, and Miguel telling how it all happened—quickly, passionately, with furious gesture—the kind and vigorous woman exerted all her skill to revive the flickering life. Soon Feliu came to aid her, while his men set to work completing the interrupted preparation of the breakfast. Flannels were heated for the friction of the frail limbs; and brandy-and-water warmed, which Carmen administered by the spoonful, skilfully as any physician,—until, at last, the little creature opened her eyes and began to sob. Sobbing still, she was laid in Carmen's warm feather-bed, well swathed in woollen wrappings. The immediate danger, at least, was over; and Feliu smiled with pride and pleasure.

Then Carmen first ventured to relate her dream; and his face became grave again. Husband and wife gazed a moment into each other's eyes, feeling together the same strange thrill— that mysterious faint creeping, as of a wind passing, which is the awe of the Unknowable. Then they looked at the child, lying there, pink-cheeked with the flush of the blood returning; and such a sudden tenderness touched them as they had known long years before, while together bending above the slumbering loveliness of lost Conchita.

—"*Que ojos!*" murmured Feliu, as he turned away,—feigning hunger. . . . (He was not hungry; but his sight had grown a little dim, as with a mist.) *Que ojos!* They were singular eyes, large, dark, and wonderfully fringed. The child's hair was yellow—it was the flash of it that had saved her; yet her eyes and brows were beautifully black. She was comely, but with such a curious, delicate comeliness—totally unlike the robust beauty of Concha. . . . At intervals she would moan a little between her sobs; and at last cried out, with a thin, shrill cry: "Maman!—oh! maman!" Then Carmen lifted her from the bed to her lap, and caressed her, and rocked her gently to and fro, as she had done many a night for Concha,—murmuring, —"*Yo seré tu madre, angel mio, dulzura mia;—seré tu madrecita, palomita mia!*" (I will be thy mother, my angel, my sweet;—I will be thy little mother, my doveling.) And the long silk fringes of the child's eyes overlapped, shadowed her little cheeks; and she slept—just as Conchita had slept long ago,— with her head on Carmen's bosom.

Feliu re-appeared at the inner door: at a sign, he approached cautiously, without noise, and looked.

—"She can talk," whispered Carmen in Spanish: "she called her mother"—*ha llamado à su madre.*

—"*Y Dios tambien la ha llamado,*" responded Feliu, with rude pathos;—"And *God also called her.*"

—"But the Virgin sent us the child, Feliu,—sent us the child for Concha's sake."

He did not answer at once; he seemed to be thinking very deeply;—Carmen anxiously scanned his impassive face.

—"Who knows?" he answered, at last;—"who knows? Perhaps she has ceased to belong to any one else." . . .

One after another, Feliu's luggers fluttered in,—bearing with them news of the immense calamity. And all the fishermen, in turn, looked at the child. Not one had ever seen her before.

V.

Ten days later, a lugger full of armed men entered the bayou, and moored at Viosca's wharf. The visitors were, for the most part, country gentlemen,—residents of Franklin and neighboring towns, or planters from the Têche country,—forming one of the numerous expeditions organized for the purpose of finding the bodies of relatives or friends lost in the great hurricane, and of punishing the robbers of the dead. They had searched numberless nooks of the coast, had given sepulture to many corpses, had recovered a large amount of jewelry, and— as Feliu afterward learned,—had summarily tried and executed several of the most abandoned class of wreckers found with ill-gotten valuables in their possession, and convicted of having mutilated the drowned. But they came to Viosca's landing only to obtain information;—he was too well known and liked to be a subject for suspicion; and, moreover, he had one good friend in the crowd,—Captain Harris of New Orleans, a veteran steamboat man and a market-contractor, to whom he had disposed of many a cargo of fresh *pompano*, sheep's-head, and Spanish-mackerel. . . . Harris was the first to step to land;— some ten of the party followed him. Nearly all had lost some relative or friend in the great catastrophe;—the gathering was serious, silent,—almost grim,—which formed about Feliu.

Mateo, who had come to the country while a boy, spoke English better than the rest of the *chénière* people;—he acted as interpreter whenever Feliu found any difficulty in comprehending or answering questions; and he told them of the child rescued that wild morning, and of Feliu's swim. His recital evoked a murmur of interest and excitement, followed by a confusion of questions. Well, they could see for themselves, Feliu said; but he hoped they would have a little patience;— the child was still weak;—it might be dangerous to startle her. "We'll arrange it just as you like," responded the captain;— "go ahead, Feliu!" . . .

All proceeded to the house, under the great trees; Feliu and Captain Harris leading the way. It was sultry and bright;— even the sea-breeze was warm; there were pleasant odors in the shade, and a soporific murmur made of leaf-speech and the hum of gnats. Only the captain entered the house with Feliu;

the rest remained without—some taking seats on a rude plank bench under the oaks—others flinging themselves down upon the weeds—a few stood still, leaning upon their rifles. Then Carmen came out to them with gourds and a bucket of fresh water, which all were glad to drink.

They waited many minutes. Perhaps it was the cool peace of the place that made them all feel how hot and tired they were: conversation flagged; and the general languor finally betrayed itself in a silence so absolute that every leaf-whisper seemed to become separately audible.

It was broken at last by the guttural voice of the old captain emerging from the cottage, leading the child by the hand, and followed by Carmen and Feliu. All who had been resting rose up and looked at the child.

Standing in a lighted space, with one tiny hand enveloped by the captain's great brown fist, she looked so lovely that a general exclamation of surprise went up. Her bright hair, loose and steeped in the sun-flame, illuminated her like a halo; and her large dark eyes, gentle and melancholy as a deer's, watched the strange faces before her with shy curiosity. She wore the same dress in which Feliu had found her—a soft white fabric of muslin, with trimmings of ribbon that had once been blue; and the now discolored silken scarf, which had twice done her such brave service, was thrown over her shoulders. Carmen had washed and repaired the dress very creditably; but the tiny slim feet were bare,—the brine-soaked shoes she wore that fearful night had fallen into shreds at the first attempt to remove them.

—"Gentlemen," said Captain Harris,—"we can find no clew to the identity of this child. There is no mark upon her clothing; and she wore nothing in the shape of jewelry—except this string of coral beads. We are nearly all Americans here; and she does not speak any English. . . . Does any one here know anything about her?"

Carmen felt a great sinking at her heart: was her new-found darling to be taken so soon from her? But no answer came to the captain's query. No one of the expedition had ever seen that child before. The coral beads were passed from hand to hand; the scarf was minutely scrutinized without avail. Somebody asked if the child could not talk German or Italian.

—"*Italiano? No!*" said Feliu, shaking his head. . . . One

of his luggermen. Gioachino Sparicio, who, though a Sicilian, could speak several Italian idioms besides his own, had already essayed.

—"She speaks something or other," answered the captain—"but no English. I couldn't make her understand me; and Feliu, who talks nearly all the infernal languages spoken down this way, says he can't make her understand him. Suppose some of you who know French talk to her a bit. . . . Laroussel, why don't you try?"

The young man addressed did not at first seem to notice the captain's suggestion. He was a tall, lithe fellow, with a dark, positive face: he had never removed his black gaze from the child since the moment of her appearance. Her eyes, too, seemed to be all for him—to return his scrutiny with a sort of vague pleasure, a half-savage confidence. . . . Was it the first embryonic feeling of race-affinity quickening in the little brain? —some intuitive, inexplicable sense of kindred? She shrank from Doctor Hecker, who addressed her in German, shook her head at Lawyer Solari, who tried to make her answer in Italian; and her look always went back plaintively to the dark, sinister face of Laroussel,—Laroussel who had calmly taken a human life, a wicked human life, only the evening before.

—"Laroussel, you're the only Creole in this crowd," said the captain; "talk to her! Talk *gumbo* to her! . . . I've no doubt this child knows German very well, and Italian too,"—he added, maliciously—"but not in the way you gentlemen pronounce it!"

Laroussel handed his rifle to a friend, crouched down before the little girl, and looked into her face, and smiled. Her great sweet orbs shone into his one moment, seriously, as if searching; and then . . . she returned his smile. It seemed to touch something latent within the man, something rare; for his whole expression changed; and there was a caress in his look and voice none of the men could have believed possible—as he exclaimed:—

—"*Fais moin bo, piti.*"

She pouted up her pretty lips and kissed his black moustache.

He spoke to her again:—

—"*Dis moin to nom, piti;—dis moin to nom, chère.*"

Then, for the first time, she spoke, answering in her argent treble:

—"Zouzoune."

All held their breath. Captain Harris lifted his finger to his lips to command silence.

—"Zouzoune? Zouzoune qui, chère?"

—"Zouzoune, ça c'est moin, Lili!"

—"C'est pas tout to nom, Lili;—dis moin, chère, to laut nom."

—"Mo pas connin laut nom."

—"Comment yé té pélé to maman, piti?"

—"Maman,—Maman 'Dèle."

—"Et comment yé té pélé to papa, chère?"

—"Papa Zulien."

—"Bon! Et comment to maman té pélé to papa?—dis ça à moin, chère?"

The child looked down, put a finger in her mouth, thought a moment, and replied:—

—"Li pélé li, 'Chéri'; li pélé li, 'Papoute.'"

—"Aïe, aïe!—c'est tout, ça?—to maman té jamain pélé li daut' chose?"

—"Mo pas connin, moin."

She began to play with some trinkets attached to his watch chain;—a very small gold compass especially impressed her fancy by the trembling and flashing of its tiny needle, and she murmured, coaxingly:—

—"Mo oulé ça! Donnin ça à moin."

He took all possible advantage of the situation, and replied at once:—

—"Oui! mo va donnin toi ça si to di moin to laut nom."

The splendid bribe evidently impressed her greatly; for tears rose to the brown eyes as she answered:

—"Mo pas capab di' ça;—mo pas capab di' laut nom. . . . Mo oulé; mo pas capab!"

Laroussel explained. The child's name was Lili,—perhaps a contraction of Eulalie; and her pet Creole name Zouzoune. He thought she must be the daughter of wealthy people; but she could not, for some reason or other, tell her family name. Perhaps she could not pronounce it well, and was afraid of being laughed at: some of the old French names were very hard for Creole children to pronounce, so long as the little ones were indulged in the habit of talking the patois; and after a certain age their mispronunciations would be made fun of in order to accustom them to abandon the idiom of the slave-nurses, and to speak only French. Perhaps, again, she was really unable to recall the name: certain memories might have been blurred in the delicate brain by the shock of that terrible night. She said her mother's name was Adèle, and her father's Julien; but these were very common names in Louisiana,—and could afford scarcely any better clew than the innocent state-ment that her mother used to address her father as "dear" (*Chéri*),—or with the Creole diminutive "little papa" (*Pa-poute*). Then Laroussel tried to reach a clew in other ways, with-out success. He asked her about where she lived,—what the place was like; and she told him about fig-trees in a court, and galleries, and *banquettes*, and spoke of a *faubou'*,—without being able to name any street. He asked her what her father used to do, and was assured that he did everything—that there was nothing he could not do. Divine absurdity of childish faith! —infinite artlessness of childish love! . . . Probably the little girl's parents had been residents of New Orleans—dwellers of the old colonial quarter,—the faubourg, the *faubou'*.

—"Well, gentlemen," said Captain Harris, as Laroussel aban-doned his cross-examination in despair,—"all we can do, now is to make inquiries. I suppose we'd better leave the child here. She is very weak yet, and in no condition to be taken to the city, right in the middle of the hot season; and nobody could care for her any better than she's being cared for here. Then, again, seems to me that as Feliu saved her life,—and that at the risk of his own,—he's got the prior claim, anyhow; and his wife is just crazy about the child—wants to adopt her. If we can find her relatives so much the better; but I say, gentlemen, let them come right here to Feliu, themselves, and thank him as he ought to be thanked, by God! That's just what I think about it."

Carmen understood the little speech;—all the Spanish charm of her youth had faded out years before; but in the one swift look of gratitude she turned upon the captain, it seemed to blossom again;—for that quick moment, she was beautiful.

"The captain is quite right," observed Dr. Hecker: "it would be very dangerous to take the child away just now." There was no dissent.

—"All correct, boys ?" asked the captain. . . . "Well, we've got to be going. By-by, Zouzoune!"

But Zouzoune burst into tears. Laroussel was going too!

—"Give her the thing, Laroussel! she gave you a kiss, any-how—more than she'd do for me," cried the captain.

Laroussel turned, detached the little compass from his watch chain, and gave it to her. She held up her pretty face for his farewell kiss. . . .

VI.

But it seemed fated that Feliu's waif should never be iden-tified;—diligent inquiry and printed announcements alike proved fruitless. Sea and sand had either hidden or effaced all the records of the little world they had engulfed: the annihila-tion of whole families, the extinction of races, had, in more than one instance, rendered vain all efforts to recognize the dead. It required the subtle perception of long intimacy to name remains tumefied and discolored by corruption and expo-sure, mangled and gnawed by fishes, by reptiles, and by birds;— it demanded the great courage of love to look upon the eyeless faces found sweltering in the blackness of cypress-shadows, under the low palmettoes of the swamps,—where gorged buz-zards started from sleep, or cotton-mouths uncoiled, hissing, at the coming of the searchers. And sometimes all who had loved the lost were themselves among the missing. The full roll-call of names could never be made out;—extraordinary mistakes were committed. Men whom the world deemed dead and buried came back, like ghosts,—to read their own epitaphs.

. . . Almost at the same hour that Laroussel was question-ing the child in Creole patois, another expedition, searching for bodies along the coast, discovered on the beach of a low islet famed as a haunt of pelicans, the corpse of a child. Some locks of bright hair still adhering to the skull, a string of red beads, a white muslin dress, a handkerchief broidered with the initials "A. L. B.,"—were secured as clews; and the little body was interred where it had been found.

And, several days before, Captain Hotard, of the relief-boat

Estelle Brousseaux, had found, drifting in the open Gulf (latitude 26° 43'; longitude 88° 17'),—the corpse of a fair-haired woman, clinging to a table. The body was disfigured beyond recognition: even the slender bones of the hands had been stripped by the nibs of the sea-birds—except one finger, the third of the left, which seemed to have been protected by a ring of gold, as by a charm. Graven within the plain yellow circlet was a date,—"JUILLET—1851"; and the names,—"ADÈLE + JULIEN,"— separated by a cross. The *Estelle* carried coffins that day: most of them were already full; but there was one for Adèle.

Who was she?—who was her Julien? . . . When the *Estelle* and many other vessels had discharged their ghastly cargoes;— when the bereaved of the land had assembled as hastily as they might for the duty of identification;—when memories were strained almost to madness in research of names, dates, incidents —for the evocation of dead words, resurrection of vanished days, recollection of dear promises,—then, in the confusion, it was believed and declared that the little corpse found on the pelican island was the daughter of the wearer of the wedding-ring: Adèle La Brierre, *née* Florane, wife of Dr. Julien La Brierre, of New Orleans, who was numbered among the missing.

And they brought dead Adèle back,—up shadowy river windings, over linked brightnesses of lake and lakelet, through many a green-glimmering bayou,—to the Creole city, and laid her to rest somewhere in the old Saint-Louis Cemetery. And upon the tablet recording her name were also graven the words:—

. . . .
Aussi à la mémoire de
son mari,
JULIEN RAYMOND LA BRIERRE,
né à la paroisse St. Landry,
le 29 Mai, MDCCCXXVIII;
et de leur fille,
EULALIE,
agée de 4 ans et 5 mois,—
Qui tous périrent
dans la grande tempête qui

balayâ L'Ile Dernière, le
10 Août, MDCCCLVI
. . . + . . .
Priez pour eux!

VII.

Yet six months afterward the face of Julien La Brierre was seen again upon the streets of New Orleans. Men started at the sight of him, as at a spectre standing in the sun. And nevertheless the apparition cast a shadow. People paused, approached, half extended a hand through old habit, suddenly checked themselves and passed on,—wondering they should have forgotten, asking themselves why they had so nearly made an absurd mistake.

It was a February day,—one of those crystalline days of our snowless Southern winter, when the air is clear and cool, and outlines sharpen in the light as if viewed through the focus of a diamond glass;—and in that brightness Julien La Brierre perused his own brief epitaph, and gazed upon the sculptured name of drowned Adèle. Only half a year had passed since she was laid away in the high wall of tombs,—in that strange colonial columbarium where the dead slept in rows, behind squared marbles lettered in black or bronze. Yet her resting-place,—in the highest range,—already seemed old. Under our Southern sun, the vegetation of cemeteries seems to spring into being spontaneously—to leap all suddenly into luxuriant life! Microscopic mossy growths had begun to mottle the slab that closed her in;—over its face some singular creeper was crawling, planting tiny reptile-feet into the chiselled letters of the inscription; and from the moist soil below speckled euphorbias were growing up to her,—and morning-glories,—and beautiful green tangled things of which he did not know the name.

And the sight of the pretty lizards, puffing their crimson pouches in the sun, or undulating athwart epitaphs, and shifting their color when approached, from emerald to ashen-gray;— the caravans of the ants, journeying to and from tiny chinks in the masonry;—the bees gathering honey from the crimson blossoms of the *crête-de-coq*, whose radicles sought sustenance, perhaps from human dust, in the decay of generations:—all that rich life of graves summoned up fancies of Resurrection, Nature's resurrection-work—wondrous transformations of flesh, marvellous transmigration of souls! . . . From some forgotten crevice of that tomb roof, which alone intervened between her and the vast light, a sturdy weed was growing. He knew that plant, as it quivered against the blue,—the *chou-gras*, as Creole children call it: its dark berries form the mocking-bird's favorite food. . . . Might not its roots, exploring darkness, have found some unfamiliar nutriment within?—might it not be that something of the dead heart had risen to purple and emerald life—in the sap of translucent leaves, in the wine of the savage berries,—to blend with the blood of the Wizard Singer,—to lend a strange sweetness to the melody of his wooing? . . .

. . . Seldom, indeed, does it happen that a man in the prime of youth, in the possession of wealth, habituated to comforts and the elegances of life, discovers in one brief week how minute his true relation to the human aggregate,—how insignificant his part as one living atom of the social organism. Seldom, at the age of twenty-eight, has one been made able to comprehend, through experience alone, that in the vast and complex Stream of Being he counts for less than a drop; and that, even as the blood loses and replaces its corpuscles, without a variance in the volume and vigor of its current, so are individual existences eliminated and replaced in the pulsing of a people's life, with never a pause in its mighty murmur. But all this, and much more, Julien had learned in seven merciless days—seven successive and terrible shocks of experience. The enormous world had not missed him; and his place therein was not void—society had simply forgotten him. So long as he had moved among them, all he knew for friends had performed their petty altruistic *rôles*,—had discharged their small human obligations,—had kept turned toward him the least selfish side of their natures,—had made with him a tolerably equitable exchange of ideas and of favors; and after his disappearance from their midst, they had duly mourned for his loss—to themselves! They had played out the final act in the unimportant drama of his life: it was really asking too much to demand a repetition. . . . Impossible to deceive himself as to the feeling his unanticipated return had aroused:—feigned pity where he had looked for sympathetic welcome; dismay where he had expected surprised delight; and, oftener, airs of resignation, or disappointment ill disguised,—always insincerity, politely masked or coldly bare. He had come back to find strangers in his home, relatives at law concerning his estate, and himself regarded as an intruder among the living,—an unlucky guest, a *revenant*. . . . How hollow and selfish a world it seemed! And yet there was love in it; he had been loved in it, unselfishly, passionately, with the love of father and of mother, of wife and child. . . . All buried!—all lost forever! . . . Oh! would to God the story of that stone were not a lie!—would to kind God he also were dead! . . .

Evening shadowed: the violet deepened and prickled itself with stars;—the sun passed below the west, leaving in his wake a momentary splendor of vermilion . . . our Southern day is not prolonged by gloaming. And Julien's thoughts darkened with the darkening, and as swiftly. For while there was yet light to see, he read another name that he used to know—the name of RAMIREZ. . . . *Nació en Cienfuegos, isla de Cuba*. . . . Wherefore born?—for what eternal purpose, Ramirez,—in the City of a Hundred Fires? He had blown out his brains before the sepulchre of his young wife. . . . It was a detached double vault, shaped like a huge chest, and much dilapidated already:—under the continuous burrowing of the crawfish it had sunk greatly on one side, tilting as if about to fall. Out from its zigzag fissurings of brick and plaster, a sinister voice seemed to come:—"*Go thou and do likewise! . . . Earth groans with her burthen even now,—the burthen of Man: she holds no place for thee!*"

VIII.

. . . That voice pursued him into the darkness of his chilly room,—haunted him in the silence of his lodging. And then began within the man that ghostly struggle between courage and despair, between patient reason and mad revolt, between weakness and force, between darkness and light, which all sensitive and generous natures must wage in their own souls at least once—perhaps many times—in their lives. Memory, in such moments, plays like an electric storm;—all involuntarily he found himself reviewing his life.

Incidents long forgotten came back with singular vividness: he saw the Past as he had not seen it while it was the Present; —remembrances of home, recollections of infancy, recurred to him with terrible intensity,—the artless pleasures and the trifling griefs, the little hurts and the tender pettings, the hopes and the anxieties of those who loved him, the smiles and tears of slaves. . . . And his first Creole pony, a present from his father the day after he had proved himself able to recite his prayers correctly in French, without one mispronunciation— without saying *crasse* for *grâce*;—and yellow Michel, who taught him to swim and to fish and to paddle a pirogue;—and the bayou, with its wonder-world of turtles and birds and creeping things;—and his German tutor, who could not pronounce the *j*;—and the songs of the cane-fields,—strangely pleasing, full of quaverings and long plaintive notes, like the call of the cranes. . . . *Tou', tou' pays blanc!* . . . Afterward Camanière had leased the place;—everything must have been changed; even the songs could not be the same. *Tou', tou' pays blanc!—Danié qui commandé.* . . .

And then Paris; and the university, with its wild under-life,— some debts, some follies; and the frequent fond letters from home to which he might have replied so much oftener;—Paris, where talent is mediocrity; Paris, with its thunders and its splendors and its seething of passion;—Paris, supreme focus of human endeavor, with its madnesses of art, its frenzied striving to express the Inexpressible, its spasmodic strainings to clutch the Unattainable, its soarings of soul-fire to the heaven of the Impossible. . . .

What a rejoicing there was at his return!—how radiant and level the long Road of the Future seemed to open before him! —everywhere friends, prospects, felicitations. Then his first serious love;—and the night of the ball at St. Martinsville,—the vision of light! Gracile as a palm, and robed at once so simply, so exquisitely in white, she had seemed to him the supreme realization of all possible dreams of beauty. . . . And his passionate jealousy; and the slap from Laroussel; and the humiliating two-minute duel with rapiers in which he learned that he had found his master. The scar was deep. Why had not Laroussel killed him then? . . . Not evil-hearted, Laroussel;—they used to salute each other afterward when they met; and Laroussel's smile was kindly. Why had he refrained from returning it? Where was Laroussel now?

For the death of his generous father, who had sacrificed so much to reform him; for the death, only a short while after, of his all-forgiving mother, he had found one sweet woman to console him with her tender words, her loving lips, her delicious caress. She had given him Zouzoune, the darling link between their lives,—Zouzoune, who waited each evening with black Églantine at the gate to watch for his coming, and to cry through all the house like a bird, "*Papa, lapé vini!— papa Zulien apé vini!*" . . . And once that she had made him very angry by upsetting the ink over a mass of business papers, and he had slapped her (could he ever forgive himself?)—she had cried, through her sobs of astonishment and pain:—"*To laimin moin?—to batté moin!*" (Thou lovest me?—thou beatest me!) Next month she would have been five years old. *To laimin moin?—to batté moin! . . .*

A furious paroxysm of grief convulsed him, suffocated him; it seemed to him that something within must burst, must break. He flung himself down upon his bed, biting the coverings in order to stifle his outcry, to smother the sounds of his despair. What crime had he ever done, oh God! that he should be made to suffer thus?—was it for this he had been permitted to live? had been rescued from the sea and carried round all the world unscathed? Why should he live to remember, to suffer, to agonize? Was not Ramirez wiser?

How long the contest within him lasted, he never knew; but ere it was done, he had become, in more ways than one, a changed man. For the first,—though not indeed for the last time,—something of the deeper and nobler comprehension of human weakness and of human suffering had been revealed to him,—something of that larger knowledge without which the sense of duty can never be fully acquired, nor the understanding of unselfish goodness, nor the spirit of tenderness. The suicide is not a coward; he is an egotist.

*

A ray of sunlight touched his wet pillow,—awoke him. He rushed to the window, flung the latticed shutters apart, and looked out.

Something beautiful and ghostly filled all the vistas,—frost-haze; and in some queer way the mist had momentarily caught and held the very color of the sky. An azure fog! Through it the quaint and checkered street—as yet but half illumined by the sun,—took tones of impossible color; the view paled away through faint bluish tints into transparent purples;—all the shadows were indigo. How sweet the morning!—how well life seemed worth living! Because the sun had shown his face through a fairy-veil of frost! . . .

Who was the ancient thinker?—was it Hermes?—who said:—

"The Sun is Laughter; for 'tis He who maketh joyous the thoughts of men, and gladdeneth the infinite world." . . .

PART III

The Shadow of the Tide

C ARMEN found that her little pet had been taught how to pray; for each night and morning when the devout woman began to make her orisons, the child would kneel beside her, with little hands joined, and in a voice sweet and clear murmur something she had learned by heart. Much as this pleased Carmen, it seemed to her that the child's prayers could not be wholly valid unless uttered in Spanish;—for Spanish was heaven's own tongue,—*la lengua de Dios, el idioma de Dios*; and she resolved to teach her to say the *Salve Maria* and the *Padre Nuestro* in Castilian,—also her own favorite prayer to the Virgin, beginning with the words, "*Madre santisima, toda dulce y hermosa.*" . . .

So Conchita—for a new name had been given to her with that terrible sea-christening—received her first lessons in Spanish; and she proved a most intelligent pupil. Before long she could prattle to Feliu;—she would watch for his return of evenings, and announce his coming with "*Aqui viene mi papacito!*"—she learned, too, from Carmen, many little caresses of speech to greet him with. Feliu's was not a joyous nature; he had his dark hours, his sombre days; yet it was rarely that he felt too sullen to yield to the little one's petting, when she would leap up to reach his neck and to coax his kiss, with— "*Dame un beso, papa!—así;—y otro! otro! otro!*" He grew to love her like his own;—was she not indeed his own, since he had won her from death? And none had yet come to dispute his claim. More and more, with the passing of weeks, months, seasons, she became a portion of his life—a part of all that he wrought for. At the first, he had had a half-formed hope that the little one might be reclaimed by relatives generous and rich enough to insist upon his acceptance of a handsome compensation; and that Carmen could find some solace in a pleasant visit to Barceloneta. But now he felt that no possible generosity could requite him for her loss; and with the unconscious selfishness of affection, he commenced to dread her identification as a great calamity.

It was evident that she had been brought up nicely. She had pretty prim ways of drinking and eating, queer little fashions of sitting in company, and of addressing people. She had peculiar notions about colors in dress, about wearing her hair; and she seemed to have already imbibed a small stock of social prejudices not altogether in harmony with the republicanism of Viosca's Point. Occasional swarthy visitors,—men of the Manilla settlements,—she spoke of contemptuously as *nègues-marrons*; and once she shocked Carmen inexpressibly by stopping in the middle of her evening prayer, declaring that she wanted to say her prayers to a *white* Virgin; Carmen's Señora de Guadalupe was only a *negra*! Then, for the first time, Carmen spoke so crossly to the child as to frighten her. But the pious woman's heart smote her the next moment for that first harsh word;—and she caressed the motherless one, consoled her, cheered her, and at last explained to her—I know not how—something very wonderful about the little figurine, something that made Chita's eyes big with awe. Thereafter she always regarded the Virgin of Wax as an object mysterious and holy.

And, one by one, most of Chita's little eccentricities were gradually eliminated from her developing life and thought. More rapidly than ordinary children, because singularly intelligent, she learned to adapt herself to all the changes of her new environment,—retaining only that indescribable something which to an experienced eye tells of hereditary refinement of habit and of mind:—a natural grace, a thorough-bred ease and elegance of movement, a quickness and delicacy of perception.

She became strong again and active—active enough to play a great deal on the beach, when the sun was not too fierce; and Carmen made a canvas bonnet to shield her head and face. Never had she been allowed to play so much in the sun before; and it seemed to do her good, though her little bare feet and hands became brown as copper. At first, it must be confessed, she worried her foster-mother a great deal by various queer misfortunes and extraordinary freaks,—getting bitten by crabs, falling into the bayou while in pursuit of "fiddlers," or losing herself at the conclusion of desperate efforts to run races at night with the moon, or to walk to the "end of the world." If she could only once get to the edge of the sky, she said, she "could climb up." She wanted to see the stars, which were the souls of good little children; and she knew that God would let her climb up. "Just what I am afraid of!"—thought Carmen to herself;—"He might let her climb up,—a little ghost!" But one day naughty Chita received a terrible lesson,—a lasting lesson, —which taught her the value of obedience.

She had been particularly cautioned not to venture into a certain part of the swamp in the rear of the grove, where the weeds were very tall; for Carmen was afraid some snake might bite the child. But Chita's bird-bright eye had discerned a gleam of white in that direction; and she wanted to know what it was. The white could only be seen from one point, behind the furthest house, where the ground was high. "Never go there," said Carmen; "there is a Dead Man there,—will bite you!" And yet, one day, while Carmen was unusually busy, Chita went there.

In the early days of the settlement, a Spanish fisherman had died; and his comrades had built him a little tomb with the surplus of the same bricks and other material brought down the bayou for the construction of Viosca's cottages. But no one, except perhaps some wandering duck hunter, had approached the sepulchre for years. High weeds and grasses wrestled together all about it, and rendered it totally invisible from the surrounding level of the marsh.

Fiddlers swarmed away as Chita advanced over the moist soil, each uplifting its single huge claw as it sidled off;—then frogs began to leap before her as she reached the thicker grass; —and long-legged brown insects sprang showering to right and left as she parted the tufts of the thickening verdure. As she went on, the bitter-weeds disappeared;—jointed grasses and sinewy dark plants of a taller growth rose above her head: she was almost deafened by the storm of insect shrilling, and the mosquitoes became very wicked. All at once something long and black and heavy wriggled almost from under her naked feet,—squirming so horribly that for a minute or two she could not move for fright. But it slunk away somewhere, and hid itself; the weeds it had shaken ceased to tremble in its wake; and her courage returned. She felt such an exquisite and fearful pleasure in the gratification of that naughty curiosity! Then, quite unexpectedly—oh! what a start it gave her!—the solitary white object burst upon her view, leprous and ghastly as the yawn of a cotton-mouth. Tombs ruin soon in Louisiana; —the one Chita looked upon seemed ready to topple down. There was a great ragged hole at one end, where wind and rain, and perhaps also the burrowing of crawfish and of worms, had loosened the bricks, and caused them to slide out of place. It seemed very black inside; but Chita wanted to know what was there. She pushed her way through a gap in the thin and rotten line of pickets, and through some tall weeds with big coarse pink flowers;—then she crouched down on hands and knees before the black hole, and peered in. It was not so black inside as she had thought; for a sunbeam slanted down through a chink in the roof; and she could see!

A brown head—without hair, without eyes, but with teeth, ever so many teeth!—seemed to laugh at her; and close to it sat a Toad, the hugest she had ever seen; and the white skin of his throat kept puffing out and going in. And Chita screamed and screamed, and fled in wild terror,—screaming all the way, till Carmen ran out to meet her and carry her home. Even when safe in her adopted mother's arms, she sobbed with fright. To the vivid fancy of the child there seemed to be some hideous relation between the staring reptile and the brown death's-head, with its empty eyes, and its nightmare-smile.

The shock brought on a fever,—a fever that lasted several days, and left her very weak. But the experience taught her to obey, taught her that Carmen knew best what was for her good. It also caused her to think a great deal. Carmen had told her that the dead people never frightened good little girls who stayed at home.

—"Madrecita Carmen," she asked, "is my mamma dead?"

—"*Pobrecita!* . . . Yes, my angel. God called her to Him, —your darling mother."

—"Madrecita," she asked again,—her young eyes growing vast with horror,—"is my own mamma now like *That?*" . . . She pointed toward the place of the white gleam, behind the great trees.

—"No, no, no! my darling!" cried Carmen, appalled herself

by the ghastly question,—"your mamma is with the dear, good, loving God, who lives in the beautiful sky,—above the clouds, my darling, beyond the sun!"

But Carmen's kind eyes were full of tears; and the child read their meaning. He who teareth off the Mask of the Flesh had looked into her face one unutterable moment:—she had seen the brutal Truth, naked to the bone!

Yet there came to her a little thrill of consolation, caused by the words of the tender falsehood; for that which she had discerned by day could not explain to her that which she saw almost nightly in her slumber. The face, the voice, the form of her loving mother still lived somewhere,—could not have utterly passed away; since the sweet presence came to her in dreams, bending and smiling over her, caressing her, speaking to her,—sometimes gently chiding, but always chiding with a kiss. And then the child would laugh in her sleep, and prattle in Creole,—talking to the luminous shadow, telling the dead mother all the little deeds and thoughts of the day. . . . Why would God only let her come at night?

. . . Her idea of God had been first defined by the sight of a quaint French picture of the Creation,—an engraving which represented a shoreless sea under a black sky, and out of the blackness a solemn and bearded gray head emerging, and a cloudy hand through which stars glimmered. God was like old Doctor de Coulanges, who used to visit the house, and talk in a voice like a low roll of thunder. . . . At a later day, when Chita had been told that God was "everywhere at the same time"—without and within, beneath and above all things,— this idea became somewhat changed. The awful bearded face, the huge shadowy hand, did not fade from her thought; but they became fantastically blended with the larger and vaguer notion of something that filled the world and reached to the stars,—something diaphanous and incomprehensible like the invisible air, omnipresent and everlasting like the high blue of heaven. . . .

II.

. . . She began to learn the life of the coast.

With her acquisition of another tongue, there came to her

also the understanding of many things relating to the world of the sea. She memorized with novel delight much that was told her day by day concerning the nature surrounding her,—many secrets of the air, many of those signs of heaven which the dwellers in cities cannot comprehend because the atmosphere is thickened and made stagnant above them—cannot even watch because the horizon is hidden from their eyes by walls, and by weary avenues of trees with whitewashed trunks. She learned, by listening, by asking, by observing also, how to know the signs that foretell wild weather:—tremendous sunsets, scuddings and bridgings of cloud,—sharpening and darkening of the sea-line,—and the shriek of gulls flashing to land in level flight, out of a still transparent sky,—and halos about the moon.

She learned where the sea-birds, with white bosoms and brown wings, made their hidden nests of sand,—and where the cranes waded for their prey,—and where the beautiful wild-ducks, plumaged in satiny lilac and silken green, found their food,—and where the best reeds grew to furnish stems for Feliu's red-clay pipe,—and where the ruddy sea-beans were most often tossed upon the shore,—and how the gray pelicans fished all together, like men—moving in far-extending semi-circles, beating the flood with their wings to drive the fish before them.

And from Carmen she learned the fables and the sayings of the sea,—the proverbs about its deafness, its avarice, its treachery, its terrific power,—especially one that haunted her for all time thereafter: *Si quieres aprender á orar, entra en el mar* (If thou wouldst learn to pray, go to the sea). She learned why the sea is salt,—how "the tears of women made the waves of the sea,"—and how the sea has "no friends,"—and how the cat's eyes change with the tides.

What had she lost of life by her swift translation from the dusty existence of cities to the open immensity of nature's freedom? What did she gain?

Doubtless she was saved from many of those little bitter-nesses and restraints and disappointments which all well-bred city children must suffer in the course of their training for the more or less factitious life of society:—obligations to remain very still with every nimble nerve quivering in dumb revolt;—the injustice of being found troublesome and being sent to bed early for the comfort of her elders;—the cruel necessity of straining her pretty eyes, for many long hours at a time, over grimy desks in gloomy school-rooms, though birds might twitter and bright winds flutter in the trees without;—the austere constraint and heavy drowsiness of warm churches, filled with the droning echoes of a voice preaching incomprehensible things;—the progressively augmenting weariness of lessons in deportment, in dancing, in music, in the impossible art of keeping her dresses unruffled and unsoiled. Perhaps she never had any reason to regret all these.

She went to sleep and awakened with the wild birds;—her life remained as unfettered by formalities as her fine feet by shoes. Excepting Carmen's old prayer-book,—in which she learned to read a little,—her childhood passed without books, —also without pictures, without dainties, without music, without theatrical amusements. But she saw and heard and felt much of that which, though old as the heavens and the earth, is yet eternally new and eternally young with the holiness of beauty,—eternally mystical and divine,—eternally weird: the unveiled magnificence of Nature's moods,—the perpetual poem hymned by wind and surge,—the everlasting splendor of the sky.

She saw the quivering pinkness of waters curled by the breath of the morning—under the deepening of the dawn—like a far fluttering and scattering of rose-leaves of fire;—

Saw the shoreless, cloudless, marvellous double-circling azure of perfect summer days—twin glories of infinite deeps inter-reflected, while the Soul of the World lay still, suffused with a jewel-light, as of vaporized sapphire;—

Saw the Sea shift color,—"change sheets,"—when the viewless Wizard of the Wind breathed upon its face, and made it green;—

Saw the immeasurable panics,—noiseless, scintillant,—which silver, summer after summer, curved leagues of beach with bodies of little fish—the yearly massacre of migrating populations, nations of sea-trout, driven from their element by terror; —and the winnowing of shark-fins,—and the rushing of porpoises,—and the rising of the *grande-écaille*, like a pillar of flame,—and the diving and pitching and fighting of the frigates and the gulls,—and the armored hordes of crabs swarming out to clear the slope after the carnage and the gorging had been done;—

Saw the Dreams of the Sky,—scudding mockeries of ridged foam,—and shadowy stratification of capes and coasts and promontories long-drawn-out,—and imageries, multicolored, of mountain frondage, and sierras whitening above sierras,— and phantom islands ringed around with lagoons of glory;—

Saw the toppling and smouldering of cloud-worlds after the enormous conflagration of sunsets,—incandescence ruining into darkness; and after it a moving and climbing of stars among the blacknesses,—like searching lamps;—

Saw the deep kindle countless ghostly candles as for mysterious night-festival,—and a luminous billowing under a black sky, and effervescences of fire, and the twirling and crawling of phosphoric foam;—

Saw the mesmerism of the Moon;—saw the enchanted tides self-heaped in muttering obeisance before her.

Often she heard the Music of the Marsh through the night: an infinity of flutings and tinklings made by tiny amphibia,— like the low blowing of numberless little tin horns, the clanking of billions of little bells;—and, at intervals, profound tones, vibrant and heavy, as of a bass-viol—the orchestra of the great frogs! And interweaving with it all, one continuous shrilling,— keen as the steel speech of a saw,—the stridulous telegraphy of crickets.

But always,—always, dreaming or awake, she heard the huge blind Sea chanting that mystic and eternal hymn, which none may hear without awe, which no musician can learn;—

Heard the hoary Preacher,—*El Pregonador*,—preaching the ancient Word, the word "as a fire, and as a hammer that breaketh the rock in pieces,"—the Elohim-Word of the Sea! . . .

Unknowingly she came to know the immemorial sympathy of the mind with the Soul of the World,—the melancholy wrought by its moods of gray, the reverie responsive to its vagaries of mist, the exhilaration of its vast exultings—days of windy joy, hours of transfigured light.

She felt,—even without knowing it,—the weight of the Silences, the solemnities of sky and sea in these low regions where all things seem to dream—waters and grasses with their

momentary wavings,—woods gray-webbed with mosses that
drip and drool,—horizons with their delusions of vapor,—
cranes meditating in their marshes,—kites floating in the high
blue. . . . Even the children were singularly quiet; and their
play less noisy—though she could not have learned the difference—than the play of city children. Hour after hour, the
women sewed or wove in silence. And the brown men,—
always barefooted, always wearing rough blue shirts,—seemed,
when they lounged about the wharf on idle days, as if they had
told each other long ago all they knew or could ever know, and
had nothing more to say. They would stare at the flickering of
the current, at the drifting of clouds and buzzards—seldom
looking at each other, and always turning their black eyes
again, in a weary way, to sky or sea. Even thus one sees the
horses and the cattle of the coast, seeking the beach to escape
the whizzing flies;—all watch the long waves rolling in, and
sometimes turn their heads a moment to look at one another,
but always look back to the waves again, as if wondering at a
mystery. . . .

How often she herself had wondered—wondered at the
multiform changes of each swell as it came in—transformations of tint, of shape, of motion, that seemed to betoken a life
infinitely more subtle than the strange cold life of lizards and
of fishes,—and sinister, and spectral. Then they all appeared to
move in order,—according to one law or impulse:—each had
its own voice, yet all sang one and the same everlasting song.
Vaguely, as she watched them and listened to them, there came
to her the idea of a unity of *will* in their motion, a unity of
menace in their utterance—the idea of one monstrous and
complex life! The sea *lived*: it could crawl backward and forward; it could speak!—it only feigned deafness and sightless-
ness for some malevolent end. Thenceforward she feared to
find herself alone with it. Was it not at her that it strove to rush,
muttering, and showing its white teeth, . . . just because it
knew that she was all by herself? . . . *Si quieres aprender á
orar, entra en el mar!* And Concha had well learned to pray.
But the sea seemed to her the one Power which God could not
make to obey Him as He pleased. Saying the creed one day, she
repeated very slowly the opening words,—"*Creo en un Dios,
padre todopoderoso, Criador del cielo y de la tierra,*"—and

paused and thought. *Creator of Heaven and Earth?* "Madrecita Carmen," she asked,—"*quien entonces hizó el mar?*" (who then made the sea?).

—"Dios, mi querida," answered Carmen.—"God, my darling. . . . All things were made by Him" (*todas las cosas fueron hechas por Él*).

Even the wicked Sea! And He had said unto it: "Thus far, and no farther." . . . Was that why it had not overtaken and devoured her when she ran back in fear from the sudden reaching out of its waves? *Thus far. . . . ?* But there were times when it disobeyed—when it rushed further, shaking the world! Was it because God was then asleep—could not hear, did not see, until too late?

And the tumultuous ocean terrified her more and more: it filled her sleep with enormous nightmare;—it came upon her in dreams, mountain-shadowing,—holding her with its spell, smothering her power of outcry, heaping itself to the stars.

Carmen became alarmed;—she feared that the nervous and delicate child might die in one of those moaning dreams out of which she had to arouse her, night after night. But Feliu, answering her anxiety with one of his favorite proverbs, suggested a heroic remedy:—

—"The world is like the sea: those who do not know how to swim in it are drowned;—and the sea is like the world," he added. . . . "Chita must learn to swim!"

And he found the time to teach her. Each morning, at sunrise, he took her into the water. She was less terrified the first time than Carmen thought she would be;—she seemed to feel confidence in Feliu; although she screamed piteously before her first ducking at his hands. His teaching was not gentle. He would carry her out, perched upon his shoulder, until the water rose to his own neck; and there he would throw her from him, and let her struggle to reach him again as best she could. The first few mornings she had to be pulled out almost at once; but after that Feliu showed her less mercy, and helped her only when he saw she was really in danger. He attempted no other instruction until she had learned that in order to save herself from being half choked by the salt water, she must not scream; and by the time she became habituated to these austere experiences, she had already learned by instinct alone how to keep

herself afloat for a while, how to paddle a little with her hands.
Then he commenced to train her to use them,—to lift them
well out and throw them forward as if reaching, to dip them
as the blade of an oar is dipped at an angle, without loud
splashing;—and he showed her also how to use her feet. She
learned rapidly and astonishingly well. In less than two months
Feliu felt really proud at the progress made by his tiny pupil: it
was a delight to watch her lifting her slender arms above the
water in swift, easy curves, with the same fine grace that marked
all her other natural motions. Later on he taught her not to
fear the sea even when it growled a little,—how to ride a swell,
how to face a breaker, how to dive. She only needed practice
thereafter; and Carmen, who could also swim, finding the
child's health improving marvellously under this new discipline, took good care that Chita should practise whenever the
mornings were not too cold, or the water too rough.

With the first thrill of delight at finding herself able to glide
over the water unassisted, the child's superstitious terror of the
sea passed away. Even for the adult there are few physical joys
keener than the exultation of the swimmer;—how much greater
the same glee as newly felt by an imaginative child,—a child,
whose vivid fancy can lend unutterable value to the most insignificant trifles, can transform a weed-patch to an Eden! . . .
Of her own accord she would ask for her morning bath, as
soon as she opened her eyes;—it even required some severity
to prevent her from remaining in the water too long. The sea
appeared to her as something that had become tame for her
sake, something that loved her in a huge rough way; a tremendous playmate, whom she no longer feared to see come
bounding and barking to lick her feet. And, little by little, she
also learned the wonderful healing and caressing power of the
monster, whose cool embrace at once dispelled all drowsiness,
feverishness, weariness,—even after the sultriest nights when
the air had seemed to burn, and the mosquitoes had filled the
chamber with a sound as of water boiling in many kettles. And
on mornings when the sea was in too wicked a humor to be
played with, how she felt the loss of her loved sport, and
prayed for calm! Her delicate constitution changed;—the soft,
pale flesh became firm and brown, the meagre limbs rounded
into robust symmetry, the thin cheeks grew peachy with richer

life; for the strength of the sea had entered into her; the sharp breath of the sea had renewed and brightened her young blood. . . .

. . . Thou primordial Sea, the awfulness of whose antiquity hath stricken all mythology dumb;—thou most wrinkled living Sea, the millions of whose years outnumber even the multitude of thy hoary motions;—thou omniform and most mysterious Sea, mother of the monsters and the gods,—whence thine eternal youth? Still do thy waters hold the infinite thrill of that Spirit which brooded above their face in the Beginning!—still is thy quickening breath an elixir unto them that flee to thee for life,—like the breath of young girls, like the breath of children, prescribed for the senescent by magicians of old,—prescribed unto weazened elders in the books of the Wizards.

III.

. . . Eighteen hundred and sixty-seven;—midsummer in the pest-smitten city of New Orleans.

Heat motionless and ponderous. The steel-blue of the sky bleached from the furnace-circle of the horizon;—the lukewarm river ran yellow and noiseless as a torrent of fluid wax. Even sounds seemed blunted by the heaviness of the air;—the rumbling of wheels, the reverberation of footsteps, fell half-toned upon the ear, like sounds that visit a dozing brain.

Daily, almost at the same hour, the continuous sense of atmospheric oppression became thickened;—a packed herd of low-bellying clouds lumbered up from the Gulf; crowded blackly against the sun; flickered, thundered, and burst in torrential rain—tepid, perpendicular—and vanished utterly away. Then, more furiously than before, the sun flamed down;— roofs and pavements steamed; the streets seemed to smoke; the air grew suffocating with vapor; and the luminous city filled with a faint, sickly odor,—a stale smell, as of dead leaves suddenly disinterred from wet mould,—as of grasses decomposing after a flood. Something saffron speckled the slimy water of the gutters; sulphur some called it; others feared even to give it a name! Was it only the wind-blown pollen of some innocuous plant? I do not know; but to many it seemed as if the Invisible Destruction were scattering visible seed! . . .

Such were the days; and each day the terror-stricken city offered up its hecatomb to death; and the faces of all the dead were yellow as flame!

"DÉCÉDÉ—;" "DÉCÉDÉE—;" "FALLECIO;"—"DIED." . . . On the door-posts, the telegraph-poles, the pillars of verandas, the lamps,—over the government letter-boxes,—everywhere glimmered the white annunciations of death. All the city was spotted with them. And lime was poured into the gutters; and huge purifying fires were kindled after sunset.

The nights began with a black heat;—there were hours when the acrid air seemed to ferment for stagnation, and to burn the bronchial tubing;—then, toward morning, it would grow chill with venomous vapors, with morbific dews,—till the sun came up to lift the torpid moisture, and to fill the buildings with oven-glow. And the interminable procession of mourners and hearses and carriages again began to circulate between the centres of life and of death;—and long trains and steamships rushed from the port, with heavy burden of fugitives.

Wealth might flee; yet even in flight there was peril. Men, who might have been saved by the craft of experienced nurses at home, hurriedly departed in apparent health, unconsciously carrying in their blood the toxic principle of a malady unfamiliar to physicians of the West and North;—and they died upon their way, by the road-side, by the river-banks, in woods, in deserted stations, on the cots of quarantine hospitals. Wiser those who sought refuge in the purity of the pine forests, or in those near Gulf Islands, whence the bright sea-breath kept ever sweeping back the expanding poison into the funereal swamps, into the misty lowlands. The watering-resorts became over-crowded;—then the fishing villages were thronged,—at least all which were easy to reach by steamboat or by lugger. And at last, even Viosca's Point,—remote and unfamiliar as it was,—had a stranger to shelter: a good old gentleman named Edwards, rather broken down in health—who came as much for quiet as for sea-air, and who had been warmly recommended to Feliu by Captain Harris. For some years he had been troubled by a disease of the heart.

Certainly the old invalid could not have found a more suitable place so far as rest and quiet were concerned. The season had early given such little promise that several men of the Point betook themselves elsewhere; and the aged visitor had two or three vacant cabins from among which to select a dwelling-place. He chose to occupy the most remote of all, which Carmen furnished for him with a cool moss bed and some necessary furniture,—including a big wooden rocking-chair. It seemed to him very comfortable thus. He took his meals with the family, spent most of the day in his own quarters, spoke very little, and lived so unobtrusively and inconspicuously that his presence in the settlement was felt scarcely more than that of some dumb creature,—some domestic animal,—some humble pet whose relation to the family is only fully comprehended after it has failed to appear for several days in its accustomed place of patient waiting,—and we know that it is dead.

IV.

Persistently and furiously, at half-past two o'clock of an August morning, Sparicio rang Dr. La Brierre's night-bell. He had fifty dollars in his pocket, and a letter to deliver. He was to earn another fifty dollars—deposited in Feliu's hands,—by bringing the Doctor to Viosca's Point. He had risked his life for that money,—and was terribly in earnest.

Julien descended in his under-clothing, and opened the letter by the light of the hall lamp. It enclosed a check for a larger fee than he had ever before received, and contained an urgent request that he would at once accompany Sparicio to Viosca's Point,—as the sender was in hourly danger of death. The letter, penned in a long, quavering hand, was signed,— "*Henry Edwards.*"

His father's dear old friend! Julien could not refuse to go,— though he feared it was a hopeless case. *Angina pectoris,*—and a third attack at seventy years of age! Would it even be possible to reach the sufferer's bedside in time? "*Duè giorno,—con vento,*"—said Sparicio. Still, he must go; and at once. It was Friday morning;—might reach the Point Saturday night, with a good wind. . . . He roused his housekeeper, gave all needful instructions, prepared his little medicine-chest;—and long

before the first rose-gold fire of day had flashed to the city
spires, he was sleeping the sleep of exhaustion in the tiny cabin
of a fishing-sloop.

. . . For eleven years Julien had devoted himself, heart and
soul, to the exercise of that profession he had first studied
rather as a polite accomplishment than as a future calling. In
the unselfish pursuit of duty he had found the only possible
consolation for his irreparable loss; and when the war came to
sweep away his wealth, he entered the struggle valorously, not
to strive against men, but to use his science against death. After
the passing of that huge shock, which left all the imposing and
splendid fabric of Southern feudalism wrecked forever, his profession stood him in good stead;—he found himself not only
able to supply those personal wants he cared to satisfy, but also
to alleviate the misery of many whom he had known in days of
opulence;—the princely misery that never doffed its smiling
mask, though living in secret, from week to week, on bread
and orange-leaf tea;—the misery that affected condescension
in accepting an invitation to dine,—staring at the face of a
watch (refused by the Mont-de-Piété) with eyes half blinded by
starvation;—the misery which could afford but one robe for
three marriageable daughters,—one plain dress to be worn in
turn by each of them, on visiting days;—the pretty misery—
young, brave, sweet,—asking for a "treat" of cakes too jocosely
to have its asking answered,—laughing and coquetting with its
well-fed wooers, and crying for hunger after they were gone.
Often and often, his heart had pleaded against his purse for
such as these, and won its case in the silent courts of Self. But
ever mysteriously the gift came,—sometimes as if from the
hand of a former slave; sometimes as from a remorseful credi-
tor, ashamed to write his name. Only yellow Victorine knew;
but the Doctor's housekeeper never opened those sphinx-lips
of hers, until years after the Doctor's name had disappeared
from the City Directory. . . .

He had grown quite thin,—a little gray. The epidemic had
burthened him with responsibilities too multifarious and ponderous for his slender strength to bear. The continual nervous
strain of abnormally protracted duty, the perpetual interruption of sleep, had almost prostrated even his will. Now he only

hoped that, during this brief absence from the city, he might find renewed strength to do his terrible task.

Mosquitoes bit savagely; and the heat became thicker;—and there was yet no wind. Sparicio and his hired boy Carmelo had been walking backward and forward for hours overhead,—urging the vessel yard by yard, with long poles, through the slime of canals and bayous. With every heavy push, the weary boy would sigh out,—"*Santo Antonio!—Santo Antonio!*" Sullen Sparicio himself at last burst into vociferations of ill-humor:— "*Santo Antonio?—Ah! santissimu e santu diavulu! . . . Sacramentu pœscite vegnu un asidente!—malidittu lu Signuri!*" All through the morning they walked and pushed, trudged and sighed and swore; and the minutes dragged by more wearily than the shuffling of their feet. "*Managgia Cristo co tutta a croce!*" . . . "*Santisimu e santu diavulu!!*"

But as they reached at last the first of the broad bright lakes, the heat lifted, the breeze leaped up, the loose sail flapped and filled; and, bending graciously as a skater, the old *San Marco* began to shoot in a straight line over the blue flood. Then, while the boy sat at the tiller, Sparicio lighted his tiny charcoal furnace below, and prepared a simple meal,—delicious yellow macaroni, flavored with goats' cheese; some fried fish, that smelled appetizingly; and rich black coffee, of Oriental fragrance and thickness. Julien ate a little, and lay down to sleep again. This time his rest was undisturbed by the mosquitoes; and when he woke, in the cooling evening, he felt almost refreshed. The *San Marco* was flying into Barataria Bay. Already the lantern in the lighthouse tower had begun to glow like a little moon; and right on the rim of the sea, a vast and vermilion sun seemed to rest his chin. Gray pelicans came flapping around the mast;—sea-birds sped hurtling by, their white bosoms rose-flushed by the western glow. . . . Again Sparicio's little furnace was at work,—more fish, more macaroni, more black coffee; also a square-shouldered bottle of gin made its appearance. Julien ate less sparingly at this second meal; and smoked a long time on deck with Sparicio, who suddenly became very good-humored, and chatted volubly in bad Spanish, and in much worse English. Then while the boy took a few hours' sleep, the Doctor helped delightedly in manœuvring the little vessel. He had been a good yachtsman in other years; and Sparicio declared he would make a good fisherman. By midnight the *San Marco* began to run with a long, swinging gait;—she had reached deep water. Julien slept soundly; the steady rocking of the sloop seemed to soothe his nerves.

—"After all," he thought to himself, as he rose from his little bunk next morning,—"something like this is just what I needed." . . . The pleasant scent of hot coffee greeted him; —Carmelo was handing him the tin cup containing it, down through the hatchway. After drinking it he felt really hungry; — he ate more macaroni than he had ever eaten before. Then, while Sparicio slept, he aided Carmelo; and during the middle of the day he rested again. He had not had so much uninter- rupted repose for many a week. He fancied he could feel himself getting strong. At supper-time it seemed to him he could not get enough to eat,—although there was plenty for everybody.

All day long there had been exactly the same wave-crease distorting the white shadow of the *San Marco's* sail upon the blue water;—all day long they had been skimming over the liq- uid level of a world so jewel-blue that the low green ribbon- strips of marsh land, the far-off fleeing lines of pine-yellow sand beach, seemed flaws or breaks in the perfected color of the universe;—all day long had the cloudless sky revealed through all its exquisite transparency that inexpressible tenderness which no painter and no poet can ever reimage,—that unutterable sweetness which no art of man may ever shadow forth, and which none may ever comprehend,—though we feel it to be in some strange way akin to the luminous and unspeakable charm that makes us wonder at the eyes of a woman when she loves.

Evening came; and the great dominant celestial tone deep- ened;—the circling horizon filled with ghostly tints,—spectral greens and grays, and pearl-lights and fish-colors. . . . Car- melo, as he crouched at the tiller, was singing, in a low, clear alto, some tristful little melody. Over the sea, behind them, lay, black-stretching, a long low arm of island-shore;—before them flamed the splendor of sun-death; they were sailing into a mighty glory,—into a vast and awful light of gold.

Shading his vision with his fingers, Sparicio pointed to the long lean limb of land from which they were fleeing, and said to La Brierre:—

—"Look-a, Doct-a! *Last-a Islan'!*"

Julien knew it;—he only nodded his head in reply, and looked the other way,—into the glory of God. Then, wishing to divert the fisherman's attention to another theme, he asked what was Carmelo singing. Sparicio at once shouted to the lad:—

—"Ha! . . . ho! Carmelo!—*Santu diavulu!* . . . . Sing-a loud-a! Doct-a lik-a! Sing-a! sing!!". . . . "He sing-a nicee," —added the boatman, with his peculiar dark smile. And then Carmelo sang, loud and clearly, the song he had been singing before,—one of those artless Mediterranean ballads, full of caressing vowel-sounds, and young passion, and melancholy beauty:—

> *"M'ama ancor, beltà fulgente,*
> *Come tu m'amasti allor;—*
> *Ascoltar non dei gente,*
> *Solo interroga il tuo cor."* . . .

—"He sing-a nicee,—mucha bueno!" murmured the fisherman. And then, suddenly,—with a rich and splendid basso that seemed to thrill every fibre of the planking,—Sparicio joined in the song:—

> *"M'ama pur d' amore eterno,*
> *Nè delitto sembri a te;*
> *T' assicuro che l' inferno*
> *Una favola sol è."* . . .

All the roughness of the man was gone! To Julien's startled fancy, the fishers had ceased to be;—lo! Carmelo was a princely page; Sparicio, a king! How perfectly their voices married together!—they sang with passion, with power, with truth, with that wondrous natural art which is the birthright of the rudest Italian soul. And the stars throbbed out in the heaven; and the glory died in the west; and the night opened its heart; and the splendor of the eternities fell all about them. Still they sang; and the *San Marco* sped on through the soft gloom, ever slightly swerved by the steady blowing of the southeast wind in her sail;—always wearing the same crimpling-frill of wave-spray about her prow,—always accompanied by the same smooth-backed swells,—always spinning out behind her the same long trail of interwoven foam. And Julien looked up. Ever the night thrilled more and more with silent twinklings;—more and more multitudinously lights pointed in the eternities;—the Evening Star quivered like a great drop of liquid white fire ready to fall; —Vega flamed as a pharos lighting the courses ethereal,—to guide the sailing of the suns, and the swarming of fleets of worlds. Then the vast sweetness of that violet night entered into his blood,—filled him with that awful joy, so near akin to sadness, which the sense of the Infinite brings,—when one feels the poetry of the Most Ancient and Most Excellent of Poets, and then is smitten at once with the contrast-thought of the sickliness and selfishness of Man,—of the blindness and brutality of cities, whereinto the divine blue light never purely comes, and the sanctification of the Silences never descends . . . furious cities, walled away from heaven. . . . Oh! if one could only sail on thus always, always through such a night— through such a star-sprinkled violet light, and hear Sparicio and Carmelo sing, even though it were the same melody always, always the same song!

. . . "Scuza, Doct-a!—look-a out!" Julien bent down, as the big boom, loosened, swung over his head. The *San Marco* was rounding into shore,—heading for her home. Sparicio lifted a huge conch-shell from the deck, put it to his lips, filled his deep lungs, and flung out into the night—thrice—a profound, mellifluent, booming horn-tone. A minute passed. Then, ghostly faint, as an echo from very far away, a triple blowing responded. . . .

And a long purple mass loomed and swelled into sight, heightened, approached—land and trees black-shadowing, and lights that swung. . . . The *San Marco* glided into a bayou,—under a high wharfing of timbers, where a bearded fisherman waited, and a woman. Sparicio flung up a rope.

The bearded man caught it by the lantern-light, and tethered the *San Marco* to her place. Then he asked, in a deep voice:

—"*Has traido al Doctor?*"

—"*Si, si!*" answered Sparicio. . . . "*Y el viejo?*"

—"*Aye! pobre!*" responded Feliu,—"*hace tres dias que esta muerto.*"

Henry Edwards was dead!

He had died very suddenly, without a cry or a word, while resting in his rocking-chair,—the very day after Sparicio had sailed. They had made him a grave in the marsh,—among the high weeds, not far from the ruined tomb of the Spanish fisherman. But Sparicio had fairly earned his hundred dollars.

V.

So there was nothing to do at Viosca's Point except to rest. Feliu and all his men were going to Barataria in the morning on business;—the Doctor could accompany them there, and take the Grand Island steamer Monday for New Orleans. With this intention Julien retired,—not sorry for being able to stretch himself at full length on the good bed prepared for him, in one of the unoccupied cabins. But he woke before day with a feeling of intense prostration, a violent headache, and such an aversion for the mere idea of food that Feliu's invitation to breakfast at five o'clock gave him an internal qualm. Perhaps a touch of malaria. In any case he felt it would be both dangerous and useless to return to town unwell; and Feliu, observing his condition, himself advised against the journey. Wednesday he would have another opportunity to leave; and in the meanwhile Carmen would take good care of him. . . . The boats departed, and Julien slept again.

The sun was high when he rose up and dressed himself, feeling no better. He would have liked to walk about the place, but felt nervously afraid of the sun. He did not remember having ever felt so broken down before. He pulled a rocking-chair to the window, tried to smoke a cigar. It commenced to make him feel still sicker, and he flung it away. It seemed to him the cabin was swaying, as the *San Marco* swayed when she first reached the deep water.

A light rustling sound approached,—a sound of quick feet treading the grass: then a shadow slanted over the threshold. In the glow of the open doorway stood a young girl,—gracile, tall,—with singularly splendid eyes,—brown eyes peeping at him from beneath a golden riot of loose hair.

—"*M'sieu-le-Docteur, maman d'mande si vous n'avez bisoin d'que'que chose?*" . . . She spoke the rude French of the fishing villages, where the language lives chiefly as a *baragouin*, mingled often with words and forms belonging to many other tongues. She wore a loose-falling dress of some light stuff, steel-gray in color;—boys' shoes were on her feet.

He did not reply;—and her large eyes grew larger for wonder at the strange fixed gaze of the physician, whose face had visibly bleached,—blanched to corpse-pallor. Silent seconds passed; and still the eyes stared—flamed as if the life of the man had centralized and focussed within them.

His voice had risen to a cry in his throat, quivered and swelled one passionate instant, and failed—as in a dream when one strives to call, and yet can only moan. . . . *She!* Her unforgotten eyes, her brows, her lips!—the oval of her face!—the dawn-light of her hair! . . . Adèle's own poise,—her own grace!—even the very turn of her neck,—even the bird-tone of her speech! . . . Had the grave sent forth a Shadow to haunt him?—could the perfidious Sea have yielded up its dead? For one terrible fraction of a minute, memories, doubts, fears, mad fancies, went pulsing through his brain with a rush like the rhythmic throbbing of an electric stream;—then the shock passed, the Reason spoke:—"Fool!—count the long years since you first saw her thus!—count the years that have gone since you looked upon her last! And Time has never halted, silly heart!— neither has Death stood still!"

. . . "*Plait-il?*"—the clear voice of the young girl asked. She thought he had made some response she could not distinctly hear.

Mastering himself an instant, as the heart faltered back to its duty, and the color remounted to his lips, he answered her in French:

—"Pardon me!—I did not hear . . . you gave me such a start!" . . . But even then another extraordinary fancy flashed through his thought;—and with the *tutoiement* of a parent to a child, with an irresistible outburst of such tenderness as almost frightened her, he cried: "Oh! merciful God!— how like her! . . . Tell me, darling, your name;—tell me who you are?" (*Dis-moi qui tu es, mignonne;—dis-moi ton nom.*)

. . . Who was it had asked her the same question, in another idiom—ever so long ago? The man with the black eyes and nose like an eagle's beak,—the one who gave her the compass. Not *this* man—no!

She answered, with the timid gravity of surprise:—

—"Chita Viosca."

He still watched her face, and repeated the name slowly,—reiterated it in a tone of wonderment:—"Chita Viosca?—Chita Viosca!"

—"*C'est à dire* . . ." she said, looking down at her feet,—"Concha—Conchita." His strange solemnity made her smile,—the smile of shyness that knows not what else to do. But it was the smile of dead Adèle.

—"Thanks, my child," he exclaimed of a sudden,—in a quick, hoarse, changed tone. (He felt that his emotion would break loose in some wild way, if he looked upon her longer.) "I would like to see your mother this evening; but I now feel too ill to go out. I am going to try to rest a little."

—"Nothing I can bring you?" she asked;—"some fresh milk?"

—"Nothing now, dear: if I need anything later, I will tell your mother when she comes."

—"Mamma does not understand French very well."

—"*No importa, Conchita;—le hablaré en Español.*"

—"*Bien, entonces!*" she responded, with the same exquisite smile. "*Adios, señor!*" . . .

But as she turned in going, his piercing eye discerned a little brown speck below the pretty lobe of her right ear,—just in the peachy curve between neck and cheek. . . . His own little Zouzoune had a birthmark like that!—he remembered the faint pink trace left by his fingers above and below it the day he had slapped her for overturning his ink-bottle. . . . "*To laimin moin?—to batté moin!*"

—"Chita!—Chita!"

She did not hear. . . . After all, what a mistake he might have made! Were not Nature's coincidences more wonderful than fiction? Better to wait,—to question the mother first, and thus make sure.

Still—there were so many coincidences! The face, the smile, the eyes, the voice, the whole charm;—then that mark,—and the fair hair. Zouzoune had always resembled Adèle so strangely! That golden hair was a Scandinavian bequest to the Florane family;—the tall daughter of a Norwegian sea-captain had once become the wife of a Florane. Viosca?—who ever knew a

Viosca with such hair? Yet again, these Spanish emigrants
sometimes married blonde German girls. . . . Might be a case
of atavism, too. Who was this Viosca? If that was his wife,—the
little brown Carmen,—whence Chita's sunny hair? . . .

And this was part of that same desolate shore whither the
Last Island dead had been drifted by that tremendous surge!
On a clear day, with a good glass, one might discern from here
the long blue streak of that ghastly coast. . . . Somewhere—
between here and there. . . . Merciful God! . . .

. . . But again! That bivouac-night before the fight at Chancellorsville, Laroussel had begun to tell him such a singular
story . . . Chance had brought them,—the old enemies,—
together; made them dear friends in the face of Death. How
little he had comprehended the man!—what a brave, true,
simple soul went up that day to the Lord of Battles! . . .
What was it—that story about the little Creole girl saved from
Last Island,—that story which was never finished? . . . Eh!
what a pain!

Evidently he had worked too much, slept too little. A decided case of nervous prostration. He must lie down, and try
to sleep. These pains in the head and back were becoming un-
bearable. Nothing but rest could avail him now.

He stretched himself under the mosquito curtain. It was
very still, breathless, hot! The venomous insects were thick;—
they filled the room with a continuous ebullient sound, as if
invisible kettles were boiling overhead. A sign of storm. . . .
Still, it was strange!—he could not perspire. . . .

Then it seemed to him that Laroussel was bending over
him—Laroussel in his cavalry uniform. "*Bon jour, camarade!
—nous allons avoir un bien mauvais temps, mon pauvre Julien.*"
How! bad weather?—"*Comment un mauvais temps?*" . . .
He looked in Laroussel's face. There was something so singular in his smile. Ah! yes,—he remembered now: it was the
wound! . . . "*Un vilain temps!*" whispered Laroussel. Then
he was gone. . . . Whither?

—"*Chéri!*" . . .

The whisper roused him with a fearful start. . . . Adèle's
whisper! So she was wont to rouse him sometimes in the old
sweet nights,—to crave some little attention for ailing Eulalie,
—to make some little confidence she had forgotten to utter

during the happy evening. . . . No, no! It was only the trees. The sky was clouding over. The wind was rising. . . . How his heart beat! how his temples pulsed! Why, this was fever! Such pains in the back and head!

Still his skin was dry,—dry as parchment,—burning. He rose up; and a bursting weight of pain at the base of the skull made him reel like a drunken man. He staggered to the little mirror nailed upon the wall, and looked. How his eyes glowed;—and there was blood in his mouth! He felt his pulse—spasmodic, terribly rapid. Could it possibly—? . . . No: this must be some pernicious malarial fever! The Creole does not easily fall a prey to the great tropical malady,—unless after a long absence in other climates. True! he had been four years in the army! But this was 1867. . . . He hesitated a moment; then, —opening his medicine-chest, he measured out and swallowed thirty grains of quinine.

Then he lay down again. His head pained more and more;— it seemed as if the cervical vertebræ were filled with fluid iron. And still his skin remained dry as if tanned. Then the anguish grew so intense as to force a groan with almost every aspiration. . . . Nausea,—and the stinging bitterness of quinine rising in his throat;—dizziness, and a brutal wrenching within his stomach. Everything began to look pink;—the light was rose-colored. It darkened more,—kindled with deepening tint. Something kept sparkling and spinning before his sight, like a firework. . . . Then a burst of blood mixed with chemical bitterness filled his mouth; the light became scarlet as claret. . . . This—this was . . . not malaria. . . .

VI.

. . . Carmen knew what it was; but the brave little woman was not afraid of it. Many a time before she had met it face to face, in Havanese summers; she knew how to wrestle with it;— she had torn Feliu's life away from its yellow clutch, after one of those long struggles that strain even the strength of love. Now she feared mostly for Chita. She had ordered the girl under no circumstances to approach the cabin.

Julien felt that blankets had been heaped upon him,—that some gentle hand was bathing his scorching face with vinegar and water. Vaguely also there came to him the idea that it was night. He saw the shadow-shape of a woman moving against the red light upon the wall;—he saw there was a lamp burning.

Then the delirium seized him: he moaned, sobbed, cried like a child,—talked wildly at intervals in French, in English, in Spanish.

—"*Mentira!*—you could not be her mother. . . . Still, if you were— And she must not come in here,—*jamas!* . . . Carmen, did you know Adèle,—Adèle Florane? So like her,— so like,—God only knows how like! . . . Perhaps I think I know;—but I do not—do not know justly, fully—how like! . . . *Si! si!—es el vómito!—yo lo conozco, Carmen!* . . . She must not die twice. . . . I died twice. . . . I am going to die again. She only once. Till the heavens be no more she will not rise. . . . *Moi, au contraire, il faut que je me lève toujours!* They need me so much;—the slate is always full; the bell will never stop. They will ring that bell for me when I am dead. . . . So will I rise again!—*resurgam!* . . . How could I save him?—could not save myself. It was a bad case,—at seventy years! . . . There! *Qui çà?*" . . .

He saw Laroussel again,—reaching out a hand to him through a whirl of red smoke. He tried to grasp it, and could not. . . . "*N'importe, mon ami,*" said Laroussel,—"*tu vas la voir bientôt.*" Who was he to see soon?—"*qui donc, Laroussel?*" But Laroussel did not answer. Through the red mist he seemed to smile;—then passed.

For some hours Carmen had trusted she could save her patient,—desperate as the case appeared to be. His was one of those rapid and violent attacks, such as often despatch their victims in a single day. In the Cuban hospitals she had seen many and many terrible examples: strong young men,—soldiers fresh from Spain,—carried panting to the fever wards at sunrise; carried to the cemeteries at sunset. Even troopers riddled with revolutionary bullets had lingered longer. . . . Still, she had believed she might save Julien's life: the burning forehead once began to bead, the burning hands grew moist.

But now the wind was moaning;—the air had become lighter, thinner, cooler. A storm was gathering in the east; and to the fever-stricken man the change meant death. . . . Impossible to bring the priest of the Caminada now; and there was no other within a day's sail. She could only pray; she had lost all hope in her own power to save.

Still the sick man raved; but he talked to himself at longer intervals, and with longer pauses between his words;—his voice was growing more feeble, his speech more incoherent. His thought vacillated and distorted, like flame in a wind.

Weirdly the past became confounded with the present; impressions of sight and of sound interlinked in fastastic affinity, —the face of Chita Viosca, the murmur of the rising storm. Then flickers of spectral lightning passed through his eyes, through his brain, with every throb of the burning arteries; then utter darkness came,—a darkness that surged and moaned, as the circumfluence of a shadowed sea. And through and over the moaning pealed one multitudinous human cry, one hideous interblending of shoutings and shriekings. . . . A woman's hand was locked in his own. . . . "Tighter," he muttered, "tighter still, darling! hold as long as you can!" It was the tenth night of August, eighteen hundred and fifty-six. . . .

—"*Chéri!*" . . .

Again the mysterious whisper startled him to consciousness, —the dim knowledge of a room filled with ruby-colored light,—and the sharp odor of vinegar. The house swung round slowly;—the crimson flame of the lamp lengthened and broadened by turns;—then everything turned dizzily fast,—whirled as if spinning in a vortex. . . . Nausea unutterable; and a frightful anguish as of teeth devouring him within,—tearing more and more furiously at his breast. Then one atrocious wrenching, rending, burning,—and the gush of blood burst from lips and nostrils in a smothering deluge. Again the vision of lightnings, the swaying, and the darkness of long ago. "Quick!—quick!—hold fast to the table, Adèle!—never let go!" . . .

. . . Up,—up,—up!—what! higher yet? Up to the red sky! Red—black-red. . . . heated iron when its vermilion dies. So, too, the frightful flood! And noiseless. Noiseless because heavy, clammy,—thick, warm, sickening . . . blood? Well might the land quake for the weight of such a tide! . . . Why did Adèle speak Spanish? Who prayed for him? . . .

—"*Alma de Cristo santísima santifícame!*

"Sangre de Cristo, embriágame!
"O buen Jesus, oye me!" . . .

Out of the darkness into—such a light! An azure haze!
Ah!—the delicious frost! . . . . All the streets were
filled with the sweet blue mist. . . . . Voiceless the
City and white;—crooked and weed-grown its narrow ways!
. . . . Old streets of tombs, these. . . . . Eh!
How odd a custom!—a Night-bell at every door. Yes, of
course!—a *night*-bell!—the Dead are Physicians of Souls: they
may be summoned only by night,—called up from the darkness and silence. . . . Yet *she?*—might he not dare to ring for
her even by day? . . . . Strange he had deemed it day!
—why, it was black, starless. . . . And it was growing queerly
cold. . . . . How should he ever find her now? It was so
black . . . so cold! . . .

—*"Chéri!"*
All the dwelling quivered with the mighty whisper.
Outside, the great oaks were trembling to their roots;—all
the shore shook and blanched before the calling of the sea.
And Carmen, kneeling at the feet of the dead, cried out,
alone in the night:
—*"O Jesus misericordioso!—tened compasion de él!"*

THE END.

TWO YEARS IN THE
FRENCH WEST INDIES

A Martinique Métisse.
(In "douillette" and "madras.")

"La façon d'être du pays est si agréable, la température si bonne, et l'on y vit dans une liberté si honnête, que je n'aye pas vu un seul homme, ny une seule femme, qui en soient revenus, en qui je n'aye remarqué une grande passion d'y retourner."

—LE PÈRE DUTERTRE (1667)

PREFACE

DURING a trip to the Lesser Antilles in the summer of 1887, the writer of the following pages, landing at Martinique, fell under the influence of that singular spell which the island has always exercised upon strangers, and by which it has earned its poetic name,—*Le Pays des Revenants.* Even as many another before him, he left its charmed shores only to know himself haunted by that irresistible regret,—unlike any other,—which is the enchantment of the land upon all who wander away from it. So he returned, intending to remain some months: but the bewitchment prevailed, and he remained two years.

Some of the literary results of that sojourn form the bulk of the present volume. Several, or portions of several, papers have been published in HARPER'S MAGAZINE; but the majority of the sketches now appear in print for the first time.

The introductory paper, entitled "A Midsummer Trip to the Tropics," consists for the most part of notes taken upon a voyage of nearly three thousand miles, accomplished in less than two months. During such hasty journeying it is scarcely possible for a writer to attempt anything more serious than a mere reflection of the personal experiences undergone; and, in spite of sundry justifiable departures from simple note-making, this paper is offered only as an effort to record the visual and emotional impressions of the moment.

My thanks are due to Mr. William Lawless, British Consul at St. Pierre, for several beautiful photographs, taken by himself, which have been used in the preparation of the illustrations.

L.H.

Philadelphia, 1889.

CONTENTS

ILLUSTRATIONS

A Midsummer Trip to the Tropics

I.

. . . A LONG, narrow, graceful steel steamer, with two masts and an orange-yellow chimney,—taking on cargo at Pier 49 East River. Through her yawning hatchways a mountainous piling up of barrels is visible below;—there is much rumbling and rattling of steam-winches, creaking of derrick-booms, groaning of pulleys as the freight is being lowered in. A breezeless July morning, and a dead heat,—87° already.

The saloon-deck gives one suggestion of past and of coming voyages. Under the white awnings long lounge-chairs sprawl here and there,—each with an occupant, smoking in silence, or dozing with head drooping to one side. A young man, awaking as I pass to my cabin, turns upon me a pair of peculiarly luminous black eyes,—creole eyes. Evidently a West Indian. . . .

The morning is still gray, but the sun is dissolving the haze. Gradually the gray vanishes, and a beautiful, pale, vapory blue—a spiritualized Northern blue—colors water and sky. A cannon-shot suddenly shakes the heavy air: it is our farewell to the American shore;—we move. Back floats the wharf, and becomes vapory with a bluish tinge. Diaphanous mists seem to have caught the sky color; and even the great red storehouses take a faint blue tint as they recede. The horizon now has a greenish glow. Everywhere else the effect is that of looking through very light-blue glasses. . . .

We steam under the colossal span of the mighty bridge; then for a little while Liberty towers above our passing,—seeming first to turn towards us, then to turn away from us, the solemn beauty of her passionless face of bronze. Tints brighten;—the heaven is glowing a little bluer. A breeze springs up. . . .

Then the water takes on another hue: pale-green lights play through it. It has begun to sound. Little waves lift up their heads as though to look at us,—patting the flanks of the vessel, and whispering to one another.

Far off the surface begins to show quick white flashes here and there, and the steamer begins to swing. . . . We are nearing Atlantic waters. The sun is high up now, almost overhead: there are a few thin clouds in the tender-colored sky,—flossy, long-drawn-out, white things. The horizon has lost its greenish glow: it is a spectral blue. Masts, spars, rigging,—the white boats and the orange chimney,—the bright deck-lines, and the snowy rail,—cut against the colored light in almost dazzling relief. Though the sun shines hot the wind is cold: its strong irregular blowing fans one into drowsiness. Also the somnolent chant of the engines—*do-do, hey! do-do hey!*—lulls to sleep.

. . . Towards evening the glaucous sea-tint vanishes,—the water becomes blue. It is full of great flashes, as of seams opening and reclosing over a white surface. It spits spray in a ceaseless drizzle. Sometimes it reaches up and slaps the side of the steamer with a sound as of a great naked hand. The wind waxes boisterous. Swinging ends of cordage crack like whips. There is an immense humming that drowns speech,—a humming made up of many sounds: whining of pulleys, whistling of riggings, flapping and fluttering of canvas, roar of nettings in the wind. And this sonorous medley, ever growing louder, has rhythm,—a *crescendo* and *diminuendo* timed by the steamer's regular swinging: like a great Voice crying out, "Whoh-oh-oh! whoh-oh-oh!" We are nearing the life-centres of winds and currents. One can hardly walk on deck against the ever-increasing breath;—yet now the whole world is blue,—not the least cloud is visible; and the perfect transparency and voidness about us make the immense power of this invisible medium seem something ghostly and awful. . . . The log, at every revolution, whines exactly like a little puppy;—one can hear it through all the roar fully forty feet away.

. . . It is nearly sunset. Across the whole circle of the Day we have been steaming south. Now the horizon is gold green. All about the falling sun, this gold-green light takes vast expansion. . . . Right on the edge of the sea is a tall, gracious ship, sailing sunsetward. Catching the vapory fire, she seems to become a phantom,—a ship of gold mist: all her spars and sails are luminous, and look like things seen in dreams.

Crimsoning more and more, the sun drops to the sea. The phantom ship approaches him,—touches the curve of his glowing face, sails right athwart it! Oh, the spectral splendor of that vision! The whole great ship in full sail instantly makes an acute silhouette against the monstrous disk,—rests there in the very middle of the vermilion sun. His face crimsons high above her top-masts,—broadens far beyond helm and bowsprit, Against this weird magnificence, her whole shape changes color: hull, masts, and sails turn black—a greenish black.

Sun and ship vanish together in another minute. Violet the night comes; and the rigging of the foremast cuts a cross upon the face of the moon.

II.

MORNING: the second day. The sea is an extraordinary blue,— looks to me something like violet ink. Close by the ship, where the foam-clouds are, it is beautifully mottled,—looks like blue marble with exquisite veinings and nebulosities. . . . Tepid wind, and cottony white clouds,—cirri climbing up over the edge of the sea all around. The sky is still pale blue, and the horizon is full of a whitish haze.

. . . A nice old French gentleman from Guadeloupe presumes to say this is not blue water;—he declares it greenish (*verdâtre*). Because I cannot discern the green, he tells me I do not yet know what blue water is. *Attendez un peu!* . . .

. . . The sky-tone deepens as the sun ascends,—deepens deliciously. The warm wind proves soporific. I drop asleep with the blue light in my face,—the strong bright blue of the noon-day sky. As I doze it seems to burn like a cold fire right through my eyelids. Waking up with a start, I fancy that everything is turning blue,—myself included. "Do you not call this the real tropical blue?" I cry to my French fellow-traveller. "*Mon Dieu! non,*" he exclaims, as in astonishment at the question;— "this is not blue!" . . . What can be *his* idea of blue, I wonder!

Clots of sargasso float by,—light-yellow sea-weed. We are nearing the Sargasso-sea,—entering the path of the trade-winds. There is a long ground-swell, the steamer rocks and rolls, and the tumbling water always seems to me growing bluer; but my friend from Guadeloupe says that this color "which I call blue" is only darkness—only the shadow of prodigious depth.

Nothing now but blue sky and what I persist in calling blue sea. The clouds have melted away in the bright glow. There is no sign of life in the azure gulf above, nor in the abyss beneath;—there are no wings or fins to be seen. Towards evening, under the slanting gold light, the color of the sea deepens into ultramarine; then the sun sinks down behind a bank of copper-colored cloud.

III.

MORNING of the third day. Same mild, warm wind. Bright blue sky, with some very thin clouds in the horizon,—like puffs of steam. The glow of the sea-light through the open ports of my cabin makes them seem filled with thick blue glass. . . . It is becoming too warm for New York clothing. . . .

Certainly the sea has become much bluer. It gives one the idea of liquefied sky: the foam might be formed of cirrus clouds compressed,—so extravagantly white it looks to-day, like snow in the sun. Nevertheless, the old gentleman from Guadeloupe still maintains this is not the true blue of the tropics!

. . . The sky does not deepen its hue to-day: it brightens it;—the blue glows as if it were taking fire throughout. Perhaps the sea may deepen its hue;—I do not believe it can take more luminous color without being set aflame. . . . I ask the ship's doctor whether it is really true that the West Indian waters are any bluer than these. He looks a moment at the sea, and replies, "*Oh* yes!" There is such a tone of surprise in his "oh" as might indicate that I had asked a very foolish question; and his look seems to express doubt whether I am quite in earnest. . . . I think, nevertheless, that this water is extravagantly, nonsensically blue!

. . . I read for an hour or two; fall asleep in the chair; wake up suddenly; look at the sea,—and cry out! This sea is impossibly blue! The painter who should try to paint it would be denounced as a lunatic. . . . Yet it is transparent; the foam-clouds, as they sink down, turn sky-blue,—a sky-blue which now looks white by contrast with the strange and violent splendor of the sea color. It seems as if one were looking into an immeasurable dyeing vat, or as though the whole ocean had been thickened with indigo. To say this is a mere reflection of the sky is nonsense!—the sky is too pale by a hundred shades for that! This must be the natural color of the water,—a blazing azure,—magnificent, impossible to describe.

The French passenger from Guadeloupe observes that the sea is "beginning to become blue."

IV.

AND the fourth day. One awakens unspeakably lazy;—this must be the West Indian languor. Same sky, with a few more bright clouds than yesterday;—always the warm wind blowing. There is a long swell. Under this trade-breeze, warm like a human breath, the ocean seems to pulse,—to rise and fall as with a vast inspiration and expiration. Alternately its blue circle lifts and falls before us and behind us;—we rise very high; we sink very low,—but always with a slow long motion. Nevertheless, the water *looks* smooth, perfectly smooth; the billowings which lift us cannot be seen;—it is because the summits of these swells are mile-broad,—too broad to be discerned from the level of our deck.

. . . Ten A.M.—Under the sun the sea is a flaming, dazzling lazulite. My French friend from Guadeloupe kindly confesses this is *almost* the color of tropical water. . . . Weeds floating by, a little below the surface, are azured. But the Guadeloupe gentleman says he has seen water still more blue. I am sorry,— I cannot believe him.

Mid-day.—The splendor of the sky is weird! No clouds above—only blue fire! Up from the warm deep color of the sea-circle the edge of the heaven glows as if bathed in greenish flame. The swaying circle of the resplendent sea seems to flash its jewel-color to the zenith.

Clothing feels now almost too heavy to endure; and the warm wind brings a languor with it as of temptation. . . . One feels an irresistible desire to drowse on deck;—the rushing speech of waves, the long rocking of the ship, the lukewarm caress of the wind, urge to slumber;—but the light is too vast to permit of sleep. Its blue power compels wakefulness. And the brain is wearied at last by this duplicated azure splendor of sky and sea. How gratefully comes the evening to us,—with its violet glooms and promises of coolness!

All this sensuous blending of warmth and force in winds and

waters more and more suggests an idea of the spiritualism of elements,—a sense of world-life. In all these soft sleepy swayings, these caresses of wind and sobbing of waters, Nature seems to confess some passional mood. Passengers converse of pleasant tempting things,—tropical fruits, tropical beverages, tropical mountain-breezes, tropical women. . . . It is a time for dreams—those day-dreams that come gently as a mist, with ghostly realization of hopes, desires, ambitions. . . . Men sailing to the mines of Guiana dream of gold.

The wind seems to grow continually warmer; the spray feels warm like blood. Awnings have to be clewed up, and wind-sails taken in;—still, there are no white-caps,—only the enormous swells, too broad to see, as the ocean falls and rises like a dreamer's breast. . . .

The sunset comes with a great burning yellow glow, fading up through faint greens to lose itself in violet light;—there is no gloaming. The days have already become shorter. . . . Through the open ports, as we lie down to sleep, comes a great whispering,—the whispering of the seas: sounds as of articulate speech under the breath,—as of women telling secrets. . . .

V.

FIFTH day out. Trade-winds from the south-east; a huge tumbling of mountain-purple waves;—the steamer careens under a full spread of canvas. There is a sense of spring in the wind to-day,—something that makes one think of the bourgeoning of Northern woods, when naked trees first cover themselves with a mist of tender green,—something that recalls the first bird-songs, the first climbings of sap to sun, and gives a sense of vital plenitude.

. . . Evening fills the west with aureate woolly clouds,—the wool of the Fleece of Gold. Then Hesperus beams like another moon, and the stars burn very brightly. Still the ship bends under the even pressure of the warm wind in her sails; and her wake becomes a trail of fire. Large sparks dash up through it continuously, like an effervescence of flame;—and queer broad clouds of pale fire swirl by. Far out, where the water is black as pitch, there are no lights: it seems as if the steamer were only grinding out sparks with her keel, striking fire with her propeller.

VI.

SIXTH day out. Wind tepid and still stronger, but sky very clear. An indigo sea, with beautiful whitecaps. The ocean color is deepening: it is very rich now, but I think less wonderful than before;—it is an opulent pansy hue. Close by the ship it looks black-blue,—the color that bewitches in certain Celtic eyes.

There is a feverishness in the air;—the heat is growing heavy; the least exertion provokes perspiration; below-decks the air is like the air of an oven. Above-deck, however, the effect of all this light and heat is not altogether disagreeable;— one feels that vast elemental powers are near at hand, and that the blood is already aware of their approach.

All day the pure sky, the deepening of sea-color, the luke-warm wind. Then comes a superb sunset! There is a painting in the west wrought of cloud-colors,—a dream of high carmine cliffs and rocks outlying in a green sea, which lashes their bases with a foam of gold. . . .

Even after dark the touch of the wind has the warmth of flesh. There is no moon; the sea-circle is black as Acheron; and our phosphor wake reappears quivering across it,—seeming to reach back to the very horizon. It is brighter to-night,—looks like another *Via Lactea*,—with points breaking through it like stars in a nebula. From our prow ripples rimmed with fire keep fleeing away to right and left into the night,—brightening as they run, then vanishing suddenly as if they had passed over a precipice. Crests of swells seem to burst into showers of sparks, and great patches of spume catch flame, smoulder through, and disappear. . . . The Southern Cross is visible—sloping backward and sidewise, as if propped against the vault of the sky: it is not readily discovered by the unfamiliarized eye; it is only after it has been well pointed out to you that you discern its position. Then you find it is only the *suggestion* of a cross— four stars set almost quadrangularly, some brighter than others.

For two days there has been little conversation on board. It may be due in part to the somnolent influence of the warm wind,—in part to the ceaseless booming of waters and roar of rigging, which drown men's voices; but I fancy it is much more due to the impressions of space and depth and vastness,—the impressions of sea and sky, which compel something akin to awe.

VII.

MORNING over the Caribbean Sea,—a calm, extremely dark-blue sea. There are lands in sight,—high lands, with sharp, peaked, unfamiliar outlines.

We passed other lands in the darkness: they no doubt resembled the shapes towering up around us now; for these are evidently volcanic creations,—jagged, coned, truncated, eccentric. Far off they first looked a very pale gray; now, as the light increases, they change hue a little,—showing misty greens and smoky blues. They rise very sharply from the sea to great heights,—the highest point always with a cloud upon it;—they thrust out singular long spurs, push up mountain shapes that have an odd scooped-out look. Some, extremely far away, seem, as they catch the sun, to be made of gold vapor; others have a madderish tone: these are colors of cloud. The closer we approach them, the more do tints of green make themselves visible. Purplish or bluish masses of coast slowly develop green surfaces; folds and wrinkles of land turn brightly verdant. Still, the color gleams as through a thin fog.

. . . The first tropical visitor has just boarded our ship: a wonderful fly, shaped like a common fly, but at least five times larger. His body is a beautiful shining black; his wings seem ribbed and jointed with silver, his head is jewel-green, with exquisitely cut emeralds for eyes.

Islands pass and disappear behind us. The sun has now risen well; the sky is a rich blue, and the tardy moon still hangs in it. Lilac tones show through the water. In the south there are a few straggling small white clouds,—like a long flight of birds. A great gray mountain shape looms up before us. We are steaming on Santa Cruz.

The island has a true volcanic outline, sharp and high: the cliffs sheer down almost perpendicularly. The shape is still vapory, varying in coloring from purplish to bright gray; but wherever peaks and spurs fully catch the sun they edge themselves with a beautiful green glow, while interlying ravines seem filled with foggy blue.

As we approach, sunlighted surfaces come out still more luminously green. Glens and sheltered valleys still hold blues and grays; but points fairly illuminated by the solar glow show just such a fiery green as burns in the plumage of certain humming-birds. And just as the lustrous colors of these birds shift according to changes of light, so the island shifts colors here and there,—from emerald to blue, and blue to gray. . . . But now we are near: it shows us a lovely heaping of high bright hills in front,—with a further coast-line very low and long and verdant, fringed with a white beach, and tufted with spidery palm-crests. Immediately opposite, other palms are poised; their trunks look like pillars of unpolished silver, their leaves shimmer like bronze.

. . . The water of the harbor is transparent and pale green. One can see many fish, and some small sharks. White butterflies are fluttering about us in the blue air. Naked black boys are bathing on the beach;—they swim well, but will not venture out far because of the sharks. A boat puts off to bring colored girls on board. They are tall, and not uncomely, although very dark;—they coax us, with all sorts of endearing words, to purchase bay rum, fruits, Florida water. . . . We go ashore in boats. The water of the harbor has a slightly fetid odor.

VIII.

VIEWED from the bay, under the green shadow of the hills overlooking it, Frederiksted has the appearance of a beautiful Spanish town, with its Romanesque piazzas, churches, many arched buildings peeping through breaks in a line of mahogany, bread-fruit, mango, tamarind, and palm trees,—an irregular mass of at least fifty different tints, from a fiery emerald to a sombre bluish-green. But on entering the streets the illusion of beauty passes: you find yourself in a crumbling, decaying town, with buildings only two stories high. The lower part, of arched Spanish design, is usually of lava rock or of brick, painted a light, warm yellow; the upper stones are most commonly left unpainted, and are rudely constructed of light timber. There are many heavy arcades and courts opening on the streets with large archways. Lava blocks have been used in paving as well as in building; and more than one of the narrow streets, as it slopes up the hill through the great light, is seen to cut its way through craggy masses of volcanic stone.

But all the buildings look dilapidated; the stucco and paint is falling or peeling everywhere; there are fissures in the walls, crumbling façades, tumbling roofs. The first stories, built with solidity worthy of an earthquake region, seem extravagantly heavy by contrast with the frail wooden superstructures. One reason may be that the city was burned and sacked during a negro revolt in 1878;—the Spanish basements resisted the fire well, and it was found necessary to rebuild only the second stories of the buildings; but the work was done cheaply and flimsily, not massively and enduringly, as by the first colonial builders.

There is great wealth of verdure. Cabbage and cocoa palms overlook all the streets, bending above almost every structure, whether hut or public building;—everywhere you see the split-ted green of banana leaves. In the court-yards you may occasionally catch sight of some splendid palm with silver-gray stem so barred as to look jointed, like the body of an annelid.

In the market-place—a broad paved square, crossed by two rows of tamarind-trees, and bounded on one side by a Spanish piazza—you can study a spectacle of savage picturesqueness. There are no benches, no stalls, no booths; the dealers stand, sit, or squat upon the ground under the sun, or upon the steps of the neighboring arcade. Their wares are piled up at their feet, for the most part. Some few have little tables, but as a rule the eatables are simply laid on the dusty ground or heaped upon the steps of the piazza—reddish-yellow mangoes, that look like great apples squeezed out of shape, bunches of ba-nanas, pyramids of bright-green cocoanuts, immense golden-green oranges, and various other fruits and vegetables totally unfamiliar to Northern eyes. . . . It is no use to ask questions —the black dealers speak no dialect comprehensible outside of the Antilles: it is a negro-English that sounds like some African tongue,—a rolling current of vowels and consonants, pouring so rapidly that the inexperienced ear cannot detach one intelligible word. A friendly white coming up enabled me to learn one phrase: "Massa, youwancocknerfoobuy?" (Master, do you want to buy a cocoanut?)

The market is quite crowded,—full of bright color under the tremendous noon light. Buyers and dealers are generally black;—very few yellow or brown people are visible in the gathering. The greater number present are women; they are very simply, almost savagely, garbed—only a skirt or petticoat, over which is worn a sort of calico short dress, which scarcely descends two inches below the hips, and is confined about the waist with a belt or a string. The skirt bells out like the skirt of a dancer, leaving the feet and bare legs well exposed; and the head is covered with a white handkerchief, twisted so as to look like a turban. Multitudes of these bare-legged black women are walking past us,—carrying bundles or baskets upon their heads, and smoking very long cigars.

They are generally short and thick-set, and walk with surprising erectness, and with long, firm steps, carrying the bosom well forward. Their limbs are strong and finely rounded. Whether walking or standing, their poise is admirable,—might be called graceful, were it not for the absence of real grace of form in such compact, powerful little figures. All year brightly colored cottonade stuffs, and the general effect of the costume in a large gathering is very agreeable, the dominant hues being pink, white, and blue. Half the women are smoking. All chatter loudly, speaking their English jargon with a pitch of voice totally unlike the English timbre: it sometimes sounds as if they were trying to pronounce English rapidly according to French pronunciation and pitch of voice.

These green oranges have a delicious scent and amazing juiciness. Peeling one of them is sufficient to perfume the skin of the hands for the rest of the day, however often one may use soap and water. . . . We smoke Porto Rico cigars, and drink West Indian lemonades, strongly flavored with rum. The tobacco has a rich, sweet taste; the rum is velvety, sugary, with a pleasant, soothing effect: both have a rich aroma. There is a wholesome originality about the flavor of these products, a uniqueness which certifies to their naif purity: something as opulent and frank as the juices and odors of tropical fruits and flowers.

The streets leading from the plaza glare violently in the strong sunlight;—the ground, almost dead-white, dazzles the eyes. . . . There are few comely faces visible,—in the streets all are black who pass. But through open shop-doors one occasionally catches glimpses of a pretty quadroon face,—with immense black eyes,—a face yellow like a ripe banana.

. . . It is now after mid-day. Looking up to the hills, or along sloping streets towards the shore, wonderful variations of foliage-color meet the eye: gold-greens, sap-greens, bluish and metallic greens of many tints, reddish-greens, yellowish-greens. The cane-fields are broad sheets of beautiful gold-green; and nearly as bright are the masses of *pomme-cannelle* frondescence, the groves of lemon and orange; while tamarind and mahoganies are heavily sombre. Everywhere palm-crests soar above the wood-lines, and tremble with a metallic shimmering in the blue light. Up through a ponderous thickness of tamarind rises the spire of the church; a skeleton of open stone-work, without glasses or lattices or shutters of any sort for its naked apertures: it is all open to the winds of heaven; it seems to be gasping with all its granite mouths for breath—panting in this azure heat. In the bay the water looks greener than ever: it is so clear that the light passes under every boat and ship to the very bottom; the vessels only cast very thin green shadows,—so transparent that fish can be distinctly seen passing through from sunlight to sunlight.

The sunset offers a splendid spectacle of pure color; there is only an immense yellow glow in the west,—a lemon-colored blaze; but when it melts into the blue there is an exquisite green light. . . . We leave to-morrow.

. . . Morning: the green hills are looming in a bluish vapor: the long faint-yellow slope of beach to the left of the town, under the mangoes and tamarinds, is already thronged with bathers,—all men or boys, and all naked: black, brown, yellow, and white. The white bathers are Danish soldiers from the barracks; the Northern brightness of their skins forms an almost startling contrast with the deep colors of the nature about them, and with the dark complexions of the natives. Some very slender, graceful brown lads are bathing with them,—lightly built as deer: these are probably creoles. Some of the black bathers are clumsy-looking, and have astonishingly long legs. . . . Then little boys come down, leading horses;—they strip, leap naked on the animals' backs, and ride into the sea,—yelling, screaming, splashing, in the morning light. Some are a fine brown color, like old bronze. Nothing could be more statuesque than the unconscious attitudes of these bronze bodies in leaping, wrestling, running, pitching shells. Their simple grace is in admirable harmony with that of Nature's green creations about them,—rhymes faultlessly with the perfect self-balance of the palms that poise along the shore. . . .

Boom! and a thunder-rolling of echoes. We move slowly out of the harbor, then swiftly towards the southeast. . . . The island seems to turn slowly half round; then to retreat from us. Across our way appears a long band of green light, reaching over the sea like a thin protraction of color from the extended spur of verdure in which the western end of the island terminates. That is a sunken reef, and a dangerous one. Lying high upon it, in very sharp relief against the blue light, is a wrecked vessel on her beam-ends,—the carcass of a brig. Her decks have been broken in; the roofs of her cabins are gone; her masts are splintered off short; her empty hold yawns naked to the sun; all her upper parts have taken a yellowish-white color, —the color of sun-bleached bone.

Behind us the mountains still float back. Their shining green has changed to a less vivid hue; they are taking bluish tones here and there; but their outlines are still sharp, and along their high soft slopes there are white specklings, which are villages and towns. These white specks diminish swiftly,—dwindle to the dimensions of salt-grains,—finally vanish. Then the island grows uniformly bluish; it becomes cloudy, vague as a dream of mountains;—it turns at last gray as smoke, and then melts into the horizon-light like a mirage.

Another yellow sunset, made weird by extraordinary black, dense, fantastic shapes of cloud. Night darkens, and again the Southern Cross glimmers before our prow, and the two Milky Ways reveal themselves,—that of the Cosmos and that ghostlier one which stretches over the black deep behind us. This alternately broadens and narrows at regular intervals, concomitantly with the rhythmical swing of the steamer. Before us the bows spout fire; behind us there is a flaming and roaring as of Phlegethon; and the voices of wind and sea become so loud that we cannot talk to one another,—cannot make our words heard even by shouting.

IX.

EARLY morning: the eighth day. Moored in another blue harbor,—a great semicircular basin, bounded by a high billowing of hills all green from the fringe of yellow beach up to their loftiest clouded summit. The land has that up-tossed look which tells a volcanic origin. There are curiously scalloped heights, which, though emerald from base to crest, still retain all the physiognomy of volcanoes: their ribbed sides must be lava under that verdure. Out of sight westward—in successions of bright green, pale green, bluish-green, and vapory gray—stretches a long chain of crater shapes. Truncated, jagged, or rounded, all these elevations are interunited by their curving hollows of land or by filaments,—very low valleys. And as they grade away in varying color through distance, these hill-chains take a curious segmented, jointed appearance, like insect forms, enormous ant-bodies. . . . This is St. Kitt's.

We row ashore over a tossing dark-blue water, and leaving the long wharf, pass under a great arch and over a sort of bridge into the town of Basse-Terre, through a concourse of brown and black people.

It is very tropical-looking; but more sombre than Frederiksted. There are palms everywhere,—cocoa, fan, and cabbage palms; many bread-fruit trees, tamarinds, bananas, Indian fig-trees, mangoes, and unfamiliar things the negroes call by incomprehensible names,—"sap-saps," "dhool-dhools." But there is less color, less reflection of light than in Santa Cruz; there is less quaintness; no Spanish buildings, no canary-colored arcades. All the narrow streets are gray or neutral-tinted; the ground has a dark ashen tone. Most of the dwellings are timber, resting on brick props, or elevated upon blocks of lava rock. It seems almost as if some breath from the enormous and always clouded mountain overlooking the town had begrimed everything, darkening even the colors of vegetation.

The population is not picturesque. The costumes are commonplace; the tints of the women's attire are dull. Browns and sombre blues and grays are commoner than pinks, yellows, and violets. Occasionally you observe a fine half-breed type—some tall brown girl walking by with a swaying grace like that of a sloop at sea;—but such spectacles are not frequent. Most of those you meet are black or a blackish brown. Many stores are kept by yellow men with intensely black hair and eyes,—men who do not smile. These are Portuguese. There are some few fine buildings; but the most pleasing sight the little town can offer the visitor is the pretty Botanical Garden, with its banyans and its palms, its monstrous lilies and extraordinary fruit-trees, and its beautiful little fountains. From some of these trees a peculiar tillandsia streams down, much like our Spanish moss,—but it is black!

. . . As we move away southwardly, the receding outlines of the island look more and more volcanic. A chain of hills and cones, all very green, and connected by strips of valley-land so low that the edge of the sea-circle on the other side of the island can be seen through the gaps. We steam past truncated hills, past heights that have the look of the stumps of peaks cut half down,—ancient fire-mouths choked by tropical verdure.

Southward, above and beyond the deep-green chain, tower other volcanic forms,—very far away, and so pale-gray as to seem like clouds. Those are the heights of Nevis,—another creation of the subterranean fires.

It draws nearer, floats steadily into definition: a great mountain flanked by two small ones; three summits; the loftiest, with clouds packed high upon it, still seems to smoke;—the second highest displays the most symmetrical crater-form I have yet seen. All are still grayish-blue or gray. Gradually through the blues break long high gleams of green.

As we steam closer, the island becomes all verdant from flood to sky; the great dead crater shows its immense wreath of perennial green. On the lower slopes little settlements are sprinkled in white, red, and brown: houses, windmills, sugar-factories, high chimneys are distinguishable;—cane-plantations unfold gold-green surfaces.

We pass away. The island does not seem to sink behind us, but to become a ghost. All its outlines grow shadowy. For a little while it continues green;—but it is a hazy, spectral green, as of colored vapor. The sea today looks almost black: the south-west wind has filled the day with luminous mist and the

phantom of Nevis melts in the vast glow, dissolves utterly. . . .
Once more we are out of sight of land,—in the centre of a
blue-black circle of sea. The water-line cuts blackly against the
immense light of the horizon,—a huge white glory that flames
up very high before it fades and melts into the eternal blue.

X.

THEN a high white shape like a cloud appears before us,—on
the purplish-dark edge of the sea. The cloud-shape enlarges,
heightens without changing contour. It is not a cloud, but an
island! Its outlines begin to sharpen,—with faintest pencillings
of color. Shadowy valleys appear, spectral hollows, phantom
slopes of pallid blue or green. The apparition is so like a mirage
that it is difficult to persuade oneself one is looking at real
land,—that it is not a dream. It seems to have shaped itself all
suddenly out of the glowing haze. We pass many miles beyond
it; and it vanishes into mist again.

. . . Another and a larger ghost; but we steam straight
upon it until it materializes,—Montserrat. It bears a family
likeness to the islands we have already passed—one dominant
height, with massing of bright crater shapes about it, and
ranges of green hills linked together by low valleys. About its
highest summit also hovers a flock of clouds. At the foot of the
vast hill nestles the little white and red town of Plymouth. The
single salute of our gun is answered by a stupendous broadside
of echoes.

Plymouth is more than half hidden in the rich foliage that
fringes the wonderfully wrinkled green of the hills at their
base;—it has a curtain of palms before it. Approaching, you
discern only one or two façades above the sea-wall, and the long
wharf projecting through an opening in the masonry, over
which young palms stand thick as canes on a sugar plantation.
But on reaching the street that descends towards the heavily
bowldered shore you find yourself in a delightfully drowsy little
burgh,—a miniature tropical town,—with very narrow paved
ways,—steep, irregular, full of odd curves and angles,—and
likewise of tiny courts everywhere sending up jets of palm-
plumes, or displaying above their stone enclosures great
candelabra-shapes of cacti. All is old-fashioned and quiet and

queer and small. Even the palms are diminutive,—slim and delicate; there is a something in their poise and slenderness like the charm of young girls who have not yet ceased to be children, though soon to become women. . . .

There is a glorious sunset,—a fervid orange splendor, shading starward into delicate roses and greens. Then black boatmen come astern and quarrel furiously for the privilege of carrying one passenger ashore; and as they scream and gesticulate, half naked, their silhouettes against the sunset seem forms of great black apes.

. . . Under steam and sail we are making south again, with a warm wind blowing south-east,—a wind very moist, very powerful, and soporific. Facing it, one feels almost cool; but the moment one is sheltered from it profuse perspiration bursts out. The ship rocks over immense swells; night falls very blackly; and there are surprising displays of phosphorescence.

XI.

. . . MORNING. A gold sunrise over an indigo sea. The wind is a great warm caress; the sky a spotless blue. We are steaming on Dominica,—the loftiest of the lesser Antilles. While the silhouette is yet all violet in distance, nothing more solemnly beautiful can well be imagined: a vast cathedral shape, whose spires are mountain peaks, towering in the horizon, sheer up from the sea.

We stay at Roseau only long enough to land the mails, and wonder at the loveliness of the island. A beautifully wrinkled mass of green and blue and gray;—a strangely abrupt peaking and heaping of the land. Behind the green heights loom the blues; behind these the grays—all pinnacled against the sky-glow—thrusting up through gaps or behind promontories. Indescribably exquisite the foldings and hollowings of the emerald coast. In glen and vale the color of cane-fields shines like a pooling of fluid bronze, as if the luminous essence of the hill tints had been dripping down and clarifying there. Far to our left, a bright green spur pierces into the now turquoise sea; and beyond it, a beautiful mountain form, blue and curved like a hip, slopes seaward, showing lighted wrinkles here and there, of green. And from the foreground, against the blue of the softly outlined shape, cocoa-palms are curving,—all sharp and shining in the sun.

. . . Another hour; and Martinique looms before us. At first it appears all gray, a vapory gray; then it becomes bluish-gray; then all green.

It is another of the beautiful volcanic family: it owns the same hill shapes with which we have already become acquainted; its uppermost height is hooded with the familiar cloud; we see the same gold-yellow plains, the same wonderful varieties of verdancy, the same long green spurs reaching out into the sea,—doubtless formed by old lava torrents. But all this is now repeated for us more imposingly, more grandiosely;—it is wrought upon a larger scale than anything we have yet seen. The semicircular sweep of the harbor, dominated by the eternally veiled summit of the Montagne Pelée (misnamed, since it is green to the very clouds), from which the land slopes down on either hand to the sea by gigantic undulations, is one of the fairest sights that human eye can gaze upon. Thus viewed, the whole island shape is a mass of green, with purplish streaks and shadowings here and there: glooms of forest-hollows, or moving umbrages of cloud. The city of St. Pierre, on the edge of the land, looks as if it had slided down the hill behind it, so strangely do the streets come tumbling to the port in cascades of masonry,—with a red billowing of tiled roofs over all, and enormous palms poking up through it,—higher even than the creamy white twin towers of its cathedral.

We anchor in limpid blue water; the cannon-shot is answered by a prolonged thunder-clapping of mountain echo.

Then from the shore a curious flotilla bears down upon us. There is one boat, two or three canoes; but the bulk of the craft are simply wooden frames,—flat-bottomed structures, made from shipping-cases or lard-boxes, with triangular ends. In these sit naked boys,—boys between ten and fourteen years of age, —varying in color from a fine clear yellow to a deep reddish-brown or chocolate tint. They row with two little square, flat pieces of wood for paddles, clutched in each hand; and these lid-shaped things are dipped into the water on either side with absolute precision, in perfect time,—all the pairs of little naked arms seeming moved by a single impulse. There is much unconscious grace in this paddling, as well as skill. Then all about the ship these ridiculous little boats begin to describe circles,—crossing and intercrossing so closely as almost to bring them into collision, yet never touching. The boys have simply come out to dive for coins they expect passengers to fling to them. All are chattering creole, laughing and screaming shrilly; every eye, quick and bright as a bird's, watches the faces of the passengers on deck. "'Tention-là!" shriek a dozen soprani. Some passenger's fingers have entered his vest-pocket, and the boys are on the alert. Through the air, twirling and glittering, tumbles an English shilling, and drops into the deep water beyond the little fleet. Instantly all the lads leap, scramble, topple head-foremost out of their little tubs, and dive in pursuit. In the blue water their lithe figures look perfectly red,—all but the soles of their upturned feet, which show nearly white. Almost immediately they all rise again: one holds up at arm's-length above the water the recovered coin, and then puts it into his mouth for safe-keeping. Coin after coin is thrown in, and as speedily brought up; a shower of small silver follows, and not a piece is lost. These lads move through the water without apparent effort, with the suppleness of fishes. Most are decidedly fine-looking boys, with admirably rounded limbs, delicately formed extremities. The best diver and swiftest swimmer, however, is a red lad;—his face is rather commonplace, but his slim body has the grace of an antique bronze.

 . . . We are ashore in St. Pierre, the quaintest, queerest, and the prettiest withal, among West Indian cities: all stone-built and stone-flagged, with very narrow streets, wooden or zinc awnings, and peaked roofs of red tile, pierced by gabled dormers. Most of the buildings are painted in a clear yellow tone, which contrasts delightfully with the burning blue ribbon of tropical sky above; and no street is absolutely level; nearly all of them climb hills, descend into hollows, curve, twist, describe sudden angles. There is everywhere a loud murmur of running water,—pouring through the deep gutters contrived between the paved thoroughfare and the absurd little sidewalks, varying in width from one to three feet. The architecture is quite old: it is seventeenth century, probably; and it reminds one a great deal of that characterizing the antiquated French quarter of New Orleans. All the tints, the forms, the vistas, would seem to have been especially selected or designed for aquarelle studies,—just to please the whim of some extravagant artist. The windows are frameless openings without glass; some have iron bars; all have heavy wooden shutters with movable slats, through which light and air can enter as through Venetian blinds. These are usually painted green or bright bluish-gray.

So steep are the streets descending to the harbor,—by flights of old mossy stone steps,—that looking down them to the azure water you have the sensation of gazing from a cliff. From certain openings in the main street—the Rue Victor Hugo—you can get something like a bird's-eye view of the harbor with its shipping. The roofs of the street below are under your feet, and other streets are rising behind you to meet the mountain roads. They climb at a very steep angle, occasionally breaking into stairs of lava rock, all grass-tufted and moss-lined.

The town has an aspect of great solidity: it is a creation of crag—looks almost as if it had been hewn out of one mountain fragment, instead of having been constructed stone by stone. Although commonly consisting of two stories and an attic only, the dwellings have walls three feet in thickness;—on one street, facing the sea, they are even heavier, and slope outward like ramparts, so that the perpendicular recesses of windows and doors have the appearance of being opened between buttresses. It may have been partly as a precaution against earthquakes, and partly for the sake of coolness, that the early colonial architects built thus;—giving the city a physiognomy so well worthy of its name,—the name of the Saint of the Rock.

And everywhere rushes mountain water,—cool and crystal clear, washing the streets;—from time to time you come to some public fountain flinging a silvery column to the sun, or showering bright spray over a group of black bronze tritons or bronze swans. The Tritons on the Place Bertin you will not readily forget;—their curving torsos might have been modelled from the forms of those ebon men who toil there tirelessly all day in the great heat, rolling hogsheads of sugar or casks of rum. And often you will note, in the course of a walk, little drinking-fountains contrived at the angle of a building, or in the thick walls bordering the bulwarks or enclosing

La Place Bertin (the Sugar Landing), St. Pierre, Martinique.

public squares: glittering threads of water spurting through lion-lips of stone. Some mountain torrent, skilfully directed and divided, is thus perpetually refreshing the city,—supplying its fountains and cooling its courts. . . . This is called the Gouyave water: it is not the same stream which sweeps and purifies the streets.

Picturesqueness and color: these are the particular and the unrivalled charms of St. Pierre. As you pursue the Grande Rue, or Rue Victor Hugo,—which traverses the town through all its length, undulating over hill-slopes and into hollows and over a bridge,—you become more and more enchanted by the contrast of the yellow-glowing walls to right and left with the jagged strip of gentian-blue sky overhead. Charming also it is to watch the cross-streets climbing up to the fiery green of the mountains behind the town. On the lower side of the main thoroughfare other streets open in wonderful bursts of blue—warm blue of horizon and sea. The steps by which these ways descend towards the bay are black with age, and slightly mossed close to the wall on either side: they have an alarming steepness,—one might easily stumble from the upper into the lower street. Looking towards the water through these openings from the Grande Rue, you will notice that the sea-line cuts across the blue space just at the level of the upper story of the house on the lower street-corner. Sometimes, a hundred feet below, you see a ship resting in the azure aperture,—seemingly suspended there in sky-color, floating in blue light. And everywhere and always, through sunshine or shadow, comes to you the scent of the city,—the characteristic odor of St. Pierre;—a compound odor suggesting the intermingling of sugar and garlic in those strange tropical dishes which creoles love. . . .

XII.

. . . A POPULATION fantastic, astonishing,—a population of the Arabian Nights. It is many-colored; but the general dominant tint is yellow, like that of the town itself—yellow in the interblending of all the hues characterizing *mulâtresse*, *capresse*, *griffe*, *quarteronne*, *métisse*, *chabine*,—a general effect of rich brownish yellow. You are among a people of half-breeds,—the finest mixed race of the West Indies.

Straight as palms, and supple and tall, these colored women and men impress one powerfully by their dignified carriage and easy elegance of movement. They walk without swinging of the shoulders;—the perfectly set torso seems to remain rigid; yet the step is a long full stride, and the whole weight is springily poised on the very tip of the bare foot. All, or nearly all, are without shoes: the treading of many naked feet over the heated pavement makes a continuous whispering sound.

. . . Perhaps the most novel impression of all is that produced by the singularity and brilliancy of certain of the women's costumes. These were developed, at least a hundred years ago, by some curious sumptuary law regulating the dress of slaves and colored people of free condition,—a law which allowed considerable liberty as to material and tint, prescribing chiefly form. But some of these fashions suggest the Orient: they offer beautiful audacities of color contrast; and the full-dress coiffure, above all, is so strikingly Eastern that one might be tempted to believe it was first introduced into the colony by some Mohammedan slave. It is merely an immense Madras handkerchief, which is folded about the head with admirable art, like a turban;—one bright end pushed through at the top in front, being left sticking up like a plume. Then this turban, always full of bright canary-color, is fastened with golden brooches,—one in front and one at either side. As for the remainder of the dress, it is simple enough: an embroidered, low-cut chemise with sleeves; a skirt or *jupe*, very long behind, but caught up and fastened in front below the breasts so as to bring the hem everywhere to a level with the end of the long chemise; and finally a *foulard*, or silken kerchief, thrown over the shoulders. These *jupes* and *foulards*, however, are exquisite in pattern and color: bright crimson, bright yellow, bright blue, bright green,—lilac, violet, rose,—sometimes mingled in plaidings or checkerings or stripings: black with orange, sky-blue with purple. And whatever be the colors of the costume, which vary astonishingly, the coiffure must be yellow—brilliant, flashing yellow: the turban is certain to have yellow stripes or yellow squares. To this display add the effect of costly and curious jewellery: immense ear-rings, each pendant being formed of five gold cylinders joined together (cylinders sometimes two inches long, and an inch at least in circumference);—a necklace of double, triple, quadruple, or quintuple rows of large hollow gold beads (sometimes smooth, but generally graven) —the wonderful *collier-choux*. Now, this glowing jewellery is not a mere imitation of pure metal: the ear-rings are worth one hundred and seventy-five francs a pair; the necklace of a Martinique quadroon may cost five hundred or even one thousand francs. . . . It may be the gift of her lover, her *doudoux*; but such articles are usually purchased either on time by small payments, or bead by bead singly until the requisite number is made up.

But few are thus richly attired: the greater number of the women carrying burdens on their heads,—peddling vegetables, cakes, fruit, ready-cooked food, from door to door,—are very simply dressed in a single plain robe of vivid colors (*douillette*) reaching from neck to feet, and made with a train, but generally girded well up so as to sit close to the figure and leave the lower limbs partly bare and perfectly free. These women can walk all day long up and down hill in the hot sun, without shoes, carrying loads of from one hundred to one hundred and fifty pounds on their heads; and if their little stock sometimes fails to come up to the accustomed weight stones are added to make it heavy enough. Doubtless the habit of carrying everything in this way from childhood has much to do with the remarkable vigor and erectness of the population. . . . I have seen a grand-piano carried on the heads of four men. With the women the load is very seldom steadied with the hand after having been once placed in position. The head remains almost motionless; but the black, quick, piercing eyes flash into every window and door-way to watch for a customer's signal. And the creole street-cries, uttered in a sonorous, far-reaching high key, interblend and produce random harmonies very pleasant to hear.

. . . "*'Cé moune-là, ça qui lè bel mango?*" Her basket of mangoes certainly weighs as much as herself. . . . "*Ça qui lè bel avocat?*" The alligator-pear—cuts and tastes like beautiful green cheese. . . . "*Ça qui lè escargot?*" Call her, if you like snails. . . . "*Ça qui lè titiri?*" Minuscule fish, of which a thousand would scarcely fill a teacup;—one of the most delicate of Martinique dishes. . . . "*Ça qui lè cannà?—Ça qui lè charbon? Ça qui lè di pain aubè?*" (Who wants ducks, charcoal, or pretty little loaves shaped like cucumbers.) . . . "*Ça qui lè pain-mi?*" A sweet maize cake in the form of a tiny sugar-loaf, wrapped in a piece of banana leaf. . . . "*Ça qui lè fromassé*" (*pharmacie*) "*lapotécai créole?*" She deals in creole roots and herbs, and all the leaves that make *tisanes* or poultices or medicines: *matriquin, feuill-corossol, balai-doux, manioc-chapelle, Marie-Perrine, graine-enba-feuill, bois-d'lhomme, zhèbe-gras, bonnet-carré, zhèbe-codeinne, zhèbe-à-femme, zhèbe-à-châtte, canne-dleau, poque, fleu-papillon, lateigne,* and a score of others you never saw or heard of before. . . . "*Ça qui lé dicaments?*" (overalls for laboring-men). . . . "*Çé moune-là, si ou pa lè acheté canari-à dans lanmain moin, moin ké crazé y.*" The vender of red clay cooking-pots;—she has only one left, if you do not buy it she will break it!

"*Hé! zenfants-la!—en deho'!*" Run out to meet her, little children, if you like the sweet rice-cakes. . . . "*Hé! gens pa' enho', gens pa' enbas, gens di galtas, moin ni bel gououôs poisson!*" Ho! people up-stairs, people downstairs, and all ye good folks who dwell in the attics,—know that she has very big and very beautiful fish to sell! . . . "*Hé! Ça qui lé mangé yonne?*"— those are "akras,"—flat yellow-brown cakes, made of pounded codfish, or beans, or both, seasoned with pepper and fried in butter. . . . And then comes the pastry-seller, black as ebony, but dressed all in white, and white-aproned and white-capped like a French cook, and chanting half in French, half in creole, with a voice like a clarinet:

> "C'est louvouier de la pâtisserie qui passe,
>   Qui té ka veillé pou' gagner son existence,
>   Toujours content,
>   Toujours joyeux.
>   Oh, qu'ils sont bons!—
>   Oh, qu'ils sont doux!"

It is the pastryman passing by, who has been up all night to gain his livelihood,—always content,—always happy. . . . Oh, how good they are (the pies)!—Oh, how sweet they are!

. . . The quaint stores bordering both sides of the street bear no names and no signs over their huge arched doors;—you must look well inside to know what business is being done. Even then you will scarcely be able to satisfy yourself as to the nature of the commerce;—for they are selling gridirons and frying-pans in the dry goods stores, holy images and rosaries in the notion stores, sweet-cakes and confectionery in the crockery stores, coffee and stationery in the millinery stores, cigars and tobacco in the china stores, cravats and laces and ribbons in the jewellery stores, sugar and guava jelly in the tobacco stores! But of all the objects exposed for sale the most attractive, because the most exotic, is a doll,—the Martinique *poupée*. There are two kinds,—the *poupée-capresse*, of which the body is covered with smooth reddish-brown leather, to imitate the tint of the *capresse* race: and the *poupée-négresse*, covered with black leather. When dressed, these dolls range in price from eleven to thirty-five francs—some, dressed to order, may cost even more; and a good *poupée-capresse* is a delightful curiosity. Both varieties of dolls are attired in the costume of the people; but the *négresse* is usually dressed the more simply. Each doll has a broidered chemise, a tastefully arranged *jupe* of bright hues, a silk *foulard*, a *collier-choux*, ear-rings of five cylinders (*zanneaux-à-clous*), and a charming little yellow-banded Madras turban. Such a doll is a perfect costume-model,—a perfect miniature of Martinique fashions, to the smallest details of material and color: it is almost too artistic for a toy.

These old costume-colors of Martinique—always relieved by brilliant yellow stripings or checkerings, except in the special violet dresses worn on certain religious occasions—have an indescribable luminosity,—a wonderful power of bringing out the fine warm tints of this tropical flesh. Such are the hues of those rich costumes Nature gives to her nearest of kin and her dearest,—her honey-lovers—her insects: these are wasp-colors. I do not know whether the fact ever occurred to the childish fancy of this strange race; but there is a creole expression which first suggested it to me;—in the patois, *pouend guêpe*, "to catch a wasp," signifies making love to a pretty colored girl. . . . And the more one observes these costumes, the more one feels that only Nature could have taught such rare comprehension of powers and harmonies among colors,— such knowledge of chromatic witchcrafts and chromatic laws.

Itinerant Pastry-seller.

"Toujours content,
Toujours joyeux."

*

. . . This evening, as I write, La Pelée is more heavily coiffed than is her wont. Of purple and lilac cloud the coiffure is,—a magnificent Madras, yellow banded by the sinking sun. La Pelée is in *costume de fête*, like a *capresse* attired for a baptism or a ball; and in her phantom turban one great star glimmers for a brooch.

XIII.

FOLLOWING the Rue Victor Hugo in the direction of the Fort, —crossing the Rivière Roxelane, or Rivière des Blanchisseuses, whose rocky bed is white with unsoaped linen far as the eye can reach,—you descend through some tortuous narrow streets into the principal marketplace.* A square—well paved and well shaded—with a fountain in the midst. Here the dealers are seated in rows;—one half of the market is devoted to fruits and vegetables; the other to the sale of fresh fish and meats. On first entering you are confused by the press and deafened by the storm of creole chatter;—then you begin to discern some order in this chaos, and to observe curious things.

In the middle of the paved square, about the market fountain, are lying boats filled with fish, which have been carried up from the water upon men's shoulders,—or, if very heavy, conveyed on rollers. . . . Such fish!—blue, rosy, green, lilac, scarlet, gold no spectral tints these, but luminous and strong like fire. Here also you see heaps of long thin fish looking like piled bars of silver,—absolutely dazzling,—of almost equal thickness from head to tail;—near by are heaps of flat pink creatures;— beyond these, again, a mass of azure backs and golden bellies. Among the stalls you can study the monsters,—twelve or fifteen feet long,—the shark, the *vierge*, the sword-fish, the *tonne*; —or the eccentricities. Some are very thin round disks, with long, brilliant, wormy feelers in lieu of fins, flickering in all directions like a moving pendent silver fringe;—others bristle with spines;—others, serpent-bodied, are so speckled as to

---

*Since this was written the market has been removed to the Savane,—to allow of the erection of a large new market-building on the old site; and the beautiful trees have been cut down.

resemble shapes of red polished granite. These are *moringues*. The *balaou, couliou, macriau, tazard, tcha-tcha, bonnique*, and *zorphi* severally represent almost all possible tints of blue and violet. The *souri* is rose-color and yellow; the *cirurgien* is black, with yellow and red stripes; the *patate*, black and yellow; the *gros-zié* is vermilion; the *couronné*, red and black. Their names are not less unfamiliar than their shapes and tints;—the *aiguille-de-mer*, or sea-needle, long and thin as a pencil;—the *Bon-Dié-manié-moin* ("the Good-God handled me"), which has something like finger-marks upon it;—the *lambi*, a huge sea-snail;—the *pisquette*, the *laline* (the Moon);—the *crapaud-de-mer*, or sea-toad, with a dangerous dorsal fin;—the *vermeil*, the *jacquot*, the *chaponne*, and fifty others. . . . As the sun gets higher, banana or balisier leaves are laid over the fish.

Even more puzzling, perhaps, are the astonishing varieties of green, yellow, and parti-colored vegetables,—and fruits of all hues and forms,—out of which display you retain only a confused general memory of sweet smells and luscious colors. But there are some oddities which impress the recollection in a particular way. One is a great cylindrical ivory-colored thing,—shaped like an elephant's tusk, except that it is not curved: this is the head of the cabbage-palm, or palmiste,—the brain of one of the noblest trees in the tropics, which must be totally destroyed to obtain it. Raw or cooked, it is eaten in a great variety of ways,—in salads, stews, fritters, or *akras*. Soon after this compact cylinder of young germinating leaves has been removed, large worms begin to appear in the hollow of the dead tree,—the *vers-palmiste*. You may see these for sale in the market, crawling about in bowls or cans: they are said, when fried alive, to taste like almonds, and are esteemed as a great luxury.

. . . Then you begin to look about you at the faces of the black, brown, and yellow people who are watching you curiously from beneath their Madras turbans, or from under the shade of mushroom-shaped hats as large as umbrellas. And as you observe the bare backs, bare shoulders, bare legs and arms and feet, you will find that the colors of flesh are even more varied and surprising than the colors of fruit. Nevertheless, it is only with fruit-colors that many of these skin-tints can be correctly compared: the only terms of comparison used by the colored people themselves being terms of this kind,—such as *peau-chapotille*, "sapota-skin." The *sapota* or *sapotille* is a juicy brown fruit with a rind satiny like a human cuticle, and just the color, when flushed and ripe, of certain half-breed skins. But among the brighter half-breeds, the colors, I think, are much more fruit-like;—there are banana-tints, lemon-tones, orange-hues, with sometimes such a mingling of ruddiness as in the pink ripening of a mango. Agreeable to the eye the darker skins certainly are, and often very remarkable—all clear tones of bronze being represented; but the brighter tints are absolutely beautiful. Standing perfectly naked at door-ways, or playing naked in the sun, astonishing children may sometimes be seen,—banana-colored or orange babies. There is one rare race-type, totally unlike the rest: the skin has a perfect gold-tone, an exquisite metallic yellow; the eyes are long, and have long silky lashes;—the hair is a mass of thick, rich, glossy curls that show blue lights in the sun. What mingling of races produced this beautiful type?—there is some strange blood in the blending,—not of coolie, nor of African, nor of Chinese, although there are Chinese types here of indubitable beauty.*

---

*I subsequently learned the mystery of this very strange and beautiful mixed race,—many fine specimens of which may also be seen in Trinidad. Three widely diverse elements have combined to form it: European, negro, and Indian,—but, strange to say, it is the most savage of these three bloods which creates the peculiar charm. . . . I cannot speak of this comely and extraordinary type without translating a passage from Dr. J. J. J. Cornilliac, an eminent Martinique physician, who recently published a most valuable series of studies upon the ethnology, climatology, and history of the Antilles. In these he writes:

. . . "When, among the populations of the Antilles, we first notice those remarkable *métis* whose olive skins, elegant and slender figures, fine straight profiles, and regular features remind us of the inhabitants of Madras or Pondicherry,—we ask ourselves in wonder, while looking at their long eyes, full of a strange and gentle melancholy (especially among the women), and at the black, rich, silky-gleaming hair curling in abundance over the temples and falling its profusion over the neck,—to what human race can belong this singular variety,—in which there is a dominant characteristic that seems indelible, and always shows more and more strongly in proportion as the type is further removed from the African element. It is the Carib blood,—blended with blood of Europeans and of blacks,—which in spite of all subsequent crossings, and in spite of the fact that it has not been renewed for more than two hundred years, still conserves as markedly as at the time of the first interblending, the race-characteristic that invariably reveals its presence in the blood of every

. . . All this population is vigorous, graceful, healthy: all you see passing by are well made—there are no sickly faces, no scrawny limbs. If by some rare chance you encounter a person who has lost an arm or a leg, you can be almost certain you are looking at a victim of the fer-de-lance,—the serpent whose venom putrefies living tissue. . . . Without fear of exaggerating facts, I can venture to say that the muscular development of the workingmen here is something which must be seen in order to be believed;—to study fine displays of it, one should watch the blacks and half-breeds working naked to the waist, —on the landings, in the gas-houses and slaughterhouses, or on the nearest plantations. They are not generally large men, perhaps not extraordinarily powerful; but they have the aspect of sculptural or even of anatomical models; they seem absolutely devoid of adipose tissue, their muscles stand out with a saliency that astonishes the eye. At a tanning-yard, while I was watching a dozen blacks at work, a young mulatto with the mischievous face of a faun walked by, wearing nothing but a clout (*lantcho*) about his loins; and never, not even in bronze, did I see so beautiful a play of muscles. A demonstrator of anatomy could have used him for a class-model;—a sculptor wishing to shape a fine Mercury would have been satisfied to take a cast of such a body without thinking of making one modification from neck to heel. "Frugal diet is the cause of this physical condition," a young French professor assures me; "all these men," he says, "live upon salt codfish and fruit." But frugal living alone could never produce such symmetry and saliency of muscles: race-crossing, climate, perpetual exercise, healthy labor—many conditions must have combined to cause it. Also it is certain that this tropical sun has a tendency to dissolve spare flesh, to melt away all superfluous tissue, leaving the muscular fibre dense and solid as mahogany.

*

---

being through whose veins it flows."—"Recherches chronologiques et historiques sur l'Origine et la Propagation de la Fièvre Jaune aux Antilles." Par J. J. J. Cornilliac. Fort-de-France: Imprimerie du Gouvernement. 1886.

But I do not think the term "olive" always indicates the color of these skins, which seemed to me exactly the tint of gold; and the hair flashes with bluish lights, like the plumage of certain black birds.

At the *mouillage*, below a green *morne*, is the bathing-place. A rocky beach rounding away under heights of tropical wood; —palms curving out above the sand, or bending half-way across it. Ships at anchor in blue water, against golden-yellow horizon. A vast blue glow. Water clear as diamond, and lukewarm.

It is about one hour after sunrise; and the higher parts of Montagne Pelée are still misty blue. Under the palms and among the lava rocks, and also in little cabins farther up the slope, bathers are dressing or undressing: the water is also dotted with heads of swimmers. Women and girls enter it well robed from feet to shoulders;—men go in very sparsely clad;— there are lads wearing nothing. Young boys—yellow and brown little fellows—run in naked, and swim out to pointed rocks that jut up black above the bright water. They climb up one at a time to dive down. Poised for the leap upon the black lava crag, and against the blue light of the sky, each lithe figure, gilded by the morning sun, has a statuesqueness and a luminosity impossible to paint in words. These bodies seem to radiate color; and the azure light intensifies the hue: it is idyllic, incredible;—Coomans used paler colors in his Pompeiian studies, and his figures were never so symmetrical. This flesh does not look like flesh, but like fruit-pulp. . . .

XIV.

. . . EVERYWHERE crosses, little shrines, wayside chapels, statues of saints. You will see crucifixes and statuettes even in the forks or hollows of trees shadowing the high-roads. As you ascend these towards the interior you will see, every mile or half-mile, some chapel, or a cross erected upon a pedestal of masonry, or some little niche contrived in a wall, closed by a wire grating, through which the image of a Christ or a Madonna is visible. Lamps are kept burning all night before these figures. But the village of Morne Rouge—some two thousand feet above the sea, and about an hour's drive from St. Pierre—is chiefly remarkable for such displays: it is a place of pilgrimage as well as a health resort. Above the village, upon the steep slope of a higher morne, one may note a singular succession of little edifices ascending to the summit,—fourteen little tabernacles, each containing a *relievo* representing some incident of Christ's

In the Cimetière du Mouillage, St. Pierre.

Passion. This is called *Le Calvaire*: it requires more than a feeble piety to perform the religious exercise of climbing the height, and saying a prayer before each little shrine on the way. From the porch of the crowning structure the village of Morne Rouge appears so far below that it makes one almost dizzy to look at it; but even for the profane one ascent is well worth making, for the sake of the beautiful view. On all the neighboring heights around are votive chapels or great crucifixes.

St. Pierre is less peopled with images than Morne Rouge, but it has several colossal ones, which may be seen from any part of the harbor. On the heights above the middle quarter, or *Centre*, a gigantic Christ overlooks the bay; and from the Morne d'Orange, which bounds the city on the south, a great white Virgin—Notre Dame de la Garde, patron of mariners—watches above the ships at anchor in the mouillage.

. . . Thrice daily, from the towers of the white cathedral, a superb chime of bells rolls its *carillon* through the town. On great holidays the bells are wonderfully rung;—the ringers are African, and something of African feeling is observable in their impressive but incantatory manner of ringing. The *bourdon* must have cost a fortune. When it is made to speak, the effect is startling: all the city vibrates to a weird sound difficult to describe,—an abysmal, quivering moan, producing unfamiliar harmonies as the voices of the smaller bells are seized and interblended by it. . . . One will not easily forget the ringing of a *bel-midi*.

. . . Behind the cathedral, above the peaked city roofs, and at the foot of the wood-clad Morne d'Orange, is the *Cimetière du Mouillage*. . . . It is full of beauty,—this strange tropical cemetery. Most of the low tombs are covered with small square black and white tiles, set exactly after the fashion of the squares on a chess-board; at the foot of each grave stands a black cross, bearing at its centre a little white plaque, on which the name is graven in delicate and tasteful lettering. So pretty these little tombs are, that you might almost believe yourself in a toy cemetery. Here and there, again, are miniature marble chapels built over the dead,—containing white Madonnas and Christs and little angels,—while flowering creepers climb and twine about the pillars. Death seems so luminous here that one thinks of it unconsciously as a soft rising from this soft green earth,—like a vapor invisible,—to melt into the prodigious day. Everything is bright and neat and beautiful; the air is sleepy with jasmine scent and odor of white lilies; and the palm —emblem of immortality—lifts its head a hundred feet into the blue light. There are rows of these majestic and symbolic trees;—two enormous ones guard the entrance;—the others rise from among the tombs,—white-stemmed, out-spreading their huge parasols of verdure higher than the cathedral towers.

Behind all this, the dumb green life of the morne seems striving to descend, to invade the rest of the dead. It thrusts green hands over the wall,—pushes strong roots underneath; —it attacks every joint of the stonework, patiently, imperceptibly, yet almost irresistibly.

. . . Some day there may be a great change in the little city of St. Pierre;—there may be less money and less zeal and less remembrance of the lost. Then from the morne, over the bulwark, the green host will move down unopposed;—creepers will prepare the way, dislocating the pretty tombs, pulling away the checkered tiling;—then will come the giants, rooting deeper,—feeling for the dust of hearts, groping among the bones;—and all that love has hidden away shall be restored to Nature,—absorbed into the rich juices of her verdure,— revitalized in her bursts of color,—resurrected in her upliftings of emerald and gold to the great sun. . . .

XV.

SEEN from the bay, the little red-white-and-yellow city forms but one multicolored streak against the burning green of the lofty island. There is no naked soil, no bare rock: the chains of the mountains, rising by successive ridges towards the interior, are still covered with forests;—tropical woods ascend the peaks to the height of four and five thousand feet. To describe the beauty of these woods—even of those covering the mornes in the immediate vicinity of St. Pierre—seems to me almost impossible;—there are forms and colors which appear to demand the creation of new words to express. Especially is this true in regard to hue;—the green of a tropical forest is something which one familiar only with the tones of Northern vegetation can form no just conception of: it is a color that conveys the idea of green fire.

You have only to follow the high-road leading out of St. Pierre by way of the Savane du Fort to find yourself, after twenty minutes' walk, in front of the Morne Parnasse, and before the verge of a high wood,—remnant of the enormous growth once covering all the island. What a tropical forest is, as seen from without, you will then begin to feel, with a sort of awe, while you watch that beautiful upclimbing of green shapes to the height of perhaps a thousand feet overhead. It presents one seemingly solid surface of vivid color,—rugose like a cliff. You do not readily distinguish whole trees in the mass;—you only perceive suggestions, dreams of trees, Doresqueries. Shapes that seem to be staggering under weight of creepers rise a hundred feet above you;—others, equally huge, are towering above these;—and still higher, a legion of monstrosities are nodding, bending, tossing up green arms, pushing out great knees, projecting curves as of backs and shoulders, intertwining mockeries of limbs. No distinct head appears except where some palm pushes up its crest in the general fight for sun. All else looks as if under a veil,—hidden and half smothered by heavy drooping things. Blazing green vines cover every branch and stem;—they form draperies and tapestries and curtains and motionless cascades—pouring down over all projections like a thick silent flood: an amazing inundation of parasitic life. . . . It is a weird and awful beauty that you gaze upon and yet the spectacle is imperfect. These woods have been decimated;—the finest trees have been cut down: you see only a ruin of what was. To see the true primeval forest, you must ride well into the interior.

The absolutism of green does not, however, always prevail in these woods. During a brief season, corresponding to some of our winter months, the forests suddenly break into a very conflagration of color, caused by the blossoming of the lianas—crimson, canary-yellow, blue, and white. There are other flowerings, indeed; but that of the lianas alone has chromatic force enough to change the aspect of a landscape.

XVI.

. . . IF it is possible for a West Indian forest to be described at
all, it could not be described more powerfully than it has been
by Dr. F. Rufz, a creole of Martinique, from one of whose
works I venture to translate the following remarkable pages:

   . . . "The sea, the sea alone, because it is the most colossal
of earthly spectacles,—only the sea can afford us any term of
comparison for the attempt to describe a *grand-bois*;—but
even then one must imagine the sea on a day of storm, suddenly immobilized in the expression of its mightiest fury. For
the summits of these vast woods repeat all the inequalities of
the land they cover; and these inequalities are mountains from
4200 to 4800 feet in height, and valleys of corresponding profundity. All this is hidden, blended together, smoothed over by
verdure, in soft and enormous undulations,—in immense billowings of foliage. Only, instead of a blue line at the horizon,
you have a green line; instead of flashings of blue, you have
flashings of green,—and in all the tints, in all the combinations
of which green is capable: deep green, light green, yellow-
green, black-green.
   "When your eyes grow weary—if it indeed be possible for
them to weary—of contemplating the exterior of these
tremendous woods, try to penetrate a little into their interior.
What an inextricable chaos it is! The sands of a sea are not
more closely pressed together than the trees are here: some
straight, some curved, some upright, some toppling,—fallen,
or leaning against one another, or heaped high upon each
other. Climbing lianas, which cross from one tree to the other,
like ropes passing from mast to mast, help to fill up all the gaps
in this treillage; and parasites—not timid parasites like ivy or
like moss, but parasites which are trees self-grafted upon trees
—dominate the primitive trunks, overwhelm them, usurp the
place of their foliage, and fall back to the ground, forming factitious weeping-willows. You do not find here, as in the great
forests of the North, the eternal monotony of birch and fir:
this is the kingdom of infinite variety;—species the most diverse
elbow each other, interlace, strangle and devour each other: all

ranks and orders are confounded, as in a human mob. The soft and tender *balisier* opens its parasol of leaves beside the *gommier*, which is the cedar of the colonies;—you see the *acomat*, the *courbaril*, the mahogany, the *tendre-à-caillou*, the ironwood . . . but as well enumerate by name all the soldiers of an army! Our oak, the balata, forces the palm to lengthen itself prodigiously in order to get a few thin beams of sunlight; for it is as difficult here for the poor trees to obtain one glance from this King of the world, as for us, subjects of a monarchy, to obtain one look from our monarch. As for the soil, it is needless to think of looking at it: it lies as far below us probably as the bottom of the sea;—it disppeared, ever so long ago, under the heaping of débris,—under a sort of manure that has been accumulating there since the creation: you sink into it as into slime; you walk upon putrefied trunks, in a dust that has no name! Here indeed it is that one can get some comprehension of what vegetable antiquity signifies;—a lurid light (*lurida lux*), greenish, as wan at noon as the light of the moon at midnight, confuses forms and lends them a vague and fantastic aspect; a mephitic humidity exhales from all parts; an odor of death prevails; and a calm which is not silence (for the ear fancies it can hear the great movement of composition and of decomposition perpetually going on) tends to inspire you with that old mysterious horror which the ancients felt in the primitive forests of Germany and of Gaul:

"'Arboribus suus horror inest.'"*

XVII.

But the sense of awe inspired by a tropic forest is certainly greater than the mystic fear which any wooded wilderness of the North could ever have created. The brilliancy of colors that seem almost preternatural; the vastness of the ocean of frondage, and the violet blackness of rare gaps, revealing its inconceived profundity; and the million mysterious sounds which

*"Enquête sur le Serpent de la Martinique (Vipère Fer-de-Lance, Bothrops Lancéolé, etc.)." Par le Docteur E. Rufz. 2 ed. 1859. Paris: Germer-Ballière. pp. 55–57 (note).

make up its perpetual murmur,—compel the idea of a creative force that almost terrifies. Man feels here like an insect,—fears like an insect on the alert for merciless enemies; and the fear is not unfounded. To enter these green abysses without a guide were folly: even with the best of guides there is peril. Nature is dangerous here: the powers that build are also the powers that putrefy; here life and death are perpetually interchanging office in the never-ceasing transformation of forces,—melting down and reshaping living substance simultaneously within the same vast crucible. There are trees distilling venom, there are plants that have fangs, there are perfumes that affect the brain, there are cold green creepers whose touch blisters flesh like fire; while in all the recesses and the shadows is a swarming of unfamiliar life, beautiful or hideous,—insect, reptile, bird,—interwarring, devouring, preying. . . . But the great peril of the forest—the danger which deters even the naturalist—is the presence of the terrible *fer-de-lance* (*trigonocephalus lanceolatus,—bothrops   lanceolatus,—craspodecephalus*),—deadliest of the Occidental thanatophidia, and probably one of the deadliest serpents of the known world.

. . . There are no less than eight varieties of it,—the most common being the dark gray, speckled with black—precisely the color that enables the creature to hide itself among the protruding roots of the trees, by simply coiling about them, and concealing its triangular head. Sometimes the snake is a clear bright yellow: then it is difficult to distinguish it from the bunch of bananas among which it conceals itself. Or the creature may be a dark yellow,—or a yellowish brown,—or the color of wine-lees, speckled pink and black,—or dead black with a yellow belly,—or black with a pink belly: all hues of tropical forest-mould, of old bark, of decomposing trees. . . . The iris of the eye is orange,—with red flashes: it glows at night like burning charcoal.

And the fer-de-lance reigns absolute king over the mountains and the ravines: he is lord of the forest and the solitudes by day, and by night he extends his dominion over the public roads, the familiar paths, the parks, the pleasure resorts. People must remain at home after dark, unless they dwell in the city itself: if you happen to be out visiting after sunset, only a mile from town, your friends will caution on anxiously not to follow

the boulevard as you go back, and to keep as closely as possible
to the very centre of the path. Even in the brightest noon you
cannot venture to enter the woods without an experienced escort; you cannot trust your eyes to detect danger: at any moment a seeming branch, a knot of lianas, a pink or gray root, a
clump of pendent yellow fruit, may suddenly take life, writhe,
stretch, spring, strike. . . . Then you will need aid indeed,
and most quickly; for within the span of a few heart-beats the
wounded flesh chills, tumefies, softens. Soon it changes color,
and begins to spot violaceously; while an icy coldness creeps
through all the blood. If the *panseur* or the physician arrives in
time, and no vein has been pierced, there is hope; but it more
often happens that the blow is received directly on a vein of
the foot or ankle,—in which case nothing can save the victim.
Even when life is saved the danger is not over. Necrosis of the
tissues is likely to set in: the flesh corrupts, falls from the bone
sometimes in tatters; and the colors of its putrefaction simulate
the hues of vegetable decay,—the ghastly grays and pinks and
yellows of trunks rotting down into the dark soil which gave
them birth. The human victim moulders as the trees moulder,
—crumbles and dissolves as crumbles the substance of the
dead palms and balatas: the Death-of-the-Woods is upon him.

To-day a fer-de-lance is seldom found exceeding six feet in
length; but the dimensions of the reptile, at least, would seem
to have been decreased considerably by man's warring upon it
since the time of Père Labat, who mentions having seen a fer-
de-lance nine feet long and five inches in diameter. He also
speaks of a *couresse*—a beautiful and harmless serpent said to
kill the fer-de-lance—over ten feet long and thick as a man's
leg; but a large couresse is now seldom seen. The negro
woodsmen kill both creatures indiscriminately; and as the
older reptiles are the least likely to escape observation, the
chances for the survival of extraordinary individuals lessen with
the yearly decrease of forest-area.

. . . But it may be doubted whether the number of deadly
snakes has been greatly lessened since the early colonial period.
Each female produces viviparously from forty to sixty young at
a birth. The favorite haunts of the fer-de-lance are to a large
extent either inaccessible or unexplored, and its multiplication
is prodigious. It is really only the surplus of its swarming that

In the Jardin des Plantes, St. Pierre.

overpours into the cane-fields, and makes the public roads dangerous after dark;—yet more than three hundred snakes have been killed in twelve months on a single plantation. The introduction of the Indian mongoos, or *mangouste* (ichneumon), proved futile as a means of repressing the evil. The mangouste kills the fer-de-lance when it has a chance; but it also kills fowls and sucks their eggs, which condemns it irrevocably with the country negroes, who live to a considerable extent by raising and selling chickens.

. . . Domestic animals are generally able to discern the presence of their deadly enemy long before a human eye can perceive it. If your horse rears and plunges in the darkness, trembles and sweats, do not try to ride on until you are assured the way is clear. Or your dog may come running back, whining, shivering: you will do well to accept his warning. The animals kept about country residences usually try to fight for their lives; the hen battles for her chickens; the bull endeavors to gore and stamp his supple enemy; the pig gives more successful combat; but the creature who fears the monster least is the brave cat. Seeing a snake, she at once carries her kittens to a place of safety, then boldly advances to the encounter. She will walk to the very limit of the serpent's striking range, and begin to feint—teasing him, startling him, trying to draw his blow. How the emerald and the topazine eyes glow then!—they are flames! A moment more and the triangular head, hissing from the coil, flashes swift as if moved by wings. But swifter still the stroke of the armed paw that dashes the horror aside, flinging it mangled in the dust. Nevertheless, pussy does not yet dare to spring;—the enemy, still active, has almost instantly reformed his coil;—but she is again in front of him, watching,— vertical pupil against vertical pupil. Again the lashing stroke; again the beautiful countering;—again the living death is hurled aside; and now the scaled skin is deeply torn,—one eye socket has ceased to flame. Once more the stroke of the serpent; once more the light, quick, cutting blow. But the trigonocephalus is blind, is stupefied;—before he can attempt to coil pussy has leaped upon him,—nailing the horrible flat head fast to the ground with her two sinewy paws. Now let him lash, writhe, twine, strive to strangle her!—in vain! he will never lift his head an instant more, and he lies still:—the keen white teeth of the cat have severed the vertebra just behind the triangular skull! . . .

XVIII.

THE Jardin des Plantes is not absolutely secure from the visits of the serpent; for the trigonocephalus goes everywhere,— mounting to the very summits of the cocoa-palms, swimming rivers, ascending walls, hiding in palm-thatched roofs, breeding in bagasse heaps. But, despite what has been printed to the contrary, this reptile fears man and hates light: it rarely shows itself voluntarily during the day. Therefore, if you desire to obtain some conception of the magnificence of Martinique vegetation, without incurring the risk of entering the high woods, you can do so by visiting the Jardin des Plantes,—only taking care to use your eyes well while climbing over fallen trees, or picking your way through dead branches. The garden is less than a mile from the city, on the slopes of the Morne Parnasse; and the primitive forest itself has been utilized in the formation of it,—so that the greater part of the garden is a primitive growth. Nature has accomplished here infinitely more than art of man (though such art has done much to lend the place its charm),—and until within a very recent time the result might have been deemed, without exaggeration, one of the wonders of the world.

A moment after passing the gate you are in twilight,— though the sun may be blinding on the white road without. All about you is a green gloaming, up through which you see immense trunks rising. Follow the first path that slopes up on your left as you proceed, if you wish to obtain the best general view of the place in the shortest possible time. As you proceed, the garden on your right deepens more and more into a sort of ravine;—on your left rises a sort of foliage-shrouded cliff; and all this in a beautiful crepuscular dimness made by the foliage of great trees meeting overhead. Palms rooted a hundred feet below you hold their heads a hundred feet above you; yet they can barely reach the light. . . . Farther on the ravine widens to frame in two tiny lakes, dotted with artificial islands, which are miniatures of Martinique, Guadeloupe, and Dominica: these are covered with tropical plants, many of which are total strangers even here: they are natives of India, Senegambia, Algeria, and the most eastern East. Arborescent ferns of unfamiliar elegance curve up from path-verge or lake-brink; and the great *arbre-du-voyageur* outspreads its colossal fan. Giant lianas droop down over the way in loops and festoons; tapering green cords, which are creepers descending to take root, hang everywhere; and parasites with stems thick as cables coil about the trees like boas. Trunks shooting up out of sight, into the green wilderness above, display no bark; you cannot guess what sort of trees they are; they are so thickly wrapped in creepers as to seem pillars of leaves. Between you and the sky, where everything is fighting for sun, there is an almost unbroken vault of leaves, a cloudy green confusion in which nothing particular is distinguishable.

You come to breaks now and then in the green steep to your left,—openings created for cascades pouring down from one mossed basin of brown stone to another,—or gaps occupied by flights of stone steps, green with mosses, and chocolate-colored by age. These steps lead to loftier paths; and all the stone-work,—the grottos, bridges, basins, terraces, steps,—are darkened by time and velveted with mossy things. . . . It is of another century, this garden: special ordinances were passed concerning it during the French Revolution (*An. II.*);—it is very quaint; it suggests an art spirit as old as Versailles, or older; but it is indescribably beautiful even now.

. . . At last you near the end, to hear the roar of falling water;—there is a break in the vault of green above the bed of a river below you; and at a sudden turn you come in sight of the cascade. Before you is the Morne itself; and against the burst of descending light you discern a precipice-verge. Over it, down one green furrow in its brow, tumbles the rolling foam of a cataract, like falling smoke, to be caught below in a succession of moss-covered basins. The first clear leap of the water is nearly seventy feet. . . . Did Josephine ever rest upon that shadowed bench near by? . . . She knew all these paths by heart: surely they must have haunted her dreams in the after-time!

Returning by another path, you may have a view of other cascades—though none so imposing. But they are beautiful; and you will not soon forget the effect of one,—flanked at its

Cascade in the Jardin des Plantes.

summit by white-stemmed palms which lift their leaves so high into the light that the loftiness of them gives the sensation of vertigo. . . . Dizzy also the magnificence of the great colonnade of palmistes and angelins, two hundred feet high, through which you pass if you follow the river-path from the cascade,—the famed *Allée des duels*. . . .

The vast height, the pillared solemnity of the ancient trees in the green dimness, the solitude, the strangeness of shapes but half seen,—suggesting fancies of silent aspiration, or triumph, or despair,—all combine to produce a singular impression of awe. . . . You are alone; you hear no human voice,—no sounds but the rushing of the river over its volcanic rocks, and the creeping of millions of lizards and tree-frogs and little toads. You see no human face; but you see all around you the labor of man being gnawed and devoured by nature,—broken bridges, sliding steps, fallen arches, strangled fountains with empty basins;—and everywhere arises the pungent odor of decay. This omnipresent odor affects one unpleasantly;—it never ceases to remind you that where Nature is most puissant to charm, there also is she mightiest to destroy.

The beautiful garden is now little more than a wreck of what it once was: since the fall of the Empire it has been shamefully abused and neglected. Some *agronome* sent out to take charge of it by the Republic, began its destruction by cutting down acres of enormous and magnificent trees,—including a superb alley of palms,—for the purpose of experimenting with roses. But the rose-trees would not be cultivated there; and the serpents avenged the demolition by making the experimental garden unsafe to enter;—they always swarm into underbrush and shrubbery after forest-trees have been cleared away. . . . Subsequently the garden was greatly damaged by storms and torrential rains; the mountain river overflowed, carrying bridges away and demolishing stone-work. No attempt was made to repair these destructions; but neglect alone would not have ruined the loveliness of the place;—barbarism was necessary! Under the present negro-radical régime orders have been given for the wanton destruction of trees older than the colony itself;—and marvels that could not be replaced in a hundred generations were cut down and converted into charcoal for the use of public institutions.

XIX.

. . . How gray seem the words of poets in the presence of this Nature! . . . The enormous silent poem of color and light—(you who know only the North do not know color, do not know light!)—of sea and sky, of the woods and the peaks, so far surpasses imagination as to paralyze it—mocking the language of admiration, defying all power of expression. That is before you which never can be painted or chanted, because there is no cunning of art or speech able to reflect it. Nature realizes your most hopeless ideals of beauty, even as one gives toys to a child. And the sight of this supreme terrestrial expression of creative magic numbs thought. In the great centres of civilization we admire and study only the results of mind,—the products of human endeavor: here one views only the work of Nature,—but Nature in all her primeval power, as in the legendary frostless morning of creation. Man here seems to bear scarcely more relation to the green life about him than the insect; and the results of human effort seem impotent by comparison with the operation of those vast blind forces which clothe the peaks and crown the dead craters with impenetrable forest. The air itself seems inimical to thought,—soporific, and yet pregnant with activities of dissolution so powerful that the mightiest tree begins to melt like wax from the moment it has ceased to live. For man merely to exist is an effort; and doubtless in the perpetual struggle of the blood to preserve itself from fermentation, there is such an expenditure of vital energy as leaves little surplus for mental exertion.

. . . Scarcely less than poet or philosopher, the artist, I fancy, would feel his helplessness. In the city he may find wonderful picturesqueness to invite his pencil, but when he stands face to face alone with Nature he will discover that he has no colors! The luminosities of tropic foliage could only be imitated in fire. He who desires to paint a West Indian forest,—a West Indian landscape,—must take his view from some great height, through which the colors come to his eye softened and subdued by distance,—toned with blues or purples by the astonishing atmosphere.

*

. . . It is sunset as I write these lines, and there are witch-crafts of color. Looking down the narrow, steep street opening to the bay, I see the motionless silhouette of the steamer on a perfectly green sea,—under a lilac sky,—against a prodigious orange light.

XX.

IN these tropic latitudes Night does not seem "to fall,"—to descend over the many-peaked land: it appears to rise up, like an exhalation, from the ground. The coast-lines darken first;—then the slopes and the lower hills and valleys become shadowed;—then, very swiftly, the gloom mounts to the heights, whose very loftiest peak may remain glowing like a volcano at its tip for several minutes after the rest of the island is veiled in black-ness and all the stars are out. . . .

. . . Tropical nights have a splendor that seems strange to northern eyes. The sky does not look so high—so far away as in the North; but the stars are larger, and the luminosity greater.

With the rising of the moon all the violet of the sky flushes;—there is almost such a rose-color as heralds northern dawn.

Then the moon appears over the mornes, very large, very bright—brighter certainly than many a befogged sun one sees in northern Novembers; and it seems to have a weird magnetism—this tropical moon. Night-birds, insects, frogs,—everything that can sing,—all sing very low on the nights of great moons. Tropical wood-life begins with dark: in the im-mense white light of a full moon this nocturnal life seems afraid to cry out as usual. Also, this moon has a singular effect on the nerves. It is very difficult to sleep on such bright nights: you feel such a vague uneasiness as the coming of a great storm gives. . . .

XXI.

YOU reach Fort-de-France, the capital of Martinique, by steamer from St. Pierre, in about an hour and a half. . . . There is an overland route—*La Trace*; but it is a twenty-five-

Departure of Steamer for Fort-de-France.

mile ride, and a weary one in such a climate, notwithstanding the indescribable beauty of the landscapes which the lofty road commands.

. . . Rebuilt in wood after the almost total destruction by an earthquake of its once picturesque streets of stone, Fort-de-France (formerly Fort-Royal) has little of outward interest by comparison with St. Pierre. It lies in a low, moist plain, and has few remarkable buildings: you can walk all over the little town in about half an hour. But the Savane,—the great green public square, with its grand tamarinds and *sabliers*,—would be worth the visit alone, even were it not made romantic by the marble memory of Josephine.

I went to look at the white dream of her there, a creation of master-sculptors. . . . It seemed to me absolutely lovely.

Sea winds have bitten it; tropical rains have streaked it: some microscopic growth has darkened the exquisite hollow of the throat. And yet such is the human charm of the figure that you almost fancy you are gazing at a living presence. . . . Perhaps the profile is less artistically real,—statuesque to the point of betraying the chisel; but when you look straight up into the sweet creole face, you can believe she lives: all the wonderful West Indian charm of the woman is there.

She is standing just in the centre of the Savane, robed in the fashion of the First Empire, with gracious arms and shoulders bare: one hand leans upon a medallion bearing the eagle profile of Napoleon. . . . Seven tall palms stand in a circle around her, lifting their comely heads into the blue glory of the tropic day. Within their enchanted circle you feel that you tread holy ground,—the sacred soil of artist and poet;—here the recollections of memoir-writers vanish away; the gossip of history is hushed for you; you no longer care to know how rumor has it that she spoke or smiled or wept: only the bewitch-ment of her lives under the thin, soft, swaying shadows of those feminine palms. . . . Over violet space of summer sea, through the vast splendor of azure light, she is looking back to the place of her birth, back to beautiful drowsy Trois-Islets,— and always with the same half dreaming, half-plaintive smile,— unutterably touching. . . .

Statue of Josephine.

XXII.

ONE leaves Martinique with regret, even after so brief a stay: the old colonial life itself, not less than the revelation of tropic nature, having in this island a quality of uniqueness, a special charm, unlike anything previously seen. . . . We steam directly for Barbadoes;—the vessel will touch at the intervening islands only on her homeward route.

. . . Against a hot wind south,—under a sky always deepening in beauty. Towards evening dark clouds begin to rise before us; and by nightfall they spread into one pitch-blackness over all the sky. Then comes a wind in immense sweeps, lifting the water,—but a wind that is still strangely warm. The ship rolls heavily in the dark for an hour or more;—then torrents of tepid rain make the sea smooth again; the clouds pass, and the violet transparency of tropical night reappears,—ablaze with stars.

At early morning a long low land appears on the horizon,— totally unlike the others we have seen; it has no visible volcanic forms. That is Barbadoes,—a level burning coral coast,—a streak of green, white-edged, on the verge of the sea. But hours pass before the green line begins to show outlines of foliage.

. . . As we approach the harbor an overhanging black cloud suddenly bursts down in illuminated rain,—through which the shapes of moored ships seem magnified as through a golden fog. It ceases as suddenly as it begun; the cloud vanishes utterly; and the azure is revealed unflecked, dazzling, wondrous. . . . It is a sight worth the whole journey,—the splendor of this noon sky at Barbadoes;—the horizon glow is almost blinding, the sea-line sharp as a razor-edge; and motionless upon the sapphire water nearly a hundred ships lie,—masts, spars, booms, cordage, cutting against the amazing magnificence of blue. . . . Meanwhile the island coast has clearly brought out all its beauties: first you note the long white winding thread-line of beach—coral and bright sand;—then the deep green fringe of vegetation through which roofs and spires project here and there, and quivering feathery heads of palms with white trunks. The general tone of this verdure is sombre green, though it is full of luster: there is a glimmer in it as of metal. Beyond all this coast-front long undulations of misty pale

Inner Basin, Bridgetown, Barbadoes.

green are visible,—far slopes of low hill and plain; the highest
curving line, the ridge of the island, bears a row of cocoa-
palms. They are so far that their stems diminish almost to invisibility: only the crests are clearly distinguishable,—like spiders
hanging between land and sky. But there are no forests: the
land is a naked unshadowed green far as the eye can reach
beyond the coast-line. There is no waste space in Barbadoes: it
is perhaps one of the most densely-peopled places on the globe
—(one thousand and thirty-five inhabitants to the square
mile);—and it sends black laborers by thousands to the other
British colonies every year,—the surplus of its population.

. . . The city of Bridgetown disappoints the stranger who
expects to find any exotic features of architecture or custom,—
disappoints more, perhaps, than any other tropical port in this
respect. Its principal streets give you the impression of walking
through an English town,—not an old-time town, but a new
one, plain almost to commonplaceness, in spite of Nelson's
monument. Even the palms are powerless to lend the place a
really tropical look;—the streets are narrow without being picturesque, white as lime roads and full of glare;—the manners,
the costumes, the style of living, the system of business are
thoroughly English;—the population lacks visible originality;
and its extraordinary activity, so oddly at variance with the
quiet indolence of other West Indian peoples, seems almost
unnatural. Pressure of numbers has largely contributed to this
characteristic; but Barbadoes would be in any event, by reason
of position alone, a busy colony. As the most-windward of the
West Indies it has naturally become not only the chief port,
but also the chief emporium of the Antilles. It has railroads,
telephones, street-cars, fire and life insurance companies, good
hotels, libraries and reading-rooms, and excellent public
schools. Its annual export trade figures for nearly $6,000,000.

The fact which seems most curious to the stranger, on his
first acquaintance with the city, is that most of this business activity is represented by black men—black merchants, shop-
keepers, clerks. Indeed, the Barbadian population, as a mass,
strikes one as the darkest in the West Indies. Black regiments
march through the street to the sound of English music,—
uniformed as Zouaves; black police, in white helmets and
white duck uniforms, maintain order; black postmen distribute

Trafalgar Square, Bridgetown, Barbadoes.

the mails; black cabmen wait for customers at a shilling an hour. It is by no means an attractive population, physically,—rather the reverse, and frankly brutal as well—different as possible from the colored race of Martinique; but it has immense energy, and speaks excellent English. One is almost startled on hearing Barbadian negroes speaking English with a strong Old Country accent. Without seeing the speaker, you could scarcely believe such English uttered by black lips; and the commonest negro laborer about the port pronounces as well as a Londoner. The purity of Barbadian English is partly due, no doubt, to the fact that, unlike most of the other islands, Barbadoes has always remained in the possession of Great Britain. Even as far back as 1676 Barbadoes was in a very different condition of prosperity from that of the other colonies, and offered a totally different social aspect—having a white population of 50,000. At that time the island could muster 20,000 infantry and 3000 horse; there were 80,000 slaves; there were 1500 houses in Bridgetown and an immense number of shops; and not less than two hundred ships were required to export the annual sugar crop alone.

But Barbadoes differs also from most of the Antilles geologically; and there can be no question that the nature of its soil has considerably influenced the physical character of its inhabitants. Although Barbadoes is now known to be also of volcanic origin,—a fact which its low undulating surface could enable no unscientific observer to suppose,—it is superficially a calcareous formation; and the remarkable effect of limestone soil upon the bodily development of a people is not less marked in this latitude than elsewhere. In most of the Antilles the white race degenerates and dwarfs under the influence of climate and environment; but the Barbadian creole—tall, muscular, large of bone—preserves and perpetuates in the tropics the strength and sturdiness of his English forefathers.

XXIII.

. . . NIGHT: steaming for British Guiana;—we shall touch at no port before reaching Demerara. . . . A strong warm gale, that compels the taking in of every awning and wind-sail. Driving tepid rain; and an intense darkness, broken only by the phosphorescence of the sea, which to-night displays extraordinary radiance.

The steamer's wake is a great broad, seething river of fire,—white like strong moonshine: the glow is bright enough to read by. At its centre the trail is brightest;—towards either edge it pales off cloudily,—curling like smoke of phosphorus. Great sharp lights burst up momentarily through it like meteors. Weirder than this strange wake are the long slow fires that keep burning about us at a distance, out in the dark. Nebulous incandescences mount up from the depths, change form, and pass;—serpentine flames wriggle by;—there are long billowing crests of fire. These seem to be formed of millions of tiny sparks, that light up all at the same time, glow for a while, disappear, reappear, and swirl away in a prolonged smouldering.

There are warm gales and heavy rain each night,—it is the hurricane season;—and it seems these become more violent the farther south we sail. But we are nearing those equinoctial regions where the calm of nature is never disturbed by storms.

. . . Morning: still steaming south, through a vast blue day. The azure of the heaven always seems to be growing deeper. There is a bluish-white glow in the horizon,—almost too bright to look at. An indigo sea. . . . There are no clouds; and the splendor endures until sunset.

Then another night, very luminous and calm. The Southern constellations burn whitely. . . . We are nearing the great shallows of the South American coast.

XXIV.

. . . It is the morning of the third day since we left Barbadoes, and for the first time since entering tropic waters all things seem changed. The atmosphere is heavy with strange mists; and the light of an orange-colored sun, immensely magnified by vapors, illuminates a greenish-yellow sea,—foul and opaque, as if stagnant. . . . I remember just such a sunrise over the Louisiana gulf-coast.

We are in the shallows, moving very slowly. The line-caster keeps calling, at regular intervals: "Quarter less five, sir!" "And a half four, sir!" . . . There is little variation in his soundings —a quarter of a fathom or half a fathom difference. The warm air has a sickly heaviness, like the air of a swamp; the water shows olive and ochreous tones alternately;—the foam is yellow in our wake. These might be the colors of a fresh-water inundation. . . .

A fellow-traveller tells me, as we lean over the rail, that this same viscous, glaucous sea washes the great penal colony of Cayenne—which he visited. When a convict dies there, the corpse, sewn up in a sack, is borne to the water, and a great bell tolled. Then the still surface is suddenly broken by fins innumerable,—black fins of sharks rushing to the hideous funeral: they know the Bell! . . .

There is land in sight—very low land,—a thin dark line suggesting marshiness; and the nauseous color of the water always deepens.

As the land draws near, it reveals a beautiful tropical appearance. The sombre green line brightens color, sharpens into a splendid fringe of fantastic evergreen fronds, bristling with palm crests. Then a mossy seawall comes into sight—dull gray stone-work, green-lined at all its joints. There is a fort. The steamer's whistle is exactly mocked by a queer echo, and the cannon-shot once reverberated—only once: there are no mountains here to multiply a sound. And all the while the water becomes a thicker and more turbid green; the wake looks more and more ochreous, the foam ropier and yellower. Vessels becalmed everywhere speck the glass-level of the sea, like insects sticking upon a mirror. It begins, all of a sudden, to rain torrentially; and through the white storm of falling drops nothing is discernible.

XXV.

AT Georgetown, steamers entering the river can lie close to the wharf;—we can enter the Government warehouses without getting wet. In fifteen minutes the shower ceases; and we leave the warehouses to find ourselves in a broad, palm-bordered street illuminated by the most prodigious day that yet shone upon our voyage. The rain has cleared the air and dissolved the mists; and the light is wondrous.

My own memory of Demerara will always be a memory of enormous light. The radiance has an indescribable dazzling

Street in Georgetown, Demerara.

force that conveys the idea of electric fire;—the horizon blinds like a motionless sheet of lightning; and you dare not look at the zenith. . . . The brightest summer-day in the North is a gloaming to this. Men walk only under umbrellas, or with their eyes down; and the pavements, already dry, flare almost unbearably.

. . . Georgetown has an exotic aspect peculiar to itself,—different from that of any West Indian city we have seen; and this is chiefly due to the presence of palm-trees. For the edifices, the plan, the general idea of the town, are modern; the white streets, laid out very broad to the sweep of the sea-breeze, and drained by canals running through their centres, with bridges at cross-streets, display the value of nineteenth-century knowledge regarding house-building with a view to coolness as well as to beauty. The architecture might be described as a tropicalized Swiss style—Swiss eaves are developed into veranda roofs, and Swiss porches prolonged and lengthened into beautiful piazzas and balconies. The men who devised these large cool halls, these admirably ventilated rooms, these latticed windows opening to the ceiling, may have lived in India; but the physiognomy of the town also reveals a fine sense of beauty in the designers: all that is strange and beautiful in the vegetation of the tropics has had a place contrived for it, a home prepared for it. Each dwelling has its garden; each garden blazes with singular and lovely color; but everywhere and always tower the palms. There are colonnades of palms, clumps of palms, groves of palms—sago and cabbage and cocoa and fan palms. You can see that the palm is cherished here, is loved for its beauty, like a woman. Everywhere you find palms, in all stages of development, from the first sheaf of tender green plumes rising above the soil to the wonderful colossus that holds its head a hundred feet above the roofs; palms border the garden walks in colonnades; they are grouped in exquisite poise about the basins of fountains; they stand like magnificent pillars at either side of gates; they look into the highest windows of public buildings and hotels.

. . . For miles and miles and miles we drive along avenues of palms—avenues leading to opulent cane-fields, traversing queer coolie villages. Rising on either side of the road to the same level, the palms present the vista of a long unbroken double

Avenue in Georgetown, Demerara.

colonnade of dead-silver trunks, shining tall pillars with deep green plume-tufted summits, almost touching, almost forming something like the dream of an interminable Moresque arcade. Sometimes for a full mile the trees are only about thirty or forty feet high; then, turning into an older alley, we drive for half a league between giants nearly a hundred feet in altitude. The double perspective lines of their crests, meeting before us and behind us in a bronze-green darkness, betray only at long intervals any variation of color, where some dead leaf droops like an immense yellow feather.

XXVI.

IN the marvellous light, which brings out all the rings of their bark, these palms sometimes produce a singular impression of subtle, fleshy, sentient life,—seem to move with a slowly stealthy motion as you ride or drive past them. The longer you watch them, the stronger this idea becomes,—the more they seem alive,—the more their long silver-gray articulated bodies seem to poise, undulate, stretch. . . . Certainly the palms of a Demerara country-road evoke no such real emotion as that produced by the stupendous palms of the Jardin des Plantes in Martinique. That beautiful, solemn, silent life up-reaching through tropical forest to the sun for warmth, for color, for power,—filled me, I remember, with a sensation of awe different from anything which I had ever experienced. . . . But even here in Guiana, standing alone under the sky, the palm still seems a creature rather than a tree,—gives you the idea of personality;—you could almost believe each lithe shape animated by a thinking force,—believe that all are watching you with such passionless calm as legend lends to beings supernatural. . . . And I wonder if some kindred fancy might not have inspired the name given by the French colonists to the male palmiste,—*angelin*. . . .

Very wonderful is the botanical garden here. It is new; and there are no groves, no heavy timber, no shade; but the finely laid-out grounds,—alternations of lawn and flower-bed,—offer everywhere surprising sights. You observe curious orange-colored shrubs; plants speckled with four different colors;

plants that look like wigs of green hair; plants with enormous broad leaves that seem made of colored crystal; plants that do not look like natural growths, but like idealizations of plants, —those beautiful fantasticalities imagined by sculptors. All these we see in glimpses from a carriage-window,—yellow, indigo, black, and crimson plants. . . . We draw rein only to observe in the ponds the green navies of the Victoria Regia,— the monster among water-lilies. It covers all the ponds and many of the canals. Close to shore the leaves are not extraordinarily large; but they increase in breadth as they float farther out, as if gaining bulk proportionately to the depth of water. A few yards off, they are large as soup-plates; farther out, they are broad as dinner-trays; in the centre of the pond or canal they have surface large as tea-tables. And all have an upturned edge, a perpendicular rim. Here and there you see the imperial flower,—towering above the leaves. . . . Perhaps, if your hired driver be a good guide, he will show you the snake-nut,—the fruit of an extraordinary tree native to the Guiana forests. This swart nut—shaped almost like a clam-shell, and halving in the same way along its sharp edges—encloses something almost incredible. There is a pale envelope about the kernel; remove it, and you find between your fingers a little viper, triangular-headed, coiled thrice upon itself, perfect in every detail of form from head to tail. Was this marvellous mockery evolved for a protective end? It is no eccentricity: in every nut the serpent-kernel lies coiled the same.

. . . Yet in spite of a hundred such novel impressions, what a delight it is to turn again cityward through the avenues of Palms, and to feel once more the sensation of being watched, without love or hate, by all those lithe, tall, silent, gracious shapes!

XXVII.

HINDOOS; coolies; men, women, and children—standing, walking, or sitting in the sun, under the shadowing of the palms. Men squatting, with hands clasped over their black knees, are watching us from under their white turbans—very steadily, with a slight scowl. All these Indian faces have the same set, stern expression, the same knitting of the brows; and the keen gaze is not altogether pleasant. It borders upon hostility; it is the look of measurement—measurement physical and moral. In the mighty swarming of India these have learned the full meaning and force of life's law as we Occidentals rarely learn it. Under the dark fixed frown the eye glitters like a serpent's.

Nearly all wear the same Indian dress; the thickly folded turban, usually white, white drawers reaching but half-way down the thigh, leaving the knees and the legs bare, and white jacket. A few don long blue robes, and wear a colored head-dress: these are babagees—priests. Most of the men look tall; they are slender and smallboned, but the limbs are well turned. They are grave—talk in low tones, and seldom smile. Those you see with heavy black beards are probably Mussulmans: I am told they have their mosques here, and that the muezzin's call to prayer is chanted three times daily on many plantations. Others shave, but the Mohammedans allow all the beard to grow. . . . Very comely some of the women are in their close-clinging soft brief robes and tantalizing veils—a costume leaving shoulders, arms, and ankles bare. The dark arm is always tapered and rounded; the silver-circled ankle always elegantly knit to the light straight foot. Many slim girls, whether standing or walking or in repose, offer remarkable studies of grace; their attitude when erect always suggests lightness and suppleness, like the poise of a dancer.

. . . A coolie mother passes, carrying at her hip a very pretty naked baby. It has exquisite delicacy of limb: its tiny ankles are circled by thin bright silver rings; it looks like a little bronze statuette, a statuette of Kama, the Indian Eros. The mother's arms are covered from elbow to wrist with silver bracelets,—some flat and decorated; others coarse, round, smooth, with ends hammered into the form of viper-heads. She has large flowers of gold in her ears, a small gold flower in her very delicate little nose. This nose ornament does not seem absurd; on these dark skins the effect is almost as pleasing as it is bizarre. This jewellery is pure metal;—it is thus the coolies carry their savings,—melting down silver or gold coin, and recasting it into bracelets, ear-rings, and nose ornaments.

. . . Evening is brief: all this time the days have been growing shorter: it will be black at 6 P.M. One does not regret it;—the glory of such a tropical day as this is almost too much to

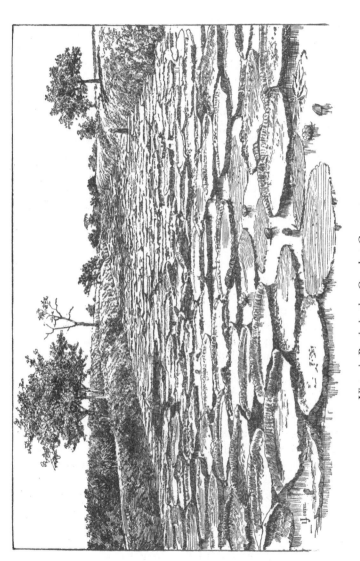

Victoria Regia in the Canal at Georgetown.

endure for twelve hours. The sun is already low, and yellow with a tinge of orange: as he falls between the palms his stare colors the world with a strange hue—such a phantasmal light as might be given by a nearly burnt-out sun. The air is full of unfamiliar odors. We pass a flame-colored bush; and an extraordinary perfume—strange, rich, sweet—envelops us like a caress: the soul of a red jasmine. . . .

. . . What a tropical sunset is this—within two days' steam-journey of the equator! Almost to the zenith the sky flames up from the sea,—one tremendous orange incandescence, rapidly deepening to vermilion as the sun dips. The indescribable intensity of this mighty burning makes one totally unprepared for the spectacle of its sudden passing: a seeming drawing down behind the sea of the whole vast flare of light. . . . Instantly the world becomes indigo. The air grows humid, weighty with vapor; frogs commence to make a queer bubbling noise; and some unknown creature begins in the trees a singular music, not trilling, like the note of our cricket, but one continuous shrill tone, high, keen, as of a thin jet of steam leaking through a valve. Strong vegetal scents, aromatic and novel, rise up. Under the trees of our hotel I hear a continuous dripping sound; the drops fall heavily, like bodies of clumsy insects. But it is not dew, nor insects; it is a thick, transparent jelly—a fleshy liquor that falls in immense drops. . . . The night grows chill with dews, with vegetable breath; and we sleep with windows nearly closed.

XXVIII.

. . . ANOTHER sunset like the conflagration of a world, as we steam away from Guiana;—another unclouded night; and morning brings back to us that bright blue in the sea-water which we missed for the first time on our approach to the main-land. There is a long swell all day, and tepid winds. But towards evening the water once more shifts its hue—takes olive tint—the mighty flood of the Orinoco is near.

Over the rim of the sea rise shapes faint pink, faint gray— misty shapes that grow and lengthen as we advance. We are nearing Trinidad.

It first takes definite form as a prolonged, undulating, pale

Demerara Coolie Girl.

gray mountain chain,—the outline of a sierra. Approaching nearer, we discern other hill summits rounding up and shouldering away behind the chain itself. Then the nearest heights begin to turn faint green—very slowly. Right before the outermost spur of cliff, fantastic shapes of rock are rising sheer from the water: partly green, partly reddish-gray where the surface remains unclothed by creepers and shrubs. Between them the sea leaps and whitens.

. . . And we begin to steam along a magnificent tropical coast,—before a billowing of hills wrapped in forest from sea to summit,—astonishing forest, dense, sombre, impervious to sun—every gap a blackness as of ink. Giant palms here and there overtop the denser foliage; and queer monster trees rise above the forest-level against the blue,—spreading out huge flat crests from which masses of lianas stream down. This forest-front has the apparent solidity of a wall, and forty-five miles of it undulate uninterruptedly by us—rising by terraces, or projecting like turret-lines, or shooting up into semblance of cathedral forms or suggestions of castellated architecture. . . . But the secrets of these woods have not been unexplored;— one of the noblest writers of our time has so beautifully and fully written of them as to leave little for any one else to say. He who knows Charles Kingsley's "At Last" probably knows the woods of Trinidad far better than many who pass them daily.

Even as observed from the steamer's deck, the mountains and forests of Trinidad have an aspect very different from those of the other Antilles. The heights are less lofty,—less jagged and abrupt,—with rounded summits; the peaks of Martinique or Dominica rise fully two thousand feet higher. The land itself is a totally different formation,—anciently being a portion of the continent; and its flora and fauna are of South America.

. . . There comes a great cool whiff of wind,—another and another;—then a mighty breath begins to blow steadily upon us,—the breath of the Orinoco. . . . It grows dark before we pass through the Ape's Mouth, to anchor in one of the calmest harbors in the world,—never disturbed by hurricanes. Over unruffled water the lights of Port-of-Spain shoot long still yellow beams. . . . The night grows chill;—the air is made

frigid by the breath of the enormous river and the vapors of
the great woods.

XXIX.

. . . SUNRISE: a morning of supernal beauty,—the sky of a
fairy tale,—the sea of a love-poem.

Under a heaven of exquisitely tender blue, the whole
smooth sea has a perfect luminous dove-color,—the horizon
being filled to a great height with greenish-golden haze,—a
mist of unspeakably sweet tint, a hue that, imitated in any
aquarelle, would be cried out against as an impossibility. As yet
the hills are nearly all gray, the forests also inwrapping them
are gray and ghostly, for the sun has but just risen above them,
and vapors hang like a veil between. Then, over the glassy level
of the flood, bands of purple and violet and pale blue and fluid
gold begin to shoot and quiver and broaden; these are the currents of the morning, catching varying color with the deepening of the day and the lifting of the tide.

Then, as the sun rises higher, green masses begin to glimmer
among the grays; the outlines of the forest summits commence
to define themselves through the vapory light, to left and right
of the great glow. Only the city still remains invisible; it lies exactly between us and the downpour of solar splendor, and the
mists there have caught such radiance that the place seems
hidden by a fog of fire. Gradually the gold-green of the horizon changes to a pure yellow; the hills take soft, rich, sensuous
colors. One of the more remote has turned a marvellous tone
—a seemingly diaphanous aureate color, the very ghost of
gold. But at last all of them sharpen bluely, show bright folds
and ribbings of green through their haze. The valleys remain
awhile clouded, as if filled with something like blue smoke; but
the projecting masses of cliff and slope swiftly change their
misty green to a warmer hue. All these tints and colors have a
spectral charm, a preternatural loveliness; everything seems
subdued, softened, semi-vaporized,—the only very sharply defined silhouettes being those of the little becalmed ships sprinkling the western water, all spreading colored wings to catch
the morning breeze.

The more the sun ascends, the more rapid the development

of the landscape out of vapory blue;—the hills all become green-faced, reveal the details of frondage. The wind fills the waiting sails—white, red, yellow,—ripples the water, and turns it green. Little fish begin to leap; they spring and fall in glittering showers like opalescent blown spray. And at last, through the fading vapor, dew-glittering red-tiled roofs reveal themselves: the city is unveiled—a city full of color, somewhat quaint, somewhat Spanish-looking—a little like St. Pierre, a little like New Orleans in the old quarter; everywhere fine tall palms.

XXX.

ASHORE, through a black swarming and a great hum of creole chatter. . . . Warm yellow narrow streets under a burning blue day;—a confused impression of long vistas, of low pretty houses and cottages, more or less quaint, bathed in sun and yellow-wash,—and avenues of shade-trees,—and low garden-walls overtopped by waving banana leaves and fronds of palms. . . . A general sensation of drowsy warmth and vast light and exotic vegetation,—coupled with some vague disappointment at the absence of that picturesque humanity that delighted us in the streets of St. Pierre, Martinique. The bright costumes of the French colonies are not visible here: there is nothing like them in any of the English islands. Nevertheless, this wonderful Trinidad is as unique ethnologically as it is otherwise remarkable among all the other Antilles. It has three distinct creole populations—English, Spanish, and French,— besides its German and Madeiran settlers. There is also a special black or half-breed element, corresponding to each creole race, and speaking the language of each; there are fifty thousand Hindoo coolies, and a numerous body of Chinese. Still, this extraordinary diversity of race elements does not make itself at once apparent to the stranger. Your first impressions, as you pass through the black crowd upon the wharf, is that of being among a population as nearly African as that of Barbadoes; and indeed the black element dominates to such an extent that upon the streets white faces look strange by contrast. When a white face does appear, it is usually under the shadow of an Indian helmet, and heavily bearded, and austere: the physiognomy of one used to command. Against the fantastic ethnic

St. James Avenue, Port-of-Spain, Trinidad.

background of all this colonial life, this strong, bearded English visage takes something of heroic relief;—one feels, in a totally novel way, the dignity of a white skin.

. . . I hire a carriage to take me to the nearest coolie village; —a delightful drive. . . . Sometimes the smooth white road curves round the slope of a forest-covered mountain;—sometimes overlooks a valley shining with twenty different shades of surface green;—sometimes traverses marvellous natural arcades formed by the interweaving and intercrossing of bamboos fifty feet high. Rising in vast clumps, and spreading out sheafwise from the soil towards the sky, the curves of their beautiful jointed stems meet at such perfect angles above the way, and on either side of it, as to imitate almost exactly the elaborate Gothic arch-work of old abbey cloisters. Above the road, shadowing the slopes of lofty hills, forests beetle in dizzy precipices of verdure. They are green—burning, flashing green —covered with parasitic green creepers and vines; they show enormous forms, or rather dreams of form, fetichistic and startling. Banana leaves flicker and flutter along the way-side; palms shoot up to vast altitudes, like pillars of white metal; and there is a perpetual shifting of foliage color, from yellow-green to orange, from reddish-green to purple, from emerald-green to black-green. But the background color, the dominant tone, is like the plumage of a green parrot.

. . . We drive into the coolie village, along a narrower way, lined with plantain-trees, bananas, flamboyants, and unfamiliar shrubs with large broad leaves. Here and there are cocoa-palms. Beyond the little ditches on either side, occupying openings in the natural hedge, are the dwellings—wooden cabins, widely separated from each other. The narrow lanes that enter the road are also lined with habitations, half hidden by banana-trees. There is a prodigious glare, an intense heat. Around, above the trees and the roofs, rise the far hill shapes, some brightly verdant, some cloudy blue, some gray. The road and the lanes are almost deserted; there is little shade; only at intervals some slender brown girl or naked baby appears at a door-way. The carriage halts before a shed built against a wall—a simple roof of palm thatch supported upon jointed posts of bamboo.

It is a little coolie temple. A few weary Indian laborers

Coolies of Trinidad.

slumber in its shadow; pretty naked children, with silver rings round their ankles, are playing there with a white dog. Painted over the wall surface, in red, yellow, brown, blue, and green designs upon a white ground, are extraordinary figures of gods and goddesses. They have several pairs of arms, brandishing mysterious things,—they seem to dance, gesticulate, threaten; but they are all very *naïf*,—remind one of the first efforts of a child with the first box of paints. While I am looking at these things, one coolie after another wakes up (these men sleep lightly) and begins to observe me almost as curiously, and I fear much less kindly, than I have been observing the gods. "Where is your babagee?" I inquire. No one seems to comprehend my question; the gravity of each dark face remains unrelaxed. Yet I would have liked to make an offering unto Siva.

. . . Outside the Indian goldsmith's cabin, palm shadows are crawling slowly to and fro in the white glare, like shapes of tarantulas. Inside, the heat is augmented by the tiny charcoal furnace which glows beside a ridiculous little anvil set into a wooden block buried level with the soil. Through a rear door come odors of unknown flowers and the cool brilliant green of banana leaves. . . . A minute of waiting in the hot silence;— then, noiselessly as a phantom, the nude-limbed smith enters by a rear door,—squats down, without a word, on his little mat beside his little anvil,—and turns towards me, inquiringly, a face half veiled by a black beard,—a turbaned Indian face, sharp, severe, and slightly unpleasant in expression. "*Vlé béras!*" explains my creole driver, pointing to his client. The smith opens his lips to utter in the tone of a call the single syllable "*Ra!*" then folds his arms.

Almost immediately a young Hindoo woman enters, squats down on the earthen floor at the end of the bench which forms the only furniture of the shop, and turns upon me a pair of the finest black eyes I have ever seen,—like the eyes of a fawn. She is very simply clad, in a coolie robe leaving arms and ankles bare, and clinging about the figure in gracious folds; her color is a clear bright brown—new bronze; her face a fine oval, and charmingly aquiline. I perceive a little silver ring, in the form of a twisted snake, upon the slender second toe of each bare foot; upon each arm she has at least ten heavy silver rings;

there are also large silver rings about her ankles; a gold flower is fixed by a little hook in one nostril, and two immense silver circles, shaped like new moons, shimmer in her ears. The smith mutters something to her in his Indian tongue. She rises, and seating herself on the bench beside me, in an attitude of perfect grace, holds out one beautiful brown arm to me that I may choose a ring.

The arm is much more worthy of attention than the rings; it has the tint, the smoothness, the symmetry, of a fine statuary's work in metal;—the upper arm, tattooed with a bluish circle of arabesques, is otherwise unadorned; all the bracelets are on the fore-arm. Very clumsy and coarse they prove to be on closer examination: it was the fine dark skin which by color contrast made them look so pretty. I choose the outer one, a round ring with terminations shaped like viper heads;—the smith inserts a pair of tongs between these ends, presses outward slowly and strongly, and the ring is off. It has a faint musky odor, not unpleasant, the perfume of the tropical flesh it clung to. I would have taken it thus; but the smith snatches it from me, heats it red in his little charcoal furnace, hammers it into a nearly perfect circle again, slakes it, and burnishes it.

Then I ask for children's *béras*, or bracelets; and the young mother brings in her own baby girl,—a little darling just able to walk. She has extraordinary eyes;—the mother's eyes magnified (the father's are small and fierce). I bargain for the single pair of thin rings on her little wrists;—while the smith is taking them off, the child keeps her wonderful gaze fixed on my face. Then I observe that the peculiarity of the eye is the size of the iris rather than the size of the ball. These eyes are not soft like the mother's, after all; they are ungentle, beautiful as they are; they have the dark and splendid flame of the eyes of a great bird—a bird of prey.

. . . She will grow up, this little maid, into a slender, graceful woman, very beautiful, no doubt; perhaps a little dangerous. She will marry, of course: probably she is betrothed even now, according to Indian custom,—pledged to some brown boy, the son of a friend. It will not be so many years before the day of their noisy wedding: girls shoot up under this sun with as swift a growth as those broad-leaved beautiful shapes which fill the open door-way with quivering emerald. And she will know the witchcraft of those eyes, will feel the temptation to use them,—perhaps to smile one of those smiles which have power over life and death.

And then the old coolie story! One day, in the yellowing cane-fields, among the swarm of veiled and turbaned workers, a word is overheard, a side glance intercepted;—there is the swirling flash of a cutlass blade; a shrieking gathering of women about a headless corpse in the sun; and passing cityward, between armed and helmeted men, the vision of an Indian prisoner, blood-crimsoned, walking very steadily, very erect, with the solemnity of a judge, the dry bright gaze of an idol. . . .

XXXI.

. . . WE steam very slowly into the harbor of St. George, Grenada, in dead silence. No cannon-signal allowed here. . . . Some one suggests that the violence of the echoes in this harbor renders the firing of cannon dangerous; somebody else says the town is in so ruinous a condition that the report of a gun would shake it down.

. . . There are heavy damp smells in the warm air as of mould, or of wet clay freshly upturned.

This harbor is a deep clear basin, surrounded and shadowed by immense volcanic hills, all green. The opening by which we entered is cut off from sight by a promontory, and hill shapes beyond the promontory;—we seem to be in the innermost ring of a double crater. There is a continuous shimmering and plashing of leaping fish in the shadow of the loftiest height, which reaches half across the water.

As it climbs up the base of the huge hill at a precipitous angle, the city can be seen from the steamer's deck almost as in a bird's-eye view. A senescent city; mostly antiquated Spanish architecture,—ponderous archways and earthquake-proof walls. The yellow buildings fronting us beyond the wharf seem half decayed; they are strangely streaked with green, look as if they had been long under water. We row ashore, land in a crowd of lazy-looking, silent blacks.

. . . What a quaint, dawdling, sleepy place it is! All these

Coolie Servant.

narrow streets are falling into ruin; everywhere the same green stains upon the walls, as of slime left by a flood; everywhere disjointed brickwork, crumbling roofs, pungent odors of mould. Yet this Spanish architecture was built to endure; those yellow, blue, or green walls were constructed with the solidity of fortress-work; the very stairs are stone; the balustrades and the railings were made of good wrought iron. In a Northern clime such edifices would resist the wear and tear of five hundred years. But here the powers of disintegration are extraordinary, and the very air would seem to have the devouring force of an acid. All surfaces and angles are yielding to the attacks of time, weather, and microscopic organisms; paint peels, stucco falls, tiles tumble, stones slip out of place, and in every chink tiny green things nestle, propagating themselves through the jointures and dislocating the masonry. There is an appalling mouldiness, an exaggerated mossiness—the mystery and the melancholy of a city deserted. Old warehouses without signs, huge and void, are opened regularly every day for so many hours; yet the business of the aged merchants within seems to be a problem;—you might fancy those gray men were always waiting for ships that sailed away a generation ago, and will never return. You see no customers entering the stores, but only a black mendicant from time to time. And high above all this, overlooking streets too steep for any vehicle, slope the red walls of the mouldering fort, patched with the viridescence of ruin.

By a road leading up beyond the city, you reach the cemetery. The staggering iron gates by which you enter it are almost rusted from their hinges, and the low wall enclosing it is nearly all verdant. Within, you see a wilderness of strange weeds, vines, creepers, fantastic shrubs run mad, with a few palms mounting above the green confusion;—only here and there a gleam of slabs with inscriptions half erased. Such as you can read are epitaphs of seamen, dating back to the years 1800, 1802, 1812. Over these lizards are running; undulations in the weeds warn you to beware of snakes; toads leap away as you proceed; and you observe everywhere crickets perched—grass-colored creatures with two ruby specks for eyes. They make a sound shrill as the scream of machinery bevelling marble. At the farther end of the cemetery is a heavy ruin that would seem to have once been part of a church: it is so covered with creeping weeds now that you only distinguish the masonry on close approach, and high trees are growing within it.

Coolie Merchant.

There is something in tropical ruin peculiarly and terribly impressive: this luxuriant, evergreen, ever-splendid Nature consumes the results of human endeavor so swiftly, buries memories so profoundly, distorts the labors of generations so grotesquely, that one feels here, as nowhere else, how ephemeral man is, how intense and how tireless the effort necessary to preserve his frail creations even a little while from the vast unconscious forces antagonistic to all stability, to all factitious equilibrium.

*

. . . A gloomy road winds high around one cliff over-looking the hollow of the bay. Following it, you pass under ex-traordinarily dark shadows of foliage, and over a blackish soil strewn with pretty bright green fruit that has fallen from above. Do not touch them even with the tip of your finger! Those are manchineel apples; with their milky juice the old Caribs were wont to poison the barbs of their parrot-feathered arrows. Over the mould, swarming among the venomous fruit, innu-merable crabs make a sound almost like the murmuring of water. Some are very large, with prodigious stalked eyes, and claws white as ivory, and a red cuirass; others, very small and very swift in their movements, are raspberry-colored; others, again, are apple-green, with queer mottlings of black and white. There is an unpleasant odor of decay in the air—vegetable decay.

Emerging from the shadow of the manchineel-trees, you may follow the road up, up, up, under beetling cliffs of plu-tonian rock that seem about to topple down upon the path-way. The rock is naked and black near the road; higher, it is veiled by a heavy green drapery of lianas, curling creepers, un-familiar vines. All around you are sounds of crawling, dull echoes of dropping; the thick growths far up waver in the breathless air as if something were moving sinuously through them. And always the odor of humid decomposition. Farther on, the road looks wilder, sloping between black rocks, through strange vaultings of foliage and night-black shadows. Its lonesomeness oppresses; one returns without regret, by rusting gate-ways and tottering walls, back to the old West Indian city rotting in the sun.

. . . Yet Grenada, despite the dilapidation of her capital and the seeming desolation of its environs, is not the least pros-perous of the Antilles. Other islands have been less fortunate: the era of depression has almost passed for Grenada; through the rapid development of her secondary cultures—coffee and cocoa—she hopes with good reason to repair some of the vast losses involved by the decay of the sugar industry.

Still, in this silence of mouldering streets, this melancholy of abandoned dwellings, this invasion of vegetation, there is a suggestion of what any West Indian port might become when the resources of the island had been exhausted, and its commerce ruined. After all persons of means and energy enough to seek other fields of industry and enterprise had taken their departure, and the plantations had been abandoned, and the warehouses closed up forever, and the voiceless wharves left to rot down into the green water, Nature would soon so veil the place as to obliterate every outward visible sign of the past. In scarcely more than a generation from the time that the last merchant steamer had taken her departure some traveller might look for the once populous and busy mart in vain: vegetation would have devoured it.

. . . In the mixed English and creole speech of the black population one can discern evidence of a linguistic transition. The original French *patois* is being rapidly forgotten or transformed irrecognizably.

Now, in almost every island the negro idiom is different. So often have some of the Antilles changed owners, moreover, that in them the negro has never been able to form a true *patois*. He had scarcely acquired some idea of the language of his first masters, when other rulers and another tongue were thrust upon him,—and this may have occurred three or four times! The result is a totally incoherent agglomeration of speech-forms—a *baragouin* fantastic and unintelligible beyond the power of any one to imagine who has not heard it. . . .

XXXII.

. . . A BEAUTIFUL fantastic shape floats to us through the morning light; first cloudy gold like the horizon, then pearly gray, then varying blue, with growing green lights;—Saint Lucia. Most strangely formed of all this volcanic family;—everywhere mountainings sharp as broken crystals. Far off the Pitons—twin peaks of the high coast—show softer contours, like two black breasts pointing against the sky. . . .

. . . As we enter the harbor of Castries, the lines of the land seem no less exquisitely odd, in spite of their rich verdure, than when viewed afar off;—they have a particular pitch of angle. . . . Other of these islands show more or less family resemblance;—you might readily mistake one silhouette for another as seen at a distance, even after several West Indian journeys. But Saint Lucia at once impresses you by its eccentricity.

Castries, drowsing under palm leaves at the edge of its curving harbor,—perhaps an ancient crater,—seems more of a village than a town: streets of low cottages and little tropic gardens. It has a handsome half-breed population: the old French colonial manners have been less changed here by English influence than in Saint Kitt's and elsewhere;—the creole *patois* is still spoken, though the costumes have changed. . . . A more beautiful situation could scarcely be imagined,—even in this tropic world. In the massing of green heights about the little town are gaps showing groves of palm beyond; but the peak summits catch the clouds. Behind us the harbor mouth seems spanned by steel-blue bars: these are lines of currents. Away, on either hand, volcanic hills are billowing to vapory distance; and in their nearer hollows are beautiful deepenings of color: ponded shades of diaphanous blue or purplish tone. . . . I first remarked this extraordinary coloring of shadows in Martinique, where it exists to a degree that tempts one to believe the island has a special atmosphere of its own. . . . A friend tells me the phenomenon is probably due to inorganic substances floating in the air,—each substance in diffusion having its own index of refraction. Substances so held in suspension by vapors would vary according to the nature of soil in different islands, and might thus produce special local effects of atmospheric tinting.

. . . We remain but half an hour at Castries; then steam along the coast to take in freight at another port. Always the same delicious color-effects as we proceed, with new and surprising visions of hills. The near slopes descending to the sea are a radiant green, with streaks and specklings of darker verdure;—the farther-rising hills faint blue, with green saliencies catching the sun;—and beyond these are upheavals of luminous gray—pearl-gray—sharpened in the silver glow of the horizon. . . . The general impression of the whole landscape is one of motion suddenly petrified,—of an earthquake surging and tossing suddenly arrested and fixed: a raging of cones and peaks and monstrous truncated shapes. . . . We approach the Pitons.

Seen afar off, they first appeared twin mammiform peaks,—

Church Street, St. George, Grenada.

naked and dark against the sky; but now they begin to brighten a little and show color,—also to change form. They take a lilaceous hue, broken by gray and green lights; and as we draw yet nearer they prove dissimilar both in shape and tint. . . . Now they separate before us, throwing long pyramidal shadows across the steamer's path. Then, as they open to our coming, between them a sea bay is revealed—a very lovely curving bay, bounded by hollow cliffs of fiery green. At either side of the gap the Pitons rise like monster pylones. And a charming little settlement, a beautiful sugar-plantation, is nestling there between them, on the very edge of the bay.

Out of a bright sea of verdure, speckled with oases of darker foliage, these Pitons from the land side tower in sombre vegetation. Very high up, on the nearer one, amid the wooded slopes, you can see houses perched; and there are bright breaks in the color there—tiny mountain pastures that look like patches of green silk velvet.

. . . We pass the Pitons, and enter another little craterine harbor, to cast anchor before the village of Choiseul. It lies on a ledge above the beach and under high hills: we land through a surf, running the boat high up on soft yellowish sand. A delicious saline scent of seaweed.

It is disappointing, the village: it is merely one cross of brief streets, lined with blackening wooden dwellings; there are no buildings worth looking at, except the queer old French church, steep-roofed and bristling with points that look like extinguishers. Over broad reaches of lava rock a shallow river flows by the village to the sea, gurgling under shadows of tamarind foliage. It passes beside the market-place—a market-place without stalls, benches, sheds, or pavements: meats, fruits, and vegetables are simply fastened to the trees. Women are washing and naked children bathing in the stream; they are bronze-skinned, a fine dark color with a faint tint of red in it. . . . There is little else to look at: steep wooded hills cut off the view towards the interior.

But over the verge of the sea there is something strange growing visible, looming up like a beautiful yellow cloud. It is an island, so lofty, so luminous, so phantom-like, that it seems a vision of the Island of the Seven Cities. It is only the form of St. Vincent, bathed in vapory gold by the sun.

. . . Evening at La Soufrière: still another semicircular bay in a hollow of green hills. Glens hold bluish shadows. The color of the heights is very tender; but there are long streaks and patches of dark green, marking watercourses and very abrupt surfaces. From the western side immense shadows are pitched brokenly across the valley and over half the roofs of the palmy town. There is a little river flowing down to the bay on the left; and west of it a walled cemetery is visible, out of which one monumental palm rises to a sublime height: its crest still bathes in the sun, above the invading shadow. Night approaches; the shade of the hills inundates all the landscape, rises even over the palm-crest. Then, black-towering into the golden glow of sunset, the land loses all its color, all its charm; forms of frondage, variations of tint, become invisible. Saint Lucia is only a monstrous silhouette; all its billowing hills, its volcanic bays, its amphitheatrical valleys, turn black as ebony.

And you behold before you a geological dream, a vision of the primeval sea: the apparition of the land as first brought forth, all peak-tossed and fissured and naked and grim, in the tremendous birth of an archipelago.

XXXIII.

HOMEWARD bound.

Again the enormous poem of azure and emerald unrolls before us, but in order inverse; again is the island-Litany of the Saints repeated for us, but now backward. All the bright familiar harbors once more open to receive us;—each lovely Shape floats to us again, first golden yellow, then vapory gray, then ghostly blue, but always sharply radiant at last, symmetrically exquisite, as if chiselled out of amethyst and emerald and sapphire. We review the same wondrous wrinkling of volcanic hills, the cities that sit in extinct craters, the woods that tower to heaven, the peaks perpetually wearing that luminous cloud which seems the breathing of each island-life,—its vital manifestation. . . .

. . . Only now do the long succession of exotic and unfamiliar impressions received begin to group and blend, to form homogeneous results,—general ideas or convictions. Strongest among these is the belief that the white race is disappearing from these islands, acquired and held at so vast a cost of blood and treasure. Reasons almost beyond enumeration have been advanced—economical, climatic, ethnical, political—all of which contain truth, yet no single one of which can wholly explain the fact. Already the white West Indian populations are diminishing at a rate that almost staggers credibility. In the island paradise of Martinique in 1848 there were 12,000 whites; now, against more than 160,000 blacks and half-breeds, there are perhaps 5000 whites left to maintain the ethnic struggle, and the number of these latter is annually growing less. Many of the British islands have been almost deserted by their former cultivators: St. Vincent is becoming desolate: Tobago is a ruin; St. Martin lies half abandoned; St. Christopher is crumbling; Grenada has lost more than half her whites; St. Thomas, once the most prosperous, the most active, the most cosmopolitan of West Indian ports, is in full decadence. And while the white element is disappearing, the dark races are multiplying as never before;—the increase of the negro and half-breed populations has been everywhere one of the startling results of emancipation. The general belief among the creole whites of the Lesser Antilles would seem to confirm the old prediction that the slave races of the past must become the masters of the future. Here and there the struggle may be greatly prolonged, but everywhere the ultimate result must be the same, unless the present conditions of commerce and production become marvellously changed. The exterminated Indian peoples of the Antilles have already been replaced by populations equally fitted to cope with the forces of the nature about them,—that splendid and terrible Nature of the tropics which consumes the energies of the races of the North, which devours all that has been accomplished by their heroism or their crimes,—effacing their cities, rejecting their civilization. To those peoples physiologically in harmony with this Nature belong all the chances of victory in the contest—already begun—for racial supremacy.

But with the disappearance of the white populations the

Castries, St. Lucia.

ethnical problem would be still unsettled. Between the black and mixed peoples prevail hatreds more enduring and more intense than any race prejudices between whites and freedmen in the past;—a new struggle for supremacy could not fail to begin, with the perpetual augmentation of numbers, the ever-increasing competition for existence. And the true black element, more numerically powerful, more fertile, more cunning, better adapted to pyrogenic climate and tropical environment, would surely win. All these mixed races, all these beautiful fruit-colored populations, seem doomed to extinction: the future tendency must be to universal blackness, if existing conditions continue—perhaps to universal savagery. Everywhere the sins of the past have borne the same fruit, have furnished the colonies with social enigmas that mock the wisdom of legislators,—a dragon-crop of problems that no modern political science has yet proved competent to deal with. Can it even be hoped that future sociologists will be able to answer them, after Nature—who never forgives—shall have exacted the utmost possible retribution for all the crimes and follies of three hundred years?

Martinique Sketches

Les Porteuses

WHEN you find yourself for the first time, upon some un-shadowed day, in the delightful West Indian city of St. Pierre,—supposing that you own the sense of poetry, the rec-ollections of a student,—there is apt to steal upon your fancy an impression of having seen it all before, ever so long ago,—you cannot tell where. The sensation of some happy dream you cannot wholly recall might be compared to this feeling. In the simplicity and solidity of the quaint architecture,—in the eccentricity of bright narrow streets, all aglow with warm coloring,—in the tints of roof and wall, antiquated by streakings and patchings of mould greens and grays,—in the startling ab-sence of window-sashes, glass, gas lamps, and chimneys,—in the blossom-tenderness of the blue heaven, the splendor of tropic light, and the warmth of the tropic wind,—you find less the impression of a scene of to-day than the sensation of some-thing that was and is not. Slowly this feeling strengthens with your pleasure in the colorific radiance of costume,—the semi-nudity of passing figures,—the puissant shapeliness of torsos ruddily swart like statue metal,—the rounded outline of limbs yellow as tropic fruit,—the grace of attitudes,—the uncon-scious harmony of groupings,—the gathering and folding and falling of light robes that oscillate with swaying of free hips,—the sculptural symmetry of unshod feet. You look up and down the lemon-tinted streets,—down to the dazzling azure bright-ness of meeting sky and sea; up to the perpetual verdure of mountain woods—wondering at the mellowness of tones, the sharpness of lines in the light, the diaphaneity of colored shad-ows; always asking memory: "When? . . . where did I see all this . . . long ago?" . . .

Then, perhaps, your gaze is suddenly riveted by the vast and solemn beauty of the verdant violet-shaded mass of the dead Volcano,—high-towering above the town, visible from all its ways, and umbraged, maybe, with thinnest curlings of cloud, —like spectres of its ancient smoking to heaven. And all at once the secret of your dream is revealed, with the rising of many a luminous memory,—dreams of the Idyllists, flowers of old Sicilian song, fancies limned upon Pompeiian walls. For a moment the illusion is delicious: you comprehend as never before the charm of a vanished world,—the antique life, the story of terra-cottas and graven stones and gracious things exhumed: even the sun is not of to-day, but of twenty centuries gone;—thus, and under such a light, walked the women of the elder world. You know the fancy absurd;—that the power of the orb has visibly abated nothing in all the eras of man,—that millions are the ages of his almighty glory; but for one instant of reverie he seemeth larger,—even that sun impossible who coloreth the words, coloreth the works of artist-lovers of the past, with the gold light of dreams.

Too soon the hallucination is broken by modern sounds, dissipated by modern sights,—rough trolling of sailors descending to their boats,—the heavy boom of a packet's signal-gun,—the passing of an American buggy. Instantly you become aware that the melodious tongue spoken by the passing throng is neither Hellenic nor Roman: only the beautiful childish speech of French slaves.

II.

BUT what slaves were the fathers of this free generation? Your anthropologists, your ethnologists, seem at fault here: the African traits have become transformed; the African characteristics have been so modified within little more than two hundred years—by interblending of blood, by habit, by soil and sun and all those natural powers which shape the mould of races,—that you may look in vain for verification of ethnological assertions. . . . No: the heel does *not* protrude;—the foot is *not* flat, but finely arched;—the extremities are not large;—all the limbs taper, all the muscles are developed; and prognathism has become so rare that months of research may not yield a single striking case of it. . . . No: this is a special race, peculiar to the island as are the shapes of its peaks,—a mountain race; and mountain races are comely. . . . Compare it with the population of black Barbadoes, where the apish grossness of African coast types has been perpetuated unchanged;—and the contrast may well astonish! . . .

III.

THE erect carriage and steady swift walk of the women who bear burdens is especially likely to impress the artistic observer: it is the sight of such passers-by which gives, above all, the antique tone and color to his first sensations;—and the larger part of the female population of mixed race are practised carriers. Nearly all the transportation of light merchandise, as well as of meats, fruits, vegetables, and food stuffs,—to and from the interior,—is effected upon human heads. At some of the ports the regular local packets are loaded and unloaded by women and girls,—able to carry any trunk or box to its destination. At Fort-de-France the great steamers of the Compagnie Générale Transatlantique, are entirely coaled by women, who carry the coal on their heads, singing as they come and go in processions of hundreds; and the work is done with incredible rapidity. Now, the creole *porteuse*, or female carrier, is certainly one of the most remarkable physical types in the world; and whatever artistic enthusiasm her graceful port, lithe walk, or half-savage beauty may inspire you with, you can form no idea, if a total stranger, what a really wonderful being she is. . . . Let me tell you something about that highest type of professional female carrier, which is to the *charbonnière*, or coaling-girl, what the thorough-bred racer is to the draught-horse,—the type of porteuse selected for swiftness and endurance to distribute goods in the interior parishes, or to sell on commission at long distances. To the same class naturally belong those country carriers able to act as porteuses of plantation produce, fruits, or vegetables,—between the nearer ports and their own interior parishes. . . . Those who believe that great physical endurance and physical energy cannot exist in the tropics do not know the creole carrier-girl.

IV.

AT a very early age—perhaps at five years—she learns to carry small articles upon her head,—a bowl of rice,—a *dobanne*, or red earthen decanter, full of water,—even an orange on a plate; and before long she is able to balance these perfectly without using her hands to steady them. (I have often seen children actually run with cans of water upon their heads, and never spill a drop.) At nine or ten she is able to carry thus a tolerably heavy basket, or a *trait* (a wooden tray with deep outward sloping sides) containing a weight of from twenty to thirty pounds; and is able to accompany her mother, sister, or cousin on long peddling journeys,—walking barefoot twelve and fifteen miles a day. At sixteen or seventeen she is a tall robust girl,—lithe, vigorous, tough,—all tendon and hard flesh;—she carries a tray or a basket of the largest size, and a burden of one hundred and twenty to one hundred and fifty pounds weight; —she can now earn about thirty francs (about six dollars) a month, *by walking fifty miles a day*, as an itinerant seller.

Among her class there are figures to make you dream of Atalanta;—and all, whether ugly or attractive as to feature, are finely shapen as to body and limb. Brought into existence by extraordinary necessities of environment, the type is a peculiarly local one,—a type of human thorough-bred representing the true secret of grace: economy of force. There are no corpulent porteuses for the long interior routes; all are built lightly and firmly as racers. There are no old porteuses;—to do the work even at forty signifies a constitution of astounding solidity. After the full force of youth and health is spent, the poor carrier must seek lighter labor;—she can no longer compete with the girls. For in this calling the young body is taxed to its utmost capacity of strength, endurance, and rapid motion.

As a general rule, the weight is such that no well-freighted porteuse can, unassisted, either "load" or "unload" (*châgé* or *déchâgé*, in creole phrase); the effort to do so would burst a blood-vessel, wrench a nerve, rupture a muscle. She cannot even sit down under her burden without risk of breaking her neck: absolute perfection of the balance is necessary for self-preservation. A case came under my own observation of a woman rupturing a muscle in her arm through careless haste in the mere act of aiding another to unload.

And no one not a brute will ever refuse to aid a woman to lift or to relieve herself of her burden;—you may see the wealthiest merchant, the proudest planter, gladly do it;—the meanness of refusing, or of making any conditions for the performance of this little kindness has only been imagined in those strange Stories of Devils wherewith the oral and uncollected literature of the creole abounds.*

V.

PREPARING for her journey, the young *màchanne* (marchande) puts on the poorest and briefest chemise in her possession, and the most worn of her light calico robes. These are all she wears. The robe is drawn upward and forward, so as to reach a little below the knee, and is confined thus by a waist-string, or a long kerchief bound tightly round the loins. Instead of a Madras or painted turban-kerchief, she binds a plain *mouchoir* neatly and closely about her head; and if her hair be long, it is combed back and gathered into a loop behind. Then, with a second mouchoir of coarser quality she makes a pad, or, as she calls it, *tòche*, by winding the kerchief round her fingers as you would coil up a piece of string;—and the soft mass, flattened with

---

* Extract from the "Story of Marie," as written from dictation:

. . . Manman-à té ni yon gouôs jà à caïe-li. Jà-la té touôp lou'de pou Marie. Cé té li menm manman là qui té kallé pouend dileau. Yon jou y pouend jà-la pou y té allé pouend dileau. Lhè manman-à rivé bò la fontaine, y pa trouvé pésonne pou châgé y. Y rété; y ka crié, "Toutt bon Chritien, vini châgé moin!"

. . . Lhé manman rété y ouè pa té ni piess bon Chritien pou châgé y. Y rété; y crié: "Pouloss, si pa ni bon Chritien, ni mauvais Chritien! toutt mauvais Chritien vini châgé moin!"

Lhè y fini di ça, y ouè yon diabe qui ka vini, ka di conm ça. "Pou moin châgé ou, ça ou ké baill moin?" Manman-là di,—y réponne, "Moin pa ni arien!" Diabe-la réponne y, "Y fau ba moin Marie pou moin pé châgé ou."

. . . This mamma had a great jar in her house. The jar was too heavy for Marie. It was this mamma herself who used to go for water. One day she took that jar to go for water. When this mamma had got to the fountain, she could not find any one to load her. She stood there, crying out, "Any good Christian, come load me!"

. . . As the mamma stood there she saw there was not a single good Christian to help her load. She stood there, and cried out: "Well, then, if there are no good Christians, there are bad Christians. Any bad Christian, come and load me!"

The moment she said that, she saw a devil coming, who said to her, "If I load you, what will you give me?" This mamma answered, and said, "I have nothing!" The devil answered her, "Must give me Marie if you want me to load you."

a patting of the hand, is placed upon her head, over the coiffure. On this the great loaded trait is poised.

She wears no shoes! To wear shoes and do her work swiftly and well in such a land of mountains would be impossible. She must climb thousands and descend thousands of feet every day,—march up and down slopes so steep that the horses of the country all break down after a few years of similar journeying. The girl invariably outlasts the horse,—though carrying an equal weight. Shoes, unless extraordinarily well made, would shift place a little with every change from ascent to descent, or the reverse, during the march,—would yield and loosen with the ever-varying strain,—would compress the toes,—produce corns, bunions, raw places by rubbing, and soon cripple the porteuse. Remember, she has to walk perhaps fifty miles between dawn and dark, under a sun to which a single hour's exposure, without the protection of an umbrella, is perilous to any European or American—the terrible sun of the tropics! Sandals are the only conceivable foot-gear suited to such a calling as hers; but she needs no sandals: the soles of her feet are toughened so as to feel no asperities, and present to sharp pebbles a surface at once yielding and resisting, like a cushion of solid caoutchouc.

Besides her load, she carries only a canvas purse tied to her girdle on the right side, and on the left a very small bottle of rum, or white *tafia*,—usually the latter, because it is so cheap. . . . For she may not always find the Gouyave Water to drink,—the cold clear pure stream conveyed to the fountains of St. Pierre from the highest mountains by a beautiful and marvellous plan of hydraulic engineering: she will have to drink betimes the common spring-water of the bamboo-fountains on the remoter high-roads; and this may cause dysentery if swallowed without a spoonful of spirits. Therefore she never travels without a little liquor.

VI.

. . . So!—She is ready: "*Châgé moin, souplè, chè!*" She bends to lift the end of the heavy trait: some one takes the other,— *yon!—dè!—toua!*—it is on her head. Perhaps she winces an instant;—the weight is not perfectly balanced; she settles it with

'Ti Marie.
(On the Route from St. Pierre to Basse-Pointe.)

her hands,—gets it in the exact place. Then, all steady,—lithe, light, half naked,—away she moves with a long springy step. So even her walk that the burden never sways; yet so rapid her motion that however good a walker you may fancy yourself to be you will tire out after a sustained effort of fifteen minutes to follow her uphill. Fifteen minutes!—and she can keep up that pace without slackening—save for a minute to eat and drink at mid-day,—for at least twelve hours and fifty-six minutes, the extreme length of a West Indian day. She starts before dawn; tries to reach her resting-place by sunset: after dark, like all her people, she is afraid of meeting *zombis.*

Let me give you some idea of her average speed under an average weight of one hundred and twenty-five pounds,— estimates based partly upon my own observations, partly upon the declarations of the trustworthy merchants who employ her, and partly on the assertion of habitants of the burghs or cities named—all of which statements perfectly agree. From St. Pierre to Basse-Pointe, by the national road, the distance is a trifle less than twenty-seven kilometres and three-quarters. She makes the transit easily in three hours and a half; and returns in the afternoon, after an absence of scarcely more than eight hours. From St. Pierre to Morne Rouge—two thousand feet up in the mountains (an ascent so abrupt that no one able to pay carriage-fare dreams of attempting to walk it)—the distance is seven kilometres and three-quarters. She makes it in little more than an hour. But this represents only the beginning of her journey. She passes on to Grande Anse, twenty-one and three-quarter kilometres away. But she does not rest there: she returns at the same pace, and reaches St. Pierre before dark. From St. Pierre to Gros-Morne the distance to be twice traversed by her is more than thirty-two kilometres. A journey of sixty-four kilometres,—daily, perhaps,—forty miles! And there are many màchannes who make yet longer trips,—trips of three or four days' duration;—these rest at villages upon their route.

VII.

SUCH travel in such a country would be impossible but for the excellent national roads,—limestone highways, solid, broad, faultlessly graded,—that wind from town to town, from hamlet to hamlet, over mountains, over ravines; ascending by zigzags to heights of twenty-five hundred feet; traversing the primeval forests of the interior; now skirting the dizziest precipices, now descending into the loveliest valleys. There are thirty-one of these magnificent routes, with a total length of 488,052 metres (more than 303 miles), whereof the construction required engineering talent of the highest order,—the building of bridges beyond counting, and devices the most ingenious to provide against dangers of storms, floods, and land-slips. Most have drinking-fountains along their course at almost regular intervals,—generally made by the negroes, who have a simple but excellent plan for turning the water of a spring through bamboo pipes to the road-way. Each road is also furnished with mile-stones, or rather kilometre-stones; and the drainage is perfect enough to assure of the highway becoming dry within fifteen minutes after the heaviest rain, so long as the surface is maintained in tolerably good condition. Well-kept embankments of earth (usually covered with a rich growth of mosses, vines, and ferns), or even solid walls of masonry, line the side that overhangs a dangerous depth. And all these highways pass through landscapes of amazing beauty,—visions of mountains so many-tinted and so singular of outline that they would almost seem to have been created for the express purpose of compelling astonishment. This tropic Nature appears to call into being nothing ordinary: the shapes which she evokes are always either gracious or odd,—and her eccentricities, her extravagances, have a fantastic charm, a grotesqueness as of artistic whim. Even where the landscape-view is cut off by high woods the forms of ancient trees—the infinite interwreathing of vine growths all on fire with violence of blossom-color,— the enormous green outbursts of balisiers, with leaves ten to thirteen feet long,—the columnar solemnity of great palmistes, —the pliant quivering exquisiteness of bamboo,—the furious splendor of roses run mad—more than atone for the loss of the horizon. Sometimes you approach a steep covered with a growth of what, at first glance, looks precisely like fine green fur: it is a first-growth of young bamboo. Or you see a hill-side covered with huge green feathers, all shelving down and overlapping as in the tail of some unutterable bird: these are baby ferns. And where the road leaps some deep ravine with a double or triple bridge of white stone, note well what delicious shapes spring up into sunshine from the black profundity on either hand! Palmiform you might hastily term them,—but no palm was ever so gracile; no palm ever bore so dainty a head of green plumes light as lace! These likewise are ferns (rare survivors, maybe, of that period of monstrous vegetation which preceded the apparition of man), beautiful tree-ferns, whose every young plume, unrolling in a spiral from the bud, at first assumes the shape of a crozier,—a crozier of emerald! Therefore are some of this species called "archbishop-trees," no doubt. . . . But one might write for a hundred years of the sights to be seen upon such a mountain road.

VIII.

IN every season, in almost every weather, the porteuse makes her journey,—never heeding rain;—her goods being protected by double and triple water-proof coverings well bound down over her trait. Yet these tropical rains, coming suddenly with a cold wind upon her heated and almost naked body, are to be feared. To any European or unacclimated white such a wetting, while the pores are all open during a profuse perspiration, would probably prove fatal: even for white natives the result is always a serious and protracted illness. But the porteuse seldom suffers in consequences: she seems proof against fevers, rheumatisms, and ordinary colds. When she does break down, however, the malady is a frightful one,—a pneumonia that carries off the victim within forty-eight hours. Happily, among her class, these fatalities are very rare.

And scarcely less rare than such sudden deaths are instances of failure to appear on time. In one case, the employer, a St. Pierre shopkeeper, on finding his *marchande* more than an hour late, felt so certain something very extraordinary must have happened that he sent out messengers in all directions to make inquiries. It was found that the woman had become a mother when only half-way upon her journey home. . . . The child lived and thrived;—she is now a pretty chocolate-colored girl of eight, who follows her mother every day from their mountain ajoupa down to the city, and back again,—bearing a little trait upon her head.

Fort-de-France, Martinique.—(Formerly Fort Royal.)

*

Murder for purposes of robbery is not an unknown crime in Martinique; but I am told the porteuses are never molested. And yet some of these girls carry merchandise to the value of hundreds of francs; and all carry money,—the money received for goods sold, often a considerable sum. This immunity may be partly owing to the fact that they travel during the greater part of the year only by day,—and usually in company. A very pretty girl is seldom suffered to journey unprotected: she has either a male escort or several experienced and powerful women with her. In the cacao season—when carriers start from Grande Anse as early as two o'clock in the morning, so as to reach St. Pierre by dawn—they travel in strong companies of twenty or twenty-five, singing on the way. As a general rule the younger girls at all times go two together,—keeping step perfectly as a pair of blooded fillies; only the veterans, or women selected for special work by reason of extraordinary physical capabilities, go alone. To the latter class belong certain girls employed by the great bakeries of Fort-de-France and St. Pierre: these are veritable caryatides. They are probably the heaviest-laden of all, carrying baskets of astounding size far up into the mountains before daylight, so as to furnish country families with fresh bread at an early hour; and for this labor they receive about four dollars (twenty francs) a month and one loaf of bread per diem. . . . While stopping at a friend's house among the hills, some two miles from Fort-de-France, I saw the local bread-carrier halt before our porch one morning, and a finer type of the race it would be difficult for a sculptor to imagine. Six feet tall,—strength and grace united throughout her whole figure from neck to heel; with that clear black skin which is beautiful to any but ignorant or prejudiced eyes; and the smooth, pleasing, solemn features of a sphinx,—she looked to me, as she towered there in the gold light, a symbolic statue of Africa. Seeing me smoking one of those long thin Martinique cigars called *bouts*, she begged one; and, not happening to have another, I gave her the price of a bunch of twenty,—ten sous. She took it without a smile, and went her way. About an hour and a half later she came back and asked for me,—to present me with the finest and largest mango I had ever seen, a monster mango. She said she wanted to see me eat it, and sat down on the ground to look on. While eating it, I learned that she had walked a whole mile out of her way under that sky of fire, just to bring her little gift of gratitude.

IX.

FORTY to fifty miles a day, always under a weight of more than a hundred pounds,—for when the trait has been emptied she puts in stones for ballast;—carrying her employer's merchandise and money over the mountain ranges, beyond the peaks, across the ravines, through the tropical forest, sometimes through by-ways haunted by the fer-de-lance,—and this in summer or winter, the season of rains or the season of heat, the time of fevers or the time of hurricanes, at a franc a day! . . . How does she live upon it?

There are twenty sous to the franc. The girl leaves St. Pierre with her load at early morning. At the second village, Morne Rouge, she halts to buy one, two, or three biscuits at a sou apiece; and reaching Ajoupa-Bouillon later in the forenoon, she may buy another biscuit or two. Altogether she may be expected to eat five sous of biscuit or bread before reaching Grande Anse, where she probably has a meal waiting for her. This ought to cost her ten sous,—especially if there be meat in her ragoût: which represents a total expense of fifteen sous for eatables. Then there is the additional cost of the cheap liquor, which she must mix with her drinking-water, as it would be more than dangerous to swallow pure cold water in her heated condition; two or three sous more. This almost makes the franc. But such a hasty and really erroneous estimate does not include expenses of lodging and clothing;—she may sleep on the bare floor sometimes, and twenty francs a year may keep her in clothes; but she must rent the floor and pay for the clothes out of that franc. As a matter of fact she not only does all this upon her twenty sous a day, but can even economize something which will enable her, when her youth and force decline, to start in business for herself. And her economy will not seem so wonderful when I assure you that thousands of men here— huge men muscled like bulls and lions—live upon an average expenditure of five sous a day. One sou of bread, two sous of manioc flour, one sou of dried codfish, one sou of tafia: such is their meal.

There are women carriers who earn more than a franc a day,—women with a particular talent for selling, who are paid on commission—from ten to fifteen per cent. These eventually make themselves independent in many instances;—they continue to sell and bargain in person, but hire a young girl to carry the goods.

X.

. . . "*Ou 'lé màchanne!*" rings out a rich alto, resonant as the tone of a gong, from behind the balisiers that shut in our garden. There are two of them—no, three—Maiyotte, Chéchelle, and Rina. Maiyotte and Chéchelle have just arrived from St. Pierre;—Rina comes from Gros-Morne with fruits and vegetables. Suppose we call them all in, and see what they have got. Maiyotte and Chéchelle sell on commission; Rina sells for her mother, who has a little garden at Gros-Morne.

. . . "*Bonjou', Maiyotte;—bonjou', Chéchelle! coument ou kallé, Rina, chè!*" . . . Throw open the folding-doors to let the great trays pass. . . . Now all three are unloaded by old Théréza and by young Adou;—all the packs are on the floor, and the water-proof wrappings are being uncorded, while Ah-Manmzell, the adopted child, brings the rum and water for the tall walkers.

. . . "Oh, what a medley, Maiyotte!" . . . Inkstands and wooden cows; purses and paper dogs and cats; dolls and cosmetics; pins and needles and soap and toothbrushes; candied fruits and smoking-caps; *pelotes* of thread, and tapes, and ribbons, and laces, and Madeira wine; cuffs, and collars, and dancing-shoes, and tobacco *sachets*. . . . But what is in that little flat bundle? Presents for your *guêpe*, if you have one. . . . *Jesis-Maïa!*—the pretty foulards! Azure and yellow in checkerings; orange and crimson in stripes; rose and scarlet in plaidings; and bronze tints, and beetle-tints of black and green.

"Chéchelle, what a *bloucoutoum* if you should ever let that tray fall—*aïe yaïe yaïe!*" Here is a whole shop of crockeries and porcelains;—plates, dishes, cups,—earthen-ware *canaris* and *dobannes*; and gift-mugs and cups bearing creole girls' names,—all names that end in ine: "Micheline," "Honorine," "Prospérine" [you will never sell that, Chéchelle: there is not a Prospérine this side of St. Pierre], "Azaline," "Leontine," "Zéphyrine," "Albertine," "Chrysaline," "Florine," "Coralline," "Alexandrine." . . . And knives and forks, and cheap spoons, and tin coffee-pots, and tin rattles for babies, and tin flutes for horrid little boys,—and pencils and note-paper and envelopes! . . .

. . . "Oh, Rina, what superb oranges!—fully twelve inches round! . . . and these, which look something like our mandarins, what do you call them?" "Zorange-macaque!" (monkey-oranges). And here are avocados—beauties!—guavas of three different kinds,—tropical cherries (which have four seeds instead of one),—tropical raspberries, whereof the entire eatable portion comes off in one elastic piece, lined with something like white silk. . . . Here are fresh nutmegs: the thick green case splits in equal halves at a touch; and see the beautiful heart within,—deep dark glossy red, all wrapped in a bright network of flat blood-colored fibre, spun over it like branching veins. . . . This big heavy red-and-yellow thing is a *pomme-cythère*: the smooth cuticle, bitter as gall, covers a sweet juicy pulp, interwoven with something that seems like cotton thread. . . . Here is a *pomme-cannelle*: inside its scaly covering is the most delicious yellow custard conceivable, with little black seeds floating in it. This larger *corossol* has almost as delicate an interior, only the custard is white instead of yellow. . . . Here are *christophines*,—great pear-shaped things, white and green, according to kind, with a peel prickly and knobby as the skin of a horned toad; but they stew exquisitely. And *mélongènes*, or egg-plants; and palmiste-pith, and *chadèques*, and *pommes-d'Haïti*,—and roots that at first sight look all alike, but they are not: there are *camanioc*, and *couscous*, and *choux-caraïbes*, and *zignames*, and various kinds of *patates* among them. Old Théréza's magic will transform these shapeless muddy things, before evening, into pyramids of smoking gold,—into odorous porridges that will look like messes of molten amber and liquid pearl;—for Rina makes a good sale.

Then Chéchelle manages to dispose of a tin coffee-pot and a big canari. . . . And Maiyotte makes the best sale of all; for the sight of a funny *biscuit* doll has made Ah-Manmzell cry and smile so at the same time that I should feel unhappy for the rest of my life if I did not buy it for her. I know I ought to get some change out of that six francs;—and Maiyotte, who is black but comely as the tents of Kedar, as the curtains of Solomon, seems to be aware of the fact.

Oh, Maiyotte, how plaintive that pretty sphinx face of yours, now turned in profile;—as if you knew you looked beautiful thus,—with the great gold circlets of your ears glittering and swaying as you bend! And why are you so long, so long untying that poor little canvas purse?—fumbling and fingering it?—is it because you want me to think of the weight of that trait and the sixty kilometres you must walk, and the heat, and the dust, and all the disappointments? Ah, you are cunning, Maiyotte! No, I do not want the change!

XI.

. . . Travelling together, the porteuses often walk in silence for hours at a time;—this is when they feel weary. Sometimes they sing,—most often when approaching their destination;—and when they chat, it is in a key so high-pitched that their voices can be heard to a great distance in this land of echoes and elevations.

But she who travels alone is rarely silent: she talks to herself or to inanimate things;—you may hear her talking to the trees, to the flowers,—talking to the high clouds and the far peaks of changing color,—talking to the setting sun!

Over the miles of the morning she sees, perchance, the mighty Piton Gélé, a cone of amethyst in the light; and she talks to it: "*Ou jojoll, oui!—moin ni envie monté assou ou, pou moin ouè bien, bien!*" (Thou art pretty, pretty, aye!—would I might climb thee, to see far, far off!)

By a great grove of palms she passes;—so thickly mustered they are that against the sun their intermingled heads form one unbroken awning of green. Many rise straight as masts; some bend at beautiful angles, seeming to intercross their long pale single limbs in a fantastic dance; others curve like bows: there is one that undulates from foot to crest, like a monster serpent poised upon its tail. She loves to look at that one,—*joli pié-bois-là!*—talks to it as she goes by,—bids it good-day.

Or, looking back as she ascends, she sees the huge blue dream of the sea,—the eternal haunter, that ever becomes larger as she mounts the road; and she talks to it: "*Mi lanmé ka gadé moin!*" (There is the great sea looking at me!) "*Màché toujou deïé moin, lanmè!*" (Walk after me, O Sea!)

Or she views the clouds of Pelée, spreading gray from the invisible summit, to shadow against the sun; and she fears the rain, and she talks to it: "*Pas mouillé moin, laplie-à! Quitté moin rivé avant mouillé moin!*" (Do not wet me, O Rain! Let me get there before thou wettest me!)

Sometimes a dog barks at her, menaces her bare limbs; and she talks to the dog: "*Chien-a, pas mòdé moin, chien—anh! Moin pa fé ou arien, chien, pou ou mòdé moin!*" (Do not bite me, O Dog! Never did I anything to thee that thou shouldst bite me, O Dog! Do not bite me, dear! Do not bite me, *doudoux!*)

Sometimes she meets a laden sister travelling the opposite way. . . . "*Coument ou yé, chè?*" she cries. (How art thou, dear?) And the other makes answer, "*Toutt douce, chè,—et ou?*" (All sweetly, dear,—and thou?) And each passes on without pausing: they have no time!

. . . It is perhaps the last human voice she will hear for many a mile. After that only the whisper of the grasses—*graïe-gras, graïe-gras!*—and the gossip of the canes—*chououa, chououa!*—and the husky speech of the *pois-Angole, ka babillé conm yon vié fenme,*—that babbles like an old woman;—and the murmur of the *filao*-trees, like the murmur of the River of the Washerwomen.

XII.

. . . Sundown approaches: the light has turned a rich yellow; —long black shapes lie across the curving road, shadows of balisier and palm, shadows of tamarind and Indian-reed, shadows of ceiba and giant-fern. And the porteuses are coming down through the lights and darknesses of the way from far Grande Anse, to halt a moment in this little village. They are going to sit down on the road-side here, before the house of the baker; and there is his great black workman, Jean-Marie, looking for them from the door-way, waiting to relieve them of their loads. . . . Jean-Marie is the strongest man in all the Champ-Flore: see what a torso,—as he stands there naked to the waist! . . . His day's work is done; but he likes to wait for the girls, though he is old now, and has sons as tall as himself. It is a habit: some say that he had a daughter once,—a por-teuse like those coming, and used to wait for her thus at that very door-way until one evening that she failed to appear, and never returned till he carried her home in his arms dead,—stricken by a serpent in some mountain path where there was none to aid. . . . The roads were not as good then as now.

. . . Here they come, the girls—yellow, red, black. See the flash of the yellow feet where they touch the light! And what impossible tint the red limbs take in the changing glow! . . . Finotte, Pauline, Médelle,—all together, as usual,—with Ti-Clé trotting behind, very tired. . . . Never mind, Ti-Clé!—you will outwalk your cousins when you are a few years older,—pretty Ti-Clé. . . . Here come Cyrillia and Zabette, and Féfé and Dodotte and Fevriette. And behind them are coming the two *chabines*,—golden girls: the twin-sisters who sell silks and threads and foulards; always together, always wearing robes and kerchiefs of similar color,—so that you can never tell which is Lorrainie and which is Édoualise.

And all smile to see Jean-Marie waiting for them, and to hear his deep kind voice calling, "*Coument ou yé, chè? coument ou kallé?*" . . . (How art thou, dear?—how goes it with thee?)

And they mostly make answer, "*Toutt douce, chè,—et ou?*" (All sweetly, dear,—and thou?) But some, overweary, cry to him, "*Ah! déchâgé moin vite, chè! moin lasse, lasse!*" (Unload me quickly, dear; for I am very, very weary.) Then he takes off their burdens, and fetches bread for them, and says foolish little things to make them laugh. And they are pleased, and laugh, just like children, as they sit right down on the road there to munch their dry bread.

. . . So often have I watched that scene! . . . Let me but close my eyes one moment, and it will come back to me,—

through all the thousand miles,—over the graves of the days. . . .

Again I see the mountain road in the yellow glow, banded with umbrages of palm. Again I watch the light feet coming,— now in shadow, now in sun,—soundlessly as falling leaves. Still I can hear the voices crying, "*Ah! déchâgé moin vite, chè!— moin lasse!*"—and see the mighty arms outreach to take the burdens away.

. . . Only, there is a change,—I know not what! . . . All vapory the road is, and the fronds, and the comely coming feet of the bearers, and even this light of sunset,—sunset that is ever larger and nearer to us than dawn, even as death than birth. And the weird way appeareth a way whose dust is the dust of generations;—and the Shape that waits is never Jean-Marie, but one darker and stronger;—and these are surely voices of tired souls who cry to Thee, thou dear black Giver of the perpetual rest, "*Ah! déchâgé moin vite, chè!—moin lasse!*"

La Grande Anse

WHILE at the village of Morne Rouge, I was frequently impressed by the singular beauty of young girls from the north-east coast—all porteuses, who passed almost daily, on their way from Grande Anse to St. Pierre and back again,—a total trip of thirty-five miles. . . . I knew they were from Grande Anse, because the village baker, at whose shop they were wont to make brief halts, told me a good deal about them: he knew each one by name. Whenever a remarkably attractive girl appeared, and I would inquire whence she came, the invariable reply (generally preceded by that peculiarly intoned French "Ah!" signifying, "Why, you certainly ought to know!") was "Grande Anse." . . . *Ah! c'est de Grande Anse, ça!* And if any commonplace, uninteresting type showed itself, it would be signalled as from somewhere else—Gros-Morne, Capote, Marigot, perhaps,—but never from Grande Anse. The Grande Anse girls were distinguishable by their clear yellow or brown skins, lithe light figures, and a particular grace in their way of dressing. Their short robes were always of bright and pleasing colors, perfectly contrasting with the ripe fruit-tint of nude limbs and faces: I could discern a partiality for white stuffs with apricot-yellow stripes, for plaidings of blue and violet, and various patterns of pink and mauve. They had a graceful way of walking under their trays, with hands clasped behind their heads, and arms uplifted in the manner of caryatides. An artist would have been wild with delight for the chance to sketch some of them. . . . On the whole, they conveyed the impression that they belonged to a particular race, very different from that of the chief city or its environs.

"Are they all banana-colored at Grande Anse?" I asked,—"and all as pretty as these?"

"I was never at Grande Anse," the little baker answered, "although I have been forty years in Martinique; but I know there is a fine class of young girls there: *il y a une belle jeunesse là, mon cher!*"

Then I wondered why the youth of Grande Anse should be any finer than the youth of other places; and it seemed to me that the baker's own statement of his never having been there might possibly furnish a clew. . . . Out of the thirty-five thousand inhabitants of St. Pierre and its suburbs, there are at least twenty thousand who never have been there, and most probably never will be. Few dwellers of the west coast visit the east coast: in fact, except among the white creoles, who represent but a small percentage of the total population, there are few persons to be met with who are familiar with all parts of their native island. It is so mountainous, and travelling is so wearisome, that populations may live and die in adjacent valleys without climbing the intervening ranges to look at one another. Grande Anse is only about twenty miles from the principal city; but it requires some considerable inducement to make the journey on horseback; and only the professional carrier-girls, plantation messengers, and colored people of peculiarly tough constitution attempt it on foot. Except for the transportation of sugar and rum, there is practically no communication by sea between the west and the north-east coast —the sea is too dangerous—and thus the populations on either side of the island are more or less isolated from each other, besides being further subdivided and segregated by the lesser mountain chains crossing their respective territories. . . . In view of all these things I wondered whether a community so secluded might not assume special characteristics within two hundred years—might not develop into a population of some yellow, red, or brown type, according to the predominant element of the original race-crossing.

II.

I HAD long been anxious to see the city of the Porteuses, when the opportunity afforded itself to make the trip with a friend obliged to go thither on some important business;—I do not think I should have ever felt resigned to undertake it alone. With a level road the distance might be covered very quickly, but over mountains the journey is slow and wearisome in the perpetual tropic heat. Whether made on horseback or in a carriage, it takes between four and five hours to go from St. Pierre to Grand Anse, and it requires a longer time to return, as the road is then nearly all uphill. The young porteuse travels almost as rapidly; and the barefooted black postman, who carries the mails in a square box at the end of a pole, is timed on leaving Morne Rouge at 4 A.M. to reach Ajoupa-Bouillon a little after six, and leaving Ajoupa-Bouillon at half-past six to reach Grande Anse at half-past eight, including many stoppages and delays on the way.

Going to Grande Anse from the chief city, one can either hire a horse or carriage at St. Pierre, or ascend to Morne Rouge by the public conveyance, and there procure a vehicle or animal, which latter is the cheaper and easier plan. About a mile beyond Morne Rouge, where the old Calebasse road enters the public highway, you reach the highest point of the journey,—the top of the enormous ridge dividing the northeast from the western coast, and cutting off the trade-winds from sultry St. Pierre. By climbing the little hill, with a tall stone cross on its summit, overlooking the Champ-Flore just here, you can perceive the sea on both sides of the island at once—*lapis lazuli* blue. From this elevation the road descends by a hundred windings and lessening undulations to the eastern shore. It sinks between mornes wooded to their summits,—bridges a host of torrents and ravines,—passes gorges from whence colossal trees tower far overhead, through heavy streaming of lianas, to mingle their green crowns in magnificent gloom. Now and then you hear a low long sweet sound like the deepest tone of a silver flute,—a bird-call, the cry of the *siffleur-de-montagne*; then all is stillness. You are not likely to see a white face again for hours, but at intervals a porteuse passes, walking very swiftly, or a field-hand heavily laden; and these salute you either by speech or a lifting of the hand to the head. . . . And it is very pleasant to hear the greetings and to see the smiles of those who thus pass,—the fine brown girls bearing trays, the dark laborers bowed under great burdens of bamboo-grass,—*Bonjou', Missié!* Then you should reply, if the speaker be a woman and pretty, "Good-day, dear" (*bonjou', chè*), or, "Good-day, my daughter" (*mafi*) even if she be old; while if the passer-by be a man, your proper reply is, "Good-day, my son" (*monfi*). . . . They are less often uttered now than in other years, these kindly greetings, but they still form part of the good and true creole manners.

The feathery beauty of the tree-ferns shadowing each brook,

A Creole Capre in Working Garb.

the grace of bamboo and arborescent grasses, seem to decrease as the road descends,—but the palms grow taller. Often the way skirts a precipice dominating some marvellous valley prospect; again it is walled in by high green banks or shrubby slopes which cut off the view; and always it serpentines so that you cannot see more than a few hundred feet of the white track before you. About the fifteenth kilometre a glorious landscape opens to the right, reaching to the Atlantic;—the road still winds very high; forests are billowing hundreds of yards below it, and rising miles away up the slopes of mornes, beyond which, here and there, loom strange shapes of mountain,—shading off from misty green to violet and faintest gray. And through one grand opening in this multicolored surging of hills and peaks you perceive the gold-yellow of cane-fields touching the sky-colored sea. Grande Anse lies somewhere in that direction. . . . At the eighteenth kilometre you pass a cluster of little country cottages, a church, and one or two large buildings framed in shade-trees—the hamlet of Ajoupa-Bouillon. Yet a little farther, and you find you have left all the woods behind you. But the road continues its bewildering curves around and between low mornes covered with cane or cocoa plants: it dips down very low, rises again, dips once more;—and you perceive the soil is changing color; it is taking a red tint like that of the land of the American cotton-belt. Then you pass the Rivière Falaise (marked *Filasse* upon old maps),—with its shallow crystal torrent flowing through a very deep and rocky channel,—and the Capote and other streams; and over the yellow rim of cane-hills the long blue bar of the sea appears, edged landward with a dazzling fringe of foam. The heights you have passed are no longer verdant, but purplish or gray,—with Pelée's cloud-wrapped enormity overtopping all. A very strong warm wind is blowing upon you—the trade-wind, always driving the clouds west: this is the sunny side of Martinique, where gray days and heavy rains are less frequent. Once or twice more the sea disappears and reappears, always over canes; and then, after passing a bridge and turning a last curve, the road suddenly drops down to the shore and into the burgh of Grande Anse.

III.

LEAVING Morne Rouge at about eight in the morning, my friend and I reached Grande Anse at half-past eleven. Everything had been arranged to make us comfortable. I was delighted with the airy corner room, commanding at once a view of the main street and of the sea—a very high room, all open to the trade-winds—which had been prepared to receive me. But after a long carriage ride in the heat of a tropical June day, one always feels the necessity of a little physical exercise. I lingered only a minute or two in the house, and went out to look at the little town and its surroundings.

As seen from the high-road, the burgh of Grande Anse makes a long patch of darkness between the green of the coast and the azure of the water: it is almost wholly black and gray—suited to inspire an etching. High slopes of cane and meadow rise behind it and on either side, undulating up and away to purple and gray tips of mountain ranges. North and south, to left and right, the land reaches out in two high promontories, mostly green, and about a mile apart—the Pointe du Rochet and the Pointe de Séguinau, or Croche-Mort, which latter name preserves the legend of an insurgent slave, a man of color, shot dead upon the cliff. These promontories form the semicircular bay of Grande Anse. All this Grande Anse, or "Great Creek," valley is an immense basin of basalt; and narrow as it is, no less than five streams water it, including the Rivière de la Grande Anse.

There are only three short streets in the town. The principal, or Grande Rue, is simply a continuation of the national road; there is a narrower one below, which used to be called the Rue de la Paille, because the cottages lining it were formerly all thatched with cane straw; and there is one above it, edging the cane-fields that billow away to the meeting of morne and sky. There is nothing of architectural interest, and all is sombre,—walls and roofs and pavements. But after you pass through the city and follow the southern route that ascends the Séguinau promontory, you can obtain some lovely landscape views—a grand surging of rounded mornes, with farther violet peaks, truncated or horned, pushing up their heads in the horizon above the highest flutterings of cane; and looking back above the town, you may see Pelée all unclouded,—not as you see it from the other coast, but an enormous ghostly silhouette, with steep sides and almost square summit, so pale as to seem transparent. Then if you cross the promontory southward, the same road will lead you into another very beautiful valley, watered by a broad rocky torrent,—the Valley of the Rivière du Lorrain. This clear stream rushes to the sea through a lofty opening in the hills; and looking westward between them, you will be charmed by the exquisite vista of green shapes piling and pushing up one behind another to reach a high blue ridge which forms the background—a vision of tooth-shaped and fantastical mountains,—part of the great central chain running south and north through nearly the whole island. It is over those blue summits that the wonderful road called *La Trace* winds between primeval forest walls.

But the more you become familiar with the face of the little town itself, the more you are impressed by the strange swarthy tone it preserves in all this splendid expanse of radiant tinting. There are only two points of visible color in it,—the church and hospital, built of stone, which have been painted yellow: as a mass in the landscape, lying between the dead-gold of the cane-clad hills and the delicious azure of the sea, it remains almost black under the prodigious blaze of light. The foundations of volcanic rock, three or four feet high, on which the frames of the wooden dwellings rest, are black; and the sea-wind appears to have the power of blackening all timber-work here through any coat of paint. Roofs and façades look as if they had been long exposed to coal-smoke, although probably no one in Grande Anse ever saw coal; and the pavements of pebbles and cement are of a deep ash-color, full of micaceous scintillation, and so hard as to feel disagreeable even to feet protected by good thick shoes. By-and-by you notice walls of black stone, bridges of black stone, and perceive that black forms an element of all the landscape about you. On the roads leading from the town you note from time to time masses of jagged rock or great bowlders protruding through the green of the slopes, and dark as ink. These black surfaces also sparkle. The beds of all the neighboring rivers are filled with dark gray stones; and many of these, broken by those violent floods which dash rocks together,—deluging the valleys, and strewing the soil of the bottomlands (*fonds*) with dead serpents,—display black cores. Bare crags projecting from the green cliffs here and there are soot-colored, and the outlying rocks of the coast offer a similar aspect. And the sand of the beach is funereally black—looks almost like powdered charcoal; and as you walk over it, sinking three or four inches every step, you are amazed by the multitude and brilliancy of minute flashes in it, like a subtle silver effervescence.

This extraordinary sand contains ninety per cent. of natural steel, and efforts have been made to utilize it industrially. Some years ago a company was formed, and a machine invented to separate the metal from the pure sand,—an immense revolving magnet, which, being set in motion under a sand shower, caught the ore upon it. When the covering thus formed by the adhesion of the steel became of a certain thickness, the simple interruption of an electric current precipitated the metal into appropriate receptacles. Fine bars were made from this volcanic steel, and excellent cutting tools manufactured from it: French metallurgists pronounced the product of peculiar excellence, and nevertheless the project of the company was abandoned. Political disorganization consequent upon the establishment of universal suffrage frightened capitalists who might have aided the undertaking under a better condition of affairs; and the lack of large means, coupled with the cost of freight to remote markets, ultimately baffled this creditable attempt to found a native industry.

Sometimes after great storms bright brown sand is flung up from the sea-depths; but the heavy black sand always reappears again to make the universal color of the beach.

IV.

BEHIND the roomy wooden house in which I occupied an apartment there was a small garden-plot surrounded with a hedge strengthened by bamboo fencing, and radiant with flowers of the *loseille-bois*,—the creole name for a sort of begonia, whose closed bud exactly resembles a pink and white dainty bivalve shell, and whose open blossom imitates the form of a butterfly. Here and there, on the grass, were nets drying, and *nasses*—curious fish-traps made of split bamboos interwoven and held in place with *mibi* stalks (the mibi is a liana heavy and tough as copper wire); and immediately behind the garden hedge appeared the white flashing of the surf. The most vivid recollection connected with my trip to Grande Anse is that of the first time that I went to the end of that garden, opened the little bamboo gate, and found myself overlooking the beach— an immense breadth of soot-black sand, with pale green patches and stripings here and there upon it—refuse of cane thatch, decomposing rubbish spread out by old tides. The one solitary boat owned in the community lay there before me, high and dry. It was the hot period of the afternoon; the town slept; there was no living creature in sight; and the booming of the surf drowned all other sounds; the scent of the warm strong sea-wind annihilated all other odors. Then, very suddenly, there came to me a sensation absolutely weird, while watching the strange wild sea roaring over its beach of black sand,—the sensation of seeing something unreal, looking at something that had no more tangible existence than a memory! Whether suggested by the first white vision of the surf over the bamboo hedge,—or by those old green tidelines on the desolation of the black beach,—or by some tone of the speaking of the sea, —or something indefinable in the living touch of the wind,— or by all of these, I cannot say;—but slowly there became defined within me the thought of having beheld just such a coast very long ago, I could not tell where,—in those child-years of which the recollections gradually become indistinguishable from dreams.

Soon as darkness comes upon Grande Anse the face of the clock in the church-tower is always lighted: you see it suddenly burst into yellow glow above the roofs and the cocoa-palms,— just like a pharos. In my room I could not keep the candle lighted because of the sea-wind; but it never occurred to me to close the shutters of the great broad windows,—sashless, of course, like all the glassless windows of Martinique;—the breeze was too delicious. It seemed full of something vitalizing that made one's blood warmer, and rendered one full of contentment—full of eagerness to believe life all sweetness. Likewise, I found it soporific—this pure, dry, warm wind. And I thought there could be no greater delight in existence than to lie down at night, with all the windows open,—and the Cross of the South visible from my pillow,—and the sea-wind pouring over the bed,—and the tumultuous whispering and muttering of the surf in one's ears,—to dream of that strange sapphire sea white-bursting over its beach of black sand.

V.

CONSIDERING that Grande Anse lies almost opposite to St. Pierre, at a distance of less than twenty miles even by the complicated windings of the national road, the differences existing in the natural conditions of both places are remarkable enough. Nobody in St. Pierre sees the sun rise, because the mountains immediately behind the city continue to shadow its roofs long after the eastern coast is deluged with light and heat. At Grande Anse, on the other hand, those tremendous sunsets which delight west coast dwellers are not visible at all; and during the briefer West Indian days Grande Anse is all wrapped in darkness as early as half-past four,—or nearly an hour before the orange light has ceased to flare up the streets of St. Pierre from the sea;—since the great mountain range topped by Pelée cuts off all the slanting light from the east valleys. And early as folks rise in St. Pierre, they rise still earlier at Grande Anse—before the sun emerges from the rim of the Atlantic: about half-past four, doors are being opened and coffee is ready. At St. Pierre one can enjoy a sea bath till seven or half-past seven o'clock, even during the time of the sun's earliest rising, because the shadow of the mornes still reaches out upon the bay;—but bathers leave the black beach of Grande Anse by six o'clock; for once the sun's face is up, the light, levelled straight at the eyes, becomes blinding. Again, at St. Pierre it rains almost every twenty-four hours for a brief while, during at least the greater part of the year; at Grande Anse it rains more moderately and less often. The atmosphere at St. Pierre is always more or less impregnated with vapor, and usually an enervating heat prevails, which makes exertion unpleasant; at Grande Anse the warm wind keeps the skin comparatively dry, in spite of considerable exercise. It is quite rare to see a heavy surf at St. Pierre, but it is much rarer not to see it at Grande Anse. . . . A curious fact concerning custom is that few white creoles care to bathe in front of the town, notwithstanding the superb beach and magnificent surf, both so inviting to one accustomed to the deep still water and rough pebbly shore of St. Pierre. The creoles really prefer their rivers as bathing-places; and when willing to take a sea bath, they will walk up and down hill for kilometres in order to reach some river mouth, so as to wash off in the fresh-water afterwards. They say that the effect of sea-salt upon the skin gives *boutons-chauds* (what we call "prickly heat"). Friends took me all the way to the mouth of the Lorrain one morning that I might have the experience of such a double bath; but after leaving the tepid sea, I must confess the plunge into the river was something terrible —an icy shock which cured me of all further desire for river baths. My willingness to let the sea-water dry upon me was regarded as an eccentricity.

VI.

IT may be said that on all this coast the ocean, perpetually moved by the blowing of the trade-winds, never rests—never hushes its roar. Even in the streets of Grande Anse, one must in breezy weather lift one's voice above the natural pitch to be heard; and then the breakers come in lines more than a mile long, between the Pointe du Rochet and the Pointe de Séguinau,—every unfurling a thunder-clap. There is no travelling by sea. All large vessels keep well away from the dangerous coast. There is scarcely any fishing; and although the sea is thick with fish, fresh fish at Grande Anse is a rare luxury. Communication with St. Pierre is chiefly by way of the national road, winding over mountain ridges two thousand feet high; and the larger portion of merchandise is transported from the chief city on the heads of young women. The steepness of the route soon kills draught-horses and ruins the toughest mules. At one time the managers of a large estate at Grande Anse attempted the experiment of sending their sugar to St. Pierre in iron carts, drawn by five mules; but the animals could not endure the work. Cocoa can be carried to St. Pierre by the porteuses, but sugar and rum must go by sea, or not at all; and the risks and difficulties of shipping these seriously affect the prosperity of all the north and north-east coast. Planters have actually been ruined by inability to send their products to market during a protracted spell of rough weather. A railroad has been proposed and planned: in a more prosperous era it might be constructed, with the result of greatly developing all the Atlantic side of the island, and converting obscure villages into thriving towns.

Sugar is very difficult to ship; rum and tafia can be handled with less risk. It is nothing less than exciting to watch a shipment of tafia from Grande Anse to St. Pierre.

A little vessel approaches the coast with extreme caution, and anchors in the bay some hundred yards beyond the breakers. She is what they call a *pirogue* here, but not at all what is called a pirogue in the United States: she has a long narrow hull, two masts, no deck; she has usually a crew of five, and can carry thirty barrels of tafia. One of the pirogue men puts a great shell to his lips and sounds a call, very mellow and deep, that can be heard over the roar of the waves far up among the hills. The shell is one of those great spiral shells, weighing seven or eight pounds—rolled like a scroll, fluted and scalloped about the edges, and pink-pearled inside,—such as are sold in America for mantle-piece ornaments,—the shell of a *lambi*. Here you can often see the lambi crawling about with its nacreous house upon its back: an enormous sea-snail with a yellowish back and rose-colored belly, with big horns and eyes in the tip of each horn—very pretty eyes, having a golden iris. This creature is a common article of food; but its thick white flesh is almost compact as cartilage, and must be pounded before being cooked.*

At the sound of the blowing of the lambi-shell, wagons descend to the beach, accompanied by young colored men running beside the mules. Each wagon discharges a certain number of barrels of tafia, and simultaneously the young men strip. They are slight, well built, and generally well muscled. Each man takes a barrel of tafia, pushes it before him into the surf, and then begins to swim to the pirogue,—impelling the barrel before him. I have never seen a swimmer attempt to

---

*   *Y batt li conm lambi*—"he beat him like a lambi"—is an expression that may often be heard in a creole court from witnesses testifying in a case of assault and battery. One must have seen a lambi pounded to appreciate the terrible picturesqueness of the phrase.

convey more than one barrel at a time; but I am told there are experts who manage as many as three barrels together,—pushing them forward in line, with the head of one against the bottom of the next. It really requires much dexterity and practice to handle even one barrel or cask. As the swimmer advances he keeps close as possible to his charge,—so as to be able to push it forward with all his force against each breaker in succession,—making it dive through. If it once glide well out of his reach while he is in the breakers, it becomes an enemy, and he must take care to keep out of its way,—for if a wave throws it at him, or rolls it over him, he may be seriously injured; but the expert seldom abandons a barrel. Under the most favorable conditions, man and barrel will both disappear a score of times before the clear swells are reached, after which the rest of the journey is not difficult. Men lower ropes from the pirogue, the swimmer passes them under his barrel, and it is hoisted aboard.

. . . Wonderful surf-swimmers these men are;—they will go far out for mere sport in the roughest kind of a sea, when the waves, abnormally swollen by the peculiar conformation of the bay, come rolling in thirty and forty feet high. Sometimes, with the swift impulse of ascending a swell, the swimmer seems suspended in air as it passes beneath him, before he plunges into the trough beyond. The best swimmer is a young capre who cannot weigh more than a hundred and twenty pounds. Few of the Grande Anse men are heavily built; they do not compare for stature and thew with those longshoremen at St. Pierre who can be seen any busy afternoon on the landing, lifting heavy barrels at almost the full reach of their swarthy arms.

. . . There is but one boat owned in the whole parish of Grande Anse,—a fact due to the continual roughness of the sea. It has a little mast and sail, and can hold only three men. When the water is somewhat less angry than usual, a colored crew take it out for a fishing expedition. There is always much interest in this event; a crowd gathers on the beach; and the professional swimmers help to bring the little craft beyond the breakers. When the boat returns after a disappearance of several hours, everybody runs down from the village to meet it. Young colored women twist their robes up about their hips, and wade out to welcome it: there is a display of limbs of all colors on such occasions, which is not without grace, that untaught grace which tempts an artistic pencil. Every *bonne* and every house-keeper struggles for the first chance to buy the fish;—young girls and children dance in the water for delight, all screaming, "*Rhalé bois-canot!*" . . . Then as the boat is pulled through the surf and hauled up on the sand, the pushing and screaming and crying become irritating and deafening; the fishermen lose patience and say terrible things. But nobody heeds them in the general clamoring and haggling and furious bidding for the *pouèsson-ououge*, the *dorades*, the *volants* (beautiful purple-backed flying-fish with silver bellies, and fins all transparent, like the wings of dragon-flies). There is great bargaining even for a young shark,—which makes very nice eating cooked after the creole fashion. So seldom can the fishermen venture out that each trip makes a memorable event for the village.

The St. Pierre fishermen very seldom approach the bay, but they do much fishing a few miles beyond it, almost in front of the Pointe du Rochet and the Roche à Bourgaut. There the best flying-fish are caught,—and besides edible creatures, many queer things are often brought up by the nets: monstrosities such as the *coffre*-fish, shaped almost like a box, of which the lid is represented by an extraordinary conformation of the jaws;—and the *barrique-de-vin* ("wine cask"), with round boneless body, secreting in a curious vesicle a liquor precisely resembling wine lees;—and the "needle-fish " (*aiguille de mer*), less thick than a Faber lead-pencil, but more than twice as long;—and huge cuttle-fish and prodigious eels. One conger secured off this coast measured over twenty feet in length, and weighed two hundred and fifty pounds—a veritable sea-serpent. . . . But even the freshwater inhabitants of Grande Anse are amazing. I have seen crawfish by actual measurement fifty centimetres long, but these were not considered remarkable. Many are said to much exceed two feet from the tail to the tip of the claws and horns. They are of an iron-black color, and have formidable pincers with serrated edges and tip-points inwardly converging, which cannot crush like the weapons of a lobster, but which will cut the flesh and make a small ugly wound. At first sight one not familiar with the crawfish of these regions can hardly believe he is not viewing some variety of gigantic lobster instead of the common fresh-water crawfish of the east coast. When the head, tail, legs, and cuirass have all been removed, after boiling, the curved trunk has still the size and weight of a large pork sausage.

These creatures are trapped by lantern-light. Pieces of manioc root tied fast to large bowlders sunk in the river are the only bait;—the crawfish will flock to eat it upon any dark night, and then they are caught with scoop-nets and dropped into covered baskets.

VII.

ONE whose ideas of the people of Grande Anse had been formed only by observing the young porteuses of the region on their way to the other side of the island, might expect on reaching this little town to find its population yellow as that of a Chinese city. But the dominant hue is much darker, although the mixed element is everywhere visible; and I was at first surprised by the scarcity of those clear bright skins I supposed to be so numerous. Some pretty children—notably a pair of twin-sisters, and perhaps a dozen school-girls from eight to ten years of age—displayed the same characteristics I have noted in the adult porteuses of Grande Anse; but within the town itself this brighter element is in the minority. The predominating race element of the whole commune is certainly colored (Grande Anse is even memorable because of the revolt of its *hommes de couleur* some fifty years ago);—but the colored population is not concentrated in the town; it belongs rather to the valleys and the heights surrounding the *chef-lieu*. Most of the porteuses are country girls, and I found that even those living in the village are seldom visible on the streets except when departing upon a trip or returning from one. An artist wishing to study the type might, however, pass a day at the bridge of the Rivière Falaise to advantage, as all the carrier-girls pass it at certain hours of the morning and evening.

But the best possible occasion on which to observe what my friend the baker called *la belle jeunesse*, is a confirmation day,—when the bishop drives to Grande Anse over the mountains, and all the population turns out in holiday garb, and the bells are tapped like tamtams, and triumphal arches—most awry to behold!—span the road-way, bearing in clumsiest lettering

A Confirmation Procession.

the welcome, *Vive Monseigneur*. On that event, the long procession of young girls to be confirmed—all in white robes, white veils, and white satin slippers—is a numerical surprise. It is a moral surprise also,—to the stranger at least; for it reveals the struggle of a poverty extraordinary with the self-imposed obligations of a costly ceremonialism.

No white children ever appear in these processions: there are not half a dozen white families in the whole urban population of about seven thousand souls; and those send their sons and daughters to St. Pierre or Morne Rouge for their religious training and education. But many of the colored children look very charming in their costume of confirmation;—you could not easily recognize one of them as the same little *bonne* who brings your morning cup of coffee, or another as the daughter of a plantation *commandeur* (overseer's assistant),—a brown slip of a girl who will probably never wear shoes again. And many of those white shoes and white veils have been obtained only by the hardest physical labor and self-denial of poor parents and relatives: fathers, brothers, and mothers working with cutlass and hoe in the snake-swarming cane-fields;—sisters walking barefooted every day to St. Pierre and back to earn a few francs a month.

. . . While watching such a procession it seemed to me that I could discern in the features and figures of the young confirmants something of a prevailing type and tint, and I asked an old planter beside me if he thought my impression correct.

"Partly," he answered; "there is certainly a tendency towards an attractive physical type here, but the tendency itself is less stable than you imagine; it has been changed during the last twenty years within my own recollection. In different parts of the island particular types appear and disappear with a generation. There is a sort of race-fermentation going on, which gives no fixed result of a positive sort for any great length of time. It is true that certain elements continue to dominate in certain communes, but the particular characteristics come and vanish in the most mysterious way. As to color, I doubt if any correct classification can be made, especially by a stranger. Your eyes give you general ideas about a red type, a yellow type, a brown type; but to the more experienced eyes of a creole, accustomed to live in the country districts, every individual of mixed race appears to have a particular color of his own. Take, for instance, the so-called capre type, which furnishes the finest physical examples of all,—you, a stranger, are at once impressed by the general red tint of the variety; but you do not notice the differences of that tint in different persons, which are more difficult to observe than shade-differences of yellow or brown. Now, to me, every capre or capresse has an individual color; and I do not believe that in all Martinique there are two half-breeds—not having had the same father and mother—in whom the tint is precisely the same."

VIII.

I THOUGHT Grande Anse the most sleepy place I had ever visited. I suspect it is one of the sleepiest in the whole world. The wind, which tans even a creole of St. Pierre to an unnatural brown within forty-eight hours of his sojourn in the village, has also a peculiarly somnolent effect. The moment one has nothing particular to do, and ventures to sit down idly with the breeze in one's face, slumber comes; and everybody who can spare the time takes a long nap in the afternoon, and little naps from hour to hour. For all that, the heat of the east coast is not enervating, like that of St. Pierre; one can take a great deal of exercise in the sun without feeling much the worse. Hunting excursions, river fishing parties, surf-bathing, and visits to neighboring plantations are the only amusements; but these are enough to make existence very pleasant at Grande Anse. The most interesting of my own experiences were those of a day passed by invitation at one of the old colonial estates on the hills near the village.

It is not easy to describe the charm of a creole interior, whether in the city or the country. The cool shadowy court, with its wonderful plants and fountain of sparkling mountain water, or the lawn, with its ancestral trees,—the delicious welcome of the host, whose fraternal easy manner immediately makes you feel at home,—the coming of the children to greet you, each holding up a velvety brown cheek to be kissed, after the old-time custom,—the romance of the unconventional chat, over a cool drink, under the palms and the ceibas,—the visible earnestness of all to please the guest, to inwrap him in a very atmosphere of quiet happiness,—combine to make a memory which you will never forget. And maybe you enjoy all this upon some exquisite site, some volcanic summit, overlooking slopes of a hundred greens,—mountains far winding in blue and pearly shadowing,—rivers singing seaward behind curtains of arborescent reeds and bamboos,—and, perhaps, Pelée, in the horizon, dreaming violet dreams under her foulard of vapors,—and, encircling all, the still sweep of the ocean's azure bending to the verge of day.

. . . My host showed or explained to me all that he thought might interest a stranger. He had brought to me a nest of the *carouge*, a bird which suspends its home, hammock-fashion, under the leaves of the banana-tree;—showed me a little fer-de-lance, freshly killed by one of his field hands; and a field lizard (*zanoli tè* in creole), not green like the lizards which haunt the roofs of St. Pierre, but of a beautiful brown bronze, with shifting tints; and eggs of the *zanoli*, little soft oval things from which the young lizards will perhaps run out alive as fast as you open the shells; and the *matoutou-falaise*, or spider of the cliffs, of two varieties, red or almost black when adult, and bluish silvery tint when young,—less in size than the tarantula, but equally hairy and venomous; and the *crabe-c'est-ma-faute* (the "Through-my-fault Crab"), having one very small and one very large claw, which latter it carries folded up against its body, so as to have suggested the idea of a penitent striking his bosom, and uttering the sacramental words of the Catholic confession, "Through my fault, through my fault, through my most grievous fault." . . . Indeed I cannot recollect one-half of the queer birds, queer insects, queer reptiles, and queer plants to which my attention was called. But speaking of plants, I was impressed by the profusion of the *zhèbe-moin-misé*—a little sensitive-plant I had rarely observed on the west coast. On the hill-sides of Grande Anse it prevails to such an extent as to give certain slopes its own peculiar greenish-brown color. It has many-branching leaves, only one inch and a half to two inches long, but which recall the form of certain common ferns; these lie almost flat upon the ground. They fold together upward from the central stem at the least touch, and the plant thus makes itself almost imperceptible;—it seems to live so, that you feel guilty of murder if you break off a leaf. It is called *Zhèbe-moin-misé*, or "Plant-did-I-amuse-myself," because it is supposed to tell naughty little children who play truant, or who delay much longer than is necessary in delivering a message, whether they deserve a whipping or not. The guilty child touches the plant, and asks, "*Ess moin amisé moin?*" (Did I amuse myself?); and if the plant instantly shuts its leaves up, that means, "Yes, you did!" Of course the leaves invariably close; but I suspect they invariably tell the truth, for all colored children, in Grande Anse at least, are much more inclined to play than work.

The kind old planter likewise conducted me over the estate. He took me through the sugar-mill, and showed me, among other more recent inventions, some machinery devised nearly two centuries ago by the ingenious and terrible Père Labat, and still quite serviceable, in spite of all modern improvements in sugar-making;—took me through the *rhummerie*, or distillery, and made me taste some colorless rum which had the aroma and something of the taste of the most delicate gin;—and finally took me into the *cases-à-vent*, or "wind-houses,"—built as places of refuge during hurricanes. Hurricanes are rare, and more rare in this century by far than during the previous one; but this part of the island is particularly exposed to such visitations, and almost every old plantation used to have one or two cases-à-vent. They were always built in a hollow, either natural or artificial, below the land-level,—with walls of rock several feet thick, and very strong doors, but no windows. My host told me about the experiences of his family in some case-à-vent during a hurricane which he recollected. It was found necessary to secure the door within by means of strong ropes; and the mere task of holding it taxed the strength of a dozen powerful men: it would bulge in under the pressure of the awful wind,—swelling like the side of a barrel; and had not its planks been made of a wood tough as hickory, they would have been blown into splinters.

I had long desired to examine a plantation drum, and see it played upon under conditions more favorable than the excitement of a holiday *caleinda* in the villages, where the amusement is too often terminated by a *voum* (general row) or a *goumage* (a serious fight);—and when I mentioned this wish to the planter he at once sent word to his commandeur, the best drummer in the settlement, to come up to the house and bring his instrument with him. I was thus enabled to make the observations necessary, and also to take an instantaneous photograph of the drummer in the very act of playing.

The old African dances, the *caleinda* and the *bélé* (which latter is accompanied by chanted improvisation) are danced on Sundays to the sound of the drum on almost every plantation in the island. The drum, indeed, is an instrument to which the country-folk are so much attached that they swear by it,— *Tambou!* being the oath uttered upon all ordinary occasions of surprise or vexation. But the instrument is quite as often called *ka*, because made out of a quarter-barrel, or *quart*,—in the patois "ka." Both ends of the barrel having been removed, a wet hide, well wrapped about a couple of hoops, is driven on, and in drying the stretched skin obtains still further tension. The other end of the ka is always left open. Across the face of the skin a string is tightly stretched, to which are attached, at intervals of about an inch apart, very short thin fragments of bamboo or cut feather stems. These lend a certain vibration to the tones.

In the time of Père Labat the negro drums had a somewhat different form. There were then two kinds of drums—a big tam-tam and a little one, which used to be played together. Both consisted of skins tightly stretched over one end of a wooden cylinder, or a section of hollow tree trunk. The larger was from three to four feet long with a diameter of fifteen to sixteen inches; the smaller, called *baboula*,* was of the same length, but only eight or nine inches in diameter. Père Labat also speaks, in his West Indian travels, of another musical instrument, very popular among the Martinique slaves of his time— "a sort of guitar" made out of a half-calabash or *couï*, covered with some kind of skin. It had four strings of silk or catgut,

---

*Moreau de Saint-Méry writes, describing the drums of the negroes of Saint Domingue: "Le plus court de ces tambours est nommé *Bamboula*, attendu qu'il est formé quelquefois d'un très-gros bambou."—"Description de la partie française de Saint Domingue," vol. i., p. 44.

and a very long neck. The tradition of this African instrument is said to survive in the modern "*banza*" (*banza nèg Guinée*).

The skilful player (*bel tambouyé*) straddles his ka stripped to the waist, and plays upon it with the finger-tips of both hands simultaneously,—taking care that the vibrating string occupies a horizontal position. Occasionally the heel of the naked foot is pressed lightly or vigorously against the skin, so as to produce changes of tone. This is called "giving heel" to the drum —*baill y talon*. Meanwhile a boy keeps striking the drum at the uncovered end with a stick, so as to produce a dry clattering accompaniment. The sound of the drum itself, well played, has a wild power that makes and masters all the excitement of the dance—a complicated double roll, with a peculiar billowy rising and falling. The creole onomatopes, *b'lip-b'lib-b'lib-b'lip*, do not fully render the roll;—for each *b'lip* or *b'lib* stands really for a series of sounds too rapidly fillipped out to be imitated by articulate speech. The tapping of a ka can be heard at surprising distances; and experienced players often play for hours at a time without exhibiting wearisomeness, or in the least diminishing the volume of sound produced.

It seems there are many ways of playing—different measures familiar to all these colored people, but not easily distinguished by anybody else; and there are great matches sometimes between celebrated *tambouyé*. The same *commandè* whose portrait I took while playing told me that he once figured in a contest of this kind, his rival being a drummer from the neighboring burgh of Marigot. . . . "*Aïe, aïe, yaïe! mon chè!—y fai tambou-à pàlé!*" said the commandè, describing the execution of his antagonist;—"my dear, he just made that drum talk! I thought I was going to be beaten for sure; I was trembling all the time—*aïe, yaïe-yaïe!* Then he got off that ka. I mounted it; I thought a moment; then I struck up the 'River-of-the-Lizard,' —*mais, mon chè, yon larivie-Léza toutt pi!*—such a River-of-the-Lizard, ah! just perfectly pure! I gave heel to that ka; I worried that ka;—I made it mad;—I made it crazy;—I made it talk;—I won!"

During some dances a sort of chant accompanies the music —a long sonorous cry, uttered at intervals of seven or eight seconds, which perfectly times a particular measure in the drum roll. It may be the burden of a song, or a mere improvisation:

"Oh! yoïe-yoïe!"

(*Drum roll.*)

"Oh! missié-à!"

(*Drum roll.*)

"Y bel tambouyé!"

(*Drum roll.*)

"Aie, ya, yaie!"

(*Drum roll.*)

"Joli tambouyé!"

(*Drum roll.*)

"Chauffé tambou-à!"

(*Drum roll.*)

"Géné tambou-à!"

(*Drum roll.*)

"Crazé tambou-à!" etc., etc.

. . . The *crieur*, or chanter, is also the leader of the dance. The caleinda is danced by men only, all stripped to the waist, and twirling heavy sticks in a mock fight. Sometimes, however —especially at the great village gatherings, when the blood becomes overheated by tafia—the mock fight may become a real one; and then even cutlasses are brought into play.

But in the old days, those improvisations which gave one form of dance its name, *bélé* (from the French *bel air*), were often remarkable rhymeless poems, uttered with natural simple emotion, and full of picturesque imagery. I cite part of one, taken down from the dictation of a common field-hand near Fort-de-France. I offer a few lines of the creole first, to indicate the form of the improvisation. There is a dancing pause at the end of each line during the performance:

Toutt fois lanmou vini lacase moin
Pou pàlé moin, moin ka reponne:
"Khé moin deja placé."
Moin ka crié, "Sécou! les voisinages!"
Moin ka crié, "Sécou! la gàde royale!"
Moin ka crié, "Sécou! la gendàmerie!
Lanmou pouend yon poignâ pou poignadé moin!"

The best part of the composition, which is quite long, might be rendered as follows:

Manner of Playing the Ka.

Each time that Love comes to my cabin
To speak to me of love, I make answer,
"My heart is already placed."
I cry out, "Help, neighbors! help!"
I cry out, "Help, *la Garde Royale!*"
I cry out, "Help, help, gendarmes!
Love takes a poniard to stab me;
How can Love have a heart so hard
To thus rob me of my health!"
When the officer of police comes to me
To hear me tell him the truth,
To have him arrest my Love;—
When I see the Garde Royale
Coming to arrest my sweet heart,
I fall down at the feet of the Garde Royale,—
I pray for mercy and forgiveness.
"Arrest me instead, but let my dear Love go!"
How, alas! with this tender heart of mine,
Can I bear to see such an arrest made!
No, no! I would rather die!
Dost not remember, when our pillows lay close together,
How we told each to the other all that our hearts
        thought? . . . etc.

The stars were all out when I bid my host good-bye;—he
sent his black servant along with me to carry a lantern and
keep a sharp watch for snakes along the mountain road.

IX.

. . . ASSUREDLY the city of St. Pierre never could have
seemed more quaintly beautiful than as I saw it on the evening
of my return, while the shadows were reaching their longest,
and sea and sky were turning lilac. Palm-heads were trembling
and masts swaying slowly against an enormous orange sunset,
—yet the beauty of the sight did not touch me! The deep level
and luminous flood of the bay seemed to me for the first time
a dead water;—I found myself wondering whether it could
form a part of that living tide by which I had been dwelling,
full of foam-lightnings and perpetual thunder. I wondered

whether the air about me—heavy and hot and full of faint leafy smells—could ever have been touched by the vast pure sweet breath of the wind from the sunrising. And I became conscious of a profound, unreasoning, absurd regret for the somnolent little black village of that bare east coast,—where there are no woods, no ships, no sunsets, . . . only the ocean roaring forever over its beach of black sand.

Un Revenant

HE who first gave to Martinique its poetical name, *Le Pays des Revenants*, thought of his wonderful island only as "The Country of Comers-back," where Nature's unspeakable spell bewitches wandering souls like the caress of a Circe,—never as the Land of Ghosts. Yet either translation of the name holds equal truth: a land of ghosts it is, this marvellous Martinique! Almost every plantation has its familiar spirits,—its phantoms: some may be unknown beyond the particular district in which fancy first gave them being;—but some belong to popular song and story,—to the imaginative life of the whole people. Almost every promontory and peak, every village and valley along the coast, has its special folk-lore, its particular tradition. The legend of Thomasseau of Perinnelle, whose body was taken out of the coffin and carried away by the devil through a certain window of the plantation-house, which cannot be closed up by human power;—the Demarche legend of the spectral horseman who rides up the hill on bright hot days to seek a friend buried more than a hundred years ago;—the legend of the *Habitation Dillon*, whose proprietor was one night mysteriously summoned from a banquet to disappear forever;—the legend of l'Abbé Piot, who cursed the sea with the curse of perpetual unrest;—the legend of Aimée Derivry of Robert, captured by Barbary pirates, and sold to become a Sultana-Validé—(she never existed, though you can find an alleged portrait in M. Sidney Daney's history of Martinique): these and many similar tales might be told to you even on a journey from St. Pierre to Fort-de-France, or from Lamentin to La Trinité, according as a rising of some peak into view, or the sudden opening of an *anse* before the vessel's approach, recalls them to a creole companion.

And new legends are even now being made; for in this remote colony, to which white immigration has long ceased,—a country so mountainous that people are born and buried in the same valley without ever seeing towns but a few hours' journey beyond their native hills, and that distinct racial types are forming within three leagues of each other,—the memory of an event or of a name which has had influence enough to send one echo through all the forty-nine miles of peaks and craters is apt to create legend within a single generation. Nowhere in the world, perhaps, is popular imagination more oddly naïve and superstitious; nowhere are facts more readily exaggerated or distorted into unrecognizability; and the forms of any legend thus originated become furthermore specialized in each separate locality where it obtains a habitat. On tracing back such a legend or tradition to its primal source, one feels amazed at the variety of the metamorphoses which the simplest fact may rapidly assume in the childish fancy of this people.

I was first incited to make an effort in this direction by hearing the remarkable story of "Missié Bon." No legendary expression is more wide-spread throughout the country than *temps coudvent Missié Bon* (in the time of the big wind of Monsieur Bon). Whenever a hurricane threatens, you will hear colored folks expressing the hope that it may not be like the *coudvent Missié Bon*. And some years ago, in all the creole police-courts, old colored witnesses who could not tell their age would invariably try to give the magistrate some idea of it by referring to the never-to-be-forgotten *temps coudvent Missié Bon.*

. . . "*Temps coudvent Missié Bon, moin té ka tété encò*" (I was a child at the breast in the time of the big wind of Missié Bon); or "*Temps coudvent Missié Bon, moin té toutt piti manmaille,—moin ka souvini y pouend caïe manman moin pòté allé.*" (I was a very, very little child in the time of the big wind of Missié Bon,—but I remember it blew mamma's cabin away.) The magistrates of those days knew the exact date of the *coudvent.*

But all I could learn about Missié Bon among the country-folk was this: Missié Bon used to be a great slave-owner and a cruel master. He was a very wicked man. And he treated his slaves so terribly that at last the Good-God (*Bon-Dié*) one day sent a great wind which blew away Missié Bon and Missié Bon's house and everybody in it, so that nothing was ever heard of them again.

It was not without considerable research that I succeeded at last in finding some one able to give me the true facts in the case of Monsieur Bon. My informant was a charming old gentleman, who represents a New York company in the city of St. Pierre, and who takes more interest in the history of his native island than creoles usually do. He laughed at the legend I had found, but informed me that I could trace it, with slight variations, through nearly every canton of Martinique.

"And now," he continued, "I can tell you the real history of 'Missié Bon,'—for he was an old friend of my grandfather; and my grandfather related it to me.

"It may have been in 1809—I can give you the exact date by reference to some old papers if necessary—Monsieur Bon was Collector of Customs at St. Pierre: and my grandfather was doing business in the Grande Rue. A certain captain, whose vessel had been consigned to my grandfather, invited him and the collector to breakfast in his cabin. My grandfather was so busy he could not accept the invitation;—but Monsieur Bon went with the captain on board the bark.

. . . "It was a morning like this; the sea was just as blue and the sky as clear. All of a sudden, while they were at breakfast, the sea began to break heavily without a wind, and clouds came up, with every sign of a hurricane. The captain was obliged to sacrifice his anchor; there was no time to land his guest: he hoisted a little jib and top-gallant, and made for open water, taking Monsieur Bon with him. Then the hurricane came; and from that day to this nothing has ever been heard of the bark nor of the captain nor of Monsieur Bon."*

"But did Monsieur Bon ever do anything to deserve the reputation he has left among the people?" I asked.

"*Ah! le pauvre vieux corps!* . . . A kind old soul who never uttered a harsh word to human being;—timid,—good-natured,

---

*What is known in the West Indies as a hurricane is happily rare; it blows with the force of a cyclone, but not always circularly; it may come from one direction, and strengthen gradually for days until its highest velocity and destructive force are reached. One in the time of Père Labat blew away the walls of a fort;—that of 1780 destroyed the lives of twenty-two thousand people in four islands: Martinique, Saint Lucia, St. Vincent, and Barbadoes.

Before the approach of such a visitation animals manifest the same signs of terror they display prior to an earthquake. Cattle assemble together, stamp, and roar; sea-birds fly to the interior; fowl seek the nearest crevice they can hide in. Then, while the sky is yet clear, begins the breaking of the sea; then darkness comes, and after it the wind.

—old-fashioned even for those old-fashioned days. . . . Never had a slave in his life!"

II.

THE legend of "Missié Bon" had prepared me to hear without surprise the details of a still more singular tradition,—that of Father Labat. . . . I was returning from a mountain ramble with my guide, by way of the Ajoupa-Bouillon road;—the sun had gone down; there remained only a blood-red glow in the west, against which the silhouettes of the hills took a velvety blackness indescribably soft; and stars were beginning to twinkle out everywhere through the violet. Suddenly I noticed on the flank of a neighboring morne—which I remembered by day as an apparently uninhabitable wilderness of bamboos, tree-ferns, and balisiers—a swiftly moving point of yellow light. My guide had observed it simultaneously;—he crossed himself, and exclaimed:

"*Moin ka couè c'est fanal Pè Labatt!*" (I believe it is the lantern of Père Labat.)

"Does he live there?" I innocently inquired.

"Live there?—why he has been dead hundreds of years! . . . *Ouill!* you never heard of Pè Labatt?" . . .

"Not the same who wrote a book about Martinique?"

"Yes,—himself. . . . They say he comes back at night. Ask mother about him;—she knows." . . .

. . . I questioned old Théréza as soon as we reached home; and she told me all she knew about "Pè Labatt." I found that the father had left a reputation far more wide-spread than the recollection of "Missié Bon,"—that his memory had created, in fact, the most impressive legend in all Martinique folk-lore.

"Whether you really saw Pè Labatt's lantern," said old Théréza, "I do not know;—there are a great many queer lights to be seen after nightfall among these mornes. Some are zombi-fires; and some are lanterns carried by living men; and some are lights burning in ajoupas so high up that you can only see a gleam coming through the trees now and then. It is not every-body who sees the lantern of Pè Labatt; and it is not good-luck to see it.

"Pè Labatt was a priest who lived here hundreds of years

ago; and he wrote a book about what he saw. He was the first person to introduce slavery into Martinique; and it is thought that is why he comes back at night. It is his penance for having established slavery here.

"They used to say, before 1848, that when slavery should be abolished, Pè Labatt's light would not be seen any more. But I can remember very well when slavery was abolished; and I saw the light many a time after. It used to move up the Morne d'Orange every clear night;—I could see it very well from my window when I lived in St. Pierre. You knew it was Pè Labatt, because the light passed up places where no man could walk. But since the statue of Notre Dame de la Garde was placed on the Morne d'Orange, people tell me that the light is not seen there any more.

"But it is seen elsewhere; and it is not good-luck to see it. Everybody is afraid of seeing it. . . . And mothers tell their children, when the little ones are naughty: '*Mi! moin ké fai Pè Labatt vini pouend ou,—oui!*' (I will make Pè Labatt come and take you away.)" . . .

What old Théréza stated regarding the establishment of slavery in Martinique by Père Labat, I knew required no investigation,—inasmuch as slavery was a flourishing institution in the time of Père Dutertre, another Dominican missionary and historian, who wrote his book,—a queer book in old French,*—before Labat was born. But it did not take me long to find out that such was the general belief about Père Labat's sin and penance, and to ascertain that his name is indeed used to frighten naughty children. *Eh! ti manmaille-là, moin ké fai Pè Labatt vini pouend ou!*—is an exclamation often heard in the vicinity of ajoupas just about the hour when all good little children ought to be in bed and asleep.

. . . The first variation of the legend I heard was on a plantation in the neighborhood of Ajoupa-Bouillon. There I was informed that Père Labat had come to his death by the bite of a snake,—the hugest snake that ever was seen in Martinique. Père Labat had believed it possible to exterminate the

---

*"Histoire Générale des Antilles . . . habités par les Français." Par le R. P. Du Tertre, de l'Ordre des Frères Prescheurs. Paris: 1661–71. 4 vols. (with illustrations) in 4to.

fer-de-lance, and had adopted extraordinary measures for its destruction. On receiving his death-wound he exclaimed, "*C'est pè toutt sépent qui té ka mòdé moin*" (It is the Father of all Snakes that has bitten me); and he vowed that he would come back to destroy the brood, and would haunt the island until there should be not one snake left. And the light that moves about the peaks at night is the lantern of Père Labat still hunting for snakes.

"*Ou pa pè suive ti limié-là piess!*" continued my informant. "You cannot follow that little light at all;—when you first see it, it is perhaps only a kilometre away; the next moment it is two, three, or four kilometres away."

I was also told that the light is frequently seen near Grande Anse, on the other side of the island,—and on the heights of La Caravelle, the long fantastic promontory that reaches three leagues into the sea south of the harbor of La Trinité.* And on my return to St. Pierre I found a totally different version of the legend;—my informant being one Manm-Robert, a kind old soul who kept a little *boutique-lapacotte* (a little booth where cooked food is sold) near the precipitous Street of the Friendships.

. . . "*Ah! Pè Labatt, oui!*" she exclaimed, at my first question, —"Pè Labatt was a good priest who lived here very long

---

*One of the lights seen on the Caravelle was certainly carried by a cattle-thief—a colossal negro who had the reputation of being a sorcerer—a *quimboiseur*. The greater part of the mountainous land forming La Caravelle promontory was at that time the property of a Monsieur Eustache, who used it merely for cattle-raising purposes. He allowed his animals to run wild in the hills; they multiplied exceedingly, and became very savage. Notwithstanding their ferocity, however, large numbers of them were driven away at night, and secretly slaughtered or sold, by somebody who used to practise the art of cattle-stealing with a lantern, and evidently without aid. A watch was set, and the thief arrested. Before the magistrate he displayed extraordinary assurance, asserting that he had never stolen from a poor man—he had stolen only from M. Eustache who could not count his own cattle—*yon richard, mon chè!* "How many cows did you steal from him?" asked the magistrate. "*Ess moin pè save?—moin té pouend yon savane toutt pleine*," replied the prisoner. (How can I tell?—I took a whole savanna-full.) . . . Condemned on the strength of his own confession, he was taken to jail. "*Moin pa ké rété la geôle*," he observed. (I shall not remain in prison.) They put him in irons, but on the following morning the irons were found lying on the floor of the cell, and the prisoner was gone. He was never seen in Martinique again.

ago. And they did him a great wrong here;—they gave him a wicked *coup d'langue* (tongue wound); and the hurt given by an evil tongue is worse than a serpent's bite. They lied about him; they slandered him until they got him sent away from the country. But before the Government 'embarked' him, when he got to that quay, he took off his shoe and he shook the dust of his shoe upon that quay, and he said: 'I curse you, O Martinique!—I curse you! There will be food for nothing, and your people will not even be able to buy it! There will be clothing material for nothing, and your people will not be able to get so much as one dress! And the children will beat their mothers! . . . You banish me;—but I will come back again.'"*

"And then what happened, Manm-Robert?"

"*Eh! fouinq! chè*, all that Pè Labatt said has come true. There is food for almost nothing, and people are starving here in St. Pierre; there is clothing for almost nothing, and poor girls cannot earn enough to buy a dress. The pretty printed calicoes (*indiennes*) that used to be two francs and a half the metre, now sell at twelve sous the metre; but nobody has any money. And if you read our papers,—*Les Colonies*, *La Defense Coloniale*,—you will find that there are sons wicked enough to beat their mothers: *oui! yche ka batt manman!* It is the malediction of Pè Labatt."

This was all that Manm-Robert could tell me. Who had related the story to her? Her mother. Whence had her mother obtained it? From her grandmother. . . . Subsequently I found many persons to confirm the tradition of the curse,— precisely as Manm-Robert had related it.

Only a brief while after this little interview I was invited to pass an afternoon at the home of a gentleman residing upon the Morne d' Orange,—the locality supposed to be especially haunted by Père Labat. The house of Monsieur M—— stands on the side of the hill, fully five hundred feet up, and in a grove of trees: an antiquated dwelling, with foundations massive as

*Y sucoué souyé y assous quai-là;—y ka di: "Moin ka maudi ou, Lanmatinique!—moin ka maudi ou! . . . Ké ni mangé pou engnien: ou pa ké pè menm acheté y! Ké ni touèle pou engnien: ou pa ké pè menm acheté yon robe! Epi yche ké batt manman. . . . Ou banni moin!—moin ké vini encò!"

the walls of a fortress, and huge broad balconies of stone. From one of these balconies there is a view of the city, the harbor, and Pelée, which I believe even those who have seen Naples would confess to be one of the fairest sights in the world. . . . Towards evening I obtained a chance to ask my kind host some questions about the legend of his neighborhood.

. . . "Ever since I was a child," observed Monsieur M——, "I heard it said that Père Labat haunted this mountain, and I often saw what was alleged to be his light. It looked very much like a lantern swinging in the hand of some one climbing the hill. A queer fact was that it used to come from the direction of Carbet, skirt the Morne d'Orange a few hundred feet above the road, and then move up the face of what seemed a sheer precipice. Of course somebody carried that light,—probably a negro; and perhaps the cliff is not so inaccessible as it looks: still, we could never discover who the individual was, nor could we imagine what his purpose might have been. . . . But the light has not been seen here now for years."

III.

AND who was Père Labat,—this strange priest whose memory, weirdly disguised by legend, thus lingers in the oral literature of the colored people? Various encyclopædias answer the question, but far less fully and less interestingly than Dr. Rufz, the Martinique historian, whose article upon him in the *Études Statistiques et Historiques* has that charm of sympathetic comprehension by which a master-biographer sometimes reveals himself a sort of necromancer,—making us feel a vanished personality with the power of a living presence. Yet even the colorless data given by dictionaries of biography should suffice to convince most readers that Jean-Baptiste Labat must be ranked among the extraordinary men of his century.

Nearly two hundred years ago—24th August, 1693—a traveller wearing the white habit of the Dominican order, partly covered by a black camlet overcoat, entered the city of Rochelle. He was very tall and robust, with one of those faces, at once grave and keen, which bespeak great energy and quick discernment. This was the Père Labat, a native of Paris, then in his thirtieth year. Half priest, half layman, one might have been tempted to surmise from his attire; and such a judgment would not have been unjust. Labat's character was too large for his calling,—expanded naturally beyond the fixed limits of the ecclesiastical life; and throughout the whole active part of his strange career we find in him this dual character of layman and monk. He had come to Rochelle to take passage for Martinique. Previously he had been professor of philosophy and mathematics at Nancy. While watching a sunset one evening from the window of his study, some one placed in his hands a circular issued by the Dominicans of the French West Indies, calling for volunteers. Death had made many wide gaps in their ranks; and various misfortunes had reduced their finances to such an extent that ruin threatened all their West Indian establishments. Labat, with the quick decision of a mind suffering from the restraints of a life too narrow for it, had at once resigned his professorship, and engaged himself for the missions.

. . . In those days, communication with the West Indies was slow, irregular, and difficult. Labat had to wait at Rochelle six whole months for a ship. In the convent at Rochelle, where he stayed, there were others waiting for the same chance,—including several Jesuits and Capuchins as well as Dominicans. These unanimously elected him their leader,—a significant fact considering the mutual jealousy of the various religious orders of that period. There was something in the energy and frankness of Labat's character which seems to have naturally gained him the confidence and ready submission of others.

. . . They sailed in November; and Labat still found himself in the position of a chief on board. His account of the voyage is amusing;—in almost everything except practical navigation, he would appear to have regulated the life of passengers and crew. He taught the captain mathematics; and invented amusements of all kinds to relieve the monotony of a two months' voyage.

. . . As the ship approached Martinique from the north, Labat first beheld the very grimmest part of the lofty coast,—the region of Macouba; and the impression it made upon him was not pleasing. "The island," he writes, "appeared to me all one frightful mountain, broken everywhere by precipices:

nothing about it pleased me except the verdure which every-where met the eye, and which seemed to me both novel and agreeable, considering the time of the year."

Almost immediately after his arrival he was sent by the Su-perior of the convent to Macouba, for acclimation; Macouba then being considered the healthiest part of the island. Who-ever makes the journey on horseback thither from St. Pierre to-day can testify to the exactitude of Labat's delightful narra-tive of the trip. So little has that part of the island changed since two centuries that scarcely a line of the father's descrip-tion would need correction to adopt it bodily for an account of a ride to Macouba in 1889.

At Macouba everybody welcomes him, pets him,—finally becomes enthusiastic about him. He fascinates and dominates the little community almost at first sight. "There is an inex-pressible charm," says Rufz,—commenting upon this portion of Labat's narrative,—"in the novelty of relations between men: no one has yet been offended, no envy has yet been excited;—it is scarcely possible even to guess whence that ill-will you must sooner or later provoke is going to come from;—there are no rivals;—there are no enemies. You are everybody's friend; and many are hoping you will continue to be only theirs." . . . Labat knew how to take legitimate advantage of this good-will;—he persuaded his admirers to rebuild the church at Macouba, according to designs made by himself.

At Macouba, however, he was not permitted to sojourn as long as the good people of the little burgh would have deemed even reasonable: he had shown certain aptitudes which made his presence more than desirable at Saint-Jacques, the great plantation of the order on the Capesterre, or Windward coast. It was in debt for 700,000 pounds of sugar,—an appalling condition in those days,—and seemed doomed to get more heavily in debt every successive season. Labat inspected every-thing, and set to work for the plantation, not merely as general director, but as engineer, architect, machinist, inventor. He did really wonderful things. You can see them for yourself if you ever go to Martinique; for the old Dominican plantation —now Government property, and leased at an annual rent of 50,000 francs—remains one of the most valuable in the colonies because of Labat's work upon it. The watercourses directed by

him still excite the admiration of modern professors of hy-
draulics; the mills he built or invented are still good;—the treatise he wrote on sugar-making remained for a hundred and
fifty years the best of its kind, and the manual of French
planters. In less than two years Labat had not only rescued the
plantation from bankruptcy, but had made it rich; and if the
monks deemed him veritably inspired, the test of time throws
no ridicule on their astonishment at the capacities of the
man. . . . Even now the advice he formulated as far back as
1720—about secondary cultures,—about manufactories to
establish,—about imports, exports, and special commercial
methods—has lost little of its value.

Such talents could not fail to excite wide-spread admiration,
—nor to win for him a reputation in the colonies beyond
precedent. He was wanted everywhere. . . . Auger, the Governor of Guadeloupe, sent for him to help the colonists in for-
tifying and defending the island against the English; and we
find the missionary quite as much at home in this new role—
building bastions, scarps, counterscarps, ravelins, etc.—as he
seemed to be upon the plantation of Saint-Jacques. We find
him even taking part in an engagement;—himself conducting
an artillery duel,—loading, pointing, and firing no less than
twelve times after the other French gunners had been killed or
driven from their posts. After a tremendous English volley, one
of the enemy cries out to him in French: "White Father, have
they told?" (*Père Blanc, ont-ils porté?*) He replies only after returning the fire with a better-directed aim, and then repeats
the mocking question: "Have they told?" "Yes, they have,"
confesses the Englishman, in surprised dismay; "but we will pay
you back for that!" . . .

. . . Returning to Martinique with new titles to distinction,
Labat was made Superior of the order in that island, and likewise Vicar-Apostolic. After building the Convent of the Mouillage, at St. Pierre, and many other edifices, he undertook that
series of voyages in the interests of the Dominicans whereof
the narration fills six ample volumes. As a traveller Père Labat
has had few rivals in his own field;—no one, indeed, seems to
have been able to repeat some of his feats. All the French and
several of the English colonies were not merely visited by him,
but were studied in their every geographical detail. Travel in

the West Indies is difficult to a degree of which strangers have little idea; but in the time of Père Labat there were few roads, —and a far greater variety of obstacles. I do not believe there are half a dozen whites in Martinique who thoroughly know their own island,—who have even travelled upon all its roads; but Labat knew it as he knew the palm of his hand, and travelled where roads had never been made. Equally well he knew Guadeloupe and other islands; and he learned all that it was possible to learn in those years about the productions and resources of the other colonies. He travelled with the fearlessness and examined with the thoroughness of a Humboldt,—so far as his limited science permitted: had he possessed the knowledge of modern naturalists and geologists he would probably have left little for others to discover after him. Even at the present time West Indian travellers are glad to consult him for information.

These duties involved prodigious physical and mental exertion, in a climate deadly to Europeans. They also involved much voyaging in waters haunted by filibusters and buccaneers. But nothing appears to daunt Labat. As for the filibusters, he becomes their comrade and personal friend;—he even becomes their chaplain, and does not scruple to make excursions with them. He figures in several sea-fights;—on one occasion he aids in the capture of two English vessels,—and then occupies himself in making the prisoners, among whom are several ladies, enjoy the event like a holiday. On another voyage Labat's vessel is captured by a Spanish ship. At one moment sabres are raised above his head, and loaded muskets levelled at his breast;—the next, every Spaniard is on his knees, appalled by a cross that Labat holds before the eyes of the captors,—the cross worn by officers of the Inquisition,—the terrible symbol of the Holy Office. "It did not belong to me," he says, "but to one of our brethren who had left it by accident among my effects." He seems always prepared in some way to meet any possible emergency. No humble and timid monk this: he has the frame and temper of those mediæval abbots who could don with equal indifference the helmet or the cowl. He is apparently even more of a soldier than a priest. When English corsairs attempt a descent on the Martinique coast at Sainte-Marie they find Père Labat waiting for them with all the negroes of the Saint-Jacques plantation, to drive them back to their ships.

For other dangers he exhibits absolute unconcern. He studies the phenomena of hurricanes with almost pleasurable interest, while his comrades on the ship abandon hope. When seized with yellow-fever, then known as the Siamese Sickness (*mal de Siam*), he refuses to stay in bed the prescribed time, and rises to say his mass. He faints at the altar; yet a few days later we hear of him on horseback again, travelling over the mountains in the worst and hottest season of the year. . . .

. . . Labat was thirty years old when he went to the Antilles;—he was only forty-two when his work was done. In less than twelve years he made his order the most powerful and wealthy of any in the West Indies,—lifted their property out of bankruptcy to rebuild it upon a foundation of extraordinary prosperity. As Rufz observes without exaggeration, the career of Père Labat in the Antilles seems to more than realize the antique legend of the labors of Hercules. Whithersoever he went, —except in the English colonies,—his passage was memorialized by the rising of churches, convents, and schools,—as well as mills, forts, and refineries. Even cities claim him as their founder. The solidity of his architectural creations is no less remarkable than their excellence of design;—much of what he erected still remains; what has vanished was removed by human agency, and not by decay; and when the old Dominican church at St. Pierre had to be pulled down to make room for a larger edifice, the workmen complained that the stones could not be separated,—that the walls seemed single masses of rock. There can be no doubt, moreover, that he largely influenced the life of the colonies during those years, and expanded their industrial and commercial capacities.

He was sent on a mission to Rome after these things had been done, and never returned from Europe. There he travelled more or less in after-years; but finally settled at Paris, where he prepared and published the voluminous narrative of his own voyages, and other curious books;—manifesting as a writer the same tireless energy he had shown in so many other capacities. He does not, however, appear to have been happy. Again and again he prayed to be sent back to his beloved Antilles, and for some unknown cause the prayer was always refused. To such a character, the restraint of the cloister must have proved a slow agony; but he had to endure it for many long years. He died at Paris in 1738, aged seventy-five.

. . . It was inevitable that such a man should make bitter enemies: his preferences, his position, his activity, his business shrewdness, his necessary self-assertion, must have created secret hate and jealousy even when open malevolence might not dare to show itself. And to these natural results of personal antagonism or opposition were afterwards superadded various resentments—irrational, perhaps, but extremely violent,—caused by the father's cynical frankness as a writer. He spoke freely about the family origin and personal failings of various colonists considered high personages in their own small world; and to this day his book has an evil reputation undeserved in those old creole communities, where any public mention of a family scandal is never forgiven or forgotten. . . . But probably even before his work appeared it had been secretly resolved that he should never be permitted to return to Martinique or Guadeloupe after his European mission. The exact purpose of the Government in this policy remains a mystery,—whatever ingenious writers may have alleged to the contrary. We only know that M. Adrien Dessalles,—the trustworthy historian of Martinique,—while searching among the old *Archives de la Marine*, found there a ministerial letter to the Intendant de Vaucresson in which this statement occurs:—

. . . "Le Père Labat shall never be suffered to return to the colonies, whatever efforts he may make to obtain permission."

IV.

ONE rises from the perusal of the "Nouveau Voyage aux Isles de l'Amérique" with a feeling approaching regret; for although the six pursy little volumes composing it—full of quaint drawings, plans, and odd attempts at topographical maps—reveal a prolix writer, Père Labat is always able to interest. He reminds you of one of those slow, precise, old-fashioned conversationalists who measure the weight of every word and never leave anything to the imagination of the audience, yet who invariably reward the patience of their listeners sooner or later by reflections of surprising profundity or theories of a totally novel description. But what particularly impresses the reader of these volumes is not so much the recital of singular incidents and facts as the revelation of the author's personality. Reading him, you divine a character of enormous force,—gifted but unevenly balanced; singularly shrewd in worldly affairs, and surprisingly credulous in other respects; superstitious and yet cynical; unsympathetic by his positivism, but agreeable through natural desire to give pleasure; just by nature, yet capable of merciless severity; profoundly devout, but withal tolerant for his calling and his time. He is sufficiently free from petty bigotry to make fun of the scruples of his brethren in the matter of employing heretics; and his account of the manner in which he secured the services of a first-class refiner for the Martinique plantation at the Fond Saint-Jacques is not the least amusing page in the book. He writes: "The religious who had been appointed Superior in Guadeloupe wrote me that he would find it difficult to employ this refiner because the man was a Lutheran. This scruple gave me pleasure, as I had long wanted to have him upon our plantation in the Fond Saint-Jacques, but did not know how I would be able to manage it. I wrote to the Superior at once that all he had to do was to send the man to me, because it was a matter of indifference to me whether the sugar he might make were Catholic or Lutheran sugar, provided it were very white."* He displays equal frankness in confessing an error or a discomfiture. He acknowledges that while Professor of Mathematics and Philosophy, he used to teach that there were no tides in the tropics; and in a discussion as to whether the *diablotin* (a now almost extinct species of West Indian nocturnal bird) were fish or flesh, and might or might not be eaten in Lent, he tells us that he was fairly worsted,—(although he could cite the celebrated myth of the "barnacle-geese" as a "fact" in justification of one's right to doubt the nature of diablotins).

One has reason to suspect that Père Labat, notwithstanding his references to the decision of the Church that diablotins were not birds, felt quite well assured within himself that they were. There is a sly humor in his story of these controversies, which would appear to imply that while well pleased at the

*Vol. iii., p. 382–3, Edition of 1722.

decision referred to, he knew all about diablotins. Moreover, the father betrays certain tendencies to gormandize not altogether in harmony with the profession of an ascetic. . . . There were parrots in nearly all of the French Antilles in those days;* and Père Labat does not attempt to conceal his fondness for—cooked parrots. (He does not appear to have cared much for them as pets: if they could not talk well, he condemned them forthwith to the pot.) "They all live upon fruits and seeds," he writes, "and their flesh contracts the odor and color of that particular fruit or seed they feed upon. They become exceedingly fat in the season when the guavas are ripe; and when they eat the seeds of the *Bois d'Inde* they have an odor of nutmeg and cloves which is delightful (*une odeur de muscade et de girofle qui fait plaisir*)." He recommends four superior ways of preparing them, as well as other fowls, for the table, of which the first and the best way is "to pluck them alive, then to make them swallow vinegar, and then to strangle them while they have the vinegar still in their throats by twisting their necks"; and the fourth way is "to skin them alive" (*de les écorcher tout en vie*). . . . "It is certain," he continues, "that these ways are excellent, and that fowls that have to be cooked in a hurry thereby obtain an admirable tenderness (*une tendreté admirable*)." Then he makes a brief apology to his readers, not for the inhumanity of his recipes, but for a display of culinary knowledge scarcely becoming a monk, and acquired only through those peculiar necessities which colonial life in the tropics imposed upon all alike. The touch of cruelty here revealed produces an impression which there is little in the entire work capable of modifying. Labat seems to have possessed but a very small quantity of altruism; his cynicism on the subject of animal suffering is not offset by any visible sympathy with human pain;—he never compassionates: you may seek in vain through all his pages for one gleam of the goodness of gentle Père Du Tertre, who, filled with intense pity for the condition of the blacks, prays masters to be merciful and just to their slaves for the love of God. Labat suggests, on the

---

*The parrots of Martinique he describes as having been green, with slate-colored plumage on the top of the head, mixed with a little red, and as having a few red feathers in the wings, throat, and tail.

other hand, that slavery is a good means of redeeming negroes from superstition and saving their souls from hell: he selects and purchases them himself for the Saint-Jacques plantation, never makes a mistake or a bad bargain, and never appears to feel a particle of commiseration for their lot. In fact, the emotional feeling displayed by Père Du Tertre (whom he mocks slyly betimes) must have seemed to him rather condemnable than praiseworthy; for Labat regarded the negro as a natural child of the devil,—a born sorcerer,—an evil being wielding occult power.

Perhaps the chapters on negro sorcery are the most astonishing in the book, displaying on the part of this otherwise hard and practical nature a credulity almost without limit. After having related how he had a certain negro sent out of the country "who predicted the arrival of vessels and other things to come,—in so far, at least, as the devil himself was able to know and reveal these matters to him," he plainly states his own belief in magic as follows:—

"I know there are many people who consider as pure imagination, and as silly stories, or positive falsehoods, all that is related about sorcerers and their compacts with the devil. I was myself for a long time of this opinion. Moreover, I am aware that what is said on this subject is frequently exaggerated; but I am now convinced it must be acknowledged that all which has been related is not entirely false, although perhaps it may not be entirely true." . . .

Therewith he begins to relate stories upon what may have seemed unimpeachable authority in those days. The first incident narrated took place, he assures us, in the Martinique Dominican convent, shortly before his arrival in the colony. One of the fathers, Père Fraise, had had brought to Martinique, "from the kingdom of Juda (?) in Guinea," a little negro about nine or ten years old. Not long afterwards there was a serious drought, and the monks prayed vainly for rain. Then the negro child, who had begun to understand and speak a little French, told his masters that he was a Rain-maker, that he could obtain them all the rain they wanted. "This proposition," says Père Labat, "greatly astonished the fathers: they consulted together, and at last, curiosity overcoming reason, they gave their consent that this unbaptized child should make some rain fall on their garden." The unbaptized child asked them if they wanted "a big or a little rain"; they answered that a moderate rain would satisfy them. Thereupon the little negro got three oranges, and placed them on the ground in a line at a short distance from one another, and bowed down before each of them in turn, muttering words in an unknown tongue. Then he got three small orange-branches, stuck a branch in each orange, and repeated his prostrations and mutterings;—after which he took one of the branches, stood up, and watched the horizon. A small cloud appeared, and he pointed the branch at it. It approached swiftly, rested above the garden, and sent down a copious shower of rain. Then the boy made a hole in the ground, and buried the oranges and the branches. The fathers were amazed to find that not a single drop of rain had fallen outside their garden. They asked the boy who had taught him this sorcery, and he answered them that among the blacks on board the slave-ship which had brought him over there were some Rain-makers who had taught him. Père Labat declares there is no question as to the truth of the occurrence: he cites the names of Père Fraise, Père Rosié, Père Temple, and Père Bournot,—all members of his own order,—as trustworthy witnesses of this incident.

Père Labat displays equal credulity in his recital of a still more extravagant story told him by Madame la Comtesse du Gênes. M. le Comte du Gênes, husband of the lady in question, and commander of a French squadron, captured the English fort of Gorea in 1696, and made prisoners of all the English slaves in the service of the factory there established. But the vessel on which these were embarked was unable to leave the coast, in spite of a good breeze: she seemed bewitched. Some of the slaves finally told the captain there was a negress on board who had enchanted the ship, and who had the power to "dry up the hearts" of all who refused to obey her. A number of deaths taking place among the blacks, the captain ordered autopsies made, and it was found that the hearts of the dead negroes were desiccated. The negress was taken on deck, tied to a gun and whipped, but uttered no cry;—the ship's surgeon, angered at her stoicism, took a hand in the punishment, and flogged her "with all his force." Thereupon she told him that inasmuch as he had abused her without reason, his heart also should be "dried up." He died next day; and his heart was found in the condition predicted. All this time the ship could not be made to move in any direction; and the negress told the captain that until he should put her and her companions on shore he would never be able to sail. To convince him of her power she further asked him to place three fresh melons in a chest, to lock the chest and put a guard over it; when she should tell him to unlock it, there would be no melons there. The captain made the experiment. When the chest was opened, the melons appeared to be there; but on touching them it was found that only the outer rind remained: the interior had been dried up,—like the surgeon's heart. Thereupon the captain put the witch and her friends ashore, and sailed away without further trouble.

Another story of African sorcery for the truth of which Père Labat earnestly vouches is the following:—

A negro was sentenced to be burned alive for witchcraft at St. Thomas in 1701: his principal crime was "having made a little figure of baked clay to speak." A certain creole, meeting the negro on his way to the place of execution, jeeringly observed, "Well, you cannot make your little figure talk any more now;—it has been broken." "If the gentleman allow me," replied the prisoner, "I will make the cane he carries in his hand speak." The creole's curiosity was strongly aroused: he prevailed upon the guards to halt a few minutes, and permit the prisoner to make the experiment. The negro then took the cane, stuck it into the ground in the middle of the road, whispered something to it, and asked the gentleman what he wished to know. "I would like to know," answered the latter, "whether the ship —— has yet sailed from Europe, and when she will arrive." "Put your ear to the head of the cane," said the negro. On doing so the creole distinctly heard a thin voice which informed him that the vessel in question had left a certain French port on such a date; that she would reach St. Thomas within three days; that she had been delayed on her voyage by a storm which had carried away her foretop and her mizzen sail; that she had such and such passengers on board (mentioning the names), all in good health. . . . After this incident the negro was burned alive; but within three days the vessel arrived in port, and the prediction or divination was found to have been absolutely correct in every particular.

. . . Père Labat in no way disapproves the atrocious sentence inflicted upon the wretched negro: in his opinion such predictions were made by the power and with the personal aid of the devil; and for those who knowingly maintained relations with the devil, he could not have regarded any punishment too severe. That he could be harsh enough himself is amply shown in various accounts of his own personal experience with alleged sorcerers, and especially in the narration of his dealings with one—apparently a sort of African doctor—who was a slave on a neighboring plantation, but used to visit the Saint-Jacques quarters by stealth to practise his art. One of the slaves of the order, a negress, falling very sick, the wizard was sent for; and he came with all his paraphernalia—little earthen pots and fetiches, etc.—during the night. He began to practise his incantations, without the least suspicion that Père Labat was watching him through a chink; and, after having consulted his fetiches, he told the sick woman she would die within four days. At this juncture the priest suddenly burst in the door and entered, followed by several powerful slaves. He dashed to pieces the soothsayer's articles, and attempted to reassure the frightened negress, by declaring the prediction a lie inspired by the devil. Then he had the sorcerer stripped and flogged in his presence.

"I had him given," he calmly observes, "about (*environ*) three hundred lashes, which flayed him (*l'écorchait*) from his shoulders to his knees. He screamed like a madman. All the negroes trembled, and assured me that the devil would cause my death. . . . Then I had the wizard put in irons, after having had him well washed with a *pimentade*,—that is to say, with brine in which pimentos and small lemons have been crushed. This causes a horrible pain to those skinned by the whip but it is a certain remedy against gangrene." . . .

And then he sent the poor wretch back to his master with a note requesting the latter to repeat the punishment,—a demand that seems to have been approved, as the owner of the negro was "a man who feared God." Yet Père Labat is obliged to confess that in spite of all his efforts, the sick negress died on the fourth day,—as the sorcerer had predicted. This fact must have strongly confirmed his belief that the devil was at the bottom of the whole affair, and caused him to doubt whether even a flogging of *about* three hundred lashes, followed by a pimentade, were sufficient chastisement for the miserable black. Perhaps the tradition of this frightful whipping may have had something to do with the terror which still attaches to the name of the Dominican in Martinique. The legal extreme punishment was twenty-nine lashes.

Père Labat also avers that in his time the negroes were in the habit of carrying sticks which had the power of imparting to any portion of the human body touched by them a most severe chronic pain. He at first believed, he says, that these pains were merely rheumatic; but after all known remedies for rheumatism had been fruitlessly applied, he became convinced there was something occult and diabolical in the manner of using and preparing these sticks. . . . A fact worthy of note is that this belief is still prevalent in Martinique!

One hardly ever meets in the country a negro who does not carry either a stick or a cutlass, or both. The cutlass is indispensable to those who work in the woods or upon plantations; the stick is carried both as a protection against snakes and as a weapon of offence and defence in village quarrels, for unless a negro be extraordinarily drunk, he will not strike his fellow with a cutlass. The sticks are usually made of a strong dense wood: those most sought after of a material termed *moudongue*,* almost as tough, but much lighter than, our hickory. On inquiring whether any of the sticks thus carried were held to possess magic powers, I was assured by many country people that there were men who knew a peculiar method of "arranging" sticks so that to touch any person with them even lightly, *and through any thickness of clothing*, would produce terrible and continuous pain.

---

*The creole word *moudongue* is said to be a corruption of *Mondongue*, the name of an African coast tribe who had the reputation of being cannibals. A Mondongue slave on the plantations was generally feared by his fellow-blacks of other tribes; and the name of the cannibal race became transformed into an adjective to denote anything formidable or terrible. A blow with a stick made of the wood described being greatly dreaded, the term was applied first to the stick, and afterward to the wood itself.

Believing in these things, and withal unable to decide whether the sun revolved about the earth, or the earth about the sun,* Père Labat was, nevertheless, no more credulous and no more ignorant than the average missionary of his time: it is only by contrast with his practical perspicacity in other matters, his worldly rationalism and executive shrewdness, that this superstitious naïveté impresses one as odd. And how singular sometimes is the irony of Time! All the wonderful work the Dominican accomplished has been forgotten by the people; while all the witchcrafts that he warred against survive and flourish openly; and his very name is seldom uttered but in connection with superstitions,—has been, in fact, preserved among the blacks by the power of superstition alone, by the belief in zombis and goblins. . . . "*Mi! ti manmaille-là, moin ké fai Pè Labatt vini pouend ou!*" . . .

V.

FEW habitants of St. Pierre now remember that the beautiful park behind the cathedral used to be called the Savanna of the White Fathers,—and the long shadowed meadow beside the Roxelane, the Savanna of the Black Fathers: the Jesuits. All the great religious orders have long since disappeared from the colony: their edifices have been either converted to other uses or demolished; their estates have passed into other hands. . . . Were their labors, then, productive of merely ephemeral results? —was the colossal work of a Père Labat all in vain, so far as the future is concerned? The question is not easily answered; but it is worth considering.

Of course the material prosperity which such men toiled to obtain for their order represented nothing more, even to their eyes, than the means of self-maintenance, and the accumulation of force necessary for the future missionary labors of the monastic community. The real ultimate purpose was, not the

---

*Accounting for the origin of the trade-winds, he writes: "I say that the Trade-Winds do not exist in the Torrid Zone merely by chance; forasmuch as the cause which produces them is very necessary, very sure, and very continuous, since they result *either from the movement of the Earth around the Sun, or from the movement of the Sun around the Earth. Whether it be the one or the other of these two great bodies which moves* . . ." etc.

acquisition of power for the order, but for the Church, of which the orders represented only a portion of the force militant; and this purpose did not fail of accomplishment. The orders passed away only when their labors had been completed, —when Martinique had become (exteriorly, at least) more Catholic than Rome itself,—after the missionaries had done all that religious zeal could do in moulding and remoulding the human material under their control. These men could scarcely have anticipated those social and political changes which the future reserved for the colonies, and which no ecclesiastical sagacity could, in any event, have provided against. It is in the existing religious condition of these communities that one may observe and estimate the character and the probable duration of the real work accomplished by the missions.

. . . Even after a prolonged residence in Martinique, its visible religious condition continues to impress one as something phenomenal. A stranger, who has no opportunity to penetrate into the home life of the people, will not, perhaps, discern the full extent of the religious sentiment; but, nevertheless, however brief his stay, he will observe enough of the extravagant symbolism of the cult to fill him with surprise. Wherever he may choose to ride or to walk, he is certain to encounter shrines, statues of saints, or immense crucifixes. Should he climb up to the clouds of the peaks, he will find them all along the way;— he will perceive them waiting for him, looming through the mists of the heights; and passing through the loveliest ravines, he will see niches hollowed out in the volcanic rocks, above and below him, or contrived in the trunks of trees bending over precipices, often in places so difficult of access that he wonders how the work could have been accomplished. All this has been done by the various property-owners throughout the country: it is the traditional custom to do it—brings good-luck! After a longer stay in the island, one discovers also that in almost every room of every dwelling—stone residence, wooden cottage, or palm-thatched ajoupa—there is a *chapelle*: that is, a sort of large bracket fastened to the wall, on which crosses or images are placed, with vases of flowers, and lamps or wax-tapers to be burned at night. Sometimes, moreover, statues are placed in windows, or above door-ways;—and all passers-by take off their hats to these. Over the porch of the cottage in a mountain

A Wayside Shrine, or Chapelle.

village, where I lived for some weeks, there was an absurd little window contrived,—a sort of purely ornamental dormer,—and in this a Virgin about five inches high had been placed. At a little distance it looked like a toy,—a child's doll forgotten there; and a doll I always supposed it to be, until one day that I saw a long procession of black laborers passing before the house, every one of whom took off his hat to it. . . . My bed-chamber in the same cottage resembled a religious museum. On the chapelle there were no less than eight Virgins, varying in height from one to sixteen inches,—a St. Joseph,—a St. John, —a crucifix,—and a host of little objects in the shape of hearts or crosses, each having some special religious significance;—while the walls were covered with framed certificates of baptism, "first-communion," confirmation, and other documents commemorating the whole church life of the family for two generations.

   . . . Certainly the first impression created by this perpetual display of crosses, statues, and miniature chapels is not pleasing, —particularly as the work is often inartistic to a degree bordering upon the grotesque, and nothing resembling art is anywhere visible. Millions of francs must have been consumed in these creations, which have the rudeness of mediævalism without its emotional sincerity, and which—amid the loveliness of tropic nature, the grace of palms, the many-colored fire of liana blossoms —jar on the æsthetic sense with an almost brutal violence. Yet there is a veiled poetry in these silent populations of plaster and wood and stone. They represent something older than the Middle Ages, older than Christianity,—something strangely distorted and transformed, it is true, but recognizably conserved by the Latin race from those antique years when every home had its beloved ghosts, when every wood or hill or spring had its gracious divinity, and the boundaries of all fields were marked and guarded by statues of gods.

   Instances of iconoclasm are of course highly rare in a country of which no native—rich or poor, white or half-breed—fails to doff his hat before every shrine, cross, or image he may happen to pass. Those merchants of St. Pierre or of Fort-de-France living only a few miles out of the city must certainly perform a vast number of reverences on their way to or from business;—I saw one old gentleman uncover his white head about twenty times in the course of a fifteen minutes' walk. I never heard of but one image-breaker in Martinique; and his act was the result of superstition, not of any hostility to popular faith or custom: it was prompted by the same childish feeling which moves Italian fishermen sometimes to curse St. Antony or to give his image a ducking in bad weather. This Martinique iconoclast was a negro cattle-driver who one day, feeling badly in need of a glass of tafia, perhaps, left the animals intrusted to him in care of a plaster image of the Virgin, with this menace (the phrase is on record):—

"*Moin ka quitté bef-là ba ou pou gàdé ba moin. Quand moin vini, si moin pa trouvé compte-moin, moin ké fouté ou vingt-nèf coudfouèt!*" (I leave these cattle with you to take care of for me. When I come back, if I don't find them all here, I'll give you twenty-nine lashes.)

Returning about half an hour later, he was greatly enraged to find his animals scattered in every direction;—and, rushing at the statue, he broke it from the pedestal, flung it upon the ground, and gave it twenty-nine lashes with his bull-whip. For this he was arrested, tried, and sentenced to imprisonment, with hard labor, for life! In those days there were no colored magistrates;—the judges were all *békés*.

"Rather a severe sentence," I remarked to my informant, a planter who conducted me to the scene of the alleged sacrilege.

"Severe, yes," he answered;—"and I suppose the act would seem to you more idiotic than criminal. But here, in Martinique, there were large questions involved by such an offence. Relying, as we have always done to some extent, upon religious influence as a factor in the maintenance of social order, the negro's act seemed a dangerous example." . . .

That the Church remains still rich and prosperous in Martinique there can be no question; but whether it continues to wield any powerful influence in the maintenance of social order is more than doubtful. A Polynesian laxity of morals among the black and colored population, and the history of race-hatreds and revolutions inspired by race-hate, would indicate that neither in ethics nor in politics does it possess any preponderant authority. By expelling various religious orders;—by establishing lay schools, lycées, and other educational

institutions where the teaching is largely characterized by aggressive antagonism to Catholic ideas;—by the removal of crucifixes and images from public buildings, French Radicalism
did not inflict any great blow upon Church interests. So far as
the white, and, one may say, the wealthy, population is concerned, the Church triumphs in her hostility to the Government schools; and to the same extent she holds an educational
monopoly. No white creole would dream of sending his children to a lay school or a lycée—notwithstanding the unques-
tionable superiority of the educational system in the latter
institutions;—and, although obliged, as the chief tax-paying
class, to bear the burden of maintaining these establishments,
the whites hold them in such horror that the Government professors are socially ostracized. No doubt the prejudice or pride
which abhors mixed schools aids the Church in this respect;
she herself recognizes race-feeling, keeps her schools unmixed,
and even in her convents, it is said, obliges the colored nuns to
serve the white! For more than two centuries every white generation has been religiously moulded in the seminaries and
convents; and among the native whites one never hears an
overt declaration of free-thought opinion. Except among the
colored men educated in the Government schools, or their foreign professors, there are no avowed free-thinkers;—and this,
not because the creole whites, many of whom have been educated in Paris, are naturally narrow-minded, or incapable of
sympathy with the mental expansion of the age, but because
the religious question at Martinique has become so intimately
complicated with the social and political one, concerning which
there can be no compromise whatever, that to divorce the
former from the latter is impossible. Roman Catholicism is an
element of the cement which holds creole society together; and
it is noteworthy that other creeds are not represented. I knew
only of one Episcopalian and one Methodist in the island,—
and heard a sort of legend about a solitary Jew whose whereabouts I never could discover;—but these were strangers.

　It was only through the establishment of universal suffrage,
which placed the white population at the mercy of its former
slaves, that the Roman Church sustained any serious injury. All
local positions are filled by blacks or men of color; no white
creole can obtain a public office or take part in legislation; and

the whole power of the black vote is ungenerously used against the interests of the class thus politically disinherited. The Church suffers in consequence: her power depended upon her intimate union with the wealthy and dominant class; and she will never be forgiven by those now in power for her sympathetic support of that class in other years. Politics yearly intensify this hostility; and as the only hope for the restoration of the whites to power, and of the Church to its old position, lies in the possibility of another empire or a revival of the monarchy, the white creoles and their Church are forced into hostility against republicanism and the republic. And political newspapers continually attack Roman Catholicism,—mock its tenets and teachings,—ridicule its dogmas and ceremonies,—satirize its priests.

In the cities and towns the Church indeed appears to retain a large place in the affection of the poorer classes;—her ceremonies are always well attended; money pours into her coffers; and one can still witness the curious annual procession of the "converted,"—aged women of color and negresses going to communion for the first time, all wearing snow-white turbans in honor of the event. But among the country people, where the dangerous forces of revolution exist, Christian feeling is almost stifled by ghastly beliefs of African origin;—the images and crucifixes still command respect, but this respect is inspired by a feeling purely fetichistic. With the political dispossession of the whites, certain dark powers, previously concealed or repressed, have obtained formidable development. The old enemy of Père Labat, the wizard (the *quimboiseur*), already wields more authority than the priest, exercises more terror than the magistrate, commands more confidence than the physician. The educated mulatto class may affect to despise him;—but he is preparing their overthrow in the dark. Astonishing is the persistence with which the African has clung to these beliefs and practices, so zealously warred upon by the Church and so mercilessly punished by the courts for centuries. He still goes to mass, and sends his children to the priest; but he goes more often to the quimboiseur and the "*magnetise*." He finds use for both beliefs, but gives large preference to the savage one,—just as he prefers the pattering of his tamtam to the music of the military band at the *Savane du Fort.* . . . And should it come to pass that Martinique be ever totally abandoned by its white population,—an event by no means improbable in the present order of things,—the fate of the ecclesiastical fabric so toil-somely reared by the monastic orders is not difficult to surmise.

VI.

FROM my window in the old Rue du Bois-Morin,—which climbs the foot of Morne Labelle by successions of high stone steps,—all the southern end of the city is visible as in a bird's-eye view. Under me is a long peaking of red-scaled roofs,—gables and dormer-windows,—with clouds of bright green here and there,—foliage of tamarind and corossolier;—westward purples and flames the great circle of the Caribbean Sea;—east and south, towering to the violet sky, curve the volcanic hills, green-clad from base to summit;—and right before me the beautiful Morne d'Orange, all palm-plumed and wood-wrapped, trends seaward and southward. And every night, after the stars come out, I see moving lights there,—lantern fires guiding the mountain-dwellers home; but I look in vain for the light of Père Labat.

And nevertheless,—although no believer in ghosts,—I see thee very plainly sometimes, thou quaint White Father, moving through winter-mists in the narrower Paris of another century; musing upon the churches that arose at thy bidding under tropic skies; dreaming of the primeval valleys changed by thy will to green-gold seas of cane,—and the strong mill that will bear thy name for two hundred years (it stands solid unto this day),—and the habitations made for thy brethren in pleasant palmy places,—and the luminous peace of thy Martinique convent,—and odor of roasting parrots fattened upon *grains de bois d'Inde* and guavas,—"*l'odeur de muscade et de girofle qui fait plaisir.*" . . .

Eh, Père Labat!—what changes there have been since thy day! The White Fathers have no place here now; and the Black Fathers, too, have been driven from the land, leaving only as a memory of them the perfect and ponderous architecture of the Perinnelle plantation-buildings, and the appellation of the river still known as the Rivière des Pères. Also the Ursulines are gone, leaving only their name on the corner of a crumbling street. And there are no more slaves; and there are new races of colors thou wouldst deem scandalous though beautiful; and there are no more parrots; and there are no more diablotins. And the grand woods thou sawest in their primitive and inviolate beauty, as if fresh from the Creator's touch in the morning of the world, are passing away; the secular trees are being converted into charcoal, or sawn into timber for the boat-builders: thou shouldst see two hundred men pulling some forest giant down to the sea upon the two-wheeled screaming thing they call a "devil" (*yon diabe*),—cric-crac!—cric-crac!—all chanting together:—

> "*Soh-soh!—yaïe-yah!*
> *Rhâlé bois-canot!*"

And all that ephemeral man has had power to change has been changed,—ideas, morals, beliefs, the whole social fabric. But the eternal summer remains,—and the Hesperian magnificence of azure sky and violet sea,—and the jewel-colors of the perpetual hills;—the same tepid winds that rippled thy cane-fields two hundred years ago still blow over Sainte-Marie;—the same purple shadows lengthen and dwindle and turn with the wheeling of the sun. God's witchery still fills this land; and the heart of the stranger is even yet snared by the beauty of it; and the dreams of him that forsakes it will surely be haunted—even as were thine own, Père Labat—by memories of its Eden-summer: the sudden leap of the light over a thousand peaks in the glory of tropic dawn,—the perfumed peace of enormous azure noons,—and shapes of palm wind-rocked in the burning of colossal sunsets,—and the silent flickering of the great fireflies through the lukewarm darkness, when mothers call their children home. . . . "*Mi fanal Pè Labatt!—mi Pè Labatt ka vini pouend ou!*"

La Guiablesse

NIGHT in all countries brings with it vaguenesses and illusions which terrify certain imaginations;—but in the tropics it produces effects peculiarly impressive and peculiarly sinister. Shapes of vegetation that startle even while the sun shines upon them assume, after his setting, a grimness,—a grotesquery, —a suggestiveness for which there is no name. . . . In the North a tree is simply tree;—here it is a personality that makes itself felt; it has a vague physiognomy, an indefinable *Me*: it is an Individual (with a capital I); it is a Being (with a capital B).

From the high woods, as the moon mounts, fantastic darknesses descend into the roads,—black distortions, mockeries, bad dreams,—an endless procession of goblins. Least startling are the shadows flung down by the various forms of palm, because instantly recognizable;—yet these take the semblance of giant fingers opening and closing over the way, or a black crawling of unutterable spiders. . . .

Nevertheless, these phasma seldom alarm the solitary and belated Bitaco: the darknesses that creep stealthily along the path have no frightful signification for him,—do not appeal to his imagination;—if he suddenly starts and stops and stares, it is not because of such shapes, but because he has perceived two specks of orange light, and is not yet sure whether they are only fire-flies, or the eyes of a trigonocephalus. The spectres of his fancy have nothing in common with those indistinct and monstrous umbrages: what he most fears, next to the deadly serpent, are human witchcrafts. A white rag, an old bone lying in the path, might be a *maléfice* which, if trodden upon, would cause his leg to blacken and swell up to the size of the limb of an elephant;—an unopened bundle of plantain leaves or of bamboo strippings, dropped by the way-side, might contain the skin of a *Soucou-yan*. But the ghastly being who doffs or dons his skin at will—and the Zombi—and the *Moun-Mò*—may be quelled or exorcised by prayer; and the lights of shrines, the white gleaming of crosses, continually remind the traveller of his duty to the Powers that save. All along the way there are shrines at intervals, not very far apart: while standing in the radiance of one niche-lamp, you may perhaps discern the glow of the next, if the road be level and straight. They are almost everywhere, —shining along the skirts of the woods, at the entrance of ravines, by the verges of precipices;—there is a cross even upon the summit of the loftiest peak in the island. And the night-walker removes his hat each time his bare feet touch the soft stream of yellow light outpoured from the illuminated shrine of a white Virgin or a white Christ. These are good ghostly company for him;—he salutes them, talks to them, tells them his pains or fears: their blanched faces seem to him full of sympathy; —they appear to cheer him voicelessly as he strides from gloom to gloom, under the goblinry of those woods which tower black as ebony under the stars. . . . And he has other companionship. One of the greatest terrors of darkness in other lands does not exist here after the setting of the sun,—the terror of *Silence*. . . . Tropical night is full of voices;—extraordinary populations of crickets are trilling; nations of tree-frogs are chanting; the *Cabri-des-bois*,* or *cra-cra*, almost deafens you with the wheezy bleating sound by which it earned its creole name; birds pipe: everything that bells, ululates, drones, clacks, guggles, joins the enormous chorus; and you fancy you see all the shadows vibrating to the force of this vocal storm. The true life of Nature in the tropics begins with the darkness, ends with the light.

And it is partly, perhaps, because of these conditions that the coming of the dawn does not dissipate all fears of the supernatural. *I ni pè zombi mênm gran'-jou* (he is afraid of ghosts even in broad daylight) is a phrase which does not sound exaggerated in these latitudes,—not, at least, to any one knowing something of the conditions that nourish or inspire weird beliefs. In the awful peace of tropical day, in the hush of the woods, the solemn silence of the hills (broken only by torrent voices that cannot make themselves heard at night), even in the amazing luminosity, there is a something apparitional and weird,— something that seems to weigh upon the world like a measureless haunting. So still all Nature's chambers are that a loud

---

*In creole, *cabritt-bois*,—("the Wood-Kid.")—a colossal cricket. Precisely at half-past four in the morning it becomes silent; and for thousands of early risers too poor to own a clock, the cessation of its song is the signal to get up.

utterance jars upon the ear brutally, like a burst of laughter in a sanctuary. With all its luxuriance of color, with all its violence of light, this tropical day has its ghostliness and its ghosts. Among the people of color there are many who believe that even at noon—when the boulevards behind the city are most deserted—the zombis will show themselves to solitary loiterers.

II.

. . . HERE a doubt occurs to me,—a doubt regarding the precise nature of a word, which I call upon Adou to explain. Adou is the daughter of the kind old capresse from whom I rent my room in this little mountain cottage. The mother is almost precisely the color of cinnamon; the daughter's complexion is brighter,—the ripe tint of an orange. . . . Adou tells me creole stories and *tim-tim*. Adou knows all about ghosts, and believes in them. So does Adou's extraordinarily tall brother, Yébé,—my guide among the mountains.

—"Adou," I ask, "what is a zombi?"

The smile that showed Adou's beautiful white teeth has instantly disappeared; and she answers, very seriously, that she has never seen a zombi, and does not want to see one.

—"*Moin pa té janmain ouè zombi,—pa 'lè ouè ça, moin!*"

—"But, Adou, child, I did not ask you whether you ever saw It;—I asked you only to tell me what It is like?" . . .

Adou hesitates a little, and answers:

—"*Zombi? Mais ça fai désòde lanuitt, zombi!*"

Ah! it is Something which "makes disorder at night." Still, that is not a satisfactory explanation. "Is it the spectre of a dead person, Adou? Is it *one who comes back?*"

—"*Non, Missié,—non; çé pa ça.*"

—"Not that? . . . Then what was it you said the other night when you were afraid to pass the cemetery on an errand,—*ça ou té ka di*, Adou?"

—"Moin té ka di: 'Moin pa lé k'allé bò cimétiè-là pa ouappò moun-mò;—moun-mò ké barré moin: moin pa sé pè vini enco.'" (*I said, "I do not want to go by that cemetery because of the dead folk;—the dead folk will bar the way, and I cannot get back again."*)

—"And you believe that, Adou?"

—"Yes, that is what they say . . . And if you go into the cemetery at night you cannot come out again: the dead folk will stop you—*moun-mò ké barré ou.*" . . .

—"But are the dead folk zombis, Adou?"

—"No; the moun-mò are not zombis. The zombis go everywhere: the dead folk remain in the graveyard. . . . Except on the Night of All Souls: then they go to the houses of their people everywhere."

—"Adou, if after the doors and windows were locked and barred you were to see entering your room in the middle of the night, a Woman fourteen feet high?" . . .

—"*Ah! pa pàlé ça!!*" . . .

—"No! tell me, Adou?"

—"Why, yes: that would be a zombi. It is the zombis who make all those noises at night one cannot understand. . . . Or, again, if I were to see a dog that high [she holds her hand about five feet above the floor] coming into our house at night, I would scream: *Mi Zombi!*"

. . . Then it suddenly occurs to Adou that her mother knows something about zombis.

—"*Ou! Manman!*"

—"*Eti!*" answers old Théréza's voice from the little outbuilding where the evening meal is being prepared, over a charcoal furnace, in an earthen canari.

—"*Missié-là ka mandé savé ça ça yé yonne zombi;—vini ti bouin!*" . . . The mother laughs, abandons her canari, and comes in to tell me all she knows about the weird word.

—"*I ni pé zombi*"—I find from old Théréza's explanations—is a phrase indefinite as our own vague expressions, "afraid of ghosts," "afraid of the dark." But the word "Zombi" also has special strange meanings. . . . "Ou passé nans grand chimin lanuitt, épi ou ka ouè gouôs difé, épi plis ou ka vini assou difé-à pli ou ka ouè difé-à ka màché: çé zombi ka fai ça. . . . Encò, chouval ka passé,—chouval ka ni anni toua patt: ça zombi." (You pass along the high-road at night, and you see a great fire, and the more you walk to get to it the more it moves away: it is the zombi makes that. . . . Or a horse *with only three legs* passes you: that is a zombi.)

—"How big is the fire that the zombi makes?" I ask.

—"It fills the whole road," answers Théréza: "*li ka rempli toutt chimin-là.* Folk call those fires the Evil Fires,—*mauvai difé*;—and if you follow them they will lead you into chasms, —*ou ké tombé adans labîme.*" . . .

And then she tells me this:

—"Baidaux was a mad man of color who used to live at St. Pierre, in the Street of the Precipice. He was not dangerous,— never did any harm;—his sister used to take care of him. And what I am going to relate is true,—*çe zhistouè veritabe!*

"One day Baidaux said to his sister: 'Moin ni yonne yche, va!—ou pa connaitt li!' [I have a child, ah!—you never saw it!] His sister paid no attention to what he said that day; but the next day he said it again, and the next, and the next, and every day after,—so that his sister at last became much annoyed by it, and used to cry out: 'Ah! mais pé guiole ou, Baidaux! ou fou pou embêté moin conm ça!—ou bien fou!' . . . But he tormented her that way for months and for years.

"One evening he went out, and only came home at midnight leading a child by the hand,—a black child he had found in the street; and he said to his sister:—

"'Mi yche-là moin mené ba ou! Tou léjou moin té ka di ou moin tini yonne yche: on pa té 'lè couè,—eh, ben! MI Y!' [Look at the child I have brought you! Every day I have been telling you I had a child: you would not believe me,—very well, LOOK AT HIM!]

"The sister gave one look, and cried out: 'Baidaux, otí ou pouend yche-là?' . . . For the child was growing taller and taller every moment. . . . And Baidaux,—because he was mad,—kept saying: 'Çé yche-moin! çé yche-moin!' [It is my child!]

"And the sister threw open the shutters and screamed to all the neighbors,—'*Sécou, sécou, sécou! Vini oué ça Baidaux mené ba moin!*' [Help! help! Come see what Baidaux has brought in here!] And the child said to Baidaux: '*Ou ni bonhè ou fou!*' [You are lucky that you are mad!] . . . Then all the neighbors came running in; but they could not see anything: the Zombi was gone." . . .

III.

. . . As I was saying, the hours of vastest light have their weirdness here;—and it is of a Something which walketh abroad under the eye of the sun, even at high noontide, that I desire to speak, while the impressions of a morning journey to the scene of Its last alleged apparition yet remains vivid in my recollection.

You follow the mountain road leading from Calebasse over long meadowed levels two thousand feet above the ocean, into the woods of La Couresse, where it begins to descend slowly, through deep green shadowing, by great zigzags. Then, at a turn, you find yourself unexpectedly looking down upon a planted valley, through plumy fronds of arborescent fern. The surface below seems almost like a lake of gold-green water,—especially when long breaths of mountain-wind set the miles of ripening cane a-ripple from verge to verge: the illusion is marred only by the road, fringed with young cocoa-palms, which serpentines across the luminous plain. East, west, and north the horizon is almost wholly hidden by surging of hills: those nearest are softly shaped and exquisitely green; above them loftier undulations take hazier verdancy and darker shadows; farther yet rise silhouettes of blue or violet tone, with one beautiful breast-shaped peak thrusting up in the midst;—while, westward, over all, topping even the Piton, is a vapory huddling of prodigious shapes—wrinkled, fissured, horned, fantastically tall. . . . Such at least are the tints of the morning. . . . Here and there, between gaps in the volcanic chain, the land hollows into gorges, slopes down into ravines;—and the sea's vast disk of turquoise flames up through the interval. Southwardly those deep woods, through which the way winds down, shut in the view. . . . You do not see the plantation buildings till you have advanced some distance into the valley;—they are hidden by a fold of the land, and stand in a little hollow where the road turns: a great quadrangle of low gray antiquated edifices, heavily walled and buttressed, and roofed with red tiles. The court they form opens upon the main route by an immense archway. Farther along ajoupas begin to line the way,—the dwellings of the field hands,—tiny cottages built with trunks of the arborescent fern or with stems of bamboo, and thatched with cane-straw: each in a little garden planted with bananas, yams, couscous, camanioc, choux-caraïbes, or other things,— and hedged about with roseaux d'Inde and various flowering shrubs.

Thereafter, only the high whispering wildernesses of cane on either hand,—the white silent road winding between its swaying cocoa-trees,—and the tips of hills that seem to glide on before you as you walk, and that take, with the deepening of the afternoon light, such amethystine color as if they were going to become transparent.

IV.

. . . IT is a breezeless and cloudless noon. Under the dazzling downpour of light the hills seem to smoke blue: something like a thin yellow fog haloes the leagues of ripening cane,—a vast reflection. There is no stir in all the green mysterious front of the vine-veiled woods. The palms of the roads keep their heads quite still, as if listening. The canes do not utter a single susurration. Rarely is there such absolute stillness among them: upon the calmest days there are usually rustlings audible, thin cracklings, faint creepings: sounds that betray the passing of some little animal or reptile—a rat or a manicou, or a zanoli or couresse,—more often, however, no harmless lizard or snake, but the deadly *fer-de-lance*. To-day, all these seem to sleep; and there are no workers among the cane to clear away the weeds, —to uproot the *pié-treffe, pié-poule, pié-balai, zhèbe-en-mè*: it is the hour of rest.

A woman is coming along the road,—young, very swarthy, very tall, and barefooted, and black-robed: she wears a high white turban with dark stripes, and a white foulard is thrown about her fine shoulders; she bears no burden, and walks very swiftly and noiselessly. . . . Soundless as shadow the motion of all these naked-footed people is. On any quiet mountain-way, full of curves, where you fancy yourself alone, you may often be startled by something you *feel*, rather than hear, behind you,—surd steps, the springy movement of a long lithe body, dumb oscillations of raiment;—and ere you can turn to look, the haunter swiftly passes with creole greeting of "bon-jou'" or "bonsouè, Missié." This sudden "becoming aware" in broad daylight of a living presence unseen is even more disquieting than that sensation which, in absolute darkness, makes one halt all breathlessly before great solid objects, whose proximity has been revealed by some mute blind emanation of force alone. But it is very seldom, indeed, that the negro or half-breed is thus surprised: he seems to divine an advent by some specialized sense,—like an animal,—and to become conscious of a look directed upon him from any distance or from behind any covert;—to pass within the range of his keen vision unnoticed is almost impossible. . . . And the approach of this woman has been already observed by the habitants of the ajoupas;—dark faces peer out from windows and door-ways;—one half-nude laborer even strolls out to the road-side under the sun to watch her coming. He looks a moment, turns to the hut again, and calls:—

—"Ou-ou! Fafa!"

—"Étí! Gabou!"

—"Vini ti bouin!—mi bel négresse!"

Out rushes Fafa, with his huge straw hat in his hand: "Otí, Gabou?"

—"Mi!"

—"Ah! quimbé moin!" cries black Fafa, enthusiastically; "fouinq! li bel!—Jésis-Maïa! li doux!" . . . Neither ever saw that woman before; and both feel as if they could watch her forever.

There is something superb in the port of a tall young mountain-griffone, or negress, who is comely and knows that she is comely: it is a black poem of artless dignity, primitive grace, savage exultation of movement. . . . "Ou marché tête enlai conm couresse qui ka passé lariviè" (*You walk with your head in the air, like the couresse-serpent swimming a river*) is a creole comparison which pictures perfectly the poise of her neck and chin. And in her walk there is also a serpentine elegance, a sinuous charm: the shoulders do not swing; the cambered torso seems immobile;—but alternately from waist to heel, and from heel to waist, with each long full stride, an indescribable undulation seems to pass; while the folds of her loose robe oscillate to right and left behind her, in perfect libration, with the free swaying of the hips. With us, only a finely trained dancer could attempt such a walk;—with the Martinique woman of color it is natural as the tint of her skin; and this allurement of motion unrestrained is most marked in those who have never worn shoes, and are clad lightly as the women of antiquity,—in two very thin and simple garments;—chemise and *robe-d'indienne*. . . . But whence is she?—of what canton? Not from Vauclin, nor from Lamentin, nor from Marigot,—from Case-Pilote or from Case-Navire: Fafa knows all the people there. Never of Sainte-Anne, nor of Sainte-Luce, nor of Sainte-Marie, nor of Diamant, nor of Gros-Morne, nor of Carbet,—the birthplace of Gabou. Neither is she of the village of the Abysms, which is in the Parish of the Preacher,—nor yet of Ducos nor of François, which are in the Commune of the Holy Ghost. . . .

V.

. . . SHE approaches the ajoupa: both men remove their big straw hats; and both salute her with a simultaneous "Bonjou', Manzell."

—"Bonjou', Missié," she responds, in a sonorous alto, without appearing to notice Gabou,—but smiling upon Fafa as she passes, with her great eyes turned full upon his face. . . . All the libertine blood of the man flames under that look;—he feels as if momentarily wrapped in a blaze of black lightning.

—"Ça ka fai moin pè," exclaims Gabou, turning his face towards the ajoupa. Something indefinable in the gaze of the stranger has terrified him.

—"*Pa ka fai moin pè—fouinq!*" (She does not make me afraid) laughs Fafa, boldly following her with a smiling swagger.

—"Fafa!" cries Gabou, in alarm. "*Fafa, pa fai ça!*"

But Fafa does not heed. The strange woman has slackened her pace, as if inviting pursuit;—another moment and he is at her side.

—"Oti ou ka rété, ché?" he demands, with the boldness of one who knows himself a fine specimen of his race.

—"Zaffai cabritt pa zaffai lapin," she answers, mockingly.

—"Mais pouki ou rhabillé toutt nouè conm ça."

—"Moin pòté deil pou name moin mò."

—"Aïe ya yaïe! . . . Non, vouè!—ça ou kallé atouèlement?"

—"Lanmou pàti: moin pàti deïë lanmou."

—"Ho!—ou ni guêpe, anh?"

—"Zanoli bail yon bal; épi maboya rentré ladans."

—"Di moin oti ou kallé, doudoux?"

—"Jouq lariviè Lezà."

—"Fouinq!—ni plis passé trente kilomett!"

—"Eh ben?—ess ou 'lè vini épi moin?"*

And as she puts the question she stands still and gazes at him;—her voice is no longer mocking: it has taken another tone,—a tone soft as the long golden note of the little brown bird they call the *siffluer-de-montagne*, the mountain-whistler. . . . yet Fafa hesitates. He hears the clear clang of the plantation bell recalling him to duty;—he sees far down the road—(*Ouill!* how fast they have been walking!)—a white and black speck in the sun: Gabou, uttering through his joined hollowed hands, as through a horn, the *ouklé*, the rally call. For an instant he thinks of the overseer's anger,—of the distance,—of the white road glaring in the dead heat: then he looks again into the black eyes of the strange woman, and answers:

—"Oui;—moin ké vini épi ou."

With a burst of mischievous laughter, in which Fafa joins, she walks on,—Fafa striding at her side. . . . And Gabou, far off, watches them go,—and wonders that, for the first time since ever they worked together, his comrade failed to answer his *ouklé*.

—"Coument yo ka crié ou, chè?" asks Fafa, curious to know her name.

—"Châché nom moin ou-menm, duviné."

But Fafa never was a good guesser,—never could guess the simplest of tim-tim.

*—"Where dost stay, dear?"
  —"Affairs of the goat are not affairs of the rabbit."
  —"But why art thou dressed all in black thus?"
  —"I wear mourning for my dead soul."
  —"*Aïe ya yaïe!* . . . No, true! . . . where art thou going now?"
  —"Love is gone: I go after love."
  —"Ho! thou hast a Wasp [lover]—eh?"
  —"The zanoli gives a ball; the *maboya* enters unasked."
  —"Tell me where thou art going, sweetheart?"
  —"As far as the River of the Lizard."
  —"*Fouinq!*—there are more than thirty kilometres!"
  —"What of that?—dost thou want to come with me?"

—"Ess Cendrine?"
—"Non, çé pa ça."
—"Ess Vitaline?"
—"Non, çé pa ça."
—"Ess Aza?"
—"Non, çé pa ça."
—"Ess Nini?"
—"Châché encò."
—"Ess Tité?"
—"Ou pa save,—tant pis pou ou!"
—"Ess Youma?"
—"Pouki ou 'lè save nom moin?—ça ou ké fai épi y?"
—"Ess Yaiya?"
—"Non, çé pa y."
—"Ess Maiyotte?"
—"Non! ou pa ké janmain trouvé y!"
—"Ess Sounoune?—ess Loulouze?"

She does not answer, but quickens her pace and begins to sing,—not as the half-breed, but as the African sings,—commencing with a low long weird intonation that suddenly breaks into fractions of notes inexpressible, then rising all at once to a liquid purling birdtone, and descending as abruptly again to the first deep quavering strain:—

> "À tè—
>> moin ka dòmi toute longue;
> Yon paillasse sé fai moin bien,
>>> Doudoux!
> À tè—
>> moin ka dòmi toute longue;
> Yon robe biésé sé fai moin bien,
>>> Doudoux!
> À tè—
>> moin ka dòmi toute longue;
> Dè jolis foulà sé fai moin bien,
>>> Doudoux!
> À tè—
>> moin ka dòmi toute longue;
> Yon joli madras sé fai moin bien,
>>> Doudoux!

À tè—
      moin ka dòmi toute longue:
Çé à tè . . ."

  . . . Obliged from the first to lengthen his stride in order to keep up with her, Fafa has found his utmost powers of walking overtaxed, and has been left behind. Already his thin attire is saturated with sweat; his breathing is almost a panting;—yet the black bronze of his companion's skin shows no moisture; her rhythmic step, her silent respiration, reveal no effort: she laughs at his desperate straining to remain by her side.

  —"Marché toujou' deïé moin,—anh, chè?—marché toujou' deïé!" . . .

And the involuntary laggard—utterly bewitched by the supple allurement of her motion, by the black flame of her gaze, by the savage melody of her chant—wonders more and more who she may be, while she waits for him with her mocking smile.

But Gabou—who has been following and watching from afar off, and sounding his fruitless ouklé betimes—suddenly starts, halts, turns, and hurries back, fearfully crossing himself at every step.

He has seen the sign by which She is known. . . .

VI.

  . . . NONE ever saw her by night. Her hour is the fulness of the sun's flood-tide: she comes in the dead hush and white flame of windless noons,—when colors appear to take a very unearthliness of intensity,—when even the flash of some colibri, bosomed with living fire, shooting hither and thither among the grenadilla blossoms, seemeth a spectral happening because of the great green trance of the land. . . .

Mostly she haunts the mountain roads, winding from plantation to plantation, from hamlet to hamlet,—sometimes dominating huge sweeps of azure sea, sometimes shadowed by mornes deep-wooded to the sky. But close to the great towns she sometimes walks: she has been seen at mid-day upon the highway which overlooks the Cemetery of the Anchorage, behind the cathedral of St. Pierre. . . . A black Woman, simply clad, of lofty stature and strange beauty, silently standing in the light, *keeping her eyes fixed upon the Sun!* . . .

VII.

DAY wanes. The further western altitudes shift their pearline gray to deep blue where the sky is yellowing up behind them; and in the darkening hollows of nearer mornes strange shadows gather with the changing of the light—dead indigoes, fuliginous purples, rubifications as of scoriæ,—ancient volcanic colors momentarily resurrected by the illusive haze of evening. And the fallow of the canes takes a faint warm ruddy tinge. On certain far high slopes, as the sun lowers, they look like thin golden hairs against the glow,—blond down upon the skin of the living hills.

Still the Woman and her follower walk together,—chatting loudly, laughing, chanting snatches of song betimes. And now the valley is well behind them;—they climb the steep road crossing the eastern peaks,—through woods that seem to stifle under burdening of creepers. The shadow of the Woman and the shadow of the man,—broadening from their feet,—lengthening prodigiously,—sometimes, mixing, fill all the way; sometimes, at a turn, rise up to climb the trees. Huge masses of frondage, catching the failing light, take strange fiery color;—the sun's rim almost touches one violet hump in the western procession of volcanic silhouettes. . . .

Sunset, in the tropics, is vaster than sunrise. . . . The dawn, upflaming swiftly from the sea, has no heralding erubescence, no awful blossoming—as in the North: its fairest hues are fawn-colors, dove-tints, and yellows,—pale yellows as of old dead gold, in horizon and flood. But after the mighty heat of day has charged all the blue air with translucent vapor, colors become strangely changed, magnified, transcendentalized when the sun falls once more below the verge of visibility. Nearly an hour before his death, his light begins to turn tint; and all the horizon yellows to the color of a lemon. Then this hue deepens, through tones of magnificence unspeakable, into orange; and the sea becomes lilac. Orange is the light of the world for a little space; and as the orb sinks, the indigo darkness comes—

not descending, but rising, as if from the ground—all within a few minutes. And during those brief minutes peaks and mornes, purpling into richest velvety blackness, appear outlined against passions of fire that rise half-way to the zenith,—enormous furies of vermilion.

. . . The Woman all at once leaves the main road,—begins to mount a steep narrow path leading up from it through the woods upon the left. But Fafa hesitates,—halts a moment to look back. He sees the sun's huge orange face sink down,—sees the weird procession of the peaks vesture themselves in blackness funereal,—sees the burning behind them crimson into awfulness; and a vague fear comes upon him as he looks again up the darkling path to the left. Whither is she now going?

—"Oti ou kallé là?" he cries.

—"Mais conm ça!—chimin tala plis cou't,—coument?"

It may be the shortest route, indeed;—but then, the fer-de-lance! . . .

—"Ni sèpent ciya,—en pile."

No: there is not a single one, she avers; she has taken that path too often not to know:

—"Pa ni sèpent piess! Moin ni coutime passé là;—pa ni piess!"

. . . She leads the way. . . . Behind them the tremendous glow deepens;—before them the gloom. Enormous gnarled forms of ceiba, balata, acoma, stand dimly revealed as they pass; masses of viny drooping things take, by the failing light, a sanguine tone. For a little while Fafa can plainly discern the figure of the Woman before him;—then, as the path zigzags into shadow, he can descry only the white turban and the white foulard;—and then the boughs meet overhead: he can see her no more, and calls to her in alarm:—

—"Oti ou?—moin pa pè ouè arien!"

Forked pending ends of creepers trail cold across his face. Huge fire-flies sparkle by,—like atoms of kindled charcoal thinkling, blown by a wind.

—"Içitt!—quimbé lanmain-moin!" . . .

How cold the hand that guides him! . . . She walks swiftly, surely, as one knowing the path by heart. It zigzags once more; and the incandescent color flames again between the trees;—the high vaulting of foliage fissures overhead, revealing the first stars. A *cabritt-bois* begins its chant. They reach the summit of the morne under the clear sky.

The wood is below their feet now; the path curves on eastward between a long swaying of ferns sable in the gloom,—as between a waving of prodigious black feathers. Through the further purpling, loftier altitudes dimly loom; and from some viewless depth, a dull vast rushing sound rises into the night. . . . Is it the speech of hurrying waters, or only some tempest of insect voices from those ravines in which the night begins? . . .

Her face is in the darkness as she stands;—Fafa's eyes are turned to the iron-crimson of the western sky. He still holds her hand, fondles it,—murmurs something to her in undertones.

—"Ess ou ainmein moin conm ça?" she asks, almost in a whisper.

Oh! yes, yes, yes! . . . more than any living being he loves her! . . . How much? Ever so much,—*gouôs conm caze!* . . . Yet she seems to doubt him,—repeating her question over and over:

—"Ess ou ainmein moin?"

And all the while,—gently, caressingly, imperceptibly,—she draws him a little nearer to the side of the path, nearer to the black waving of the ferns, nearer to the great dull rushing sound that rises from beyond them:

—"Ess ou ainmein moin?"

—"Oui, oui!" he responds,—"ou save ça!—oui, chè doudoux, ou save ça!" . . .

And she, suddenly,—turning at once to him and to the last red light, the goblin horror of her face transformed,—shrieks with a burst of hideous laughter:

—"*Atò, bô!*"*

For the fraction of a moment he knows her name:—then, smitten to the brain with the sight of her, reels, recoils, and, backward falling, crashes two thousand feet down to his death upon the rocks of a mountain torrent.

---

*"Kiss me now!"

La Vérette

O NE returning from the country to the city in the Carnival
season is lucky to find any comfortable rooms for rent. I
have been happy to secure one even in a rather retired street,—
so steep that it is really dangerous to sneeze while descending
it, lest one lose one's balance and tumble right across the town.
It is not a fashionable street, the Rue du Morne Mirail; but,
after all, there is no particularly fashionable street in this extraordinary city, and the poorer the neighborhood, the better
one's chance to see something of its human nature.

One consolation is that I have Manm-Robert for a next-
door neighbor, who keeps the best bouts in town (those long
thin Martinique cigars of which a stranger soon becomes fond),
and who can relate more queer stories and legends of old times
in the island than anybody else I know of. Manm-Robert is
yon màchanne làpacotte, a dealer in such cheap articles of food
as the poor live upon: fruits and tropical vegetables, manioc-
flour, "macadam" (a singular dish of rice stewed with salt
fish—*diri épi coubouyon lamori*), akras, etc.; but her bouts
probably bring her the largest profit—they are all bought up by
the békés. Manm-Robert is also a sort of doctor: whenever any
one in the neighborhood falls sick she is sent for, and always
comes, and very often cures,—as she is skilled in the knowledge and use of medicinal herbs, which she gathers herself
upon the mornes. But for these services she never accepts any
remuneration: she is a sort of Mother of the poor in her immediate vicinity. She helps everybody, listens to everybody's
troubles, gives everybody some sort of consolation, trusts
everybody, and sees a great deal of the thankless side of human
nature without seeming to feel any the worse for it. Poor as
she must really be she appears to have everything that everybody wants; and will lend anything to her neighbors except a
scissors or a broom, which it is thought bad-luck to lend. And,
finally, if anybody is afraid of being bewitched (*quimboisé*)
Manm-Robert can furnish him or her with something that will
keep the bewitchment away. . . .

II.

February 15th.

. . . ASH-WEDNESDAY. The last masquerade will appear this afternoon, notwithstanding; for the Carnival lasts in Martinique a day longer than elsewhere.

All through the country districts since the first week of January there have been wild festivities every Sunday—dancing on the public highways to the pattering of tamtams,—African dancing, too, such as is never seen in St. Pierre. In the city, however, there has been less merriment than in previous years;— the natural gaiety of the population has been visibly affected by the advent of a terrible and unfamiliar visitor to the island, —*La Vérette*: she came by steamer from Colon.

. . . It was in September. Only two cases had been reported when every neighboring British colony quarantined against Martinique. Then other West Indian colonies did likewise. Only two cases of small-pox. "But there may be two thousand in another month," answered the governors and the consuls to many indignant protests. Among West Indian populations the malady has a signification unknown in Europe or the United States: it means an exterminating plague.

Two months later the little capital of Fort-de-France was swept by the pestilence as by a wind of death. Then the evil began to spread. It entered St. Pierre in December, about Christmas time. Last week 173 cases were reported; and a serious epidemic is almost certain. There were only 8500 inhabitants in Fort-de-France; there are 28,000 in the three quarters of St. Pierre proper, not including her suburbs; and there is no saying what ravages the disease may make here.

III.

. . . THREE o'clock, hot and clear. . . . In the distance there is a heavy sound of drums, always drawing nearer: *tam!—tam!—tamtamtam!* The Grande Rue is lined with expectant multitudes; and its tiny square,—the Batterie d'Esnotz,—thronged with békés. *Tam!—tam!—tamtamtam!* . . . In our own street the people are beginning to gather at door-ways, and peer out of windows,—prepared to descend to the main thoroughfare at the first glimpse of the procession.

—"*Oti masque-à?*" Where are the maskers?

It is little Mimi's voice: she is speaking for two besides herself, both quite as anxious as she to know where the maskers are,—Maurice, her little fair-haired and blue-eyed brother, three years old; and Gabrielle, her child-sister, aged four,—two years her junior.

Every day I have been observing the three, playing in the door-way of the house across the street. Mimi, with her brilliant white skin, black hair, and laughing black eyes, is the prettiest, —though all are unusually pretty children. Were it not for the fact that their mother's beautiful brown hair is usually covered with a violet foulard, you would certainly believe them white as any children in the world. Now there are children whom every one knows to be white, living not very far from here, but in a much more silent street, and in a rich house full of servants, —children who resemble these as one *fleur-d'amour* blossom resembles another;—there is actually another Mimi (though she is not so called at home) so like this Mimi that you could not possibly tell one from the other,—except by their dress. And yet the most unhappy experience of the Mimi who wears white satin slippers was certainly that punishment given her for having been once caught playing in the street with this Mimi, who wears no shoes at all. What mischance could have brought them thus together?—and the worst of it was they had fallen in love with each other at first sight! . . . It was not because the other Mimi must not talk to nice little colored girls, or that this one may not play with white children of her own age: it was because there are cases. . . . It was not because the other children I speak of are prettier or sweeter or more intelligent than these now playing before me;—or because the finest microscopist in the world could or could not detect any imaginable race difference between those delicate satin skins. It was only because human nature has little changed since the day that Hagar knew the hate of Sarah, and the thing was grievous in Abraham's sight because of his son. . . .

. . . The father of these children loved them very much: he had provided a home for them,—a house in the Quarter of the

Fort, with an allowance of two hundred francs monthly; and he died in the belief their future was secured. But relatives fought the will with large means and shrewd lawyers, and won! . . . Yzore, the mother, found herself homeless and penniless, with three children to care for. But she was brave;— she abandoned the costume of the upper class forever, put on the douillette and the foulard,—the attire that is a confession of race,—and went to work. She is still comely, and so white that she seems only to be masquerading in that violet head-dress and long loose robe. . . .

—"*Vini ouè!—vini ouè!*" cry the children to one another,— "come and see!" The drums are drawing near;—everybody is running to the Grande Rue. . . .

IV.

Tam!—tam!—tamtamtam! . . . The spectacle is interesting from the Batterie d'Esnotz. High up the Rue Peysette,—up all the precipitous streets that ascend the mornes,—a far gathering of showy color appears: the massing of maskers in rose and blue and sulphur-yellow attire. . . . Then what a *degringolade* begins!—what a tumbling, leaping, cascading of color as the troupes descend. Simultaneously from north and south, from the Mouillage and the Fort, two immense bands enter the Grande Rue;—the great dancing societies these,—the *Sans-souci* and the *Intrépides.* They are rivals; they are the composers and singers of those Carnival songs,—cruel satires most often, of which the local meaning is unintelligible to those unacquainted with the incident inspiring the improvisation,—of which the words are too often coarse or obscene,—whose burdens will be caught up and re-echoed through all the burghs of the island. Vile as may be the motive, the satire, the malice, these chants are preserved for generations by the singular beauty of the airs; and the victim of a Carnival song need never hope that his failing or his wrong will be forgotten: it will be sung of long after he is in his grave.

. . . Ten minutes more, and the entire length of the street is thronged with a shouting, shrieking, laughing, gesticulating host of maskers. Thicker and thicker the press becomes;—the drums are silent: all are waiting for the signal of the general

Rue Victor Hugo (Formerly Grande Rue), St. Pierre.

dance. Jests and practical jokes are being everywhere perpetrated; there is a vast hubbub, made up of screams, cries, chattering, laughter. Here and there snatches of Carnival song are being sung:—"*Cambronne, Cambronne;*" or "*Ti fenm-là doux, li doux, li doux!*" . . . "Sweeter than sirup the little woman is";—this burden will be remembered when the rest of the song passes out of fashion. Brown hands reach out from the crowd of masks, pulling the beards and patting the faces of white spectators. . . . "*Moin connaitt ou, chè!—moin connaitt ou, doudoux! ba moin ti d'mi franc!*" It is well to refuse the half-franc,—though you do not know what these maskers might take a notion to do to-day. . . . Then all the great drums suddenly boom together; all the bands strike up; the mad medley kaleidoscopes into some sort of order; and the immense processional dance begins. From the Mouillage to the Fort there is but one continuous torrent of sound and color: you are dazed by the tossing of peaked caps, the waving of hands, and twinkling of feet;—and all this passes with a huge swing,—a regular swaying to right and left. . . . It will take at least an hour for all to pass; and it is an hour well worth passing. Band after band whirls by; the musicians all garbed as women or as monks in canary-colored habits;—before them the dancers are dancing backward, with a motion as of skaters; behind them all leap and wave hands as in pursuit. Most of the bands are playing creole airs,—but that of the *Sans-souci* strikes up the melody of the latest French song in vogue,—*Petits amoureux aux plumes* ("Little feathered lovers"*). Everybody now seems to know

---

*"Petits amoureux aux plumes,
     Enfants d'un brillant séjour,
Vous ignorez l'amertume,
     Vous parlez souvent d'amour: . . .
Vous méprisez la dorure,
     Les salons, et les bijoux;
Vous chérissez la Nature,
     Petits oiseaux, becquetez-vous!

"Voyez làbas, dans cette église,
     Auprès d'un confessional,
Le prêtre, qui veut faire croire à Lise,
     Qu'un baiser est un grand mal;—
Pour prouver à la mignonne
     Qu'un baiser bien fait, bien doux,

this song by heart; you hear children only five or six years old singing it: there are pretty lines in it, although two out of its four stanzas are commonplace enough, and it is certainly the air rather than the words which accounts for its sudden popularity.

V.

. . . EXTRAORDINARY things are happening in the streets through which the procession passes. Pest-smitten women rise from their beds to costume themselves,—to mask faces already made unrecognizable by the hideous malady,—and stagger out to join the dancers. . . . They do this in the Rue Long-champs, in the Rue St. Jean-de-Dieu, in the Rue Peysette, in the Rue de Petit Versailles. And in the Rue Ste.-Marthe there are three young girls sick with the disease, who hear the blowing of the horns and the pattering of feet and clapping of hands in chorus;—they get up to look through the slats of their windows on the masquerade,—and the creole passion of the dance comes upon them. "*Ah!*" cries one,—"*nou ké bien amieusé nou!—c'est zaffai si nou mò!*" [We will have our fill of fun: what matter if we die after!] And all mask, and join the

---

N'a jamais damné personne
Petits oiseaux, becquetez-vous!"

[*Translation.*]
Little feathered lovers, cooing,
    Children of the radiant air,
Sweet your speech,—the speech of wooing;
    Ye have ne'er a grief to bear!
Gilded ease and jewelled fashion
    Never own a charm for you;
Ye love Nature's truth with passion,
    Pretty birdlings, bill and coo!

See that priest who, Lise confessing,
    Wants to make the girl believe
That a kiss without a blessing
    Is a fault for which to grieve!
Now to prove, to his vexation,
    That no tender kiss and true
Ever caused a soul's damnation,
    Pretty birdlings, bill and coo!

rout, and dance down to the Savane, and over the river-bridge into the high streets of the Fort, carrying contagion with them! . . . No extraordinary example, this: the ranks of the dancers hold many and many a *verrettier*.

VI.

. . . THE costumes are rather disappointing,—though the mummery has some general characteristics that are not unpicturesque;—for example, the predominance of crimson and canary-yellow in choice of color, and a marked predilection for pointed hoods and high-peaked head-dresses. Mock religious costumes also form a striking element in the general tone of the display,—Franciscan, Dominican, or Penitent habits,—usually crimson or yellow, rarely sky-blue. There are no historical costumes, few eccentricities or monsters: only a few "vampire-bat" head-dresses abruptly break the effect of the peaked caps and the hoods. . . . Still there are some decidedly local ideas in dress which deserve notice,—the *congo*, the *bébé* (or *ti-man-maille*), the *ti nègue gouos-sirop* ("little molasses-negro"); and the *diablesse*.

The congo is merely the exact reproduction of the dress worn by workers on the plantations. For the women, a gray calico shirt and coarse petticoat of percaline; with two coarse handkerchiefs (*mouchoirs fatas*), one for her neck, and one for the head, over which is worn a monstrous straw hat;—she walks either barefoot or shod with rude native sandals, and she carries a hoe. For the man the costume consists of a gray shirt of rough material, blue canvas pantaloons, a large mouchoir fatas to tie around his waist, and a *chapeau Bacoué*,—an enormous hat of Martinique palm-straw. He walks barefooted and carries a cutlass.

The sight of a troupe of young girls *en bébé*, in baby-dress, is really pretty. This costume comprises only a loose, embroidered chemise, lace-edged pantalettes, and a child's cap; the whole being decorated with bright ribbons of various colors. As the dress is short and leaves much of the lower limbs exposed, there is ample opportunity for display of tinted stockings and elegant slippers.

The "molasses-negro" wears nothing but a cloth around his

loins;—his whole body and face being smeared with an atrocious mixture of soot and molasses. He is supposed to represent the original African ancestor.

The *devilesses* (*diablesses*) are few in number; for it requires a very tall woman to play deviless. These are robed all in black, with a white turban and white foulard; they wear black masks. They also carry *boms* (large tin cans), which they allow to fall upon the pavement from time to time; and they walk barefoot. . . . The deviless (in true Bitaco idiom, "*guiablesse*") represents a singular Martinique superstition. It is said that sometimes at noonday, a beautiful negress passes silently through some isolated plantation,—smiling at the workers in the cane-fields,—tempting men to follow her. But he who follows her never comes back again; and when a field hand mysteriously disappears, his fellows say, "*Y té ka ouè la Guiablesse!*" . . . The tallest among the devilesses always walks first, chanting the question, "*Jou ouvè?*" (Is it yet daybreak?) And all the others reply in chorus, "*Jou pa'ncò ouvè.*" (It is not yet day.)

—The masks worn by the multitude include very few grotesques: as a rule, they are simply white wire masks, having the form of an oval and regular human face;—and they disguise the wearer absolutely, although they can be seen through perfectly well from within. It struck me at once that this peculiar type of wire mask gave an indescribable tone of ghostliness to the whole exhibition. It is not in the least comical; it is neither comely nor ugly; it is colorless as mist,—expressionless, void, dead;—it lies on the face like a vapor, like a cloud,—creating the idea of a spectral vacuity behind it. . . .

VII.

. . . Now comes the band of the *Intrépides*, playing the *bouèné*. It is a dance melody,—also the name of a *mode* of dancing, peculiar and unrestrained;—the dancers advance and retreat face to face; they hug each other, press together, and separate to embrace again. A very old dance, this,—of African origin; perhaps the same of which Père Labat wrote in 1722:—

—"It is not modest. Nevertheless, it has not failed to become so popular with the Spanish Creoles of America, and so much in vogue among them, that it now forms the chief of their amusements, and that it enters even into their devotions. They dance it even in their Churches, and in their Processions; and the Nuns seldom fail to dance it Christmas Night, upon a stage erected in their Choir and immediately in front of their iron grating, which is left open, so that the People may share in the joy manifested by these good souls for the birth of the Saviour."*   . . .

VIII.

. . . EVERY year, on the last day of the Carnival, a droll ceremony used to take place called the "Burial of the Bois-bois,"— the bois-bois being a dummy, a guy, caricaturing the most unpopular thing in city life or in politics. This bois-bois, after having been paraded with mock solemnity through all the ways of St. Pierre, was either interred or "drowned,"—flung into the sea. . . . And yesterday the dancing societies had announced their intention to bury a *bois-bois laverette*,—a manikin that was to represent the plague. But this bois-bois does not make its appearance. *La Vérette* is too terrible a visitor to be made fun of, my friends;—you will not laugh at her, because you dare not. . . .

No: there is one who has the courage,—a yellow goblin crying from behind his wire mask, in imitation of the màchannes: "*Ça qui 'lè quatòze graines laverette pou yon sou?*" (Who wants to buy fourteen verette-spots for a sou?)

Not a single laugh follows that jest. . . . And just one week from to-day, poor mocking goblin, you will have a great many more than *quatorze graines*, which will not cost you even a sou, and which will disguise you infinitely better than the mask you now wear;—and they will pour quick-lime over you, ere

---

*. . . "Cette danse est opposée à la pudeur. Avec tout cela, elle ne laisse pas d'être tellement du goût des Espagnols Créolles de l'Amérique, & si fort en usage parmi eux, qu'elle fait la meilleure partie de leurs divertissements, & qu'elle entre même dans leurs devotions. Ils la dansent même dans leurs Églises & à leurs processions; et les Religieuses ne manquent guère de la danser la Nuit de Noël, sur un théatre élevé dans leur Chœur, vis-à-vis de leur grille, qui est ouverte, afin que le Peuple aît sa part dans la joye que ces bonnes âmes témoignent pour la naissance du Sauveur."

ever they let you pass through this street again—in a seven franc coffin! . . .

IX.

AND the multicolored clamoring stream rushes by,—swerves off at last through the Rue des Ursulines to the Savane,—rolls over the new bridge of the Roxelane to the ancient quarter of the Fort.

All of a sudden there is a hush, a halt;—the drums stop beating, the songs cease. Then I see a sudden scattering of goblins and demons and devilesses in all directions: they run into houses, up alleys,—hide behind door-ways. And the crowd parts; and straight through it, walking very quickly, comes a priest in his vestments, preceded by an acolyte who rings a little bell. *C'est Bon-Dié ka passé!* ("It is the Good-God who goes by!") The father is bearing the "viaticum" to some victim of the pestilence: one must not appear masked as a devil or a deviless in the presence of the Bon-Dié.

He goes by. The flood of maskers recloses behind the ominous passage;—the drums boom again; the dance recommences; and all the fantastic mummery ebbs swiftly out of sight.

X.

NIGHT falls;—the maskers crowd to the ball-rooms to dance strange tropical measures that will become wilder and wilder as the hours pass. And through the black streets, the Devil makes his last Carnival-round.

By the gleam of the old-fashioned oil lamps hung across the thoroughfares I can make out a few details of his costume. He is clad in red, wears a hideous blood-colored mask, and a cap of which the four sides are formed by four looking-glasses;—the whole head-dress being surmounted by a red lantern. He has a white wig made of horse-hair, to make him look weird and old,—since the Devil is older than the world! Down the street he comes, leaping nearly his own height,—chanting words without human signification,—and followed by some three hundred boys, who form the chorus to his chant—all clapping hands together and giving tongue with a simultaneity that testifies how strongly the sense of rhythm enters into the natural musical feeling of the African,—a feeling powerful enough to impose itself upon all Spanish-America, and there create the unmistakable characteristics of all that is called "creole music."

—"Bimbolo!"
—"Zimabolo!"
—"Bimbolo!"
—"Zimabolo!"
—"Et zimbolo!"
—"Et bolo-po!"

—sing the Devil and his chorus. His chant is cavernous, abysmal,—booms from his chest like the sound of a drum beaten in the bottom of a well. . . . *Ti manmaille-là, baill moin lavoix!* ("Give me voice, little folk,—give me voice!") And all chant after him, in a chanting like the rushing of many waters, and with triple clapping of hands:—"*Ti manmaille-là, baill moin lavoix!*" . . . Then he halts before a dwelling in the Rue Peysette, and thunders:—

—"*Eh! Marie-sans-dent!—Mi! diabe-là derhò!*"

That is evidently a piece of spite-work: there is somebody living there against whom he has a grudge. . . . "*Hey! Marie-without-teeth! look! the Devil is outside!*" And the chorus catch the clue.

DEVIL.—"*Eh! Marie-sans-dent!*" . . .
CHORUS.—"*Marie-sans-dent! mi!—diabe-là derhò!*"
D.—"*Eh! Marie-sans-dent!*" . . .
C.—"*Marie-sans-dent! mi!—diabe-à derhò!*"
D.—"*Eh! Marie-sans-dent!*" . . . etc.

The Devil at last descends to the main street, always singing the same song;—I follow the chorus to the Savanna, where the rout makes for the new bridge over the Roxelane, to mount the high streets of the old quarter of the Fort; and the chant changes as they cross over:—

DEVIL.—"*Oti ouè diabe-là passé lariviè?*" (Where did you see the Devil going over the river?) And all the boys repeat the words, falling into another rhythm with perfect regularity and ease:—"*Oti ouè diabe-là passé lariviè?*"

DEVIL.—"*Oti ouè diabe?*" . . .
CHORUS.—"*Oti ouè diabe-là passé lariviè?*"

Quarter of the Fort, St. Pierre (overlooking the Rivière Roxelane).

D.—"*Oti ouè diabe?*"
C.—"*Oti ouè diabe-là passi lariviè?*"
D.—"*Oti ouè diabe?*" . . . etc.

About midnight the return of the Devil and his following arouses me from sleep:—all are chanting a new refrain, "The Devil and the zombis sleep anywhere and everywhere!" (*Diabe épi zombi ka dòmi tout-pàtout.*) The voices of the boys are still clear, shrill, fresh,—clear as a chant of frogs;—they still clap hands with a precision of rhythm that is simply wonderful,—making each time a sound almost exactly like the bursting of a heavy wave:—

Devil.—"*Diabe épi zombi.*" . . .
Chorus.—"*Diabe épi zombi ka dòmi tout-pàtout!*"
D.—"*Diabe épi zombi.*" . . .
C.—"*Diabe épi zombi ka dòmi tout-pàtout!*"
D.—"*Diabe épi zombi.*" . . . etc.

. . . What is this after all but the old African method of chanting at labor. The practice of carrying the burden upon the head left the hands free for the rhythmic accompaniment of clapping. And you may still hear the women who load the transatlantic steamers with coal at Fort-de-France thus chanting and clapping. . . .

Evidently the Devil is moving very fast; for all the boys are running;—the pattering of bare feet upon the pavement sounds like a heavy shower. . . . Then the chanting grows fainter in distance; the Devil's immense basso becomes inaudible;—one only distinguishes at regular intervals the *crescendo* of the burden,—a wild swelling of many hundred boy-voices all rising together,—a retreating storm of rhythmic song, wafted to the ear in gusts, in *rafales* of contralto. . . .

XI.

February 17th.

. . . Yzore is a *calendeuse.*

The calendeuses are the women who make up the beautiful Madras turbans and color them; for the amazingly brilliant yellow of these head-dresses is not the result of any dyeing process: they are all painted by hand. When purchased the Madras is simply a great oblong handkerchief, having a pale green or pale pink ground, and checkered or plaided by intersecting bands of dark blue, purple, crimson, or maroon. The calendeuse lays the Madras upon a broad board placed across her knees,—then, taking a camel's-hair brush, she begins to fill in the spaces between the bands with a sulphur-yellow paint, which is always mixed with gum-arabic. It requires a sure eye, very steady fingers, and long experience to do this well. . . . After the Madras has been "calendered" (*calendé*) and has become quite stiff and dry, it is folded about the head of the purchaser after the comely Martinique fashion,—which varies considerably from the modes popular in Guadeloupe or Cayenne,—is fixed into the form thus obtained; and can thereafter be taken off or put on without arrangement or disarrangement, like a cap. The price for calendering a Madras is now two francs and fifteen sous;—and for making-up the turban, six sous additional, except in Carnival-time, or upon holiday occasions, when the price rises to twenty-five sous. . . . The making-up of the Madras into a turban is called "tying a head" (*marré yon tête*); and a prettily folded turban is spoken of as "a head well tied" (*yon tête bien marré*). . . . However, the profession of calendeuse is far from being a lucrative one: it is two or three days' work to calender a single Madras well. . . .

But Yzore does not depend upon calendering alone for a living: she earns much more by the manufacture of *moresques* and of *chinoises* than by painting Madras turbans. . . . Everybody in Martinique who can afford it wears moresques and chinoises. The moresques are large loose comfortable pantaloons of thin printed calico (*indienne*),—having colored designs representing birds, frogs, leaves, lizards, flowers, butterflies, or kittens,—or perhaps representing nothing in particular, being simply arabesques. The chinoise is a loose body-garment, very much like the real Chinese blouse, but always of brightly colored calico with fantastic designs. These things are worn at home during siestas, after office-hours, and at night. To take a nap during the day with one's ordinary clothing on means always a terrible drenching from perspiration, and an after-feeling of exhaustion almost indescribable—best expressed, perhaps, by the local term: *corps écrasé*. Therefore, on entering one's room for the siesta, one strips, puts on the light moresques and the chinoise, and dozes in comfort. A suit of this sort is very neat, often quite pretty, and very cheap (costing only about six francs);—the colors do not fade out in washing, and two good suits will last a year. . . . Yzore can make two pair of moresques and two chinoises in a single day upon her machine.

. . . I have observed there is a prejudice here against treadle machines;—the creole girls are persuaded they injure the health. Most of the sewing-machines I have seen among this people are operated by hand,—with a sort of little crank. . . .

XII.

February 22d.

. . . OLD physicians indeed predicted it; but who believed them? . . .

It is as though something sluggish and viewless, dormant and deadly, had been suddenly upstirred to furious life by the wind of robes and tread of myriad dancing feet,—by the crash of cymbals and heavy vibration of drums! Within a few days there has been a frightful increase of the visitation, an almost incredible expansion of the invisible poison: the number of new cases and of deaths has successively doubled, tripled, quadrupled. . . .

. . . Great caldrons of tar are kindled now at night in the more thickly peopled streets,—about one hundred paces apart, each being tended by an Indian laborer in the pay of the city: this is done with the idea of purifying the air. These sinister fires are never lighted but in times of pestilence and of tempest: on hurricane nights, when enormous waves roll in from the fathomless sea upon one of the most fearful coasts in the world, and great vessels are being driven ashore, such is the illumination by which the brave men of the coast make desperate efforts to save the lives of shipwrecked men, often at the cost of their own.*

---

*During a hurricane, several years ago, a West Indian steamer was disabled at a dangerously brief distance from the coast of the island by having her propeller fouled. Some broken and drifting rigging had become wrapped around it. One of the crew, a Martinique mulatto, tied a rope about his waist, took his knife between his teeth, dived overboard, and in that tremendous sea performed the difficult feat of disengaging the propeller, and thus saving the

XIII.

February 23d.

A COFFIN passes, balanced on the heads of black men. It holds the body of Pascaline Z——, covered with quicklime.

She was the prettiest, assuredly, among the pretty shop-girls of the Grande Rue,—a rare type of *sang-mêlée.* So oddly pleasing, the young face, that once seen, you could never again dissociate the recollection of it from the memory of the street. But one who saw it last night before they poured quick-lime upon it could discern no features,—only a dark brown mass, like a fungus, too frightful to think about.

. . . And they are all going thus, the beautiful women of color. In the opinion of physicians, the whole generation is doomed. . . . Yet a curious fact is that the young children of octoroons are suffering least: these women have their children vaccinated,—though they will not be vaccinated themselves. I see many brightly colored children, too, recovering from the disorder: the skin is not pitted, like that of the darker classes; and the rose-colored patches finally disappear altogether, leaving no trace.

. . . Here the sick are wrapped in banana leaves, after having been smeared with a certain unguent. . . . There is an immense demand for banana leaves. In ordinary times these leaves —especially the younger ones, still unrolled, and tender and soft beyond any fabric possible for man to make—are used for poultices of all kinds, and sell from one to two sous each, according to size and quality.

XIV.

February 29th.

. . . THE whites remain exempt from the malady.

One might therefore hastily suppose that liability to contagion would be diminished in proportion to the excess of white blood over African; but such is far from being the case;—St. Pierre is losing its handsomest octoroons. Where the proportion

---

steamer from otherwise certain destruction. . . . This brave fellow received the Cross of the Legion of Honor. . . .

of white to black blood is 116 to 8, as in the type called *mame-louc*;—or 122 to 4, as in the *quarteronné* (not to be confounded with the *quarteron* or quadroon);—or even 127 to 1, as in the *sang-mêlé*, the liability to attack remains the same, while the chances of recovery are considerably less than in the case of the black. Some few striking instances of immunity appear to offer a different basis for argument; but these might be due to the social position of the individual rather than to any constitutional temper: wealth and comfort, it must be remembered, have no small prophylactic value in such times. Still,—although there is reason to doubt whether mixed races have a constitutional vigor comparable to that of the original parent-races,— the liability to diseases of this class is decided less, perhaps, by race characteristics than by ancestral experience. The white peoples of the world have been practically inoculated, vaccinated, by experience of centuries;—while among these visibly mixed or black populations the seeds of the pest find absolutely fresh soil in which to germinate, and its ravages are therefore scarcely less terrible than those it made among the American-Indian or the Polynesian races in other times. Moreover, there is an unfortunate prejudice against vaccination here. People even now declare that those vaccinated die just as speedily of the plague as those who have never been;—and they can cite cases in proof. It is useless to talk to them about averages of immunity, percentage of liability, etc.;—they have seen with their own eyes persons who had been well vaccinated die of the verette, and that is enough to destroy their faith in the system. . . . Even the priests, who pray their congregations to adopt the only known safeguard against the disease, can do little against this scepticism.

XV.

March 5th.

. . . THE streets are so narrow in this old-fashioned quarter that even a whisper is audible across them; and after dark I hear a great many things,—sometimes sounds of pain, sobbing, despairing cries as Death makes his nightly round,—sometimes, again, angry words, and laughter, and even song,—always one

melancholy chant: the voice has that peculiar metallic timbre
that reveals the young negress:—

> "*Pauv' ti Lélé,*
> *Pauv' ti Lélé!*
> *Li gagnin doulè, doulè, doulè,—*
> *Li gagnin doulè*
> *Tout-pàtout!*"

I want to know who little Lélé was, and why she had pains "all
over";—for however artless and childish these creole songs
seem, they are invariably originated by some real incident. And
at last somebody tells me that "poor little Lélé" had the reputation in other years of being the most unlucky girl in St. Pierre;
whatever she tried to do resulted only in misfortune;—when it
was morning she wished it were evening, that she might sleep
and forget; but when the night came she could not sleep for
thinking of the trouble she had had during the day, so that she
wished it were morning. . . .

More pleasant it is to hear the chatting of Yzore's children
across the way, after the sun has set, and the stars come out. . . .
Gabrielle always wants to know what the stars are:—

—"*Ça qui ka clairé conm ça, manman?*" (What is it that
shines like that?)

And Yzore answers:—

—"*Ça, mafi,—c'est ti limiè Bon-Dié.*" (Those are the little
lights of the Good-God.)

—"It is so pretty,—eh, mamma? I want to count them."

—"You cannot count them, child."

—"One—two—three—four—five—six—seven." Gabrielle
can only count up to seven. "*Moin peide!*—I am lost, mamma!"

The moon comes up;—she cries:—"*Mi! manman!—gàdé
gouôs difé qui adans ciel-à!* Look at the great fire in the sky!"

—"It is the Moon, child! . . . Don't you see St. Joseph in
it, carrying a bundle of wood?"

—"Yes, mamma! I see him! . . . A great big bundle of
wood!" . . .

But Mimi is wiser in moon-lore: she borrows half a franc
from her mother "to show to the Moon." And holding it up
before the silver light, she sings:—

—"Pretty Moon, I show you my little money;—now let me always have money so long as you shine!"*

Then the mother takes them up to bed;—and in a little while there floats to me, through the open window, the murmur of the children's evening prayer:—

> "Ange-gardien
> Veillez sur moi;
>
> *   *   *   *
>
> Ayez pitié de ma faiblesse;
> Couchez-vous sur mon petit lit;
> Suivez-moi sans cesse."† . . .

I can only catch a line here and there. . . . They do not sleep immediately;—they continue to chat in bed. Gabrielle wants to know what a guardian-angel is like. And I hear Mimi's voice replying in creole:—

—"*Zange-gàdien, c'est yon jeine fi, toutt bel.*" (The guardian-angel is a young girl, all beautiful.)

A little while, and there is silence; and I see Yzore come out, barefooted, upon the moonlit balcony of her little room,—looking up and down the hushed street, looking at the sea, looking up betimes at the high flickering of stars,—moving her lips as in prayer. . . . And, standing there white-robed, with her rich dark hair loose-falling, there is a weird grace about her that recalls those long slim figures of guardian-angels in French religious prints. . . .

XVI.

March 6th.

THIS morning Manm-Robert brings me something queer,—something hard tied up in a tiny piece of black cloth, with a string attached to hang it round my neck. I must wear it, she says.

---

*"*Bel laline, moin ka montré ou ti pièce moin!—ba moin làgent toutt temps ou ka clairé!*" . . . This little invocation is supposed to have most power when uttered on the first appearance of the new moon.

†"Guardian-angel, watch over me;—have pity upon my weakness; lie down on my little bed with me; follow me whithersoever I go." . . . The prayers are always said in French. Metaphysical and theological terms cannot be rendered in the patois; and the authors of creole catechisms have always been obliged to borrow and explain French religious phrases in order to make their texts comprehensible.

—"*Ça ça yé, Manm-Robert?*"

—"*Pou empêché ou pouend laverette,*" she answers. It is to keep me from catching the *verette!* . . . And what is inside it?

—"*Toua graines maïs, épi dicamfre.*" (Three grains of corn, with a bit of camphor!) . . .

XVII.

March 8th.

. . . RICH households throughout the city are almost helpless for the want of servants. One can scarcely obtain help at any price: it is true that young country-girls keep coming into town to fill the places of the dead; but these new-comers fall a prey to the disease much more readily than those who preceded them. And such deaths often represent more than a mere derangement in the mechanism of domestic life. The creole *bonne* bears a relation to the family of an absolutely peculiar sort,—a relation of which the term "house-servant" does not convey the faintest idea. She is really a member of the household: her association with its life usually begins in childhood, when she is barely strong enough to carry a dobanne of water up-stairs; —and in many cases she has the additional claim of having been born in the house. As a child, she plays with the white children,—shares their pleasures and presents. She is very seldom harshly spoken to, or reminded of the fact that she is a servitor: she has a pet name;—she is allowed much familiarity,—is often permitted to join in conversation when there is no company present, and to express her opinion about domestic affairs. She costs very little to keep; four or five dollars a year will supply her with all necessary clothing;—she rarely wears shoes;— she sleeps on a little straw mattress (*paillasse*) on the floor, or perhaps upon a paillasse supported upon an "elephant" (*léfan*) —two thick square pieces of hard mattress placed together so as to form an oblong. She is only a nominal expense to the family; and she is the confidential messenger, the nurse, the chamber-maid, the water-carrier,—everything, in short, except cook and washer-woman. Families possessing a really good bonne would not part with her on any consideration. If she has been brought up in the household, she is regarded almost as a kind of adopted child. If she leave that household to make a home of her own, and have ill-fortune afterwards, she will not be afraid to return with her baby, which will perhaps be received and brought up as she herself was, under the old roof. The stranger may feel puzzled at first by this state of affairs; yet the cause is not obscure. It is traceable to the time of the formation of creole society—to the early period of slavery. Among the Latin races,—especially the French,—slavery preserved in modern times many of the least harsh features of slavery in the antique world,—where the domestic slave, entering the *familia*, actually became a member of it.

XVIII.

March 10th.

. . . YZORE and her little ones are all in Manm-Robert's shop;—she is recounting her troubles,—fresh troubles: forty-seven francs' worth of work delivered on time, and no money received. . . . So much I hear as I enter the little *boutique* myself, to buy a package of "bouts."

—"*Assise!*" says Manm-Robert, handing me her own chair;—she is always pleased to see me, pleased to chat with me about creole folk-lore. Then observing a smile exchanged between myself and Mimi, she tells the children to bid me good-day:—"*Allé di bonjou' Missié-à!*"

One after another, each holds up a velvety cheek to kiss. And Mimi, who has been asking her mother the same question over and over again for at least five minutes without being able to obtain an answer, ventures to demand of me on the strength of this introduction:—

—"*Missié, oti masque-à?*"

—"*Y ben fou, pouloss!*" the mother cries out;—"Why, the child must be going out of her senses! . . . *Mimi pa 'mbêté moune conm ça!—pa ni piess masque: c'est la-vérette qui ni.*" (Don't annoy people like that!—there are no maskers now; there is nothing but the verette!)

[You are not annoying me at all, little Mimi; but I would not like to answer your question truthfully. I know where the maskers are,—most of them, child; and I do not think it would be well for you to know. They wear no masks now; but if you were to see them for even one moment, by some extraordinary accident, pretty Mimi, I think you would feel more frightened than you ever felt before.] . . .

—*"Toutt lanuite y k'anni rêvé masque-à,"* continues Yzore. . . . I am curious to know what Mimi's dreams are like;—wonder if I can coax her to tell me. . . .

XIX.

. . . I HAVE written Mimi's last dream from the child's dictation:—*

—"I saw a ball," she says. "I was dreaming: I saw everybody dancing with masks on;—I was looking at them. And all at once saw that the folks who were dancing were all made of pasteboard. And I saw a commandeur: he asked me what I was doing there. I answered him: 'Why, I saw a ball, and I came to look—what of it?' He answered me:—'Since you are so curious to come and look at other folks' business, you will have to stop here and dance too!' I said to him:—'No! I won't dance with people made of pasteboard;—I am afraid of them!' . . . And I ran and ran and ran,—I was so much afraid. And I ran into a big garden, where I saw a big cherry-tree that had only leaves upon it; and I saw a man sitting under the cherry-tree. He asked me:—'What are you doing here?' I said to him:—'I am trying to find my way out.' He said:—'You must stay here.' I said:—'No, no!'—and I said, in order to be able to get

---

*—"Moin té ouè yon bal;—moin rêvé: moin té ka ouè toutt moune ka dansé masqué; moin té ka gàdé. Et toutt-à-coup moin ka ouè c'est bon-homme-cáton ka dansé. Et moin ka ouè yon Commandé: y ka mandé moin ça moin ka fai là. Moin reponne y conm ça:—'Moin ouè yon bal, moin gàdé—coument!' Y ka réponne moin:—'Pisse ou si quirièse pou vini gàdé baggaïe moune, faut rété là pou dansé 'tou.' Moin réponne y:—'Non! moin pa dansé épi bonhomme-càton!—moin pè!' . . . Et moin ka couri, moin ka couri, moin ka couri à fòce moin té ni pè. Et moin rentré adans grand jàdin; et moin ouè gouôs pié-cirise qui té chàgé anni feuill; et moin ka ouè yon nhomme as-sise enba cirise-à. Y mandé moin:—'Ça ou ka fai là?' Moin di y:—'Moin ka châché chimin pou moin allé.' Y di moin:—'Faut rété içitt.' Et moin di y:—'Non!'—et pou chappé cò moin, moin di y:—'Allé enhaut-là: ou ké ouè yon bel bal,—toutt bonhomme-càton ka dansé, épi yon Commandè-en-càton ka coumandé yo.' . . . Epi moin levé, à fòce moin té pè." . . .

away:—'Go up there!—you will see a fine ball: all pasteboard people dancing there, and a pasteboard commandeur commanding them!' . . . And then I got so frightened that I awoke." . . .

. . . "And why were you so afraid of them, Mimi?" I ask.

—"*Pace yo té toutt vide endedans!*" answers Mimi. (*Because they were all hollow inside!*)

xx.

March 19th.

. . . THE death-rate in St. Pierre is now between three hundred and fifty and four hundred a month. Our street is being depopulated. Every day men come with immense stretchers,—covered with a sort of canvas awning,—to take somebody away to the *lazaretto*. At brief intervals, also, coffins are carried into houses empty, and carried out again followed by women who cry so loud that their sobbing can be heard a great way off.

. . . Before the visitation few quarters were so densely peopled: there were living often in one small house as many as fifty. The poorer classes had been accustomed from birth to live as simply as animals,—wearing scarcely any clothing, sleeping on bare floors, exposing themselves to all changes of weather, eating the cheapest and coarsest food. Yet, though living under such adverse conditions, no healthier people could be found, perhaps, in the world,—nor a more cleanly. Every yard having its fountain, almost everybody could bathe daily,—and with hundreds it was the custom to enter the river every morning at daybreak, or to take a swim in the bay (the young women here swim as well as the men). . . . But the pestilence, entering among so dense and unprotected a life, made extraordinarily rapid havoc; and bodily cleanliness availed little against the contagion. Now all the bathing resorts are deserted,—because the lazarettos infect the bay with refuse, and because the clothing of the sick is washed in the Roxelane.

. . . Guadeloupe, the sister colony, now sends aid;—the sum total is less than a single American merchant might give to a charitable undertaking: but it is a great deal for Guadeloupe to give. And far Cayenne sends money too; and the mother-country will send one hundred thousand francs.

XXI.

March 20th.

. . . THE infinite goodness of this colored population to one
another is something which impresses with astonishment those
accustomed to the selfishness of the world's great cities. No one
is suffered to go to the pest-house who has a bed to lie upon,
and a single relative or tried friend to administer remedies;—
the multitude who pass through the lazarettos are strangers,—
persons from the country who have no home of their own, or
servants who are not permitted to remain sick in houses of employers. . . . There are, however, many cases where a mistress
will not suffer her bonne to take the risks of the pest-house,—
especially in families where there are no children: the domestic
is carefully nursed; a physician hired for her, remedies purchased for her. . . .

But among the colored people themselves the heroism displayed is beautiful, is touching,—something which makes one
doubt all accepted theories about the natural egotism of
mankind, and would compel the most hardened pessimist to
conceive a higher idea of humanity. There is never a moment's
hesitation in visiting a stricken individual: every relative, and
even the most intimate friends of every relative, may be seen
hurrying to the bedside. They take turns at nursing, sitting up
all night, securing medical attendance and medicines, without
ever a thought of the danger,—nay, of the almost absolute certainty of contagion. If the patient have no means, all contri-
bute: what the sister or brother has not, the uncle or the aunt,
the godfather or godmother, the cousin, brother-in-law or
sister-in-law, may be able to give. No one dreams of refusing
money or linen or wine or anything possible to give, lend, or
procure on credit. Women seem to forget that they are beautiful, that they are young, that they are loved,—to forget everything but the sense of that which they hold to be duty. You see
young girls of remarkably elegant presence,—young colored
girls well educated and *élevées-en-chapeau** (that is to say,

---

*Lit.,—"brought-up-in-a-hat." To wear the madras is to acknowledge one-
self of color;—to follow the European style of dressing the hair, and adopt the
costume of the white creoles indicates a desire to affiliate with the white class.

brought up like white creole girls, dressed and accomplished like them), voluntarily leave rich homes to nurse some poor mulatress or capresse in the indigent quarters of the town, because the sick one happens to be a distant relative. They will not trust others to perform this for them;—they feel bound to do it in person. I heard such a one say, in reply to some earnest protest about thus exposing herself (she had never been vaccinated):
—"*Ah! quand il s'agit du devoir, la vie ou la mort c'est pour moi la même chose.*"

. . . But without any sanitary law to check this self-immolation, and with the conviction that in the presence of duty, or what is believed to be duty, "life or death is the same thing," or ought to be so considered,—you can readily imagine how soon the city must become one vast hospital.

XXII.

. . . By nine o'clock, as a general rule, St. Pierre becomes silent: every one here retires early and rises with the sun. But sometimes, when the night is exceptionally warm, people continue to sit at their doors and chat until a far later hour; and on such a night one may hear and see curious things, in this period of plague. . . .

It is certainly singular that while the howling of a dog at night has no ghastly signification here (nobody ever pays the least attention to the sound, however hideous), the moaning and screaming of cats is believed to bode death; and in these times folks never appear to feel too sleepy to rise at any hour and drive them away when they begin their cries. . . . To-night—a night so oppressive that all but the sick are sitting up—almost a panic is created in our street by a screaming of cats;—and long after the creatures have been hunted out of sight and hearing, everybody who has a relative ill with the prevailing malady continues to discuss the omen with terror.

. . . Then I observe a colored child standing barefooted in the moonlight, with her little round arms uplifted and hands joined above her head. A more graceful little figure it would be hard to find as she appears thus posed; but, all unconsciously, she is violating another superstition by this very attitude; and the angry mother shrieks:—

—"*Ti manmaille-là!—tiré lanmain-ou assous tête-ou, foute! pisse moin encò là! . . . Espéré moin allé lazarett avant metté lanmain conm ça!*" (Child, take down your hands from your head . . . because I am here yet! Wait till I go to the lazaretto before you put up your hands like that!)

For it was the savage, natural, primitive gesture of mourning, —of great despair.

. . . Then all begin to compare their misfortunes, to relate their miseries;—they say grotesque things,—even make jests about their troubles. One declares:—

—"*Si moin té ka venne chapeau, à fòce moin ni malhè, toutt manman sé fai yche yo sans tête.*" (I have that ill-luck, that if I were selling hats all the mothers would have children without heads!)

—Those who sit at their doors, I observe, do not sit, as a rule, upon the steps, even when these are of wood. There is a superstition which checks such a practice. "*Si ou assise assous pas-lapòte, ou ké pouend doulè toutt moune.*" (If you sit upon the door-step, you will take the pain of all who pass by.)

XXIII.

March 30th.

GOOD FRIDAY. . . .

The bells have ceased to ring,—even the bells for the dead; the hours are marked by cannon-shots. The ships in the harbor form crosses with their spars, turn their flags upside down. And the entire colored population put on mourning:—it is a custom among them centuries old.

You will not perceive a single gaudy robe to-day, a single cal-endered Madras: not a speck of showy color is visible through all the ways of St. Pierre. The costumes donned are all similar to those worn for the death of relatives: either full mourning,—a black robe with violet foulard, and dark violet-banded head-kerchief; or half-mourning,—a dark violet robe with black foulard and turban;—the half-mourning being worn only by those who cannot afford the more sombre costume. From my window I can see long processions climbing the mornes about the city, to visit the shrines and crucifixes, and to pray for the cessation of the pestilence.

. . . Three o'clock. Three cannon-shots shake the hills: it is the supposed hour of the Saviour's death. All believers—whether in the churches, on the highways, or in their homes—bow down and kiss the cross thrice, or, if there be no cross, press their lips three times to the ground or the pavement, and utter those three wishes which if expressed precisely at this traditional moment will surely, it is held, be fulfilled. Immense crowds are assembled before the crosses on the heights, and about the statue of Notre Dame de la Garde.

. . . There is no hubbub in the streets; there is not even the customary loud weeping to be heard as the coffins go by. One must not complain to-day, nor become angry, nor utter unkind words,—any fault committed on Good Friday is thought to obtain a special and awful magnitude in the sight of Heaven. . . . There is a curious saying in vogue here. If a son or daughter grow up vicious,—become a shame to the family and a curse to the parents,—it is observed of such:—"*Ça, c'est yon péché Vendredi-Saint!*" (Must be a *Good Friday sin!*)

There are two other strange beliefs connected with Good Friday. One is that it always rains on that day,—that the sky weeps for the death of the Saviour; and that this rain, if caught in a vessel, will never evaporate or spoil, and will cure all diseases.

The other is that only Jesus Christ died precisely at three o'clock. Nobody else ever died exactly at that hour;—they may die a second before or a second after three, but never exactly at three.

XXIV.

March 31st.

. . . HOLY SATURDAY morning;—nine o'clock. All the bells suddenly ring out; the humming of the *bourdon* blends with the thunder of a hundred guns: this is the *Gloria*! . . . At this signal it is a religious custom for the whole coast-population to enter the sea, and for those living too far from the beach to bathe in the rivers. But rivers and sea are now alike infected;—all the linen of the lazarettos has been washed therein; and to-day there are fewer bathers than usual.

But there are twenty-seven burials. Now they are burying the dead two together: the cemeteries are overburdened. . . .

XXV.

. . . IN most of the old stone houses you will occasionally see spiders of terrifying size,—measuring across perhaps as much as six inches from the tip of one out-stretched leg to the tip of its opposite fellow, as they cling to the wall. I never heard of any one being bitten by them; and among the poor it is deemed unlucky to injure or drive them away. . . . But early this morning Yzore swept her house clean, and ejected through the door-way quite a host of these monster insects. Manm-Robert is quite dismayed:—

—"*Jesis-Maïa!*—ou 'lè malhè encò pou fai ça, chè? (You want to have still more bad luck, that you do such a thing?)

And Yzore answers:—

—"*Toutt moune içitt pa ni yon sou!—gouôs conm ça fil za-grignin, et moin pa menm mangé! Epi laverette encò. . . . Moin couè toutt ça ka pòté malhè!*" (No one here has a sou!—heaps of cobwebs like that, and nothing to eat yet; and the verette into the bargain. . . . I think those things bring bad luck.)

—"Ah! you have not eaten yet!" cries Manm-Robert. "*Vini épi moin!*" (Come with me!)

And Yzore—already feeling a little remorse for her treatment of the spiders—murmurs apologetically as she crosses over to Manm-Robert's little shop:—"*Moin pa tchoué yo; moin chassé yo—ké vini encò.*" (I did not kill them; I only put them out;—they will come back again.)

But long afterwards, Manm-Robert remarked to me that they never went back. . . .

XXVI.

April 5th.

—"*Toutt bel bois ka allé,*" says Manm-Robert. (All the beautiful trees are going.) . . . I do not understand.

—"*Toutt bel bois—toutt bel moune ka allé,*" she adds, interpretatively. (All the "beautiful trees,"—all the handsome people,—are passing away.) . . . As in the speech of the world's primitive poets, so in the creole patois is a beautiful woman compared with a comely tree: nay, more than this, the name of the object is actually substituted for that of the living being. *Yon bel bois* may mean a fine tree: it more generally signifies a graceful woman: this is the very comparison made by Ulysses looking upon Nausicaa, though more naïvely expressed. . . . And now there comes to me the recollection of a creole ballad illustrating the use of the phrase,—a ballad about a youth of Fort-de-France sent to St. Pierre by his father to purchase a stock of dobannes,* who, falling in love with a handsome colored girl, spent all his father's money in buying her presents and a wedding outfit:—

> "Moin descenne Saint-Piè
> Acheté dobannes
> Auliè ces dobannes
> C'est yon *bel-bois* moin mennein monté!"

("I went down to Saint-Pierre to buy dobannes: instead of the dobannes, 'tis a pretty tree—a charming girl—that I bring back with me.")

—"Why, who is dead now, Manm-Robert?"

—"It is little Marie, the porteuse, who has got the vérette. She is gone to the lazaretto."

XXVII.

April 7th.

—*Toutt bel bois ka allé.* . . . News has just come that Ti Marie died last night at the lazaretto of the Fort: she was attacked by what they call the *lavérette-pouff*,—a form of the disease which strangles its victim within a few hours.

Ti Marie was certainly the neatest little màchanne I ever knew. Without being actually pretty, her face had a childish charm which made it a pleasure to look at her;—and she had a clear chocolate-red skin, a light compact little figure, and a remarkably symmetrical pair of little feet which had never felt the pressure of a shoe. Every morning I used to hear her passing cry, just about daybreak:—"*Qui 'lè café?—qui 'lè sirop?*" (Who

---

*Red earthen-ware jars for keeping drinking-water cool. The origin of the word is probably to be sought in the name of the town, near Marseilles, where they are made,—"Aubagne."

wants coffee?—who wants syrup?) She looked about sixteen: but was a mother. "Where is her husband?" I ask. "*Nhomme-y mò laverette 'tou.*" (Her man died of the verette also.) "And the little one, her *yche*?" "Y lazarett." (At the lazaretto.) . . . But only those without friends or relatives in the city are suffered to go to the lazaretto;—Ti Marie cannot have been of St. Pierre?

—"No: she was from Vauclin," answers Manm-Robert. "You do not often see pretty red girls who are natives of St. Pierre. St. Pierre has pretty *sang-mêlées.* The pretty red girls mostly come from Vauclin. The yellow ones, who are really *belbois,* are from Grande Anse: they are banana-colored people there. At Gros-Morne they are generally black." . . .

XXVIII.

. . . IT appears that the red race here, the *race capresse*, is particularly liable to the disease. Every family employing capresses for house-servants loses them;—one family living at the next corner has lost four in succession. . . .

The tint is a cinnamon or chocolate color;—the skin is naturally clear, smooth, glossy: it is of the capresse especially that the term "sapota-skin" (*peau-chapoti*) is used,—coupled with all curious creole adjectives to express what is comely,—*jojoll, beaujoll,** etc. The hair is long, but bushy; the limbs light and strong, and admirably shaped. . . . I am told that when transported to a colder climate, the capre or capresse partly loses this ruddy tint. Here, under the tropic sun, it has a beauty only possible to imitate in metal. . . . And because photography cannot convey any idea of this singular color, the capresse

---

*I may cite in this relation one stanza of a creole song—very popular in St. Pierre—celebrating the charms of a little capresse:—

> "Moin toutt jeine,
> Gouôs, gouâs, vaillant,
> Peau di chapoti
> Ka fai plaisi;—
> Lapeau moin
> Li bien poli;
> Et moin ka plai
> Mênm toutt nhomme grave!"

hates a photograph.—"*Moin pas nouè*," she says;—"*moin ouóuge: ou fai moin nouè nans pòtrait-à.*" (I am not black: I am red:—you make me black in that portrait.) It is difficult to make her pose before the camera: she is red, as she avers, beautifully red; but the malicious instrument makes her gray or black—*nouè conm poule-zo-nouè* ("black as a black-boned hen!").

. . . And this red race is disappearing from St. Pierre—doubtless also from other plague-stricken centres.

XXIX.

April 10th.

. . . MANM-ROBERT is much annoyed and puzzled because the American steamer—the *bom-mangé*, as she calls it—does not come. It used to bring regularly so many barrels of potatoes and beans, so much lard and cheese and garlic and dried pease—everything, almost, of which she keeps a stock. It is now nearly eight weeks since the cannon of a New York steamer aroused the echoes of the harbor. Every morning Manm-Robert has been sending out her little servant Louis to see if there is any sign of the American packet:—"*Allé ouè Batterie d'Esnotz si bom-mangé-à pas vini.*" But Louis always returns with the same rueful answer:—

—"*Manm-Robert, pa ni piess bom-mangé*" (there is not so much as a bit of a *bom-mangé*).

. . . "No more American steamers for Martinique:" that is the news received by telegraph! The disease has broken out among the shipping; the harbors have been declared infected. United States mail-packets drop their Martinique mails at St. Kitt's or Dominica, and pass us by. There will be suffering

---

—Which might be freely rendered thus:—

> "I am dimpled, young,
> Round-limbed, and strong,
> With sapota-skin
> That is good to see:
> All glossy-smooth
> Is this skin of mine;
> And the gravest men
> Like to look at me!"

now among the *canotiers*, the *caboteurs*, all those who live by stowing or unloading cargo;—great warehouses are being closed up, and strong men discharged, because there will be nothing for them to do.

. . . They are burying twenty-five *verettiers* per day in the city.

But never was this tropic sky more beautiful;—never was this circling sea more marvellously blue;—never were the mornes more richly robed in luminous green, under a more golden day. . . . And it seems strange that Nature should remain so lovely. . . .

. . . Suddenly it occurs to me that I have not seen Yzore nor her children for some days; and I wonder if they have moved away. . . . Towards evening, passing by Manm-Robert's, I ask about them. The old woman answers me very gravely:—

—"*Atò, mon chè, c'est Yzore qui ni lavérette!*"

The mother has been seized by the plague at last. But Manm-Robert will look after her; and Manm-Robert has taken charge of the three little ones, who are not now allowed to leave the house, for fear some one should tell them what it were best they should not know. . . . *Pauv ti manmaille!*

XXX.

April 13th.

. . . STILL the vérette does not attack the native whites. But the whole air has become poisoned; the sanitary condition of the city becomes unprecedentedly bad; and a new epidemic makes its appearance,—typhoid fever. And now the békés begin to go, especially the young and strong; and the bells keep sounding for them, and the tolling bourdon fills the city with its enormous hum all day and far into the night. For these are rich; and the high solemnities of burial are theirs—the coffin of acajou, and the triple ringing, and the Cross of Gold to be carried before them as they pass to their long sleep under the palms,—saluted for the last time by all the population of St. Pierre, standing bareheaded in the sun. . . .

. . . Is it in times like these, when all the conditions are febrile, that one is most apt to have queer dreams?

Last night it seemed to me that I saw that Carnival dance again,—the hooded musicians, the fantastic torrent of peaked caps, and the spectral masks, and the swaying of bodies and waving of arms,—but soundless as a passing of smoke. There were figures I thought I knew;—hands I had somewhere seen reached out and touched me in silence;—and then, all suddenly, a Viewless Something seemed to scatter the shapes as leaves are blown by a wind. . . . And waking, I thought I heard again,—plainly as on that last Carnival afternoon,—the strange cry of fear:—"*C'est Bon-Dié ka passé!*" . . .

XXXI.

April 20th.

. . . VERY early yesterday morning Yzore was carried away under a covering of quick-lime: the children do not know; Manm-Robert took heed they should not see. They have been told their mother has been taken to the country to get well,— that the doctor will bring her back soon. . . . All the furniture is to be sold at auction to pay the debts;—the landlord was patient, he waited four months; the doctor was kindly: but now these must have their due. Everything will be bidden off, except the chapelle, with its Virgin and angels of porcelain: *yo pa ka pè venne Bon-Dié* (the things of the Good-God must not be sold). And Manm-Robert will take care of the little ones.

The bed—a relic of former good-fortune,—a great Martinique bed of carved heavy native wood,—a *lit-à-bateau* (boat-bed), so called because shaped almost like a barge, perhaps— will surely bring three hundred francs;—the armoire, with its mirror doors, not less than two hundred and fifty. There is little else of value: the whole will not fetch enough to pay all the dead owes.

XXXII.

April 28th.

—*Tam-tam-tam!*—*tam-tam-tam!* . . . It is the booming of the auction-drum from the Place: Yzore's furniture is about to change hands.

The children start at the sound, so vividly associated in their minds with the sights of Carnival days, with the fantastic mirth of the great processional dance: they run to the sunny street, calling to each other,—*Vini ouè!*—they look up and down. But there is a great quiet in the Rue du Morne Mirail;—the street is empty.

. . . Manm-Robert enters very weary: she has been at the sale, trying to save something for the children, but the prices were too high. In silence she takes her accustomed seat at the worn counter of her little shop; the young ones gather about her, caress her;—Mimi looks up laughing into the kind brown face, and wonders why Manm-Robert will not smile. Then Mimi becomes afraid to ask where the maskers are,—why they do not come. But little Maurice, bolder and less sensitive, cries out:—

—"*Manm-Robert, oti masque-à?*"

Manm-Robert does not answer;—she does not hear. She is gazing directly into the young faces clustered about her knee, —yet she does not see them: she sees far, far beyond them,— into the hidden years. And, suddenly, with a savage tenderness in her voice, she utters all the dark thought of her heart for them:—

—"*Toua ti blancs sans lesou!—quitté moin châché papa-ou qui adans cimétiè pou vini pouend ou tou!*" (Ye three little pen-niless white ones!—let me go call your father, who is in the cemetery, to come and take you also away!)

Les Blanchisseuses

WHOEVER stops for a few months in St. Pierre is certain, sooner or later, to pass an idle half-hour in that charming place of Martinique idlers,—the beautiful Savane du Fort,—and, once there, is equally certain to lean a little while over the mossy parapet of the river-wall to watch the *blanchisseuses* at work. It has a curious interest, this spectacle of primitive toil: the deep channel of the Roxelane winding under the palm-crowned heights of the Fort; the blinding whiteness of linen laid out to bleach for miles upon the huge bowlders of porphyry and prismatic basalt; and the dark bronze-limbed women, with faces hidden under immense straw hats, and knees in the rushing torrent,—all form a scene that makes one think of the earliest civilizations. Even here, in this modern colony, it is nearly three centuries old; and it will probably continue thus at the Rivière des Blanchisseuses for fully another three hundred years. Quaint as certain weird Breton legends whereof it reminds you, —especially if you watch it before daybreak while the city still sleeps,—this fashion of washing is not likely to change. There is a local prejudice against new methods, new inventions, new ideas,—several efforts at introducing a less savage style of washing proved unsuccessful; and an attempt to establish a steam-laundry resulted in failure. The public were quite con-tented with the old ways of laundrying, and saw no benefits to be gained by forsaking them;—while the washers and ironers engaged by the laundry proprietor at higher rates than they had ever obtained before soon wearied of in-door work, abandoned their situations, and returned with a sense of relief to their ancient way of working out in the blue air and the wind of the hills, with their feet in the mountain-water and their heads in the awful sun.

. . . It is one of the sights of St. Pierre,—this daily scene at the River of the Washerwomen: everybody likes to watch it;—the men, because among the blanchisseuses there are not a few decidedly handsome girls; the women, probably because a woman feels always interested in woman's work. All the white bridges of the Roxelane are dotted with lookers-on during fine

Rivière des Blanchisseuses.

days, and particularly in the morning, when every bonne on her way to and from the market stops a moment to observe or to greet those blanchisseuses whom she knows. Then one hears such a calling and clamoring,—such an intercrossing of cries from the bridge to the river, and the river to the bridge. . . . "Ouill! Noémi!" . . . "Coument ou yé, chè?" . . . "Eh! Pascaline!" . . . "Bonjou', Youtte!—Dédé!—Fifi!—Henrillia!" . . . "Coument ou kallé, Cyrillia?" . . . "Toutt douce, chè!—et Ti Mémé?" . . . "Y bien;—oti Ninotte?" . . . "Bo ti manmaille pou moin, chè—ou tanne?" . . . But the bridge leading to the market of the Fort is the poorest point of view; for the better classes of blanchisseuses are not there: only the lazy, the weak, or non-professionals—house-servants, who do washing at the river two or three times a month as part of their family-service—are apt to get so far down. The experienced professionals and early risers secure the best places and choice of rocks; and among the hundreds at work you can discern something like a physical gradation. At the next bridge the women look better, stronger; more young faces appear; and the further you follow the river-course towards the Jardin des Plantes, the more the appearance of the blanchisseuses improves,—so that within the space of a mile you can see well exemplified one natural law of life's struggle,—the best chances to the best constitutions.

You might also observe, if you watch long enough, that among the blanchisseuses there are few sufficiently light of color to be classed as bright mulatresses;—the majority are black or of that dark copper-red race which is perhaps superior to the black creole in strength and bulk; for it requires a skin insensible to sun as well as the toughest of constitutions to be a blanchisseuse. A porteuse can begin to make long trips at nine or ten years; but no girl is strong enough to learn the washing-trade until she is past twelve. The blanchisseuse is the hardest worker among the whole population;—her daily labor is rarely less than thirteen hours; and during the greater part of that time she is working in the sun, and standing up to her knees in water that descends quite cold from the mountain peaks. Her labor makes her perspire profusely; and she can never venture to cool herself by further immersion without serious danger of pleurisy. The trade is said to kill all who continue at it beyond a certain number of years:—"*Nou ka mò toutt dleau*" (we all die of the water), one told me, replying to a question. No feeble or light-skinned person can attempt to do a single day's work of this kind without danger; and a weak girl, driven by necessity to do her own washing, seldom ventures to go to the river. Yet I saw an instance of such rashness one day. A pretty sang-mêlée, per-haps about eighteen or nineteen years old,—whom I after-wards learned had just lost her mother and found herself thus absolutely destitute,—began to descend one of the flights of stone steps leading to the river, with a small bundle upon her head; and two or three of the blanchisseuses stopped their work to look at her. A tall capresse inquired mischievously:—

—"*Ou vini pou pouend yon bain?*" (Coming to take a bath?) For the river is a great bathing-place.

—"*Non; moin vini lavé.*" (No; I am coming to wash.)

—"*Aïe! aïe! aïe!—y vini lavé!*" . . . And all within hearing laughed together. "Are you crazy, girl?—*ess ou fou?*" The tall capresse snatched the bundle from her, opened it, threw a gar-ment to her nearest neighbor, another to the next one, dividing the work among a little circle of friends, and said to the stranger, "Non ké lavé toutt ça ba ou bien vite, chè,—va, amisé ou!" (We'll wash this for you very quickly, dear—go and amuse your-self!) These kind women even did more for the poor girl;—they subscribed to buy her a good breakfast, when the food-seller—the màchanne-mangé—made her regular round among them, with fried fish and eggs and manioc flour and bananas.

II.

ALL of the multitude who wash clothing at the river are not professional blanchisseuses. Hundreds of women, too poor to pay for laundrying, do their own work at the Roxelane;—and numerous bonnes there wash the linen of their mistresses as a regular part of their domestic duty. But even if the profession-als did not always occupy a certain well-known portion of the channel, they could easily be distinguished from others by their rapid and methodical manner of work, by the ease with which immense masses of linen are handled by them, and, above all, by their way of whipping it against the rocks. Furthermore, the greater number of professionals are likewise teachers, mistresses (*bou'geoises*), and have their apprentices beside them,—young girls from twelve to sixteen years of age. Among these *apprenti*, as they are called in the patois, there are many attractive types, such as idlers upon the bridges like to look at.

If, after one year of instruction, the apprentice fails to prove a good washer, it is not likely she will ever become one; and there are some branches of the trade requiring a longer period of teaching and of practice. The young girl first learns simply to soap and wash the linen in the river, which operation is called "rubbing" (*frotté* in creole);—after she can do this pretty well, she is taught the curious art of whipping it (*fessé*). You can hear the sound of the fessé a great way off, echoing and re-echoing among the mornes: it is not a sharp smacking noise, as the name might seem to imply, but a heavy hollow sound exactly like that of an axe splitting dry timber. In fact, it so closely resembles the latter sound that you are apt on first hearing it to look up at the mornes with the expectation of seeing woodmen there at work. And it is not made by striking the linen with anything, but only by lashing it against the sides of the rocks. . . . After a piece has been well rubbed and rinsed, it is folded up into a peculiar sheaf-shape, and seized by the closely gathered end for the fessé. Then the folding process is repeated on the reverse, and the other end whipped. This process expels suds that rinsing cannot remove: it must be done very dexterously to avoid tearing or damaging the material. By an experienced hand the linen is never torn; and even pearl and bone buttons are much less often broken than might be supposed. The singular echo is altogether due to the manner of folding the article for the fessé.

After this, all the pieces are spread out upon the rocks, in the sun, for the "first bleaching" (*pouèmiè lablanie*). In the evening they are gathered into large wooden trays or baskets, and carried to what is called the "lye-house" (*lacaïe lessive*)—overlooking the river from a point on the Fort bank opposite to the higher end of the Savane. Here each blanchisseuse hires a small or a large vat, or even several,—according to the quantity of work done,—at two, three, or ten sous, and leaves her washing to steep in lye (*coulé* is the creole word used) during the night. There are watchmen to guard it. Before daybreak it is rinsed in warm water; then it is taken back to the river,—is rinsed again, ready for ironing. To press and iron well is the most difficult part of the trade. When an apprentice is able to iron a gentleman's shirt nicely, and a pair of white pantaloons, she is considered to have finished her time;—she becomes a journey-woman (*ouvouïyé*).

Even in a country where wages are almost incredibly low, the blanchisseuse earns considerable money. There is no fixed scale of prices: it is even customary to bargain with these women beforehand. Shirts and white pantaloons figure at six and eight cents in laundry bills; but other washing is much cheaper. I saw a lot of thirty-three pieces—including such large ones as sheets, bed-covers, and several douillettes (the long Martinique trailing robes of one piece from neck to feet)—for which only three francs was charged. Articles are frequently stolen or lost by house-servants sent to do washing at the river; but very seldom indeed by the regular blanchisseuses. Few of them can read or write or understand owners' marks on wearing apparel; and when you see at the river the wilderness of scattered linen, the seemingly enormous confusion, you cannot understand how these women manage to separate and classify it all. Yet they do this admirably,—and for that reason perhaps more than any other, are able to charge fair rates;—it is false economy to have your washing done by the house-servant;—with the professionals your property is safe. And cheap as her rates are, a good professional can make from twenty-five to thirty francs a week; averaging fully a hundred francs a month,—as much as many a white clerk can earn in the stores of St. Pierre, and quite as much (considering local differences in the purchasing power of money) as $60 per month would represent in the United States.

Probably the ability to earn large wages often tempts the blanchisseuse to continue at her trade until it kills her. The "water-disease," as she calls it (*maladie-dleau*), makes its appearance after middle-life: the feet, lower limbs, and abdomen swell enormously, while the face becomes almost fleshless;—then, gradually tissues give way, muscles yield, and the whole physical structure crumbles.

Nevertheless, the blanchisseuse is essentially a sober liver,—never a drunkard. In fact, she is sober from rigid necessity: she would not dare to swallow one mouthful of spirits while at work with her feet in the cold water;—everybody else in Martinique, even the little children, can drink rum; the blanchisseuse cannot, unless she wishes to die of a congestion. Her strongest refreshment is *mabi*,—a mild, effervescent, and, I think, rather disagreeable, beer made from molasses.

III.

ALWAYS before daybreak they rise to work, while the vapors of the mornes fill the air with scent of mouldering vegetation,—clayey odors,—grassy smells: there is only a faint gray light, and the water of the river is very chill. One by one they arrive, barefooted, under their burdens built up tower-shape on their trays;—silently as ghosts they descend the steps to the riverbed, and begin to unfold and immerse their washing. They greet each other as they come, then become silent again; there is scarcely any talking: the hearts of all are heavy with the heaviness of the hour. But the gray light turns yellow; the sun climbs over the peaks: light changes the dark water to living crystal; and all begin to chatter a little. Then the city awakens; the currents of its daily life circulate again,—thinly and slowly at first, then swiftly and strongly,—up and down every yellow street, and through the Savane, and over the bridges of the river. Passers-by pause to look down, and cry "*bonjou', chè!*" Idle men stare at some pretty washer, till she points at them and cries:—"*Gadé Missié-à ka guetté nou!—anh!—anh!—anh!*" And all the others look up and repeat the groan—"*anh!—anh!—anh!*" till the starers beat a retreat. The air grows warmer; the sky blue takes fire: the great light makes joy for the washers; they shout to each other from distance to distance, jest, laugh, sing. Gusty of speech these women are: long habit of calling to one another through the roar of the torrent has given their voices a singular sonority and force: it is well worth while to hear them sing. One starts the song,—the next joins her; then another and another, till all the channel rings with the melody from the bridge of the Jardin des Plantes to the Pont-bois:—

> "C'est moin qui té ka lavé,
>   Passé, raccommodé:
>   Y té néf hè disouè

> Ou metté moin derhò,—
> Yche moin assous bouas moin;—
> Laplie té ka tombé—
> Léfan moin assous tête moin!
> Doudoux, ou m'abandonne!
> Moin pa ni pèsonne pou soigné moin."*

. . . A melancholy chant—originally a Carnival improvisation made to bring public shame upon the perpetrator of a cruel act;—but it contains the story of many of these lives—the story of industrious affectionate women temporarily united to brutal and worthless men in a country where legal marriages are rare. Half of the creole songs which I was able to collect during a residence of nearly two years in the island touch upon the same sad theme. Of these, "Chè Manman Moin," a great favorite still with the older blanchisseuses, has a simple pathos unrivalled, I believe, in the oral literature of this people. Here is an attempt to translate its three rhymeless stanzas into prose; but the childish sweetness of the patois original is lost:—

CHÈ MANMAN MOIN.

I.

. . . "Dear mamma, once you were young like I;—dear papa, you also have been young;—dear great elder brother, you too have been young. Ah! let me cherish this sweet friendship!—so sick my heart is—yes, 'tis very, very ill, this heart of mine: love, only love can make it well again." . . .

II.

"O cursed eyes he praised that led me to him! O cursed lips of mine which ever repeated his name! O cursed moment in which I gave up my heart to the ingrate who no longer knows how to love." . . .

III.

"Doudoux, you swore to me by Heaven!—doudoux, you swore to me by your faith! . . . And now you cannot come to me? . . . Oh! my heart is withering with pain! . . . I was passing by the cemetery;—

---

*It was I who washed and ironed and mended;—at nine o'clock at night thou didst put me out-of-doors, with my child in my arms,—the rain was falling,—with my poor straw mattress upon my head! . . . Doudoux! thou dost abandon me! . . . I have none to care for me.

I saw my name upon a stone—all by itself. I saw two white roses; and in a moment one faded and fell before me. . . . So my forgotten heart will be!" . . .

The air is not so charming, however, as that of a little song which every creole knows, and which may be often heard still at the river: I think it is the prettiest of all creole melodies. "To-to-to" (patois for the French *toc*) is an onomatope for the sound of knocking at a door.

> "*To, to, to!*—'Ça qui là?'
> —'C'est moin-mênme, lanmou;—
> Ouvé lapott ba moin!'

> "*To, to, to!*—'Ça qui là?'
> —'C'est moin-mênme lanmou,
> Qui ka ba ou khè moin!'

> "*To, to, to!*—'Ça qui là?'
> —'C'est moin-mênme lanmou;
> Laplie ka mouillé moin!' "

[*To-to-to.* . . . "Who taps there?"—"'Tis mine own self Love: open the door for me."

To-to-to. . . . "Who taps there?"—"'Tis mine own self Love, who give my heart to thee."

To-to-to. . . . "Who taps there?"—"'Tis mine own self Love: open thy door to me;—the rain is wetting me!" . . .]

. . . But it is more common to hear the blanchisseuses singing merry, jaunty, sarcastic ditties,—Carnival compositions,—in which the African sense of rhythmic melody is more marked:—"Marie-Clémence maudi," "Loéma tombé," "Quand ou ni ti mari jojoll."*

—At mid-day the màchanne-mangé comes, with her girls,—carrying trays of fried fish, and *akras*, and cooked beans, and bottles of mabi. The blanchisseuses buy, and eat with their feet in the water, using rocks for tables. Each has her little tin cup to drink her mabi in. . . . Then the washing and the chanting and the booming of the fessé begin again. Afternoon wanes;—school-hours close; and children of many beautiful colors

---

*See Appendix for specimens of creole music.

come to the river, and leap down the steps crying, "*Eti! man-man!*"—"*Sésé!*"—"*Nenneine!*" calling their elder sisters, mothers, and godmothers: the little boys strip naked to play in the water a while. . . . Towards sunset the more rapid and active workers begin to gather in their linen, and pile it on trays. Large patches of bald rock appear again. . . . By six o'clock almost the whole bed of the river is bare;—the women are nearly all gone. A few linger a while on the Savane, to watch the last-comer. There is always a great laugh at the last to leave the channel: they ask her if she has not forgotten "to lock up the river."

—"*Ou fèmé lapòte lariviè, chè—anh?*"

—"*Ah! oui, chè!—moin fèmé y, ou tanne?—moin ni laclé-à!*" (Oh yes, dear. I locked it up,—you hear?—I've got the key!)

But there are days and weeks when they do not sing,—times of want or of plague, when the silence of the valley is broken only by the sound of linen beaten upon the rocks, and the great voice of the Roxelane, which will sing on when the city itself shall have ceased to be, just as it sang one hundred thousand years ago. . . . "Why do they not sing to-day?" I once asked during the summer of 1887,—a year of pestilence. "*Yo ka pensé toutt lanmizè yo,—toutt lapeine yo,*" I was answered. (They are thinking of all their trouble, all their misery.) Yet in all seasons, while youth and strength stay with them, they work on in wind and sun, mist and rain, washing the linen of the living and the dead,—white wraps for the newly born, white robes for the bride, white shrouds for them that pass into the Great Silence. And the torrent that wears away the ribs of the perpetual hills wears away their lives,—sometimes slowly, slowly as black basalt is worn,—sometimes suddenly,—in the twinkling of an eye.

For a strange danger ever menaces the blanchisseuse,—the treachery of the stream! . . . Watch them working, and observe how often they turn their eyes to the high north-east, to look at Pelée. Pelée gives them warning betimes. When all is sunny in St. Pierre, and the harbor lies blue as lapis-lazuli, there may be mighty rains in the region of the great woods and the valleys of the higher peaks; and thin streams swell to raging floods which burst suddenly from the altitudes, rolling down rocks and trees and wreck of forests, uplifting crags, devastating slopes. And sometimes, down the ravine of the Roxelane, there comes a roar as of eruption, with a rush of foaming water like a moving mountain-wall; and bridges and buildings vanish with its passing. In 1865 the Savane, high as it lies above the river-bed, was flooded;—and all the bridges were swept into the sea.

So the older and wiser blanchisseuses keep watch upon Pelée; and if a blackness gather over it, with lightnings breaking through, then—however fair the sun shine on St. Pierre—the alarm is given, the miles of bleaching linen vanish from the rocks in a few minutes, and every one leaves the channel. But it has occasionally happened that Pelée gave no such friendly signal before the river rose: thus lives have been lost. Most of the blanchisseuses are swimmers, and good ones,—I have seen one of these girls swim almost out of sight in the harbor, during an idle hour;—but no swimmer has any chances in a rising of the Roxelane: all overtaken by it are stricken by rocks and drift;— *yo crazé*, as a creole term expresses it,—a term signifying to crush, to bray, to dash to pieces.

. . . Sometimes it happens that one who has been absent at home for a brief while returns to the river only to meet her comrades fleeing from it,—many leaving their linen behind them. But she will not abandon the linen intrusted to her: she makes a run for it,—in spite of warning screams,—in spite of the vain clutching of kind rough fingers. She gains the river-bed;—the flood has already reached her waist, but she is strong; she reaches her linen,—snatches it up, piece by piece, scattered as it is—"one!—two!—five!—seven!";—there is a roaring in her ears—"eleven!—thirteen!" she has it all . . . but now the rocks are moving! For one instant she strives to reach the steps, only a few yards off;—another, and the thunder of the deluge is upon her,—and the crushing crags,—and the spinning trees. . . .

Perhaps before sundown some canotier may find her floating far in the bay,—drifting upon her face in a thousand feet of water,—with faithful dead hands still holding fast the property of her employer.

La Pelée

THE first attempt made to colonize Martinique was abandoned almost as soon as begun, because the leaders of the expedition found the country "too rugged and too mountainous," and were "terrified by the prodigious number of serpents which covered its soil." Landing on June 25, 1635, Olive and Duplessis left the island after a few hours' exploration, or, rather, observation, and made sail for Guadeloupe,—according to the quaint and most veracious history of Père Dutertre, of the Order of Friars-Preachers.

A single glance at the topographical map of Martinique would suffice to confirm the father's assertion that the country was found to be *trop haché et trop montueux*: more than two-thirds of it is peak and mountain;—even to-day only 42,445 of its supposed 98,782 hectares have been cultivated; and on page 426 of the last "Annuaire" (1887) I find the statement that in the interior there are extensive Government lands of which the area is "not exactly known." Yet mountainous as a country must be which—although scarcely forty-nine miles long and twenty miles in average breadth—remains partly unfamiliar to its own inhabitants after nearly three centuries of civilization (there are not half a dozen creoles who have travelled all over it), only two elevations in Martinique bear the name *montagne*. These are La Montagne Pelée, in the north, and La Montagne du Vauclin, in the south. The term *morne*, used throughout the French West Indian colonies to designate certain altitudes of volcanic origin, a term rather unsatisfactorily translated in certain dictionaries as "a small mountain," is justly applied to the majority of Martinique hills, and unjustly sometimes even to its mightiest elevation,—called Morne Pelé, or Montagne Pelée, or simply "La Montagne," according, perhaps, to the varying degree of respect it inspires in different minds. But even in the popular nomenclature one finds the orography of Martinique, as well as of other West Indian islands, regularly classified by *pitons*, *mornes*, and *monts* or *montagnes*. Mornes usually have those beautiful and curious forms which bespeak volcanic origin even to the unscientific observer: they are most often pyramidal or conoid up to a certain height; but have summits either rounded or truncated;—their sides, green with the richest vegetation, rise from valley-levels and coast-lines with remarkable abruptness, and are apt to be curiously ribbed or wrinkled. The pitons, far fewer in number, are much more fantastic in form;—volcanic cones, or volcanic upheavals of splintered strata almost at right angles,—sometimes sharp of line as spires, and mostly too steep for habitation. They are occasionally mammiform, and so symmetrical that one might imagine them artificial creations,—particularly when they occur in pairs. Only a very important mass is dignified by the name *montagne*: there are, as I have already observed, but two thus called in all Martinique,—Pelée, the head and summit of the island; and La Montagne du Vauclin, in the south-east. Vauclin is inferior in height and bulk to several mornes and pitons of the north and north-west,—and owes its distinction probably to its position as centre of a system of ranges: but in altitude and mass and majesty, Pelée far outranks everything in the island, and well deserves its special appellation, "La Montagne."

No description could give the reader a just idea of what Martinique is, configuratively, so well as the simple statement that, although less than fifty miles in extreme length, and less than twenty in average breadth, there are upwards of *four hundred mountains* in this little island, or of what at least might be termed mountains elsewhere. These again are divided and interpeaked, and bear hillocks on their slopes;—and the lowest hillock in Martinique is fifty metres high. Some of the peaks are said to be totally inaccessible: many mornes are so on one or two or even three sides. Ninety-one only of the principal mountains have been named; and among these several bear similar appellations: for example, there are two Mornes-Rouges, one in the north and one in the south; and there are four or five Gros-Mornes. All the elevations belong to six great groups, clustering about or radiating from six ancient volcanic centres,— 1. La Pelée; 2. Pitons du Carbet; 3. Roches Carrées;* 4. Vauclin;

*Also called *La Barre de l'Isle*,—a long high mountain-wall interlinking the northern and southern system of ranges,—and only two metres broad at the summit. The "Roches-Carrées" display a geological formation unlike anything discovered in the rest of the Antillesian system, excepting in Grenada,— columnar or prismatic basalts. . . . In the plains of Marin curious petrifac-

5. Marin; 6. Morne de la Plaine. Forty-two distinct mountain-masses belong to the Carbet system alone,—that of Pelée including but thirteen; and the whole Carbet area has a circumference of 120,000 metres,—much more considerable than that of Pelée. But its centre is not one enormous pyramidal mass like that of "La Montagne": it is marked only by a group of five remarkable porphyritic cones,—the Pitons of Carbet;—while Pelée, dominating everything, and filling the north, presents an aspect and occupies an area scarcely inferior to those of Ætna.

—Sometimes, while looking at La Pelée, I have wondered if the enterprise of the great Japanese painter who made the Hundred Views of Fusiyama could not be imitated by some creole artist equally proud of his native hills, and fearless of the heat of the plains or the snakes of the slopes. A hundred views of Pelée might certainly be made: for the enormous mass is omnipresent to dwellers in the northern part of the island, and can be seen from the heights of the most southern mornes. It is visible from almost any part of St. Pierre,—which nestles in a fold of its rocky skirts. It overlooks all the island ranges, and overtops the mighty Pitons of Carbet by a thousand feet;—you can only lose sight of it by entering gorges, or journeying into the valleys of the south. . . . But the peaked character of the whole country, and the hot moist climate, oppose any artistic undertaking of the sort suggested: even photographers never dream of taking views in the further interior, nor on the east coast. Travel, moreover, is no less costly than difficult: there are no inns or places of rest for tourists; there are, almost daily, sudden and violent rains, which are much dreaded (since a thorough wetting, with the pores all distended by heat, may produce pleurisy); and there are serpents! The artist willing to devote a few weeks of travel and study to Pelée, in spite of these annoyances and risks, has not yet made his appearance in Martinique.*

---

tions exist;—I saw a honey-comb so perfect that the eye alone could scarcely divine the transformation.

*Thibault de Chanvallon, writing of Martinique in 1751, declared:—"All possible hinderances to study are encountered here (*tout s'oppose à l'étude*): if the Americans [creoles] do not devote themselves to research, the fact must

Huge as the mountain looks from St. Pierre, the eye under-estimates its bulk; and when you climb the mornes about the town, Labelle, d'Orange, or the much grander Parnasse, you are surprised to find how much vaster Pelée appears from these summits. Volcanic hills often seem higher, by reason of their steepness, than they really are; but Pelée deludes in another manner. From surrounding valleys it appears lower, and from adjacent mornes higher than it really is: the illusion in the for-mer case being due to the singular slope of its contours, and the remarkable breadth of its base, occupying nearly all the northern end of the island; in the latter, to misconception of the comparative height of the eminence you have reached, which deceives by the precipitous pitch of its sides. Pelée is not very remarkable in point of altitude, however: its height was estimated by Moreau de Jonnés at 1600 metres; and by others at between 4400 and 4500 feet. The sum of the various imper-fect estimates made justify the opinion of Dr. Cornilliac that the extreme summit is over 5000 feet above the sea—perhaps 5200.* The clouds of the summit afford no indication to eyes accustomed to mountain scenery in northern countries; for in these hot moist latitudes clouds hang very low, even in fair weather. But in bulk Pelée is grandiose: it spurs out across the island from the Caribbean to the Atlantic: the great chains of mornes about it are merely counter-forts; the Piton Pierreux and the Piton Pain-à-Sucre (*Sugar-loaf Peak*), and other elevations

---

not be attributed solely to indifference or indolence. On the one hand, the overpowering and continual heat,—the perpetual succession of mornes and acclivities,—the difficulty of entering forests rendered almost inaccessible by the lianas interwoven across all openings, and the prickly plants which oppose a barrier to the naturalist,—the continual anxiety and fear inspired by serpents also;—on the other hand, the disheartening necessity of having to work alone, and the discouragement of being unable to communicate one's ideas or dis-coveries to persons having similar tastes. And finally, it must be remembered that these discouragements and dangers are never mitigated by the least hope of personal consideration, or by the pleasure of emulation,—since such study is necessarily unaccompanied either by the one or the other in a country where nobody undertakes it."—(*Voyage à la Martinique.*) . . . The conditions have scarcely changed since De Chanvallon's day, despite the creation of Govern-ment roads, and the thinning of the high woods.

*Humboldt believed the height to be not less than 800 *toises* (1 toise=6 ft. 4.73 inches), or about 5115 feet.

Foot of La Pelée, behind the Quarter of the Fort.

varying from 800 to 2100 feet, are its volcanic children. Nearly
thirty rivers have their birth in its flanks,—besides many ther-
mal springs, variously mineralized. As the culminant point of
the island, Pelée is also the ruler of its meteorologic life,—
cloud-herder, lightning-forger, and rain-maker. During clear
weather you can see it drawing to itself all the white vapors of
the land,—robbing lesser eminences of their shoulder-wraps
and head-coverings;—though the Pitons of Carbet (3700 feet)
usually manage to retain about their middle a cloud-clout,—a
lantchô. You will also see that the clouds run in a circle about
Pelée,—gathering bulk as they turn by continual accessions
from other points. If the crater be totally bare in the morning,
and shows the broken edges very sharply against the blue, it is
a sign of foul rather than of fair weather to come.*

Even in bulk, perhaps, Pelée might not impress those who
know the stupendous scenery of the American ranges; but none
could deny it special attractions appealing to the senses of form
and color. There is an imposing fantasticality in its configuration worth months of artistic study: one does not easily tire of
watching its slopes undulating against the north sky,—and the
strange jagging of its ridges,—and the succession of its terraces
crumbling down to other terraces, which again break into
ravines here and there bridged by enormous buttresses of basalt:
an extravaganza of lava-shapes overpitching and cascading into
sea and plain. All this is verdant wherever surfaces catch the sun:
you can divine what the frame is only by examining the dark
and ponderous rocks of the torrents. And the hundred tints of
this verdure do not form the only colorific charms of the landscape. Lovely as the long upreaching slopes of cane are,—and
the loftier bands of forest-growths, so far off that they look like
belts of moss,—and the more tender-colored masses above,

---

*There used to be a strange popular belief that however heavily veiled by
clouds the mountain might be prior to an earthquake, these would always vanish with the first shock. But Thibault de Chanvallon took pains to examine
into the truth of this alleged phenomenon; and found that during a number of
earthquake shocks the clouds remained over the crater precisely as usual. . . .
There was more foundation, however, for another popular belief, which still
exists,—that the absolute purity of the atmosphere about Pelée, and the perfect exposure of its summit for any considerable time, might be regarded as an
omen of hurricane.

wrinkling and folding together up to the frost-white clouds of the summit,—you will be still more delighted by the shadow-colors,—opulent, diaphanous. The umbrages lining the wrinkles, collecting in the hollows, slanting from sudden projections, may become before your eyes almost as unreally beautiful as the land-scape colors of a Japanese fan;—they shift most generally dur-ing the day from indigo-blue through violets and paler blues to final lilacs and purples; and even the shadows of passing clouds have a faint blue tinge when they fall on Pelée.

. . . Is the great volcano dead? . . . Nobody knows. Less than forty years ago it rained ashes over all the roofs of St. Pierre;—within twenty years it has uttered mutterings. For the moment, it appears to sleep; and the clouds have dripped into the cup of its highest crater till it has become a lake, several hundred yards in circumference. The crater occupied by this lake—called L'Étang, or "The Pool"—has never been active within human memory. There are others,—difficult and dan-gerous to visit because opening on the side of a tremendous gorge; and it was one of these, no doubt, which has always been called *La Souffrière*, that rained ashes over the city in 1851.

The explosion was almost concomitant with the last of a series of earthquake shocks, which began in the middle of May and ended in the first week of August,—all much more severe in Guadeloupe than in Martinique. In the village Au Prêcheur, lying at the foot of the western slope of Pelée, the people had been for some time complaining of an oppressive stench of sulphur,—or, as chemists declared it, sulphuretted hydrogen, —when, on the 4th of August, much trepidation was caused by a long and appalling noise from the mountain,—a noise compared by planters on the neighboring slopes to the hollow roaring made by a packet blowing off steam, but infinitely louder. These sounds continued through intervals until the following night, sometimes deepening into a rumble like thunder. The mountain guides declared: "*C'est la Souffrière qui bout!*" (the Souffrière is boiling); and a panic seized the negroes of the neighboring plantations. At 11 P.M. the noise was terri-ble enough to fill all St. Pierre with alarm; and on the morning of the 6th the city presented an unwonted aspect, compared by creoles who had lived abroad to the effect of a great hoar-frost. All the roofs, trees, balconies, awnings, pavements, were covered with a white layer of ashes. The same shower blanched the roofs of Morne Rouge, and all the villages about the chief city,—Carbet, Fond-Corré, and Au Prêcheur; also whitening the neighboring country: the mountain was sending up columns of smoke or vapor; and it was noticed that the Rivière Blanche, usually of a glaucous color, ran black into the sea like an out-pouring of ink, staining its azure for a mile. A committee appointed to make an investigation, and prepare an official report, found that a number of rents had either been newly formed, or suddenly become active, in the flank of the mountain: these were all situated in the immense gorge sloping westward from that point now known as the Morne de la Croix. Several were visited with much difficulty,—members of the commission being obliged to lower themselves down a succession of precipices with cords of lianas; and it is noteworthy that their researches were prosecuted in spite of the momentary panic created by another outburst. It was satisfactorily ascertained that the main force of the explosion had been exerted within a perimeter of about one thousand yards; that various hot springs had suddenly gushed out,—the temperature of the least warm being about 37° Réaumur (116° F.);—that there was no change in the configuration of the mountain;—and that the terrific sounds had been produced only by the violent outrush of vapor and ashes from some of the rents. In hope of allaying the general alarm, a creole priest climbed the summit of the volcano, and there planted the great cross which gives the height its name and still remains to commemorate the event.

There was an extraordinary emigration of serpents from the high woods, and from the higher to the lower plantations,—where they were killed by thousands. For a long time Pelée continued to send up an immense column of white vapor; but there were no more showers of ashes; and the mountain gradually settled down to its present state of quiescence.

II.

FROM St. Pierre, trips to Pelée can be made by several routes;—the most popular is that by way of Morne Rouge and the Calebasse; but the summit can be reached in much less time by making the ascent from different points along the coast-road to Au Prêcheur,—such as the Morne St. Martin, or a well-known path further north, passing near the celebrated hot springs (*Fontaines Chaudes*). You drive towards Au Prêcheur, and begin the ascent on foot, through cane-plantations. . . . The road by which you follow the north-west coast round the skirts of Pelée is very picturesque:—you cross the Roxelane, the Rivière des Pères, the Rivière Sèche (whose bed is now occupied only by a motionless torrent of rocks);—passing first by the suburb of Fond-Corré, with its cocoa groves, and broad beach of iron-gray sand,—a bathing resort;—then Pointe Prince, and the Fond de Canonville, somnolent villages that occupy wrinkles in the hem of Pelée's lava robe. The drive ultimately rises and lowers over the undulations of the cliff, and is well shadowed along the greater part of its course: you will admire many huge *fromagers*, or silk-cotton trees, various heavy lines of tamarinds, and groups of *flamboyants* with thick dark feathery foliage, and cassia-trees with long pods pending and blackening from every branch, and hedges of *campêche*, or logwood, and calabash-trees, and multitudes of the pretty shrubs bearing the fruit called in creole *raisins-bò-lanmè*, or "sea-side grapes." Then you reach Au Prêcheur: a very antiquated village, which boasts a stone church and a little public square with a fountain in it. If you have time to cross the Rivière du Prêcheur, a little further on, you can obtain a fine view of the coast, which, rising suddenly to a grand altitude, sweeps round in a semicircle over the Village of the Abysses (*Aux Abymes*),— whose name was doubtless suggested by the immense depth of the sea at that point. . . . It was under the shadow of those cliffs that the Confederate cruiser *Alabama* once hid herself, as a fish hides in the shadow of a rock, and escaped from her pursuer, the *Iroquois*. She had long been blockaded in the harbor of St. Pierre by the Northern man-of-war,—anxiously awaiting a chance to pounce upon her the instant she should leave French waters;—and various Yankee vessels in port were to send up rocket-signals should the *Alabama* attempt to escape under cover of darkness. But one night the privateer took a creole pilot on board, and steamed out southward, with all her lights masked, and her chimneys so arranged that neither smoke nor sparks could betray her to the enemy in the offing. However, some Yankee vessels near enough to discern her movements through the darkness at once shot rockets south; and the *Iro-quois* gave chase. The *Alabama* hugged the high shore as far as Carbet, remaining quite invisible in the shadow of it: then she suddenly turned and recrossed the harbor. Again Yankee rockets betrayed her manœuvre to the *Iroquois*; but she gained Aux Abymes, laid herself close to the enormous black cliff, and there remained indistinguishable; the *Iroquois* steamed by north without seeing her. Once the Confederate cruiser found her enemy well out of sight, she put her pilot ashore and escaped into the Dominica channel. The pilot was a poor mulatto, who thought himself well paid with five hundred francs!

. . . The more popular route to Pelée by way of Morne Rouge is otherwise interesting. . . . Anybody not too much afraid of the tropic sun must find it a delightful experience to follow the mountain roads leading to the interior from the city, as all the mornes traversed by them command landscapes of extraordinary beauty. According to the zigzags of the way, the scenery shifts panoramically. At one moment you are looking down into valleys a thousand feet below; at another, over luminous leagues of meadow or cane-field, you see some far crowding of cones and cratered shapes—sharp as the teeth of a saw, and blue as sapphire,—with further eminences ranging away through pearline color to high-peaked remotenesses of vapory gold. As you follow the windings of such a way as the road of the Morne Labelle, or the Morne d'Orange, the city disappears and reappears many times,—always diminishing, till at last it looks no bigger than a chess-board. Simultaneously distant mountain shapes appear to unfold and lengthen;—and always, always the sea rises with your rising. Viewed at first from the bulwark (*boulevard*) commanding the roofs of the town, its horizon-line seemed straight and keen as a knife-edge;—but as you mount higher, it elongates, begins to curve; and gradually the whole azure expanse of water broadens out roundly like a disk. From certain very lofty summits further inland you behold the immense blue circle touching the sky all round you,—except where a still greater altitude, like that of Pelée or the Pitons, breaks the ring; and this high vision of the sea has a phantasmal effect hard to describe, and due to vapory conditions of the atmosphere. There are bright cloudless days when, even as seen from the city, the ocean-verge has a spectral vagueness; but on any day, in any season, that you ascend to a point dominating the sea by a thousand feet, the rim of the visible world takes a ghostliness that startles,—because the prodigious light gives to all near shapes such intense sharpness of outline and vividness of color.

Yet wonderful as are the perspective beauties of those mountain routes from which one can keep St. Pierre in view, the road to Morne Rouge surpasses them, notwithstanding that it almost immediately leaves the city behind, and out of sight. Excepting only *La Trace*,—the long route winding over mountain ridges and between primitive forests south to Fort-de-France,—there is probably no section of national highway in the island more remarkable than the Morne Rouge road. Leaving the Grande Rue by the public conveyance, you drive out through the Savane du Fort, with its immense mango and tamarind trees, skirting the Roxelane. Then reaching the boulevard, you pass high Morne Labelle,—and then the Jardin des Plantes on the right, where white-stemmed palms are lifting their heads two hundred feet,—and beautiful Parnasse, heavily timbered to the top;—while on your left the valley of the Roxelane shallows up, and Pelée shows less and less of its tremendous base. Then you pass through the sleepy, palmy, pretty Village of the Three Bridges (*Trois Ponts*),—where a Fahrenheit thermometer shows already three degrees of temperature lower than at St. Pierre;—and the national road, making a sharp turn to the right, becomes all at once very steep—so steep that the horses can mount only at a walk. Around and between the wooded hills it ascends by zigzags,—occasionally overlooking the sea,—sometimes following the verges of ravines. Now and then you catch glimpses of the road over which you passed half an hour before undulating far below, looking narrow as a tape-line,—and of the gorge of the Roxelane,—and of Pelée, always higher, now thrusting out long spurs of green and purple land into the sea. You drive under cool shadowing of mountain woods—under waving bamboos like enormous ostrich feathers dyed green,—and exquisite tree-ferns thirty to forty feet high,—and imposing ceibas, with strangely buttressed trunks,—and all sorts of broad-leaved forms: cachibous, balisiers, bananiers. . . . Then you reach a plateau covered with cane, whose yellow expanse is bounded on the right by a demilune of hills sharply angled as crystals;—on the left it dips seaward; and before you Pelée's head towers over the shoulders of intervening mornes. A strong cool wind is blowing; and the horses can trot a while. Twenty minutes, and the road, leaving the plateau, becomes steep again;—you are approaching the volcano over the ridge of a colossal spur. The way turns in a semicircle,—zigzags,— once more touches the edge of a valley,—where the clear fall might be nearly fifteen hundred feet. But narrowing more and more, the valley becomes an ascending gorge; and across its chasm, upon the brow of the opposite cliff, you catch sight of houses and a spire seemingly perched on the verge, like so many birds'-nests,—the village of Morne Rouge. It is two thousand feet above the sea; and Pelée, although looming high over it, looks a trifle less lofty now.

One's first impression of Morne Rouge is that of a single straggling street of gray-painted cottages and shops (or rather booths), dominated by a plain church, with four pursy-bodied palmistes facing the main porch. Nevertheless, Morne Rouge is not a small place, considering its situation;—there are nearly five thousand inhabitants; but in order to find out where they live, you must leave the public road, which is on a ridge, and explore the high-hedged lanes leading down from it on either side. Then you will find a veritable city of little wooden cottages,—each screened about with banana-trees, Indian-reeds, and *pommiers-roses*. You will also see a number of handsome private residences —country-houses of wealthy merchants; and you will find that the church, though uninteresting exteriorly, is rich and impressive within: it is a famous shrine, where miracles are alleged to have been wrought. Immense processions periodically wend their way to it from St. Pierre,—starting at three or four o'clock in the morning, so as to arrive before the sun is well up. . . . But there are no woods here,—only fields. An odd tone is given to the lanes by a local custom of planting hedges of what are termed *roseaux d'Inde*, having a dark-red foliage; and there is a visible fondness for ornamental plants with crimson leaves. Otherwise the mountain summit is somewhat bare; trees have a scrubby aspect. You must have noticed while ascending that the palmistes became smaller as they were situated higher: at Morne Rouge they are dwarfed,—having a short stature, and very thick trunks.

heavy rains and hurricanes, begins on July 15th, is no more trustworthy than the contradictory declarations of Martinique authors who have attempted to define the vague and illusive limits of the tropic seasons. Still, the Government report on the subject is more satisfactory than any: according to the "Annuaire," there are these seasons:—

1. *Saison fraîche.* December to March. Rainfall, about 475 millimetres.

2. *Saison chaude et sèche.* April to July. Rainfall, about 140 millimetres.

3. *Saison chaude et pluvieuse.* July to November. Rainfall average, 1121 millimetres.

Other authorities divide the *saison chaude et sèche* into two periods, of which the latter, beginning about May, is called the *Renouveau*; and it is at least true that at the time indicated there is a great burst of vegetal luxuriance. But there is always rain, there are almost always clouds, there is no possibility of marking and dating the beginnings and the endings of weather in this country where the barometer is almost useless, and the thermometer mounts in the sun to twice the figure it reaches in the shade. Long and patient observation has, however, established the fact that during the hivernage, if the heavy showers have a certain fixed periodicity,—falling at mid-day or in the heated part of the afternoon,—Pelée is likely to be clear early in the morning; and by starting before daylight one can then have good chances of a fine view from the summit.

IV.

AT five o'clock of a September morning, warm and starry, I leave St. Pierre in a carriage with several friends, to make the ascent by the shortest route of all,—that of the Morne St. Martin, one of Pelée's western counterforts. We drive north along the shore for about half an hour; then, leaving the coast behind, pursue a winding mountain road, leading to the upper plantations, between leagues of cane. The sky begins to brighten as we ascend, and a steely glow announces that day has begun on the other side of the island. Miles up, the crest of the volcano cuts sharp as a saw-edge against the growing light: there is not a cloud visible. Then the light slowly yellows behind the vast

Village of Morne Rouge, Martinique.

In spite of the fine views of the sea, the mountain-heights, and the valley-reaches, obtainable from Morne Rouge, the place has a somewhat bleak look. Perhaps this is largely owing to the universal slate-gray tint of the buildings,—very melancholy by comparison with the apricot and banana yellows tinting the walls of St. Pierre. But this cheerless gray is the only color which can resist the climate of Morne Rouge, where people are literally dwelling in the clouds. Rolling down like white smoke from Pelée, these often create a dismal fog; and Morne Rouge is certainly one of the rainiest places in the world. When it is dry everywhere else, it rains at Morne Rouge. It rains at least three hundred and sixty days and three hundred and sixty nights of the year. It rains almost invariably once in every twenty-four hours; but oftener five or six times. The dampness is phenomenal. All mirrors become patchy; linen moulds in one day; leather turns white; woollen goods feel as if saturated with moisture; new brass becomes green; steel crumbles into red powder: wood-work rots with astonishing rapidity; salt is quickly transformed into brine; and matches, unless kept in a very warm place, refuse to light. Everything moulders and peels and decomposes; even the frescos of the church-interior lump out in immense blisters; and a microscopic vegetation, green or brown, attacks all exposed surfaces of timber or stone. At night it is often really cold;—and it is hard to understand how, with all this dampness and coolness and mouldiness, Morne Rouge can be a healthy place. But it is so, beyond any question: it is the great Martinique resort for invalids; strangers debilitated by the climate of Trinidad or Cayenne come to it for recuperation.

Leaving the village by the still uprising road, you will be surprised, after a walk of twenty minutes northward, by a magnificent view,—the vast valley of the Champ-Flore, watered by many torrents, and bounded south and west by double, triple, and quadruple surging of mountains,—mountains broken, peaked, tormented-looking, and tinted (*irisées*, as the creoles say) with all those gemtones distance gives in a West Indian atmosphere. Particularly impressive is the beauty of one purple cone in the midst of this many-colored chain: the Piton Gélé. All the valley-expanse of rich land is checkered with alternations of meadow and cane and cacao,—except northwestwardly, where woods billow out of sight beyond a curve. Facing this

landscape, on your left, are mornes of various heig among which you will notice La Calebasse, overtopping thing but Pelée shadowing behind it;—and a grass-grow leads up westward from the national highway towards th cano. This is the Calebasse route to Pelée.

III.

ONE must be very sure of the weather before undertakin ascent of Pelée; for if one merely selects some particular l day in advance, one's chances of seeing anything fron summit are considerably less than an astronomer's chan being able to make a satisfactory observation of the next sit of Venus. Moreover, if the heights remain even clouded, it may not be safe to ascend the Morne de la Cr a cone-point above the crater itself, and ordinarily inv from below. And a cloudless afternoon can never be pred from the aspect of deceitful Pelée: when the crater edge quite clearly cut against the sky at dawn, you may be tole certain there will be bad weather during the day; and they are all bare at sundown, you have no good reaso believe they will not be hidden next morning. Hundred tourists, deluded by such appearances, have made the weary in vain,—found themselves obliged to return without ha seen anything but a thick white cold fog. The sky may ren perfectly blue for weeks in every other direction, and Pe head remain always hidden. In order to make a successfu cent, one must not wait for a period of dry weather,—one m thus wait for years! What one must look for is a certain pe dicity in the diurnal rains,—a regular alternation of sun cloud; such as characterizes a certain portion of the *hiverna* or rainy summer season, when mornings and evenings are fectly limpid, with very heavy sudden rains in the middle of day. It is of no use to rely on the prospect of a dry spell. Th is no really dry weather, notwithstanding there recurs—in bo —a *Saison de la Sécheresse*. In fact, there are no distinc marked seasons in Martinique:—a little less heat and rain fr October to July, a little more rain and heat from July to Oct ber: that is about all the notable difference! Perhaps the offic notification by cannon-shot that the hivernage, the season

cone; and one of the most beautiful dawns I ever saw reveals on our right an immense valley through which three rivers flow. This deepens very quickly as we drive; the mornes about St. Pierre, beginning to catch the light, sink below us in distance; and above them, southwardly, an amazing silhouette begins to rise,—all blue,—a mountain wall capped with cusps and cones, seeming high as Pelée itself in the middle, but sinking down to the sea-level westward. There are a number of extraordinary acuminations; but the most impressive shape is the nearest,—a tremendous conoidal mass crowned with a group of peaks, of which two, taller than the rest, tell their name at once by the beauty of their forms,—the Pitons of Carbet. They wear their girdles of cloud, though Pelée is naked to-day. All this is blue: the growing light only deepens the color, does not dissipate it;—but in the nearer valleys gleams of tender yellowish green begin to appear. Still the sun has not been able to show himself;—it will take him some time yet to climb Pelée.

Reaching the last plantation, we draw rein in a village of small wooden cottages,—the quarters of the field hands,—and receive from the proprietor, a personal friend of my friends, the kindest welcome. At his house we change clothing and prepare for the journey;—he provides for our horses, and secures experienced guides for us,—two young colored men belonging to the plantation. Then we begin the ascent. The guides walk before, barefoot, each carrying a cutlass in his hand and a package on his head—our provisions, photographic instruments, etc.

The mountain is cultivated in spots up to twenty-five hundred feet; and for three-quarters of an hour after leaving the planter's residence we still traverse fields of cane and of manioc. The light is now strong in the valley; but we are in the shadow of Pelée. Cultivated fields end at last; the ascending path is through wild cane, wild guavas, guinea-grass run mad, and other tough growths, some bearing pretty pink blossoms. The forest is before us. Startled by our approach, a tiny fer-de-lance glides out from a bunch of dead wild-cane, almost under the bare feet of our foremost guide, who as instantly decapitates it with a touch of his cutlass. It is not quite fifteen inches long, and almost the color of the yellowish leaves under which it had been hiding. . . . The conversation turns on snakes as we make our first halt at the verge of the woods.

Hundreds may be hiding around us; but a snake never shows himself by daylight except under the pressure of sudden alarm. We are not likely, in the opinion of all present, to meet with another. Every one in the party, except myself, has some curious experience to relate. I hear for the first time about the alleged inability of the trigonocephalus to wound except at a distance from his enemy of not less than one-third of his length; —about M. A——, a former director of the Jardin des Plantes, who used to boldly thrust his arm into holes where he knew snakes were, and pull them out,—catching them just behind the head and wrapping the tail round his arm,—and place them alive in a cage without ever getting bitten;—about M. B——, who, while hunting one clay, tripped in the coils of an immense trigonocephalus, and ran so fast in his fright that the serpent, entangled round his leg, could not bite him;—about M. C——, who could catch a fer-de-lance by the tail, and "crack it like a whip" until the head would fly off;—about an old white man living in the Champ-Flore, whose diet was snake-meat, and who always kept in his ajoupa "a keg of salted serpents" (*yon ka sèpent-salé*);—about a monster eight feet long which killed, near Morne Rouge, M. Charles Fabre's white cat, but was also killed by the cat after she had been caught in the folds of the reptile;—about the value of snakes as protectors of the sugar-cane and cocoa-shrub against rats;—about an unsuccessful effort made, during a plague of rats in Guadeloupe, to introduce the fer-de-lance there;—about the alleged power of a monstrous toad, the *crapaud-ladre*, to cause the death of the snake that swallows it;—and, finally, about the total absence of the idyllic and pastoral elements in Martinique literature, as due to the presence of reptiles everywhere. "Even the flora and fauna of the country remain to a large extent unknown,"—adds the last speaker, an amiable old physician of St. Pierre,—"because the existence of the fer-de-lance renders all serious research dangerous in the extreme."

My own experiences do not justify my taking part in such a conversation;—I never saw alive but two very small specimens of the trigonocephalus. People who have passed even a considerable time in Martinique may have never seen a fer-de-lance except in a jar of alcohol, or as exhibited by negro snake-catchers, tied fast to a bamboo. But this is only because strangers rarely travel much in the interior of the country, or find themselves on country roads after sundown. It is not correct to suppose that snakes are uncommon even in the neighborhood of St. Pierre: they are often killed on the bulwarks behind the city and on the verge of the Savane; they have been often washed into the streets by heavy rains; and many washer-women at the Roxelane have been bitten by them. It is considered very dangerous to walk about the bulwarks after dark;—for the snakes, which travel only at night, then descend from the mornes towards the river. The Jardin des Plantes shelters great numbers of the reptiles; and only a few clays prior to the writing of these lines a colored laborer in the garden was stricken and killed by a fer-de-lance measuring one metre and sixty-seven centimetres in length. In the interior much larger reptiles are sometimes seen: I saw one freshly killed measuring six feet five inches, and thick as a man's leg in the middle. There are few planters in the island who have not some of their hands bitten during the cane-cutting and cocoa-gathering seasons;—the average annual mortality among the class of *travailleurs* from serpent bite alone is probably fifty*,—always fine young men or women in the prime of life. Even among the wealthy whites deaths from this cause are less rare than might be supposed: I know one gentleman, a rich citizen of St. Pierre, who in ten years lost three relatives by the trigonocephalus,—the wound having in each case been received in the neighborhood of a vein. When the vein has been pierced, cure is impossible.

V.

. . . We look back over the upreaching yellow fan-spread of cane-fields, and winding of tortuous valleys, and the sea expanding beyond an opening in the west. It has already broadened surprisingly, the sea,—appears to have risen up, not as a horizontal plane, but like an immeasurable azure precipice: what will it look like when we shall have reached the top? Far down we can distinguish a line of field-hands—the whole *atelier*, as it is called, of a plantation—slowly descending a slope, hewing the

---

*"De la piqûre du serpent de la Martinique," par Auguste Charriez, Médecin de la Marine. Paris: Moquet, 1875.

canes as they go. There is a woman to every two men, a binder (*amarreuse*): she gathers the canes as they are cut down, binds them with their own tough long leaves into a sort of sheaf, and carries them away on her head;—the men wield their cutlasses so beautifully that it is a delight to watch them. One cannot often enjoy such a spectacle nowadays; for the introduction of the piece-work system has destroyed the picturesqueness of plantation labor throughout the island, with rare exceptions. Formerly the work of cane-cutting resembled the march of an army;—first advanced the cutlassers in line, naked to the waist; then the amarreuses, the women who tied and carried; and behind these the *ka*, the drum,—with a paid *crieur* or *crieuse* to lead the song;—and lastly the black Commandeur, for general. And in the old days, too, it was not unfrequent that the sudden descent of an English corsair on the coast converted this soldiery of labor into veritable military: more than one attack was repelled by the cutlasses of a plantation atelier.

At this height the chatting and chanting can be heard, though not distinctly enough to catch the words. Suddenly a voice, powerful as a bugle, rings out,—the voice of the Commandeur: he walks along the line, looking, with his cutlass under his arm. I ask one of our guides what the cry is:—

—"*Υ ka coumandé yo pouend gàde pou sèpent,*" he replies. (He is telling them to keep watch for serpents.) The nearer the cutlassers approach the end of their task, the greater the danger: for the reptiles, retreating before them to the last clump of cane, become massed there, and will fight desperately. Regularly as the ripening-time, Death gathers his toll of human lives from among the workers. But when one falls, another steps into the vacant place,—perhaps the Commandeur himself: these dark swordsmen never retreat; all the blades swing swiftly as before; there is hardly any emotion; the travailleur is a fatalist. . . .*

---

*M. Francard Bayardelle, overseer of the Prèsbourg plantation at Grande Anse, tells me that the most successful treatment of snakebite consists in severe local cupping and bleeding; the immediate application of twenty to thirty leeches (when these can be obtained), and the administration of alkali as an internal medicine. He has saved several lives by these methods.

The negro *panseur's* method is much more elaborate and, to some extent, mysterious. He cups and bleeds, using a small *couï*, or half-calabash, in lieu of

VI.

. . . WE enter the *grands-bois*,—the primitive forest,—the "high woods."

As seen with a field-glass from St. Pierre, these woods present only the appearance of a band of moss belting the volcano, and following all its corrugations,—so densely do the leafy crests intermingle. But on actually entering them, you find yourself at once in green twilight, among lofty trunks uprising everywhere like huge pillars wrapped with vines;—and the interspaces between these bulks are all occupied by lianas and parasitic creepers,—some monstrous,—veritable parasite-trees, —ascending at all angles, or dropping straight down from the tallest crests to take root again. The effect in the dim light is that of innumerable black ropes and cables of varying thicknesses stretched taut from the soil to the tree-tops, and also from branch to branch, like rigging. There are rare and remarkable trees here,—acomats, courbarils, balatas, ceibas or fromagers, acajous, gommiers;—hundreds have been cut down by charcoal-makers; but the forest is still grand. It is to be regretted that the Government has placed no restriction upon the barbarous destruction of trees by the *charbonniers*, which is going on throughout the island. Many valuable woods are rapidly disappearing. The courbaril, yielding a fine-grained, heavy, chocolate-colored timber; the balata, giving a wood even heavier, denser, and darker; the acajou, producing a rich red wood, with a strong scent of cedar; the bois-de-fer; the bois d'Inde; the superb acomat,—all used to flourish by tens of thousands upon these volcanic slopes, whose productiveness is eighteen times greater than that of the richest European soil. All Martinique furniture used to be made of native woods; and

---

a glass; and then applies cataplasms of herbs,—orange-leaves, cinnamon-leaves, clove-leaves *chardon-béni*, *charpentier*, perhaps twenty other things, all mingled together;—this poulticing being continued every day for a month. Meantime the patient is given all sorts of absurd things to drink, in tafia and sour-orange juice—such as old clay pipes ground to powder, or *the head of the fer-de-lance itself*, roasted dry and pounded. . . . The plantation negro has no faith in any other system of cure but that of the panseur;—he refuses to let the physician try to save him, and will scarcely submit to be treated even by an experienced white overseer.

the colored cabinet-makers still produce work which would probably astonish New York or London manufacturers. But to-day the island exports no more hard woods: it has even been found necessary to import much from neighboring islands;—and yet the destruction of forests still goes on. The domestic fabrication of charcoal from forest-trees has been estimated at 1,400,000 hectolitres per annum. Primitive forest still covers the island to the extent of 21.37 per cent.; but to find precious woods now, one must climb heights like those of Pelée and Carbet, or penetrate into the mountains of the interior.

Most common formerly on these slopes were the gommiers, from which canoes of a single piece, forty-five feet long by seven wide, used to be made. There are plenty of gommiers still; but the difficulty of transporting them to the shore has latterly caused a demand for the gommiers of Dominica. The dimensions of canoes now made from these trees rarely exceed fifteen feet in length by eighteen inches in width: the art of making them is an inheritance from the ancient Caribs. First the trunk is shaped to the form of the canoe, and pointed at both ends; it is then hollowed out. The width of the hollow does not exceed six inches at the widest part; but the cavity is then filled with wet sand, which in the course of some weeks widens the excavation by its weight, and gives the boat perfect form. Finally gunwales of plank are fastened on; seats are put in—generally four;—and no boat is more durable nor more swift.

. . . We climb. There is a trace rather than a foot-path;—no visible soil, only vegetable detritus, with roots woven over it in every direction. The foot never rests on a flat surface,—only upon surfaces of roots; and these are covered, like every protruding branch along the route, with a slimy green moss, slippery as ice. Unless accustomed to walking in tropical woods, one will fall at every step. In a little while I find it impossible to advance. Our nearest guide, observing my predicament, turns, and without moving the bundle upon his head, cuts and trims me an excellent staff with a few strokes of his cutlass. This staff not only saves me from dangerous slips, but also serves at times to probe the way; for the further we proceed, the vaguer the path becomes. It was made by the *chasseurs-de-choux* (cabbage-hunters),—the negro mountaineers who live by furnishing

La Montagne Pelée. As seen from Grande Anse.

heads of young cabbage-palm to the city markets; and these men also keep it open,—otherwise the woods would grow over it in a month. Two chasseurs-de-choux stride past us as we advance, with their freshly gathered palm-salad upon their heads, wrapped in cachibou or balisier leaves, and tied with lianas. The palmiste-franc easily reaches a stature of one hundred feet; but the young trees are so eagerly sought for by the chasseurs-de-choux that in these woods few reach a height of even twelve feet before being cut.

. . . Walking becomes more difficult;—there seems no termination to the grands-bois: always the same faint green light, the same rude natural stair-way of slippery roots,—half the time hidden by fern leaves and vines. Sharp ammoniacal scents are in the air; a dew, cold as ice-water, drenches our clothing. Unfamiliar insects make trilling noises in dark places; and now and then a series of soft clear notes ring out, almost like a thrush's whistle: the chant of a little tree-frog. The path becomes more and more overgrown; and but for the constant excursions of the cabbage-hunters, we should certainly have to cutlass every foot of the way through creepers and brambles. More and more amazing also is the interminable interweaving of roots: the whole forest is thus spun together—not underground so much as overground. These tropical trees do not strike deep, although able to climb steep slopes of porphyry and basalt: they send out great far-reaching webs of roots,—each such web interknotting with others all round it, and these in turn with further ones; while between their reticulations lianas ascend and descend: and a nameless multitude of shrubs as tough as india-rubber push up, together with mosses, grasses, and ferns. Square miles upon square miles of woods are thus interlocked and interbound into one mass solid enough to resist the pressure of a hurricane; and where there is no path already made, entrance into them can only be effected by the most dexterous cutlassing.

An inexperienced stranger might be puzzled to understand how this cutlassing is done. It is no easy feat to sever with one blow a liana thick as a man's arm; the trained cutlasser does it without apparent difficulty: moreover, he cuts horizontally, so as to prevent the severed top presenting a sharp angle and proving afterwards dangerous. He never appears to strike hard,—only to give light taps with his blade, which flickers continually about him as he moves. Our own guides in cutlassing are not at all inconvenienced by their loads; they walk perfectly upright, never stumble, never slip, never hesitate, and do not even seem to perspire: their bare feet are prehensile. Some creoles in our party, habituated to the woods, walk nearly as well in their shoes; but they carry no loads.

. . . At last we are rejoiced to observe that the trees are becoming smaller;—there are no more colossal trunks;—there are frequent glimpses of sky: the sun has risen well above the peaks, and sends occasional beams down through the leaves. Ten minutes, and we reach a clear space,—a wild savane, very steep, above which looms a higher belt of woods. Here we take another short rest.

Northward the view is cut off by a ridge covered with herbaceous vegetation;—but to the south-west it is open, over a gorge of which both sides are shrouded in sombre green— crests of trees forming a solid curtain against the sun. Beyond the outer and lower cliff valley-surfaces appear miles away, flinging up broad gleams of cane-gold; further off greens disappear into blues, and the fantastic masses of Carbet loom up far higher than before. St. Pierre, in a curve of the coast, is a little red-and-yellow semicircular streak, less than two inches long. The interspaces between far mountain chains,—masses of pyramids, cones, single and double humps, queer blue angles as of raised knees under coverings,—resemble misty lakes: they are filled with brume;—the sea-line has vanished altogether. Only the horizon, enormously heightened, can be discerned as a circling band of faint yellowish light,—auroral, ghostly,— almost on a level with the tips of the Pitons. Between this vague horizon and the shore, the sea no longer looks like sea, but like a second hollow sky reversed. All the landscape has unreal beauty:—there are no keen lines; there are no definite beginnings or endings; the tints are half-colors only;—peaks rise suddenly from mysteries of bluish fog as from a flood; land melts into sea the same hue. It gives one the idea of some great aquarelle unfinished,—abandoned before tones were deepened and details brought out.

VII.

WE are overlooking from this height the birthplaces of several rivers; and the rivers of Pelée are the clearest and the coolest of the island.

From whatever direction the trip be undertaken, the ascent of the volcano must be made over some one of those many immense ridges sloping from the summit to the sea west, north, and east,—like buttresses eight to ten miles long,—formed by ancient lava-torrents. Down the deep gorges between them the cloud-fed rivers run,—receiving as they descend the waters of countless smaller streams gushing from either side of the ridge. There are also cold springs,—one of which furnishes St. Pierre with her *Eau-de-Gouyave* (guava-water), which is always sweet, clear, and cool in the very hottest weather. But the water of almost every one of the seventy-five principal rivers of Martinique is cool and clear and sweet. And these rivers are curious in their way. Their average fall has been estimated at nine inches to every six feet;—many are cataracts;—the Rivière de Case-Navire has a fall of nearly 150 feet to every fifty yards of its upper course. Naturally these streams cut for themselves channels of immense depth. Where they flow through forests and between mornes, their banks vary from 1200 to 1600 feet high,—so as to render their beds inaccessible; and many enter the sea through a channel of rock with perpendicular walls from 150 to 200 feet high. Their waters are necessarily shallow in normal weather; but during rain-storms they become torrents thunderous and terrific beyond description. In order to comprehend their sudden swelling, one must know what tropical rain is. Col. Boyer Peyreleau, in 1823, estimated the annual rainfall in these colonies at 150 inches on the coast, to 350 on the mountains,—while the annual fall at Paris was only eighteen inches. The character of such rain is totally different from that of rain in the temperate zone: the drops are enormous, heavy like hailstones,—one will spatter over the circumference of a saucer! —and the shower roars so that people cannot hear each other speak without shouting. When there is a true storm, no roofing seems able to shut out the cataract; the best-built houses leak in all directions; and objects but a short distance off become invisible behind the heavy curtain of water. The ravages of such rain may be imagined! Roads are cut away in an hour; trees are overthrown as if blown down;—for there are few West Indian trees which plunge their roots even as low as two feet; they merely extend them over a large diameter; and isolated trees will actually slide under rain. The swelling of rivers is so sudden that washer-women at work in the Roxelane and other streams have been swept away and drowned without the least warning of their danger; the shower occurring seven or eight miles off.

Most of these rivers are well stocked with fish, of which the *tétart, banane, loche,* and *dormeur* are the principal varieties. The tétart (best of all) and the loche climb the torrents to the height of 2500 and even 3000 feet: they have a kind of pneumatic sucker, which enables them to cling to rocks. Under stones in the lower basins crawfish of the most extraordinary size are taken; some will measure thirty-six inches from claw to tail. And at all the river-mouths, during July and August, are caught vast numbers of *titiri**,—tiny white fish, of which a thousand might be put into one teacup. They are delicious when served in oil,—infinitely more delicate than the sardine. Some regard them as a particular species: others believe them to be only the fry of larger fish,—as their periodical appearance and disappearance would seem to indicate. They are often swept by millions into the city of St. Pierre, with the flow of mountain-water which purifies the streets: then you will see them swarming in the gutters, fountains, and bathing-basins; —and on Saturdays, when the water is temporarily shut off to allow of the pipes being cleansed, the titiri may die in the gutters in such numbers as to make the air offensive.

The mountain-crab, celebrated for its periodical migrations, is also found at considerable heights. Its numbers appear to have been diminished extraordinarily by its consumption as an article of negro diet; but in certain islands those armies of crabs described by the old writers are still occasionally to be

---

*The sheet-lightnings which play during the nights of July and August are termed in creole *Zéclai-titiri,* or "titiri-lightnings";—it is believed these give notice that the titiri have begun to swarm in the rivers. Among the colored population there exists an idea of some queer relation between the lightning and the birth of the little fish;—it is commonly said, "*Zéclai-à ka fai yo écloré*" (the lightning hatches them).

seen. The Père Dutertre relates that in 1640, at St. Christophe, thirty sick emigrants, temporarily left on the beach, were attacked and devoured alive during the night by a similar species of crab. "They descended from the mountains in such multitude," he tells us, "that they were heaped higher than houses over the bodies of the poor wretches . . . whose bones were picked so clean that not one speck of flesh could be found upon them." . . .

VIII.

. . . WE enter the upper belt of woods—green twilight again. There are as many lianas as ever: but they are less massive in stem;—the trees, which are stunted, stand closer together; and the web-work of roots is finer and more thickly spun. These are called the *petits-bois* (little woods), in contradistinction to the grands-bois, or high woods. Multitudes of balisiers, dwarf-palms, arborescent ferns, wild guavas, mingle with the lower growths on either side of the path, which has narrowed to the breadth of a wheel-rut, and is nearly concealed by protruding grasses and fern leaves. Never does the sole of the foot press upon a surface large as itself,—always the slippery backs of roots crossing at all angles, like loop-traps, over sharp fragments of volcanic rock or pumice-stone. There are abrupt descents, sudden acclivities, mud-holes, and fissures;—one grasps at the ferns on both sides to keep from falling; and some ferns are spiked sometimes on the under surface, and tear the hands. But the barefooted guides stride on rapidly, erect as ever under their loads,—chopping off with their cutlasses any branches that hang too low. There are beautiful flowers here,—various unfamiliar species of lobelia;—pretty red and yellow blossoms belonging to plants which the creole physician calls *Bromeliaceæ*; and a plant like the *Guy Lussacia* of Brazil, with violet-red petals. There is an indescribable multitude of ferns,—a very museum of ferns! The doctor, who is a great woodsman, says that he never makes a trip to the hills without finding some new kind of fern; and he had already a collection of several hundred.

The route is continually growing steeper, and makes a number of turns and windings: we reach another bit of savane, where we have to walk over black-pointed stones that resemble

Arborescent Ferns on a Mountain Road.

slag;—then more petits-bois, still more dwarfed, then another
opening. The naked crest of the volcano appears like a peaked
precipice, dark-red, with streaks of green, over a narrow but terrific chasm on the left: we are almost on a level with the crater,
but must make a long circuit to reach it, through a wilderness of
stunted timber and bush. The creoles call this undergrowth
razié: it is really only a prolongation of the low jungle which
carpets the high forests below, with this difference, that there
are fewer creepers and much more fern. . . . Suddenly we
reach a black gap in the path about thirty inches wide—half
hidden by the tangle of leaves,—*La Fente*. It is a volcanic fissure
which divides the whole ridge, and is said to have no bottom:
for fear of a possible slip, the guides insist upon holding our
hands while we cross it. Happily there are no more such clefts;
but there are mud-holes, snags, roots, and loose rocks beyond
counting. Least disagreeable are the *bourbiers*, in which you
sink to your knees in black or gray slime. Then the path descends into open light again;—and we find ourselves at the
Étang,—in the dead Crater of the Three Palmistes.

An immense pool, completely encircled by high green walls
of rock, which shut out all further view, and shoot up, here and
there, into cones, or rise into queer lofty humps and knobs.
One of these elevations at the opposite side has almost the
shape of a blunt horn: it is the Morne de la Croix. The scenery
is at once imposing and sinister: the shapes towering above the
lake and reflected in its still surface have the weirdness of
things seen in photographs of the moon. Clouds are circling
above them and between them;—one descends to the water,
haunts us a moment, blurring everything; then rises again. We
have travelled too slow; the clouds have had time to gather.

I look in vain for the Three Palmistes which gave the crater
a name: they were destroyed long ago. But there are numbers
of young ones scattered through the dense ferny covering of
the lake-slopes,—just showing their heads like bunches of great
dark-green feathers.

—The estimate of Dr. Rufz, made in 1851, and the estimate
of the last "Annuaire" regarding the circumference of the lake,
are evidently both at fault. That of the "Annuaire," 150 metres,
is a gross error: the writer must have meant the diameter,—

following Rufz, who estimated the circumference at something over 300 paces. As we find it, the Étang, which is nearly circular, must measure 200 yards across;—perhaps it has been greatly swollen by the extraordinary rains of this summer. Our guides say that the little iron cross projecting from the water about two yards off was high and dry on the shore last season. At present there is only one narrow patch of grassy bank on which we can rest, between the water and the walls of the crater.

The lake is perfectly clear, with a bottom of yellowish shallow mud, which rests—according to investigations made in 1851—upon a mass of pumice-stone mixed in places with ferruginous sand; and the yellow mud itself is a detritus of pumice-stone. We strip for a swim.

Though at an elevation of nearly 5000 feet, this water is not so cold as that of the Roxelane, nor of other rivers of the north-west and north-east coasts. It has an agreeable fresh taste, like dew. Looking down into it, I see many larvæ of the *maringouin*, or large mosquito: no fish. The maringouins themselves are troublesome,—whirring around us and stinging. On striking out for the middle, one is surprised to feel the water growing slightly warmer. The committee of investigation in 1851 found the temperature of the lake, in spite of a north wind, 20.5 Centigrade, while that of the air was but 19 (about 69 F. for the water, and 66.2 for the air). The depth in the centre is over six feet; the average is scarcely four.

Regaining the bank, we prepare to ascend the Morne de la Croix. The circular path by which it is commonly reached is now under water; and we have to wade up to our waists. All the while clouds keep passing over us in great slow whirls. Some are white and half-transparent; others opaque and dark gray;—a dark cloud passing through a white one looks like a goblin. Gaining the opposite shore, we find a very rough path over splintered stone, ascending between the thickest fern-growths possible to imagine. The general tone of this fern is dark green; but there are paler cloudings of yellow and pink,—due to the varying age of the leaves, which are pressed into a cushion three or four feet high, and almost solid enough to sit upon. About two hundred and fifty yards from the crater edge, the path rises above this tangle, and zigzags up the morne, which now appears twice as lofty as from the lake, where we had a curiously foreshortened view of it. It then looked scarcely a hundred feet high; it is more than double that. The cone is green to the top with moss, low grasses, small fern, and creeping pretty plants, like violets, with big carmine flowers. The path is a black line: the rock laid bare by it looks as if burned to the core. We have now to use our hands in climbing; but the low thick ferns give a good hold. Out of breath, and drenched in perspiration, we reach the apex,—the highest point of the island. But we are curtained about with clouds,—moving in dense white and gray masses: we cannot see fifty feet away.

The top of the peak has a slightly slanting surface of perhaps twenty square yards, very irregular in outline;—southwardly the morne pitches sheer into a frightful chasm, between the converging of two of those long corrugated ridges already described as buttressing the volcano on all sides. Through a cloud-rift we can see another crater-lake twelve hundred feet below—said to be five times larger than the Étang we have just left: it is also of more irregular outline. This is called the *Étang Sec*, or "Dry Pool," because dry in less rainy seasons. It occupies a more ancient crater, and is very rarely visited: the path leading to it is difficult and dangerous,—a natural ladder of roots and lianas over a series of precipices. Behind us the Crater of the Three Palmistes now looks no larger than the surface on which we stand;—over its further boundary we can see the wall of another gorge, in which there is a third crater-lake. West and north are green peakings, ridges, and high lava walls steep as fortifications. All this we can only note in the intervals between passing of clouds. As yet there is no landscape visible southward;—we sit down and wait.

IX.

. . . Two crosses are planted nearly at the verge of the precipice; a small one of iron; and a large one of wood—probably the same put up by the Abbé Lespinasse during the panic of 1851, after the eruption. This has been splintered to pieces by a flash of lightning; and the fragments are clumsily united with cord. There is also a little tin plate let into a slit in a black post: it bears a date,—*8 April, 1867*. . . . The volcanic vents, which were active in 1851, are not visible from the peak: they are in the gorge descending from it, at a point nearly on a level with the Étang Sec.

The ground gives out a peculiar hollow sound when tapped, and is covered with a singular lichen,—all composed of round overlapping leaves about one-eighth of an inch in diameter, pale green, and tough as fish-scales. Here and there one sees a beautiful branching growth, like a mass of green coral: it is a gigantic moss. *Cabane-Jésus* ("bed-of-Jesus") the patois name is: at Christmas-time, in all the churches, those decorated cribs in which the image of the Child-Saviour is laid are filled with it. The creeping crimson violet is also here. Fireflies with bronze-green bodies are crawling about;—I notice also small frogs, large gray crickets, and a species of snail with a black shell. A solitary humming-bird passes, with a beautiful blue head, flaming like sapphire.

All at once the peak vibrates to a tremendous sound from somewhere below. . . . It is only a peal of thunder; but it startled at first, because the mountain rumbles and grumbles occasionally. . . . From the wilderness of ferns about the lake a sweet long low whistle comes—three times;—a *siffleur-de-montagne* has its nest there.

There is a rain-storm over the woods beneath us: clouds now hide everything but the point on which we rest; the crater of the Palmistes becomes invisible. But it is only for a little while that we are thus befogged: a wind comes, blows the clouds over us, lifts them up and folds them like a drapery, and slowly whirls them away northward. And for the first time the view is clear over the intervening gorge,—now spanned by the rocket-leap of a perfect rainbow.

. . . Valleys and mornes, peaks and ravines,—succeeding each other swiftly as surge succeeds surge in a storm,—a weirdly tossed world, but beautiful as it is weird: all green the foreground, with all tints of green, shadowing off to billowy distances of purest blue. The sea-line remains invisible as ever: you know where it is only by the zone of pale light ringing the double sphericity of sky and ocean. And in this double blue void the island seems to hang suspended: far peaks seem to come up from nowhere, to rest on nothing—like forms of mirage. Useless to attempt photography;—distances take the same color as the sea. Vauclin's truncated mass is recognizable only by the shape of its indigo shadows. All is vague, vertiginous;—the land still seems to quiver with the prodigious forces that up-heaved it.

High over all this billowing and peaking tower the Pitons of Carbet, gem-violet through the vapored miles,—the tallest one filleted with a single soft white band of cloud. Through all the wonderful chain of the Antilles you might seek in vain for other peaks exquisite of form as these. Their beauty no less surprises the traveller today than it did Columbus three hundred and eighty-six years ago, when—on the thirteenth day of June, 1502 —his caravel first sailed into sight of them, and he asked his Indian guide the name of the unknown land, and the names of those marvellous shapes. Then, according to Pedro Martyr de Anghiera, the Indian answered that the name of the island was Madiana; that those peaks had been venerated from immemorial time by the ancient peoples of the archipelago as the birthplace of the human race; and that the first brown habitants of Madiana, having been driven from their natural heritage by the man-eating pirates of the south—the cannibal Caribs,— remembered and mourned for their sacred mountains, and gave the names of them, for a memory, to the loftiest summits of their new home,—Hayti. . . . Surely never was fairer spot hallowed by the legend of man's nursing-place than the valley blue-shadowed by those peaks,—worthy, for their gracious femininity of shape, to seem the visible breasts of the All-nourishing Mother,—dreaming under this tropic sun.

Touching the zone of pale light north-east, appears a beautiful peaked silhouette,—Dominica. We had hoped to perceive Saint Lucia; but the atmosphere is too heavily charged with vapor to-day. How magnificent must be the view on certain extraordinary days, when it reaches from Antigua to the Grenadines —over a range of three hundred miles! But the atmospheric conditions which allow of such a spectacle are rare indeed. As a general rule, even in the most unclouded West Indian weather, the loftiest peaks fade into the light at a distance of one hundred miles.

A sharp ridge covered with fern cuts off the view of the northern slopes: one must climb it to look down upon Macouba. Macouba occupies the steepest slope of Pelée, and the grimmest part of the coast: its little *chef-lieu* is industrially famous for the manufacture of native tobacco, and historically for the ministrations of Père Labat, who rebuilt its church. Little change has taken place in the parish since his time. "Do you know Macouba?" asks a native writer;—"it is not Pelion upon Ossa, but ten or twelve Pelions side by side with ten or twelve Ossæ, interseparated by prodigious ravines. Men can speak to each other from places whence, by rapid walking, it would require hours to meet;—to travel there is to experience on dry land the sensation of the sea."

With the diminution of the warmth provoked by the exertion of climbing, you begin to notice how cool it feels;—you could almost doubt the testimony of your latitude. Directly east is Senegambia: we are well south of Timbuctoo and the Sahara,—on a line with southern India. The ocean has cooled the winds; at this altitude the rarity of the air is northern; but in the valleys below the vegetation is African. The best alimentary plants, the best forage, the flowers of the gardens, are of Guinea;—the graceful date-palms are from the Atlas region: those tamarinds, whose thick shade stifles all other vegetal life beneath it, are from Senegal. Only, in the touch of the air, the vapory colors of distance, the shapes of the hills, there is a something not of Africa: that strange fascination which has given to the island its poetic creole name,—*le Pays des Revenants*. And the charm is as puissant in our own day as it was more than two hundred years ago, when Père Dutertre wrote:—"I have never met one single man, nor one single woman, of all those who came back therefrom, in whom I have not remarked a most passionate desire to return thereunto."

Time and familiarity do not weaken the charm, either for those born among these scenes who never voyaged beyond their native island, or for those to whom the streets of Paris and the streets of St. Pierre are equally well known. Even at a time when Martinique had been forsaken by hundreds of her ruined planters, and the paradise-life of the old days had become only a memory to embitter exile,—a Creole writes:—

—"Let there suddenly open before you one of those vistas, or *anses*, with colonnades of cocoa-palm—at the end of which you see smoking the chimney of a sugar-mill, and catch a glimpse of the hamlet of negro cabins (*cases*);—or merely picture to yourself one of the most ordinary, most trivial scenes: nets being hauled by two ranks of fishermen; a *canot*, waiting for the *em-bellie* to make a dash for the beach; even a negro bending under the weight of a basket of fruits, and running along the shore to get to market;—and illuminate that with the light of our sun! What landscapes!—O Salvator Rosa! O Claude Lorrain, —if I had your pencil! . . . Well do I remember the day on which, after twenty years of absence, I found myself again in presence of these wonders;—I feel once more the thrill of delight that made all my body tremble, the tears that came to my eyes. It was my land, my own land, that appeared so beautiful." . . .*

X.

AT the beginning, while gazing south, east, west, to the rim of the world, all laughed, shouted, interchanged the quick delight of new impressions: every face was radiant. . . . Now all look serious;—none speak. The first physical joy of finding oneself on this point in violet air, exalted above the hills, soon yields to other emotions inspired by the mighty vision and the colossal peace of the heights. Dominating all, I think, is the consciousness of the awful antiquity of what one is looking upon,—such a sensation, perhaps, as of old found utterance in that tremendous question of the Book of Job:—"*Wast thou brought forth before the hills?*" . . . And the blue multitude of the peaks, the perpetual congregation of the mornes, seem to chorus in the vast resplendence,—telling of Nature's eternal youth, and the passionless permanence of that about us and beyond us and beneath,—until something like the fulness of a great grief begins to weigh at the heart. . . . For all this astonishment of beauty, all this majesty of light and form and color, will surely endure,—marvellous as now,—after we shall have lain down to sleep where no dreams come, and may never arise from the dust of our rest to look upon it.

*Dr. E. Rufz: "Études historiques," vol. i., p. 189.

'Ti Canotié

ONE might almost say that commercial time in St. Pierre
is measured by cannon-shots,—by the signal-guns of
steamers. Every such report announces an event of extreme
importance to the whole population. To the merchant it is a
notification that mails, money, and goods have arrived;—to
consuls and Government officials it gives notice of fees and
dues to be collected;—for the host of lightermen, longshoremen, port laborers of all classes, it promises work and pay;—
for all it signifies the arrival of food. The island does not feed
itself: cattle, salt meats, hams, lard, flour, cheese, dried fish, all
come from abroad,—particularly from America. And in the
minds of the colored population the American steamer is so intimately associated with the idea of those great tin cans in which
food-stuffs are brought from the United States, that the onomatope applied to the can, because of the sound outgiven by it
when tapped,—*bom!*—is also applied to the ship itself. The
English or French or Belgian steamer, however large, is only
known as *packett-à*, *batiment-là*; but the American steamer is
always the "bom-ship"—*batiment-bom-à*; or, the "food-ship"
—*batiment-mangé-à*. . . . You hear women and men asking
each other, as the shock of the gun flaps through all the town,
"*Mi! gadé ça qui là, chè?*" And if the answer be, "*Mais c'est
bom-là, chè,—bom-mangé-à ka rivé*" (Why, it is the bom, dear,—
the food-bom that has come), great is the exultation.

Again, because of the sound of her whistle, we find a steamer
called in this same picturesque idiom, *batiment-cône*, —"the
horn-ship." There is even a song, of which the refrain is:—

> "Bom-là rivé, chè,—
> Batiment-cône-là rivé."

. . . But of all the various classes of citizens, those most
joyously excited by the coming of a great steamer, whether she
be a "bom" or not,—are the *'ti canotié*, who swarm out immediately in little canoes of their own manufacture to dive for
coins which passengers gladly throw into the water for the
pleasure of witnessing the graceful spectacle. No sooner does a

steamer drop anchor—unless the water be very rough indeed —than she is surrounded by a fleet of the funniest little boats imaginable, full of naked urchins screaming creole.

These *'ti canotié*—these little canoe-boys and professional divers—are, for the most part, sons of boatmen of color, the real *canotiers*. I cannot find who first invented the *'ti canot*: the shape and dimensions of the little canoe are fixed according to a tradition several generations old; and no improvements upon the original model seem to have ever been attempted, with the sole exception of a tiny water-tight box contrived sometimes at one end, in which the *palettes*, or miniature paddles, and various other trifles may be stowed away. The actual cost of material for a canoe of this kind seldom exceeds twenty-five or thirty cents; and, nevertheless, the number of canoes is not very large—I doubt if there be more than fifteen in the harbor;—as the families of Martinique boatmen are all so poor that twenty-five sous are difficult to spare, in spite of the certainty that the little son can earn fifty times the amount within a month after owning a canoe.

For the manufacture of a canoe an American lard-box or kerosene-oil box is preferred by reason of its shape; but any well-constructed shipping-case of small size would serve the purpose. The top is removed; the sides and the corners of the bottom are sawn out at certain angles; and the pieces removed are utilized for the sides of the bow and stern,—sometimes also in making the little box for the paddles, or palettes, which

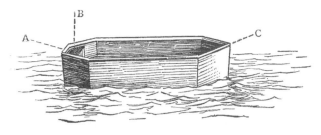

'TI CANOT.
A, *stern*;—B, *little box for the palettes, etc.*;—C, *prow*.

are simply thin pieces of tough wood about the form and size of a cigar-box lid. Then the little boat is tarred and varnished: it cannot sink,—though it is quite easily upset. There are no seats. The boys (there are usually two to each canot) simply squat down in the bottom,—facing each other. They can paddle with surprising swiftness over a smooth sea; and it is a very pretty sight to witness one of their prize contests in racing,— which take place every 14th of July. . . .

II.

. . . IT was five o'clock in the afternoon: the horizon beyond the harbor was turning lemon-color;—and a thin warm wind began to come in weak puffs from the south-west,—the first breaths to break the immobility of the tropical air. Sails of vessels becalmed at the entrance of the bay commenced to flap lazily: they might belly after sundown.

The *La Guayra* was in port, lying well out: her mountainous iron mass rising high above the modest sailing craft moored in her vicinity,—barks and brigantines and brigs and schooners and barkentines. She had lain before the town the whole afternoon, surrounded by the entire squadron of *'ti canots*; and the boys were still circling about her flanks, although she had got up steam and was lifting her anchor. They had been very lucky, indeed, that afternoon,—all the little canotiers;—and even many yellow lads, not fortunate enough to own canoes, had swum out to her in hope of sharing the silver shower falling from her saloon-deck. Some of these, tired out, were resting themselves by sitting on the slanting cables of neighboring ships. Perched naked thus,—balancing in the sun, against the blue of sky or water, their slender bodies took such orange from the mellowing light as to seem made of some self-luminous substance, —flesh of sea-fairies. . . .

Suddenly the *La Guayra* opened her steam-throat and uttered such a moo that all the mornes cried out for at least a minute after;—and the little fellows perched on the cables of the sailing craft tumbled into the sea at the sound and struck out for shore. Then the water all at once burst backward in immense frothing swirls from beneath the stern of the steamer; and there arose such a heaving as made all the little canoes dance. The *La Guayra* was moving. She moved slowly at first, making a great fuss as she turned round: then she began to settle down to her journey very majestically,—just making the water pitch a little behind her, as the hem of a woman's robe tosses lightly at her heels while she walks.

And, contrary to custom, some of the canoes followed after her. A dark handsome man, wearing an immense Panama hat, and jewelled rings upon his hands, was still throwing money; and still the boys dived for it. But only one of each crew now plunged; for, though the *La Guayra* was yet moving slowly, it was a severe strain to follow her, and there was no time to be lost.

The captain of the little band—black Maximilien, ten years old, and his comrade Stéphane—nicknamed *Ti Chabin*, because of his bright hair,—a slim little yellow boy of eleven— led the pursuit, crying always, "*Encò, Missié,—encò!*" . . .

The *La Guayra* had gained fully two hundred yards when the handsome passenger made his final largess,—proving himself quite an expert in flinging coin. The piece fell far short of the boys, but near enough to distinctly betray a yellow shimmer as it twirled to the water. That was gold!

In another minute the leading canoe had reached the spot, the other canotiers voluntarily abandoning the quest—for it was little use to contend against Maximilien and Stéphane, who had won all the canoe contests last 14th of July. Stéphane, who was the better diver, plunged.

He was much longer below than usual, came up at quite a distance, panted as he regained the canoe, and rested his arms upon it. The water was so deep there, he could not reach the coin the first time, though he could see it: he was going to try again,—it was gold, sure enough.

—"*Fouinq! ça fond içitt!*" he gasped.

Maximilien felt all at once uneasy. Very deep water, and perhaps sharks. And sunset not far off! The *La Guayra* was diminishing in the offing.

—"*Boug-là 'lé fai nou néyé!—laissé y, Stéphane!*" he cried. (The fellow wants to drown us. *Laissé*—leave it alone.)

But Stéphane had recovered breath, and was evidently resolved to try again. It was gold!

—"*Mais ça c'est lò!*"

—"*Assez, non!*" screamed Maximilien. "*Pa plongé 'ncò, moin ka di ou! Ah! foute!*" . . .

Stéphane had dived again!

. . . And where were the others? "*Bon-Dié, gadé oti yo yé!*" They were almost out of sight,—tiny specks moving shoreward. . . . The *La Guayra* now seemed no bigger than the little packet running between St. Pierre and Fort-de-France.

Up came Stéphane again, at a still greater distance than before,—holding high the yellow coin in one hand. He made for the canoe, and Maximilien paddled towards him and helped him in. Blood was streaming from the little diver's nostrils, and blood colored the water he spat from his mouth.

—"*Ah! moin té ka di ou laissé y!*" cried Maximilien, in anger and alarm. . . . "*Gàdé, gàdé sang-à ka coulé nans nez ou,—nans bouch ou! . . . Mi oti lézautt!*"

Lézautt, the rest, were no longer visible.

—"*Et mi oti nou yé!*" cried Maximilien again. They had never ventured so far from shore.

But Stéphane answered only, "*C'est ló!*" For the first time in his life he held a piece of gold in his fingers. He tied it up in a little rag attached to the string fastened about his waist,—a purse of his own invention,—and took up his paddles, coughing the while and spitting crimson.

—"*Mi! mi!—mi oti nou yé!*" reiterated Maximilien. "*Bon-Dié!* look where we are!"

The Place had become indistinct;—the light-house, directly behind half an hour earlier, now lay well south: the red light had just been kindled. Seaward, in advance of the sinking orange disk of the sun, was the *La Guayra*, passing to the horizon. There was no sound from the shore: about them a great silence had gathered,—the Silence of seas, which is a fear. Panic seized them: they began to paddle furiously.

But St. Pierre did not appear to draw any nearer. Was it only an effect of the dying light, or were they actually moving towards the semicircular cliffs of Fond-Corré? . . . Maximilien began to cry. The little chabin paddled on,—though the blood was still trickling over his breast.

Maximilien screamed out to him:—

—"*Ou pa ka pagayé,—anh?—ou ni bousoin dòmi?*" (Thou dost not paddle, eh?—thou wouldst go to sleep?)

—"*Si! moin ka pagayé,—epi fò!*" (I am paddling, and hard, too!) responded Stéphane. . . .

—"*Ou ka pagayé!—ou ka menti!*" (Thou art paddling!—thou liest!) vociferated Maximilien. . . . "And the fault is all thine. I cannot, all by myself, make the canoe to go in water like this! The fault is all thine: I told thee not to dive, thou stupid!"

—"*Ou fou!*" cried Stéphane, becoming angry. "*Moin ka pagayé!*" (I am paddling.)

—"Beast! never may we get home so! Paddle, thou lazy;— paddle, thou nasty!"

—"*Macaque* thou!—monkey!"

—"*Chabin!*—must be chabin, for to be stupid so!"

—"Thou black monkey!—thou species of *ouistiti!*"

—"Thou tortoise-of-the-land!—thou slothful more than *molocoye!*"

—"Why, thou cursed monkey, if thou sayest I do not paddle, thou dost not know how to paddle!" . . .

. . . But Maximilien's whole expression changed: he suddenly stopped paddling, and stared before him and behind him at a great violet band broadening across the sea northward out of sight; and his eyes were big with terror as he cried out:—

—"*Mais ni qui chose douóle içitt!*" . . . There is something queer, Stéphane; there is something queer." . . .

—"Ah! you begin to see now, Maximilien!—it is the current!"

—"A devil-current, Stéphane. . . . We are drifting: we will go to the horizon!" . . .

To the horizon—"*nou kallé lhorizon!*"—a phrase of terrible picturesqueness. . . . In the creole tongue, "to the horizon" signifies to the Great Open—into the measureless sea.

—"*C'est pa lapeine pagayé atouèlement*" (It is no use to paddle now), sobbed Maximilien, laying down his palettes.

—"*Si! si!*" said Stéphane, reversing the motion: "paddle with the current."

—"With the current! It runs to La Dominique!"

—"*Pouloss,*" phlegmatically returned Stéphane,—"*ennou!*— let us make for La Dominique!"

—"Thou fool!—it is more than past forty kilometres. . . . *Stéphane, mi! gadé!—mi qui gouôs requ'em!*"

A long black fin cut the water almost beside them, passed, and vanished,—a *requin* indeed! But, in his patois, the boy almost re-echoed the name as uttered by quaint Père Dutertre, who, writing of strange fishes more than two hundred years ago, says it is called REQUIEM, because for the man who findeth himself alone with it in the midst of the sea, surely a requiem must be sung.

—"Do not paddle, Stéphane!—do not put thy hand in the water again!"

III.

. . . THE *La Guayra* was a point on the sky-verge;—the sun's face had vanished. The silence and the darkness were deepening together.

—"*Si lanmè ka vini plis fò, ça nou ké fai?*" (If the sea roughens, what are we to do?) asked Maximilien.

—"Maybe we will meet a steamer," answered Stéphane: "the *Orinoco* was due to-day."

—"And if she pass in the night?"

—"They can see us." . . .

—"No, they will not be able to see us at all. There is no moon."

—"They have lights ahead."

—"I tell thee, they will not see us at all,—*pièss! pièss! pièss!*"

—"Then they will hear us cry out."

—"No,—we cannot cry so loud. One can hear nothing but a steam-whistle or a cannon, with the noise of the wind and the water and the machine. . . . Even on the Fort-de-France packet one cannot hear for the machine. And the machine of the *Orinoco* is more big than the church of the 'Centre.'"

—"Then we must try to get to La Dominique."

. . . They could now feel the sweep of the mighty current; —it even seemed to them that they could hear it,—a deep low whispering. At long intervals they saw lights,—the lights of houses in Pointe-Prince, in Fond-Canonville,—in Au Prêcheur. Under them the depth was unfathomed:—hydrographic charts mark it *sans-fond*. And they passed the great cliffs of Aux Abymes, under which lies the Village of the Abysms.

The red glare in the west disappeared suddenly as if blown out;—the rim of the sea vanished into the void of the gloom; —the night narrowed about them, thickening like a black fog.

And the invisible, irresistible power of the sea was now bearing them away from the tall coast,—over profundities unknown,—over the *sans-fond*—out "to the horizon."

IV.

. . . BEHIND the canoe a long thread of pale light quivered and twisted: bright points from time to time mounted up, glowered like eyes, and vanished again;—glimmerings of faint flame wormed away on either side as they floated on. And the little craft no longer rocked as before;—they felt another and a larger motion,—long slow ascents and descents enduring for minutes at a time;—they were riding the great swells,—*riding the horizon!*

Twice they were capsized. But happily the heaving was a smooth one, and their little canoe could not sink: they groped for it, found it, righted it, and climbed in, and baled out the water with their hands.

From time to time they both cried out together, as loud as they could,—"*Sucou!—sucou!—sucou!*"—hoping that some one might be looking for them. . . . The alarm had indeed been given; and one of the little steam-packets had been sent out to look for them,—with torch-fires blazing at her bows; but she had taken the wrong direction.

—"Maxmilien," said Stéphane, while the great heaving seemed to grow vaster,—"*fau nou ka prié Bon-Dié.*" . . .

Maximilien answered nothing.

—"*Fau prié Bon-Dié*" (We must pray to the Bon-Dié), repeated Stéphane.

—"*Pa lapeine, li pas pè ouè nou atò!*" (It is not worth while: He cannot see us now) answered the little black. . . . In the immense darkness even the loom of the island was no longer visible.

—"O Maximilien!—*Bon-Dié ka ouè toutt, ka connaitt toutt*" (He sees all; He knows all), cried Stéphane.

—"*Y pa pè ouè non pièss atouèlement, moin ben sur!*" (He cannot see us at all now,—I am quite sure) irreverently responded Maximilien. . . .

—"Thou thinkest the Bon-Dié like thyself!—He has not eyes like thou," protested Stéphane. "*Li pas ka tini coulè; li pas ka tini zié*" (He has not color; He has not eyes), continued the boy, repeating the text of his catechism,—the curious creole catechism of old Père Goux, of Carbet. [Quaint priest and quaint catechism have both passed away.]

—"*Moin pa save si li pa ka tini coulè*" (I know not if He has not color), answered Maximilien. "But what I well know is that if He has not eyes, He cannot see. . . . *Fouinq!*—how idiot!"

—"Why, it is in the Catechism," cried Stéphane. . . . "'*Bon-Dié, li conm vent: vent tout-patout, et nou pa save ouè li;—li ka touché nou,—li ka boulvésé lanmè.*'" (The Good-God is like the Wind: the Wind is everywhere, and we cannot see It;—It touches us,—It tosses the sea.)

—"If the Bon-Dié is the Wind," responded Maximilien, "then pray thou the Wind to stay quiet."

—"The Bon-Dié is not the Wind," cried Stéphane: "He is *like* the Wind, but He is not the Wind." . . .

—"*Ah! soc-soc!—fouinq!* . . . More better past praying to care we be not upset again and eaten by sharks."

*　　*　　*　　*　　*　　*　　*

. . . Whether the little chabin prayed either to the Wind or to the Bon-Dié, I do not know. But the Wind remained very quiet all that night,—seemed to hold its breath for fear of ruffling the sea. And in the Mouillage of St. Pierre furious American captains swore at the Wind because it would not fill their sails.

v.

PERHAPS, if there had been a breeze, neither Stéphane nor Maximilien would have seen the sun again. But they saw him rise.

Light pearled in the east, over the edge of the ocean, ran around the rim of the sky and yellowed: then the sun's brow appeared;—a current of gold gushed rippling across the sea before him;—and all the heaven at once caught blue fire from horizon to zenith. Violet from flood to cloud the vast recumbent form of Pelée loomed far behind,—with long reaches of mountaining: pale grays o'ertopping misty blues. And in the north another lofty shape was towering,—strangely jagged and peaked and beautiful,—the silhouette of Dominica: a sapphire

saw! . . . No wandering clouds:—over far Pelée only a shadowy piling of nimbi. . . . Under them the sea swayed dark as
purple ink—a token of tremendous depth. . . . Still a dead
calm, and no sail in sight.

—"*Ça c'est la Dominique*," said Maximilien,—"*Ennou pou
ouivage-à!*"

They had lost their little palettes during the night;—they
used their naked hands, and moved swiftly. But Dominica was
many and many a mile away. Which was the nearer island, it
was yet difficult to say;—in the morning sea-haze, both were
vapory,—difference of color was largely due to position. . . .

Sough!—sough!—sough!—A bird with a white breast passed
overhead; and they stopped paddling to look at it,—a gull. Sign
of fair weather!—it was making for Dominica.

—"*Moin ni ben faim*," murmured Maximilien. Neither had
eaten since the morning of the previous day,—most of which
they had passed sitting in their canoe.

—"*Moin ni anni soif*," said Stéphane. And besides his thirst
he complained of a burning pain in his head, always growing
worse. He still coughed, and spat out pink threads after each
burst of coughing.

The heightening sun flamed whiter and whiter: the flashing
of waters before his face began to dazzle like a play of lightning. . . . Now the islands began to show sharper lines,
stronger colors; and Dominica was evidently the nearer;—for
bright streaks of green were breaking at various angles through
its vapor-colored silhouette, and Martinique still remained all
blue.

. . . Hotter and hotter the sun burned; more and more
blinding became his reverberation. Maximilien's black skin suffered least; but both lads, accustomed as they were to remaining
naked in the sun, found the heat difficult to bear. They would
gladly have plunged into the deep water to cool themselves,
but for fear of sharks;—all they could do was to moisten their
heads, and rinse their mouths with sea-water.

Each from his end of the canoe continually watched the
horizon. Neither hoped for a sail, there was no wind; but they
looked for the coming of steamers,—the *Orinoco* might pass,
or the English packet, or some one of the small Martinique
steamboats might be sent out to find them.

Yet hours went by; and there still appeared no smoke in the ring of the sky,—never a sign in all the round of the sea, broken only by the two huge silhouettes. . . . But Dominica was certainly nearing;—the green lights were spreading through the luminous blue of her hills.

. . . Their long immobility in the squatting posture began to tell upon the endurance of both boys,—producing dull throbbing aches in thighs, hips, and loins. . . . Then, about mid-day, Stéphane declared he could not paddle any more;—it seemed to him as if his head must soon burst open with the pain which filled it: even the sound of his own voice hurt him,—he did not want to talk.

VI.

. . . AND another oppression came upon them,—in spite of all the pains, and the blinding dazzle of waters, and the biting of the sun: the oppression of drowsiness. They began to doze at intervals,—keeping their canoe balanced in some automatic way,—as cavalry soldiers, overweary, ride asleep in the saddle.

But at last, Stéphane, awaking suddenly with a paroxysm of coughing, so swayed himself to one side as to overturn the canoe; and both found themselves in the sea.

Maximilien righted the craft, and got in again; but the little chabin twice fell back in trying to raise himself upon his arms. He had become almost helplessly feeble. Maximilien, attempting to aid him, again overturned the unsteady little boat; and this time it required all his skill and his utmost strength to get Stéphane out of the water. Evidently Stéphane could be of no more assistance;—the boy was so weak he could not even sit up straight.

—"*Aïe! ou ké jété nou encò,*" panted Maximilien,—"*metté ou toutt longue.*"

Stéphane slowly let himself down, so as to lie nearly all his length in the canoe,—one foot on either side of Maximilien's hips. Then he lay very still for a long time,—so still that Maximilien became uneasy.

—"*Ou ben malade?*" he asked. . . . Stéphane did not seem to hear: his eyes remained closed.

—"Stéphane!" cried Maximilien, in alarm,—"Stéphane!"

—"*C'est lò, papoute,*" murmured Stéphane, without lifting his eyelids.—"*ça c'est lò!—ou pa janmain ouè yon bel pièce conm ça?*" (It is gold, little father. . . . Didst thou ever see a pretty piece like that? . . . No, thou wilt not beat me, little father? —no, *papoute!*)

—"*Ou ka dòmi, Stéphane?*"—queried Maximilien, wondering,—"art asleep?"

But Stéphane opened his eyes and looked at him so strangely! Never had he seen Stéphane look that way before.

—"*Ça ou ni, Stéphane?*—what ails thee?—*aïe! Bon-Dié, Bon-Dié!*"

—"*Bon-Dié!*"—muttered Stéphane, closing his eyes again at the sound of the great Name,—"He has no color;—He is like the Wind." . . .

—"Stéphane!" . . .

—"He feels in the dark;—He has not eyes." . . .

—"*Stéphane, pa pàlé ça!!*"

—"He tosses the sea. . . . He has no face;—He lifts up the dead . . . and the leaves." . . .

—"*Ou fou!*" cried Maximilien, bursting into a wild fit of sobbing,—"Stéphane, thou art mad!"

And all at once he became afraid of Stéphane,—afraid of all he said,—afraid of his touch,—afraid of his eyes, . . . he was growing like a *zombi!*

But Stephane's eyes remained closed;—he ceased to speak.

. . . About them deepened the enormous silence of the sea;—low swung the sun again. The horizon was yellowing: day had begun to fade. Tall Dominica was now half green; but there yet appeared no smoke, no sail, no sign of life.

And the tints of the two vast Shapes that shattered the rim of the light shifted as if evanescing,—shifted like tones of West Indian fishes,—of *pisquette* and *congre*,—of *caringue* and *gouôs-zié* and *balaou*. Lower sank the sun;—cloud-fleeces of orange pushed up over the edge of the west;—a thin warm breath caressed the sea,—sent long lilac shudderings over the flanks of the swells. Then colors changed again: violet richened to purple;— greens blackened softly;—grays smouldered into smoky gold.

And the sun went down.

VII.

AND they floated into the fear of the night together. Again the ghostly fires began to wimple about them: naught else was visible but the high stars.

Black hours passed. From minute to minute Maximilien cried out:—"*Sucou! sucou!*" Stéphane lay motionless and dumb: his feet, touching Maximilien's naked hips, felt singularly cold.

. . . Something knocked suddenly against the bottom of the canoe,—knocked heavily—making a hollow loud sound. It was not Stéphane;—Stéphane lay still as a stone: it was from the depth below. Perhaps a great fish passing.

It came again,—twice,—shaking the canoe like a great blow. Then Stéphane suddenly moved,—drew up his feet a little,—made as if to speak:—"*Ou* . . ."; but the speech failed at his lips,—ending in a sound like the moan of one trying to call out in sleep;—and Maximilien's heart almost stopped beating. . . . Then Stéphane's limbs straightened again; he made no more movement;—Maximilien could not even hear him breathe. . . . All the sea had begun to whisper.

A breeze was rising;—Maximilien felt it blowing upon him. All at once it seemed to him that he had ceased to be afraid,—that he did not care what might happen. He thought about a cricket he had one day watched in the harbor,—drifting out with the tide, on an atom of dead bark,—and he wondered what had become of it. Then he understood that he himself was the cricket,—still alive. But some boy had found him and pulled off his legs. There they were,—his own legs, pressing against him: he could still feel the aching where they had been pulled off; and they had been dead so long they were now quite cold. . . . It was certainly Stéphane who had pulled them off. . . .

The water was talking to him. It was saying the same thing over and over again,—louder each time, as if it thought he could not hear. But he heard it very well:—"*Bon-Dié, li conm vent . . . li ka touché nou . . . nou pa save ouè li.*" (But why had the Bon-Dié shaken the wind?) "*Li pa ka tini zié,*" answered the water. . . . *Ouille!*—He might all the same care not to upset folks in the sea! . . . *Mi!* . . .

But even as he thought these things, Maximilien became aware that a white, strange, bearded face was looking at him: the Bon-Dié was there,—bending over him with a lantern,—talking to him in a language he did not understand. And the Bon-Dié certainly had eyes,—great gray eyes that did not look wicked at all. He tried to tell the Bon-Dié how sorry he was for what he had been saying about him;—but found he could not utter a word. He felt great hands lift him up to the stars, and lay him down very near them,—just under them. They burned blue-white, and hurt his eyes like lightning:—he felt afraid of them. . . . About him he heard voices,—always speaking the same language, which he could not understand. . . . "*Poor little devils!—poor little devils!*" Then he heard a bell ring; and the Bon-Dié made him swallow something nice and warm;—and everything became black again. The stars went out! . . .

. . . Maximilien was lying under an electric-light on board the great steamer *Rio de Janeiro*, and dead Stéphane beside him. . . . It was four o'clock in the morning.

La Fille de Couleur

NOTHING else in the picturesque life of the French colonies of the Occident impresses the traveller on his first arrival more than the costumes of the women of color. They surprise the æsthetic sense agreeably;—they are local and special: you will see nothing resembling them among the populations of the British West Indies; they belong to Martinique, Guadeloupe, Désirade, Marie-Galante, and Cayenne,—in each place differing sufficiently to make the difference interesting, especially in regard to the head-dress. That of Martinique is quite Oriental;—more attractive, although less fantastic than the Cayenne coiffure, or the pretty drooping mouchoir of Guadeloupe.

These costumes are gradually disappearing, for various reasons,—the chief reason being of course the changes in the social condition of the colonies during the last forty years. Probably the question of health had also something to do with the almost universal abandonment in Martinique of the primitive slave-dress,—*chemise* and *jupe*,—which exposed its wearer to serious risks of pneumonia; for as far as economical reasons are concerned, there was no fault to find with it: six francs could purchase it when money was worth more than it is now. The douillette, a long trailing dress, one piece from neck to feet, has taken its place.* But there was a luxurious variety of the jupe costume which is disappearing because of its cost; there is no money in the colonies now for such display:—I refer to the celebrated attire of the pet slaves and *belles affranchies* of the old colonial days. A full costume,—including violet or crimson "petticoat" of silk or satin; chemise with half-sleeves, and much embroidery and lace; "trembling-pins" of gold (*zépingue tremblant*) to attach the folds of the brilliant Madras turban; the great necklace of three or four strings of gold beads bigger

---

*The brightly colored douillettes are classified by the people according to the designs of the printed calico:—*robe-à-bambou,—robe-à-bouquet,—robe-arc-en-ciel,—robe-à-carreau,*—etc., according as the pattern is in stripes, flower-designs, "rainbow" bands of different tints, or plaidings. *Ronde-en-ronde* means a stuff printed with disk-patterns, or link-patterns of different colors,—each joined with the other. A robe of one color only is called a *robe-uni.*

than peas (*collier-choux*); the ear-rings, immense but light as egg-shells (*zanneaux-à-clous* or *zanneaux-chenilles*); the bracelets (*portes-bonheur*); the studs (*boutons-à-clous*); the brooches, not only for the turban, but for the chemise, below the folds of the showy silken foulard or shoulder-scarf,—would sometimes represent over five thousand francs expenditure. This gorgeous attire is becoming less visible every year: it is now rarely worn except on very solemn occasions,—weddings, baptisms, first communions, confirmations. The *da* (nurse) or "porteuse-de-baptême" who bears the baby to church, holds it at the baptismal font, and afterwards carries it from house to house in order that all the friends of the family may kiss it, is thus attired; but nowadays, unless she be a professional (for there are professional *das*, hired only for such occasions), she usually borrows the jewellery. If tall, young, graceful, with a rich gold tone of skin, the effect of her costume is dazzling as that of a Byzantine Virgin. I saw one young da who, thus garbed, scarcely seemed of the earth and earthly;—there was an Oriental something in her appearance difficult to describe,—something that

---

The general laws of contrasts observed in the costume require the silk foulard, or shoulder-kerchief, to make a sharp relief with the color of the robe, thus:—

Robe.	Foulard.
Yellow	Blue.
Dark blue	Yellow.
Pink	Green.
Violet	Bright red.
Red	Violet.
Chocolate (cacoa)	Pale blue.
Sky blue	Pale rose.

These refer, of course, to dominant or ground colors, as there are usually several tints in the foulard as well as the robe. The painted Madras should always be bright yellow. According to popular ideas of good dressing, the different tints of skin should be relieved by special choice of color in the robe, as follows:—

Capresse (a clear red skin) should wear	Pale yellow.
Mulatresse (according to shade)	Rose. / Blue. / Green.
Négresse	White. / Scarlet, or any violent color.

made you think of the Queen of Sheba going to visit Solomon. She had brought a merchant's baby, just christened, to receive the caresses of the family at whose house I was visiting; and when it came to my turn to kiss it, I confess I could not notice the child: I saw only the beautiful dark face, coiffed with orange and purple, bending over it, in an illumination of antique gold. . . . What a da! . . . She represented really the type of

The Martinique Turban, or "Madras Calendé."

that *belle affranchie* of other days, against whose fascination special sumptuary laws were made: romantically she imaged for me the supernatural god-mothers and Cinderellas of the creole fairy-tales. For these become transformed in the West Indian folklore,—adapted to the environment, and to local idealism:

Cinderella, for example, is changed to a beautiful métisse, wearing a quadruple *collier-choux, zépingues tremblants*, and all the ornaments of a da.* Recalling the impression of that dazzling *da*, I can even now feel the picturesque justice of the fabulist's description of Cinderella's creole costume: *Ça té ka baille ou mal ziè!*—(it would have given you a pain in your eyes to look at her!)

. . . Even the every-day Martinique costume is slowly changing. Year by year the "calendeuses"—the women who paint and fold the turbans—have less work to do;—the colors of the *douillette* are becoming less vivid;—while more and more young colored girls are being *élevées en chapeau* ("brought up in a hat")—*i.e.*, dressed and educated like the daughters of the whites. These, it must be confessed, look far less attractive in the latest Paris fashion, unless white as the whites themselves: on the other hand, few white girls could look well in *douillette* and *mouchoir*,—not merely because of color contrast, but because they have not that amplitude of limb and particular cambering of the torso peculiar to the half-breed race, with its large bulk and stature. Attractive as certain coolie women are, I observed that all who have adopted the Martinique costume look badly in it: they are too slender of body to wear it to advantage.

Slavery introduced these costumes, even though it probably did not invent them; and they were necessarily doomed to pass away with the peculiar social conditions to which they belonged. If the population clings still to its *douillettes, mouchoirs*, and *foulards*, the fact is largely due to the cheapness of such attire. A girl can dress very showily indeed for about twenty francs—shoes excepted;—and thousands never wear shoes. But the fashion will no doubt have become cheaper and uglier within another decade.

---

* . . . "Vouèla Cendrillon evec yon bel ròbe velou grande lakhè. . . . Ça té ka bail ou mal ziè. Li té tini bel zanneau dans zòreill li, quate-tou-chou, bouoche, bracelet, tremblant,—toutt sòte bel baggaïe conm ça.". . .—[*Conte Cendrillon,—d'après Turiault*.]

—"There was Cendrillon with a beautiful long trailing robe of velvet on her! . . . It was enough to hurt one's eyes to look at her. She had beautiful rings in her ears, and a collier-choux of four rows, brooches, *tremblants*, bracelets,—everything fine of that sort."—[Story of Cinderella in Turiault's Creole Grammar.]

The Guadeloupe Head-dress.

At the present time, however, the stranger might be sufficiently impressed by the oddity and brilliancy of these dresses
to ask about their origin,—in which case it is not likely that he
will obtain any satisfactory answer. After long research I found
myself obliged to give up all hope of being able to outline the
history of Martinique costume,—partly because books and
histories are scanty or defective, and partly because such an
undertaking would require a knowledge possible only to a specialist. I found good reason, nevertheless, to suppose that these
costumes were in the beginning adopted from certain fashions
of provincial France,—that the respective fashions of Guadeloupe, Martinique, and Cayenne were patterned after modes
still worn in parts of the mother-country. The old-time garb
of the *affranchie*—that still worn by the *da*—somewhat recalls
dresses worn by the women of Southern France, more particularly about Montpellier. Perhaps a specialist might also trace
back the evolution of the various creole coiffures to old forms
of head-dresses which still survive among the French country-
fashions of the south and south-west provinces;—but local
taste has so much modified the original style as to leave it unrecognizable to those who have never studied the subject. The
Martinique fashion of folding and tying the Madras, and of
calendering it, are probably local; and I am assured that the
designs of the curious semi-barbaric jewellery were all invented
in the colony, where the *collier-choux* is still manufactured by
local goldsmiths. Purchasers buy one, two, or three *grains*, or
beads, at a time, and string them only on obtaining the requisite number. . . . This is the sum of all that I was able to learn
on the matter; but in the course of searching various West
Indian authors and historians for information, I found something far more important than the origin of the *douillette* or
the *collier-choux*: the facts of that strange struggle between nature and interest, between love and law, between prejudice and
passion, which forms the evolutional history of the mixed race.

II.

CONSIDERING only the French peasant colonist and the West
African slave as the original factors of that physical evolution

Young Mulattress.

visible in the modern *fille-de-couleur*, it would seem incredible;
—for the intercrossing alone could not adequately explain all
the physical results. To understand them fully, it will be necessary to bear in mind that both of the original races became
modified in their lineage to a surprising degree by conditions
of climate and environment.

The precise time of the first introduction of slaves into Martinique is not now possible to ascertain,—no record exists on
the subject; but it is probable that the establishment of slavery
was coincident with the settlement of the island. Most likely the
first hundred colonists from St. Christophe, who landed, in 1635,
near the bay whereon the city of St. Pierre is now situated,
either brought slaves with them, or else were furnished with

negroes very soon after their arrival. In the time of Père Dutertre (who visited the colonies in 1640, and printed his history of the French Antilles at Paris in 1667) slavery was already a flourishing institution,—the foundation of the whole social structure. According to the Dominican missionary, the Africans then in the colony were decidedly repulsive; he describes the women as "hideous" (*hideuses*). There is no good reason to charge Dutertre with prejudice in his pictures of them. No writer of the century was more keenly sensitive to natural beauty than the author of that "Voyage aux Antilles" which inspired Chateaubriand, and which still, after two hundred and fifty years, delights even those perfectly familiar with the nature of the places and things spoken of. No other writer and traveller of the period possessed to a more marked degree that sense of generous pity which makes the unfortunate appear to us in an illusive, almost ideal aspect. Nevertheless, he asserts that the negresses were, as a general rule, revoltingly ugly, —and, although he had seen many strange sides of human nature (having been a soldier before becoming a monk), was astonished to find that miscegenation had already begun. Doubtless the first black women thus favored, or afflicted, as the case might be, were of the finer types of negresses; for he notes remarkable differences among the slaves procured from different coasts and various tribes. Still, these were rather differences of ugliness than aught else: they were all repulsive;— only some were more repulsive than others.* Granting that the first mothers of mulattoes in the colony were the superior rather than the inferior physical types,—which would be a perfectly natural supposition,—still we find their offspring worthy in his eyes of no higher sentiment than pity. He writes in his chapter entitled "*De la naissance honteuse des mulastres*":—

---

*It is quite possible, however, that the slaves of Dutertre's time belonged for the most part to the uglier African tribes; and that later supplies may have been procured from other parts of the slave coast. Writing half a century later, Père Labat declares having seen freshly disembarked blacks handsome enough to inspire an artist:—"*J'en ai vu des deux sexes faits à peindre, et beaux par merveille*" (vol. iv., chap. vii.). He adds that their skin was extremely fine, and of velvety softness;—"*le velours n'est pas plus doux.*" . . . Among the 30,000 blacks yearly shipped to the French colonies, there were doubtless many representatives of the finer African races.

Plantation Coolie Woman in Martinique Costume.

—"They have something of their Father and something of their Mother,—in the same wise that Mules partake of the qualities of the creatures that engendered them: for they are neither all white, like the French; nor all black, like the Negroes, but have a livid tint, which comes of both." . . .

To-day, however, the traveller would look in vain for a *livid* tint among the descendants of those thus described: in less than two centuries and a half the physical characteristics of the race have been totally changed. What most surprises is the rapidity of the transformation. After the time of Père Labat, Europeans never could "have mistaken little negro children for monkeys." Nature had begun to remodel the white, the black, and half-breed according to environment and climate: the descendant of the early colonists ceased to resemble his

Coolie Half-breed.

fathers; the creole negro improved upon his progenitors;[*] the mulatto began to give evidence of those qualities of physical and mental power which were afterwards to render him dangerous to the integrity of the colony itself. In a temperate climate such a change would have been so gradual as to escape observation for a long period;—in the tropics it was effected with a quickness that astounds by its revelation of the natural forces at work.

—"Under the sun of the tropics," writes Dr. Rufz, of Martinique, "the African race, as well as the European, becomes greatly modified in its reproduction. Either race gives birth to a totally new being.

[*]"Leur sueur n'est pas fétide comme celle des nègres de la Guinée," writes the traveller Dauxion-Lavaysse, in 1813.

The Creole African came into existence as did the Creole white. And just as the offspring of Europeans who emigrated to the tropics from different parts of France displayed characteristics so identical that it was impossible to divine the original race-source,—so likewise the Creole negro —whether brought into being by the heavy thick-set Congo, or the long slender black of Senegambia, or the suppler and more active Mandingo,— appeared so remodelled, homogeneous, and adapted in such wise to his environment that it was utterly impossible to discern in his features anything of his parentage, his original kindred, his original source. . . . The transformation is absolute. All that can be asserted is: 'This is a white Creole; this is a black Creole';—or, 'This is a European white; this is an African black';—and furthermore, after a certain number of years passed in the tropics, the enervated and discolored aspect of the European may create uncertainty as to his origin. But with very few exceptions the primitive African, or, as he is termed here, the 'Coast Black' (*le noir de la Côte*), can be recognized at once. . . .

Country-girl—Pure Negro Race.

. . . "The Creole negro is gracefully shaped, finely proportioned: his limbs are lithe, his neck long;—his features are more delicate, his lips less thick, his nose less flattened, than those of the African;—he has the Carib's large and melancholy eye, better adapted to express the emotions. . . . Rarely can you discover in him the sombre fury of the African, rarely a surly and savage mien: he is brave, chatty, boastful. His skin has not the same tint as his father's, —it has become more satiny; his hair remains woolly, but it is a finer wool; . . . all his outlines are more rounded;— one may perceive that the cellular tissue predominates, as in cultivated plants, of which the ligneous and savage fibre has become transformed." . . .*

This new and comelier black race naturally won from its masters a more sympathetic attention than could have been vouchsafed to its progenitors; and the consequences in Martinique and elsewhere seemed to have evoked the curious Article 9 of the *Code Noir* of 1665,—enacting, first, that free men who should have one or two children by slave women, as well as the slave-owners permitting the same, should be each condemned to pay two thousand pounds of sugar; secondly, that if the violator of the ordinance should be himself the owner of the mother and father of her children, the mother and the children should be confiscated for the profit of the Hospital, and deprived for their lives of the right to enfranchisement. An exception, however, was made to the effect that if the father were unmarried at the period of his concubinage, he could escape the provisions of the penalty by marrying, "according to the rites of the Church," the female slave, who would thereby be enfranchised, and her children "rendered free and legitimate." Probably the legislators did not imagine that the first portion of the article could prove inefficacious, or that any violator of the ordinance would seek to escape the penalty by those means offered in the provision. The facts, however, proved the reverse. Miscegenation continued; and Labat notices two cases of marriage between whites and blacks,—describing the off-

---

*Dr. E. Rufz: "Études historiques et statistiques sur la population de la Martinique." St. Pierre: 1850. Vol. i., pp. 148–50.

It has been generally imagined that the physical constitution of the black race was proof against the deadly climate of the West Indies. The truth is that the freshly imported Africans died of fever by thousands and tens-of-thousands; —the creole-negro race, now so prolific, represents only the fittest survivors in the long and terrible struggle of the slave element to adapt itself to the new environment. Thirty thousand negroes a year were long needed to supply the French colonies. Between 1700 and 1789 no less than 900,000 slaves were imported by San Domingo alone;—yet there were less than half that number left in 1789. (See Placide Justin's history of Santo Domingo, p. 147.) The entire slave population of Barbadoes had to be renewed every sixteen years, according to estimates: the loss to planters by deaths of slaves (reckoning the value of a slave at only £20 sterling) during the same period was £1,600,000 ($8,000,000). (Burck's "History of European Colonies," vol. ii., p. 141; French edition of 1767.)

spring of one union as "very handsome little mulattoes." These legitimate unions were certainly exceptional,—one of them was dissolved by the ridicule cast upon the father;—but illegitimate unions would seem to have become common within a very brief time after the passage of the law. At a later day they were to become customary. The Article 9 was evidently at fault; and in March, 1724, the Black Code was reinforced by a new ordinance, of which the sixth provision prohibited marriage as well as concubinage between the races.

It appears to have had no more effect than the previous law, even in Martinique, where the state of public morals was better than in Santo Domingo. The slave race had begun to exercise an influence never anticipated by legislators. Scarcely a century had elapsed since the colonization of the island; but in that time climate and civilization had transfigured the black woman. "After one or two generations," writes the historian Rufz, "the *Africaine*, reformed, refined, beautified in her descendants, transformed into the creole negress, commenced to exert a fascination irresistible, capable of winning anything (*capable de tout obtenir*)."* Travellers of the eighteenth century were confounded by the luxury of dress and of jewellery displayed by swarthy beauties in St. Pierre. It was a public scandal to European eyes. But the creole negress or mulattress, beginning to understand her power, sought for higher favors and privileges than silken robes and necklaces of gold beads: she sought to obtain, not merely liberty for herself, but for her parents, brothers, sisters,—even friends. What successes she achieved in this regard may be imagined from the serious statement of creole historians that if human nature had been left untrammelled to follow its better impulses, slavery would have ceased to exist a century before the actual period of emancipation! By 1738, when the white population had reached its maximum (15,000),† and colonial luxury had arrived at its greatest height, the question of voluntary enfranchisement was becoming very grave. So omnipotent the charm of half-breed beauty that masters were becoming the slaves of their slaves. It was not only the creole *negress* who had appeared to play a

*Rufz: "Études," vol. i., p. 236.
†I am assured it has now fallen to a figure not exceeding 5000.

part in this strange drama which was the triumph of nature over interest and judgment: her daughters, far more beautiful, had grown up to aid her, and to form a special class. These women, whose tints of skin rivalled the colors of ripe fruit, and whose gracefulness—peculiar, exotic, and irresistible—made them formidable rivals to the daughters of the dominant race, were no doubt physically superior to the modern *filles-de-couleur*. They were results of a natural selection which could have taken place in no community otherwise constituted;—the offspring of the union between the finer types of both races. But that which only slavery could have rendered possible began to endanger the integrity of slavery itself: the institutions upon which the whole social structure rested were being steadily sapped by the influence of half-breed girls. Some new, severe, extreme policy was evidently necessary to avert the already visible peril. Special laws were passed by the Home-Government to check enfranchisement, to limit its reasons or motives; and the power of the slave woman was so well comprehended by the Métropole that an extraordinary enactment was made against it. It was decreed that whosoever should free a woman of color would have to pay to the Government *three times her value as a slave!*

Thus heavily weighted, emancipation advanced much more slowly than before, but it still continued to a considerable extent. The poorer creole planter or merchant might find it impossible to obey the impulse of his conscience or of his affection, but among the richer classes pecuniary considerations could scarcely affect enfranchisement. The country had grown wealthy; and although the acquisition of wealth may not evoke generosity in particular natures, the enrichment of a whole class develops pre-existing tendencies to kindness, and opens new ways for its exercise. Later in the eighteenth century, when hospitality had been cultivated as a gentleman's duty to fantastical extremes, —when liberality was the rule throughout society,—when a notary summoned to draw up a deed, or a priest invited to celebrate a marriage, might receive for fee five thousand francs in gold,—there were certainly many emancipations. . . . "Even though interest and public opinion in the colonies," says a historian,[*] "were adverse to enfranchisement, the private feeling

[*] Rufz: "Études," vol. ii., pp. 311, 312.

of each man combated that opinion;—Nature resumed her sway in the secret places of hearts;—and as local custom permitted a sort of polygamy, the rich man naturally felt himself bound in honor to secure the freedom of his own blood. . . . It was not a rare thing to see legitimate wives taking care of the natural children of their husbands,—becoming their godmothers (*s'en faire les marraines*)." . . . Nature seemed to laugh all these laws to scorn, and the prejudices of race! In vain did the wisdom of legislators attempt to render the condition of the enfranchised more humble,—enacting extravagant penalties for the blow by which a mulatto might avenge the insult of a white,—prohibiting the freed from wearing the same dress as their former masters or mistresses wore;—"the *belles affranchies* found, in a costume whereof the negligence seemed a very inspiration of voluptuousness, means of evading that social inferiority which the law sought to impose upon them:—they began to inspire the most violent jealousies."*

III.

WHAT the legislators of 1685 and 1724 endeavored to correct did not greatly improve with the abolition of slavery, nor yet with those political troubles which socially deranged colonial life. The *fille-de-couleur*, inheriting the charm of the *belle affranchie*, continued to exert a similar influence, and to fulfil an almost similar destiny. The latitude of morals persisted,— though with less ostentation: it has latterly contracted under the pressure of necessity rather than through any other influences. Certain ethical principles thought essential to social integrity elsewhere have always been largely relaxed in the tropics; and—excepting, perhaps, Santo Domingo—the moral standard in Martinique was not higher than in the other French colonies. Outward decorum might be to some degree maintained; but there was no great restraint of any sort upon private lives: it was not uncommon for a rich man to have many "natural" families; and almost every individual of means had children of color. The superficial character of race prejudices

*Rufz: "Études," vol. i., p. 237.

was everywhere manifested by unions, which although never mentioned in polite converse, were none the less universally known; and the "irresistible fascination" of the half-breed gave the open lie to pretended hate. Nature, in the guise of the *belle affranchie*, had mocked at slave codes;—in the *fille-de-couleur* she still laughed at race pretensions, and ridiculed the fable of physical degradation. To-day the situation has not greatly changed; and with such examples on the part of the cultivated race, what could be expected from the other? Marriages are rare;—it has been officially stated that the illegitimate births are sixty per cent.; but seventy-five to eighty per cent. would probably be nearer the truth. It is very common to see in the local papers such announcements as: *Enfants légitimes*, 1 (one birth announced); *enfants naturels*, 25.

In speaking of the *fille-de-couleur* it is necessary also to speak of the extraordinary social stratification of the community to which she belongs. The official statement of 20,000 "colored" to the total population of between 173,000 and 174,000 (in which the number of pure whites is said to have fallen as low as 5,000) does not at all indicate the real proportion of mixed blood. Only a small element of unmixed African descent really exists; yet when a white creole speaks of the *gens-de-couleur* he certainly means nothing darker than a mulatto skin. Race classifications have been locally made by sentiments of political origin: at least four or five shades of visible color are classed as negro. There is, however, some natural truth at the bottom of this classification: where African blood predominates, the sympathies are likely to be African; and the turning-point is reached only in the true mulatto, where, allowing the proportions of mixed blood to be nearly equal, the white would have the dominant influence in situations more natural than existing politics. And in speaking of the *filles-de-couleur*, the local reference is always to women in whom the predominant element is white: a white creole, as a general rule, deigns only thus to distinguish those who are nearly white,—more usually he refers to the whole class as mulattresses. Those women whom wealth and education have placed in a social position parallel with that of the daughters of creole whites are in some cases allowed to pass for white,—or at the very worst, are only referred to in a whisper as being *de couleur*. (Needless to say, these are totally beyond the range of the present considerations: there is nothing to be further said of them except that they can be classed with the most attractive and refined women of the entire tropical world.) As there is an almost infinite gradation from the true black up to the brightest *sang-mêlé*, it is impossible to establish any color-classification recognizable by the eye alone; and whatever lines of demarcation can be drawn between castes must be social rather than ethnical. In this sense we may accept the local Creole definition of *fille-de-couleur* as signifying, not so much a daughter of the race of visible color, as the half-breed girl destined from her birth to a career like that of the *belle affranchie* of the old régime;—for the moral cruelties of slavery have survived emancipation.

Physically, the typical *fille-de-couleur* may certainly be classed, as white creole writers have not hesitated to class her, with the "most beautiful women of the human race."* She has inherited not only the finer bodily characteristics of either parent race, but a something else belonging originally to neither, and created by special climatic and physical conditions,—a grace, a suppleness of form, a delicacy of extremities (so that all the lines described by the bending of limbs or fingers are parts of clean curves), a satiny smoothness and fruit-tint of skin,—solely West Indian. . . . Morally, of course, it is much more difficult to describe her; and whatever may safely be said refers rather to the fille-de-couleur of the past than of the present half-century. The race is now in a period of transition: public education and political changes are modifying the type, and it is impossible to guess the ultimate consequence, because it is impossible to safely predict what new influences may yet be brought to affect its social development. Before the present era of colonial decadence, the character of the fille-de-couleur was not what it is now. Even when totally uneducated, she had a peculiar charm,—that charm of childishness which has power to win sympathy from the rudest natures. One could not but feel attracted towards this *naïf* being, docile as an infant, and

* *La race de sang-mêlé, issue des blancs et des noirs, est éminement civilizable. Comme types physiques, elle fournit dans beaucoup d'individus, dans ses femmes en général, les plus beaux specimens de la race humaine.*—"Le Préjugé de Race aux Antilles Françaises." Par G. Souquet-Basiège. St. Pierre, Martinique: 1883. pp. 661–62.

as easily pleased or as easily pained,—artless in her goodnesses as in her faults, to all outward appearance;—willing to give her youth, her beauty, her caresses to some one in exchange for the promise to love her,—perhaps also to care for a mother, or a younger brother. Her astonishing capacity for being delighted with trifles, her pretty vanities and pretty follies, her sudden veerings of mood from laughter to tears,—like the sudden rainbursts and sunbursts of her own passionate climate: these touched, drew, won, and tyrannized. Yet such easily created joys and pains did not really indicate any deep reserve of feeling: rather a superficial sensitiveness only,—like the *zhèbe-m'amisé*, or *zhèbe-manmzelle*, whose leaves close at the touch of a hair. Such human manifestations, nevertheless, are apt to attract more in proportion as they are more visible,—in proportion as the soul-current, being less profound, flows more audibly. But no hasty observation could have revealed the whole character of the fille-de-couleur to the stranger, equally charmed and surprised: the creole comprehended her better, and probably treated her with even more real kindness. The truth was that centuries of deprivation of natural rights and hopes had given to her race—itself fathered by passion unrestrained and mothered by subjection unlimited—an inherent scepticism in the duration of love, and a marvellous capacity for accepting the destiny of abandonment as one accepts the natural and the inevitable. And that desire to please—which in the fille-de-couleur seemed to prevail above all other motives of action (maternal affection excepted)—could have appeared absolutely natural only to those who never reflected that even sentiment had been artificially cultivated by slavery.

She asked for so little,—accepted a gift with such childish pleasure,—submitted so unresistingly to the will of the man who promised to love her. She bore him children—such beautiful children!—whom he rarely acknowledged, and was never asked to legitimatize;—and she did not ask perpetual affection notwithstanding,—regarded the relation as a necessarily temporary one, to be sooner or later dissolved by the marriage of her children's father. If deceived in all things,—if absolutely ill-treated and left destitute, she did not lose faith in human nature: she seemed a born optimist, believing most men good; —she would make a home for another and serve him better

Capresse.

than any slave. . . . "*Née de l'amour*," says a creole writer, "*la fille-de-couleur vit d'amour, de rires, et d'oublis.*"* . . .

Then came the general colonial crash! . . . You cannot see its results without feeling touched by them. Everywhere the weird beauty, the immense melancholy of tropic ruin. Magnificent terraces, once golden with cane, now abandoned to weeds and serpents;—deserted plantation-homes, with trees rooted in the apartments and pushing up through the place of the roofs;—grass-grown alleys ravined by rains;—fruit-trees strangled by lianas;—here and there the stem of some splendid palmiste, brutally decapitated, naked as a mast;—petty frail growths of banana-trees or of bamboo slowly taking the place of century-old forest giants destroyed to make charcoal. But beauty enough remains to tell what the sensual paradise of the old days must have been, when sugar was selling at 52.

And the fille-de-couleur has also changed. She is much less humble and submissive,—somewhat more exacting: she comprehends better the moral injustice of her position. The almost extreme physical refinement and delicacy, bequeathed to her by the freedwomen of the old régime, are passing away: like a conservatory plant deprived of its shelter, she is returning to a more primitive condition,—hardening and growing perhaps less comely as well as less helpless. She perceives also in a vague way the peril of her race: the creole white, her lover and protector, is emigrating;—the domination of the black becomes more and more probable. Furthermore, with the continual increase of the difficulty of living, and the growing pressure of population, social cruelties and hatreds have been developed such as her ancestors never knew. She is still loved; but it is alleged that she rarely loves the white, no matter how large the sacrifices made for her sake, and she no longer enjoys that rep-

---

*Turiault: "Étude sur le langage Créole de la Martinique." Brest: 1874. . . . On page 136 he cites the following pretty verses in speaking of the *fille-de-couleur*:—

> L'Amour prit soin de la former
> Tendre, naïve, et caressante,
> Faite pour plaire, encore plus pour aimer,
> Portant tous les traits précieux
> Du caractère d'une amante,
> Le plaisir sur sa bouche et l'amour dans ses yeux.

utation of fidelity accorded to her class in other years. Probably the truth is that the fille-de-couleur never had at any time capacity to bestow that quality of affection imagined or exacted as a right. Her moral side is still half savage: her feelings are still those of a child. If she does not love the white man according to his unreasonable desire, it is certain at least that she loves him as well as he deserves. Her alleged demoralization is more apparent than real;—she is changing from an artificial to a very natural being, and revealing more and more in her sufferings the true character of the luxurious social condition that brought her into existence. As a general rule, even while questioning her fidelity, the creole freely confesses her kindness of heart, and grants her capable of extreme generosity and devotedness to strangers or to children whom she has an opportunity to care for. Indeed, her natural kindness is so strikingly in contrast with the harder and subtler character of the men of color that one might almost feel tempted to doubt if she belong to the same race. Said a creole once, in my hearing:— "The gens-de-couleur are just like the *tourlouroux*:* one must pick out the females and leave the males alone." Although perhaps capable of a double meaning, his words were not lightly uttered;—he referred to the curious but indubitable fact that the character of the colored woman appears in many respects far superior to that of the colored man. In order to understand this, one must bear in mind the difference in the colonial history of both sexes; and a citation from General Romanet,[†] who visited Martinique at the end of the last century, offers a clue to the mystery. Speaking of the tax upon enfranchisement, he writes:—

—"The governor appointed by the sovereign delivers the certificates of liberty,—on payment by the master of a sum usually equivalent to the value of the subject. Public interest frequently justifies him in making the price of the slave proportionate to the desire or the interest manifested by the master. It can be readily understood that the tax upon the liberty of the women ought to be higher than that of the men:

*A sort of land-crab;—the female is selected for food, and, properly cooked, makes a delicious dish;—the male is almost worthless.

[†]"Voyage à la Martinique." Par J. R., Général de Brigade. Paris: An. XII., 1804. Page 106.

the latter unfortunates having no greater advantage than that of being useful;—the former know how to please: they have those rights and privileges which the whole world allows to their sex; they know how to make even the fetters of slavery serve them for adornments. They may be seen placing upon their proud tyrants the same chains worn by themselves, and making them kiss the marks left thereby: the master becomes the slave, and purchases another's liberty only to lose his own."

Long before the time of General Romanet, the colored male slave might win liberty as the guerdon of bravery in fighting against foreign invasion, or might purchase it by extraordinary economy, while working as a mechanic on extra time for his own account (he always refused to labor with negroes); but in either case his success depended upon the possession and exercise of qualities the reverse of amiable. On the other hand, the bondwoman won manumission chiefly through her power to excite affection. In the survival and perpetuation of the fittest of both sexes these widely different characteristics would obtain more and more definition with successive generations.

I find in the "Bulletin des Actes Administratifs de la Martinique" for 1831 (No. 41) a list of slaves to whom liberty was accorded *pour services rendus à leurs maîtres.* Out of the sixty-nine enfranchisements recorded under this head, there are only two names of male adults to be found,—one an old man of sixty;—the other, called Laurencin, the betrayer of a conspiracy. The rest are young girls, or young mothers and children;— plenty of those singular and pretty names in vogue among the creole population,—Acélie, Avrillette, Mélie, Robertine, Célianne, Francillette, Adée, Catharinette, Sidollie, Céline, Coraline;—and the ages given are from sixteen to twenty-one, with few exceptions. Yet these liberties were asked for and granted at a time when Louis Philippe had abolished the tax on manumissions. . . . The same "Bulletin" contains a list of liberties granted to colored men, *pour service accompli dans la milice,* only!

Most of the French West Indian writers whose works I was able to obtain and examine speak severely of the *hommes-de-couleur* as a class,—in some instances the historian writes with a very violence of hatred. As far back as the commencement of the eighteenth century, Labat, who, with all his personal oddities, was undoubtedly a fine judge of men, declared:—"The mulattoes are as a general rule well made, of good stature, vigorous, strong, adroit, industrious, and daring (*hardis*) beyond all conception. They have much vivacity, but are given to their pleasures, fickle, proud, deceitful (*cachés*), wicked, and capable of the greatest crimes." A San Domingo historian, far more prejudiced than Père Labat, speaks of them "as physically superior, though morally inferior to the whites": he wrote at a time when the race had given to the world the two best swordsmen it has yet perhaps seen,—Saint-Georges and Jean-Louis.

Commenting on the judgment of Père Labat, the historian Borde observes:—"The wickedness spoken of by Père Labat doubtless relates to their political passions only; for the women of color are, beyond any question, the best and sweetest persons in the world—*à coup sûr, les meilleurs et les plus douces personnes qu'il y ait au monde.*"—("Histoire de l'Ile de la Trinidad," par M. Pierre Gustave Louis Borde, vol. i., p. 222.) The same author, speaking of their goodness of heart, generosity to strangers and the sick, says "they are born Sisters of Charity";—and he is not the only historian who has expressed such admiration of their moral qualities. What I myself saw during the epidemic of 1887–88 at Martinique convinced me that these eulogies of the women of color are not extravagant. On the other hand, the existing creole opinion of the men of color is much less favorable than even that expressed by Père Labat. Political events and passions have, perhaps, rendered a just estimate of their qualities difficult. The history of the *hommes-de-couleur* in all the French colonies has been the same;—distrusted by the whites, who feared their aspirations to social equality, distrusted even more by the blacks (who still hate them secretly, although ruled by them), the mulattoes became an Ishmaelitish clan, inimical to both races, and dreaded of both. In Martinique it was attempted, with some success, to manage them by according freedom to all who would serve in the militia for a certain period with credit. At no time was it found possible to compel them to work with blacks; and they formed the whole class of skilled city workmen and mechanics for a century prior to emancipation.

. . . To-day it cannot be truly said of the *fille-de-couleur* that her existence is made up of "love, laughter, and forgettings."

She has aims in life,—the bettering of her condition, the higher education of her children, whom she hopes to free from the curse of prejudice. She still clings to the white, because through him she may hope to improve her position. Under other conditions she might even hope to effect some sort of reconciliation between the races. But the gulf has become so much widened within the last forty years, that no *rapprochement* now appears possible; and it is perhaps too late even to restore the lost prosperity of the colony by any legislative or commercial reforms. The universal creole belief is summed up in the daily-repeated cry: "*C'est un pays perdu!*" Yearly the number of failures increase; and more whites emigrate;—and with every bankruptcy or departure some fille-de-couleur is left almost destitute, to begin life over again. Many a one has been rich and poor several times in succession;—one day her property is seized for debt;—perhaps on the morrow she finds some one able and willing to give her a home again. . . . Whatever comes, she does not die for grief, this daughter of the sun: she pours out her pain in song, like a bird. Here is one of her little improvisations,—a song very popular in both Martinique and Guadeloupe, though originally composed in the latter colony:—

—"Good-bye Madras!
Good-bye foulard!
Good-bye pretty calicoes!
Good-bye collier-choux!
That ship
Which is there on the buoy,
It is taking
My doudoux away.

—"Very good-day,
Monsieur the Consignee.
I come
To make one little petition.
My doudoux
Is going away.
Alas! I pray you
Delay his going."

—"Adiéu Madras!
Adiéu foulard!
Adiéu dézinde!
Adiéu collier-choux!
Batiment-là
Qui sou labouè-là,
Li ka mennein
Doudoux-à-moin allé.

—"Bien le-bonjou',
Missié le Consignataire.
Moin ka vini
Fai yon ti pétition;
Doudoux-à-moin
Y ka pati,—
T'enprie, hélas!
Rétàdé li."

[He answers kindly in French: the *békés* are always kind to these gentle children.]

—"My dear child,	—"Ma chère enfant
It is too late.	Il est trop tard,
The bills of lading	Les connaissements
Are already signed;	Sont déjà signés,
The ship	Le batiment
Is already on the buoy.	Est déjà sur la bouée;
In an hour from now	Dans une heure d'içi,
They will be getting her under way."	Ils vont appareiller."
—"When the foulards came. . . .	—"Foulard rivé,
I always had some;	Moin té toujou tini;
When the Madras-kerchiefs came,	Madras rivé,
I always had some;	Moin té toujou tini;
When the printed calicoes came,	Dézindes rivé,
I always had some.	Moin té toujou tini.
. . . That second officer	—Capitaine sougonde
Is such a kind man!	C'est yon bon gàçon!
"Everybody has	"Toutt moune tini
Somebody to love;	Yon moune yo aimé;
Everybody has	Toutt moune tini
Somebody to pet;	Yon moune yo chéri;
Everybody has	Toutt moune tini
A sweetheart of her own.	Yon doudoux à yo.
I am the only one	Jusse moin tou sèle
Who cannot have that,—I!"	Pa tini ça,—moin!"

. . . On the eve of the *Fête Dieu*, or Corpus Christi festival, in all these Catholic countries, the city streets are hung with banners and decorated with festoons and with palm branches; and great altars are erected at various points along the route of the procession, to serve as resting-places for the Host. These are called *reposoirs*; creole patois, "*reposouè Bon-Dié.*" Each wealthy man lends something to help to make them attractive,—rich plate, dainty crystal, bronzes, paintings, beautiful models of ships or steamers, curiosities from remote parts of the world. . . . The procession over, the altar is stripped, the valuables are returned to their owners: all the splendor disappears. . . . And the spectacle of that evanescent magnificence, repeated year by year, suggested to this proverb-loving people a similitude for the unstable fortune of the fille-de-couleur:—*Fortune milatresse c'est reposouè Bon-Dié.* (The luck of the mulattress is the resting-place of the Good-God).

Bête-Ni-Pié

St. Pierre is in one respect fortunate beyond many tropical cities;—she has scarcely any mosquitoes, although there are plenty of mosquitoes in other parts of Martinique, even in the higher mountain villages. The flood of bright water that pours perpetually through all her streets, renders her comparatively free from the pest;—nobody sleeps under a mosquito bar.

Nevertheless, St. Pierre is not exempt from other peculiar plagues of tropical life; and you cannot be too careful about examining your bed before venturing to lie down, and your clothing before you dress;—for various disagreeable things might be hiding in them: a spider large as a big crab, or a scorpion or a *mabouya* or a centipede,—or certain large ants whose bite burns like the pricking of a red-hot needle. No one who has lived in St. Pierre is likely to forget the ants. . . . There are three or four kinds in every house;—the *fourmi fou* (mad ant), a little speckled yellowish creature whose movements are so rapid as to delude the vision; the great black ant which allows itself to be killed before it lets go what it has bitten; the venomous little red ant, which is almost too small to see; and the small black ant which does not bite at all,—are usually omnipresent, and appear to dwell together in harmony. They are pests in kitchens, cupboards, and safes; but they are scavengers. It is marvellous to see them carrying away the body of a great dead roach or centipede,—pulling and pushing together like trained laborers, and guiding the corpse over obstacles or around them with extraordinary skill. . . . There was a time when ants almost destroyed the colony,—in 1751. The plantations devastated by them are described by historians as having looked as if desolated by fire. Underneath the ground in certain places, layers of their eggs two inches deep were found extending over acres. Infants left unwatched in the cradle for a few hours were devoured alive by them. Immense balls of living ants were washed ashore at the same time on various parts of the coast (a phenomenon repeated within the memory of creoles now living in the northeast parishes). The Government vainly offered rewards for the best means of destroying the insects; but the plague gradually disappeared as it came.

None of these creatures can be prevented from entering a dwelling;—you may as well resign yourself to the certainty of meeting with them from time to time. The great spiders (with the exception of those which are hairy) need excite no alarm or disgust;—indeed they are suffered to live unmolested in many houses, partly owing to a belief that they bring good-luck, and partly because they destroy multitudes of those enormous and noisome roaches which spoil whatever they cannot eat. The scorpion is less common; but it has a detestable habit of lurking under beds; and its bite communicates a burning fever. With far less reason, the mabouya is almost equally feared. It is a little lizard about six inches long, and ashen-colored;—it haunts only the interior of houses, while the bright-green lizards dwell only upon the roofs. Like other reptiles of the same order, the mabouya can run over or cling to polished surfaces; and there is a popular belief that if frightened, it will leap at one's face or hands and there fasten itself so tightly that it cannot be dislodged except by cutting it to pieces. Moreover, its feet are supposed to have the power of leaving certain livid and ineffaceable marks upon the skin of the person to whom it attaches itself:—*ça ka ba ou lota*, say the colored people. Nevertheless, there is no creature more timid and harmless than the mabouya.

But the most dreaded and the most insolent invader of domestic peace is the centipede. The water system of the city banished the mosquito; but it introduced the centipede into almost every dwelling. St. Pierre has a plague of centipedes. All the covered drains, the gutters, the crevices of fountain-basins and bathing-basins, the spaces between floor and ground, shelter centipedes. And the *bête-à-mille-pattes* is the terror of the barefooted population:—scarcely a day passes that some child or bonne or workman is not bitten by the creature.

The sight of a full-grown centipede is enough to affect a strong set of nerves. Ten to eleven inches is the average length of adults; but extraordinary individuals much exceeding this dimension may be sometimes observed in the neighborhood of distilleries (*rhommeries*) and sugar-refineries. According to age, the color of the creature varies from yellowish to black;—

the younger ones often have several different tints; the old ones are uniformly jet-black, and have a carapace of surprising toughness,—difficult to break. If you tread, by accident or design, upon the tail, the poisonous head will instantly curl back and bite the foot through any ordinary thickness of upper-leather.

As a general rule the centipede lurks about the courtyards, foundations, and drains by preference; but in the season of heavy rains he does not hesitate to move upstairs, and make himself at home in parlors and bedrooms. He has a provoking habit of nestling in your *moresques* or your *chinoises*,—those wide light garments you put on before taking your siesta or retiring for the night. He also likes to get into your umbrella,—an article indispensable in the tropics; and you had better never open it carelessly. He may even take a notion to curl himself up in your hat, suspended on the wall—(I have known a trigono-cephalus to do the same thing in a country-house). He has also a singular custom of mounting upon the long trailing dresses (douillettes) worn by Martinique women,—and climbing up very swiftly and lightly to the wearer's neck, where the prickling of his feet first betrays his presence. Sometimes he will get into bed with you and bite you, because you have not resolution enough to lie perfectly still while he is tickling you. . . . It is well to remember before dressing that merely shaking a garment may not dislodge him;—you must examine every part very patiently,—particularly the sleeves of a coat and the legs of pantaloons.

The vitality of the creature is amazing. I kept one in a bottle without food or water for thirteen weeks, at the end of which time it remained active and dangerous as ever. Then I fed it with living insects, which it devoured ravenously;—beetles, roaches, earthworms, several *lepismæ*, even one of the dangerous-looking millepedes, which have a great resemblance in outward structure to the centipede, but a thinner body, and more numerous limbs,—all seemed equally palatable to the prisoner. . . . I knew an instance of one, nearly a foot long, remaining in a silk parasol for more than four months, and emerging unexpectedly one day, with aggressiveness undiminished, to bite the hand that had involuntarily given it deliverance.

In the city the centipede has but one natural enemy able to

cope with him,—the hen! The hen attacks him with delight, and often swallows him, head first, without taking the trouble to kill him. The cat hunts him, but she is careful never to put her head near him;—she has a trick of whirling him round and round upon the floor so quickly as to stupefy him: then, when she sees a good chance, she strikes him dead with her claws. But if you are fond of your cat you will let her run no risks, as the bite of a large centipede might have very bad results for your pet. Its quickness of movement demands all the quickness of even the cat for self-defence. . . . I know of men who have proved themselves able to seize a fer-de-lance by the tail, whirl it round and round, and then flip it as you would crack a whip,—whereupon the terrible head flies off; but I never heard of any one in Martinique daring to handle a living centipede.

There are superstitions concerning the creature which have a good effect in diminishing his tribe. If you kill a centipede, you are sure to receive money soon; and even if you dream of killing one it is good-luck. Consequently, people are glad of any chance to kill centipedes,—usually taking a heavy stone or some iron utensil for the work;—a wooden stick is not a good weapon. There is always a little excitement when a *bête-ni-pié* (as the centipede is termed in the patois) exposes itself to death; and you may often hear those who kill it uttering a sort of litany of abuse with every blow, as if addressing a human enemy:—"*Quitté moin tchoué ou, maudi!—quitté moin tchoué ou, scelerat!—quitté moin tchoué ou, Satan!—quitté moin tchoué ou, abonocio!*" etc. (Let me kill you, accursed! scoundrel! Satan! abomination!)

The patois term for the centipede is not a mere corruption of the French *bête-à-mille-pattes*. Among a population of slaves, unable to read or write,* there were only the vaguest conceptions of numerical values; and the French term bête-à-mille-pattes was not one which could appeal to negro imagination. The slaves themselves invented an equally vivid name, *bête-anni-pié* (the Beast-which-is-all-feet); *anni* in creole signifying "only," and in such a sense "all." Abbreviated by subsequent usage to *bête-'ni-pié*, the appellation has amphibology;

---

*According to the Martinique "Annuaire" for 1887, there were even then, out of a total population of 173,182, no less than 125,366 unable to read and write.

—for there are two words *ni* in the patois, one signifying "to have," and the other "naked." So that the creole for a centipede might be translated in three ways,—"the Beast-which-is-all-feet"; or, "the Naked-footed Beast"; or, with fine irony of affirmation, "the Beast-which-has-feet."

II.

WHAT is the secret of that horror inspired by the centipede? . . . It is but very faintly related to our knowledge that the creature is venomous;—the results of the bite are only temporary swelling and a brief fever;—it is less to be feared than the bite of other tropical insects and reptiles which never inspire the same loathing by their aspect. And the shapes of venomous creatures are not always shapes of ugliness. The serpent has elegance of form as well as attractions of metallic tinting;— the tarantula, or the *matoutou-falaise*, have geometrical beauty. Lapidaries have in all ages expended rare skill upon imitations of serpent grace in gold and gems;—a princess would not scorn to wear a diamond spider. But what art could utilize successfully the form of the centipede? It is a form of absolute repulsiveness,—a skeleton-shape half defined:—the suggestion of some old reptile-spine astir, crawling with its fragments of ribs.

No other living thing excites exactly the same feeling produced by the sight of the centipede,—the intense loathing and peculiar fear. The instant you see a centipede you feel it is absolutely necessary to kill it; you cannot find peace in your house while you know that such a life exists in it: perhaps the intrusion of a serpent would annoy and disgust you less. And it is not easy to explain the whole reason of this loathing. The form alone has, of course, something to do with it,—a form that seems almost a departure from natural laws. But the form alone does not produce the full effect, which is only experienced when you see the creature in motion. The true horror of the centipede, perhaps, must be due to the monstrosity of its movement, —multiple and complex, as of a chain of pursuing and interdevouring lives: there is something about it that makes you recoil, as from a sudden corrupt swarming-out. It is confusing,—a series of contractings and lengthenings and undulations so rapid as to allow of being only half seen: it alarms also, because the thing seems perpetually about to disappear, and because you know that to lose sight of it for one moment involves the very unpleasant chance of finding it upon you the next,—perhaps between skin and clothing.

But this is not all:—the sensation produced by the centipede is still more complex—complex, in fact, as the visible organization of the creature. For, during pursuit,—whether retreating or attacking, in hiding or fleeing,—it displays a something which seems more than instinct: calculation and cunning,—a sort of malevolent intelligence. It knows how to delude, how to terrify, —it has marvellous skill in feinting;—it is an abominable juggler. . . .

III.

I AM about to leave my room after breakfast, when little Victoire who carries the meals up-stairs in a wooden tray, screams out:—"*Gadé, Missié! ni bête-ni-pié assous dos ou!*" There is a thousand-footed beast upon my back!

Off goes my coat, which I throw upon the floor;—the little servant, who has a nervous horror of centipedes, climbs upon a chair. I cannot see anything upon the coat, nevertheless;—I lift it by the collar, turn it about very cautiously—nothing! Suddenly the child screams again; and I perceive the head close to my hand;—the execrable thing had been hiding in a perpendicular fold of the coat, which I drop only just in time to escape getting bitten. Immediately the centipede becomes invisible. Then I take the coat by one flap, and turn it over very quickly: just as quickly does the centipede pass over it in the inverse direction, and disappear under it again. I have had my first good look at him: he seems nearly a foot long,—has a greenish-yellow hue against the black cloth,—and pink legs, and a violet head;—he is evidently young. . . . I turn the coat a second time: same disgusting manœuvre. Undulations of livid color flow over him as he lengthens and shortens;—while running his shape is but half apparent; it is only as he makes a half pause in doubling round and under the coat that the panic of his legs becomes discernible. When he is fully exposed they move with invisible rapidity,—like a vibration;—you can see only a sort of pink haze extending about him,—something to which you would no more dare advance your finger than to the vapory halo edging a circular saw in motion. Twice more I turn and re-turn the coat with the same result;—I observe that the centipede always runs towards my hand, until I withdraw it: he feints!

With a stick I uplift one portion of the coat after another; and suddenly perceive him curved under a sleeve,—looking quite small!—how could he have seemed so large a moment ago? . . . But before I can strike him he has flickered over the cloth again, and vanished; and I discover that he has the power of *magnifying himself*,—dilating the disgust of his shape at will: he invariably amplifies himself to face attack. . . .

It seems very difficult to dislodge him; he displays astonishing activity and cunning at finding wrinkles and folds to hide in. Even at the risk of damaging various things in the pockets, I stamp upon the coat;—then lift it up with the expectation of finding the creature dead. But it suddenly rushes out from some part or other, looking larger and more wicked than ever,—drops to the floor, and charges at my feet: a sortie! I strike at him unsuccessfully with the stick: he retreats to the angle between wainscoting and floor, and runs along it fast as a railroad train,—dodges two or three pokes,—gains the door-frame,—glides behind a hinge, and commences to run over the wall of the stair-way. There the hand of a black servant slaps him dead.

—"Always strike at the head," the servant tells me; "never tread on the tail. . . . This is a small one: the big fellows can make you afraid if you do not know how to kill them."

. . . I pick up the carcass with a pair of scissors. It does not look formidable now that it is all contracted;—it is scarcely eight inches long,—thin as card-board, and even less heavy. It has no substantiality, no weight;—it is a mere appearance, a mask; a delusion. . . . But remembering the spectral, cunning, juggling something which magnified and moved it but a moment ago,—I feel almost tempted to believe, with certain savages, that there are animal shapes inhabited by goblins. . . .

IV.

—"Is there anything still living and lurking in old black drains of Thought,—any bigotry, any prejudice, anything in the moral world whereunto the centipede may be likened?"

—"Really, I do not know," replied the friend to whom I had put the question; "but you need only go as far as the vegetable world for a likeness. Did you ever see anything like this?" he added, opening a drawer and taking therefrom something revolting, which, as he pressed it in his hand, looked like a long thick bundle of dried centipedes.

—"Touch them," he said, holding out to me the mass of articulated flat bodies and bristling legs.

—"Not for anything!" I replied, in astonished disgust. He laughed, and opened his hand. As he did so, the mass expanded. . . .

—"Now look," he exclaimed!

Then I saw that all the bodies were united at the tails—grew together upon one thick flat annulated stalk . . . a plant!— "But here is the fruit," he continued, taking from the same drawer a beautifully embossed ovoid nut, large as a duck's egg, ruddy-colored, and so exquisitely varnished by nature as to resemble a rosewood carving fresh from the hands of the cabinet-maker. In its proper place among the leaves and branches, it had the appearance of something delicious being devoured by a multitude of centipedes. Inside was a kernel, hard and heavy as iron-wood; but this in time, I was told, falls into dust: though the beautiful shell remains always perfect.

Negroes call it the *coco-macaque.*

Ma Bonne

I CANNOT teach Cyrillia the clock;—I have tried until both of us had our patience strained to the breaking-point. Cyrillia still believes she will learn how to tell the time some day or other;—I am certain that she never will. "*Missié,*" she says, "*lézhè pa aïen pou moin: c'est minitt ka fouté moin yon travail!*" —the hours do not give her any trouble; but the minutes are a frightful bore! And nevertheless, Cyrillia is punctual as the sun;—she always brings my coffee and a slice of corossol at five in the morning precisely. Her clock is the *cabritt-bois.* The great cricket stops singing, she says, at half-past four: the cessation of its chant awakens her. . . .

—"*Bonjou', Missié. Coument ou passé lanuitt?*"—"Thanks, my daughter, I slept well."—"The weather is beautiful: if Missié would like to go to the beach, his bathing-towels are ready."— "Good! Cyrillia; I will go." . . . Such is our regular morning conversation.

Nobody breakfasts before eleven o'clock or thereabout; but after an early sea-bath, one is apt to feel a little hollow during the morning, unless one take some sort of refreshment. Cyrillia always prepares something for me on my return from the beach,—either a little pot of fresh cocoa-water, or a *cocoyage*, or a *mabiyage*, or a *bavaroise.*

The *cocoyage* I like the best of all. Cyrillia takes a green cocoanut, slices off one side of it so as to open a hole, then pours the opalescent water into a bowl, adds to it a fresh egg, a little Holland gin, and some grated nutmeg and plenty of sugar. Then she whips up the mixture into effervescence with her *baton-lélé.* The *baton-lélé* is an indispensable article in every creole home: it is a thin stick which is cut from a young tree so as to leave at one end a whorl of branch-stumps sticking out at right angles like spokes;—by twirling the stem between the hands, the stumps whip up the drink in a moment.

The *mabiyage* is less agreeable, but is a popular morning drink among the poorer classes. It is made with a little white rum and a bottle of the bitter native root-beer called *mabi.*

The taste of *mabi* I can only describe as that of molasses and water flavored with a little cinchona bark.

The *bavaroise* is fresh milk, sugar, and a little Holland gin or rum,—mixed with the baton-lélé until a fine thick foam is formed. After the *cocoyage*, I think it is the best drink one can take in the morning; but very little spirit must be used for any of these mixtures. It is not until just before the mid-day meal that one can venture to take a serious stimulant,—*yon ti ponch*, —rum and water, sweetened with plenty of sugar or sugar syrup.

The word *sucre* is rarely used in Martinique,—considering that sugar is still the chief product;—the word *doux*, "sweet," is commonly substituted for it. *Doux* has, however, a larger range of meaning: it may signify syrup, or any sort of sweets,— duplicated into *doudoux*, it means the corossole fruit as well as a sweetheart. *Ça qui lè doudoux?* is the cry of the corossole-seller. If a negro asks at a grocery store (*graisserie*) for *sique* instead of for *doux*, it is only because he does not want it to be supposed that he means syrup;—as a general rule, he will only use the word *sique* when referring to quality of sugar wanted, or to sugar in hogsheads. *Doux* enters into domestic consumption in quite remarkable ways. People put sugar into fresh milk, English porter, beer, and cheap wine;—they cook various vegetables with sugar, such as peas; they seem to be particularly fond of sugar-and-water and of *d'leau-pain*,—bread-and-water boiled, strained, mixed with sugar, and flavored with cinnamon. The stranger gets accustomed to all this sweetness without evil results. In a northern climate the consequence would probably be at least a bilious attack; but in the tropics, where salt fish and fruits are popularly preferred to meat, the prodigal use of sugar or sugar-syrups appears to be decidedly beneficial.

. . . After Cyrillia has prepared my *cocoyage*, and rinsed the bathing-towels in fresh-water, she is ready to go to market, and wants to know what I would like to eat for breakfast. "Anything creole, Cyrillia;—I want to know what people eat in this country." She always does her best to please me in this respect,—almost daily introduces me to some unfamiliar dishes, something odd in the way of fruit or fish.

II.

CYRILLIA has given me a good idea of the range and character of *mangé-Créole*; and I can venture to write something about it after a year's observation. By *mangé-Créole* I refer only to the food of the people proper, the colored population; for the *cuisine* of the small class of wealthy whites is chiefly European, and devoid of local interest:—I might observe, however, that the fashion of cooking is rather Provençal than Parisian;—rather of southern than of northern France.

Meat, whether fresh or salt, enters little into the nourishment of the poorer classes. This is partly, no doubt, because of the cost of all meats; but it is also due to natural preference for fruits and fish. When fresh meat is purchased, it is usually to make a stew or *daube*;—probably salt meats are more popular; and native vegetables and manioc flour are preferred to bread. There are only two popular soups which are peculiar to the creole cuisine,—*calalou*, a gombo soup, almost precisely similar to that of Louisiana; and the *soupe-d'habitant*, or "country soup." It is made of yams, carrots, bananas, turnips, *choux-caraïbes*, pumpkins, salt pork, and pimento, all boiled together;—the salt meat being left out of the composition on Fridays.

The great staple, the true meat of the population, is salt codfish, which is prepared in a great number of ways. The most popular and the rudest preparation of it is called "Ferocious" (*féroce*); and it is not at all unpalatable. The codfish is simply fried, and served with vinegar, oil, pimento;—manioc flour and avocados being considered indispensable adjuncts. As manioc flour forms a part of almost every creole meal, a word of information regarding it will not be out of place here.

Everybody who has heard the name probably knows that the manioc root is naturally poisonous, and that the toxic elements must be removed by pressure and desiccation before the flour can be made. Good manioc flour has an appearance like very coarse oatmeal; and is probably quite as nourishing. Even when dear as bread, it is preferred, and forms the flour of the population, by whom the word *farine* is only used to signify manioc flour: if wheat-flour be referred to it is always qualified as "French flour" (*farine-Fouance*). Although certain flours are regularly advertised as American in the local papers, they are still *farine-Fouance* for the population, who call everything foreign French. American beer is *biè-Fouance*; American canned peas, *ti-pois-Fouance*; any white foreigner who can talk French is *yon béké-Fouance*.

Usually the manioc flour is eaten uncooked:* merely poured into a plate, with a little water and stirred with a spoon into a thick paste or mush,—the thicker the better;—*dleau passé farine* (more water than manioc flour) is a saying which describes the condition of a very destitute person. When not served with fish, the flour is occasionally mixed with water and refined molasses (*sirop-battrie*): this preparation, which is very nice, is called *cousscaye*. There is also a way of boiling it with molasses and milk into a kind of pudding. This is called *matêté*; children are very fond of it. Both of these names, *cousscaye* and *matêté*, are alleged to be of Carib origin: the art of preparing the flour itself from manioc root is certainly an inheritance from the Caribs, who bequeathed many singular words to the creole patois of the French West Indies.

Of all the preparations of codfish with which manioc flour is eaten, I preferred the *lamori-bouilli*,—the fish boiled plain, after having been steeped long enough to remove the excess of salt; and then served with plenty of olive-oil and pimento. The people who have no home of their own, or at least no place to cook, can buy their food already prepared from the *màchannes lapacotte*, who seem to make a specialty of *macadam* (codfish stewed with rice) and the other two dishes already referred to. But in every colored family there are occasional feasts of *lamori-au-laitt*, codfish stewed with milk and potatoes; *lamori-au-grattin*, codfish boned, pounded with toast crumbs, and boiled with butter, onions, and pepper into a mush;—*coubouyon-lamori*, codfish stewed with butter and oil;—*bachamelle*, codfish boned and stewed with potatoes, pimentos, oil, garlic, and butter.

Pimento is an essential accompaniment to all these dishes, whether it be cooked or raw: everything is served with plenty

---

*There is record of an attempt to manufacture bread with one part manioc flour to three of wheat flour. The result was excellent; but no serious effort was ever made to put the manioc bread on the market.

of pimento,—*en pile, en pile piment.* Among the various kinds I can mention only the *piment-café,* or "coffee-pepper," larger but about the same shape as a grain of Liberian coffee, violet-red at one end; the *piment-zouèseau,* or bird-pepper, small and long and scarlet;—and the *piment-capresse,* very large, pointed at one end, and bag-shaped at the other. It takes a very deep red color when ripe, and is so strong that if you only break the pod in a room, the sharp perfume instantly fills the apartment. Unless you are as well trained as any Mexican to eat pimento, you will probably regret your first encounter with the *capresse.*

Cyrillia told me a story about this infernal vegetable.

III.

ZHISTOUÈ PIMENT.

Té ni yon manman qui té ni en pile, en pile yche; et yon jou y pa té ni aïen pou y té baill yche-là mangé. Y té ka lévé bon matin-là sans yon sou: y pa sa ça y té douè fai,—là y té ké baill latête. Y allé lacaïe macoumè-y, raconté lapeine-y. Macoumè baill y toua chopine farine-manioc. Y allé lacaill lautt macoumè, qui baill y yon grand trai piment. Macoumè-là di y venne trai-piment-à, épi y té pè acheté lamori,—pisse y ja té ni farine. Madame-là di: "Mèçi, macoumè;"—y di y bonjou'; épi y allé lacaïe-y.

PIMENTO STORY.

There was once a mamma who had ever so many children; and one day she had nothing to give those children to eat. She had got up very early that morning, without a sou in the world: she did not know what to do: she was so worried that her head was upset. She went to the house of a woman-friend, and told her about her trouble. The friend gave her three *chopines* [three pints] of manioc flour. Then she went to the house of another female friend, who gave her a big trayful of pimentos. The friend told her to sell that tray of pimentos: then she could buy some codfish,—since she already had some manioc flour. The good-wife said: "Thank you, *macoumè,*" —she bid her good-day, and then went to her own house.

Lhè y rivé àcaïe y limé difè: y metté canari épi dleau assous difé-à; épi y cassé toutt piment-là et metté yo adans canari-à assous difé.

Lhè y ouè canari-à ka bouï, y pouend *baton-lélé*, épi y lélé piment-à: aloss y ka fai yonne calalou-piment. Lhè calalou-piment-là té tchouitt, y pouend chaque zassiett yche-li; y metté calalou yo fouète dans zassiett-là; y metté tamari fouète, assou, épi ta-y. Épi lhè calalou-là té bien fouète, y metté farine nans chaque zassiett-là. Épi y crié toutt moune vini mangé. Toutt moune vini metté yo à-tabe.

Pouèmiè bouchée mari-à pouend, y rété,—y crié: "Aïe! ouaill! mafenm!" Fenm-là réponne mari y: "Ouaill! mon-mari!" Cés ti manmaille-là crié: "Ouaill! manman!" Manman-à réponne:—"Ouaill! yches-moin!" . . . Yo toutt pouend couri, quitté caïe-là sèle,—épi yo toutt tombé la-riviè à touempé bouche yo. Cés ti manmaille-là bouè dleau sitellement jusse temps yo toutt néyé: té ka rété anni manman-là épi papa-là. Yo té

The moment she got home, she made a fire, and put her *canari* [earthen pot] full of water on the fire to boil: then she broke up the pimentos and put them into the canari on the fire.

As soon as she saw the canari boiling, she took her *baton-lélé*, and beat up all those pimentos: then she made a *pimento-calalou*. When the pimento-calalou was well cooked, she took each one of the children's plates, and poured their calalou into the plates to cool it; she also put her husband's out to cool, and her own. And when the calalou was quite cool, she put some manioc flour into each of the plates. Then she called to everybody to come and eat. They all came, and sat down to table.

The first mouthful that husband took he stopped and screamed:—"*Aïe! ouaill!* my wife!" The woman answered her husband: "*Ouaill!* my husband!" The little children all screamed: "*Ouaill!* mamma!" Their mamma answered: "*Ouaill!* my children!" . . . They all ran out, left the house empty; and they tumbled into the river to steep their mouths. Those little children just drank water and drank water till they were all là, bò lariviè, qui té ka pleiré. Moin té ka passé à lhè-à;— moin ka mandé yo: "Ça zautt ni?"

drowned: there was nobody left except the mamma and the papa. They stayed there on the river-bank, and cried. I was passing that way just at that time;—I asked them: "What ails you people?"

Nhomme-là lévé: y baill moin yon sèle coup d'piè, y voyé moin lautt bò lariviè— ou ouè moin vini pou conté ça ba ou.

That man got up and gave me just one kick that sent me right across the river; I came here at once, as you see, to tell you all about it. . . .

IV.

. . . It is no use for me to attempt anything like a detailed description of the fish Cyrillia brings me day after day from the Place du Fort: the variety seems to be infinite. I have learned, however, one curious fact which is worth noting: that, as a general rule, the more beautifully colored fish are the least palatable, and are sought after only by the poor. The *perroquet*, black, with bright bands of red and yellow; the *cirurgien*, blue and black; the *patate*, yellow and black; the *moringue*, which looks like polished granite; the *souri*, pink and yellow; the vermilion *Gouôs-zie*; the rosy *sade*; the red *Bon-Dié-manié-moin* ("the-Good-God-handled-me")—it has two queer marks as of great fingers; and the various kinds of all-blue fish, *balaou*, *conliou*, etc., varying from steel-color to violet,—these are seldom seen at the tables of the rich. There are exceptions, of course, to this and all general rules: notably the *couronné*, pink spotted beautifully with black,—a sort of Redfish, which never sells less than fourteen cents a pound; and the *zorphi*, which has exquisite changing lights of nacreous green and purple. It is said, however, that the zorphi is sometimes poisonous, like the *bécunne*; and there are many fish which, although not venomous by nature, have always been considered dangerous. In the time of Père Dutertre it was believed these fish ate the apples of the manchineel-tree, washed into the sea by rains;—to-day it is popularly supposed that they are rendered occasionally poisonous by eating the barnacles attached to copper-plating of ships. The *tazard*, the *lune*, the *capitaine*, the *dorade*, the *perroquet*, the *couliou*, the *congre*, various crabs, and even the *tonne*,—all are dangerous unless perfectly fresh: the least decomposition seems to develop a mysterious poison. A singular phenomenon regarding the poisoning occasionally produced by the bécunne and dorade is that the skin peels from the hands and feet of those lucky enough to survive the terrible colics, burnings, itchings, and delirium, which are early symptoms. Happily these accidents are very rare, since the markets have been properly inspected: in the time of Dr. Rufz, they would seem to have been very common,—so common that he tells us he would not eat fresh fish without being perfectly certain where it was caught and how long it had been out of the water.

The poor buy the brightly colored fish only when the finer qualities are not obtainable at low rates; but often and often the catch is so enormous that half of it has to be thrown back into the sea. In the hot moist air, fish decomposes very rapidly; it is impossible to transport it to any distance into the interior; and only the inhabitants of the coast can indulge in fresh fish,—at least sea-fish.

Naturally, among the laboring class the question of quality is less important than that of quantity and substance, unless the fish-market be extraordinarily well stocked. Of all fresh fish, the most popular is the *tonne*, a great blue-gray creature whose flesh is solid as beef; next come in order of preferment the flying-fish (*volants*), which often sell as low as four for a cent;—then the *lambi*, or sea-snail, which has a very dense and nutritious flesh;—then the small whitish fish classed as *sàdines*;—then the blue-colored fishes according to price, *couliou*, *balaou*, etc.;—lastly, the shark, which sells commonly at two cents a pound. Large sharks are not edible; the flesh is too hard; but a young shark is very good eating indeed. Cyrillia cooked me a slice one morning: it was quite delicate, tasted almost like veal.

The quantity of very small fish sold is surprising. With ten sous the family of a laborer can have a good fish-dinner: a pound of *sàdines* is never dearer than two sous;—a pint of manioc flour can be had for the same price; and a big avocado sells for a sou. This is more than enough food for any one person; and by doubling the expense one obtains a proportionately greater quantity—enough for four or five individuals.

Old Market-place of the Fort, St. Pierre.—(Removed in 1888.)

The *sàdines* are roasted over a charcoal fire, and flavored with a sauce of lemon, pimento, and garlic. When there are no *sàdines*, there are sure to be *coulious* in plenty,—small *coulious* about as long as your little finger: these are more delicate, and fetch double the price. With four sous' worth of *coulious* a family can have a superb *blaffe*. To make a *blaffe* the fish are cooked in water, and served with pimento, lemon, spices, onions, and garlic; but without oil or butter. Experience has demonstrated that *coulious* make the best *blaffe*; and a *blaffe* is seldom prepared with other fish.

V.

THERE are four dishes which are the holiday luxuries of the poor:—*manicou, ver-palmiste, zandouille*, and *poule-épi-diri*.*

The *manicou* is a brave little marsupial, which might be called the opossum of Martinique: it fights, although overmatched, with the serpent, and is a great enemy to the fieldrat. In the market a manicou sells for two francs and a half at cheapest: it is generally salted before being cooked.

The great worm, or caterpillar, called *ver-palmiste* is found in the heads of cabbage-palms,—especially after the cabbage has been cut out, and the tree has begun to perish. It is the grub of a curious beetle, which has a proboscis of such form as suggested the creole appellation, *léfant*: the "elephant." These worms are sold in the Place du Fort at two sous each: they are spitted and roasted alive, and are said to taste like almonds. I have never tried to find out whether this be fact or fancy; and I am glad to say that few white creoles confess a liking for this barbarous food.

The *zandouilles* are delicious sausages made with pigbuff,—

---

*I must mention a surreptitious dish, *chatt*;—needless to say the cats are not sold, but stolen. It is true that only a small class of poor people eat cats; but they eat so many cats that cats have become quite rare in St. Pierre. The custom is purely superstitious: it is alleged that if you eat cat seven times, or if you eat seven cats, no witch, wizard, or *quimboiseur* can ever do you any harm; and the cat ought to be eaten on Christmas Eve in order that the meal be perfectly efficacious. . . . The mystic number "seven" enters into another and a better creole superstition;—if you kill a serpent, seven great sins are forgiven to you: *ou ké ni sept grands péchés effacé.*

and only seen in the market on Sundays. They cost a franc and a half each; and there are several women who have an established reputation throughout Martinique for their skill in making them. I have tasted some not less palatable than the famous London "pork-pies." Those of Lamentin are reputed the best in the island.

But *poule-épi-diri* is certainly the most popular dish of all: it is the dearest, as well, and poor people can rarely afford it. In Louisiana an almost similar dish is called *jimbalaya*: chicken cooked with rice. The Martiniquais think it such a delicacy that an over-exacting person, or one difficult to satisfy, is reproved with the simple question:—"*Ça ou lè 'ncò—poule-épi-diri?*" (What more do you want, great heavens!—chicken-and-rice?) Naughty children are bribed into absolute goodness by the promise of poule-épi-diri:—

> —"*Aïe! chè, bò doudoux!*
> *Doudoux ba ou poule-épi-diri;*
> *Aïe! chè, bò doudoux!*". . .

(*Aïe*, dear! kiss *doudoux!*—*doudoux* has rice-and-chicken for you!—*aïe*, dear! kiss *doudoux!*)

How far rice enters into the success of the dish above mentioned I cannot say; but rice ranks in favor generally above all cereals; it is at least six times more in demand than maize. *Diri-doux*, rice boiled with sugar, is sold in prodigious quantities daily,—especially at the markets, where little heaps of it, rolled in pieces of banana or *cachibou* leaves, are retailed at a cent each. *Diri-aulaitt*, a veritable rice-pudding, is also very popular; but it would weary the reader to mention one-tenth of the creole preparations into which rice enters.

VI.

EVERYBODY eats *akras*;—they sell at a cent apiece. The akra is a small fritter or pancake, which may be made of fifty different things,—among others codfish, titiri, beans, brains, *choux-caraïbes*, little black peas (*poix-zié-nouè*, "black-eyed peas"), or of crawfish (*akra-cribîche*). When made of carrots, bananas, chicken, palm-cabbage, etc., and sweetened, they are called *marinades.* On first acquaintance they seem rather greasy for so hot a climate; but one learns, on becoming accustomed to tropical conditions, that a certain amount of oily or greasy food is both healthy and needful.

First among popular vegetables are beans. Red beans are preferred; but boiled white beans, served cold with vinegar and plenty of oil, form a favorite salad. Next in order of preferment come the *choux-caraïbes, patates, zignames, camanioc,* and *cousscouche*: all immense roots,—the true potatoes of the tropics. The camanioc is finer than the choux-caraïbe, boils whiter and softer: in appearance it resembles the manioc root very closely, but has no toxic element. The cousscouche is the best of all: the finest Irish potato boiled into sparkling flour is not so good. Most of these roots can be cooked into a sort of mush, called *migan*: such as *migan-choux,* made with the choux-caraïbe; *migan-zignames,* made with yams; *migan-cousscouche,* etc.,—in which case crabs or shrimps are usually served with the *migan.* There is a particular fondness for the little rosy crab called *tourlouroux,* in patois *touloulou. Migan* is also made with bread-fruit. Very large bananas or plantains are boiled with codfish, with *daubes,* or meat stews, and with eggs. The bread-fruit is a fair substitute for vegetables. It must be cooked very thoroughly, and has a dry potato taste. What is called the *fleu-fouitt-à-pain,* or "bread-fruit flower"—a long pod-shaped solid growth, covered exteriorly with tiny seeds closely set as pin-heads could be, and having an interior pith very elastic and resistant,—is candied into a delicious sweetmeat.

VII.

THE consumption of bananas is enormous: more bananas are eaten than vegetables; and more banana-trees are yearly being cultivated. The negro seems to recognize instinctively that economical value of the banana to which attention was long since called by Humboldt, who estimated that while an acre planted in wheat would barely support three persons, an acre planted in banana-trees would nourish fifty.

Bananas and plantains hold the first place among fruits in popular esteem;—they are cooked in every way, and served with almost every sort of meat or fish. What we call bananas in the United States, however, are not called bananas in Martinique, but figs (*figues*). Plantains seem to be called *bananes*. One is often surprised at popular nomenclature: *choux* may mean either a sort of root (*choux-caraïbe*), or the top of the cabbage-palm; *Jacquot* may mean a fish; *cabane* never means a cabin, but a bed; *crickett* means not a cricket, but a frog; and at least fifty other words have equally deceptive uses. If one desires to speak of real figs—dried figs—he must say *figues-Fouance* (French figs): otherwise nobody will understand him. There are many kinds of bananas here called *figues*;—the four most popular are the *figues-bananes*, which are plantains, I think; the *figues-makouenga*, which grow wild, and have a red skin; the *figues-pommes* (apple-bananas), which are large and yellow; and the *ti-figues-dessè* (little-dessert-bananas), which are to be seen on all tables in St. Pierre. They are small, sweet, and always agreeable, even when one has no appetite for other fruits.

It requires some little time to become accustomed to many tropical fruits, or at least to find patience as well as inclination to eat them. A large number, in spite of delicious flavor, are provokingly stony: such as the ripe guavas, the cherries, the barbadines; even the corrossole and *pomme-cannelle* are little more than huge masses of very hard seeds buried in pulp of exquisite taste. The *sapota*, or *sapodilla*, is less characterized by stoniness, and one soon learns to like it. It has large flat seeds, which can be split into two with the finger-nail; and a fine white skin lies between these two halves. It requires some skill to remove entire this little skin, or pellicle, without breaking it: to do so is said to be a test of affection. Perhaps this bit of folk-lore was suggested by the shape of the pellicle, which is that of a heart. The pretty fille-de-couleur asks her doudoux:—"*Ess ou ain-mein moin?—pouloss tiré ti lapeau-là sans cassé-y.*" Woe to him if he breaks it! . . . The most disagreeable fruit is, I think, the *pomme-d'Haiti*, or Haytian apple: it is very attractive exteriorly; but has a strong musky odor and taste which nauseates. Few white creoles ever eat it.

Of the oranges, nothing except praise can be said; but there are fruits that look like oranges, and are not oranges, that are far more noteworthy. There is the *chadèque*, which grows here to fully three feet in circumference, and has a sweet pink pulp;

and there is the "forbidden-fruit" (*fouitt-défendu*), a sort of cross between the orange and the chadèque, and superior to both. The colored people declare that this monster fruit is the same which grew in Eden upon the fatal tree: *c'est ça mênm qui fai moune ka fai yche conm ça atouèlement!* The fouitt-défendu is wonderful, indeed, in its way; but the fruit which most surprised me on my first acquaintance with it was the *zabricôt*.

—"*Ou lè yon zabricôt?*" (Would you like an apricot?) Cyrillia asked me one day. I replied that I liked apricots very much,—wanted more than one. Cyrillia looked astonished, but said nothing until she returned from market, and put on the table *two* apricots, with the observation:—"*Ça ké fai ou malade mangé toutt ça!*" (You will get sick if you eat all that.) I could not eat even half of one of them. Imagine a plum larger than the largest turnip, with a skin like a russet apple, solid sweet flesh of a carrot-red color, and a nut in the middle bigger than a duck's egg and hard as a rock. These fruits are aromatic as well as sweet to the taste: the price varies from one to four cents each, according to size. The tree is indigenous to the West Indies; the aborigines of Hayti had a strange belief regarding it. They alleged that its fruits formed the nourishment of the dead; and however pressed by hunger, an Indian in the woods would rather remain without food than strip one of these trees, lest he should deprive the ghosts of their sustenance. . . . No trace of this belief seems to exist among the colored people of Martinique.

Among the poor such fruits are luxuries: they eat more mangoes than any other fruits excepting bananas. It is rather slobbery work eating a common mango, in which every particle of pulp is threaded fast to the kernel: one prefers to gnaw it when alone. But there are cultivated mangoes with finer and thicker flesh which can be sliced off, so that the greater part of the fruit may be eaten without smearing and sucking. Among grafted varieties the *mangue* is quite as delicious as the orange. Perhaps there are nearly as many varieties of mangoes in Martinique as there are varieties of peaches with us: I am acquainted, however, with only a few,—such as the *mango-Bassignac*;—*mango-pêche* (or peach-mango);—*mango-vert* (green mango), very large and oblong;—*mango-grêffé*;—*mangotine*, quite

Bread-fruit Tree.

round and small;—*mango-quinette*, very small also, almost egg-shaped;—*mango-Zézé*, very sweet, rather small, and of flattened form;—*mango-d'or* (golden mango), worth half a franc each;—*mango-Lamentin*, a highly cultivated variety;— and the superb *Reine-Amélie* (or Queen Amelia), a great yellow fruit which retails even in Martinique at five cents apiece.

VIII.

. . . "*Ou c'est bonhomme càton?—ou c'est zimage, non?*" (Am I a pasteboard man, or an image, that I do not eat?) Cyrillia wants to know. The fact is that I am a little overfed; but the stranger in the tropics cannot eat like a native, and my abstemiousness is a surprise. In the North we eat a good deal for the sake of caloric; in the tropics, unless one be in the habit of taking much physical exercise, which is a very difficult thing to do, a generous appetite is out of the question. Cyrillia will not suffer me to live upon *mangé-Créole* altogether; she insists upon occasional beefsteaks and roasts, and tries to tempt me with all kinds of queer delicious desserts as well,—particularly those cakes made of grated cocoanut and sugar-syrup (*tablett-coco-rapé*) of which a stranger becomes very fond. But, nevertheless, I cannot eat enough to quiet Cyrillia's fears.

Not eating enough is not her only complaint against me. I am perpetually doing something or other which shocks her. The Creoles are the most cautious livers in the world, perhaps;—the stranger who walks in the sun without an umbrella, or stands in currents of air, is for them an object of wonder and compassion. Cyrillia's complaints about my recklessness in the matter of hygiene always terminate with the refrain: "*Yo pa fai ça içi*"— (People never do such things in Martinique.) Among such rash acts are washing one's face or hands while perspiring, taking off one's hat on coming in from a walk, going out immediately after a bath, and washing my face with soap. "Oh, Cyrillia! what foolishness!—why should I not wash my face with soap?" "Because it will blind you," Cyrillia answers: "*ça ké tchoué limiè zié ou*" (it will kill the light in your eyes). There is no cleaner person than Cyrillia; and, indeed among the city people, the daily bath is the rule in all weathers; but soap is never used on the face by thousands, who, like Cyrillia, believe it will " kill the light of the eyes."

One day I had been taking a long walk in the sun, and returned so thirsty that all the old stories about travellers suffering in waterless deserts returned to memory with new significance;—visions of simooms arose before me. What a delight to see and to grasp the heavy, red, thick-lipped *dobanne*, the water-jar, dewy and cool with the exudation of the *Eau-de-Gouyave* which filled it to the brim,—*toutt vivant*, as Cyrillia says, "all alive"! There was a sudden scream,—the water-pitcher was snatched from my hands by Cyrillia with the question: "*Ess ou lè tchoué cò-ou?—Saint Joseph!*" (Did I want to kill my body?) . . . The Creoles use the word "body" in speaking of anything that can happen to one,—"hurt one's body," "tire one's body," "marry one's body," "bury one's body," etc.;—I wonder whether the expression originated in zealous desire to prove a profound faith in the soul. . . . Then Cyrillia made me a little punch with sugar and rum, and told me I must never drink fresh-water after a walk unless I wanted to kill my body. In this matter her advice was good. The immediate result of a cold drink while heated is a profuse and icy perspiration, during which currents of air are really dangerous. A cold is not dreaded here, and colds are rare; but pleurisy is common, and may be the consequence of any imprudent exposure.

I do not often have the opportunity at home of committing even an unconscious imprudence; for Cyrillia is ubiquitous, and always on the watch lest something dreadful should happen to me. She is wonderful as a house-keeper as well as a cook: there is certainly much to do, and she has only a child to help her, but she always seems to have time. Her kitchen apparatus is of the simplest kind: a charcoal furnace constructed of bricks, a few earthenware pots (*canari*), and some gridirons;—yet with these she can certainly prepare as many dishes as there are days in the year. I have never known her to be busy with her *canari* for more than an hour; yet everything is kept in perfect order. When she is not working, she is quite happy in sitting at a window, and amusing herself by watching the life of the street,—or playing with a kitten, which she has trained so well that it seems to understand everything she says.

IX.

WITH darkness all the population of the island retire to their homes;—the streets become silent, and the life of the day is done. By eight o'clock nearly all the windows are closed, and the lights put out;—by nine the people are asleep. There are no evening parties, no night amusements, except during rare theatrical seasons and times of Carnival; there are no evening visits: active existence is almost timed by the rising and setting of the sun. . . . The only pleasure left for the stranger of evenings is a quiet smoke on his balcony or before his door: reading is out of the question, partly because books are rare, partly because lights are bad, partly because insects throng about every lamp or candle. I am lucky enough to have a balcony, broad enough for a rocking-chair; and sometimes Cyrillia and the kitten come to keep me company before bedtime. The kitten climbs on my knees; Cyrillia sits right down upon the balcony.

One bright evening, Cyrillia was amusing herself very much by watching the clouds: they were floating high; the moonlight made them brilliant as frost. As they changed shape under the pressure of the trade-wind, Cyrillia seemed to discover wonderful things in them: sheep, ships with sails, cows, faces, perhaps even *zombis.*

—"*Travaill Bon-Dié joli,—anh?*" (Is not the work of the Good-God pretty?) she said at last. . . . "There was Madame Rémy, who used to sell the finest *foulards* and Madrases in St. Pierre;—she used to study the clouds. She drew the patterns of the clouds for her *foulards:* whenever she saw a beautiful cloud or a beautiful rainbow, she would make a drawing of it in color at once; and then she would send that to France to have *foulards* made just like it. . . . Since she is dead, you do not see any more pretty *foulards* such as there used to be." . . .

—"Would you like to look at the moon with my telescope, Cyrillia?" I asked. "Let me get it for you."

—"Oh no, no!" she answered, as if shocked.

—"Why?"

—"*Ah! faut pa gàdé baggaïe Bon-Dié conm ça!*" (It is not right to look at the things of the Good-God that way.)

I did not insist. After a little silence, Cyrillia resumed:—

—"But I saw the Sun and the Moon once fighting together: that was what people call an *eclipse*,—is not that the word? . . . They fought together a long time: I was looking at them. We put a *terrine* full of water on the ground, and looked into the water to see them. And the Moon is stronger than the Sun!—yes, the Sun was obliged to give way to the Moon. . . . Why do they fight like that?"

—"They don't, Cyrillia."

—"Oh yes, they do. I saw them! . . . And the Moon is much stronger than the Sun!"

I did not attempt to contradict this testimony of the eyes. Cyrillia continued to watch the pretty clouds. Then she said:—

—"Would you not like to have a ladder long enough to let you climb up to those clouds, and see what they are made of?"

—"Why, Cyrillia, they are only vapor,—brume: I have been in clouds."

She looked at me in surprise, and, after a moment's silence, asked, with an irony of which I had not supposed her capable:—

—"Then you are the Good-God?"

—"Why, Cyrillia, it is not difficult to reach clouds. You see clouds always upon the top of the Montagne Pelée;—people go there. I have been there—in the clouds."

—"Ah! those are not the same clouds: those are not the clouds of the Good-God. You cannot touch the sky when you are on the Morne de la Croix."

—"My dear Cyrillia, there is no sky to touch. The sky is only an appearance."

—"*Anh, anh, anh!* No sky!—you say there is no sky? . . . Then, what is that up there?'

—"That is air, Cyrillia, beautiful blue air."

—"And what are the stars fastened to?"

—"To nothing. They are suns, but so much further away than our sun that they look small."

—"No, they are not suns! They have not the same form as the sun. . . . You must not say there is no sky: it is wicked! But you are not a Catholic!"

—"My dear Cyrillia, I don't see what that has to do with the sky."

—"Where does the Good-God stay, if there be no sky? And where is heaven?—and where is hell?"

—"Hell in the sky, Cyrillia?"

—"The Good-God made heaven in one part of the sky, and hell in another part, for bad people. . . . Ah! you are a Protestant;—you do not know the things of the Good-God! That is why you talk like that."

—"What is a Protestant, Cyrillia?"

—"You are one. The Protestants do not believe in religion,—do not love the Good-God."

—"Well, I am neither a Protestant nor a Catholic, Cyrillia."

—"Oh! you do not mean that; you cannot be a *maudi*, an accursed. There are only the Protestants, the Catholics, and the accursed. You are not a *maudi*, I am sure. But you must not say there is no sky" . . .

—"But, Cyrillia"—

—"No: I will not listen to you:—you are a Protestant. Where does the rain come from, if there is no sky?" . . .

—"Why, Cyrillia, . . . the clouds" . . .

—"No, you are a Protestant. . . . How can you say such things? There are the Three Kings and the Three Valets,—the beautiful stars that come at Christmas-time,—there, over there —all beautiful, and big, big, big! . . . And you say there is no sky!"

—"Cyrillia, perhaps I am a *maudi*."

—"No, no! You are only a Protestant. But do not tell me there is no sky: it is wicked to say that!"

—"I won't say it any more, Cyrillia—there! But I will say there are no *zombis*."

—"I know you are not a *maudi*;—you have been baptized."

—"How do you know I have been baptized?"

—"Because, if you had not been baptized you would see *zombis* all the time, even in broad day. All children who are not baptized see *zombis*." . . .

X.

CYRILLIA's solicitude for me extends beyond the commonplaces of hygiene and diet into the uncertain domain of matters ghostly. She fears much that something might happen to me through the agency of wizards, witches (*sociès*), or *zombis*. Especially zombis. Cyrillia's belief in zombis has a solidity that renders argument out of the question. This belief is part of her inner nature,—something hereditary, racial, ancient as Africa, as characteristic of her people as the love of rhythms and melodies totally different from our own musical conceptions, but possessing, even for the civilized, an inexplicable emotional charm.

Zombi!—the word is perhaps full of mystery even for those who made it. The explanations of those who utter it most often are never quite lucid: it seems to convey ideas darkly impossible to define,—fancies belonging to the mind of another race and another era,—unspeakably old. Perhaps the word in our own language which offers the best analogy is "goblin": yet the one is not fully translated by the other. Both have, however, one common ground on which they become indistinguishable,—that region of the supernatural which is most primitive and most vague; and the closest relation between the savage and the civilized fancy may be found in the fears which we call childish,—of darkness, shadows, and things dreamed. One form of the *zombi*-belief—akin to certain ghostly superstitions held by various primitive races—would seem to have been suggested by nightmare,—that form of nightmare in which familiar persons become slowly and hideously transformed into malevolent beings. The *zombi* deludes under the appearance of a travelling companion, an old comrade—like the desert spirits of the Arabs—or even under the form of an animal. Consequently the creole negro fears everything living which he meets after dark upon a lonely road,—a stray horse, a cow, even a dog; and mothers quell the naughtiness of their children by the threat of summoning a zombi-cat or a zombi-creature of some kind. "*Zombi ké nana ou*" (the zombi will gobble thee up) is generally an effectual menace in the country parts, where it is believed zombis may be met with any time after sunset. In the city it is thought that their regular hours are between two and four o'clock in the morning. At least so Cyrillia says:—

—"Dèzhè, toua-zhè-matin: c'est lhè zombi. Yo ka sòti dèzhè, toua zhè: c'est lhè yo. A quattrhè yo ka rentré;—angelus ka sonné." (At four o'clock they go back where they came from, before the *Angelus* rings.) Why?

—"*C'est pou moune pas joinne yo dans larue*" (So that people may not meet with them in the street), Cyrillia answers.

—"Are they afraid of the people, Cyrillia?" I asked.

—"No, they are not afraid; but they do not want people to know their business" (*pa lè moune ouè zaffai yo*).

Cyrillia also says one must not look out of the window when a dog howls at night. Such a dog may be a *mauvais vivant* (evil being): "If he sees me looking at him he will say, '*Ou tropp quirièse quitté cabane ou pou gàdé zaffai lezautt.*'" (You are too curious to leave your bed like that to look at other folks' business.)

—"And what then, Cyrillia?"

—"Then he will put out your eyes,—*y ké coqui zié ou,*— make you blind."

—"But, Cyrillia," I asked one day, "did you ever see any zombis?"

—"How? I often see them! . . . They walk about the room at night;—they walk like people. They sit in the rocking-chairs and rock themselves very softly, and look at me. I say to them:—'What do you want here?—I never did any harm to anybody. Go away!' Then they go away."

—"What do they look like?"

—"Like people,—sometimes like beautiful people (*bel moune*). I am afraid of them. I only see them when there is no light burning. While the lamp burns before the Virgin they do not come. But sometimes the oil fails, and the light dies."

In my own room there are dried palm leaves and some withered flowers fastened to the wall. Cyrillia put them there. They were taken from the *reposoirs* (temporary altars) erected for the last Corpus Christi procession: consequently they are blessed, and ought to keep the zombis away. That is why they are fastened to the wall, over my bed.

Nobody could be kinder to animals than Cyrillia usually shows herself to be: all the domestic animals in the neighborhood impose upon her;—various dogs and cats steal from her impudently, without the least fear of being beaten. I was therefore very much surprised to see her one evening catch a flying beetle that approached the light, and deliberately put its head in the candle-flame. When I asked her how she could be so cruel, she replied:—

—"*Ah! ou pa connitt choïe pays-ci.*" (You do not know Things in this country.)

The Things thus referred to I found to be supernatural Things. It is popularly believed that certain winged creatures which circle about candles at night may be *engagés* or *envoyés* —wicked people having the power of transformation, or even zombis "sent" by witches or wizards to do harm. "There was a woman at Tricolore," Cyrillia says, "who used to sew a great deal at night; and a big beetle used to come into her room and fly about the candle, and bother her very much. One night she managed to get hold of it, and she singed its head in the candle. Next day, a woman who was her neighbor came to the house with her head all tied up. '*Ah! macoumè,*' asked the sewing-woman, '*ça ou ni dans guiôle-ou?*' And the other answered, very angrily, '*Ou ni toupet mandé moin ça moin ni dans guiôle moin!—et cété ou qui té brilé guiôle moin nans chandelle-ou hiè-souè.*'" (You have the impudence to ask what is the matter with my mouth! and you yourself burned my mouth in your candle last night.)

Early one morning, about five o'clock, Cyrillia, opening the front door, saw a huge crab walking down the street. Probably it had escaped from some barrel; for it is customary here to keep live crabs in barrels and fatten them,—feeding them with maize, mangoes, and, above all, green peppers: nobody likes to cook crabs as soon as caught; for they may have been eating manchineel apples at the river-mouths. Cyrillia uttered a cry of dismay on seeing that crab; then I heard her talking to herself: —"*I* touch it?—never! it can go about its business. How do I know it is not *an arranged crab* (*yon crabe rangé*), or an *envoyé?*—since everybody knows I like crabs. For two sous I can buy a fine crab and know where it comes from." The crab went on down the street: everywhere the sight of it created consternation; nobody dared to touch it; women cried out at it, "*Miserabe!—envoyé Satan!—allez, maudi!*"—some threw holy water on the crab. Doubtless it reached the sea in safety. In the evening Cyrillia said: "I think that crab was a little zombi;—I am going to burn a light all night to keep it from coming back."

Another day, while I was out, a negro to whom I had lent two francs came to the house, and paid his debt. Cyrillia told me when I came back, and showed me the money carefully enveloped in a piece of brown paper; but said I must not touch it,—she would get rid of it for me at the market. I laughed at her fears; and she observed: "You do not know negroes, Missié! —negroes are wicked, negroes are jealous! I do not want you to touch that money, because I have not a good opinion about this affair."

After I began to learn more of the underside of Martinique life, I could understand the source and justification of many similar superstitions in simple and uneducated minds. The negro sorcerer is, at worst, only a poisoner; but he possesses a very curious art which long defied serious investigation, and in the beginning of the last century was attributed, even by whites, to diabolical influence. In 1721, 1723, and 1725, several negroes were burned alive at the stake as wizards in league with the devil. It was an era of comparative ignorance; but even now things are done which would astonish the most sceptical and practical physician. For example, a laborer discharged from a plantation vows vengeance; and the next morning the whole force of hands—the entire *atelier*—are totally disabled from work. Every man and woman on the place is unable to walk; everybody has one or both legs frightfully swollen. *Yo té ka pilé malifice*: they have trodden on a "malifice." What is the "malifice"? All that can be ascertained is that certain little prickly seeds have been scattered all over the ground, where the barefooted workers are in the habit of passing. Ordinarily, treading on these seeds is of no consequence; but it is evident in such a case that they must have been prepared in a special way,—soaked in some poison, perhaps snake-venom. At all events, the physician deems it safest to treat the inflammations after the manner of snake wounds; and after many days the hands are perhaps able to resume duty.

XI.

WHILE Cyrillia is busy with her *canari*, she talks to herself or sings. She has a low rich voice,—sings strange things, things that have been forgotten by this generation,—creole songs of the old days, having a weird rhythm and fractions of tones that are surely African. But more generally she talks to herself, as all the Martiniquaises do: it is a continual murmur as of a stream.

At first I used to think she was talking to somebody else, and would call out:—

—"*Épi quiless moune ça ou ka pàlé-à?*"

But she would always answer:—"*Moin ka pàlé anni cò moin*" (I am only talking to my own body), which is the creole expression for talking to oneself.

—"And what are you talking so much to your own body about, Cyrillia?"

—"I am talking about my own little affairs" (*ti zaffai-moin*). . . . That is all that I could ever draw from her.

But when not working, she will sit for hours looking out of the window. In this she resembles the kitten: both seem to find the same silent pleasure in watching the street, or the green heights that rise above its roofs,—the Morne d'Orange. Occasionally at such times she will break the silence in the strangest way, if she thinks I am not too busy with my papers to answer a question:—

—"*Missié?*"—timidly.

—"Eh?"

—"*Di moin, chè, ti manmaille dans pays ou, toutt piti, piti—ess ça pàlé Anglais?*" (Do the little children in my country—the very, very little children—talk English?)

—"Why, certainly, Cyrillia."

—"*Toutt piti, piti?*"—with growing surprise.

—"Why, of course!"

—"*C'est drôle, ça!*" (It is queer, that!) She cannot understand it.

—"And the little *manmaille* in Martinique, Cyrillia—*toutt piti, piti,*—don't they talk creole?"

—"*Oui; mais toutt moune ka pâlé nègue: ça facile.*" (Yes; but anybody can talk negro—that is easy to learn.)

XII.

CYRILLIA's room has no furniture in it: the Martinique bonne lives as simply and as rudely as a domestic animal. One thin mattress covered with a sheet, and elevated from the floor only by a léfant, forms her bed. The *léfant*, or "elephant," is composed of two thick square pieces of coarse hard mattress stuffed with shavings, and placed end to end. Cyrillia has a good pillow, however,—*bourré épi flèches-canne*,—filled with the plumes of the sugar-cane. A cheap trunk with broken hinges contains her modest little wardrobe: a few *mouchoirs*, or kerchiefs, used for head-dresses, a spare *douillette*, or long robe, and some tattered linen. Still she is always clean, neat, fresh-looking. I see a pair of sandals in the corner,—such as the women of the country sometimes wear—wooden soles with a leather band for the instep, and two little straps; but she never puts them on. Fastened to the wall are two French prints— lithographs: one representing Victor Hugo's *Esmeralda* in prison with her pet goat; the other, Lamartine's *Laurence* with her fawn. Both are very old and stained and bitten by the *bête-à-ciseau*, a species of *lepisma*, which destroys books and papers, and everything it can find exposed. On a shelf are two bottles, —one filled with holy water; another with *tafia camphrée* (camphor dissolved in tafia), which is Cyrillia's sole remedy for colds, fevers, headaches—all maladies not of a very fatal de-scription. There are also a little woollen monkey, about three inches high—the dusty plaything of a long-dead child;—an im-age of the Virgin, even smaller;—and a broken cup with fresh bright blossoms in it, the Virgin's flower-offering;—and the Virgin's invariable lamp—a night-light, a little wick floating on olive-oil in a tiny glass.

I know that Cyrillia must have bought these flowers—they are garden flowers—at the Marchè du Fort. There are always old women sitting there who sell nothing else but bouquets for the Virgin,—and who cry out to passers-by:—"*Gagné ti bouquet pou Viège-ou, chè!* . . . Buy a nosegay, dear, for your Virgin;—she is asking you for one;—give her a little one, *chè cocott*." . . . Cyrillia says you must not smell the flowers you give the Virgin: it would be stealing from her. . . . The little lamp is always lighted at six o'clock. At six o'clock the Virgin is supposed to pass through all the streets of St. Pierre, and wherever a lamp burns before her image, she enters there and blesses that house. "*Faut limé lampe ou pou fai la-Viège passé dans caïe-ou*," says Cyrillia. (You must light the lamp to make the Virgin come into your house.) . . . Cyrillia often talks to her little image, exactly as if it were a baby,—calls it pet names, —asks if it is content with the flowers.

This image of the Virgin is broken: it is only half a Virgin,—the upper half. Cyrillia has arranged it so, nevertheless, that had I not been very inquisitive I should never have divined its mishap. She found a small broken powder-box without a lid,—probably thrown negligently out of a boudoir window by some wealthy beauty: she filled this little box with straw, and fixed the mutilated image upright within it, so that you could never suspect the loss of its feet. The Virgin looks very funny, thus peeping over the edge of her little box,—looks like a broken toy, which a child has been trying to mend. But this Virgin has offerings too: Cyrillia buys flowers for her, and sticks them all round her, between the edge of the powder-box and the straw. After all, Cyrillia's Virgin is quite as serious a fact as any image of silver or of ivory in the homes of the rich: probably the prayers said to her are more simply beautiful, and more direct from the heart, than many daily murmured before the *chapelles* of luxurious homes. And the more one looks at it, the more one feels that it were almost wicked to smile at this little broken toy of faith.

—"Cyrillia, *mafi*," I asked her one day, after my discovery of the little Virgin,—"would you not like me to buy a *chapelle* for you?" The *chapelle* is the little bracket-altar, together with images and ornaments, to be found in every creole bedroom.

—"*Mais non, Missié*," she answered, smiling, "*moin aimein ti Viège moin, pa lè gagnin dautt*. I love my little Virgin: do not want any other. I have seen much trouble: she was with me in my trouble;—she heard my prayers. It would be wicked for me to throw her away. When I have a sou to spare, I buy flowers for her;—when I have no money, I climb the mornes, and pick pretty buds for her. . . . But why should Missié want to buy me a *chapelle?*—Missié is a Protestant?"

—"I thought it might give you pleasure, Cyrillia."

—"No, Missié, I thank you; it would not give me pleasure. But Missié could give me something else which would make me very happy— I often thought of asking Missié . . . but—"

—"Tell me what it is, Cyrillia."

She remained silent a moment, then said:—

—"Missié makes photographs. . . ."

—"You want a photograph of yourself, Cyrillia?"

—"Oh! no, Missié, I am too ugly and too old. But I have a

daughter. She is beautiful—*yon bel bois*,—like a beautiful tree, as we say here. I would like so much to have her picture taken."

A photographic instrument belonging to a clumsy amateur suggested this request to Cyrillia. I could not attempt such work successfully; but I gave her a note to a photographer of much skill; and a few days later the portrait was sent to the house. Cyrillia's daughter was certainly a comely girl,—tall and almost gold-colored, with pleasing features; and the photograph looked very nice, though less nice than the original. Half the beauty of these people is a beauty of tint,—a tint so exquisite sometimes that I have even heard white creoles declare no white complexion compares with it: the greater part of the charm remaining is grace,—the grace of movement; and neither of these can be rendered by photography. I had the portrait framed for Cyrillia, to hang up beside her little pictures.

When it came, she was not in; I put it in her room, and waited to see the effect. On returning, she entered there; and I did not see her for so long a time that I stole to the door of the chamber to observe her. She was standing before the portrait, —looking at it, talking to it as if it were alive. "*Yche moin, yche moin! . . . Oui! ou toutt bel!—yche moin bel.*" (My child, my child! . . . Yes, thou art all beautiful: my child is beautiful.) All at once she turned—perhaps she noticed my shadow, or felt my presence in some way: her eyes were wet;—she started, flushed, then laughed.

—"Ah! Missié, you watch me;—*ou guetté moin. . . .* But she is my child. Why should I not love her? . . . She looks so beautiful there."

—"She is beautiful, Cyrillia;—I love to see you love her."

She gazed at the picture a little longer in silence;—then turned to me again, and asked earnestly:—

—"*Pouki yo pa ka fai pòtrai pàlé—anh? . . . pisse yo ka tiré y toutt samm ou: c'est ou-menm! . . . Yo douè fai y palé 'tou.*"

(Why do they not make a portrait talk,—tell me? For they draw it just all like you!—it is yourself: they ought to make it talk.)

—"Perhaps they will be able to do something like that one of these days, Cyrillia."

—"Ah! that would be so nice. Then I could talk to her.

C'est yon bel moune moin fai—y bel, joli moune! . . . Moin sé causé épi y." . . .

. . . And I, watching her beautiful childish emotion, thought:—Cursed be the cruelty that would persuade itself that one soul may be like another,—that one affection may be replaced by another,—that individual goodness is not a thing apart, original, untwinned on earth, but only the general characteristic of a class or type, to be sought and found and utilized at will! . . . Self-cursèd he who denies the divinity of love! Each heart, each brain in the billions of humanity,—even so surely as sorrow lives,—feels and thinks in some special way unlike any other; and goodness in each has its unlikeness to all other goodness,—and thus its own infinite preciousness; for however humble, however small, it is something all alone, and God never repeats his work. No heart-beat is cheap, no gentleness is despicable, no kindness is common; and Death, in removing a life—the simplest life ignored,—removes what never will reappear through the eternity of eternities,—since every being is the sum of a chain of experiences infinitely varied from all others. . . . To some Cyrillia's happy tears might bring a smile: to me that smile would seem the unforgivable sin against the Giver of Life! . . .

"Pa combiné, chè!"

MORE finely than any term in our tongue does the French word *frisson* express that faint shiver—as of a ghostly touch thrilling from hair to feet—which intense pleasure sometimes gives, and which is felt most often and most strongly in childhood, when the imagination is still so sensitive and so powerful that one's whole being trembles to the vibration of a fancy. And this electric word best expresses, I think, that long thrill of amazed delight inspired by the first knowledge of the tropic world,—a sensation of weirdness in beauty, like the effect, in child-days, of fairy tales and stories of phantom isles.

For all unreal seems the vision of it. The transfiguration of all things by the stupendous light and the strange vapors of the West Indian sea,—the interorbing of flood and sky in blinding azure,—the sudden springs of gem-tinted coast from the ocean,—the iris-colors and astounding shapes of the hills,—the unimaginable magnificence of palms,—the high woods veiled and swathed in vines that blaze like emerald: all remind you in some queer way of things half forgotten,—the fables of enchantment. Enchantment it is indeed—but only the enchantment of that Great Wizard, the Sun, whose power you are scarcely beginning to know.

And into the life of the tropical city you enter as in dreams one enters into the life of a dead century. In all the quaint streets—over whose luminous yellow façades the beautiful burning violet of the sky appears as if but a few feet away—you see youth good to look upon as ripe fruit; and the speech of the people is soft as a coo; and eyes of brown girls caress you with a passing look. . . . Love's world, you may have heard, has few restraints here, where Nature ever seems to cry out, like the swart seller of corossoles:—"*Ça qui lè doudoux?*" . . .

How often in some passing figure does one discern an ideal almost realized, and forbear to follow it with untired gaze only when another, another, and yet another, come to provoke the same æsthetic fancy,—to win the same unspoken praise! How often does one long for artist's power to fix the fleeting lines,

498

to catch the color, to seize the whole exotic charm of some special type! . . . One finds a strange charm even in the timbre of these voices,—these half-breed voices, always with a tendency to contralto, and vibrant as ringing silver. What is that mysterious quality in a voice which has power to make the pulse beat faster, even when the singer is unseen? . . . do only the birds know?

. . . It seems to you that you could never weary of watching this picturesque life,—of studying the costumes, brilliant with butterfly colors,—and the statuesque semi-nudity of laboring hundreds,—and the untaught grace of attitudes,—and the simplicity of manners. Each day brings some new pleasure of surprise;—even from the window of your lodging you are ever noting something novel, something to delight the sense of oddity or beauty. . . . Even in your room everything interests you, because of its queerness or quaintness: you become fond of the objects about you,—the great noiseless rocking-chairs that lull to sleep;—the immense bed (*lit-à-bateau*) of heavy polished wood, with its richly carven sides reaching down to the very floor;—and its invariable companion, the little couch or *sopha*, similarly shaped but much narrower, used only for the siesta;—and the thick red earthen vessels (*dobannes*) which keep your drinking-water cool on the hottest days, but which are always filled thrice between sunrise and sunset with clear water from the mountain,—*dleau toutt vivant*, "all alive"; —and the *verrines*, tall glass vases with stems of bronze in which your candle will burn steadily despite a draught;—and even those funny little angels and Virgins which look at you from their bracket in the corner, over the oil lamp you are presumed to kindle nightly in their honor, however great a heretic you may be. . . . You adopt at once, and without reservation, those creole home habits which are the result of centuries of experience with climate,—abstention from solid food before the middle of the day, repose after the noon meal;—and you find each repast an experience as curious as it is agreeable. It is not at all difficult to accustom oneself to green pease stewed with sugar, eggs mixed with tomatoes, salt fish stewed in milk, palmiste pith made into salad, grated cocoa formed into rich cakes, and dishes of titiri cooked in oil,—the minuscule fish, of which a thousand will scarcely fill a saucer. Above all, you are astonished by the endless variety of vegetables and fruits, of all conceivable shapes and inconceivable flavors.

And it does not seem possible that even the simplest little recurrences of this antiquated, gentle home-life could ever prove wearisome by daily repetition through the months and years. The musical greeting of the colored child, tapping at your door before sunrise,—"*Bonjou', Missié,*"—as she brings your cup of black hot coffee and slice of corossole;—the smile of the silent brown girl who carries your meals up-stairs in a tray poised upon her brightly coiffed head, and who stands by while you dine, watching every chance to serve, treading quite silently with her pretty bare feet;—the pleasant manners of the *màchanne* who brings your fruit, the *porteuse* who delivers your bread, the *blanchisseuse* who washes your linen at the river,—and all the kindly folk who circle about your existence, with their trays and turbans, their *foulards* and *douillettes*, their primitive grace and creole chatter: these can never cease to have a charm for you. You cannot fail to be touched also by the amusing solicitude of these good people for your health, because you are a stranger: their advice about hours to go out and hours to stay at home,—about roads to follow and paths to avoid on account of snakes,—about removing your hat and coat, or drinking while warm. . . . Should you fall ill, this solicitude intensifies to devotion; you are tirelessly tended;—the good people will exhaust their wonderful knowledge of herbs to get you well,—will climb the mornes even at midnight, in spite of the risk of snakes and fear of zombis, to gather strange plants by the light of a lantern. Natural joyousness, natural kindliness, heart-felt desire to please, childish capacity of being delighted with trifles,—seem characteristic of all this colored population. It is turning its best side towards you, no doubt; but the side of the nature made visible appears none the less agreeable because you suspect there is another which you have not seen. What kindly inventiveness is displayed in contriving surprises for you, or in finding some queer thing to show you, —some fantastic plant, or grotesque fish, or singular bird! What apparent pleasure in taking trouble to gratify,—what innocent frankness of sympathy! . . . Childishly beautiful seems the readiness of this tinted race to compassionate: you do not reflect that it is also a savage trait, while the charm of its novelty is yet upon you. No one is ashamed to shed tears for the death of a pet animal; any mishap to a child creates excitement, and evokes an immediate volunteering of services. And this compassionate sentiment is often extended, in a semi-poetical way, even to inanimate objects. One June morning, I remember, a three-masted schooner lying in the bay took fire, and had to be set adrift. An immense crowd gathered on the wharves; and I saw many curious manifestations of grief,—such grief, perhaps, as an infant feels for the misfortune of a toy it imagines to possess feeling, but not the less sincere because unreasoning. As the flames climbed the rigging, and the masts fell, the crowd moaned as though looking upon some human tragedy; and everywhere one could hear such strange cries of pity as, "*Pauv' malhérè!*" (poor unfortunate), "*pauv' diabe!*" . . . "*Toutt baggaïe-y pou allé, cassé!*" (All its things-to-go-with are broken!) sobbed a girl, with tears streaming clown her cheeks. . . . She seemed to believe it was alive. . . .

. . . And day by day the artlessness of this exotic humanity touches you more;—day by day this savage, somnolent, splendid Nature—delighting in furious color—bewitches you more. Already the anticipated necessity of having to leave it all some day—the far-seen pain of bidding it farewell—weighs upon you, even in dreams.

II.

READER, if you be of those who have longed in vain for a glimpse of that tropic world,—tales of whose beauty charmed your childhood, and made stronger upon you that weird mesmerism of the sea which pulls at the heart of a boy,—one who had longed like you, and who, chance-led, beheld at last the fulfilment of the wish, can swear to you that the magnificence of the reality far excels the imagining. Those who know only the lands in which all processes for the satisfaction of human wants have been perfected under the terrible stimulus of necessity, can little guess the witchery of that Nature ruling the zones of color and of light. Within their primeval circles, the earth remains radiant and young as in that preglacial time whereof some transmitted memory may have created the hundred traditions of an Age of Gold. And the prediction of a paradise to come,—a phantom realm of rest and perpetual light: may this not have been but a sum of the remembrances and the yearnings of man first exiled from his heritage,—a dream born of the great nostalgia of races migrating to people the pallid North? . . .

. . . But with the realization of the hope to know this magical Nature you learn that the actuality varies from the preconceived ideal otherwise than in surpassing it. Unless you enter the torrid world equipped with scientific knowledge extraordinary, your anticipations are likely to be at fault. Perhaps you had pictured to yourself the effect of perpetual summer as a physical delight,—something like an indefinite prolongation of the fairest summer weather ever enjoyed at home. Probably you had heard of fevers, risks of acclimatization, intense heat, and a swarming of venomous creatures; but you may nevertheless believe you know what precautions to take; and published statistics of climatic temperature may have persuaded you that the heat is not difficult to bear. By that enervation to which all white dwellers in the tropics are subject you may have understood a pleasant languor,—a painless disinclination to effort in a country where physical effort is less needed than elsewhere, —a soft temptation to idle away the hours in a hammock, under the shade of giant trees. Perhaps you have read, with eyes of faith, that torpor of the body is favorable to activity of the mind, and therefore believe that the intellectual powers can be stimulated and strengthened by tropical influences:—you suppose that enervation will reveal itself only as a beatific indolence which will leave the brain free to think with lucidity, or to revel in romantic dreams.

III.

You are not at first undeceived;—the disillusion is long delayed. Doubtless you have read the delicious idyl of Bernardin de Saint-Pierre (this is not Mauritius, but the old life of Mauritius was wellnigh the same); and you look for idyllic personages among the beautiful humanity about you,—for idyllic scenes among the mornes shadowed by primeval forest, and the valleys threaded by a hundred brooks. I know not whether the faces and forms that you seek will be revealed to you;—but you will not be able to complain for the lack of idyllic loveliness in the commonest landscape. Whatever artistic knowledge you possess will merely teach you the more to wonder at the luxuriant purple of the sea, the violet opulence of the sky, the violent beauty of foliage greens, the lilac tints of evening, and the color-enchantments distance gives in an atmosphere full of iridescent power,—the amethysts and agates, the pearls and ghostly golds, of far mountainings. Never, you imagine, never could one tire of wandering through those marvellous valleys,—of climbing the silent roads under emeraldine shadow to heights from which the city seems but a few inches long, and the moored ships tinier than gnats that cling to a mirror,—or of swimming in that blue bay whose clear flood stays warm through all the year.* Or, standing alone, in some aisle of colossal palms, where humming-birds are flashing and shooting like a showering of jewel-fires, you feel how weak the skill of poet or painter to fix the sensation of that white-pillared imperial splendor;—and you think you know why creoles exiled by necessity to colder lands may sicken for love of their own,—die of home-yearning, as did many a one in far Louisiana, after the political tragedies of 1848. . . .

. . . But you are not a creole, and must pay tribute of suffering to the climate of the tropics. You will have to learn that a temperature of 90° Fahr. in the tropics is by no means the same thing as 90° Fahr. in Europe or the United States;—that the mornes cannot be climbed with safety during the hotter hours of the afternoon;—that by taking a long walk you incur serious danger of catching a fever;—that to enter the high woods, a path must be hewn with the cutlass through the creepers and vines and undergrowth,—among snakes, venomous insects, venomous plants, and malarial exhalations;—that the finest blown dust is full of irritant and invisible enemies;—that it is

---

*Rufz remarks that the first effect of this climate of the Antilles is a sort of general physical excitement, an exaltation, a sense of unaccustomed strength, —which begets the desire of immediate action to discharge the surplus of nervous force. "Then all distances seem brief;—the greatest fatigues are braved without hesitation."—*Études*.

folly to seek repose on a sward, or in the shade of trees,—particularly under tamarinds. Only after you have by experience become well convinced of these facts can you begin to comprehend something general in regard to West Indian conditions of life.

IV.

. . . SLOWLY the knowledge comes. . . . For months the vitality of a strong European (the American constitution bears the test even better) may resist the debilitating climate: perhaps the stranger will flatter himself that, like men habituated to heavy labor in stifling warmth,—those toiling in mines, in foundries, in engine-rooms of ships, at iron-furnaces,—so he too may become accustomed, without losing his strength, to the continuous draining of the pores, to the exhausting force of this strange motionless heat which compels change of clothing many times a day. But gradually he finds that it is not heat alone which is debilitating him, but the weight and septic nature of an atmosphere charged with vapor, with electricity, with unknown agents not less inimical to human existence than propitious to vegetal luxuriance. If he has learned those rules of careful living which served him well in a temperate climate, he will not be likely to abandon them among his new surroundings; and they will help him, no doubt,—particularly if he be prudent enough to avoid the sea-coast at night, and all exposure to dews or early morning mists, and all severe physical strain. Nevertheless, he becomes slowly conscious of changes extraordinary going on within him,—in especial, a continual sensation of weight in the brain, daily growing, and compelling frequent repose;—also a curious heightening of nervous sensibility to atmospheric changes, to tastes and odors, to pleasure and pain. Total loss of appetite soon teaches him to follow the local custom of eating nothing solid before mid-day, and enables him to divine how largely the necessity for caloric enters into the food-consumption of northern races. He becomes abstemious, eats sparingly, and discovers his palate to have become oddly exacting—finds that certain fruits and drinks are indeed, as the creoles assert, appropriate only to particular physical conditions corresponding with particular hours of the day. Corossole is only to be eaten in the morning, after black coffee;—vermouth is good to drink only between the hours of nine and half-past ten;—rum or other strong liquor only before meals or after fatigue;—claret or wine only during a repast, and then very sparingly,—for, strangely enough, wine is found to be injurious in a country where stronger liquors are considered among the prime necessaries of existence.

And he expected, at the worst, to feel lazy, to lose some physical energy! But this is no mere languor which now begins to oppress him;—it is a sense of vital exhaustion painful as the misery of convalescence: the least effort provokes a perspiration profuse enough to saturate clothing, and the limbs ache as from muscular overstrain;—the lightest attire feels almost insupportable;—the idea of sleeping even under a sheet is torture, for the weight of a silken handkerchief is discomfort. One wishes one could live as a savage,—naked in the heat. One burns with a thirst impossible to assuage—feels a desire for stimulants, a sense of difficulty in breathing, occasional quickenings of the heart's action so violent as to alarm. Then comes at last the absolute dread of physical exertion. Some slight relief might be obtained, no doubt, by resigning oneself forthwith to adopt the gentle indolent manners of the white creoles, who do not walk when it is possible to ride, and never ride if it is equally convenient to drive;—but the northern nature generally refuses to accept this ultimate necessity without a protracted and painful struggle.

 . . . Not even then has the stranger fully divined the evil power of this tropical climate, which remodels the characters of races within a couple of generations,—changing the shape of the skeleton,—deepening the cavities of the orbits to protect the eye from the flood of light,—transforming the blood,—darkening the skin. Following upon the nervous modifications of the first few months come modifications and changes of a yet graver kind;—with the loss of bodily energy ensues a more than corresponding loss of mental activity and strength. The whole range of thought diminishes, contracts,—shrinks to that narrowest of circles which surrounds the physical self, the inner ring of merely material sensation: the memory weakens appallingly;—the mind operates faintly, slowly, incoherently,—almost as in dreams. Serious reading, vigorous thinking,

become impossible. You doze over the most important project;
—you fall fast asleep over the most fascinating of books.

Then comes the vain revolt, the fruitless desperate striving
with this occult power which numbs the memory and enchants
the will. Against the set resolve to think, to act, to study, there
is a hostile rush of unfamiliar pain to the temples, to the eyes,
to the nerve centres of the brain; and a great weight is somewhere in the head, always growing heavier: then comes a
drowsiness that overpowers and stupefies, like the effect of a
narcotic. And this obligation to sleep, to sink into coma, will
impose itself just so surely as you venture to attempt any mental work in leisure hours, after the noon repast, or during the
heat of the afternoon. Yet at night you can scarcely sleep.
Repose is made feverish by a still heat that keeps the skin
drenched with thick sweat, or by a perpetual, unaccountable,
tingling and prickling of the whole body-surface. With the approach of morning the air grows cooler, and slumber comes,—
a slumber of exhaustion, dreamless and sickly; and perhaps
when you would rise with the sun you feel such a dizziness,
such a numbness, such a torpor, that only by the most intense
effort can you keep your feet for the first five minutes. You experience a sensation that recalls the poet's fancy of death-in-
life, or old stories of sudden rising from the grave: it is as
though all the electricity of will had ebbed away,—all the vital
force evaporated, in the heat of the night. . . .

V.

It might be stated, I think, with safety, that for a certain class
of invalids the effect of the climate is like a powerful stimulant,
—a tonic medicine which may produce astonishing results
within a fixed time,—but which if taken beyond that time will
prove dangerous. After a certain number of months, your first
enthusiasm with your new surroundings dies out;—even Nature ceases to affect the senses in the same way: the *frisson* ceases
to come to you. Meanwhile you may have striven to become as
much as possible a part of the exotic life into which you have
entered,—may have adopted its customs, learned its language.
But you cannot mix with it mentally;—you circulate only as an
oil-drop in its current. You still feel yourself alone.

The very longest West Indian day is but twelve hours fifty-six minutes;—perhaps your first dissatisfaction was evoked by the brevity of the days. There is no twilight whatever; and all activity ceases with sundown: there is no going outside of the city after dark, because of snakes;—club life here ends at the hour it only begins abroad;—there is no visiting of evenings; after the seven o'clock dinner, every one prepares to retire. And the foreigner, accustomed to make evening a time for social intercourse, finds no small difficulty in resigning himself to this habit of early retiring. The natural activity of a European or American mind requires some intellectual exercise,—at least some interchange of ideas with sympathetic natures; the hours during the suspension of business after noon, or those following the closing of offices at sunset, are the only ones in which busy men may find time for such relaxation; and these very hours have been always devoted to restorative sleep by the native population ever since the colony began. Naturally, therefore, the stranger dreads the coming of the darkness, the inevitable isolation of long sleepless hours. And if he seek those solaces for loneliness which he was wont to seek at home,—reading, study,—he is made to comprehend, as never before, what the absence of all libraries, lack of books, inaccessibility of all reading-matter, means for the man of the nineteenth century. One must send abroad to obtain even a review, and wait months for its coming. And this mental starvation gnaws at the brain more and more as one feels less inclination and less capacity for effort, and as that single enjoyment, which at first rendered a man indifferent to other pleasures,—the delight of being alone with tropical Nature,—becomes more difficult to indulge. When lethargy has totally mastered habit and purpose, and you must at last confess yourself resigned to view Nature from your chamber, or at best from a carriage window,—then, indeed, the want of all literature proves a positive torture. It is not a consolation to discover that you are an almost solitary sufferer, —from climate as well as from mental hunger. With amazement and envy you see young girls passing to walk right across the island and back before sunset, under burdens difficult for a strong man to lift to his shoulder;—the same journey on horseback would now weary you for days. You wonder of what flesh and blood can these people be made,—what wonderful vitality lies in those slender woman-bodies, which, under the terrible sun, and despite their astounding expenditure of force, remain cool to the sight and touch as bodies of lizards and serpents! And contrasting this savage strength with your own weakness, you begin to understand better how mighty the working of those powers which temper races and shape race habits in accordance with environment.

. . . Ultimately, if destined for acclimatation, you will cease to suffer from these special conditions; but ere this can be, a long period of nervous irritability must be endured; and fevers must thin the blood, soften the muscles, transform the Northern tint of health to a dead brown. You will have to learn that intellectual pursuits can be persisted in only at risk of life;—that in this part of the world there is nothing to do but to plant cane and cocoa, and make rum, and cultivate tobacco,—or open a magazine for the sale of Madras handkerchiefs and foulards,— and eat, drink, sleep, perspire. You will understand why the tropics settled by European races produce no sciences, arts, or literature,—why the habits and the thoughts of other centuries still prevail where Time itself moves slowly as though enfeebled by the heat.

And with the compulsory indolence of your life, the long exacerbation of the nervous system, will come the first pain of nostalgia,—the first weariness of the tropics. It is not that Nature can become ever less lovely to your sight; but that the tantalization of her dangerous beauty, which you may enjoy only at a safe distance, exasperates at last. The colors that at first bewitched will vex your eyes by their violence;—the creole life that appeared so simple, so gentle, will reveal dulnesses and discomforts undreamed of. You will ask yourself how much longer can you endure the prodigious light, and the furnace heat of blinding blue days, and the void misery of sleepless nights, and the curse of insects, and the sound of the mandibles of enormous roaches devouring the few books in your possession. You will grow weary of the grace of the palms, of the gemmy colors of the ever-clouded peaks, of the sight of the high woods made impenetrable by lianas and vines and serpents. You will weary even of the tepid sea, because to enjoy it as a swimmer you must rise and go out at hours while the morning air is still chill and heavy with miasma;—you will weary, above all, of tropic fruits, and feel that you would gladly pay a hundred francs for the momentary pleasure of biting into one rosy juicy Northern apple.

VI.

. . . BUT if you believe this disillusion perpetual,—if you fancy the old bewitchment has spent all its force upon you,—you do not know this Nature. She is not done with you yet: she has only torpefied your energies a little. Of your willingness to obey her, she takes no cognizance;—she ignores human purposes, knows only molecules and their combinations; and the blind blood in your veins,—thick with Northern heat and habit,—is still in dumb desperate rebellion against her.

Perhaps she will quell this revolt forever,—thus:—

One day, in the second hour of the afternoon, a few moments after leaving home, there will come to you a sensation such as you have never known before: a sudden weird fear of the light.

It seems to you that the blue sky-fire is burning down into your brain,—that the flare of the white pavements and yellow walls is piercing somehow into your life,—creating an unfamiliar mental confusion,—blurring out thought. . . . Is the whole world taking fire? . . . The flaming azure of the sea dazzles and pains like crucible-glow;—the green of the mornes flickers and blazes in some amazing way. . . . Then dizziness inexpressible: you grope with eyes shut first—afraid to open them again in that stupefying torrefaction,—moving automatically,—vaguely knowing you must get out of the flaring and flashing,—somewhere, anywhere away from the white wrath of the sun, and the green fire of the hills, and the monstrous color of the sea. . . . Then, remembering nothing, you find yourself in bed,—with an insupportable sense of weight at the back of the head,—a pulse beating furiously,—and a strange sharp pain at intervals stinging through your eyes. . . . And the pain grows, expands,—fills all the skull,—forces you to cry out,—replaces all other sensations except a weak consciousness, vanishing and recurring, that you are very sick, more sick than ever before in all your life.

*

. . . And with the tedious ebbing of the long fierce fever, all the heat seems to pass from your veins. You can no longer imagine, as before, that it would be delicious to die of cold;—you shiver even with all the windows closed;—you feel currents of air,—imperceptible to nerves in a natural condition,—which shock like a dash of cold water, whenever doors are opened and closed; the very moisture upon your forehead is icy. What you now wish for are stimulants and warmth. Your blood has been changed;—tropic Nature has been good to you: she is preparing you to dwell with her.

. . . Gradually, under the kind nursing of those colored people,—among whom, as a stranger, your lot will probably be cast,—you recover strength; and perhaps it will seem to you that the pain of lying a while in the Shadow of Death is more than compensated by this rare and touching experience of human goodness. How tirelessly watchful,—how naïvely sympathetic, —how utterly self-sacrificing these women-natures are! Patiently, through weeks of stifling days and sleepless nights,— cruelly unnatural to them, for their life is in the open air,—they struggle to save without one murmur of fatigue, without heed to their most ordinary physical wants, without a thought of recompense;—trusting to their own skill when the physician abandons hope,—climbing to the woods for herbs when medicines prove without avail. The dream of angels holds nothing sweeter than this reality of woman's tenderness.

And simultaneously with the return of force, you may wonder whether this sickness has not sharpened your senses in some extraordinary way,—especially hearing, sight, and smell. Once well enough to be removed without danger, you will be taken up into the mountains somewhere,—for change of air; and there it will seem to you, perhaps, that never before did you feel so acutely the pleasure of perfumes,—of color-tones,—of the timbre of voices. You have simply been acclimated. . . . And suddenly the old fascination of tropic Nature seizes you again,—more strongly than in the first days;—the *frisson* of delight returns; the joy of it thrills through all your blood,— making a great fulness at your heart as of unutterable desire to give thanks. . . .

VII.

. . . MY friend Felicien had come to the colony fresh from the region of the Vosges, with the muscles and energies of a mountaineer, and cheeks pink as a French country-girl's;—he had never seemed to me physically adapted for acclimation; and I feared much for him on hearing of his first serious illness. Then the news of his convalescence came to me as a grateful surprise. But I did not feel reassured by his appearance the first evening I called at the little house to which he had been removed, on the brow of a green height overlooking the town. I found him seated in a *berceuse* on the veranda. How wan he was, and how spectral his smile of welcome,—as he held out to me a hand that seemed all of bone!

. . . We chatted there a while. It had been one of those tropic days whose charm interpenetrates and blends with all the subtler life of sensation, and becomes a luminous part of it forever,—steeping all after-dreams of ideal peace in supernal glory of color,—transfiguring all fancies of the pure joy of being. Azure to the sea-line the sky had remained since morning; and the trade-wind, warm as a caress, never brought even one gauzy cloud to veil the naked beauty of the peaks.

And the sun was yellowing,—as only over the tropics he yellows to his death. Lilac tones slowly spread through sea and heaven from the west;—mornes facing the light began to take wondrous glowing color,—a tone of green so fiery that it looked as though all the rich sap of their woods were phosphorescing. Shadows blued;—far peaks took tinting that scarcely seemed of earth,—iridescent violets and purples interchanging through vapor of gold. . . . Such the colors of the *carangue*, when the beautiful tropic fish is turned in the light, and its gem-greens shift to rich azure and prism-purple.

Reclining in our chairs, we watched the strange splendor from the veranda of the little cottage,—saw the peaked land slowly steep itself in the aureate glow,—the changing color of the verdured mornes, and of the sweep of circling sea. Tiny birds, bosomed with fire, were shooting by in long curves, like embers flung by invisible hands. From far below, the murmur of the city rose to us,—a stormy hum. So motionless we remained that the green and gray lizards were putting out their heads from behind the columns of the veranda to stare at us,—as if wondering whether we were really alive. I turned my head suddenly to look at two queer butterflies; and all the lizards hid themselves again. *Papillon-lanmò,*—Death's butterflies,—these were called in the speech of the people: their broad wings were black like blackest velvet;—as they fluttered against the yellow light, they looked like silhouettes of butterflies. Always through my memory of that wondrous evening,—when I little thought I was seeing my friend's face for the last time,—there slowly passes the black palpitation of those wings. . . .

. . . I had been chatting with Felicien about various things which I thought might have a cheerful interest for him; and more than once I had been happy to see him smile. . . . But our converse waned. The ever-magnifying splendor before us had been mesmerizing our senses,—slowly overpowering our wills with the amazement of its beauty. Then, as the sun's disk —enormous,—blinding gold—touched the lilac flood, and the stupendous orange glow flamed up to the very zenith, we found ourselves awed at last into silence.

The orange in the west deepened into vermilion. Softly and very swiftly night rose like an indigo exhalation from the land,— filling the valleys, flooding the gorges, blackening the woods, leaving only the points of the peaks a while to catch the crimson glow. Forests and fields began to utter a rushing sound as of torrents, always deepening,—made up of the instrumentation and the voices of numberless little beings: clangings as of hammered iron, ringings as of dropping silver upon a stone, the dry bleatings of the *cabritt-bois,* and the chirruping of treefrogs; and the *ki-i-i-i-i-i* of crickets. Immense trembling sparks began to rise and fall among the shadows,—twinkling out and disappearing all mysteriously: these were the fire-flies awakening. Then about the branches of the *bois-canon* black shapes began to hover, which were not birds—shapes flitting processionally without any noise; each one in turn resting a moment as to nibble something at the end of a bough;—then yielding place to another, and circling away, to return again from the other side . . . the *guimbos,* the great bats.

But we were silent, with the emotion of sunset still upon us:

that ghostly emotion which is the transmitted experience of a race,—the sum of ancestral experiences innumerable,—the mingled joy and pain of a million years. . . . Suddenly a sweet voice pierced the stillness,—pleading:—

—"*Pa combiné, chè!—pa combiné conm ça!*" (Do not think, dear!—do not think like that!)

. . . Only less beautiful than the sunset she seemed, this slender half-breed, who had come all unperceived behind us, treading soundlessly with her slim bare feet. . . . "And you, Missié," she said to me, in a tone of gentle reproach;—"you are his friend! why do you let him think? It is thinking that will prevent him getting well."

Combiné in creole signifies to think intently, and therefore to be unhappy,—because, with this artless race, as with children, to think intensely about anything is possible only under great stress of suffering.

—"*Pa combiné,—non, chè*," she repeated, plaintively, stroking Felicien's hair. "It is thinking that makes us old. . . . And it is time to bid your friend good-night.". . .

—"She is so good," said Felicien, smiling to make her pleased;—"I could never tell you how good. But she does not understand. She believes I suffer if I am silent. She is contented only when she sees me laugh; and so she will tell me creole stories by the hour to keep me amused, as if I were a child.". . .

As he spoke she slipped an arm about his neck.

—"*Doudoux*," she persisted;—and her voice was a dove's coo,—"*Si ou ainmein moin, pa combiné—non!*"

And in her strange exotic beauty, her savage grace, her supple caress, the velvet witchery of her eyes,—it seemed to me that I beheld a something imaged, not of herself, nor of the moment only,—a something weirdly sensuous: the Spirit of tropic Nature made golden flesh, and murmuring to each lured wanderer:—"*If thou wouldst love me, do not think!*" . . .

Yé

A LMOST every night, just before bedtime, I hear some group of children in the street telling stories to each other. Stories, enigmas or *tim-tim*, and songs, and round games, are the joy of child-life here,—whether rich or poor. I am particularly fond of listening to the stories,—which seem to me the oddest stories I ever heard.

I succeeded in getting several dictated to me, so that I could write them;—others were written for me by creole friends, with better success. To obtain them in all their original simplicity and naïve humor of detail, one should be able to write them down in short-hand as fast as they are related: they lose greatly in the slow process of dictation. The simple mind of the native story-teller, child or adult, is seriously tried by the inevitable interruptions and restraints of the dictation method; —the reciter loses spirit, becomes soon weary, and purposely shortens the narrative to finish the task as soon as possible. It seems painful to such a one to repeat a phrase more than once, —at least in the same way; while frequent questioning may irritate the most good-natured in a degree that shows how painful to the untrained brain may be the exercise of memory and steady control of imagination required for continuous dictation. By patience, however, I succeeded in obtaining many curiosities of oral literature,—representing a group of stories which, whatever their primal origin, have been so changed by local thought and coloring as to form a distinctively Martinique folk-tale circle. Among them are several especially popular with the children of my neighborhood; and I notice that almost every narrator embellishes the original plot with details of his own, which he varies at pleasure.

I submit a free rendering of one of these tales,—the history of Yé and the Devil. The whole story of Yé would form a large book,—so numerous the list of his adventures; and this adventure seems to me the most characteristic of all. Yé is the most curious figure in Martinique folk-lore. Yé is the typical Bitaco, —or mountain negro of the lazy kind,—the country black whom city blacks love to poke fun at. As for the Devil of Martinique folk-lore, he resembles the *travailleur* at a distance; but when you get dangerously near him, you find that he has red eyes and red hair, and two little horns under his *chapeau-Bacouè*, and feet like an ape, and fire in his throat. *Y ka sam yon gouôs, gouôs macaque.* . . .

II.

Ça qui pa té connaitt Yé? . . . Who is there in all Martinique who never heard of Yé? Everybody used to know the old rascal. He had every fault under the sun;—he was the laziest negro in the whole island; he was the biggest glutton in the whole world. He had an amazing number* of children; and they were most of the time all half dead for hunger.

Well, one day Yé went out to the woods to look for something to eat. And he walked through the woods nearly all day, till he became ever so tired; but he could not find anything to eat. He was just going to give up the search, when he heard a queer crackling noise,—at no great distance. He went to see what it was,—hiding himself behind the big trees as he got nearer to it.

All at once he came to a little hollow in the woods, and saw a great fire burning there,—and he saw a Devil sitting beside the fire. The Devil was roasting a great heap of snails; and the sound Yé had heard was the crackling of the snail-shells. The Devil seemed to be very old;—he was sitting on the trunk of a bread-fruit tree; and Yé took a good long look at him. After Yé had watched him for a while, Yé found out that the old Devil was quite blind.

The Devil had a big calabash in his hand full of *feroce*,—that is to say, boiled salt codfish and manioc flour, with ever so many pimentos (*épi en pile piment*),—just what negroes like Yé are most fond of. And the Devil seemed to be very hungry; and the food was going so fast down his throat that it made Yé unhappy to see it disappearing. It made him so unhappy that he felt at last he could not resist the temptation to steal from the old blind Devil. He crept quite close up to the Devil without making any noise, and began to rob him. Every time the

---

*In the patois, "*yon rafale yche*,"—a "whirlwind of children."

Devil would lift his hand to his mouth, Yé would slip his own fingers into the calabash, and snatch a piece. The old Devil did not even look puzzled;—he did not seem to know anything; and Yé thought to himself that the old Devil was a great fool. He began to get more and more courage;—he took bigger and bigger handfuls out of the calabash;—he ate even faster than the Devil could eat. At last there was only one little bit left in the calabash. Yé put out his hand to take it,—and all of a sudden the Devil made a grab at Yé's hand and caught it! Yé was so frightened he could not even cry out, *Aïe-yaïe!* The Devil finished the last morsel, threw down the calabash, and said to Yé in a terrible voice:—"*Atò, saff!—ou c'est ta moin!*" (I've got you now, you glutton;—you belong to me!) Then he jumped on Yé's back, like a great ape, and twisted his legs round Yé's neck, and cried out:—

—"Carry me to your cabin,—and walk fast!"

. . . When Yé's poor children saw him coming, they wondered what their papa was carrying on his back. They thought it might be a sack of bread or vegetables or perhaps a *régime* of bananas,—for it was getting dark, and they could not see well. They laughed and showed their teeth and danced and screamed: "Here's papa coming with something to eat!—papa's coming with something to eat!" But when Yé had got near enough for them to see what he was carrying, they yelled and ran away to hide themselves. As for the poor mother, she could only hold up her two hands for horror.

When they got into the cabin the Devil pointed to a corner, and said to Yé:—"Put me down there!" Yé put him down. The Devil sat there in the corner and never moved or spoke all that evening and all that night. He seemed to be a very quiet Devil indeed. The children began to look at him.

But at breakfast-time, when the poor mother had managed to procure something for the children to eat,—just some bread-fruit and yams,—the old Devil suddenly rose up from his corner and muttered:—

—"*Manman mò!—papa mò!—toutt yche mò!*" (Mamma dead!—papa dead!—all the children dead!)

And he blew his breath on them, and they all fell down stiff as if they were dead—*raidi-cadave!* Then the Devil ate up everything there was on the table. When he was done, he filled the pots and dishes with dirt, and blew his breath again on Yé and all the family, and muttered:—

—"*Toutt moune lévé!*" (Everybody get up!)

Then they all got up. Then he pointed to all the plates and dishes full of dirt, and said to them:—*

—"*Gobe-moin ça!*"

And they had to gobble it all up, as he told them.

After that it was no use trying to eat anything. Every time anything was cooked, the Devil would do the same thing. It was thus the next day, and the next, and the day after, and so every day for a long, long time.

Yé did not know what to do; but his wife said she did. If she was only a man, she would soon get rid of that Devil. "Yé," she insisted, "go and see the Bon-Dié [the Good-God], and ask him what to do. I would go myself if I could; but women are not strong enough to climb the great morne."

So Yé started off very, very early one morning, before the peep of day, and began to climb the Montagne Pelée. He climbed and walked, and walked and climbed, until he got at last to the top of the Morne de la Croix.† Then he knocked at the sky as loud as he could till the Good-God put his head out of a cloud and asked him what he wanted:—

—"*Eh bien!—ça ou ni, Yé? ça ou lè?*"

When Yé had recounted his troubles, the Good-God said:—

—"*Pauv ma pauv!* I knew it all before you came, Yé. I can tell you what to do; but I am afraid it will be no use—you will never be able to do it! Your gluttony is going to be the ruin of you, poor Yé! Still, you can try. Now listen well to what I am going to tell you. First of all, you must not eat anything before you get home. Then when your wife has the children's dinner ready, and you see the Devil getting up, you must cry out:— '*Tam ni pou tam ni bé!*' Then the Devil will drop down dead. Don't forget not to eat anything—*ou tanne?*" . . .

Yé promised to remember all he was told, and not to eat

---

*In the original:—"Y té ka monté assous tabe-là, épi y té ka fai caca adans toutt plats-à, adans toutt zassiett-là."

†A peaklet rising above the verge of the ancient crater now filled with water.

anything on his way down;—then he said good-bye to the
Bon-Dié (*bien conm y faut*), and started. All the way he kept
repeating the words the Good-God had told him: "*Tam ni
pou tam ni bé!—tam ni pou tam ni bé!*"—over and over again.

But before reaching home he had to cross a little stream;
and on both banks he saw wild guava-bushes growing, with
plenty of sour guavas upon them;—for it was not yet time for
guavas to be ripe. Poor Yé was hungry! He did all he could to
resist the temptation, but it proved too much for him. He
broke all his promises to the Bon-Dié: he ate and ate and ate
till there were no more guavas left,—and then he began to eat
zicaques and green plums, and all sorts of nasty sour things, till
he could not eat any more.

By the time he got to the cabin his teeth were so on edge
that he could scarcely speak distinctly enough to tell his wife to
get the supper ready.

And so while everybody was happy, thinking that they were
going to be freed from their trouble, Yé was really in no condition to do anything. The moment the supper was ready, the
Devil got up from his corner as usual, and approached the
table. Then Yé tried to speak; but his teeth were so on edge
that instead of saying,—"*Tam ni pou tam ni bé*," he could only
stammer out:—

—"*Anni toqué Diabe-là cagnan.*"

This had no effect on the Devil at all: he seemed to be used
to it! He blew his breath on them all, sent them to sleep, ate
up all the supper, filled the empty dishes with filth, awoke Yé
and his family, and ordered them as usual:—

—"*Gobe-moin ça!*" And they had to gobble it up,—every bit
of it.

The family nearly died of hunger and disgust. Twice more
Yé climbed the Montagne Pelée; twice more he climbed the
Morne de la Croix; twice more he disturbed the poor Bon-
Dié, all for nothing!—since each time on his way down he
would fill his paunch with all sorts of nasty sour things, so that
he could not speak right. The Devil remained in the house
night and day;—the poor mother threw herself down on the
ground, and pulled out her hair,—so unhappy she was!

But luckily for the poor woman, she had one child as cunning as a rat,—* a boy called Ti Fonté (Little Impudent), who bore his name well. When he saw his mother crying so much, he said to her:—

—"Mamma, send papa just once more to see the Good-God: I know something to do!"

The mother knew how cunning her boy was: she felt sure he meant something by his words;—she sent old Yé for the last time to see the Bon-Dié.

Yé used always to wear one of those big long coats they call *lavalasses*;—whether it was hot or cool, wet or dry, he never went out without it. There were two very big pockets in it— one on each side. When Ti Fonté saw his father getting ready to go, he jumped *floup!* into one of the pockets and hid himself there. Yé climbed all the way to the top of the Morne de la Croix without suspecting anything. When he got there the little boy put one of his ears out of Yé's pocket,—so as to hear everything the Good-God would say.

This time he was very angry,—the Bon-Dié: he spoke very crossly; he scolded Yé a great deal. But he was so kind for all that,—he was so generous to good-for-nothing Yé, that he took the pains to repeat the words over and over again for him:—"*Tam ni pou tam ni bé.*" . . . And this time the Bon-Dié was not talking to no purpose: there was somebody there well able to remember what he said. Ti Fonté made the most of his chance;—he sharpened that little tongue of his; he thought of his mamma and all his little brothers and sisters dying of hunger down below. As for his father, Yé did as he had done before—stuffed himself with all the green fruit he could find.

The moment Yé got home and took off his coat, Ti Fonté jumped out, *plapp!*—and ran to his mamma, and whispered:—

—"Mamma, get ready a nice, big dinner!—we are going to have it all to ourselves to-day: the Good-God didn't talk for nothing,—I heard every word he said!"

Then the mother got ready a nice *calalou-crabe*, a *ton-ton-banane*, a *matété-cirique*,—several calabashes of *cousscaye*, two *régimes-figues* (bunches of small bananas),—in short, a very

---

*The great field-rat of Martinique is, in Martinique folk-lore, the symbol of all cunning, and probably merits its reputation.

fine dinner indeed, with a *chopine* of tafia to wash it all well down.

The Devil felt as sure of himself that day as he had always felt, and got up the moment everything was ready. But Ti Fonté got up too, and yelled out just as loud as he could:—

—"*Tam ni pou tam ni bé!*"

At once the Devil gave a scream so loud that it could be heard right down to the bottom of hell,—and he fell dead.

Meanwhile, Yé, like the old fool he was, kept trying to say what the Bon-Dié had told him, and could only mumble:—

—"*Anni toqué Diabe-là cagnan!*"

He would never have been able to do anything;—and his wife had a great mind just to send him to bed at once, instead of letting him sit down to eat all those nice things. But she was a kind-hearted soul; and so she let Yé stay and eat with the children, though he did not deserve it. And they all ate and ate, and kept on eating and filling themselves until daybreak— *pauv piti!*

But during this time the Devil had begun to smell badly, and he had become swollen so big that Yé found he could not move him. Still, they knew they must get him out of the way somehow. The children had eaten so much that they were all full of strength—*yo té plein lafòce*; and Yé got a rope and tied one end round the Devil's foot; and then he and the children—all pulling together—managed to drag the Devil out of the cabin and into the bushes, where they left him just like a dead dog. They all felt themselves very happy to be rid of that old Devil.

But some days after old good-for-nothing Yé went off to hunt for birds. He had a whole lot of arrows with him. He suddenly remembered the Devil, and thought he would like to take one more look at him. And he did.

Fouinq! what a sight! The Devil's belly had swelled up like a morne: it was yellow and blue and green,—looked as if it was going to burst. And Yé, like the old fool he always was, shot an arrow up in the air, so that it fell down and stuck into the Devil's belly. Then he wanted to get the arrow, and he climbed up on the Devil, and pulled and pulled till he got the arrow out. Then he put the point of the arrow to his nose,—just to see what sort of a smell dead Devils had.

The moment he did that, his nose swelled up as big as the refinery-pot of a sugar-plantation.

Yé could scarcely walk for the weight of his nose; but he had to go and see the Bon-Dié again. The Bon-Dié said to him:—

—"Ah! Yé, my poor Yé, you will live and die a fool!—you are certainly the biggest fool in the whole world! . . . Still, I must try to do something for you;—I'll help you anyhow to get rid of that nose! . . . I'll tell you how to do it. To-morrow morning, very early, get up and take a big *taya* [whip], and beat all the bushes well, and drive all the birds to the Roche de la Caravelle. Then you must tell them that I, the Bon-Dié, want them to take off their bills and feathers, and take a good bath in the sea. While they are bathing, you can choose a nose for yourself out of the heap of bills there."

Poor Yé did just as the Good-God told him; and while the birds were bathing, he picked out a nose for himself from the heap of beaks,—and left his own refinery-pot in its place.

The nose he took was the nose of the *coulivicou.** And that is why the *coulivicou* always looks so much ashamed of himself even to this day.

III.

. . . POOR Yé!—you still live for me only too vividly outside of those strange folk-tales of eating and of drinking which so cruelly reveal the long slave-hunger of your race. For I have seen you cutting cane on peak slopes above the clouds;—I have seen you climbing from plantation to plantation with your cutlass in your hand, watching for snakes as you wander to look for work, when starvation forces you to obey a master, though born with the resentment of centuries against all

---

*The *coulivicou,* or "Colin Vicou," is a Martinique bird with a long meagre body, and an enormous bill. It has a very tristful and taciturn expression. . . . *Maig conm yon coulivicou,* "thin as a coulivicou," is a popular comparison for the appearance of anybody much reduced by sickness.

masters;—I have seen you prefer to carry two hundred-weight of bananas twenty miles to market, rather than labor in the fields;—I have seen you ascending through serpent-swarming woods to some dead crater to find a cabbage-palm,—and always hungry,—and always shiftless! And you are still a great fool, poor Yé!—and you have still your swarm of children,—your *rafale yche*;—and they are famished; for you have taken into your *ajoupa* a Devil who devours even more than you can earn,—even your heart, and your splendid muscles, and your poor artless brain,—the Devil Tafia! . . . And there is no Bon-Dié to help you rid yourself of him now: for the only Bon-Dié you ever really had, your old creole master, cannot care for you any more, and you cannot care for yourself. Mercilessly moral, the will of this enlightened century has abolished forever that patriarchal power which brought you up strong and healthy on scanty fare, and scourged you into its own idea of righteousness, yet kept you innocent as a child of the law of the struggle for life. But you feel that law now;—you are a citizen of the Republic! you are free to vote, and free to work, and free to starve if you prefer it, and free to do evil and suffer for it;—and this new knowledge stupefies you so that you have almost forgotten how to laugh!

Lys

IT is only half-past four o'clock: there is the faintest blue light of beginning day,—and little Victoire already stands at the bedside with my wakening cup of hot black fragrant coffee. What! so early? . . . Then with a sudden heart-start I remember this is my last West Indian morning. And the child—her large timid eyes all gently luminous—is pressing something into my hand.

Two vanilla beans wrapped in a morsel of banana-leaf,—her poor little farewell gift! . . .

Other trifling souvenirs are already packed away. Almost everybody that knows me has given me something. Manm-Robert brought me a tiny packet of orange-seeds,—seeds of a "gift-orange": so long as I can keep these in my vest-pocket I will never be without money. Cyrillia brought me a package of *bouts*, and a pretty box of French matches, warranted inextinguishable by wind. Azaline, the blanchisseuse, sent me a little pocket looking-glass. Cerbonnie, the *màchanne*, left a little cup of guava jelly for me last night. Mimi—dear child!—brought me a little paper dog! It is her best toy; but those gentle black eyes would stream with tears if I dared to refuse it. . . . Oh, Mimi! what am I to do with a little paper dog? And what am I to do with the chocolate-sticks and the cocoanuts and all the sugar-cane and all the cinnamon-apples? . . .

II.

. . . TWENTY minutes past five by the clock of the Bourse. The hill shadows are shrinking back from the shore;—the long wharves reach out yellow into the sun;—the tamarinds of the Place Bertin, and the pharos for half its height, and the red-tiled roofs along the bay are catching the glow. Then, over the light-house—on the outermost line depending from the southern yardarm of the semaphore—a big black ball suddenly runs up like a spider climbing its own thread. . . . *Steamer from the South!* The packet has been sighted. And I have not yet been able to pack away into a specially purchased wooden box all the fruits and vegetable curiosities and odd little presents sent to me. If Radice the boatman had not come to help me, I should never be able to get ready; for the work of packing is being continually interrupted by friends and acquaintances coming to say good-bye. Manm-Robert brings to see me a pretty young girl—very fair, with a violet foulard twisted about her blonde head. It is little Basilique, who is going to make her *pouémiè communion*. So I kiss her, according to the old colonial custom, once on each downy cheek;—and she is to pray to *Notre Dame du Bon Port* that the ship shall bear me safely to far-away New York.

And even then the steamer's cannon-call shakes over the town and into the hills behind us, which answer with all the thunder of their phantom artillery.

III.

. . . THERE is a young white lady, accompanied by an aged negress, already waiting on the south wharf for the boat;—evidently she is to be one of my fellow-passengers. Quite a pleasing presence: slight graceful figure,—a face not precisely pretty, but delicate and sensitive, with the odd charm of violet eyes under black eyebrows. . . .

A friend who comes to see me off tells me all about her. Mademoiselle Lys is going to New York to be a governess,—to leave her native island forever. A story sad enough, though not more so than that of many a gentle creole girl. And she is going all alone; for I see her bidding good-bye to old Titine,—kissing her. "*Adié encò, chè;—Bon-Dié ké béni ou!*" sobs the poor servant, with tears streaming down her kind black face. She takes off her blue shoulder-kerchief, and waves it as the boat recedes from the wooden steps.

. . . Fifteen minutes later, Mademoiselle and I find ourselves under the awnings shading the saloon-deck of the *Guadeloupe*. There are at least fifty passengers,—many resting in chairs, lazy-looking Demerara chairs with arm-supports immensely lengthened so as to form rests for the lower limbs. Overhead, suspended from the awning frames, are two tin cages containing parrots;—and I see two little greenish monkeys, no bigger than squirrels, tied to the wheel-hatch,—two *sakiwinkis.* These are from the forests of British Guiana. They keep up a continual thin sharp twittering, like birds,—all the while circling, ascending, descending, retreating or advancing to the limit of the little ropes attaching them to the hatch.

The *Guadeloupe* has seven hundred packages to deliver at St. Pierre: we have ample time,—Mademoiselle Violet-Eyes and I,—to take one last look at the "Pays des Revenants."

I wonder what her thoughts are, feeling a singular sympathy for her,—for I am in that sympathetic mood which the natural emotion of leaving places and persons one has become fond of, is apt to inspire. And now at the moment of my going,—when I seem to understand as never before the beauty of that tropic Nature, and the simple charm of the life to which I am bidding farewell,—the question comes to me: "Does she not love it all as I do,—nay, even much more, because of that in her own existence which belongs to it?" But as a child of the land, she has seen no other skies,—fancies, perhaps, there may be brighter ones. . . .

. . . Nowhere on this earth, Violet-Eyes!—nowhere beneath this sun! . . . Oh! the dawnless glory of tropic morning!—the single sudden leap of the giant light over the purpling of a hundred peaks,—over the surging of the mornes! And the early breezes from the hills,—all cool out of the sleep of the forests, and heavy with vegetal odors thick, sappy, savage-sweet!—and the wild high winds that run ruffling and crumpling through the cane of the mountain slopes in storms of papery sound!—

And the mighty dreaming of the woods,—green-drenched with silent pouring of creepers,—dashed with the lilac and yellow and rosy foam of liana flowers!—

And the eternal azure apparition of the all-circling sea,—that as you mount the heights ever appears to rise perpendicularly behind you,—that seems, as you descend, to sink and flatten before you!—

And the violet velvet distances of evening;—and the swaying of palms against the orange-burning,—when all the heaven seems filled with vapors of a molten sun! . . .

IV.

How beautiful the mornes and azure-shadowed hollows in the jewel clearness of this perfect morning! Even Pelée wears only her very lightest head-dress of gauze; and all the wrinklings of her green robe take unfamiliar tenderness of tint from the early sun. All the quaint peaking of the colored town—sprinkling the sweep of blue bay with red and yellow and white-of-cream— takes a sharpness in this limpid light as if seen through a dia-mond lens; and there above the living green of the familiar hills I can see even the faces of the statues—the black Christ on his white cross, and the White Lady of the Morne d'Orange— among upcurving palms. . . . It is all as though the island were donning its utmost possible loveliness, exerting all its witchery,—seeking by supremest charm to win back and hold its wandering child,—Violet-Eyes over there! . . . She is looking too.

I wonder if she sees the great palms of the Voie du Parnasse, —curving far away as to bid us adieu, like beautiful bending women. I wonder if they are not trying to say something to her; and I try myself to fancy what that something is:—

—"Child, wilt thou indeed abandon all who love thee! . . . Listen!—'tis a dim grey land thou goest unto,—a land of bitter winds,—a land of strange gods,—a land of hardness and bar-renness, where even Nature may not live through half the cy-cling of the year! Thou wilt never see us there. . . . And there, when thou shalt sleep thy long sleep, child, that land will have no power to lift thee up;—vast weight of stone will press thee down forever;—until the heavens be no more thou shalt not awake! . . . But here, darling, our loving roots would seek for thee, would find thee: thou shouldst live again!—we lift, like Aztec priests, the blood of hearts to the Sun!" . . .

V.

. . . It is very hot. . . . I hold in my hand a Japanese paper-fan with a design upon it of the simplest sort: one jointed green bamboo, with a single spurt of sharp leaves, cutting across a pale blue murky double streak that means the horizon above a sea. That is all. Trivial to my Northern friends this design might seem; but to me it causes a pleasure bordering on pain. . . . I know so well what the artist means; and they could not know, unless they had seen bamboos,—and bamboos peculiarly situated. As I look at this fan I know myself descending the Morne Parnasse by the steep winding road; I have the sense of windy heights behind me, and forest on either hand, and before me the blended azure of sky and sea with one bamboo-spray swaying across it at the level of my eyes. Nor is this all;—I have the every sensation of the very moment,—the vegetal odors, the mighty tropic light, the warmth, the intensity of irreproducible color. . . . Beyond a doubt, the artist who dashed the design on this fan with his miraculous brush must have had a nearly similar experience to that of which the memory is thus aroused in me, but which I cannot communicate to others.

. . . And it seems to me now that all which I have tried to write about the *Pays des Revenants* can only be for others, who have never beheld it,—vague like the design upon this fan.

VI.

Brrrrrrrrrr! . . . The steam-winch is lifting the anchor; and the *Guadeloupe* trembles through every plank as the iron torrent of her chain-cable rumbles through the hawse-holes. . . . At last the quivering ceases;—there is a moment's silence; and Violet-Eyes seems trying to catch a last glimpse of her faithful *bonne* among the ever-thickening crowd upon the quay. . . . Ah! there she is—waving her foulard. Mademoiselle Lys is waving a handkerchief in reply. . . .

Suddenly the shock of the farewell gun shakes heavily through our hearts, and over the bay,—where the tall mornes catch the flapping thunder, and buffet it through all their circle in tremendous mockery. Then there is a great whirling and whispering of whitened water behind the steamer—another,— another; and the whirl becomes a foaming stream: the mighty propeller is playing! . . . All the blue harbor swings slowly round;—and the green limbs of the land are pushed out further on the left, shrink back upon the right;—and the mountains are moving their shoulders. And then the many-tinted façades,—and the tamarinds of the Place Bertin,—and the

Basse-terre, St. Kitt's.

light-house,—and the long wharves with their throng of turbaned women,—and the cathedral towers,—and the fair
palms,—and the statues of the hills,—all veer, change place,
and begin to float away . . . steadily, very swiftly.

Farewell, fair city,—sun-kissed city,—many-fountained city!
—dear yellow-glimmering streets,—white pavements learned
by heart,—and faces ever looked for,—and voices ever loved!
Farewell, white towers with your golden-throated bells!—
farewell, green steeps, bathed in the light of summer everlasting!—craters with your coronets of forest!—bright mountain
paths upwinding 'neath pomp of fern and angelin and feathery
bamboo!—and gracious palms that drowse above the dead!
Farewell, soft-shadowing majesty of valleys unfolding to the
sun,—green golden cane-fields ripening to the sea! . . .

. . . The town vanishes. The island slowly becomes a green
silhouette. So might Columbus first have seen it from the deck
of his caravel,—nearly four hundred years ago. At this distance
there are no more signs of life upon it than when it first became
visible to his eyes: yet there are cities there,—and toiling,—and
suffering,—and gentle hearts that knew me. . . . Now it is
turning blue,—the beautiful shape!—becoming a dream. . . .

VII.

AND Dominica draws nearer,—sharply massing her hills against the vast light in purple nodes and gibbosities and denticulations. Closer and closer it comes, until the green of its heights breaks through the purple here and there,—in flashings and ribbings of color. Then it remains as if motionless a while;—then the green lights go out again,—and all the shape begins to recede sideward towards the south.

. . . And what had appeared a pearl-grey cloud in the north slowly reveals itself as another island of mountains,—hunched and horned and mammiform: Guadeloupe begins to show her double profile. But Martinique is still visible;—Pelée still peers high over the rim of the south. . . . Day wanes;—the shadow of the ship lengthens over the flower-blue water. Pelée changes aspect at last,—turns pale as a ghost,—but will not fade away. . . .

. . . The sun begins to sink as he always sinks to his death in the tropics,—swiftly,—too swiftly!—and the glory of him makes golden all the hollow west,—and bronzes all the flickering wave-backs. But still the gracious phantom of the island will not go,—softly haunting us through the splendid haze. And always the tropic wind blows soft and warm;—there is an indescribable caress in it! Perhaps some such breeze, blowing from Indian waters, might have inspired that prophecy of Islam concerning the Wind of the Last Day,—that "Yellow Wind, softer than silk, balmier than musk,"—which is to sweep the spirits of the just to God in the great Winnowing of Souls. . . .

Then into the indigo night vanishes forever from my eyes the ghost of Pelée; and the moon swings up,—a young and lazy moon, drowsing upon her back, as in a hammock. . . . Yet a few nights more, and we shall see this slim young moon erect,—gliding upright on her way,—coldly beautiful like a fair Northern girl.

VIII.

AND ever through tepid nights and azure days the *Guadeloupe* rushes on,—her wake a river of snow beneath the sun, a torrent of fire beneath the stars,—steaming straight for the North.

Under the peaking of Montserrat we steam,—beautiful Montserrat, all softly wrinkled like a robe of greenest velvet fallen from the waist!—breaking the pretty sleep of Plymouth town behind its screen of palms . . . young palms, slender and full of grace as creole children are;—

And by tall Nevis, with her trinity of dead craters purpling through ocean-haze;—by clouded St. Christopher's mountain-giant;—past ghostly St. Martin's, far-floating in fog of gold, like some dream of the Saint's own Second Summer;—

Past low Antigua's vast blue harbor,—shark-haunted, bounded about by huddling of little hills, blue and green;—

Past Santa Cruz, the "Island of the Holy Cross,"—all radiant with verdure though wellnigh woodless,—nakedly beautiful in the tropic light as a perfect statue;—

Past the long cerulean reaching and heaping of Porto Rico on the left, and past hopeless St. Thomas on the right,—old St. Thomas, watching the going and the coming of the commerce that long since abandoned her port,—watching the ships once humbly solicitous for patronage now turning away to the Spanish rival, like ingrates forsaking a ruined patrician;—

And the vapory Vision of St. John;—and the grey ghost of Tortola,—and further, fainter, still more weirdly dim, the aureate phantom of Virgin Gorda.

IX.

THEN only the enormous double-vision of sky and sea.

The sky: a cupola of blinding blue, shading down and paling into spectral green at the rim of the world,—and all fleckless, save at evening. Then, with sunset, comes a light gold-drift of little feathery cloudlets into the West,—stippling it as with a snow of fire.

The sea: no flower-tint may now make any comparison for the splendor of its lucent color. It has shifted its hue;—for we have entered into the Azure Stream: it has more than the magnificence of burning cyanogen. . . .

But, at night, the Cross of the South appears no more. And other changes come, as day succeeds to day,—a lengthening of the hours of light, a longer lingering of the after-glow,—a cooling of the wind. Each morning the air seems a little cooler, a little rarer;—each noon the sky looks a little paler, a little further away—always heightening, yet also more shadowy, as if its color, receding, were dimmed by distance,—were coming more faintly down from vaster altitudes.

. . . Mademoiselle is petted like a child by the lady passengers. And every man seems anxious to aid in making her voyage a pleasant one. For much of which, I think, she may thank her eyes!

X.

A DIM morning and chill;—blank sky and sunless waters: the sombre heaven of the North with colorless horizon rounding in a blind grey sea. . . . What a sudden weight comes to the heart with the touch of the cold mist, with the spectral melancholy of the dawn!—and then what foolish though irrepressible yearning for the vanished azure left behind!

. . . The little monkeys twitter plaintively, trembling in the chilly air. The parrots have nothing to say: they look benumbed, and sit on their perches with eyes closed.

. . . A vagueness begins to shape itself along the verge of the sea, far to port: that long heavy clouding which indicates the approach of land. And from it now floats to us something ghostly and frigid which makes the light filmy and the sea shadowy as a flood of dreams,—the fog of the Jersey coast.

At once the engines slacken their respiration. The *Guadeloupe* begins to utter her steam-cry of warning,—regularly at intervals of two minutes,—for she is now in the track of all the ocean vessels. And from far away we can hear a heavy knelling,—the booming of some great fog-bell.

. . . All in a white twilight. The place of the horizon has vanished;—we seem ringed in by a wall of smoke. . . . Out of this vapory emptiness—very suddenly—an enormous steamer rushes, towering like a hill—passes so close that we can see faces, and disappears again, leaving the sea heaving and frothing behind her.

*

. . . As I lean over the rail to watch the swirling of the wake, I feel something pulling at my sleeve: a hand,—a tiny black hand,—the hand of a *sakiwinki*. One of the little monkeys, straining to the full length of his string, is making this dumb appeal for human sympathy;—the bird-black eyes of both are fixed upon me with the oddest look of pleading. Poor little tropical exiles! I stoop to caress them; but regret the impulse a moment later: they utter such beseeching cries when I find myself obliged to leave them again alone! . . .

. . . Hour after hour the *Guadeloupe* glides on through the white gloom,—cautiously, as if feeling her way; always sounding her whistle, ringing her bells, until at last some brown-winged bark comes flitting to us out of the mist, bearing a pilot. . . . How strange it must all seem to Mademoiselle who stands so silent there at the rail!—how weird this veiled world must appear to her, after the sapphire light of her own West Indian sky, and the great lazulite splendor of her own tropic sea!

But a wind comes!—it strengthens,—begins to blow very cold. The mists thin before its blowing; and the wan blank sky is all revealed again with livid horizon around the heaving of the iron-grey sea.

. . . Thou dim and lofty heaven of the North,—grey sky of Odin,—bitter thy winds and spectral all thy colors!—they that dwell beneath thee know not the glory of Eternal Summer's green,—the azure splendor of southern day!—but thine are the lightnings of Thought illuminating for human eyes the interspaces between sun and sun. Thine the generations of might,—the strivers, the battlers,—the men who make Nature tame!—thine the domain of inspiration and achievement,—the larger heroisms, the vaster labors that endure, the higher knowledge, and all the witchcrafts of science! . . .

But in each one of us there lives a mysterious Something which is Self, yet also infinitely more than Self,—incomprehensibly multiple,—the complex total of sensations, impulses, timidities belonging to the unknown past. And the lips of the little stranger from the tropics have become all white, because that Something within her,—ghostly bequest from generations who loved the light and rest and wondrous color of a more radiant world,—now shrinks all back about her girl's heart with fear of this pale grim North. . . . And lo!—opening mile-wide in dream-grey majesty before us,—reaching away, through measureless mazes of masting, into remotenesses all vapor-veiled,—the mighty perspective of New York harbor! . . .

Thou knowest it not, this gloom about us, little maiden;— 'tis only a magical dusk we are entering,—only that mystic dimness in which miracles must be wrought! . . . See the marvellous shapes uprising,—the immensities, the astonishments! And other greater wonders thou wilt behold in a little while, when we shall have become lost to each other forever in the surging of the City's million-hearted life! . . . 'Tis all shadow here, thou sayest?—Ay, 'tis twilight, verily, by contrast with that glory out of which thou camest, Lys—twilight only,—but the Twilight of the Gods! . . . *Adié, chè!—Bon-Dié ké béni ou!* . . .

SOME CREOLE MELODIES

MORE than a hundred years ago Thibault de Chanvallon expressed his astonishment at the charm and wonderful sense of musical rhythm characterizing the slave-songs and slave-dances of Martinique. The rhythmical sense of the negroes especially impressed him. "I have seen," he writes, "seven or eight hundred negroes accompanying a wedding-party to the sound of song: they would all leap up in the air and come down together;—the movement was so exact and general that the noise of their fall made but a single sound."

An almost similar phenomenon may be witnessed any Carnival season in St. Pierre,—while the Devil makes his nightly round, followed by many hundred boys clapping hands and leaping in chorus. It may also be observed in the popular malicious custom of the *pillard*, or, in creole, *piyà*. Some person whom it is deemed justifiable and safe to annoy, may suddenly find himself followed in the street by a singing chorus of several hundred, all clapping hands and dancing or running in perfect time, so that all the bare feet strike the ground together. Or the *pillard-chorus* may even take up its position before the residence of the party disliked, and then proceed with its performance. An example of such a *pillard* is given further on, in the song entitled *Loéma tombé*. The improvisation by a single voice begins the *pillard*,—which in English might be rendered as follows:—

(*Single voice*)	You little children there!—you who were by the river-side!
	Tell me truly this:—Did you see Loéma fall?
	Tell me truly this—
(*Chorus, opening*)	Did you see Loéma fall?
(*Single voice*)	Tell me truly this—
(*Chorus*)	Did you see Loéma fall?
(*Single voice, more rapidly*)	Tell me truly this—
(*Chorus, more quickly*)	Loéma fall!
(*Single voice*)	Tell me truly this—

(*Chorus*)   Loéma fall!
(*Single voice*)   Tell me truly this—
(*Chorus, always more quickly, and more loudly, all the hands
clapping together like a fire of musketry*) Loéma fall! etc.

The same rhythmic element characterizes many of the games
and round dances of Martinique children;—but, as a rule, I
think it is perceptible that the sense of time is less developed in
the colored children than in the black.

The other melodies which are given as specimens of Martinique music show less of the African element,—the nearest
approach to it being in *Tant sirop*; but all are probably creations of the mixed race. *Marie-Clémence* is a Carnival satire
composed not more than four years ago. *To-to-to* is very old—
dates back, perhaps, to the time of the *belles-affranchies*. It is
seldom sung now except by survivors of the old régime: the
sincerity and tenderness of the emotion that inspired it—the
old sweetness of heart and simplicity of thought,—are passing
forever away.

To my friend, Henry Edward Krehbiel, the musical lecturer
and critic,—at once historian and folklorist in the study of
race-music,—and to Mr. Frank van der Stucken, the New York
musical composer, I owe the preparation of these four melodies
for voice and piano-forte. The arrangements of *To-to-to* and
Loéma tombé are Mr. Van der Stucken's.

"TO-TO-TO."

(Creole words.)

MARIE-CLÉMENCE.
(*Creole words.*)

Ma - rie Clémence maudi, La - mo-ri fritt li

mau-di, Collier-choux li mau-di, Toutt baggaïe li mau-di.

Toutt baggaïe li mau-di. Aïe !... La-gué moin, lagué moin,

la-gué moin !   Moin ké né - yé cò moin, Moin ké né- yé

cò   moin,   En - ba gouôs pile ouôche là.

TANT SIROP EST DOUX
(*Negro-French.*)

Tant si - rop est doux, Ma- de - lein - e ! Tant si - rop - là

doux!   doux! Ne fai pas tant de bruit, Ma-de-leine, Ne

fai pas tant de bruit, Ma-de-leine, La mai - son n'est pas à

nous, Ma - de-leine, La mai - son n'est pas à   nous.

LOÉMA TOMBÉ.

(*Creole words.*)

Allegro moderato.

Cé   ti manmaille-là! Zautt té bô - la - ri - vié,— Ou'a di moin

conm' ça: Si ouè Lo - é - ma tom - bé! Ou'a di moin conm' ça:

Ref. continued ad lib.

growing more and more rapid.

Lo - é - ma tom - bé! Ou'a di moin conm' ça: Lo - é - ma tom-

bé! Ou'a di moin conm' ça: Lo - é - ma tom - bé!

YOUMA

The Story of a West-Indian Slave

To my friend
JOSEPH S. TUNISON

Youma

THE *da*, during old colonial days, often held high rank in rich Martinique households. The *da* was usually a Creole negress,—more often, at all events, of the darker than of the lighter hue,—more commonly a *capresse* than a *mestive*; but in her particular case the prejudice of color did not exist. The *da* was a slave; but no freedwoman, however beautiful or cultivated, could enjoy social privileges equal to those of certain *das*. The *da* was respected and loved as a mother: she was at once a foster-mother and nurse. For the Creole child had two mothers: the aristocratic white mother who gave him birth; the dark bond-mother who gave him all care,—who nursed him, bathed him, taught him to speak the soft and musical speech of slaves, took him out in her arms to show him the beautiful tropic world, told him wonderful folk-stories of evenings, lulled him to sleep, attended to his every possible want by day or by night. It was not to be wondered at that during infancy the *da* should have been loved more than the white mother: when there was any marked preference it was nearly always in the *da's* favor. The child was much more with her than with his real mother: she alone satisfied all his little needs; he found her more indulgent, more patient, perhaps even more caressing, than the other. The *da* was herself at heart a child, speaking a child-language, finding pleasure in childish things,—artless, playful, affectionate; she comprehended the thoughts, the impulses, the pains, the faults of the little one as the white mother could not always have done: she knew intuitively how to soothe him upon all occasions, how to amuse him, how to excite and caress his imagination;—there was absolute harmony between their natures,—a happy community of likes and dislikes,—a perfect sympathy in the animal joy of being. Later on, when the child had become old enough to receive his first lessons from a tutor or governess, to learn to speak French, the affection for the *da* and the affection for the mother began to differentiate in accordance with mental expansion; but, though the mother might be more loved, the *da* was not less cherished than before. The love of the nurse lasted through life; and the relation of the *da* to the family seldom ceased,—except in those cruel instances where she was only "hired" from another slave-holder.

In many cases the family *da* had been born upon the estate: —under the same roof she might serve as nurse for two generations. More often it would happen, that as the family multiplied and divided,—as the sons and daughters, growing up, became themselves fathers and mothers,—she would care for all their children in turn. She ended her days with her masters: although she was legally property, it would have been deemed almost an infamy to sell her. When freed by gratitude—*pour services rendus*,—she did not care to make a home of her own: freedom had small value for her except in the event of her outliving those to whom she was attached. She had children of her own, for whom she would have desired freedom rather than for herself, and for whom she might rightfully ask it, since she had sacrificed so much of her own maternal pleasures for the sake of others' children. She was unselfish and devoted to a degree which compelled gratitude even from natures of iron;— she represented the highest development of natural goodness possible in a race mentally undeveloped, kept half savage by subservience, but physically refined in a remarkable manner by climate, environment, and all those mysterious influences which form the characteristics of Creole peoples.

The *da* is already of the past. Her special type was a product of slavery, largely created by selection: the one creation of slavery perhaps not unworthy of regret,—one strange flowering amid all the rank dark growths of that bitter soil. The atmosphere of freedom was not essentially fatal to the permanence of the type; but with freedom came many unlooked-for changes: a great industrial depression due to foreign rivalry and new discoveries,—a commercial crisis, in brief,—accompanied the establishment of universal suffrage, the subordination of the white element to the black by a political upheaval, and the total disintegration of the old social structure. The transformation was too violent for good results; the abuse of political powers too speedily and indiscriminately conferred, intensified the old hates and evolved new ones: the races drew forever apart when they needed each other most. Then the increasing difficulty of existence quickly developed egotism: generosity and prosper-

ity departed together; Creole life shrank into narrower channels; and the character of all classes visibly hardened under
pressure of necessities previously unknown.

    . . . . There are really no more *das*: there are now only *gar-
diennes* or *bonnes*—nurses who can seldom keep a place more
than three months. The loyalty and simplicity of the *da* have
become traditions: vain to seek for any parallels among the
new generation of salaried domestics! But of those who used
to be *das*, several survive, and still bear the name, which, once
conferred, is retained through life as an honorific title. Some
are yet to be seen in Saint Pierre. . . . There is a very fine
house on the seaward side of the Grande Rue, for example, on
whose marble door-step one may be observed almost every fine
morning,—a very aged negress, who loves the sun. That is Da
Siyotte. Gentlemen of wealth and high position, merchants and
judges, salute her as they pass by. You might see the men of the
family,—the gray old father and his handsome sons,—pause to
chat a moment with her before going to their offices. You
might see young ladies bend down and kiss her before taking
their places in the carriage for a drive. You would find,—could
you linger long enough,—that all visitors greet her with a smile,
and a kindly query:—"*Coument ou yé, Da Siyotte?*" . . . .
Woe to the stranger who should speak rudely to her, under the
impression that she is only a servant! . . . . "*Si elle n'est qu'une
domestique,*" said the master of the house, rebuking such a
one,—"*alors vous n'êtes qu'un valet!*" For to insult the *da*, is to
insult the household. When she dies, she will have such a funeral as money alone could not obtain,—a funeral of the *pre-
mière classe*, attended by the richest and proudest of the city.
There are planters who will ride that day twenty miles over the
mornes to act as pall-bearers. There are ladies who rarely tread
pavement, who seldom go out except in their own vehicles,—
but who will follow the coffin of that old negress on foot, in
the hot sun, all the way to the *Cimetière du Mouillage*. And
they will inter their *da* in the family vault, while the crowns
of the great palms quiver to the *bourdon*.

I.

THERE are old persons still living in Saint Pierre who remember Youma, a tall *capresse*, the property of Madame Léonie Peyronnette. The servant was better known than the mistress;—for Madame Peyronnette went out little after the loss of her husband, a wealthy merchant, who had left her in more than comfortable circumstances.

Youma was a pet slave, and also the godchild of Madame Peyronnette: it was not uncommon during the old régime for Creole ladies to become godmothers of little slaves. Douceline, the mother of Youma, had been purchased as a *da* for Madame Peyronnette's only child, Aimée—and had died when Aimée was nearly five years old. The two children were nearly the same age, and seemed much attached to each other: after Douceline's death, Madame Peyronnette resolved to bring up the little capresse as a playmate for her daughter.

The dispositions of the two children were noticeably different; and with their growth, the difference became more marked. Aimée was demonstrative and affectionate, sensitive and passionate,—quick to veer from joy to grief, from tears to smiles. Youma, on the contrary, was almost taciturn, seldom betrayed emotion: she would play silently when Aimée screamed, and scarcely smile when Aimée laughed so violently as to frighten her mother. In spite of these differences of organization, or perhaps because of them, the two got along together very well: they had never a serious quarrel, and were first separated only when Aimée, at the age of nine, was sent to a convent to receive an education more finished than it was thought that private teachers were capable of giving. Aimée's grief at parting from her playmate was not assuaged by the assurance that she would find at school nicer companions than a young capresse; —Youma, who had certainly more to lose by the change, remained outwardly calm,—"*était d'une conduite irréprochable,*" said Madame Peyronnette, too fine an observer to attribute the "irreproachable conduct" to insensibility.

The friends continued to see each other, however; for Madame Peyronnette drove to the convent in her carriage regularly every Sunday, always taking Youma with her; and Aimée seemed scarcely less delighted to see her former playmate than to see her mother. During the first summer vacation and the Christmas holidays, the companionship of childhood was naïvely resumed; and the mutual affection survived the subsequent natural change of relation: though nominally a *bonne*, who addressed Aimée as a mistress, Youma was treated almost as a foster-sister. And when Mademoiselle had finished her studies, the young slave-maid remained her confidante, and to some extent her companion. Youma had never learned to read and write; Madame Peyronnette believed that to educate her would only make her dissatisfied with the scope of a destiny out of which no effort could elevate her; but the girl had a natural intelligence which compensated her lack of mental training in many respects: she knew what to do and how to speak upon all occasions. She had grown up into a superb woman,—certainly the finest capresse of the arrondissement. Her tint was a clear deep red;—there was in her features a soft vague beauty, —a something that suggested the indefinable face of the Sphinx, especially in profile;—her hair, though curly as a black fleece, was long and not uncomely; she was graceful furthermore, and very tall. At fifteen she had seemed a woman; at eighteen she was taller by head and shoulders than her young mistress; and Mademoiselle Aimée, though not below the average stature, had to lift up her eyes, when they walked out together, to look into Youma's face. The young *bonne* was universally admired: she was one of those figures that a Martiniquais would point out with pride to a stranger as a type of the beauty of the mixed race. Even in slave days, the Creole did not refuse himself the pleasure of admiring in human skin those tones none fear to praise in bronze or gold: he frankly confessed them exquisite;—æsthetically, his "color prejudice" had no existence. There were few young whites, nevertheless, who would have presumed to tell their admiration to Youma: there was something in the eyes and the serious manner of the young slave that protected her quite as much as the moral power of the family in which she had been brought up.

Madame Peyronnette was proud of her servant, and took pleasure in seeing her attired as handsomely as possible in the brilliant and graceful costume then worn by the women of color. In regard to dress, Youma had no reason to envy any of the freed class: she had all that a capresse could wish to wear, according to local ideas of color contrast,—*jupes* of silk and of satin,—*robes-dézindes* with head-dresses and foulards to match, —azure with orange, red with violet, yellow with bright blue, green with rose. On particular occasions, such as the first communion of Aimée, the *fête* of madame, a ball, a wedding to which the family were invited, Youma's costume was magnificent. With her trailing *jupe* of orange satin attached just below the bosom, and exposing above it the laced and embroidered chemise, with half-sleeves leaving the braceleted arms bare, and fastened at the elbow with gold clasps (*boutons-à-clous*);—her neck-kerchief (*mouchouè-en-lai*) of canary yellow striped with green and blue;—her triple necklace of graven gold beads (*collier-chou*);—her flashing ear-pendants (*zanneaux-à-clou*), each a packet of thick gold cylinders interjoined;—her yellow-banded Madras turban, dazzling with jewelry,—"trembling-pins," chainlets, quivering acorns of gold (*broches-à-gland*),— she might have posed to a painter for the Queen of Sheba. There were various pretty presents from Aimée among Youma's ornaments; but the greater part of the jewelry had been purchased for her by Madame Peyronnette, in a series of New-Year gifts. Youma was denied no pleasure which it was thought she might reasonably wish for,—except liberty.

Perhaps Youma had never given herself any trouble on the subject; but Madame Peyronnette had thought a good deal about it, and had made up her mind. Twice she refused the girl's liberty to Mademoiselle Aimée, in spite of earnest prayers and tears. The refusal was prompted by motives which Aimée was then too young fully to comprehend. Madame Peyronnette's real intention was that Youma should be enfranchised so soon as it could render her any happier to be free. For the time being, her slavery was a moral protection: it kept her legally under the control of those who loved her most; it guarded her against dangers she yet knew nothing of;—above all, it prevented the possibility of her forming a union not approved by her mistress. The godmother had plans of her own for the girl's future: she intended that Youma should one day marry a thrifty and industrious freedman,—somebody able to make a good home for her, a shipwright, cabinet-maker, builder, master mechanic of some kind;—and in such an event she was to have her liberty,—perhaps a small dowry besides. In the meanwhile she was certainly as happy as it was possible to make her.

. . . . At nineteen Aimée made a love-match,—marrying M. Louis Desrivières, a distant cousin, some ten years older. M. Desrivières had inherited a prosperous estate on the east coast; but, like many wealthy planters, passed the greater part of the year by preference in the city; and it was to his mother's residence in the Quartier du Fort that he led his young bride. Youma, in accordance with Aimée's wish, accompanied her to her new home. It was not so far from Madame Peyronnette's dwelling in the Grande Rue to the home of the Desrivières in the Rue de la Consolation that either the daughter or the god-daughter could find the separation painful.

. . . . Thirteen months later, Youma, attired like some Oriental princess, carried to the baptismal font a baby girl, whose advent into the little colonial world was recorded in the Archives de la Marine,—"*Lucile-Aimée-Francillette-Marie, fille du sieur Raoul-Ernest-Louis Desrivières, et de dame Adélaïde-Hortense-Aimée Peyronnette.*" Then Youma became the *da* of little Mayotte. It is by the last of the names conferred at christening that the child is generally called and known,—or, rather, by some Creole diminutive of that name. . . . The diminutive of Marie is Mayotte.

In both families Mayotte was thought to resemble her father more than her mother: she had his gray eyes, and brown hair,—that bright hair which with children of the older colonial families darkens to apparent black as they grow up. She gave promise of becoming pretty.

Another year passed, during which no happier household could have been found: then, with cruel suddenness, Aimée was taken away by death. She had gone out with her husband in an open carriage, for a drive on the beautiful mountain-route called *La Trace*; leaving Youma with the child at home. On their return journey, one of those chilly and torrential rains which at certain seasons accompany an unexpected storm, overtook them when far from any place of shelter, and in the middle of an afternoon that had been unusually warm. Both were drenched in a moment; and a strong north-east wind, springing up, blew

full upon them the whole way home. The young wife, naturally delicate, was attacked with pleurisy; and in spite of all possible aid, expired before the next sunrise.

And Youma robed her for the last time, tenderly and deftly
as she had robed her for her first ball in pale blue, and for her
wedding day all in vapory white. Only now, Aimée was robed
all in black, as dead Creole mothers are.

M. Desrivières had loved his young wife passionately: he had
married with a fresh heart, and a character little hardened by
contact with the rougher side of existence. The trial was a terrible one;—for a time it was feared that he could not survive it.
When he began at last to recover from the serious illness caused
by his grief, he found it impossible to linger in his home, with
its memories: he went as soon as possible to his plantation, and
tried to busy himself there, making from time to time brief visits
to the city to see his child, whom Madame Peyronnette insisted
on caring for. But Mayotte proved delicate, like her mother; and
during a season of epidemic, some six months later, Madame
Peyronnette decided that it would be better to send her to the
country, to her father, in charge of Youma. Anse-Marine was
known to be one of the healthiest places in the colony; and the
child began to gain strength there, as the sensitive-plant—
zhèbe-mamisé—toughens in the warm sea-wind.

II.

It is a long ride from Saint Pierre over the mountains to the
plantation of Anse-Marine,—formerly owned by the Desrivières; but the fatigue of six hours in the saddle under a tropic sun
is not likely to be felt by one susceptible to those marvellous
beauties in which the route abounds. Sometimes it rises almost
to those white clouds that nearly always veil the heads of the
great peaks;—sometimes it slopes down through the green twilight of primitive forests;—sometimes it overlooks vast depths
of valley walled in by mountains of strange shapes and tints;—
sometimes it winds over undulations of cane-covered land,
beyond whose yellow limit appears the vapory curve of an almost
purple sea.

Perhaps, for hours together, you see no motion but that of
leaves and their shadows,—hear only the sound of your horse's

hoofs, or the papery rustling of cane waved by the wind,—or, from the verge of some green chasm veiled by tree-ferns, the long low flute-call of an unknown bird. But, sooner or later, at a turn of the way, you come upon something of more human interest,—some living incident full of exotic charm: such as a caravan of young colored girls, barefooted and bare-armed, transporting on their heads to market the produce of a *cacao-yère*; or a negro running by under an amazing load of bread-fruits or *régimes-bananes*.

Perhaps you may meet a troop of black men drawing to the coast upon a *diabe* or "devil,"—which is a low strong vehicle with screaming axles,—a *gommier* already hollowed out and shapen for a canoe: those behind pushing, and those before pulling all together, while a drummer beats his *ka* on the bottom of the unfinished boat, to the measure of their song: "*Bom! ti canot!—allé châché!—méné vini!—Bom! ti canot!*" . . . .

Or perhaps you encounter a band of woodmen, sawing into planks by the roadside some newly felled tree, with a core yellow as saffron, or vermilion-red,—a tree of which you do not know the name. It has been lifted upon a strong timber framework; and three men wield the long saw,—one above, two below,—all with their shirts off. The torso of the man above is orange-yellow: one of the sawyers below is cinnamon-color, the other a shining black as of lacquer: all are sculpturally muscled; and they sing as they saw:—

> "Aïe! dos calé,
> Aïe!
> Aïe! dos calé!
> Aïe, scié bois,
> Aïe!
> Pou nou allé.". . . .

. . . . Such incidents become rarer as you begin the long descent, through cane-fields and *cacaoyères*, from the wooded heights to the further sea,—leaving shadows and coolness behind to ride over lands all uncovered to the sun; but the immense peace charms like a caress, and the magnificent expansions of the view console for the seeming absence of human life. Behind you, and to north and south, the mornes heighten their semicircle above the undulating leagues of yellow cane,—and beyond them sharper summits loom, all violet,—and over the violet tower successive surgings of paler peaks and cusps and jagged ridges,—phantom blues and pearls. Before you, over the yellow miles, purples the far crescent of sea under its horizon curve,—a band of upward-fading opal light;—and a strong warm wind is blowing in your face. You ride on, sometimes up a low wide hill, sometimes over a plateau,—more often down a broad incline,—the sea alternately vanishing and reappearing, —and leave the main road at last to follow a way previously hidden by rising ground,—a plantation road, bordered with cocoa-palms. It brings you by long windings, between canes that shut off the view on either hand, to one of the prettiest valleys in the world. At least you will deem it so, as you draw rein at the verge of a morne, to admire the almost perfect half-round of softly wrinkled hills opening to the sea,—whose foam-line stretches like a snowy quivering thread between two green peaks, over a band of ebon beach;—and the golden expanse of canes below;—and the river dividing it, broadening between fringes of bamboo, to reach the breakers;—and the tenderness of shadows blue-tinted by vapors, the flickering of sunlight in the silver of cascades, the touching of sky and sea beyond all. Last, you will notice the plantation buildings on a knoll below, in a grove of cocoa-palms:—the long yellow-painted mill, with its rumbling water-wheel and tall chimney;—the *rhommerie*;— the sugar-house;—the village of thatched cabins, with banana leaves fluttering in tiny gardens;—the single-story residence of the planter, built to resist winds and earthquakes;—the cottage of the overseer;—the hurricane-house, or *case-à-vent*;—and the white silhouette of a high wooden cross at the further entrance to the little settlement.

All this was once the property of the Desrivières,—the whole valley from shore to hill-top: the *atelier* numbered nearly one hundred and fifty hands. Since then, the plantation has been sold and resold many times,—exploited with varying fortune by foreigners as well as Creoles;—and nevertheless there have been so few changes that the place itself probably looks just as it looked fifty years, or even a hundred years ago.

But at the time when the Desrivières owned Anse-Marine, plantation life offered an aspect very different to that which it presents to-day. On this estate in particular, it was patriarchal and picturesque to a degree scarcely conceivable by one who knows the colony only since the period inaugurated by emancipation. The slaves were treated very much like children: it was a traditional family policy to sell only those who could not be controlled without physical punishment. Each adult was allowed a small garden, which he might cultivate as he pleased, —half-days being allotted twice in every week for that purpose; and the larger part of the money received for the produce, the slave was permitted to retain. Legally a slave could own nothing, yet several of the Desrivières hands were known to have economized creditable sums, with the encouragement of their owner. Work was performed with song, to the music of the drum;—there were holidays, and evenings of privileged dancing. The great occasion of the year was the *fête* of Madame Desrivières, the mother of the young planter, the old mistress (*tétesse*),—a day of *bamboulas* and *caleindas*,—when all the slaves were received by the lady on the veranda: each kissed her hand and each found in it a silver coin. But it was a delight for the visitor, especially if a European, to watch even the common incidents of this colonial country life, so full of exotic oddities and unconscious poetry.

The routine of each day opened with an amusing scene,— the morning inspection of the feet of the children. These, up to the age of nine or ten, had little to do but to play and eat. They were under the charge of the *infirmière*, Tanga, an old African woman, who, aided by her daughters, prepared their simple food, and looked after them while their mothers were in the fields. Soon after sun-rise, Tanga, accompanied by the overseer, would assemble them, and make them sit down in line on the long plank benches under the awning of the infirmary building: then at the command, "*Lévé piézautt!*" they would all hold up their little feet together, and the inspection would begin. Whenever Tanga's sharp eye detected the small round swelling which betrays the presence of a *chique*, the child was sent to the infirmary for immediate treatment, and the mother's name taken down by the overseer for reprimand,—every mother being held responsible for a *chique* allowed to remain in her child's foot overnight. There was so much tickling and laughing and screaming at these inspections, that Tanga always had to frighten the children several times before the examination could be finished.

Another morning scene of interest was the departure of a singing caravan of women and girls, carrying to market on their heads various products of the plantation: cocoa, coffee, cassia; and fruits,—cocoa-nuts, and *mangues*, oranges and bananas, corossols (custard-apples) and "cinnamon-apples" (*pommes cannelles*).

Then a merry event, which occurred almost weekly, was the sortie of the gommier,—a huge canoe nearly sixty feet long, made from a single extraordinary tree. It had no rudder, but a bow at either end, so as to move equally well in either direction; and benches for a dozen paddlers, with a raised seat in the centre for a drummer. It had two *commandeurs*, one at each bow;—it could carry a dozen barrels of rum and six or seven casks of sugar;—and it was used chiefly for transporting these products to the small vessels from Saint Pierre, which dared not venture near the dangerous surf. The gommier itself could only be launched from a sloping cradle built expressly for it over deep water in the hollow of a projecting cliff. When the freight had been stowed and the rowers were in their seats, the drummer beat a signal; blocks were removed, cables loosed, and the long craft shot into the sea,—all its paddles smiting the water simultaneously, in time to the rhythm of the *tamtam*, or the *tambou-belai*.

Every Sunday afternoon the Père Kerambrun came on horseback from the neighboring village to catechise the negro children. It was usually in the sugar house that he held his little class,—the broad doors being thrown open front and rear to admit the sea-breeze, and the sun would throw in spidery shadows of palm-heads on the floor. The old priest knew how to teach the little ones in their own tongue,—repeating over and over again each question and answer of the Creole catechism, till the children learned them by heart, and could chant them like a refrain.

—"*Coument ou ka crié fi Bon-Dié?*" the father would ask. (How do you call the Son of the Good-God?)

Then all the child voices, repeating the question and its answer, would shrill in unison:—

"*Coument ou ka crié fi Bon-Dié?—Nou ka crié li Zézou-Chri.*"

—"*Et ça y fai pou nou-zautt, fi Bon-Dié-à?*" (And what did He do for us, that Son of the good God?)

—"*Et ça y fai pou nou-zautt, fi Bon-Dié-à?—Li payé pou nou p'allé dans len-fé; li baill toutt sang-li pou ça.*" (He paid for us not to go to hell; He gave all His blood for that.)

—"*Et quilé priè qui pli meillè-adans toutt priè nou ka fai?*" (And what is the best prayer among all the prayers we say?)

—"*Et quilé priè qui pli meillè adans toutt priè nou ka fai?— C'est Note Pè,*

—"*pace Zézou-Chri
montré nou li!*"

—all would sing together. (It is the *Notre Père,*—the Lord's prayer,—because Jesus Christ showed us how to say it.)

And at the end of each day's task,—when the lambi-shell was blown for the last time to summon all from the fields and the mill buildings, there was the patriarchal spectacle of evening prayer,—an old colonial custom. The master and his overseer, standing by the cross erected before the little village of the plantation, waited for all the hands to assemble. Each man came, bearing the regulation bundle of forage for the animals, and laying the package of herbs before him, removed his hat. Then all, women and men, would kneel down and re-peat in unison the *Je vous salue, Marie,* the *Notre Père,* and the Creed,—as the stars thrilled out, and the yellow glow died behind the peaks.

. . . . Often, when the nights were clear and warm, the slaves would assemble after the evening meal, to hear stories told by the *libres-de-savane* (old men and women exempted from physical labor),—those curious stories which composed the best part of the unwritten literature of a people forbidden to read. In those days, such oral literature gave delight to adults as well as to children, to *békés* as well as to negroes: it even ex-erted some visible influence upon colonial character. Every *da* was a story-teller. Her recitals first developed in the white child intrusted to her care the power of fancy,—Africanizing it, per-haps, to a degree that after-education could not totally remove, —creating a love of the droll and the extraordinary. One did not weary of hearing these stories often repeated;—for they were told with an art impossible to describe; and the little songs or refrains belonging to each—sometimes composed of African words, more often of nonsense-rhymes imitating the *bamboula* chants and *caleinda* improvisations,—held a weird charm which great musicians have confessed. And furthermore, in these *contes créoles*,—whether of purely African invention, or merely African adaptation of old-world folk-lore and fable,—the local color is marvellous: there is such a reflection of colonial thought and life as no translation can preserve. The scenes are laid among West Indian woods and hills, or sometimes in the quaintest quarter of an old colonial port. The European cottage of folk-tale becomes the tropical *case* or *ajoupa*, with walls of bamboo and roof of dried cane-leaves;—the Sleeping Beauties could never be discovered in their primeval forest but by some *nègue-marron* or *chasseu-chou*;—the Cinderellas and Princesses appear as beautiful half-breed girls, wearing a costume never seen in picture-books;—the fairies of old-world myth are changed into the Bon-Dié or the Virgin Mary;—the Bluebeards and giants turn into *quimboiseurs* and devils;—the devils themselves (except when they yawn to show the fire in their throats) so closely resemble the half-nude *travailleurs*, with their canvas trousers and *mouchouè-fautas* and other details of costume, as not to be readily recognized: it requires keen inspection to detect the diabolic signs,—the red hair, crimson eyes, and hornroots under the shadowing of the enormous "mule-food hat" or the *chapeau-bacoué*.

Then the Bon-Dié, the "good God," figures as the best and kindest of old *békés*,—an affable gray planter whose *habitation* lies somewhere in the clouds over the *Montagne Pelée*: you can see his "sheep" and his "*choux-caraïbes*" sometimes in the sky. And the breaker of enchantments is the parish priest,—*Missié labbé*,—who saves pretty naughty girls by passing his stole about their necks. . . . It was at Anse-Marine that Youma found most of the tales she recounted to Mayotte, when the child became old enough to take delight in them.

. . . . So the life had been in the valley plantation for a hundred years, with little varying. Doubtless there were shadows in it,—sorrows which never found utterance,—happenings that never had mention in the verses of any *chantrelle*,—days without song or laughter, when the fields were silent. . . . But the tropic sun ever flooded it with dazzling color; and great moons made rose-light over it; and always, always, out of the purple vastness of the sea, a mighty breath blew pure and warm upon it,—the breath of the winds that are called unchanging: *les Vents Alizés.*

III.

IN the morning Youma usually took Mayotte to the river to bathe,—in a clear shallow pool curtained with bamboos, where there were many strange little fish to be seen;—sometimes in the evening, an hour before the sunsetting, she would take her to the sea-beach, to enjoy the breeze and watch the tossing of the surf. But during the heat of the day, the child was permitted to view the wonder-world of the plantation only from the verandas of the house; and the hours seemed long. The cutting of the cane in the neighboring fields to the playing of the drum,—the coming and going of the wagons creaking under their loads of severed stems,—the sharpening of cutlasses at the grindstone,—the sweet smell of the *vesou*,—the rumble of the machines,—the noisy foaming of the little stream turning the wheel of the mill: all the sights and odors and sounds of plantation life filled her with longing to be out amidst them. What tantalized her most was the spectacle of the slave children playing on the grass-plot and about the buildings,—playing funny games in which she longed to join.

—"I wish I was a little negress," she said one day, as she watched them from the porch.

—"Oh!" exclaimed Youma in astonishment. . . . "and why?"

—"Because then you would let me run and roll in the sun."

—"But the sun does not hurt little negroes and negresses; and the sun would make you very sick, doudoux. . . ."

—"And that is why I wish I was a little negress."

—"It is not nice to wish that!" declared Youma, severely.

—"Why is it not nice?"

—"Fie! . . . . wish to be an ugly little negress!"

—"You are a negress, da,—or nearly the same thing,—and you are not ugly at all. You are beautiful, da; you look like chocolate."

—"Is it not much prettier to look like cream?"

—"No: I like chocolate better than cream. . . . tell me a story, da."

It was the only way to keep her quiet. She was four years old, and had developed an extraordinary passion for stories. The story *Montala*, of the wizard orange-tree which grew to heaven;—the story *Mazin-lin-guin*, of the proud girl who married a goblin;—the story of the Zombi-bird whose feathers were colored "with the colors of other days,"—the bird that sang in the stomachs of those who ate it, and then made itself whole again;—the story of La Belle, whose godmother was the Virgin; —the story of Pié-Chique-à, who learned to play the fiddle after the devil's manner;—the story of Colibri, the Humming-Bird, who once owned the only drum there was in the world, and would not lend it when the Bon-Dié wanted to make a road, although the negroes said they could not work without a drum;—the story of Nanie Rosette, the greedy child, who sat down upon the Devil's Rock and could not get up again, so that her mother had to hire fifty carpenters to build a house over her before midnight;—the wonderful story of Yé, who found an old blind devil roasting snails in the woods, and stole the food out of the old devil's calabash, but was caught by him, and obliged to carry him home and feed him for ever so long . . . . these and many more such tales had been told to little Mayotte already, with the effect of stimulating her appetite for more. If these tales did not form the supreme pleasure of her stay at the plantation, they at least enhanced and colored all her other pleasures,—spreading about reality an atmosphere deliciously unreal,—imparting a fantastic personality to lifeless things,—filling the shadows with *zombis*,—giving speech to shrubs and trees and stones . . . . even the canes talked to her, *chououa-chououa*, like old whispering Babo, the *libre-de-savane*. Each habitant of the plantation,—from the smallest black child to tall Gabriel, or "Gabou," the *commandeur* of all,— realized for her some figure of the *contes*; and each spot of hill or shore or ravine visited in her morning walks with Youma, furnished her with the scenery for some impossible episode. . . .

*

—"Mayotte!" exclaimed Youma;—"you know one must not tell stories in the daytime, unless one wants to see *zombis* at night!"

—"No, da! . . . . tell me one. . . . I am not afraid, da."

—"Oh! the little liar! . . . . You are afraid,—very much afraid of *zombis*. And if I tell you a story you will see them tonight."

—"Doudoux-da, no!—tell me one. . . ."

—"You will not wake me up to-night, and tell me you see *zombis*?"

—"No, da—I promise."

—"Well, then, for this once,"—said Youma, uttering the traditional words which announce that the Creole story-teller is ready,—"*bobonne fois?*"

—"*Toua fois bel conte!*" cried the delighted child. And Youma began:—

DAME KÉLÉMENT.

Long, long ago there lived an old woman who everybody said was a witch, and in league with the devil. And nearly all the bad things said about her were true.

One day a poor little girl lost her way in the woods. After she had walked until she could not walk any more, she sat down and began to cry. She cried for a long, long time.

All about her she could see nothing but trees and lianas;—all the ground was covered with slippery green roots; and the trees were so high, and the lianas so woven between them, that there was very little light. She was lost in the *grands bois*—the great woods which swarm with serpents. . . .

All at once, while she sat there crying, she heard strange sounds quite near her,—sounds of singing and dancing.

She got up and walked towards the sounds. Looking through the trees she saw the same old woman that people used to talk about, riding on *balai-zo*,* and dancing round and round in a ring with ever so many serpents and *crapaud-làde*,—great ugly toads. And they were all singing:

Kingué,
Kingué;

---

*A broom made of the branches of a shrub called *guiyantine*.

Vonvon
Malato,
Vloum-voum!
Jambi,
Kingué,
Tou galé,
Zo galé,
Vloum!

The little girl stood there stupid with fright: she could not even cry any more.

But the old woman had seen the leaves move; and she came with a sort of fire playing all round her, and asked the little girl:—

—"What are you doing in the *razié*?"*

—"Mother, I lost my way in the woods.". . . .

—"Then, my child, you must come to the house with me. . . . You might undo me, unravel me, destroy me if you had a chance."

The little girl did not understand all that the old woman said; for the wicked old creature was talking about matters that only sorcerers know.

By the time they got to the house, the poor child was very tired: she sat down on a calabash which served the witch for a chair. Then she saw the old woman light two fires on the earth floor, with torch-gum,—which smells like incense. On one fire she placed a big pot full of *manman-chou*, *camagnoic*, yams, christophines, bananas, devil's egg-plants (*melongène-diabe*), and many herbs the little girl did not know the names of. On the other fire she began to broil some toads, and an earth-lizard,—*zanoli-tè*.

At noon the old woman swallowed all that as if it was nothing at all;—then she looked at the little girl, who was nearly dead for hunger, and said to her:—

—"Until you can tell me what name I am called by, you will not get anything to eat." . . . . Then she went away, leaving the little girl alone.

The little girl began to weep. Suddenly she felt something touching her. It was a big serpent,—the biggest she had ever seen. She was so frightened that she almost died;—then she cried out:—

—"*Oti papa moin?—oti manman moin?*
Latitolé ké mangé moin!"

But the serpent did not do her any harm: he only rubbed his head fondly against her shoulder, and sang:—

Razié: the lower growths which occupy the ground under forest-trees, or cover the soil in places where the trees have been cleared away.

—"*Bennemè, bennepè,—tambou belai!*
Tche p'accoutoumé tambou belai!"

The little girl cried out louder than before:—

—"*Oti papa moin?—oti manman moin?*
Latitolé ké mangé moin!"

But the serpent, still rubbing his head fondly against her, answered, singing very softly:—

—"*Bennepè, bennemè,—tambou belai!*
Tche p'accoutoumé tambou belai!"

Then when he saw she had become less afraid, he lifted his head close to her ear, and whispered something.

The moment she heard it she ran out of the house and into the woods again. There she began to ask all the animals she met to tell her the old witch's name.

She asked every four-footed beast;—she asked all the lizards and the birds. But they did not know.

She came to a big river, and she asked all the fishes. The fishes, one after another, made answer to her that they did not know. But the *cirique*, the river crab that is yellow like a plantain,—the cirique knew. The cirique was the only one in the whole world who knew the name. The name was *Dame Kélément.*

. . . . Then the child ran back to the house with all her might; her little stomach was paining her so that she felt she could not bear the pain much longer. The old woman was already at the house, scraping some magnioc to make flour and *cassave.* . . . The little girl walked up to her, and said:

—"Give me to eat, *Dame Kélément.*"

Two flashes of fire leaped from the witch's eyes: she gave such a start that she nearly broke her head against the iron-stones that she balanced her pots on.

—"Child! you have got the better of me!" she screamed. "Take everything!—take it, take it!—eat, eat, eat!—all in the house is yours!"

Then she sprang through the door quick as a powder-flash: she seemed to fly through the fields and woods. . . . And she ran straight to the river;—for it was deep under the bed of the river that the Devil had buried the name which he had given her. She stood on the bank, and chanted:—

—"*Loche,* O loche!—was it you who told that my name was Dame Kélément?"

Then the loche, that is black like the black stones of the stream, lifted up its head, and cried:—

—"No, mamma!—no, mamma!—it was not I who told that your name was Dame Kélément."

—"*Titiri*, O titiri!—tell me, was it any among you who told that my name was Dame Kélément?"

Then the titiri, the tiny transparent titiri, answered all together, clinging to the stones:—

—"No, mamma!—no, mamma!—none of us ever said that your name was Dame Kélément."

—"*Cribîche*, O cribîche!—was it you who told that my name was Dame Kélément?"

Then the cribîche, the great crawfish of the river, lifted up his head and his claws, and made answer:—

—"No, mamma!—no, mamma!—it was not I who said that your name was Dame Kélément."

—"*Tétart*, O tétart!—was it you who said that my name was Dame Kélément?"

And the tétart, that is gray like the gray rocks of iron to which it holds fast, made answer, saying:—

—"No, mamma!—no, mamma!—it was not I who told them that your name was Dame Kélément."

—"*Dormeur*, O dormeur!—was it you who told that my name was Dame Kélément?"

And the dormeur, the lazy dormeur, that sleeps in the shadow of the rocks, awoke and rose and made answer:—

—"No, mamma!—no, mamma!—it was not I who told them that your name was Dame Kélément."

—"*Matavalé*, O matavalé!—was it you that said my name was Dame Kélément?"

And the matavalé, the shining matavalé, that flashes like copper when the sun touches his scales, opened his mouth and answered:—

—"No, mamma!—no, mamma!—I never said that your name was Dame Kélément!"

—"*Milet!*—*bouc!*—*pisquette!*—*zangui!*—*zhabitant!*—was it any one among you who told that my name was Dame Kélément?"

But they all cried out:—

—"No, no, no, mamma!—none of us ever said that your name was Dame Kélément."

—"*Cirique*, O cirique!—was it you who said my name was Dame Kélément?"

Then the cirique lifted up his eyes and his yellow claws, and screamed:—

—"Yes, you old wretch!—yes, you old witch!—yes, you old malediction!—yes, it was I who said that your name was Dame Kélément!". . . .

The moment she heard those words she stamped on the ground so hard that the Devil heard her, and opened a great hole at her feet; and she leaped into it head-first. And the ground closed over her. Two days after, there grew up from the place a clump of the weed they call *arrête-nègue*,—the plant that is all thorns.

Now while this was happening, the serpent had turned into a man;—for the old witch had changed a man into that serpent. He took the little girl by the hand, and led her to her mother.

But they came back again next day to search the old woman's cabin. They found in it seven casks filled with the bones of dead people; and also ever so much silver and gold,—more than enough to make the little girl rich. When she got married, there was the finest wedding ever seen in this country.

. . . . Mayotte's morning visits to the river with Youma had furnished her with material for the imaginative scenery of the last part of this foolish little story, which delighted her so much that she made her nurse repeat it over and over again. She had seen the crawfish show their heads above the pools; she had caught the *titiri* in her little hands; she knew by sight the *loche* and the *tétart*, the *matavalé* and the *zhabitant*, the *dormeur* and the *cirique*. She also knew—by painful experience— the *arrête-nègue*. Dame Kélément, she fancied, must have had a face like old Tanga's when angry; and the little girl who lost her way in the woods must have looked just like a certain little black girl whom Tanga often had to scold, and who used to cry in the most extraordinary way: "*Aïe-yaïe-yaïe-yaïe-yaïe-yaïe!*"

But in the midst of her ecstasy, a faint fear came to her with the recollection of Youma's warning. . . .

—"Da," she asked, timidly, "I will not see zombis to-night, will I?"

—"Ah! you must not ask me to tell stories in the daytime any more," said Youma, guardedly.

—"But tell me, I won't see them tonight,—will I?"

—"If you see them," replied Youma, without mercy, "call me!—I will make them go away."

IV.

YOUMA was alone in the house that night with the child; for M. Desrivières had ridden over to Sainte-Marie, and the servants occupied an adjoining building. . . . She was roused from her sleep by hearing the child cry:—

—"*Da, oh da!—moin pè!*"

The tiny lamp left burning before the images of the saints had gone out;—little Mayotte was afraid.

—"*Pa pè,*"—called Youma, quickly rising to caress her,—"*mi da-ou, chè.*"

—"Oh! there is Something in the room, *da!*" said the child. She had heard stealthy sounds.

—"No, doudoux; you have been dreaming. . . . Da will light the lamp for you."

She felt for the matches on the little night-table,—could not find them,—remembered she had left them in the adjoining salon,—moved towards the door;—and her foot suddenly descended upon something that sent a cold shock through all her blood,—something clammy and chill, that lived! Instantly she threw all the weight of her lithe strong body upon that foot—the left: she never could tell why;—perhaps the impulse was instinctive. Under her naked sole the frigid life she strove to crush writhed with a sudden power that nearly threw her down; and in the same moment she felt something wind round her ankle, over her knee, wrapping the flesh from heel to thigh with bruising force . . . . the folds of a serpent!

—"*Tambou!*" she muttered between her teeth,—and hardened her muscles against the tightening coil, and strengthened the pressure of her foot upon the unseen enemy. . . . The foot of the half-breed, never deformed by shoes, retains prehensile power,—grasps like a hand;—the creature writhed in vain to escape. Already the cold terror had passed; and Youma felt only the calm anger of resolve: hers was one of those semi-savage natures wherein fear rarely lives beyond the first moment of nervous surprise. She called softly to the little one.

—"*Ti doudoux?*"

—"Da?"

—"Do not move till I tell you: stay in bed; there is a *bête* in the room."

—"*Aïe, aïe!*" sobbed the frightened child,—"what is it, da?"

—"Do not be afraid, cocotte: I am holding it, and it cannot bite you, unless you get up. I am going to call for Gabriel: do not stir, dear."

And Youma called, with all the power of her clear voice:

—"*Sucou!—sucou! Eh! Gabou!*". . . .

—"What is it?—what is it, da?" sobbed the little girl.

—"Do not cry like that, or I will get angry! How can I see what it is in the dark?". . . .

She called again and again for aid. . . . *Bon-Dié!* how powerful the creature was!—the pressure of the coil became a numbing pain. Her strength was already beginning to weaken under the obstinate, icy, ever-increasing constriction. What if the cramp should come to help it? . . . . Or was it the entering of venom into her blood that made those strange tinglings and tremblings? . . . . She had not felt herself stricken;—but only the month before a plantation-hand had been bitten in the dark without feeling it; and they could not save him. . . . "*Eh! Gabou!*". . . . Even the servants in the pavilion seemed to sleep like dead. And if the child should leave the bed in spite of her warning? . . . .

—"Oh! they are coming, da!" cried Mayotte. "Gabou is coming!" She had seen the flash of his lantern through the slatted shutters. "But the door is locked, da!"

—"Stay in bed, Mayotte!—if you move it will bite you!" The salon filled with voices and sound of feet; then there was a pushing at the bedroom door.

—"It is locked," called Youma; —"break it!—smash it in!—I cannot move!"

. . . . A crash!—the room filled with a flare of lanterns; and Youma saw that the livid throat was under her foot;—the hideous head vainly strained at her heel.

—"*Pa bouèné piess!*" cried the voice of the commandeur. "Do not stir for your life, my girl! Keep still for your life! Stay just as you are!"

She stood like a bronze. Gabriel was beside her, his naked cutlass in his hand. . . . "*Quim fò! quim fò!—pas bouèné piess, piess, piess!*". . . . Then she saw the gleam of his steel pass, and the severed head leap to the wainscoting, where it fell gaping,—the eyes still burning like sparks of charcoal. In the same moment the coil loosed and dropped, and Youma lifted her foot;—the body of the reptile lashed the planking, twisted, strove to crawl as if to join the head;—again and again the cutlass descended, and each lopped fragment nevertheless moved.

—"Are you hurt, my daughter?" a kind voice asked,—the voice of M. Desrivières: he had seen it all.

—"*Pa couè maîte*," she answered, looking at her foot. But she did not know. He led her to a chair, knelt down and began the examination himself; while Mayotte climbed to Youma's neck, clinging and kissing and crying: "Did he bite you, dear da?—did he bite you ?" . . . . "No, doudoux; no, cocotte: do not be afraid!" She was telling the truth unawares: the serpent had never been able to use his fangs; but the seaming of his coil remained upon the smooth red skin as if branded. . . . Gabriel had dropped his cutlass and detached the long *mouchoir-fautas* about his waist to make a ligature: he was the *panseur* of the plantation.

—"Never mind, my son," said M. Desrivières: "she has not been bitten."

Gabriel stood dumb for astonishment.

Meanwhile the room had filled with armed plantation-hands, and a clamor of exclamations: . . . . "*Die Seignè! qui sépent!*" . . . . "*Mi tête-là ka lè modé toujou!*" . . . . "*C'est guiabe mènm!*" . . . . "*Moceauà ka rimié pou yo joinne!*" . . . . "*Aïe! Youma tchoque!—ouill papa!*" . . . . And a serpent nearly six feet in length! No one had ever heard of such a feat before. When Youma told how it happened,—very simply and very calmly,—there was a dead hush of admiration. It was first broken by the rough basso of the commandeur, exclaiming:— "*Ouaill! ou brave, mafi!—foute! ou sévè!*" . . . . "Severe," the negro's strongest adjective to qualify courage, retains in his patois something of quaint and reverential meaning,— something of that sense which survives in our own modern application of it to art and truth: the Creole now rarely uses it except in irony, but Gabriel uttered it with unconscious exquisiteness; and M. Desrivières himself applauded.

—"*Doudoux-da-moin!*" cried Mayotte, smothering her nurse with caresses;—"*ti cocotte-da-moin! . . . . Mais bo y, papoute!—bo y!*" she pleaded, to M. Desrivières. He smiled and kissed Youma's forehead.

—"And it was all my fault," declared Mayotte, beginning to sob again: "I made her tell me stories in the daytime."

But that serpent was no zombi: they found his trail and followed it to a hole which some rat had gnawed in the planking of the salon, under a sideboard.

V.

FROM that night Youma became the object of a sort of cult at Anse-Marine;—there is no quality the black admires so much as physical courage. The entire *atelier* began to evince for her a respect almost fetichistic. The girl's heroism had conquered any petty dislikes which her city manners and natural reserve might have provoked, and had hopelessly crushed the small jealousies of house-servants who imagined themselves supplanted by a stranger in the master's home. These now only sought to obtain her good-will, to win her smile;—the plantation declared itself proud of her,—boasted of her prowess to the slaves of neighboring estates;—the hands saluted her when she passed, as if she were a mistress; and the improvisors of the *caleinda* chants celebrated her praises in their *belai*. Even the overseer, M. de Comislles, though a rigid disciplinarian, no longer addressed her as *mafi*, "my daughter," but as *Manzell*, —Manzell Youma.

But what secretly pleased her above all was the attention of Gabriel. Gabriel appeared to have taken a sudden fancy to her. Although the busiest man on the estate, he found time to show his friendship by little kindnesses and courtesies of which one could scarcely have believed so rude a nature capable. He invented opportunities to meet her during the mid-day respite from labor, and of evenings,—before or after making his nightly round to see that all the regulations of cleanliness and good order had been obeyed in every cabin,—that clothing had been washed, and refuse removed. His visits were necessarily brief;—they were also strangely silent: he rarely spoke, except when asked a direct question, or when teased by Mayotte into taking her on his knees and answering her prattle. More usually he would simply seat himself on the veranda close to Youma's rocking-chair, and listen to her chat with the child, or her story-telling,—seldom even turning his face

towards her, but seeming to watch the noisy life of the *cases*.
But almost at every visit he would bring something for the
child,—knowing she would share it with her *da*,—some gift of
fruit gathered in his own garden: such as a bunch of *figues*,
which are tiny dessert bananas scarcely two inches long;—or a
zabricot (tropical apricot),—that singular fruit the ancient
Haytians held sacred as the food of ghosts,—a colossal plum,
as large as the largest turnip, with musky vermilion flesh, and a
kernel big as a duck's egg;—or an odorous branch cut from a
zorange-macaque tree, heavy with mandarines;—or a *fouitt-
defendu*,—the same, according to Creole tradition, which Eve
was tempted by the Serpent to eat,—a sort of huge orange
larger than a pumpkin, with a luscious pink pulp. . . . One
day,—the day of Mayotte's *fête*,—Gabriel brought a very
pretty present: a basket he had himself woven of bamboo strips
and liana stems, filled with samples of almost everything the
estate produced. There was a beautiful little sugar-loaf,—a
package of *batons-caco*, or sticks of chocolate,—a little *couï*, or
half-calabash, filled with brown sugar,—a can of refined
syrup,—a *pain-mi*, or boiled-maize cake, sweetened, and
wrapped in a piece of balisier leaf tied with a *ti-liane-razié*;—
some *tablettes* of grated cocoa candied in liquid sugar;—and a
nice bundle of Chambéry cane, tied with a cane leaf. . . . Another day, when Youma had taken the child to the river for her
morning bath, she found there, fixed upon the bank beside the
little pool, a broad and handsome rustic bench, built of the
long tough stems of the *pommier-rose*, with split bamboos for
the back and the seat: Gabriel had made it, working at night,
and had carried it to the river before daybreak, as a surprise for
Youma.

. . . . Silent as Gabriel's visits were, they began to exert an
influence on Youma. She found in them an unfamiliar pleasure,
—became accustomed to look for them with unconscious
eagerness;—even felt vaguely unhappy when he did not come.
And yet, after having failed to see him for a longer time than
usual, she never asked what had prevented his visit;—she
would not have confessed, even to herself, that she feared his
indifference. He, on the other hand, never offered an explanation. The two strange natures comprehended each other with-

out speech,—drew and dominated each other in a dumb, primitive, half-savage way.

. . . . He brought one afternoon a fine *sapota*,—that fruit in whose smooth flushed swarthy skin Creole fancy finds the semblance of half-breed beauty. Within its flat black seed, between the two halves of the kernel, lies a pellicle,—creamy, fragile, and shaped like a heart,—which it requires dexterity to remove without breaking. Lovers challenge each other to do it as a test of affection.

—"Mayotte," said Youma, after they had eaten the fruit together,—"I want to see if you love me." . . . . She cracked the flinty shell of a seed between her teeth,—then tried to remove the pellicle, and broke it.

—"Oh, da !" cried the child, "it is not true!—you know I love you." . . . .

—"*Piess, piess!*" declared Youma, teasing her;—"you do not love me one bit!"

But Gabriel asked for a seed, and she gave him one. Rude and hard as his fingers were, he took out the little heart intact, and gave it to Mayotte.

—"*Ou ouè!*" he said, maliciously;—"*da ou ainmein moin passé ou!*" (Your da loves me better than you.)

—"It is not true!—no, *cocotte!*" Youma assured the child. But she did not feel sure of what she said.

. . . . When the cane-cutting season was over, Gabriel asked and obtained leave to go to La Trinité one holiday morning. He returned at evening, later than the hour at which he was accustomed to find the young *capresse* on the veranda; but she was still there. Seeing him approach, she rose with the child asleep in her arms, and put her finger to her lips.

"*Quimbé!*" whispered Gabriel, slipping into Youma's hand something flat and square, wrapped in tissue-paper: then, without another word, he strode away to his quarters.

When Mayotte had been put to bed, Youma looked at the packet. . . . A little card-board box: within it, upon a layer of pink cotton, shone two large light circles of plain gold,— barbaric ear-rings such as are only made by colonial goldsmiths, but well suited to the costume and bronze skin of the race of color. . . . Youma already possessed far finer jewelry; but Gabriel had walked thirty kilometres for these.

He smiled as he passed by her window in the morning and saw them shimmering in her ears. Her acceptance of the gift signified assent to a question unspoken,—the question which civilized men most fear to ask, but which the Creole slave could ask without words.

VI.

—"WHAT is it, my son?" said M. Desrivières, as Gabriel, who had asked to speak with him alone, stood nervously twirling a great straw hat between his fingers.

—"*Maître*," he began, shyly,—"*moin ainmein ti bonne ou.*" . . . .

—"Youma?" queried M. Desrivières in surprise.

—"*Mais oui, maître.*"

—"Is Youma willing to marry you?"

—"*Mais oui, maître.*"

For a few moments M. Desrivières could make no reply: the possibility of a union between the two had never occurred to him, and Gabriel's revelation almost shocked him. The *commandeur* was certainly one of the finest physical men of his race,—young, industrious, intelligent; but he would make a rough mate indeed for a girl brought up as Youma had been. She was also a slave, without education; but she had received a domestic training that gave her a marked superiority above her class, and she had moral qualities more delicate by far than those of Gabriel. . . . Above all, she had been the companion of Aimée's childhood, and afterwards her friend rather than her servant: the influence of Aimée's had done much for her; —something of Aimée's manner, and of Aimée's thought, had become a part of her own. . . . No; Madame Peyronnette would never hear of such a union: the mere idea of it would revolt her like a brutality!

—"But, Gabriel," he answered at last, "Youma does not belong to me. She belongs to my mother-in-law."

—"Master, I know she belongs to Madame Peyronnette," said Gabriel, making the rim of his *chapeau-bacouè* revolve still more quickly;—"but I thought you would like to do something for me."

The planter smiled at the suggestion. . . . He had often expressed to Gabriel the wish to see him marry,—had even promised to give him a handsome wedding when he should have made a choice. But Gabriel seemed in no haste to choose. Then it became known that, while he remained indifferent to the girls of Anse-Marine, he was in the habit of making furtive visits to a neighboring estate; and M. Desrivières himself went there to discover the object of those visits. He found it in the person of a handsome *griffone*; and, wishing to give Gabriel an agreeable surprise, bought the girl for fifteen hundred francs, and brought her back with him. But from the day that she belonged to the plantation, Gabriel paid no further attention to her whatever. Secretly, he resented his master's intermeddling in the matter; and nevertheless, in spite of that episode, it now seemed to him quite natural to beg M. Desrivières to buy Youma for him. . . . The planter, however, felt no anger;— the incident rather amused him. He valued Gabriel highly, and understood him well:—a nature impatient of control, but capable of exerting it to an extraordinary degree. As a *commandeur* he was inestimable; as a *travailleur* he would have been almost impossible to manage. His former owner, a *petit blanc*, had been glad to sell him, with the frank assurance that he was "sullen, incorrigible, and dangerous." De Comislles, who purchased him, knew it was a case of "fine stock" unappreciated; and often boasted of the bargain he had made.

—"I cannot buy her for you, my son," said M. Desrivières, kindly. "Youma is not for sale. Madame Peyronnette will not sell her at any price,—even to me. . . . I am going to the city to-morrow, and will ask my mother-in-law if she will let Youma marry you: that is all I can do."

Gabriel ceased to twirl his hat: he stood silent for a little while, with his eyes cast down, and a decidedly sinister expression in his face. He had never thought that Youma's fate might not be decided even by M. Desrivières's wealth and influence: a suspicion that the planter's assurances were false, momentarily darkened his thoughts. Then he looked up, bowed to M. Desrivières, and with a hoarsely muttered "*Mèçi, maître*," withdrew.

*

—"It is Youma who will suffer the most," thought M.
Desrivières.

VII.

MADAME PEYRONNETTE'S decision was just what M. Desrivières had expected. She was even more astonished by Youma's
choice than he had been,—could only attribute it to a fascination purely physical, or, as she termed it, animal: the one peril
among all others that she had especially feared for Youma. She
even reproached her son-in-law,—held him responsible for the
affair; and finally insisted upon Youma's immediate return to
the city. She did not wish that another should be Mayotte's
nurse; but whether Mayotte remained at Anse-Marine or not,
Youma should return. It was time at all events that the child
should begin to learn something more important than sucking
sugar-cane and playing with little negroes;—besides, she had
become quite strong, and the city was exceptionally healthy.
Youma might continue to live with the Desrivières at the Fort;
but a girl innocent enough to become enamoured of the first
common negro who made love to her, needed looking after;
and Madame Peyronnette intended to make sure that no more
such things should happen. . . . M. Desrivières offered no
opposition to his mother-in-law's wishes; he announced his intention to return to town himself as soon as possible, and
bring Mayotte and her nurse with him.

. . . . To Youma this decision brought a shock of pain that
stupefied her too much for tears. Then, with the instinctive,
automatic resentment that sudden pain provokes, came to her
also for the first time the full keen sense of the fact that she was
a slave,—helpless to resist the will that struck her. Every disappointment she had ever known,—each constraint, reprimand,
refusal, suppression of an impulse, every petty pang she had
suffered since a child,—crowded to her memory, scorched it,
blackened it; filled her with the delusion that she had been unhappy all her life, and with a hot secret anger against the long
injustice imagined, breaking down her good sense, and her
trained habit of cheerful resignation. In that instant she almost

hated her godmother, hated M. Desrivières, hated everybody
. . . . except Gabriel. At his advent into her life, something
long held in subjection within her,—something like a darker
passionate second soul, full of strange impulses and mysterious
emotions,—had risen to meet him, bursting its bonds, and
winning mastery at last: the nature of the savage race whose
blood dominated in her veins.

Its earlier rebellions had produced no graver result than occasional secret fits of melancholy,—beginning after Aimée's
departure to school, when Youma was first taken into an existence high-hedged about in those days with formalities extraordinary. Except during the evenings of a brief theatrical season,
and the occasion of a select ball, the Creole ladies remained
almost cloistered in their homes from Sunday to Sunday,
scarcely leaving their apartments except to go to church,—
never entering a store under any circumstances, and having
even the smallest details of their shopping done for them by
slaves. Enervated by a climate that would probably have exterminated the European element within a few generations but
for the constant infusion of fresh blood from abroad, the white
women of the colonies could adapt themselves without pain to
this life of cool and elegant seclusion. But Youma was of the race
of sun-lovers. The very privileges accorded her, the very training
given to her as a sort of adopted child, had tended rather to
contract her natural life than to expand it. In the country she
had found larger opportunities for out-door enjoyment, and
freedom from formal restraints of a certain kind; but even in
the country her existence was confined by her duty as a nurse,
—compressed into the small sphere of a child's requirements.
Youma was too young to be *da*. For the *da* there were no pleasures. The responsibilities of such a place,—requiring nothing
less than absolute self-sacrifice,—were confided as a rule only to
slaves who had been mothers, who had fulfilled the natural
destiny of woman. But Youma had scarcely ceased to be a child,
when she found herself again sentenced to act, think, and speak
as a child,—for the sake of a child not her own. Her magnificent
youth dumbly protested against this perpetual constraint. Despite that sense of personal dignity Madame Peyronnette had
spared no pains to cultivate in her,—the feeling of having social superiority among her class,—she sometimes found herself

envying the lot of others who would have gladly changed places with her: the girls who travelled singing over the sunny mountain roads, the negresses working in the fields, chanting *belai* to the tapping of the *ka*. Youma felt a painful pleasure in watching them. She suffered so much from the weariness of physical inaction;—she was so tired of living in shadow, of resting in rocking-chairs, of talking baby talk,—just as in other years she had been tired of dwelling behind closed shutters, and broidering and sewing in a half-light, and hearing conversations which she could not understand. Still, at such moments, she had judged herself ungrateful,— almost wicked,—and battled with her discontent, and conquered it,—until Gabriel came.

Gabriel! . . . . He seemed to open to her a new world full of all that her being longed for,—light, and joy, and melody: he appeared to her in some way blended with the freedom of air and sun, of river and sea,—fresh scents of wood and field,— the long blue shadows of morning,—the rose-light of tropical moonrise,—and the songs of the *chantrelles*,— and the merriment of dances under the cocoa-palms to the throbbing thunder of the drums. Gabriel, so calm, so strong, so true! her man of all men, made for her by the Bon-Dié;—Gabriel, who, though a slave, could compel the esteem of his master;—Gabriel, for whom she prayed each night, and laid before the Virgin's image her little offering of wild flowers;—Gabriel, with whom she would be so happy, even in the poorest of *ajoupas*,—for whom she would gladly give liberty if she had it, or even her life if it could do him service! . . . . She wished to be beautiful—and they said she was beautiful (*yon bel-bois*, like a shapely tree, like a young palm)—only for his sake. . . . And they were going to take him from her,—pretending that he was not good enough for her (as if *they* could know!),—because they wanted her to remain with them always, to suffer for them always, to live in darkness and silence, like a *manicou*. And they had the power to be cruel to her, to take him away from her! The world was all wrong,—wrong at least for her. Whomsoever she loved was taken from her; first her mother, Douceline; then Aimée Desrivières;—now Gabriel.

. . . . It was the morning after his arrival from the city that M. Desrivières had called her aside to tell her: she had just returned from the river with Mayotte, after giving the child her morning bath. He had spoken kindly, but very frankly,—in a way that left no hope possible.

For a long time she sat speechless and motionless in her room: then, obeying the child's wish, went out with her upon the veranda. The day was exquisitely clear, with a tepid wind from the sea. Above her, on the nearer side of the valley, sounded the mellow booming of a *tambou-belai*, and a chorus of African song. A troop of field-hands were making a new path to the summit of one of the mornes; the old path having been washed away by recent heavy rains. The overseer had surveyed the course for it, marked out the zigzag with stretched cords; and the workers were slowly descending in a double line,—all singing,—all the hoes and rammers keeping time to the drum rhythm. Sometimes the men would throw up their hoes in the air and catch them again, or exchange them in a fling, without losing the measure of the movement. And there was a girl,— young Chrysaline,—carrying a tray with tin cups, *dobannes* of water, and a pitcher of liquor;—serving drink all round at intervals; for the work was hot. . . . Youma looked for a tall figure in blue cotton shirt and white canvas trousers at the head of the column. But Gabriel was not visible. Another was acting in his place, overseeing the task, and keeping a watch for serpents,—a black man, Marius.

Only three days more; and she would have to leave Anse-Marine,—would see Gabriel no more. . . . They were going to return to the dull hot city in the dullest and hottest month of the year. . . . Did Gabriel know? . . . . Or was it because he knew, that she did not see him among the workers? She felt that if he knew, he would contrive some chance to speak with her. . . .

Even as this feeling came, Gabriel appeared before the house,—made her a sign to leave the child and come to him.

He laid his hand caressingly upon her shoulder, and whispered:—

—"The master told me all this morning . . . . he is going to take you away from us?"

—"Yes," she answered, sadly;—"we are going back to the city."

—"When?"

—"Monday coming."

—"It is only Thursday," he said, with a peculiar smile. . . . "Doudoux, you know that once they have you back in the city again, they will never let you see me, never!—yes, you know it!"

—"But, Gabriel," she answered, with a choking in her voice,—hurt by the tone of pleading in his words: "what can I do?—you know there is not any way."

—"There *is* a way," he interrupted, almost roughly.

Wondering, she looked at him,—a new vague hope dawning in her large eyes.

—"There is a way, my girl," he repeated,—"if you are brave. Look!"

He pointed beyond the valley, over the sea to the north-east, where loomed a shape of phantasmal beauty,—a vision only seen in fairest weather. Out of the purpling ocean circle, the silhouette of Dominica towered against the amethystine day,—with crown of ghostly violet peaks, and clouds far curled upon them, like luminous wool of gold.

—"*Doudoux, in one night!*". . . . he whispered, watching her face.

She caught his meaning . . . . Freedom for the slave who could set his foot on British soil!

—"Gabriel!" called the voice of M. de Comislles.

—"*Eti!*" he shouted in answer. . . . "Think about it, my girl,—*chongé, chongé bien, chè!*"

—"Gabriel!" again cried the voice of the overseer.

—"*Ka vini!*" called Gabriel, running towards the summons.

. . . . She returned to her accustomed place on the veranda, where Mayotte was playing with a black kitten. She scarcely heard the child's laughter, and joyous callings to her to look when the little animal performed some droll prank,—answered mechanically as if half awake: her gaze continued fixed upon the shining apparition in the horizon, that tempted her will with its vapory loveliness. Slowly, while she gazed, it took diaphanous pallor,—began to fade into the vast light. Then, as the sun climbed higher, it passed mysteriously away: there remained only the clear-colored circling sea, the rounded spotlessness of the summer heaven. . . . But the luminous violet memory of it lingered with her,— burned into her thought.

She did not see Gabriel again that day. He seemed to avoid her purposely,—to give her time to reflect.

VIII.

. . . . NEVER a doubt of Gabriel's ability to carry out his project entered her mind: the possibilities of pursuit and capture, of encountering a *rafale* in that awful channel—or even worse; for the hurricane season had set in,—gave her little concern. What danger could she not brave for his sake?—anywhere with him she would feel secure.

But slowly the exaltation of her fancy began to calm. The totally unexpected suggestion of a means to frustrate the will of others, and to win all that she desired, had cooled the passion of her disappointment; and, with its cooling, her natural power of just reflection gradually returned. Then she felt afraid, —afraid of something in herself that she knew was wrong. For even in the first moment, the proposal of Gabriel had vaguely smitten her conscience,—startled her moral sense before she could weigh, however hastily, the results of abandoning her friends, her birthplace, her duties,—of declassing herself forever,—of losing the esteem of all who put trust in her. But now as she thought,—seriously thought,—she knew that a shame rose and tingled in her face. . . .

No—no—no!—it was not true that her life had been all unhappiness. She began to recall,—in shining soft succession,— many delightful days. Days of her childhood, above all,—with Aimée, when they played together in the great court of Madame Peyronnette's house in the high street—the beautiful sunny court with its huge-leaved queer plants and potted palms,—where the view of the splendid bay lay all open in blue light from the Grosse-Roche to Fond Corré;—with ships coming and going over the horizon, or drowsily swaying at anchor,—the court where each morning they used to feed the *zanolis*, the little green lizards of the *tonnelle*, who flashed down from the green vault of climbing vines to eat the crumbs thrown them! . . . . Aimée, who shared all things with her,—even when a tall young lady. Aimée, whose dying hand clasped hers with such loving trust,—whose dying lips had whispered:—"*Youma, O Youma! you will love my child?— Youma, you will never leave her, whatever happens, while she is little?—promise, dear Youma!*". . . . And she had— promised. . . .

She saw again the face of Madame Peyronnette, smiling under its bands of silver hair,—smiling as when Youma felt her cheek stroked by the fine white hand that glimmered with rings;—as when she heard the gentle assurance:—"You are my daughter, too, child—my beautiful dark daughter-in-God! You must be happy;—I want you to be happy!" . . . . And had she not really tried to make her so,—contrived for her,— planned for her,—expended much for her sake, that she might never have the right to envy others of her class? . . . . And Youma thought of all the gifts, the New-Year surprises,—the perpetual comfort. She had always had a room apart,—a room overlooking the *tonnelle* with its vines and pommes-de-liane, where the humming-birds circled in gleams of crimson and emerald,—a little chamber full of sea-wind: she had never been allowed to lie on a simple mattress unrolled upon the floor, like a common domestic.

For Aimée's sake she had found scarcely less consideration in her second home, from Madame Desrivières and her son. And ever since Aimée's death, the kindness of M. Desrivières had been that of a father. He had trusted her to such a degree that he had never noticed Gabriel's visits.

. . . . What would all these think of her? To whom did she owe most?—to them, whom she had known so long, and the kind lady who had brought her up with her own child, after having named her at the baptismal font; or to Gabriel, whom she had known only for one season? . . . . Ah! never,—not even for his sake, could she be false to them!—the good God would never forgive her! . . . . But Gabriel did not know: if he knew, he could not ask her to fly with him.

. . . . Once more the darker side of her nature was quelled,—sank back sobbing to its old place. The cruel pain remained: but she lay down to rest that night with a strong re-solve to seek Gabriel as soon as possible, and to say *No*.

*

And nevertheless her heart sank a little next morning, when
Gabriel, striding by as she was taking the child to the river,
said, in a low, hurried tone:—

—"Go to the beach this evening, at four o'clock. I will see
you there. The gommier leaves for La Trinité with a cargo."

Then he was gone, before she could answer a word.

IX.

A STRANGE coast is that on which the valley of Anse-Marine
opens,—a coast of fantastic capes and rocks with sinister appellations, in which the Devil's name is sometimes mentioned.
Black iron ore forms the high cliffs; but countless creepers tap-
estry them, and lianas everywhere dangle down to meet the
shore fringe of *patate-bò-lanmè*,—the vivid green sea-vine,—
crawling over a sand black as powdered jet. (Its thick leaves
when broken show a sap white as milk; and it bears a beautiful
carmine cup-shaped flower.) The waves are very long, very
heavy;—they crumble over with a crash that deafens, and
ghostly uptossings of foam as of waving hands. The sea is never
quiet there: north and south the *falaises* perpetually loom
through a haze of tepid spray,—rising like smoke to the sun. . . .
There is a Creole legend that it was not so in other years;—that
a priest, mocked by fishermen, shook his black robe against
the sea, and cursed it with the curse of eternal unrest. And the
fishing-boats and the spread nets rotted on the beach, while
men vainly waited for the sea to calm. . . . The foam-line
never vanishes through the year: it only broadens or narrows,
as the surf becomes, under the pressure of the trade-winds,
more or less dangerous. Sometimes it whitens far up the river
mouths, leaps to the summit of the cliffs, and shakes all the
land,—though there is scarcely a breeze, and not one cloud in
the sky. At such a time you will see that far out, even to the
horizon, the flood is blue as lapis lazuli, and smooth as a mirror: the thunder and the foaming do not extend beyond the
coast. That is a *raz-de-marée*,—a *raz-de-marée du fond*: the sea
swinging from the depths,—rocking from the bottom. This
spectacle may endure two, three, four days; and then cease
mysteriously as it began.

For the *travailleur* of the eastern plantations, the only barrier between slavery and freedom was this wild sea. There were but few boats on the coast;—north of La Trinité, there were but few points from which a boat could be safely launched. But at Anse-Marine there was one such place,—a sort of natural cove in a promontory projecting into deep water from the southern end of the valley-opening, and curving so as to give a lee side. It was thence the *gommier* was launched to the sound of the drum; and a little boat was also kept there in a shed,—the master's private boat,—seldom used. This Gabriel knew how to handle well.

. . . . Before the hour appointed Youma took Mayotte to the beach: the great heat of the day was spent, the strong wind was almost cool, and the cliffs were throwing shadow. A visit to this shore was a delight for the child. There were no pretty little shells like those thrown up by the tide at the Grosse Roche of Saint Pierré, and the surf was too strong to permit of her wading, as she would have wished to do. But it was a joy to see it tumbling and flashing; and the black sand was full of funny yellow hairy-legged crabs, and little sea-roaches—*ravett-lanmè*—which had spades in their tails, to dig holes with;—and sometimes one might meet a baby turtle, just out of the egg, making its way to the water.

The children came soon after,—black and yellow, brown and red,—all in charge of Tanga's daughters, Zoune and Gambi, to see the gommier go out. The little ones were not allowed to venture fairly into the water for fear of accidents; but they could gambol on the skirts of the surf to their hearts' content. They screamed and leaped all together whenever a big wave would chase up the sand, whirling and hissing about their little bare feet.

Then the wagons appeared, moving along the cliff road, with their loads of rum and sugar: it was hard work for the mules, strong and fat as they were. . . . Youma heard Gabriel's voice urging them on,—helping the drivers.

Then a slim brown boy, naked as a bronze, appeared on horseback,—coming down to the beach at a gallop, riding without a saddle. It was the overseer's little groom, going to give M. de Comislles's horse a bath in the surf. The boy was scarcely more than a child, and the animal,—a black Porto Rico stallion,—very spirited; but the two knew each other. As the surf reached the horse's knees, the lad leaped down, and began to wash him. Then an immense breaker bursting, whelmed both almost out of sight in a quivering woolly sheet of foam. The horse seemed to like it, never moved: there was no fear for the boy,—he could swim like a *couliou*. He played about the horse, patted him, hugged his neck, threw water on him: when a heavy breaker came he would cling to the stallion's mane.

"*Yo kallé! yo kallé!*" cried the children at last, as a drum-roll vibrated from the launching-place: the freight had been stowed, the crew were in their places, the *tambouyé* on his perch. It was the signal to let go—"*lagué toutt*"; and all eyes turned to see the gommier rush into the water; and everybody shouted as she reached it safely, pitched, steadied again with the first plunge of the paddles, and started on her journey, to the merry measure of *Madame lézhabitant*. The children stopped their play to watch;—and from the cliffs sounded a clapping of hands, and women's laughter, and jocose screams of *adié*,—as the long craft shot away to the open,—till the chant of the crew was lost in the voice of the surf, and the faces ceased to be distinguishable. Even then, for a minute or two the booming of the drum could be heard; but the gommier soon rounded the long point, and passed out of sight, making south. . . . The event of the day was over.

Tanga's daughters gathered their little flock, and left the beach;—the boy in the surf leaped to the horse's back, turned him, and off they went up the valley at a gallop,—shining like a group in metal,—to dry themselves in wind and sun;—the lookers-on disappeared from the cliffs;—and the empty wagons turned back rumbling to the plantation. . . . Youma still lingered, to Mayotte's great satisfaction. The child had found a cocoa-nut—empty, shrunken, and blackened by long pitching about in the waves. She amused herself by rolling it into the surf, and seeing it cast out again—always at some distance from where it had been thrown in;—and this so much diverted her that she did not notice Gabriel hastening towards them. . . . But Youma advanced to meet him.

—"*Doudoux-moin*," he said, breathing quickly with the hurry of his coming, as he took her hand in both his own,—"listen well to what I am going to tell you. . . . The gommier has gone;—there will be no boat to pursue us: we can go to-night if you will be brave. . . . To-morrow we can be free,—to-morrow morning, doudoux!"

—"Ah! Gabriel. . . ." she began. But he would not hear her: he spoke on so earnestly, so rapidly, that she could not interrupt him, telling her his hopes, his plans. He had a little money,—knew what he was going to do. They would buy a little place in the country,—(it was a beautiful country there, and everything was cheap, and there were no serpents!)—he could build a little house himself,—plant a fruit garden. . . . The master's boat was ready for their escape;—wind and sea were in their favor;—there would be no moon till after midnight;—there was nothing to fear. And with the coming sunrise they would be free.

He spoke of his love for her,—of the life they might live together,—of liberty as he imagined it,—of their children who would be free,—with naïve power of persuasion, and with a fulness that revealed how earnestly and long he had nourished his dream,—vividly imaging his thought by those strange Creole words which, like tropic lizards, change color with position. Not until he had said all that was in his heart, could Youma answer him, with the tears running down her cheeks:—

—"Oh! Gabriel! I cannot go!—do not tell me any more; I cannot go!" . . . .

Then she stopped,—struck dumb by the sudden change in his face. As he dropped her hand, there was an expression in his eyes she had never seen before. But he did not fix them upon her: he turned, and folded his arms, and stared at the sea.

—"Doudoux," she went on,—"you would not let me speak. . . . I did as you told me;—I thought it all over,—over and over again. And the more I thought about it, the more I felt it could not be. . . . And you would not give me a chance to tell you,"—she repeated, pleadingly,—touching his arm,—trying to draw his look again.

But he did not answer,—stood rigid and grim as the black rock behind him,—looking always to the horizon, where the place of his hope had been,—free Dominica, with its snakeless valleys,—all viewless now, veiled by the vapors of evening.

—"Gabriel," she persisted, caressingly,—"listen, dou-doux." . . . .

—"Ah! you will not come?" he said at last,—"you will not come?" . . . . There was almost a menace in his voice, as he turned the wrath of his eyes upon her.

—"I cannot go, doudoux," she repeated, with gentle force. "Listen to me. . . . you know I love you?"

—"*Pa pàlé ça!—pa lapeine!*" he answered, bitterly. . . . "I offer you all that I have;—it is not enough for you. . . . I give you the chance to be free with me, and you tell me you prefer to remain a slave."

—"Oh, Gabriel!" she sobbed,—"can you reproach me like that? You know in your heart whether I love you."

—"Then you are afraid,—afraid of the sea?"

—"It is not that." . . . .

—"*Ouill, mafi!*—I thought you brave!"

—"Gabriel," she cried, almost fiercely, "I am not afraid of anything except of doing wrong,—I am afraid of the Bon-Dié only."

—"*Qui Bon-Dié ça?*" he scoffed,—"the Bon-Dié of the békés?—the Bon-Dié of Manm-Peyronnette?"

—"You shall not talk that kind of talk to me, Gabriel!" she exclaimed, with eyes blazing,—"it brings bad luck!"

He looked at her in surprise at the sudden change in her manner, as, for the first time, her will rose to match his own.

—"*Ça ka pòté malhè, ou tenne?*" she repeated, meeting his gaze and mastering it. He turned sullenly to the sea again, and let her speak,—listening restively to her passionate explana-tion. . . . Afraid?—how little he knew her heart! But she had forgotten, because of him, what it was wicked to forget. She had done wrong even to think of going with him,—forsaking the godmother who had brought her up from an infant,—deserting the mistress who had cared for her like a daughter,—abandoning the child confided to her care, the child of Madame Desrivières, the child who loved her so much, who would suffer so much to lose her,—might even die; for she knew of a little one who had died for grief at having lost her *da*. No: it would be cruel,—it would be wicked, to leave her in such a way. . . .

—"And you leave me for a child, Youma,—a child not your own?" cried Gabriel. "You talk as if you were the only nurse in the world: there are plenty of *das*."

—"Not like me," said Youma,—"not at least for her. I have been mother to her since her own mother died. . . . But it is not the child only, Gabriel;—it is what I owe to those who loved and trusted me all these years.". . . . And the old sweetness came back into her voice, while she asked:—"Doudoux, could you think me true, and see me thankless and false to those who have been good to me all my life?"

—"Good to you!" he burst out, with sudden bitterness. "Do you think them good because they do not happen to be bad? How good to you? Because they dress you beautifully,—give you a *belle jupe*, a calendered *madras*, a *collier-choux*, and put gold upon you that folks may cry:—'See how madame . . . . see how monsieur is generous to a slave!' Give them?—no!— lend them only,—put them upon you for a showing: they are not yours! You can own nothing; you are a slave; you are naked as a worm before the law! You have no right to anything,—no, not even to what I gave you;—you have no right to become the wife of the man you choose;—you would have no right, if a mother, to care for your own child,—though you give half your life, all your youth, to nursing children of békés. . . . No, Youma, you were not brought up like your mistress's daughter. Why were you never taught what white ladies know? —why were you never shown how to read and write?—why are you kept a slave? . . . . Good to you? It was to their interest, my girl!—it repays them to-day,—since it keeps you with them,—when you could be free with me."

—"No, no, doudoux," protested the girl,—"you are not just! You do not know my godmother; you do not know what she has been for me;—you could never make me believe she has not been generous and kind! . . . . Do you think, Gabriel, that people can be good only for a motive?—do you think M. Desrivières has not been kind to you?"

—"There are good *békés*, Youma;—there are masters who are better masters than others: there is no good master!"

—"Oh, Gabriel!—and M. Desrivières?"

—"Do you believe slavery is a good thing,—a right thing, Youma?"

She could not answer him directly. The ethical question of slavery had first been brought to her mind in a vague way by her recent disappointment;—previously the subject would have seemed to her one of those into which it was not quite proper to inquire doubtingly.

—"I think it is wicked to be cruel to slaves," she replied. . . . "But since the good God arranged it so that there should be slaves and masters, doudoux. . . ."

—"*Ou trop sott—ou trop enfant!*"—he cried out, and held his peace; feeling that it were vain to argue with her,—that what he called her folly and her childishness separated them far more than the will of a mistress. Her idea of duty to her god-mother, of duty to the child, appeared to be mingled in some way with her idea of religion,—to which the least light allusion would provoke her anger. He could comprehend it only as a sort of mental weakness created by béké-teaching. To his own thinking, slavery was a kind of trickery,—the duping of blacks by whites; and it was simply because they could not dupe him, that they had given him a position entailing no physical labor, and in which he could feel himself more free than others. He did not feel grateful therefor: it seemed to him that no possible kindnesses, no imaginable indulgences on the part of a master could deserve the voluntary sacrifice of a chance for liberty by the slave. Though really possessing a rude intelligence above his comrades, Gabriel shared many savage traits of his race,—traits that three hundred years of colonial servitude could hardly modify: among others, the hatred of all constraint,—reasonable or unreasonable. Still the Creole *bitaco* prefers hungry liberty to any comfort obtainable by hired labor;—his refusal to work for wages necessitated the importation of coolies, yet he can do the work of three;—he is capable of prodigious physical effort; he will carry on his head twenty miles to town a load of vegetables of his own weight, or twenty-four bread-fruits; he will cutlass his way through forest to the very summit of peaks to find particular herbs and cabbage-palm for the market; he will do anything extraordinary to avoid being under orders,—martyrize his body by herculean efforts to escape control. . . . This spirit in Gabriel had been temporarily softened by the profits and petty dignity of his position,—by the ambition of being one day able to settle on his own land in some wild place, and live independent of everybody;—but not the least of the reasons which made him valuable at Anse-Marine was his confidence of being able to escape when he pleased. . . . And, nevertheless, judging Youma by himself, the very motive she had urged for her refusal seemed to him the one of all others he could not reason with her against, because he coupled it with his own ideas of the supernatural,—likened it to certain dark superstitions of which he knew the extraordinary power. Through her kind-heartedness, the *békés* had been able to impose upon her mind;—and tenderness of heart, except to him and for him alone, he deemed childish and foolish. . . . "*C'est bon khè crabe qui lacause y pa ni tête*," says the negro proverb.—(It is because of the crab's good heart that he lacks a head.)

Nevertheless he himself had a heart,—though a rough one;—and it was moved by the sight of Youma's silent tears which his anger and his reproaches had caused. He loved her well in his hard way; and all his tenacity of will set itself against the losing of her. She had denied his wish; and he knew her strength of resolve,—yet with time he might find another way to make her his own. Something would depend on herself,—on such influence as she might have with her mistress; but he relied more upon the probability of a social change. Hopeless as he had pictured the future for Youma, he was far from believing it hopeless. Echoes of the words and work of philanthropists had reached him: he knew how and why the English slaves had received their freedom;—he knew also something of which he could not speak, even in a whisper, to Youma. . . . From plantation to plantation there had passed a secret message,—framed in African speech for the ears of those chosen to know and fearless to do;—already, even within the remotest valleys of the colony, hearts had been strangely stirred by the blowing of the great wind of Emancipation. . . .

—"Doudoux-moin!" he suddenly entreated, in a tone of tenderness such as she had never heard him use,—"*pa pleiré conm ça, chè,—non!*" And she felt him drawing her close in a contrite caress. . . . "It was not with you, little heart, that I was angry!—listen: there are things you do not know, child; but I believe you—you are doing what you think is right. . . .

Pa pleiré,—non!—ti bigioule moin! . . . Listen: since you will not come, I will not go;—I will stay here at Anse-Marine. . . . *Pa pleiré, doudoux!*"

A little while she sobbed in his embrace without replying; then she murmured:—

—"I shall be more happy, doudoux, to know that you do not go. . . . But it is not a time to be angry, dear, when we must say good-bye for always."

—"Ah! my little wasp! will you let them choose another husband for you, when they have you back in Saint Pierre?" he asked, with a smile of confidence.

—"Gabriel!" she cried, passionately,—"they can never do that! . . . . If they will not let me have you, doudoux, I will remain forever as I am. . . . No!—they cannot do that!"

—"*Bon, ti khè-moin!*—then it is not good-bye for always. . . . Wait!"

She looked up, wondering. . . . But in the same moment, Mayotte, tired of playing with her cocoa-nut, and seeing Gabriel, ran to them screaming, "Gabou!—Gabou!"—and clung delightedly to the commandeur's knee.

—"No!—go and play a little while longer," said Youma. "Gabou is too tired to be pulled about."

—"Are you, Gabou?" asked Mayotte straining her little head back to look up to his face. And without waiting for his answer, she went on to tell him:—"Oh! Gabou! we are going back to town with *papoute!*"

—"He knows that," said Youma; "go and play."

—"But, da, I am tired!" she answered, discontentedly, still clinging to Gabriel's knee, expecting him to toss her up in his arms. . . . "*Pouend moin!*" she coaxed,—"take me up!—take me up!"

—"*Pauv piti, màgré ça!*" exclaimed Gabriel, lifting her to the level of his great bronze face,—"you do not care one bit that you are going to leave Gabou and all your dear friends at Anse-Marine,—*piess, piess, piti mechante!*—you do not love Gabou!"

—"Yes, I do!" she cooed, patting his dark cheeks,—"I do love you, Gabou!"

—"*Allé!—ti souyé!*—you love Gabou to play with you: that

is all! And Gabou has no time to play with you now;—Gabou must go and see what everybody is doing, before it is time to sound the *cònelambi.* . . . *Bo!*—*Adié, cocotte.*"

He placed her in her nurse's arms, and kissed Youma also,—but on the forehead only, as he had seen M. Desrivières do . . . . because of the child. . . . "*Adié, ti khè!*"

—"*Pou toujou?*" she murmured, almost inaudibly, vainly struggling with the emotion which stifled her voice,—"for always?"

—"*Ah! non, chè!*" he answered, smiling to give her hope. . . . "*Mône pa k'encontré;—moune k'encontré toujou.*"

(Only the mornes never meet;—folk always meet again.)

X.

. . . . WOULD she ever see him again? she asked herself unceasingly through all her wakefulness of that night,—her last save one at Anse-Marine. But always came the self-answer of tears. . . . She heard the number of the hour at which she might have fled with him to freedom, and hour after hour, tingled out by the little bronze salon timepiece through its vaulted glass. She closed her eyes,—and still, as through their shut lids, saw the images of the evening: the figure of Gabriel, and Mayotte playing with her cocoa-nut, and the velvet shadowing of the black cliffs on the black sand, and a white sheeting and leaping of surf,—silent like breakings of cloud. They went and came,—distorted and vanished and returned again with startling vividness, as if they would never fade utterly away. Only in the first hours of the morning there began for her that still soft darkness which is rest from thought.

But again a little while, and her mind wakened to the fancy of a voice calling her name,—faintly, as from a great distance,—a voice remembered as in a dream one holds remembrance of dreams gone before.

Then she became aware of a face,—the face of a beautiful brown woman looking at her with black soft eyes,—smiling under the yellow folds of a *madras* turban,—and lighted by a light that came from nowhere,—that was only a memory of some long-dead morning. And through the dimness round about it a soft blue radiance grew,—the ghost of a day; and she knew the face and murmured to it:—"*Doudoux-manman.*". . . .

. . . . They two were walking somewhere she had been long ago,—somewhere among mornes: she felt the guiding of her mother's hand as when a child.

And before them as they went, something purple and vague and vast rose and spread,—the enormous spectre of the sea, rounding to the sky. And in the pearliness over its filmy verge there loomed again the vision of the English island, with long shreddings of luminous cloud across its violet peaks. . . . Slowly it brightened and slowly changed its color as she gazed; and all the peaks flushed crimson to their tips,—like a budding of wondrous roses from sea to sun. . . .

And Douceline, softly speaking, as to an infant, said:—

—"*Travail Bon-Dié toutt joli, anh?*"—(Is it not all-pretty, the work of the good God?)

—"Oh! my little jewel-mamma,—*ti-bijou-manman!*—oh! my little-heart-mamma,—*ti-khè-manman!* . . . . I must not go!" . . . .

. . . . But Douceline was no longer with her,—and the shining shadow of the island had also passed away,—and she heard the voice of Mayotte crying . . . . somewhere behind trees.

And she hastened there, and found her, under some huge growth that spread out coiling roots far and wide: one could not discern what tree it was for the streaming weight of lianas upon it. The child had plucked a sombre leaf, and was afraid, —something so strange had trickled upon her fingers.

—"It is only the blood-liana," said Youma: "they dye with it." . . . .

—"But it is warm," said the child,—still full of fear. . . . Then both became afraid because of a heavy pulsing sound, dull as the last flappings of a cannon-echo among the mornes. The earth shook with it. And the light began to fail,—dimmed into a red gloom, as when the sun dies.

—"It is the tree!" gasped Mayotte,—"*the heart of a tree!*"

But they could not go: a weird numbness weighed their feet to the ground.

And suddenly the roots of the tree bestirred with frightful

life, and reached out writhing to wrap about them;—and the black gloom of branches above them became a monstrous swarming;—and the ends of the roots and the ends of the limbs had eyes. . . .

. . . . And through the ever-deepening darkness came the voice of Gabriel, crying,—"*It is a Zombi!—I cannot cut it!*"

XI.

THE season of heavy humid heat and torrential rains,—the long *hivernage*,—had passed with its storms;—and the season of north-east winds, when the heights grow cool;—and the season of dryness, when the peaks throw off their wrappings of cloud. It was the *renouveau*, the most delicious period of the year,—that magical spring-time of the tropics, when the land suddenly steeps itself in iridescent vapor, and all distances become jewel-tinted, while nature renews her saps after the bleaching and withering of the dry months, and rekindles all her colors. The forests covered themselves at once with fruit and flowers; the shrivelled lianas revived their luminous green, put forth new million tendrils, and over the heights of the *grands bois* poured down cataracts of blue, white, pink, and yellow blossom. The palmistes and the angelins appeared to grow suddenly taller as they shook off their dead plumes;—an aureate haze hung over the valleys of ripe cane;—and mountain roads began to turn green almost to their middle under the immense invasion of new-born grasses, herbs, and little bushes. . . . Mosses and lichens sprouted everywhere upon surfaces of stone or timber unprotected by paint;—grasses shot up through the jointing of basaltic pavements; and, simultaneously, tough bright plants burst into life from all the crevices of walls and roofs, attacking even the solid masonry of fortifications, compelling man to protect his work. An infinite variety: ferns and capillaria and vines that sink their tendrils into the hardest rock;—the *thé-miraille*, and the *mousse-miraille*; the *pourpier* and the wild guava; the *fleuri-Noël*, the Devil's tobacco (*tabac-diabe*), and the *lakhératt*;—even little trees, that must be removed at once for the safety of dwellings, —such as the young *fromager* or silk-cotton,—rose from wall tops and roofs,—branching from the points of gables,—

rooting upon ridges and cornices. . . . The enormous cone
of Pelée, which through the weeks of north winds had outlined the cusps of its cratered head against the blue light, once
more drew down the clouds about it, and changed the tawny
tone of its wrinkled slopes to lush green. Soft thunders rolled
among the hills; tepid dashes of rain refreshed the earth at
intervals;—the air grew sweet with balsamic scents;—the color
of the sky itself deepened.

But though the land might put forth all its bewitchment,
the hearts of the colonists were heavy. For the first time in
many years the magnificent crop was being gathered with difficulty: there were mills silent for the want of arms to feed
them. For the first time in centuries the slave might refuse to
obey, and the master fear to punish. The Republic had been
proclaimed; and the promise of emancipation had aroused in
the simple minds of the negroes a ferment of fantastic ideas,—
free gifts of plantations,—free donations of wealth,—perpetual
repose unearned,—paradise life for all. They had seen the
common result of freedom accorded for services exceptional;—
they were familiar with the life of the free classes;—but such
evidence had small value for them: the liberty given by the *béké*
resembled in nothing that peculiar quality of liberty to be accorded by the Republic!

They had dangerous advisers, unfortunately, to nourish such
imaginings: men of color who foresaw in the coming social
transformation larger political opportunities. The situation
had totally changed since the time when slaves and freedmen
fought alike on the side of the planters against Rochambeau
and republicanism, against the *bourgeoisie* and the *patriotes*.
The English capture of the island had justified that distrust of
the first Revolution shown by the *hommes de couleur*, and had
preserved the old régime for another half-century. But during
that half-century the free class of color had obtained all the
privileges previously refused it by prejudice or by caution; and
the interests of the *gens de couleur* had ceased to be inseparably
identified with those of the whites. They had won all that was
possible to win by the coalition; and they now knew the institution of slavery doomed beyond hope, not by the mere fiat of
a convention, but by the opinion of the nineteenth century.
And the promise of universal suffrage had been given. There

were scarcely twelve thousand whites;—there were one hundred and fifty thousand blacks and half-breeds.

Yet there was nothing in the aspect or attitude of the slave population which could fully have explained to a stranger the alarm of the whites. The subject race had not only been physically refined by those extraordinary influences of climate and environment which produce the phenomena of creolization; but the more pleasing characteristics of the original savage nature,—its emotional artlessness, its joyousness, its kindliness, its quickness to sympathy, its capacity to find pleasure in trifles,—had been cultivated and intensified by slavery. The very speech of the population,—the curious patois shaped in the mould of a forgotten African tongue, and liquefied with fulness of long vowel sounds,—caressed the ear like the cooing of pigeons. . . . Even to-day the stranger may find in the gentler traits of this exotic humanity an indescribable charm,—despite all those changes of character wrought by the vastly increased difficulties of life under the new conditions. Only the Creole knows by experience the darker possibilities of the same semi-savage nature: its sudden capacities of cruelty,—its blind exaltations of rage,—its stampede-furies of destruction.

. . . . Before the official announcement of political events reached the colony, the negroes,—through some unknown system of communication swifter than government vessels,—knew their prospects, knew what was being done for them, felt themselves free. A prompt solution of the slavery question was more than desirable;—delay was becoming dangerous. There were as yet no hostile manifestations;—but the slave-owners,—knowing the history of those sudden uprisings which revealed an unsuspected power of organization and a marvellous art of secrecy,—felt the air full of menace, and generally adopted a policy of caution and forbearance. But in a class accustomed to command there will always be found men whose anger makes light of prudence, and whose resolve challenges all consequences. Such a one among the planters of 1848 dared to assert his rights even on the eve of emancipation;—chastised with his own hand the slave who refused to work, and sent him to the city prison to await the judgment of a law that might at any moment become obsolete.

His rashness precipitated the storm. The *travailleurs* began to leave the plantations, and to mass in armed bands upon the heights overlooking Saint Pierre. The populace of the city rose in riot, burst into the cutlass stores and seized the weapons, surrounded the jail and demanded the release of the prisoner. . . . "*Si ou pa lagué y, ké ouè!—nou ké fai toutt nègue'bitation descenne!*" That terrible menace first revealed the secret understanding between the slaves of the port and the blacks of the plantation;—the officers of the law recoiled before the threat, and turned their prisoner loose.

But the long-suppressed passion of the subject class was not appeased: the mob continued to parade the streets, uttering cries never heard before,—"*Mort aux blancs!—À bas les békés!*" . . . . feeling secured from military interference by the recognized cowardice of a republican governor. Evening found the riot still unquelled,—the whites imprisoned in their residences, or fleeing for refuge to the ships in the harbor. And those dwelling on the hills, keeping watch, heard all through the night the rallying *ouklé* of negroes striding by, armed with cutlasses and bamboo pikes and bottles filled with sand. Twenty-four hours later, the whole slave-population of the island was in revolt; and the towns were threatened with a general descent of the *travailleurs*.

XII.

ANOTHER day found the situation still more sinister. All business was suspended; every store and warehouse closed; even the markets remained empty; the bakeries had been pillaged, and provisions had become almost unobtainable. A rumor was abroad that emancipation had been voted,—that the news was being concealed,—that the official proclamation of freedom could only be enforced by an appeal to arms. . . .

Prior to the outbreak there had been a fierce heat of political excitement, created by the republican election. The white slave-holders had voted for a freed-man faithful to their interests; the men of color had used their freshly acquired privileges to secure representation in the person of a noted French abolitionist. Pictures of him had been distributed by thousands, together with republican cockades and tiny tricolored flags: the people kissed the pictures with tears of enthusiasm and shouts of "*Vive papa!*"—the colored children waved the little flags and cried: "*Vive la République!*"—some were so young they could only cry, "*Vive la 'Ipipi!*" And the complete victory of the *hommes de couleur* only intensified the exaltation. . . . But after the affair of the jail, the children ceased to appear in the streets with their little flags; and there was no longer a distribution of cockades, but a distribution of cutlasses—new cutlasses, for they had to be sharpened, and all the grindstones were in requisition.

. . . . It became more and more perilous for the whites to show themselves in the streets. They watched for chances to get to the ships, under the protection of their own slaves or of loyal freedmen, having influence with the populace, knowing every dark face in it. But after mid-day such faithful servants began to find their devotion unavailing: strange negroes were mingling with the rioters,—savage-looking men, whom the city domestics had never seen before, and who replied to the assurance "*C'est yon bon, béké*" (this is a *good* white) only by abuse or violence. Armed bands incessantly paraded,—beating drums,—chanting,—shouting "*À bas les békés!*"—watching for a fugitive to challenge with the phrase,—"*Eh! citoyen . . . . citoyenne . . . . arrête! Je te parle!*"—affecting French speech for the pleasure of the insulting *tutoiement.* They peered for white faces at windows, cursed them, clamored: "*Mi! ausouè-à ké de-brayé ou!*"—gesturing with knives as if opening fish. Some great aggressive movement seemed to be preparing; and the *travailleurs* were always massing upon the heights. The whites who could not flee, feeling their lives in danger,—tried to prepare for defence: in some houses the women and girls made ball-cartridges. Slaves betrayed these preparations; and a rumor circulated that the békés were secretly organizing to attack the mob. . . . The time was long past when the whites could suppress a riot, and hang men of color to the mango-trees of the Batterie d'Esnotz; but what they had done in other days was remembered against them.

It was in the Quarter of the Fort,—the most ancient part of the city, situated on an eminence, and isolated by the Rivière Roxelane,—that the white Creoles found themselves least safe from attack. It was especially difficult for them to reach the ships: the bridges and all approaches to the shore being crowded with armed negroes. The greater number of the houses were small, and could offer little protection if besieged;—and many persons preferred to leave their own homes and seek asylum in the few large dwellings of the district. Among such were the Desrivières family, who found refuge with their relatives the De Kersaints. The De Kersaint residence was unusually roomy,— not more than two full stories high, but long, broad, and built with the solidity of a stronghold. It stood at the verge of the old quarter, in a steeply sloping street, descending westward so as to leave a great half-disk of sea visible above the roofs, and ascending eastward to join a country road leading to the interior. The windows of the rear overlooked vast canefields, extending far up the flanks of the Montagne Pelée, whose clouded crest towered fifteen miles away.

There were more than thirty persons assembled for safety at the De Kersaints'—mostly wives and daughters of relatives; and there was serious alarm among these. In the forenoon the servants had deserted the house,—one of them, a negress, irritated by some reproach, had left with the threat: "*Ausouè ou ké ouè—attenne!*" (Wait! you will see to-night!) M. de Kersaint, an old gentleman of seventy, who, seconded by his son, had made the fugitives as comfortable as was possible, strove to calm their fears. He believed the night would bring nothing worse than a great increase of noise and menace: he did not think the leaders of the city populace intended more than intimidation. There might be a general descent of the plantation hands,—that would be a graver danger; but there were five hundred troops in the neighboring barracks. No criminal violence had yet occurred in the quarter: it was reported that a gentleman had been killed in the other end of the city,—but there were so many wild reports!

. . . . As a fact, the whites of the Fort,—mostly deserted by their slaves and domestics,—knew little of what was going on even in their immediate vicinity. Things that for two hundred years had been done in darkness and secrecy were now being done openly in the light. An occult power had suddenly assumed unquestioned sway,—the power of the African sorcerer.

Under the tamarinds of the Place du Fort, a *quimboiseur* plied his ghastly calling,—selling amulets, selling fetiches, selling magical ointments made of the grease of serpents. Before him

stood an open cask filled with tafia mingled with gunpowder
and thickened with bodies of crushed wasps. About him
crowded the black men of the port,—the half-nude *gabarriers*,
wont to wield oars twenty-five feet long;—the herculean
nèguegouôs-bois, brutalized by the labor of paddling their massive and awkward craft;—tough *canotiers*, whose skins of
bronze scarcely bead in the hottest summer sun;—the crews of
the *yôles* and the *sabas* and the *gommiers*;—the men of the
cooperies, and the cask rollers, and the stowers;—and the fishers of *tonne*,—and the fishers of sharks. "*Ça qui lè?*" shouted
the quimboiseur, serving out the venom in cups of tin,—"*Ça
qui lè vini bouè y?* . . . . Who will drink it, the Soul of a
Man?—the Spirit of Combat?—the Essence of Falling to
Rise?—the Heart-Mover?—the Hell-Breaker?" . . . . And
they clamored for it, swallowed it—the wasps and the gunpowder and the alcohol,—drinking themselves into madness.

. . . . Sunset yellowed the sky,—filled the horizon with
flare of gold;—the sea changed its blue to lilac;—the mornes
brightened their vivid green to a tone so luminous that they
seemed turning phosphorescent. Rapidly the glow crimsoned,
—shadows purpled; and night spread swiftly from the east,—
black-violet and full of stars.

Even as the last vermilion light began to fade, there sounded
from the Place du Fort a long, weird, hollow call, that echoed
sobbingly through all the hills like an enormous moan. Then
another,—from the Mouillage;—another,—from the river-
mouth;—and others, interblending, from the *pirogues* and the
gabarres and the *sabas* of the harbor: the blowing of a hundred
lambi-shells,—the negroes of the city calling to their brethren
of the hills. . . . So still, the fishers of sharks, from the black
coast of Prêcheur, call the *travailleurs* of the heights to descend and divide the flesh.

And other moaning signals responded faintly,—from the
valley of the Roxelane and the terraces of Perrinelle,—from
the Morne d'Orange and the Morne Mirail and the Morne Labelle: the *travailleurs* were coming! . . . . And from the
marketplace, where by lantern-light the sorcerer still gave out
his *léssence-brisé-lenfè*, and his amulets and grease of serpents,
began to reverberate ominously the heavy pattering of a
tamtam.

Barricaded within their homes, the whites of the lower city could hear the tumult of the gathering. . . . Masters and slaves alike were haunted by a dream of blood and fire,—the memory of Hayti.

XIII.

AT the De Kersaints' all the apartments of the upper floor had been given up to the fugitives, except one front room where the men remained on watch: many of the women and young girls preferred to sit up with them rather than seek repose. Downstairs all the windows and doors had been securely closed; and it was decided to extinguish all lights during the passing of a mob. Then was converse on the events of the preceding day, the late election, prospects of emancipation, the history of former uprisings,—some of which the older men remembered well,—and on the character of negroes. This topic brought out a series of anecdotes,—some sinister, but mostly droll. A planter in the little assembly related a story about one of his own slaves who had saved enough money to buy a cow. At the first announcement of the political change in France he took the cow out of the field and tied it to the porch of his master's house. "*Pouki ou marré vache lanmaison?*" (Why do you tie the cow to the house?) asked the planter. . . . "*Moin ka marré vache lanmaison, maîte, pace yo ka proclamé la repiblique—pisse you fois repiblique-à proclamé, zaffai ta yon c'est ta toutt*"(Master, I tie the cow to the house because they proclaim the Republic,—for once that the Republic is proclaimed, the belongings of one are the belongings of everybody). In spite of the general anxiety, this narrative provoked laughter. Then, the conversation taking another turn, M. Desrivières told the story of Youma and the serpent,—there being many present who had not heard of the incident before. The young capresse, who sat with Mayotte on her knees, arose with the child, and left the apartment before M. Desrivières had ended his recital. A few minutes later he followed her into the adjoining room, called her away from the little one, and said to her, in an undertone which could not reach the child's ears:—

—"Youma, my daughter, the street is very quiet now; and I think it will be better for you to leave the child with my mother, and pass the night with our colored neighbors. . . . I can open the door for you."

—"Why, master?" . . . . She had never asked him why before.

—"*Mafi*," he answered, with a caress in his eyes, "I cannot ask you to stay with us to-night. There is danger for all of us," he added, sinking his voice to a whisper: "we may be attacked."

—"That is why I wish to stay, master." . . . . This time she spoke aloud and firmly.

—"Oh! papa!" cried Mayotte, coming between them,—"do not send her anywhere!—I want her to tell me stories!"

—"Little egotist!" said M. Desrivières, stooping to kiss her,— "and if Youma wishes to go?" . . . .

—"You do not,—do you, *da?*" asked the child in surprise. She imagined herself at a sort of evening pleasure party.

—"I will stay to tell you stories," said Youma . . . . M. Desrivières pressed her hand, and left her with the child.

. . . . As M. Desrivières announced, the street had become very quiet. It was one of the most retired: during the day there had been no gatherings in it;—some bands of negroes had passed from time to time shouting "*À bas les békés!*"—but since nightfall the disorderly element had disappeared. White citizens ventured to open their windows and look abroad. They heard the blowing of the lambi-shells without guessing its meaning,—imagined some fresh excitement in the direction of the harbor. Nevertheless, all became more anxious. The rushing of the water along the steep gutters,—the mountain water purifying every street,—seemed to sound unusually loud.

—"It always makes a great noise in this street," said M. de Kersaint,—"there is so much incline."

—"I think we are all more or less nervous to-night," said another gentleman.

But Youma, suddenly returning alone to the room where the men conversed, pointed to the windows, and exclaimed:—

—"It is not the water!"

The ears of the half-breed have a singular keenness to sounds. . . . All talk ceased: the men held their breath to listen.

XIV.

A HEAVY murmur, as of far surf, filled the street,—slowly loudened,—became a dull unbroken roar. From the heights it seemed to approach, and with it a glow, as of conflagration. . . . At once in every house the lights were extinguished, the windows closed, the doors secured;—the street became desolate as a cemetery. But from behind the slatted shutters of upper rooms all could watch the brightening of the light, hear the coming of the roar. . . .

—"*Yo ka vini!*" cried Youma.

And into the high street suddenly burst a storm of clamorings, a blaze of torch fires,—as a dense mass of black men in canvas trousers, hundreds naked to the waist, came moving at a run: the downpour of the *travailleurs*. Under the shock of their bare feet the dwellings trembled:—through all the walls a vibration passed, as of a faint earthquake. . . . If they would only go by!

Hundreds had already passed; and still the rushing vision seemed without end, the cascading of great straw hats interminable;—and over the torrent of it the steel of pikes and plantation forks and brandished cutlasses flickered in the dancing of torch fires. But there came an unexpected halt,—a struggling and shouldering, a stifling pressure,—a half lull in the tempest of shouting; while the street filled with a sinister odor of alcohol,—a stench of *tafia*. Evidently the mob was drunk, and being so, doubly dangerous. . . . . Some one had given an order, which nobody could fully hear; a stentorian voice repeated it, as the tumult subsided: "*Là!—làmênm!— caïe béké!*" All the black faces turned to the dwelling of the De Kersaints; and all the black throats roared again. Unfortunately the imposing front of the building,—the only two-story edifice in a street of cottages,—had signalled out its proprietors as rich békés. To be a béké, a white and to be rich, was, in the belief of the simple *travailleur* at least, to be an aristocrat, an enemy of emancipation,—most likely a slave-holder. . . . . "*Fouillé là!*" the same immense voice pealed—(Search there!); —and the whole house shook to a furious knocking at the main entrance, of which the massive double doors were secured by an iron bar, as well as by lock and bolt. "*Ouvé!—ouvé ba nou!*" (Open for us!) shouted the crowd.

M. de Kersaint unfastened a shutter of one of the upper front rooms, and looked down upon the mob. It was an appalling mob,—there were nightmare-faces in it. Most of the visages were unfamiliar; but some he could recognize—faces of the port: many of the roughest city class had joined the *travailleurs* before their descent. There were women also in the mob,—gesticulating, screaming: some were plantation negresses; others were not,—and these were the worst. . . .

—"*Ça oulé, méfi?*" asked M. de Kersaint.

The first time they could not hear him for the uproar; but it soon calmed at the sight of the white-haired béké at the window: everybody wanted to listen. M. de Kersaint was not seriously alarmed;—he did not believe the crowd could dare more than a brutal manifestation,—what in the patois is termed a *voum*. He repeated in Creole:—

—"What do you want, my sons?" . . . . It was thus the béké addressed the slave;—in his lips the word *monfi* had an almost patriarchal meaning of affection and protection: its use survives even in these republican years. But as uttered in that moment by M. de Kersaint, it fell upon the political passion of the mob like oil on fire.

—"*Ou sé pè-nou, anh?*"—laughed a mocker: "Are you our father? . . . . There are no more 'my sons': there are only citizens,—*anni cittoyen!*"

—"*Y trop souyé!—y trop malin!*" screamed a woman's voice. "He wants to flatter us, the old béké!—he is too sly!"

—"*Cittoyens, pouloss,*" responded M. de Kersaint. "Why do you want to break into my house? Have I ever done harm to any of you?"

—"You have arms in the house!" answered the same menacing voice that had first directed the attention of the populace to the dwelling. It rang from the chest of a very tall negro, who seemed to be the leader of the riot: he wore only a straw hat and cotton trousers, and carried a cutlass. All at once M. de Kersaint remembered having seen him before,—working on the plantation of Fond-Laillet, as commandeur.

—"Sylvain, my son," answered M. de Kersaint, "we have no arms here. But we have women and children here. We have nothing to do with your wrongs."

—"*Ouvé ba nou!*"

—"None of you have any right to enter my house."

—"*Ouvé ba nou!*"

—"You have no right.". . . .

—"Ah! we will take the right," shouted the leader; and a general roar went up,—thousands of excited voices reiterating the demand, "*Ouvé ba nou!*"

The white head withdrew from the window, and a young face appeared at it,—dark, handsome, and resolute;—the head of the younger De Kersaint.

—"*Tas de charognes!*" shouted the young man,—"yes, we have arms; and we know how to use them! The first one of you who enters this house, I shall make his black brains leap!"

He had a single loaded pistol: there was not another weapon in the building. He counted on the cowardice of the mob. But the negroes knew, or thought they knew, the truth: the old béké had not lied to them;—they were not afraid.

—"*Bon! nou ké ouè!*" menaced the leader. . . . "*Ennou!*" he cried, turning to the crowd, "*crazé caïe-là!*" Almost in the same instant, a stone shot by some powerful hand whirred by the head of the younger De Kersaint, and crashed into the furniture of the apartment. Vainly the shutters were bolted: a second missile dashed them open again;—a third shivered those of the next window. Stone followed stone. There were several persons severely injured;—a lady was stricken senseless;—a gentleman's shoulder fractured. And the cry of the crowd was for more stones—"*Ba nou ouôches! ba ouôches!*"—because the central pavement before the house was a rough cement, affording scanty material for missiles. But the lower cross-street was paved with rounded rocks from the river-bed;—a line of negresses formed from the point of attack to the corner at the cry of "*Fai lachaîne!*"—and the disjointed pavement was passed up along the line by apronfuls. There was perfect order in this system of supplying projectiles: the black women had been trained for generations to "make the chain" when transporting stone from the torrents to the site of a building, or the place of a protection-wall.

Then the stone shower became terrific,—pulverizing furniture, bursting partitions, shattering chamber doors. . . . How the Creole negro can fling a stone may be comprehended only by those who have seen him, on mountain roads, bring down fruit from trees growing at inaccessible heights. . . . All the shutters of the upper front rooms had already ceased to exist;—the inmates had sought refuge in the rear apartments. But the shutters of the windows of the ground-floor, being very heavy, solid, and partly protected with iron, continued to resist; and the doors of the great arch-way defied the brawny pressure of all the shoulders pushed against them.

—"*Méné pié-bois içi!—pié-bois—pié-bois!*" cried the men, straining to burst the doors, under cover of the bombardment; and the cry passed up the street toward the mountain slope. . . . From within the house it was no longer possible to observe what the mob were doing;—the windows were unapproachable. But such a shout suddenly made itself heard from the street that it was evident something new had occurred. . . . "Ah! the soldiers!" joyfully exclaimed Madame de Kersaint.

She was mistaken. The fresh excitement had been caused by the appearance of the *pié-bois*,—a weighty log carried by a crew of twenty men,—all crying "*Ba laï!—ba laï!*" Then those pushing at the doors fell back to give the battering-ram full play.

The men chanted as they swung it. . . . "*Soh-soh!—yaïe-yah! Rhâlé fò!*" And all the house shook to the enormous blow.

—"*Soh-soh!—yaïe-yah! Rhâlé fò!*" Bolts and locks burst;—the framework itself loosened in a showering of mortar;—the broad iron bar within still held, but it had bent like a bow, and the doors had yielded fully five inches.

—"*Soh-soh!—yaïe-yah! Rhâlé fò!*" A clang of broken metal; an explosion of splintered timber,—and the doors were down. The arch-way rang out the clap of their fall like a cannon-shot; the log-bearers dropped their log;—a brute roar of exultation acclaimed the feat. . . . Within, all was black.

There was a moment's hesitation;—the darkness and the voidness intimidated. "*Pòté flambeau vini!*" shouted the chief to the torch-bearers, reaching for a light . . . . "*ba moin! ba moin!*" He snatched one, and leaped forward, brandishing his weapon in the other hand. But precisely as he passed the threshold, a stunning report pealed through the archway; and the tall negro staggered, dropping torch and cutlass,—flung up both naked arms, reeled half round, and fell on his back, dead. The younger De Kersaint had kept his word.

The negroes at the entrance would have turned back in panic; but the pressure from behind, the rush of blind fury, was resistless; and the van of the populace was hurled into the arch-way,—struggling, howling, striking, stumbling over the corpse and the broken doors,—and with such an impetus that many fell. . . . The younger De Kersaint had not thought of retreat, even when the gentlemen who had descended with him, finding resistance hopeless, were remounting to the upper rooms: he still stood at the foot of the stairs with his empty pistol,—believing himself able to hold back the invasion, to terrorize by moral force. But terror may become a blind rage, even in the slave,—when made desperate by the necessity of confronting a pistol muzzle; and the blacks flung themselves on the young man with the very fury of fear. He had time only to dash his useless weapon in the face of the foremost, as a bayonet fastened to a pole passed through his body: then he sank without one cry under such a mad slashing of cutlasses that strikers wounded each other in their frenzy. . . . Simultaneously a double-barrelled gun, loaded with ball, was fired from the entrance at those reascending the stair-way,—both barrels together,—and M. Desrivières fell. He expired almost instantly, before his comrades could drag him into a room, of which the doors were at once barricaded with all the heavy furniture available;—the entire charge had entered his back, shattering the spine.

. . . . Then, after the momentary panic, came the reaction of hate, the mob thirst of vengeance;—traditional hate of the white intensified by the passions of the hour; vengeance for the fear inspired, for the killing of their leader, for all fancied or remembered wrongs. But the apartments of the ground-floor were empty: the békés had retreated to the upper rooms, whither it might be dangerous to pursue them;—perhaps they had arms in reserve for the last extremity. It was at all events certain they could not escape. The windows of the rear were high, and looked down upon a plantation road skirting cane-fields, where armed blacks were on the watch; and the side walls

were solid masonry without a single opening. Neither was escape possible by way of the roof,—elevated fully twenty feet
above the tiles of adjoining cottages;—the békés were helpless!
. . . . But no one now offered to lead the assault. There were
only clamorings,—hideous threats,—utterances that seemed
the conception of cannibals in delirium. . . . Meanwhile the
body of the dead leader, raised upon a broken door for a litter,
was being paraded through the streets by torch-light: armed
men ran beside the corpse, pointing to the pink brain oozing
from the wound, and crying:—"*Mi!—yo k'assassiné nou! yo ka
tchoué fouè nou!*" . . . . The excitement became maniacal;
but one voice,—a woman's, the voice of the wife of dead Sylvain, shrieked clearly through it all:—

—"*Metté difé, zautt!—brilé toutt béké!*"

And the mob caught up the cry,—stormed it through the
street. "*Difé!—metté difé!*" . . . . But what if the békés
should make a desperate rush upon the incendiaries? . . . .
"*Oté lescalié!*" some one suggested, and settled all hesitations.
There were arms enough to tear down any stair-way in five
minutes: it took less time for the rioters to obey the suggestion. They pulled away the stairs;—they smashed the wreck into
kindling-wood, piled it on the tiles of the hall-way, and fired it
with torches. The balustrade was of mahogany, but the steps
were *bois du nord*,—yellow pine, resinous and light. . . . "*Ka
pleine gomme!—ka brilé bien!*". . . . Simultaneously the furniture of the lower rooms was demolished;—everything they
contained was heaped upon the fire,—combustible or incom-
bustible: portraits, curtains, *verrines*, bronzes, mats, mirrors,
hangings. . . . "*Sacré tonnè, nou ké brilé toutt!—Ké ouè!*"
. . . . There were sounds of affright overhead,—of feet wildly
running,—of furniture being dragged away from doors;—
there were shrieks. . . . "*Ouaill!*—not so brave now, the
cursed békés!". . . . Then faces appeared through the smoke,
looking down,—a gray-haired lady, striving to be heard, to
speak to some heart;—a young mother dumbly pointing to
her infant. Two black arms reached up toward her in savage
mockery, and a negress hoarsely screamed: "*Ba moin li!—
moin sé vlopé enlai y conm chatrou!*—miming the cuttle-fish
devouring its prey! A burst of obscene laughter followed the
infamous jest. . . . But the heat and smoke became

unendurable;—the incendiaries retreated,—mostly to the street,—a few to the cane-fields in the rear, to watch for any possible attempts at escape. There was no more stone-throwing: the flingers were weary; and the mob was content to watch the progress of its vengeance. The shrieks could still be heard: they were answered by gibes and curses.

The arch-way reddened,—lighted,—began to glow like a furnace, forcing by its heat a general falling back from the entrance . . . . And soon the crackling within became a low roar, like the sound of a torrent;—all the *rez-de-chaussée* was seized by the flame. It put long yellow tongues through the windows;—they serpentined about the masonry, licked the key-stones and the wall above them,—striving to climb;—began to devour the framework of the shutters. . . . And, at intervals, from street to street, sounded the sinister melancholy blowing of the great sea-shells.

Over all the roofs of the city the voice of an immense bell began to peal,—rapidly, continuously: the *bourdon* of the cathedral was tolling the tocsin. One after another the bells of the lesser churches joined in the alarm. But, for the first time, the pumps remained in their station-houses;—the black firemen ignored the summons! And still the soldiers,—though muttering mutiny,—were rigidly confined to their barracks by superior order. Yet the Governor* knew the city was at the mercy of a negro mob,—knew the white population in peril of massacre. The order seemed incredible to those who read it with their eyes;—it remains one of the stupefying facts of French colonial history,—one of the many, not of the few, which appear to justify the white Creole's undying hate of Republicanism.

. . . . Fanned by a south breeze, the flames assailed the rear more rapidly than the front rooms of the besieged dwelling,—destroying communication between them by devouring the lobbies connected with the wrecked end of the stairway. And, through the outpouring of smoke, men began to drop or leap from back windows,—abandoning the women and children,—goaded by the swift menace of the hideous death of fire. On the side of the street there could have been no hope; —on that of the fields there were fewer enemies: there was one

---

*Rostoland, maréchal de camp, gouverneur provisoire.

desperate chance. Of those who took it, the first two were killed almost as soon as they touched the ground;—the third, a French stranger, although frightfully wounded, was able to run for his life nearly two hundred yards before being overtaken and despatched. But two others could profit by the incident;— gaining the high canes, they fled at a crouching run between the stems,—doubling,—twisting,—and were quickly lost to view . . . . "*Béké lacampagne mênm!*"—cried the disappointed pursuers:—"*yo ka fenne kanne!*" Only a country Creole could have known the trick, successfully practised by maroon negroes—*fenne kanne* (splitting the cane). . . . Darkness and the terror of serpents aided their flight.

Some chivalrous men,—M. de Kersaint was of these,— refused that desperate chance; remained to give the consolation of their presence to the helpless women,—mothers and wives, and young girls delicately bred, into the perfumed quiet of whose existence no shadow of fear had ever fallen before. . . . There were still nearly thirty souls within the flaming house; and the soldiers were still confined to their barracks!

The smoke being blown to the north, the view of the burning dwelling continued almost unobscured on the street side;—but as yet, since the stone-throwing began, no one had appeared at the front windows. The rabble watched and wondered: it seemed as if all communication between the front and rear of the besieged house had already been cut off, so that the last scene of the tragedy would remain hidden from them—a brutal disappointment! The first frenzy had exhausted itself: there remained only that revolting apathy which in savage natures follows the perpetration of a monstrous act;—the tempest of outcries subsided to a low tide-roar of excited converse. . . .

—"They are women and children who scream like that."

—"Malediction! they are békés—let them all roast together!"

—"*Ouill papa!*—they burned enough of us when they had the power to do it."

—"Yes! they burned poor negresses for sorcery. The priest who confessed them said they were innocent."

—"*Ah! c'est taille-Toto ça!*"—that was in the old times!"

—"Old times! We don't forget. These are the new times, *monfi!*"

—"*C'est jusse!* . . . . We are fighting for our liberty now."

—"Houlo!". . . . A new roar went up:—there was an apparition at one of the windows.

—"*Mi! yon négresse!*"

—"It is the *da!—Jesis-Maïa!*"

—"*Pé!—pé zautt!*"

—"Pé!" . . . . The word ran from mouth to mouth;—almost a hush followed its passage through the crowd, a hush of malignant expectation;—then Youma's powerful contralto rang out with the distinctness of a bugle-call.

—"*Eh! tas de capons!*" she cried, fearlessly,—"cowards afraid to face men! Do you believe you will win your liberty by burning women and children? . . . . Who were the mothers of you ?"

—"We are burning békés," screamed a negress in response: "they kill us; we kill them. *C'est jusse!*"

—"You lie!" cried Youma. "The békés never murdered women and children."

—"They did!" vociferated a mulatto in the mob, better dressed than his fellows;—"they did! In seventeen hundred and twenty-one! In seventeen hundred and twenty-five!" . . . .

—"*Aïe, macaque!*" mocked Youma. "So you burn negresses now for imitation! What have the negresses done to you, Ape?"

—"They are with the békés."

—"You were with the békés yesterday, the day before yesterday, and always,—every one of you. The békés gave you to eat,—the békés gave you to drink,—the békés cared for you when you were sick. . . . The békés gave *you* freedom, O you traitor mulatto!—gave you a name, *saloprie!*—gave you the clothes you wear, ingrate! *You!*—you are not fighting for your liberty, liar!—the békés gave it to you long ago for your black mother's sake! . . . . *Fai doctè, milatt!*—I know you! . . . . coward without a family, without a race!—*fai filosofe*, O you renegade, who would see a negress burn because a negress was your mother!—*Allé!—bâtà-béké!*". . . .

Then Youma could not make herself heard: a fresh outburst of vociferation drowned her voice. But her reproaches had struck home in at least one direction: she had touched and stirred the smouldering contempt, the secret jealous hate of the black for the freedman of color; and the mulatto's discomfiture was hailed by yells of ironical laughter. In the same moment there was a violent pushing and swaying;—some one was forcing his way to the front through all the pressure,—rapidly, furiously, —smiting with his elbows, battering with his shoulders: a giant *capre*. . . . He freed himself, and sprang into the clear space before the flaming building,— making his cutlass flicker about his head,—and shouted:—

—"*Nou pa ka brilé négresse!*". . . .

The mulatto put to scorn advanced and would have spoken; —ere he could utter a word, the travailleur, with a sudden backward blow of his unarmed hand, struck him to the ground.

—"*A moin! méfouè!*" thundered the tall new-comer;— "Stand by me, brothers!—we do not burn negresses!"

And Youma knew it was Gabriel who stood there alone,— colossal, menacing, magnificent,—daring the hell about him for her sake. . . .

—"*Ni raison! ni raison!*" responded numbers. . . . "*Non! nou pa ka brilé négresse! . . . . Châché léchelle!*" Gabriel had forced sympathy,—wrung some sentiment of compassion from those wild-beast hearts. . . . "*Pòté léchelle vini!—içi yon léchelle!*" was clamored through the crowd . . . . "a ladder!— a ladder!"

Five minutes,—and a ladder touched the window. Gabriel himself ascended it,—reached the summit,—put out his iron hand. Even as he did so, Youma, stooping to the sill, lifted Mayotte from behind it.

The child was stupid with terror;—she did not know him.

—"Can you save her?" asked Youma,—holding up the little fair-haired girl.

Gabriel could only shake his head; the street sent up so frightful a cry. . . .

—"*Non!—non!—non!—non!—pa lè yche-béké!—janmain yche-béké!*"

—"Then you cannot save me!" cried Youma, clasping the child to her bosom,—"*janmain! janmain, mon ami!*"

—"Youma, in the name of God . . . ."

—"In the name of God you ask me to be a coward! . . . . Are you vile, Gabriel?—are you base? . . . . Save myself and leave the child to burn? . . . . Go!"

—"Leave the *béké's yche!*—leave it!—leave it, girl!" shouted a hundred voices.

—"*Moin!*" cried Youma, retreating beyond the reach of

Gabriel's hand,—"*moin!* . . . . Never shall I leave it,—never! I shall go to God with it."

—"Burn with it, then!" howled the negroes . . . . "down with that ladder! down with it, down with it!" Gabriel had barely time to save himself, when the ladder was dragged away. All the first fury of the riot seemed to have been rekindled by the sight of the child;—again broke forth the tempest of maledictions.

But it calmed: there was another reaction. . . . Gabriel had men to strive with him. They forced the ladder once more into position;—they formed a desperate guard about it with their cutlasses;—they called to Youma to descend. . . . She only waved her hand in disdain: she knew she could not save the child.

And the fierce heat below began to force back the guard at the foot of the ladder. . . . Suddenly Gabriel uttered a curse of despair. Touched by a spirt of flame, the ladder itself had ignited,—and was burning furiously.

Youma remained at the window. There was now neither hate nor fear in her fine face: it was calm as in the night when Gabriel had seen her stand unmoved with her foot on the neck of the serpent.

Then a sudden light flared up behind her, and brightened. Against it her tall figure appeared, as in the Chapel of the Anchorage Gabriel had seen, against a background of gold, the figure of *Notre Dame du Bon Port.* . . . Still her smooth features expressed no emotion. Her eyes were bent upon the blond head hiding against her breast;—her lips moved;—she was speaking to the child. . . . Little Mayotte looked up one moment into the dark and beautiful bending face,—and joined her slender hands, as if to pray.

But with a piteous cry, she clung to Youma's bosom again. For the thick walls quivered as walls quiver when a hurricane blows;—and there were shrieks,—frantic, heart-sickening, from the rear,—and a noise of ruining, as of smothered thunder. Youma drew off her foulard of yellow silk, and wrapped it about the head of the child: then began to caress her with calm tenderness,—murmuring to her,—swaying her softly in her arms,—all placidly, as though lulling her to sleep. Never to Gabriel's watching eyes had Youma seemed so beautiful.

Another minute—and he saw her no more. The figure and the light vanished together, as beams and floor and roof all quaked down at once into darkness. . . . Only the skeleton of stone remained,—black-smoking to the stars.

And stillness came,—a stillness broken only by the hissing and crepitation of the stifled fire, the booming of the tocsin, the far blowing of the great sea-shells. The victims had ceased to shriek;—the murderers stood appalled by the ghastliness of their consummated crime.

Then, from below, the flames wrestled out again,—crimsoning the smoke whirls, the naked masonry, the wreck of timbers. They wriggled upward, lengthening, lapping together,—lifted themselves erect,—grew taller, fiercer,— twined into one huge fluid spire of tongues that flapped and shivered high into the night. . . .

The yellowing light swelled, expanded from promontory to promontory, palpitated over the harbor,—climbed the broken slopes of the dead volcano leagues through the gloom. The wooded mornes towered about the city in weird illumination, —seeming loftier than by day,—blanching and shadowing alternately with the soaring and sinking of the fire;—and at each huge pulsing of the glow, the white cross of their central summit stood revealed, with the strange passion of its black Christ.

. . . . And the same hour, from the other side of the world,—a ship was running before the sun, bearing the Republican gift of liberty and promise of universal suffrage to the slaves of Martinique.

SELECTED JOURNALISM

SOME STRANGE EXPERIENCE

THE REMINISCENCES OF A GHOST-SEER,

Being the Result of a Chat on the Kitchen-Stairs

"THEY do say the dead never come back again," she observed half dreamingly; "but then I have seen such queer things!"

She was a healthy, well built country girl, whom the most critical must have called good looking; robust and ruddy, despite the toil of life in a boarding-house kitchen, but with a strangely thoughtful expression in her large dark eyes, as though she were ever watching the motions of somebody who cast no shadow, and was invisible to all others. Spiritualists were wont to regard her as a strong "medium," although she had a peculiar dislike of being so regarded. She had never learned to read or write, but possessed naturally a wonderful wealth of verbal description, a more than ordinarily vivid memory, and a gift of conversation which would have charmed an Italian *improvisatore*. These things we learned during an idle half hour passed one summer's evening in her company on the kitchen stairs; while the boarders lounged on the porch in the moonlight, and the hall lamp created flickering shadows along the varnished corridors, and the hungry rats held squeaking carnival in the dark dining-room. To the weird earnestness of the story-teller, the melody of her low, soft voice, and the enthralling charm of her conversation, we can not attempt to do justice; nor shall we even undertake to report her own mysterious narrative word for word, but only to convey to the reader those impressions of it which linger in the writer's memory.

"The first thing I can remember about ghost-people," she said, "happened to me when I was quite a little child. It was in Bracken County, Kentucky, on a farm, between Dover and Augusta—about half way between the towns—for I remember a great big stone that was set up on the road just above the farm, which they called the "Half-way Stone," and it had a big letter H cut on it. The farm-house was away back from the river, in a lonely place, among woods of beech and sugartrees; and was one of the weirdest old buildings you ever saw. It was built before there were any nails used out West; so you can imagine how old it was; and I heard that the family who first built it had many a terrible fight with the Indians. Before the house ran a rocky lane full of gutters and mud holes; and behind it was a great apple orchard, where very few apples grew, because no one took care of the trees. Great slimy, creeping plants had grown up about them, and strangled them; and the pathways were almost grown over with high weeds, and strong rank grass; and owls lived in some of the trees, but the family seemed to be afraid to shoot them. At the end of the orchard yawned a great, deep well, unused for many years; cats and dogs and rabbits had found graves in the fetid black water; the stones were green with moss and slime; the bucket was covered with moss; and great black snakes which lived in holes in the sides of the well used to wriggle out on sunny days and blink their wicked, shiny eyes at the house. This well was at the mouth of a deep hollow, choked up with elder-brush and those creeping plants that can never be killed, and there were black-snakes, garter-snakes and dry-land moccasins living there. Near the hollow on the other side flowed a clear "branch" of water over a bed of soft blue clay, which we used to roll into "slate pencils" and make mud pies of. One time we wanted to make a little mill-dam there, to drown some geese in, and while digging into the blue clay with a grubbing-hoe we found four great big Mexican dollars buried there. We did not know what they were then, and we brought them to the farm-house, where they took them from us. Some time afterwards two men came and bought the piece of ground where we had found the money, and they set to digging; but nothing more was ever found there.

"The farm house looked as if it had been built a hundred years ago, but those who built it built well and strong, for it was sound from roof to foundation. Many of the big trees in the orchard, planted by them, had rotted and died, and the bark was peeling off over nests of the gray wood-lice that burrowed under it; but the old house was still strong. It was a very queer, antiquated structure, with ghostly looking gables, and great limestone chimneys towered up at each end of it. There were four big rooms, two up stairs and two down stairs, and a little kitchen built against the house, making a fifth room; there were five old-fashioned doors of heavy planking, and there were eight or ten narrow windows, with ever so many tiny panes of glass in them. The house was built of heavy sarsaparilla logs, with floors of black walnut, and walls ceiled with blue ash; and there were no shelves, but only recesses in the walls—small, square recesses, where books and little things were kept. The clapboards were fastened down on the roof with wooden pegs, and the flooring was pegged down to the sleepers. Between the planking and the logs of the south room on the first floor there was an old Revolutionary musket built into the wall. The north room, next to this, was never occupied.

"I remember that room well; for the door was often open, although no one of the family ever entered it since an old lady named Frankie Boyd had died there, years before, of consumption. She had lingered a long time, and coughed a great deal, and used to spit on the wall beside the bed. The bed was an old-time piece of furniture, with posters; and all the furniture was old-fashioned. There was an old-fashioned clothes-chest with legs; an old-fashioned rocking-chair, with great heavy rockers; and an old-fashioned spinning-wheel. One of the old lady's dresses, a black dress, still hung on the wall where she had placed it the last time she had took it off; but it had become so old and moth-eaten that a touch would have crumbled it like so much burnt paper. The dust was thick on the floor, so thick that the foot would leave an impression in it; and the windows were yellow like parchment for want of cleaning.

"They said that the old lady used to walk about that room, and that no one could sleep there. Doors used to open and shut without the touch of human hands; and all night long the sound of the rocking-chair rocking, and of the spinning-wheel humming, could be heard through the house. That was why nobody ever went into that room. But the ghost of Frankie Boyd was not the only ghost there. The house had once been owned by the Paddy family, and Lee Paddy, the 'old man,' and all his children, had died in the room used when I was there for a kitchen, and had been buried in the family graveyard, on the north side of the house, under the shadow of a great locust tree. After Frankie Boyd died the house fell into the hands of her nephew, a man named Bean, who had a rich father, a scientific old gentleman, in Lewis County. Both father and son were queer people, and the old man's eccentricity at one time nearly lost him his life. Some one killed an immense black-snake on his farm, and the scientific Mr. Bean had it cooked for dinner after the manner of cooking salmon. Then he invited a friendly neighbor to dine with him. They say that the neighbor was delighted with the repast, and declared that he had never eaten finer salmon. But when old Bean told him that he had eaten a black snake which John killed yesterday morning, the shock nearly killed him, and he staggered home to get his shotgun. Bean did not dare to leave his home for weeks afterwards.

"After the death of Frankie Boyd, the old farmhouse in Bracken County of course became a weirder and ghostlier place than ever—a scary place, as the slaves around there used to call it. It was a dreadfully creaky place, and no one could pass out or down the old staircase without making a prodigious creaking and crackling. Now at all hours of the day or night those stairs creaked and creaked, and doors opened and banged, and steps echoed overhead in the rooms upstairs. I was a very little girl then and had a little boy-playmate, who used to run about with me all over the farm, digging in the blue clay, running after the fowls, watching the great snakes that glided about the noisome well, climbing the strangled apple trees in search of withered and shrunken apples, and throwing pebbles at the great, ugly horned owls that used to sit there among the creepers, blinking with their great yellow eyes. We did not know why the house was haunted by such odd noises; and the old negro servants were strictly forbidden to tell us anything about the queer things that walked about there. But, nevertheless, we had a perfect horror of the house; we dreaded to be left in it alone; we never entered it on sunny days, except at meal time, and when foul weather forced us to stay in-doors the folks often found us sitting down and crying in a corner. We could not at first tell why we cried, further than that we were afraid of something undefinable—a vague fear always weighed upon us like a nightmare. They told us to go up stairs, one evening after dark, and we had to go without a light. Something came after us, and stepped up the stairs behind us, and touched our heads, and followed us into the room, and seemed to sob and moan. We screamed with fear, and the folks ran up with a lantern and took us down stairs again. Some one used also to play with the rusty old musket that had been built into the wall, and would get under the black walnut floor, knocking loudly and long; and all the time the rocking-chair creaked and thumped in the north room. Bean had got used to it all; but he seldom went up stairs, and the books in the old recesses became black with layers of clammy dust, and the spiders spun thick, glutinous webs across the windows.

"It came to pass about six months after the dead had followed us into the dark room upstairs, that a great storm came down through the woods, wrestling with the ancient trees, tearing away the serpent-creepers in the garden, swelling the springs to torrents, and the old farm-house rattled through all its dry bones. The great limestone chimneys and the main building stood the test bravely: but the little kitchen building where all the Paddy family had died, was shattered from clapboards to doorstep. It had been built in a very curious fashion, a fashion passed away and forgotten; and the cunning of modern house builders could not rebuild it. So they pulled it down, log by log, and brought destruction upon many spider colonies, and mice nests, and serpent holes; building a new pinewood structure in its place, with modern doors and windows. And from that time the strange noises ceased and the dead seemed to rest, except in the room where the yellow spittle had dried upon the walls and the old-fashioned furniture had become hoary with years of dust. The steps on the staircase died away forever, and the knocking beneath the floor ceased.

"But I must not forget to tell you one more curious thing about the place. There was a hen-house near the grave of the Paddy family; and the hens were great in multitude, and laid eggs by hundreds. Somehow or other we could scarcely ever get any eggs for all that. The hens were thin, spectral birds, which looked as if they had been worn out by anxiety and disappointment. Something or other used to steal their eggs the moment they were laid; and what it was no one ever pretended to know. The old negro cook hinted that the ghosts of the Paddy family sucked the eggs; but as we could never find even an egg-shell, this supposition did not hold good. Traps were laid for pole-cats, weasels, coons, and every variety of wild egg-thieves; but none were ever seen there or caught; and the poultry ceased to propagate their species, so that fresh relays of poultry had to be purchased ever and anon. I don't know whether the old farm-house still stands or whether Bachelor Bean has been gathered to his fathers, for it is many years since I left there to live with friends at Dover.

"I had another experience, of a much more unpleasant kind, I think, during the time I remained at Dover. All the country round there is hilly; and there are two broad turnpike roads winding out of the city—one called the Maysville pike, the other the Dover pike, running from Dover beyond Minerva. Now, both of the pikes have been the scene of violent death; and both are said to be haunted. Of the latter fact I have the testimony of my own eyes—which, I make bold to remark, are very sharp eyes.

"About four miles from Dover, on the Maysville pike, the road, following the winding of the hills, crosses a rude bridge of rocks and timber over a swift stream, and curves into the shape of a gigantic horse-shoe. This place is called 'Horse-shoe Bend,' is situated between two hills, and is wild and 'scary' in the extreme. Since the occurrence which gave a specter to Horse-shoe Bend, few have the courage to pass the spot after nightfall; and those who must, put spurs to their horses and gallop by as though the Devil were riding behind them; for the specter of a suicide haunts the bend.

"I can't well remember when it happened, but I do not think it was more than half a dozen years ago; and I even forget the man's name. I only know that he was a married man, pretty well-to-do, and lived at Rock Springs, below Augusta. One day he left his home on business, and was detained in town beyond his usual hour for returning. It was a bright, frosty winter's night; the pike was white and hard as iron, and his horse's hoofs made merry music on the long trot home, until he saw his farm-house and its shadow lying black and sharp on the fields, and the blood-red glow of the wood fire in the great limestone fireplace. Then it occurred to him, strangely enough, to dismount, tie his horse to a tree, and creep softly up to the window. His wife sat by the fire, but not alone; the arm of a stranger was about her waist, and the fingers of a stranger were playing with her hair. Then he turned, sick at heart, from the window, and crept along in the shadows to where his horse stood, and mounted and rode away, recklessly, madly, furiously. People who looked out of their windows as he passed say they never saw man ride so before. The hard pike flashed into fire under the iron hoofs of the flying horse, the rider cursed like a fiend, and the great watch-dogs in the farmhouses howled as though a specter were sweeping by. Neither horse nor horseman ever returned. Some little school children next morning passing by Horse-shoe Bend, in the golden light of the early sun, saw the farmer hanging from a tree by his bridle rein; and the horse laying by the side of the road, dead, and frozen like his rider. Preacher Holton and Sam Berry cut down the body; but the specter of the suicide has never left the spot. They say the only way to make the spirit of a suicide rest is to bury the body with a stake driven through it. I don't know whether that is true; but I know that every time I passed Horse-shoe Bend I could see the farmer leaning against a tree, dressed in his gray winter suit, and the horse lying down by the side of the road. You could see the very woof of the cloth, the very hair of the black horse; yet the moment you got near enough to touch the specter with the hand, it passed away like the flame of a candle blown out. I have often seen it.

"I don't know very much about the history of the apparition which haunts the other pike; I have forgotten the name, but I have seen the thing which walks there. About three miles from Dover, on the way to Minerva, is a toll gate, and about a mile and a half above the toll gate is a place called Firman's Woods, a hilly place, with trees. In a hollow by the side of the road at this point, a farmer was murdered for his money, and his body flung into the brush. He had ridden over that road a hundred times, and paid many a toll at the toll-gate; everybody knew his grizzled beard and broad-brimmed hat when he passed by. On the night of the murder he had disposed of some stock and was returning home with a well filled pocket-book, when he met another horseman traveling toward Minerva. Perhaps he was incautious with his new acquaintance; perhaps he foolishly displayed the greasy pocket-book, fat with rolls of green bills, for on reaching Firman's Woods the stranger stabbed him to the heart with a bowie-knife, hid the corpse in the hollow, and galloped off with the dead man's money. The victim of the murder has never found the sleepy rest of death. A spectral rider gallops nightly along the pike, sometimes flying past the toll-gate invisible, his horse's hoofs echoing loud and sharply of cold nights, and splashing through the mud with a soggy sound on rainy evenings. But he is only seen at Firman's Woods—a shadowy figure, headless and horrible. I have seen it, and beheld it dissolve like the flame of a candle in a strong current of wind.

"The most frightful experience I ever had—at least the one which frightened me most—was in the town of Minerva. I was working for a family there as cook, and my room was a dark and shadowy apartment, in the back of the building. It had a window, but the window gave scarcely any light, because it faced a higher building across the alley, and had not been cleaned for years. I thought there was something queer about the room, because the first day I came to the house Joe —— took me up stairs with a candle in his hand, and said, 'You won't be afraid to sleep here, will you?' Well, I said, 'No.'"

[Here we ventured to ask the narrator what Joe's other name was, but she objected, for private reasons, to mention it, and we had to content ourselves with the fact that Joe was the proprietor of the house and a man of family.]

"I worked there only one day. When supper was over, and the dishes had been washed up, and every thing put in order, I went up-stairs to bed. I remember that I felt afraid—I could not tell why—to blow the candle out; but I thought the folks would scold me for wasting candles, so I blew it out at last, and crept into bed, and tried to pull the covers up over me. I found I could not move them at first; they seemed to be nailed to the foot of the bed. Then I gave a very strong pull, and succeeded in getting the clothes up, although it seemed as if a heavy weight had been lying on them. Suddenly I felt a distinct pull back— something was pulling the clothes off of the bed. I pulled them back again, and they were again pulled off. Of course I felt frightened; but I had seen and heard strange things before, and concluded to lie down quietly and let the clothes be, because I thought that if I would let the Thing alone, it would let me alone. And at last I fell asleep.

"I don't know how long I slept; but I had a hideous nightmare, and awoke panting in the dark, feeling that something was in the room with me. About a minute afterward it put its fingers on my mouth, and then stroked my nose. I thought of getting up, but I was too frightened to move; when I felt an immense hand placed on my chest, pressing me down to the bed—a hand so vast that it covered me from shoulder to shoulder, and felt heavier than iron. I was too frightened to faint, too spell-bound to scream, too powerless to move under that giant pressure. And with the pressure came horror, a horror of hell, unspeakably awful, worse than the ghastly enchantment of a thousand nightmares. I remember that I would have wished to die but for the hideous fancy that my ghost would go out in the dark to that awful Thing. The hand was suddenly removed, and I shrieked like a maniac in the dungeon of a lunatic asylum. Every one heard that shriek; and they came running up with lights and white faces. They showed me the doors and the windows securely fastened, and showed me that no human being had been in the room besides myself; but I did not need to be told that. I left the house next day.

"There was something of the same kind in a house in Lexington, where I used to live. It had once been owned by a lady named Jane ——, a slaveholder in the days before the war; but she had passed to the place of Shadows, and her house had fallen into other hands. Still her sins haunted it—haunted it horribly. They say that one winter's night, many years ago, she had whipped a negro slave to death with her own hands for some trifling act of disobedience. He was a powerful man, but they had stripped and securely tied him so that resistance was impossible, and the woman beat him with a leather strap, dipped in water, for eight consecutive hours. And the body died and was buried under the floor, and became green with rottenness; but the ghost of the man walked about and groaned, and tormented all who lived in the building. The woman used to sit on her doorstep all night crying in the moonshine, while the ghost groaned within. At last she moved away, and died in another neighborhood; but even when I was there the specter used to pull the bedclothing off the beds down stairs, if any one dared to sleep there.

"I have seen and heard many odd things of this kind; and once I saw what they call a wraith or a double, but I don't think you would find them so interesting as my last experience in a Cincinnati house. It was on West Fifth street, and I was working there both as cook and chambermaid. There was a story connected with the house, which I never knew correctly, and will therefore not attempt to relate, beyond that a certain young girl died there and came back afterwards. But I was not told about this circumstance until I had worked there for some time. It happened one evening, about dusk, that I went up stairs to one of the bed-rooms on an errand; and I saw a young lady, all in white, standing before the mirror, tall and silent. The sun had set the color of blood that evening, and a faint rosy-glow still mingled with the gloomy gray, so that objects were plainly discernible and sharply outlined. Now, as I had left all the boarders at supper, I thought on first entering the room that the figure before the mirror must be that of some lady visitor, whose coming I had not known. I stood for a moment and looked at her, but did not see any face, for her back was turned to me, and, as she seemed unusually tall, I thought that the blackness of her hair was lost in the blackness of the shadows above the mirror. But it suddenly occurred to me to glance at the mirror. I did so. There was the figure, tall, silent and white, but there was no face or head visible. I approached to touch the white shadow; it vanished like the flame of a candle vanishes, or as the breath vanishes from the mirror that has been breathed upon.

"People call me a medium, sometimes, and ask me to sit in dark circles and help to call up spirits. I have always refused— do you wonder at it? I tell you the truth, sir, when I say that far from refusing to leave the dead alone, I would be only too happy if they would leave me alone."

Cincinnati Commercial, September 26, 1875

LEVEE LIFE

HAUNTS AND PASTIMES OF THE ROUSTABOUTS.

Their Original Songs and Peculiar Dances.

ALONG the river-banks on either side of the levee slope, where the brown water year after year climbs up to the ruined side-walks, and pours into the warehouse cellars, and paints their grimy walls with streaks of water-weed green, may be studied a most curious and interesting phase of life—the life of a community within a community,—a society of wanderers who have haunts but not homes, and who are only connected with the static society surrounding them by the common bond of State and municipal law. It is a very primitive kind of life; its lights and shadows are alike characterized by a half savage simplicity; its happiness or misery is almost purely animal; its pleasures are wholly of the hour, neither enhanced nor lessened by anticipations of the morrow. It is always pitiful rather than shocking; and it is not without some little charm of its own—the charm of a thoughtless existence, whose virtues are all original, and whose vices are for the most part foreign to it. A great portion of this levee-life haunts also the subterranean hovels and ancient frame buildings of the district lying east of Broadway to Culvert street, between Sixth and Seventh streets. But, on a cool spring evening, when the levee is bathed in moonlight, and the torch-basket lights dance redly upon the water, and the clear air vibrates to the sonorous music of the deep-toned steam-whistle, and the sound of wild banjo-thrumming floats out through the open doors of the levee dance-houses, then it is perhaps that one can best observe the peculiarities of this grotesquely-picturesque roustabout life.

Probably less than one-third of the stevedores and 'long-shoremen employed in our river traffic are white; but the calling now really belongs by right to the negroes, who are by far the best roustabouts and are unrivaled as firemen. The white stevedores are generally tramps, willing to work only through the fear of the Work-house; or, some times laborers unable to obtain other employment, and glad to earn money for the time being at any employment. On board the boats, the whites and blacks mess separately and work under different mates, there being on an average about twenty-five roustabouts to every boat which unloads at the Cincinnati levee. Cotton boats running on the Lower Mississippi, will often carry sixty or seventy deck-hands, who can some seasons earn from forty-five dollars to sixty dollars per month. On the Ohio boats, the average wages paid to roustabouts will not exceed $30 per month. 'Longshoremen earn fifteen and twenty cents per hour, according to the season. These are frequently hired by Irish contractors, who undertake to unload a boat at so much per package; but the first-class boats generally contract with the 'longshoremen directly through the mate, and sometimes pay twenty-five cents per hour for such labor. "Before Freedom," as the colored folks say, white laborers performed most of the roustabout labor on the steamboats; the negroes are now gradually monopolizing the calling, chiefly by reason of their peculiar fitness for it. Generally speaking they are the best porters in the world; and in the cotton States, it is not uncommon, we are told, to see negro levee hands for a wager, carry five-hundred-pound cotton-bales on their backs to the wharf boat. River men, to-day, are recognizing the superior value of negro labor in steamboat traffic, and the colored roustabouts are now better treated, probably, than they have been since the war. Under the present laws, too, they are better protected. It used at one time to be a common thing for some ruffianly mate to ship sixty or seventy stevedores, and, after the boat had taken in all her freight, to hand the poor fellows their money and land them at some small town, or even in the woods, hundreds of miles from their home. This can be done no longer with legal impunity.

Roustabout life in the truest sense is, then, the life of the colored population of the Rows, and, partly, of Bucktown—blacks and mulattoes from all parts of the States, but chiefly from Kentucky and Eastern Virginia, where most of them appear to have toiled on the plantations before Freedom; and echoes of the old plantation life still live in their songs and their pastimes. You may hear old Kentucky slave songs chanted nightly on the steamboats, in that wild, half-melancholy key peculiar to the natural music of the African race; and you may see the old slave dances nightly performed to the air of some ancient Virginia-reel in the dance-houses of Sausage Row, or the "ball-rooms" of Bucktown. There is an intense uniqueness about all this pariah existence; its boundaries are most definitely fixed; its enjoyments are wholly sensual, and many of them are marked by peculiarities of a strictly local character. Many of their songs, which have never appeared in print, treat of levee life in Cincinnati, of all the popular steamboats running on the "Muddy Water," and of the favorite roustabout haunts on the river bank and in Bucktown. To collect these curious songs, or even all the most popular of them, would be a labor of months, and even then a difficult one, for the colored roustabouts are in the highest degree suspicious of a man who approaches them with a note-book and pencil. Occasionally, however, one can induce an intelligent steamboatman to sing a few river songs by an innocent bribe in the shape of a cigar or a drink, and this we attempted to do with considerable success during a few spare evenings last week, first, in a popular roustabout haunt on Broadway, near Sixth, and afterward in a dingy frame cottage near the corner of Sixth and Culvert streets. Unfortunately some of the most curious of these songs are not of a character to admit of publication in the columns of a daily newspaper; but others which we can present to our readers may prove interesting. Of these the following song, "Number Ninety-Nine," was at one time immensely popular with the steamboatmen. The original resort referred to was situated on Sixth and Culvert street, where Kirk's building now stands. We present the song with some necessary emendations:

> "You may talk about yer railroads,
>   Yer steamboats and can-*el*
> If 't hadn't been for Liza Jane
>   There wouldn't a bin no hell.
>   Chorus—Oh, ain't I gone, gone, gone,
>   Oh, ain't I gone, gone, gone,
>   Oh, ain't I gone, gone, gone,
>   Way down de ribber road.
>
> "Whar do you get yer whisky?
>   Whar do you get yer rum?

I got it down in Bucktown,
　　At Number Ninety-nine.
　　　　Chorus—Oh, ain't I gone, gone, gone, &c.

"I went down to Bucktown,
　　Nebber was dar before,
Great big niggah knocked me down,
　　But Katy barred the door.
　　　　Chorus—Oh, ain't I gone, gone, gone, &c.

"She hugged me, she kissed me,
　　She tole me not to cry;
She said I wus de sweetest thing
　　Dat ebber libbed or died.
　　　　Chorus—Oh, ain't I gone, gone, gone, &c.
　*　　*　　*　　*　　*　　*
"Yonder goes the Wildwood,
　　She's loaded to the guards,
But yonder comes the Fleetwood,
　　An' she's the boat for me.
　　　　Chorus—Oh, ain't I gone, gone, gone, &c."

The words, "'Way down to Rockingham," are sometimes substituted in the chorus, for "'way down de ribber road."

One of the most popular roustabout songs now sung on the Ohio is the following. The air is low, and melancholy, and when sung in unison by the colored crew of a vessel leaving or approaching port, has a strange, sad sweetness about it which is very pleasing. The two-fold character of poor Molly, at once good and bad, is somewhat typical of the stevedore's sweetheart:

Molly was a good gal and a bad gal, too.
　　　　Oh Molly, row, gal.
Molly was a good gal and a bad gal, too,
　　　　Oh Molly, row, gal.

I'll row dis boat and I'll row no more,
　　　　Row, Molly, row, gal.
I'll row dis boat, and I'll go on shore,
　　　　Row, Molly, row, gal.

Captain on the biler deck a-heaving of the lead,
　　　Oh Molly, row, gal.
Calling to the pilot to give her, "Turn ahead,"
　　　Row, Molly, row, gal.

Here is another to a slow and sweet air. The chorus, when well sung, is extremely pretty:

　Shawneetown is burnin' down,
　　　　Who tole you so?
　Shawneetown is burnin' down,
　　　　Who tole you so?

　Cythie, my darlin' gal,
　　　　Who tole you so?
　Cythie, my darlin' gal,
　　　　How do you know?

Chorus—Shawneetown is burnin', &c.

How the h——l d'ye 'spect me to hold her,
　　　　Way down below?
I've got no skin on either shoulder,
　　　　Who tole you so?

Chorus—Shawneetown is burnin', &c.

De houses dey is all on fire,
　　　　Way down below.
De houses dey is all on fire,
　　　　Who tole you so?

Chorus—Shawneetown is burnin', &c.

My old missus tole me so,
　　　　Way down below.
An' I b'lieve what ole missus says,
　　　　Way down below.

Chorus—Shawneetown is burnin', &c.

The most melancholy of all these plaintive airs is that to which the song "Let her go by" is commonly sung. It is generally sung on leaving port, and sometimes with an affecting pathos inspired of the hour, while the sweethearts of the singers watch the vessel gliding down stream.

I'm going away to New Orleans!
　　Good-bye, my lover, good-bye!
I'm going away to New Orleans!
　　Good-bye, my lover, good-bye!
　　　Oh, let her go by!

She's on her way to New Orleans!
　　Good-bye, my lover, good-bye!
She bound to pass the Robert E. Lee,
　　Good-bye, my lover, good-bye!
　　　Oh, let her go by!

I'll make dis trip and I'll make no more!
　　Good-bye, my lover, good-bye!
I'll roll dese barrels, I'll roll no more!
　　Good-bye, my lover, good-bye!
　　　Oh, let her go by!

An' if you are not true to me,
　　Farewell, my lover, farewell!
An' if you are not true to me,
　　Farwell, my lover, farewell!
　　　Oh, let her go by!

The next we give is of a somewhat livelier description. It has, we believe, been printed in a somewhat different form in certain song books. We give it as it was sung to us in a Broadway saloon:

I come down the mountain,
　　An' she come down the lane,
An' all that I could say to her
　　Was, "Good bye, 'Liza Jane."

Chorus—Farewell, 'Liza Jane!
Farewell, 'Liza Jane!
Don't throw yourself away, for I
Am coming back again.

I got up on a house-top,
　　An' give my horn a blow;
Thought I heerd Miss Dinah say,
　　"Yonder comes your beau."
[Chorus.]

Ef I'd a few more boards,
    To build my chimney higher,
I'd keep aroun' the country gals,
    Chunkin' up the fire.
[Chorus.]

The following are fragments of rather lengthy chants, the words being almost similar in both, but the choruses and airs being very different. The air of the first is sonorous and regularly slow, like a sailor's chant when heaving anchor; the air of the next is quick and lively.

"Belle-a-Lee's got no time,
    Oh, Belle! oh, Belle!
Robert E. Lee's got railroad time,
    Oh, Belle! oh, Belle!

"Wish I was in Mobile Bay,
    Oh, Belle! oh, Belle!
Rollin' cotton by de day,
    Oh, Belle! oh, Belle!
*   *   *   *   *   *

"I wish I was in Mobile Bay,
Rollin' cotton by de day,
    Stow'n' sugar in de hull below,
      Below, belo-ow,
    Stow'n' sugar in de hull below!

"De Natchez is a new boat; she's just in her prime,
Beats any oder boat on de New Orleans line.
      Stow'n' sugar in de hull below, &c.

"Engineer, t'rough de trumpet, given de firemen news,
Couldn't make steam for de fire in de flues.
      Stow'n' sugar in de hull below, &c.

"Cap'n on de biler deck, a scratchin' of his head,
Hollers to de deck hand to heave de larbo'rd lead.
      Stow'n' sugar in de hull below, &c.

Perhaps the prettiest of all these songs is "The Wandering Steamboatman," which, like many other roustabout songs, rather frankly illustrates the somewhat loose morality of the calling:

> I am a wandering steamboatman,
>   And far away from home;
> I fell in love with a pretty gal,
>   And she in love with me.
>
> She took me to her parlor
>   And cooled me with her fan;
> She whispered in her mother's ear:
>   "I love the steamboatman."

The mother entreats her daughter not to become engaged to the stevedore. "You know," she says, "that he is a steamboatman, and has a wife at New Orleans." But the steamboatman replies, with great nonchalance:

> If I've a wife at New Orleans
>   I'm neither tied nor bound;
> And I'll forsake my New Orleans wife
>   If you'll be truly mine.

Another very curious and decidedly immoral song is popular with the loose women of the "Rows." We can only give one stanza:

> I hev a roustabout for my man—
> Livin' with a white man for a sham,
>   Oh, leave me alone,
>   Leave me alone,
> I'd like you much better if you'd leave me alone.

But the most famous songs in vogue among the roustabouts is "Limber Jim," or "Shiloh." Very few know it all by heart, which is not wonderful when we consider that it requires something like twenty minutes to sing "Limber Jim" from beginning to end, and that the whole song, if printed in full, would fill two columns of the Commercial. The only person in the city who can sing the song through, we believe, is a colored laborer living near Sixth and Culvert streets, who "run on the river" for years, and acquired so much of a reputation by singing "Limber Jim," that he has been nicknamed after the mythical individual aforesaid, and is now known by no other name. He keeps a little resort in Bucktown, which is known as "Limber Jim's," and has a fair reputation for one dwelling in that locality. Jim very good-naturedly sang the song for us a few nights ago, and we took down some of the most striking verses for the benefit of our readers. The air is wonderfully quick and lively, and the chorus is quite exciting. The leading singer sings the whole song, excepting the chorus, "Shiloh," which dissyllable is generally chanted by twenty or thirty voices of abysmal depth at the same time with a sound like the roar of twenty Chinese gongs struck with tremendous force and precision. A great part of "Limber Jim" is very profane, and some of it not quite fit to print. We can give only about one-tenth part of it. The chorus is frequently accompanied with that wonderfully rapid slapping of thighs and hips known as "patting Juba."

> Nigger an' a white man playing seven-up,
> White man played an ace; an' nigger feared to take it up,
> White man played ace an' nigger played a nine,
> White man died, an' nigger went blind.
>> Limber Jim,
>>> [All.] Shiloh!
>> Talk it agin,
>>> [All.] Shiloh!
>> Walk back in love,
>>> [All.] Shiloh!
>> You turtle-dove,
>>> [All.] Shiloh!

> Went down the ribber, couldn't get across;
> Hopped on a rebel louse; thought 'twas a hoss,
> Oh lor', gals, 't ain't no lie,
> Lice in Camp Chase big enough to cry.—
>> Limber Jim, &c.

> Bridle up a rat, sir; saddle up a cat.
> Please han' me down my Leghorn hat,
> Went to see widow; widow warn't home;
> Saw to her daughter,—she gave me honeycomb.
>> Limber Jim, &c.

> Jay-bird sittin' on a swinging limb,
> Winked at me an' I winked at him,

Up with a rock an' struck him on the shin,
G—d d—n yer soul, don't wink again.
      Limber Jim, &c.

Some folks says that a rebel can't steal,
I found twenty in my corn-fiel',
Sich pullin' of shucks an' tearin of corn!—
Nebber saw the like since I was born.
      Limber Jim, &c.

John Morgan come to Danville and cut a mighty dash,
Las' time I saw him, he was under whip an' lash;
'Long come a rebel at a sweepin' pace,
Whar 're ye goin', Mr. Rebel? "I'm goin' to Camp Chase."
      Limber Jim, &c.

Way beyond de sun and de moon,
White gal tole me I were too soon.
White gal tole me I come too soon,
An' nigger gal called me an ole d—d fool.
      Limber Jim, &c.

Eighteen pennies hidden in a fence,
Cynthiana gals ain't got no sense;
Every time they go from home
Comb thar heads wid an ole jaw bone.
      Limber Jim, &c.

Had a little wife an' didn' inten' to keep her;
Showed her a flatboat an' sent her down de ribber;
Head like a fodder-shock, mouf like a shovel,
Put yerself wid yaller gal, put yerself in trouble.
      Limber Jim, &c.

I went down to Dinah's house, Dinah was in bed,
Hoisted de window an' poked out her head;
T'rowed, an' I hit her in de eyeball,—bim;
"Walk back, Mr. Nigger; don't do dat agin."
      Limber Jim, &c.

Gambling man in de railroad line,
Saved my ace an' played my nine;

If you want to know my name,
My name's High-low-jack-in-the-game.
   Limber Jim,
     Shiloh!
   Talk it agin,
     Shiloh!
   You dancing girl,
     Shiloh!
   Sure's you're born,
     Shiloh!

Grease my heel with butter in the fat,
I can talk to Limber Jim better'n dat.
   Limber Jim,
     Shiloh!
   Limber Jim,
     Shiloh!
   Walk back in love,
     Shiloh!
   My turtle dove,
     Shiloh!

[Patting Juba]—And you can't go yonder,
   Limber Jim!
     And you can't go yonder,
   Limber Jim!
     And you can't go-oo-o!

One fact worth mentioning about these negro singers is, that they can mimic the Irish accent to a degree of perfection which an American, Englishman or German could not hope to acquire. At the request of Patrolman Tighe and his partner, the same evening that we interviewed Limber Jim, a very dark mulatto, named Jim Delaney, sang for us in capital style that famous Irish ditty known as "The hat me fahther wor-re." Yet Jim, notwithstanding his name, has little or no Irish blood in his veins; nor has his companion, Jim Harris, who joined in the rollicking chorus:

   " 'Tis the raylics of ould dacency,
    The hat me fahther wor-r-re."

Jim Delaney would certainly make a reputation for Irish specialties in a minstrel troupe; his mimicry of Irish character is absolutely perfect, and he possesses a voice of great flexibility, depth and volume. He "runs" on the river.

On the southeast corner of Culvert and Sixth streets, opposite to the house in which we were thus entertained by Limber Jim and his friends, stands Kirk's building, now occupied jointly by Kirk and Ryan. Two stories beneath this building is now the most popular dance-house of the colored steamboatmen and their "girls." The building and lot belong to Kirk; but Ryan holds a lease on the basement and half of the upper building. Recently the landlord and the leaseholder had a falling out, and are at bitter enmity; but Ryan seems to have the upper hand in the matter, and is making considerable money from the roustabouts. He has closed up the old side entrance, admission to the ball-room being now obtainable only through the bar-room, and the payment of ten cents. A special policeman has been wisely hired by the proprietor to preserve order below, and the establishment is, generally speaking, well conducted for an establishment of the kind. The amount of patronage it receives depends almost wholly upon the condition of the river traffic; during the greater part of the week the attendance is somewhat slim, but when the New Orleans boats come in the place is crowded to overflowing. Beside the admittance fee of ten cents, an additional dime is charged to all the men for every set danced—the said dime to be expended in "treating partners." When the times are hard and money scarce, the girls often pay the fees for their men in order to make up sets.

With its unplastered and windowless limestone walls; sanded floor; ruined ceiling, half plank, half cracked plaster; a dingy black counter in one corner, and rude benches ranged along the walls, this dancing-room presented rather an outlandish aspect when we visited it. At the corner of the room opposite "the bar," a long bench was placed, with its face to the wall; and upon the back of this bench, with their feet inwardly reclining upon the seat, sat the musicians. A well-dressed, neatly-built mulatto picked the banjo, and a somewhat lighter colored musician led the music with a fiddle, which he played remarkably well and with great spirit. A short, stout negress, illy dressed, with a rather good-natured face and a bed shawl tied about her head, palyed the bass viol, and that with no inexperienced band. This woman is known to the police as Anna Nun.

The dancers were in sooth a motley crew: the neat dresses of the girls strongly contrasting with the rags of the poorer roustabouts, some of whom were clad only in shirt, pants and shocking hats. Several wickedly handsome women were smoking stogies. Bill Williams, a good-natured black giant, who keeps a Bucktown saloon, acted for a while as Master of Ceremonies. George Moore, the colored Democrat who killed, last election day, the leader of a party who attacked his house, figured to advantage in the dance, possessing wonderful activity in spite of his heavy bulk. The best performer on the floor was a stumpy little roustabout named Jem Scott, who is a marvelous jig-dancer, and can waltz with a tumbler full of water on his head without spilling a drop. One fourth of the women present were white, including two girls only about seventeen years old, but bearing physiognomical evidence of precocious vice. The best-looking girl in the room was a tall, lithe quadroon named Mary Brown, with auburn hair, gray eyes, a very fair skin, and an air of quiet innocence wholly at variance with her reputation. A short, supple mulatto girl, with a blue ribbon in her hair, who attracted considerable admiration, and was famous for dancing "breakdowns," had but recently served a term in the penitentiary for grand larceny. Another woman present, a gigantic negress, wearing a red plaid shawl, and remarkable for an immense head of frizzly hair, was, we were informed, one of the most adroit thieves known to the police. It was a favorite trick of hers to pick a pocket while dancing, and hide the stolen money in her hair.

"How many of those present do you suppose carry knives?" we asked Patrolman Tighe.

"All of them," was the reply. "All the men, and women, too, carry knives or razors; and many of them pistols as well. But they seldom quarrel, except about a girl. Their great vice is thieving; and the fights down here are generally brought about by white roughs who have no business in this part of town except crime."

The musicians struck up that weird, wild, lively air, known perhaps to many of our readers as the "Devil's Dream," and in which "the musical ghost of a cat chasing the spectral ghost of a rat" is represented by a succession of "miauls" and "squeaks" on the fiddle. The dancers danced a double quadrille, at first, silently and rapidly; but warming with the wild spirit of the music, leaped and shouted, swinging each other off the floor, and keeping time with a precision which shook the building in time to the music. The women, we noticed, almost invariably embraced the men about the neck in swinging, the men clasping them about the waist. Sometimes the men advancing leaped and crossed legs with a double shuffle, and with almost sightless rapidity. Then the music changed to an old Virginia reel, and the dancing changing likewise, presented the most grotesque spectacle imaginable. The dancing became wild; men patted juba and shouted, the negro women danced with the most fantastic grace, their bodies describing almost incredible curves forward and backward; limbs intertwined rapidly in a wrestle with each other and with the music; the room presented a tide of swaying bodies and tossing arms, and flying hair. The white female dancers seemed heavy, cumbersome, ungainly by contrast with their dark companions; the spirit of the music was not upon them; they were abnormal to the life about them. Once more the music changed—to some popular negro air, with the chorus—

> "Don't get weary,
> I'm goin' home."

The musicians began to sing; the dancers joined in; and the dance terminated with a roar of song, stamping of feet, "patting juba," shouting, laughing, reeling. Even the curious spectators involuntarily kept time with their feet; it was the very drunkenness of music, the intoxication of the dance. Amid such scenes does the roustabout find his heaven; and this heaven is certainly not to be despised.

The great dancing resort for steamboatmen used to be Pickett's, on Sausage Row; but year after year the river came up and flooded all the grimy saloons on the Rows, and, departing, left behind it alluvial deposits of yellow mud, and the Spirit of Rheumatic Dampness. So, about two months ago, Pickett rented out his old quarters, partly as a barber-shop, partly as a shooting-gallery, and moved into the building, No. 91 Front street, between Ludlow and Lawrence. He has had the whole building renovated throughout, and painted the front very handsomely. The basement on the river side is now used for a dancing-room; but the room is very small, and will not accommodate half of the dancers who used to congregate in the old building. The upper part of the building the old man rents out to river men and their wives or mistresses, using the second floor for a restaurant and dining-rooms, which are very neatly fitted up. Whatever may have been the old man's sins, Pickett has a heart full of unselfish charity sufficient to cover them all. Year after year, through good or ill-fortune, he has daily fed and maintained fifty or sixty homeless and needy steamboatmen. Sometimes when the river trade "looks up," and all the boats are running on full time, some grateful levee hand repays his benefactor, but it is very seldom. And the old man never asks for it or expects it; he only says: "Boys, when you want to spend your money, spend it here." Although now very old, and almost helpless from a rupture, Pickett has yet but to rap on the counter of his saloon to enforce instantaneous quiet. The roustabouts will miss the old man when he is gone—the warm corner to sleep in, the simple but plentiful meal when out of a berth, and the rough kindness of his customary answer to a worthless, hungry, and shivering applicant for food and lodging, "G—d d—n you, you don't deserve it; but come in and behave yourself." The day is not far off when there will be great mourning along the levee.

With the exception of Ryan's dance-house, and one or two Bucktown lodging-houses, the roustabouts generally haunt the Rows, principally Sausage Row, from Broadway to Ludlow street. Rat Row, from Walnut to Main, is more especially the home of the white tramps and roustabouts. Here is situated the celebrated "Blazing Stump," otherwise called St. James Restaurant, which is kept by a Hollander, named Venneman. Venneman accommodates only white men, and endeavors to keep an orderly house; but the "Blazing Stump" must always remain a resort for thieves, burglars, and criminals of every description. The "Stump" is No. 13 Rat Row. No. 16 is a lodging house for colored roustabouts, kept by James Madison. No. 12 is a policy shop, although it pretends to be a saloon; and the business is so cunningly conducted that the police can not, without special privilege, succeed in closing up the business. No. 10, which used to be known as Buckner's, is another haunt for colored roustabouts. They have a pet crow attached to the establishment, which is very plucky, and can whip all the cats and dogs in the neighborhood. It waddles about on the sidewalk of sunny days, pecking fiercely at any stranger who meddles with it, but the moment it sees the patrolmen coming along the levee it runs into the house.

No. 7—Goodman's clothing store—is said to be a "fence." At the west end of the row is Captain Dilg's celebrated hostelry, a popular and hospitable house, frequented by pilots and the most respectable class of river men. At the eastern terminus of the row is the well known Alhambra saloon, a great resort for colored steamboatmen, where large profits are realized on cigars and whisky of the cheapest kind. The contractors who hire roustabouts frequently have a private understanding with the proprietor of some levee coffee-house or saloon, and always go there to pay off their hands. Then the first one treats, then another, and so on until all the money just made by a day's heavy labor is lying in the counter drawer, and the roustabouts are helplessly boozy.

Of the two rows Sausage Row is perhaps the most famous. No. 1 is kept by old Barney Hodke, who has made quite a reputation by keeping a perfectly orderly house in a very disorderly neighborhood. No. 2 is Cottonbrook's clothing store, *alias* the "American Clothing Store," whereof the proprietor is said to have made a fortune by selling cheap clothing to the negro stevedores. No. 3 is Mrs. Sweeney's saloon and boarding-house, an orderly establishment for the entertainment of river men. No. 4 is an eating- and lodging-house for roustabouts, kept by Frank Fortner, a white man. No. 6 is a barber-shop for colored folks, with a clothing-store next to it. No. 7 is a house of ill-fame, kept by a white woman, Mary Pearl, who boards several unfortunate white girls. This is a great resort for colored men.

No. 8 is Maggie Sperlock's. Maggie has another saloon in Bucktown. She is a very fat and kindhearted old mulatto woman, who is bringing up half a dozen illegitimate children, abandoned by their parents. One of these, a very pretty boy, is said to be the son of a white lady, who moves in good society, by a colored man.

No. 9 is now Chris. Meyer's; it was known as "Schwabe Kate's" when Meyer's wife lived. This is the great resort for German tramps.

Next in order comes a barber-shop and shooting-gallery—"Long Branch" and "Saratoga." These used to be occupied by Pickett.

A few doors east of this is Chas. Redman's saloon, kept by a crippled soldier. This is another great roustabout haunt, where robberies are occasionally committed. And a little further east is Pickett's new hotel. On these two rows Officers Brazil and Knox have made no less than two hundred and fifty-six arrests during the past two years. The most troublesome element is, of course, among the white tramps.

A number of the colored river men are adroit thieves; these will work two or three months and then "lay off" until all their money has found its way to whisky-shops and brothels. The little clothing and shoe stores along the levee are almost daily robbed of some articles by such fellows, who excel in ingenious confidence dodges. A levee hand with extinct cigar will, for example, walk into a shoe shop with a "Say, bohss, giv a fellah a light." While the "bohss" is giving a light to the visitor, who always takes care to stand between the proprietor and the doorway, a confederate sneaks off with a pair of shoes. A fellow called "China Robinson," who hangs about Madison's is said to be famous at such tricks. The police officers, however, will not allow any known sluggard or thief to loaf about the levee for more than thirty days without employment. There is always something to do for those who wish to do it, and roustabouts who persist in idleness and dirt, after one or two friendly warnings, get sent to the Work-house.

Half of the colored 'longshoremen used at one time to wear only a coat and pants, winter and summer; but now they are a little more careful of themselves, and fearful of being sent to the Work-house to be cleaned up. Consequently, when Officer Brazil finds a very ragged and dirty specimen of levee life on the Row, he has seldom occasion to warn him more than once to buy himself a shirt and a change of garments.

Generally speaking, the women give very little trouble. Some of the white girls now living in Pickett's barracks or in Bucktown brothels are of respectable parentage. Two of the most notorious are sisters, who have a sad history. They are yet rather handsome. All these women are morphine eaters, and their greatest dread is to be sent to the Work-house, and being thus deprived of this stimulant. Some who were sent to the Work-house, we were told, had died there from want of it. The white girls of the Row soon die, however, under any circumstances; their lives are often fairly burnt out with poisonous whisky and reckless dissipation before they have haunted the levee more than two or three years. After a fashion, the roustabouts treat their women kindly, with a rough good nature that is peculiar to them; many of the women are really married. But faithfulness to a roustabout husband is considered quite an impossible virtue on the levee. The stevedores are mostly too improvident and too lazy to support their "gals." While the men are off on a trip, a girl will always talk about what she will be able to buy "when my man comes back—if he has any money." When the lover does comes back, sometimes after a month's absence, he will perhaps present his "gal" with fifty cents, or at most a dollar, and thinks he has done generously by her. We are speaking in general terms, of course, and alluding to the mass of the colored roustabouts who "run on the river" all their lives, and have no other calling. It is needless to say that there are thrifty and industrious stevedores who support their families well, and will finally leave the river for some more lucrative employment.

Such is a glimpse of roustabout life. They know of no other life; they can understand no other pleasures. Their whole existence is one vision of anticipated animal pleasure or of animal misery; of giant toil under the fervid summer sun; of toil under the icy glare of the winter moon; of fiery drinks and drunken dreams; of the madness of music and the intoxication of fantastic dances; of white and dark mistresses awaiting their coming at the levees, with waving of brightly colored garments; of the deep music of the great steam whistles; of the torch-basket fires redly dancing upon the purple water, the white stars sailing overhead, the passing lights of well known cabins along the dark river banks, and the mighty panting of the iron heart of the great vessel, bearing them day after day and night after night to fresh scenes of human frailty, and nearer to that Dim Levee slope, where weird boats ever discharge ghostly freight, and depart empty.

Cincinnati Commercial, March 17, 1876

BLACK VARIETIES

THE MINSTRELS OF THE ROW

Picturesque Scenes Without Scenery—

Physiognomical Studies at Pickett's

THE attractive novelty of theatricals at old Pickett's tavern, on the levee, by real negro minstrels, with amateur dancing performances by roustabouts and their "girls," has already created considerable interest in quarters where one would perhaps least expect to find it; and the patrolmen of the Row nightly escort fashionably dressed white strangers to No. 91 Front street. The theater has two entrances, one through the neat, spotlessly clean bar-room on the Front street side, the other from the sidewalk on the river side. The theater is also the ball-room; and when the ancient clock behind the black bar in the corner announces in senile, metallically-husky tones the hour of 12, the footlights are extinguished, the seats cleared away, and the audience quickly form into picturesque sets for wild dances.

It is a long, low room, with a staircase at the southwest corner, ascending to the saloon above; an unplastered ceiling of clean white pine plank, resembling an inverted section of steamboat deck, a black wooden bar at the southeast corner, and rude wooden benches of unpainted plank arranged along the walls and across the room from the bar to the stage. This stage consists of a wooden platform, elevated about a yard from the floor; and the little room under the staircase at the left side serves as the green-room. Tallow dips, placed about a foot apart, serve for footlights. Strips of white muslin sewed together form the curtains, which are attached by rings to a metal rod in the ceiling, and open and close much after the manner of the curtains of an old-fashioned, four-posted bedstead. These curtains were made by a mild-mannered brown girl called Annie, remarkable for deep, dark eyes, light, wavy hair, and wonderful curves of mouth, chin and neck; but poor Annie is no better than she ought to be, and loves to smoke a great, black, brier-root pipe.

Ere the curtain rose we found it extremely interesting to glance over the motley audience, largely made up of women less fair, but not less frail than Annie.

A sharp-faced Irish girl, with long fawn-colored hair and hard gray eyes; a pretty and ruddy-faced young white woman, very neatly built and fashionably dressed, the wife of a colored bar-keeper; a white brunette, with unpleasantly deep-set black eyes and long curly hair, who feigns to have colored blood in her veins; a newly arrived white blonde, who last week followed a roustabout hither from Ironton through some strange and vain infatuation; the notorious Adams sisters; a young Cincinnati woman of evil repute, whose parents live but a few squares up town, and have not for years exchanged word or look with their daughter, though she almost daily passes by the old home; and one Gretchen-faced woman, with rather regular features and fair hair, who has lately deserted a good home at Portsmouth to become the mistress of a stevedore—these comprised the white women present. Excepting the bar-keeper's little white wife, they evidently preferred to sit together. But the pictur-esqueness of the spectacle was rendered all the more striking by the contrast.

Every conceivable hue possible to the human skin might be studied in the dense and motley throng that filled the hall. There were full-blooded black women, solidly built, who were smoking stogies, and wore handkerchiefs of divers colors twined about their curly pates, after the old Southern fashion. Some of these were evidently too poor to own a whole dress, and ap-peared in petticoat and calico waist alone; but the waists had been carefully patched and washed, and the white petticoats were spotlessly clean and crisp with starch. Others were re-markably well dressed—excepting their ornaments, which were frequently of a character calculated to provoke a smile. One little negro woman had a flat locket with a brilliantly-colored picture painted on it, and at least six inches in diameter, sus-pended from her ebon neck by a golden chain. Gold or imita-tion, yellow and glittering, flashed everywhere in ear pendants against dusky cheeks, in massive rings upon strong black hands, in fair chains coiling about brown necks or clasping bare brown arms.

It is a mystery how many of these women, who can not

afford to buy two dresses, or who have to borrow decent attire to go out of doors, can refuse to part with their jewelry in almost any extremity, but we have been reliably assured that such is the case. As a rule these levee girls do not invest in bogus jewelry. It was curious to observe the contrast of physical characteristics among the lighter-hued women; girls with almost fair skins frequently possessing wooly hair; dark mulattoes on the contrary often having light, floating, wavy locks. One mulatto girl present wore her own hair—frizzly and thick as the mane of a Shetland pony—flowing down to her waist in gipsy style. Where turbans were not worn among the fairer skinned, the hair was generally confined with a colored ribbon. At least three-fourths of the audience were women, and of these one-third, perhaps, were smoking—several of the white girls were chewing. Of the men present, the greater number were roustabouts, in patched attire, often of the most fantastic description. Four musicians played lively old-time banjo tunes before the stage, and through the half-open door at the other end of the theater glimpses were visible of an expanse of purple, star-studded sky, a more deeply purple expanse of rippling river, the dark rolling outline of the Kentucky hills, and a long line of yellow points of light, scattered along the curving shore as far as the eye could reach. From without, the cool, sweet river air occasionally crept in by gentle breaths, and from within, the dim light of trembling candle-flame, the blue wreaths of heavy tobacco smoke, the sound of vociferous laughter and the notes of wild music, all floated out together into the white moonlight.

The little stage curtain rose, or, rather, parted, upon a scene originally ludicrous in itself, which evoked a shout of mingled glee and amusement from the expectant audience. The six performers were, with one exception, very dark men, with pronounced negro features; but they had exaggerated their natural physiognomical characteristics by a lavish expenditure of burnt cork and paint. The mouths of the end-men grinned from ear to ear; their eyes appeared monstrous, and their attire could not have been done justice to by any ordinary play-bill artist. It was a capital get up in its line, such as white minstrels could hardly hope to equal. The three principal performers were professionals from Louisville. The right end man had a tambourine with a silver rim, which he unfortunately smashed during the evening by knocking it against his pate, and as a tambourine performer he can not have many white rivals, tapping the instrument against his hand, elbow, knee, head, foot, with a rapidity which almost defied the eye to follow it.

After the first musical performance minstrel jokes were in order, including odd conundrums, "hits" at the patrolmen, and miscellaneous jokes of a humorous, but always innocent description. Here is a specimen:

"How dy'e feel to-night, Mr. Royal?"

"I feel's as if I was in de clouds; an' angels pouring 'lasses all over me."

"Well, Mr. Royal, I want to prepose a kolumdrum to you. Kin you spell 'blind pig' with two letters?"

"Cou'se I kin. Blind pig?—let's see!—pig? P-g, pig."

"Wrong, sir; wrong. B-l-i-n-d, blind, p-i-g, pig—blind pig. Thar's an 'i' in pig, an' you left out the eye."

"But if he's got an eye, he can't be a blind pig." [Roars of laughter.]

"Hev' you got a wife, Mr. Moore?"

"Yes."

"Isn't it sweet to hev' a nice little wife?"

"Yes."

"When you git up in de morning she kin give you a s-t-r-o-n-g cup of coffee."

"Yes."

"An' give you nice, strong butter?"

"No; not strong butter."

"An' give you a nice, strong hug?"

"Yes."

"An' kiss you at the door, and say, 'By-by, baby; dream of me?'"

"Yes."

"An' when y'ar just gone out the front way, open de back door an' let a great big black niggar in de back way?"

Then they sung a song, with a roaring chorus, called "Cahve de Possum," after which came more jokes, and then a most comical scene—really the best performance of the evening—between two men, one attired as a woman, with an enormously exaggerated "pull-back," and the other costumed as a journeyman whitewasher. The effects of this scene upon the audience was extremely interesting. The women not only laughed but screamed and leaped in their seats, to fall back and laugh till the tears ran down their cheeks. A well built young black woman named Lucy Mason, whose face still bore the scars of a recent razor-slash, then came upon the stage, attired in a short petticoat with scalloped edges; striped stockings, which displayed a pair of solid, well-turned legs; and boy's brogans. She danced a break-down very fairly, and was several times called out. Then a little roustabout, from New Orleans, danced a jig; and the performance closed with a lengthy but very comical extravaganza entitled "Damon and Pythias." To the curious visitor, however, the merits of the performance, although an excellent one, were far less entertaining than the spectacle of the enjoyment which it occasioned—the screams of laughter and futile stuffing of handkerchiefs in laughing mouths, the tears of merriment, the innocent appreciation of the most trivial joke, the stamping of feet and leaping, and clapping of hands—a very extravaganza of cachination.

Midnight twanged out from the ancient clock, laughter was heard only in occasional chuckles, a roustabout extinguished the footlights with his weatherbeaten hat, the bar became thronged with dusky drinkers, and the musicians put their instruments by. Then the room suddenly vibrated in every fiber of its pine-planking to a long, deeply swelling sound, which suddenly hushed the chatter like a charm. Half of the hearts in the room beat a little faster—hearts well trained to recognize the Voices of the River; and the sound grew stronger and sweeter, like an unbroken roll of soft, rich, deep thunder. "The Wildwood," shouted a score of voices at once, and the throng rushed out on the levee to watch the great white boat steaming up in the white moonlight, with a weird train of wreathing smoke behind her, and dark lovers of swarthy levee girls on board.

Cincinnati Commercial, April 9, 1876

GIBBETED

EXECUTION OF A YOUTHFUL MURDERER.

SHOCKING TRAGEDY AT DAYTON.

A Broken Rope and a Double Hanging.

Sickening Scenes Behind the Scaffold-Screen.

THE execution of James Murphy, yesterday afternoon, at Dayton, for the murder of Colonel William Dawson, in that city, on the night of August 31, 1875, was an event, it must be said, which the people of Montgomery County had long looked forward to with no small degree of satisfaction. The murder was of itself peculiarly atrocious, from the fact that it was actually committed without a shadow of provocation. The victim was a worthy and popular citizen, and the feeling of the public in regard to the crime was sufficiently evinced in the fact that the city authorities, subsequent to the arrest of Murphy, were obliged to call out the militia that the claim of legal justice to deal with the criminal might be protected. Colonel Dawson, it may be remembered, was murdered apparently for no other reason than that he refused a drunken party permission to intrude upon the quiet enjoyments of a private wedding party. The Colonel was Superintendent of the Champion Plow Works, at Dayton, and the bridegroom being an employe of the company, the Colonel had, by request, assumed the management of the wedding ball. When Murphy was refused admittance, he induced one of his companions, Lewis Meyers, to entice the Colonel out of doors on the pretext of getting a drink; and soon after the invitation had been accepted, Murphy struck Dawson, and during the subsequent scuffle, suddenly plunged a long knife up to the haft in the Colonel's left side. The victim of this cowardly assault lived but a few moments afterward, and died without being able to positively identify his assassin.

Circumstantial evidence, notwithstanding, clearly pointed to Murphy as the criminal, and to Meyers as his accomplice; the former being sentenced to death, and the latter, being convicted of manslaughter, to a term of two years in the State Penitentiary. Sentence was passed on the 28th of April, the jury having disagreed upon the first trial, in February, which necessitated a second.

The youth of the prisoner—he was only nineteen years of age—did not, strange as it may seem, excite any marked degree of sympathy for his miserable fate. He was a fair skinned, brown haired, beardless lad, with rather large features, a firm, vicious mouth; sullen, steady gray eyes, shadowed by a habitual frown; a rather bold forehead, half concealed by a mass of curly locks, brushed down,—a face, in short, that, notwithstanding its viciousness, was not devoid of a certain coarse regularity. His parents were hard-working Irish people, but in his own features showed little evidence of Celtic blood.

Perhaps the dogged obstinacy of the prisoner in denying, almost to the last, his evident crime, had no little to do with the state of public feeling in regard to him. Moreover, he had long been notorious in the city as a worthless loafer and precocious ruffian, perpetually figuring in some street fight, drunken brawl or brutal act of violence. For a considerable period of time, previous to the murder of Colonel Dawson, he had been the boasted leader of a band of young roughs, from nineteen to twenty years of age, who were known in Dayton as the "chain-gang."

The boy's mother had died while he was yet young; but he did not lack a home, and the affection of an old father, and of brothers and sisters—the latter of whom he is said to have cruelly abused in fits of drunken passion. In this connection it would of course be in order, religiously, to discourse upon the results of neglecting early admonitions; and, philosophically, upon the evidence that the unfortunate lad had inherited an evil disposition, whereof the tendencies were not to be counteracted by any number of admonitions. But the facts in the case, as they appeared to the writer, were simply that a poor, ignorant, passionate boy, with a fair, coarse face, had in the heat of drunken anger taken away the life of a fellow-being, and paid the penalty of his brief crime, by a hundred days of mental torture, and a hideous death.

Perhaps there are many readers of this article, who may have perused and shuddered at the famous tale of the "Iron Shroud." You may remember that the victim, immured in the walls of a dungeon, lighted by seven windows, finds that each successive day of his imprisonment, one of the windows disappears forever. There are first seven, then six, then five, then four, then three, then two, then but one—dim and shadowy;—and then the night-black darkness that prefigures the formless gloom of the Shadow of Death. And through the thick darkness booms, hour after hour, the abysmal tones of a giant bell, announcing to the victim the incessant approach of the fearful midnight when the walls shall crush his bones to shapelessness. No one ever read that tale of the Castle of Tolfi without experiencing such horrors as make the flesh creep. Yet the agony therein depicted by a cunning writer is, after all, but a very slight exaggeration of the torture to which condemned criminals are periodically subjected in our prisons—not for seven days, forsooth, but for one hundred. This is the mercy of the law!—to compel the wretched victim to await the slow but inevitable approach of the grimmest and most ignominious of deaths for one hundred days. Fancy the ghastly mental computation of time which he must make to his own heart—"ninety-nine—ninety-eight—ninety-seven—ninety-six—ninety-five," until at last the allotment of life is reduced to a miserable seven days, as frightfully speedy as those of the Man in the Iron Shroud. And then the black scaffold with the blacker mystery below the drop, the sea of curious and unsympathetic faces, the moment of supreme suspense after his eyes are veiled from the light of the world by the sable hood. But this pyramid of agony is not absolutely complete until apexed by the vision of a fragile rope, the sudden hush of horror, and the bitterest period of agony twice endured. It is cruel folly to assert that because the criminal be ignorant, uneducated, phlegmatic, unimaginative, he is incapable of acutely feeling the torture of hideous suspense. That was asserted, nevertheless, and frequently asserted yesterday, by spectators of the execution. We did not think so. The victim was young and strong, a warm-blooded, passionate boy, with just that coarse animal vitality which makes men cling most strongly to life, as a thing to be enjoyed in the mere fact of possession—the mere ability to hear, see, feel.

The incidents of the prisoner's jail life during the last week —how he ate, drank, smoked, talked—might be very fully dwelt on as matters of strictly local interest, but may be briefly dismissed in these columns. There is, however, one story connected with that jail-life too strange and peculiar to be omitted. It seems that young Murphy learned to entertain a special affection for Tom Hellriggle, a Deputy Sheriff of Montgomery County, who had attended him kindly since his removal from the jail-room to a cell on the third floor, which opened in the rear of the scaffold. One night recently, Murphy said to Hellriggle, confidentially: "I knew I was going to be hanged, long ago. Do you know that I knew it before I was sentenced?"

"Why, how did you know that?" curiously asked the deputy.

Then the lad told him that during the intervals of the trials, one night between 12 and 1 o'clock, he heard the voice of a woman crying weirdly and wildly in the darkness, and so loudly that the sound filled all the jail-room, and that many of the men awoke and shuddered.

"You remember that, don't you?" asked the lad.

"I do," said the deputy; "and I also remember that there was no living woman in the jail-room that night."

"So," continued the boy, "they asked me if I heard it, and I said yes; but I pretended I did not know what it was. I believe I said no human being could cry so fearfully as that. But I did know what it was, Tom—*I saw the woman.*"

"Who was it?" asked Tom, earnestly.

"It was my mother. And I knew why she cried so strangely. She was crying for me."

There are few men who enter the condemned cell and leave it for the gallows without having entertained during the interval a strong desire to take their own lives, and are for the most part deterred from so doing rather by the religious dread of a dim and vague Something after death, than by any physical fear. So it appears to have been with Murphy. When all hope, except the hope of pardon from the All-forgiving Father, was dead within him, and the Governor of Ohio had refused to grant a reprieve or commutation of sentence, then the prisoner listened much more calmly to the admonitions of Father Murphy, a fat, kindly, red-cheeked Irish priest, who took a heartfelt interest in the "spiritual welfare" of his namesake. He soon expressed repentance for his crime, and even agreed to confess all publically—an act, all the circumstances properly considered, which really evinced more manhood than the act of "dying game" with the secret.

Shortly afterward he handed to Deputy Sheriff Hellriggle a small, keen knife, which he had managed to conceal, despite all the vigilance of his guards. "I would not take my own life, now," he said, "though I were to be hung twice over." Yet at the time the poor fellow probably had little idea that he would actually suffer the penalty of the law twice. It was evident, however, that he had frequently premeditated suicide, as in a further conversation with his guard he pointed out certain ingenious and novel modes of self-destruction which he had planned. That the criminal possessed no ordinary amount of nerve and self-control under the most trying circumstances, can not for a moment be questioned; nor can it be truthfully averred that his courage was merely the result of stolid phlegm and natural insensibility. None of the family, indeed, appear to inherit over-sensitive organizations, as a glance at the faces of the visitors to the condemned cell sufficiently satisfied us. When James' oldest brother, a ruddily-featured young man of twenty, visited the prisoner day before yesterday, he mounted the black scaffold erected outside the cell-door, and, after a few humorous remarks, actually executed a double-shuffle dance upon the trap-door, until Sheriff Patton, hearing the noise, at once turned him out of the corridor. But James' actions in jail, his last farewell to his relations, his sensitiveness in regard to certain reports afloat concerning his past career, and lastly, the very fact that his nerve did finally yield under a fearful and wholly unexpected pressure, all tend to show that his nature was by no means so brutally unfeeling as had been alleged.

The scaffold had been erected at the rear end of the central corridor of the jail hospital ward in the third story of the building, immediately without the cell-room in which the prisoner had been confined subsequent to his removal from the gloomier jail-room below, where he had heard the loud knocking of the carpenter's hammers, and the hum of saws—sounds of which the grim significance was fully recognized by him without verbal interpretation. "Ah, they are putting up the gallows!" he said: "The noise don't frighten me much, though." To the reporter who visited the long, white corridors by lamp-light, with the tall, black-draped and ebon-armed apparition at its further end, these preparations for an execution under roof, instead of beneath the clear sky, and in the pure air, seemed somewhat strange and mysteriously horrible. It is scarcely necessary to describe the mechanism of the scaffold, further than to observe that the trap-door was closed by curved bolts, the outer ends of which were inserted into or withdrawn from shallow sockets in the framework at either side of the door, by foot-pressure upon a lever, which connected with the inner ends of the bolts, and worked them like the handles of huge pincers. The rope did, however, attract considerable attention from all who examined it previous to the execution. It seemed no thicker than a strong clothes-line, though actually three eighths of an inch, and appeared wholly unequal to the task for which it had been expressly manufactured from unbleached hemp. Yet Sheriff Gerard, of Putnam County, who had officiated at five executions, and was considered an authority upon such matters, had had it well tested with a keg of nails and other heavy weights, and believed it sufficiently strong. A bucket of water was supended to it for some twenty-four hours, in order to remove its slight elasticity. But the bucket turned slowly around at intervals, and, under the constant pressure and motion, it seems that the rope became worn and weakened at the point of its insertion into the crossbeam. The drop-length was regulated to three feet and a half.

The unfortunate boy's mental impressions, yesterday morning, must assuredly have consisted of a strange and confused vision of solemn images and mysterious events. From the opening door of his cell he could plainly perceive every mechanical detail of the black gibbet, with its dismal hangings of sable muslin. Sisters of Charity, in dark robes; solemn-faced priests, with snowy Roman collars; Sheriffs and Deputy Sheriffs of austere countenance, which appeared momentarily to become yet more severe; policemen in full dress whispering in knots along the white corridor, a score of newspaper correspondents and reporters scattered through the crowd, writing and questioning and occasionally stealing peeps at the prisoner through the open door; calm-visaged physicians consulting together over open watches, as though eager to feel the last pulsations of the dying heart; undertakers, professional, cool and sad, gathered about a long, handsome black walnut coffin, adorned with silver crosses, which stood in the corner of one hospital room—these and other figures thronged the scene of death and disgrace while without a bright sun and a clear sky appeared for the last time to the wandering eyes of the condemned. He had early in the morning gone through the necessary formal preparations of being shaved, bathing, and putting on the neat suit of black cloth for which he had been measured a few days before. He had slept soundly all night; after having listened to the merry music of the city band, playing before the columned Court-house, but his sleep was probably consequent upon physical and mental exhaustion from haunting fear, rather than a natural and healthy slumber. He had risen at 7 o'clock, made a full confession in presence of the Sheriff, heard mass, listened to Father Murphy's admonitions, ate a light breakfast, and smoked several cigars. Father Murphy's admonitions, delivered in simple language, and a strong old-country brogue, seemed to us passive listeners somewhat peculiar, especially when he stated that the "flesh and blood of Jesus Christ, which not even the angels were worthy to eat," would give strength to the poor lad "to meet his God at half-past 1 o'clock." But if ever religious faith comforted the last moments of a young criminal, it did in this instance; and it was owing to the kindly but powerful efforts of the little priest that the youth made a full public confession of his crime. This is the confession:

MONTGOMERY COUNTY JAIL,
DAYTON, O., August 24, 1876.
To Warren Munger and Elihu Thompson, my Attorneys:

I will now say to you, and the public in general, that ever since you became my attorneys, at all times until to-day, I have denied that I struck and killed William Dawson, for which crime I am now under sentence of death. This statement I have made you in the mistaken hope and belief that it might do me some good, and I therefore put the blame on another person—Charles Tredtin. Now that all hope is gone, I have to say that you have done all you could for me as my attorneys, and that I feel satisfied with your efforts in my behalf. I am willing now to make public all I know about the murder of Colonel William Dawson, and I desire to make the statement, for I am now about to die, and do not want to die with a lie upon my lips. I do not wish Tredtin to be pointed out as long as he lives as the person who stabbed Colonel Dawson; and I desire also that justice may be done Meyers, who is entirely innocent, and was not connected in any way with the killing of Dawson. The following are the facts:

On the evening of the murder, Jim Allen, John Petty, George Petty, Charles Hooven and myself were at a dance on McClure street. From there I and Hooven and George Petty went down the street to Barlow's Hall, where there was a dance going on, but of which we did not know until we arrived there. We went in and went up to the bar, and had a drink of beer. About fifteen minutes after this, Gerdes and I started up to get into the ball-room, but before we started Kline, Petty and Tredtin had gone up. When we got within two or three steps of the top of the first stairway I met Brunner there on duty as door-keeper, and he asked me if I had a pass. I told him no, and then he said, "You'll have to go down stairs." I said, "All right." Then Dawson grabbed hold of me and said, "Get down, or I'll throw you down." I jerked away from him, laughed at him, and went down stairs. Then Gerdes and I went and saw the man who got married, and asked him if he couldn't let me up stairs. He said, "Yes, of course I can;" and then I went up with Gerdes and the man who got married, and he told Brunner to let me in. We went into the ball-room, where Kline, Tredtin and Petty were standing. Then Kline said, "Where's that big son of a bitch that was going to throw you down stairs?" and I said, "What do you want to know for?" He then said, "I want to know." Then I said, "There he is; whatever you want to say to him, say it." Then Kline said, "Oh, you big son of a bitch!" After about half an hour Petty and I went down stairs to the bar-room. Gerdes, Tredtin and Kline came down there, where I saw them, but whether they came together or not I don't know. Kline, Petty and I drank beer together. We all five then went back up stairs. Dawson and Meyers went down stairs, into the bar-room; then we five followed on down, and went out at the side door on the street. We then began talking about the occurrence on the stairway between Dawson and myself, and some one said, but I don't recollect who it was, "Damn him, we'll get him before morning." I don't recollect that there was anything more said. Meyers was not with us then on the street, or at all in any way connected with us or our party that evening. All five of us then went back together up stairs, where we saw Meyers and Dawson. We staid there some five or ten minutes, when we saw Meyers and Dawson go down stairs and then we five followed after them, and saw them go out of the side door on to the street, and we followed them out. Kline said to me and Petty, near the corner of the side street and Fifth street, "You go down this side of the street and we'll go down the other." Petty and I followed after Meyers and Dawson, some distance behind them, while Kline, Gerdes and Tredtin went across to the north side of the street, and went down west on that side of Fifth street. We saw Meyers and Dawson try to get in at the big gate at Weidner's, and Pearl street. When we came together Dawson sort of turned around, and I struck him with both fists in the breast; Petty struck Meyers, and Meyers caught hold of a post and prevented himself from falling into the gutter, and then straightened himself up and ran away eastward, and Petty started across the street as soon as Meyers ran. My strokes in Dawson's breast staggered him, and he didn't recover himself until after Meyers and Petty had left. About the time Dawson recovered himself, Kline and Tredtin run in and struck Dawson too. My passions were now aroused. I drew my knife out of my inside breast coat pocket and stabbed Colonel Dawson. I did it on the instant, and took no second thought about it. I do not remember of hearing Dawson say anything before or after I cut him. He may have said something, but I did not hear him. The purpose of our party of five in following Meyers and Dawson out was to lick them both. I saw Gerdes about the middle of the street coming towards us, but he didn't get up to us. Which way Kline and Tredtin went I do not know. Dawson started east on Fifth street on a run. I was facing the east when I cut Dawson. After Dawson run I was alone on the sidewalk, when Frank came up and struck at me with his club. I dodged him and struck at him with my knife, but don't know whether I cut his clothes or not. I then wheeled and started to run west. As I run he threw his club at me, and as I started to run across the street, I fell over the hitching-post in front of Weidner's, and there I dropped my cap and knife. Frank fired at me with a pistol, and shot at me just as I fell. I got up and started to run across the street, and Frank fired a second time at me as I was about to enter the alley on the north side of Fifth street. I stood in the alley awhile, and then I went home to my father's house, where I was afterward arrested by the police. Whisky and bad company have been the ruination of me, and the cause of all my bad luck. I had drank a good deal that night of beer and whisky.

This is a true and correct statement about the murder, and is all I wish to say about the matter.

JAMES MURPHY.

He also dictated a letter of thanks to Sheriff Patton, his deputies, and all who had been kind to him during his confinement. Sheriff Patton himself paid for the prisoner's coffin, a very neat one.

At half-past one o'clock, Deputy Sheriff Freeman appeared at the door of the cell-room, which opened directly upon the ladder leading to the scaffold, and observed in a low, steady voice: "Time's up, Jim; the Sheriff wants you." The prisoner immediately responded, "All right; I am ready;" and walked steadily up the steps of the ladder, accompanied by Fathers Murphy and Carey. His arms had been pinioned at the elbows by a strong bandage of black calico. Probably he looked at that moment younger and handsomer than he had ever appeared before; and a hum of audible surprise at his appearance passed through the spectators. Accompanied by his confessor and Father Carey he walked steadily to the front of the platform; and after looking quietly and calmly upon the faces below, spoke in a deep, clear, bold voice, pausing between each sentence to receive some suggestion from the priest at his side.

"Gentlemen, I told a lie in the Court-house by saying Tredtin was guilty.

"I think I am guilty"—with a determined nod of the head.

"I return thanks to Sheriff Patton, his deputies and all my friends.

"I forgive all my enemies and ask their forgiveness.

"If there is any one here who has any hard feelings towards me, I ask their forgiveness.

"This is my last request.

"Gentlemen, I want all young men to take warning by me. Drink and bad company brought me here to-day.

"And I ask the forgiveness of Mrs. Dawson and her children, whom I injured in passion, when I did not know what I was doing.

"I believe Jesus Christ will save me."

Sheriff Patton then read in a quiet, steady voice, the death-warrant. It was heavily bordered in black, and bore a great sable seal. "It is my solemn duty," said the Sheriff, "to execute the sentence passed upon you by the Court:

"State of Ohio, Montgomery County—To William Patton, Sheriff: Whereas, at the January Term, 1876, of the Court of Common Pleas, within and for the County of Montgomery and State of Ohio, to-wit, on the 28th day of April, 1876, upon a full and impartial trial, one James Murphy, now in your custody, was found guilty of deliberate and premeditated murder of one William Dawson, in manner and

form as found in a true bill of indictment by the grand jury on the
30th day of October, 1875; and whereas the Court aforesaid, at the
term aforesaid, to-wit: on the 12th day of May, 1876, upon the conviction aforesaid, ordered, adjudged and sentenced the said James Murphy to be imprisoned in the County jail until the 25th day of August,
1876, and that on that day, between the hours of 10 A.M. and 4 P.M.,
he be taken from said jail, and hanged by the neck until he be dead,
this is therefore to command that you keep the said James Murphy in
safe and secure custody until said day, August 25th, 1876; and that on
said day, between said hours, you take said James Murphy, and in the
place and manner provided by law, hang him by the neck until he be
dead. Of this warrant, and all your proceedings thereon, you shall
make due return forthwith thereafter.

"Witness: JOHN S. ROBERTSON, Clerk of said Court.

"And the seal thereof of the city of Dayton, in said county, this
20th day of June, 1876.

"[Seal Court of Common Pleas]

"JOHN S. ROBERTSON, Clerk."

In the meantime Deputy Sheriff Freeman adjusted the thin
noose about the prisoner's neck, and pinioned his lower limbs.
"James Murphy, good-bye, and may God bless you!" observed
Patton in a whisper, handing the black cap to a deputy. At this
moment the representative of the Commercial succeeded in
obtaining admittance to the little audience of physicians in rear
of the scaffold; and took up his position immediately to the left
of the trap-door. The next instant the Sheriff pressed the lever
with his foot, the drop opened as though in electric response,
the thin rope gave way at the crossbeam above, and the body
of the prisoner fell downward and backward on the floor of the
corridor, behind the scaffold screen. "My God, my God!"
cried Freeman, with a subdued scream; "give me that other
rope, quick." It had been laid away for use "in case the first
rope should break," we were told.

The poor young criminal had fallen on his back, apparently
unconscious, with the broken rope around his neck, and the
black cap vailing his eyes. The reporter knelt beside him and
felt his pulse. It was beating slowly and regularly. Probably the
miserable boy thought then, if he could think at all, that he
was really dead—dead in darkness, for his eyes were vailed—
dead and blind to this world, but about to open his eyes upon

another. The awful hush immediately following his fall might have strengthened this dim idea. But then came gasps, and choked sobs from the spectators; the hurrying of feet, and the horrified voice of Deputy Freeman calling, "For God's sake, get me that other rope, quick!" Then a pitiful groan came from beneath the black cap.

"My God! Oh, my God!"

"Why, I ain't dead—I ain't dead!"

"Are you hurt, my child?" inquired Father Murphy.

"No, father, I'm not dead; I'm not hurt. What are they going to do with me?"

No one had the heart to tell him, lying there blind and helpless and ignorant even of what had occurred. The reporter, who still kept his hand on the boy's wrist, suddenly felt the pulsation quicken horribly, the rapid beating of intense fear; the youth's whole body trembled violently.

"His pulse is one hundred and twenty," whispered a physician.

"What's the good of leaving me here in this misery?" cried the lad. "Take me out of this, I tell you."

In the meantime they had procured the other rope—a double thin rope with two nooses—and fastened it strongly over the crossbeam. The prisoner had fallen through the drop precisely at 1:44½ P.M.; the second noose was ready within four minutes later. Then the deputies descended from the platform and lifted the prostrate body up.

"Don't carry me," groaned the poor fellow, "I can walk— let me walk."

But they carried him up again, Father Murphy supporting his head. The unfortunate wanted to see the light once more, to get one little glimpse at the sun, the narrow world within the corridor, and the faces before the scaffold. They took off his ghastly mask while the noose was being readjusted. His face was livid, his limbs shook with terror, and he suddenly seized Deputy Freeman by the coat, saying in a husky whisper, "What are you going to do with me?" They tried to unfasten his hand, but it was the clutch of death-fear. Then the little Irish priest whispered firmly in his ear, "Let go my son; let go, like a man—be a man; die like a man." And he let go. But they had to support him at arm's length while the Sheriff pressed the trap-lever—six and one-half minutes after the first fall. It was humanely rapid work then.

The body fell heavily, with a jerk, turned about once, rocked backward and forward, and became almost still. From the corridor only the head was visible—turned from the audience. Father Murphy sprinkled holy water upon the victim. The jugular veins became enlarged, and the neck visibly swelled below the black cap. At this time the pulse was beating steadily at 100; the wrist felt hot and moist, and we noticed the hand below it tightly clutched a little brass crucifix, placed there by the priest at the last moment. Gradually the pulse became fainter. Five minutes later, Dr. Crum, the jail physician, holding the right wrist, announced it at eighty-four. In ten minutes from the moment of the drop it sunk to sixty. In sixteen minutes the heart only fluttered, and the pulse became imperceptible. In seventeen minutes Dr. Crum, after a stethoscopic examination, made the official announcement of death.

The body was at once cut down by Sheriff Patton, and deposited in the handsome coffin designed for it. Half an hour later we returned to the jail, and examined the dead face. It was perfectly still, as the face of a sleeper, calm and undisfigured. It was perhaps slightly swollen, but quite natural, and betrayed no evidence of pain. The rope had cut deeply into the flesh of the neck, and the very texture of the hemp was redly imprinted on the skin. A medical examination showed the neck to have been broken.

Cincinnati Commercial, August 26, 1876

DOLLY

AN IDYL OF THE LEVEE

"THE Lord only," once observed Officer Patsy Brazil, "knows what Dolly's real name is."

Dolly was a brown, broad-shouldered girl of the levee, with the lithe strength of a pantheress in her compactly-knit figure, and owning one of those peculiar faces which at once attract and puzzle by their very uniqueness—a face that possessed a strange comeliness when viewed at certain angles, especially half-profile, and that would have seemed very soft and youthful but for the shadow of its heavy black brows, perpetually knitted Medusa-wise, as though by everlasting pain, above a pair of great, dark, keen, steady eyes. It was a face, perhaps, rather Egyptian than aught else; fresh with a youthful roundness, and sweetened by a sensitive, passionate, pouting mouth.

Moreover, Dolly's odd deportment and peculiar attire were fancifully suggestive of those wanton Egyptian women whose portraits were limned on mighty palace walls by certain ancient and forgotten artists—some long-limbed, gauze-clad girls who seem yet to move with a snakish and fantastic grace; others, strong-limbed and deep-bosomed, raimented in a single, close-fitting robe, and wearing their ebon hair loosely flowing in a long thick mass. Dolly appeared to own the elfish grace of the former, together with the more mortal form of the latter. She must have made her own dresses, for no such dresses could have been purchased with love or with money, they were very antique and very graceful. Her favorite dress, a white robe, with a zig-zag border of purple running around the bottom, fitted her almost closely from shoulder to knee, following the sinuous outline of her firm figure, and strongly recalling certain pictures in the Egyptian Department of a famous German work upon the Costumes of Antiquity. Of course Dolly knew nothing of Antiquity or of Egypt—in fact she could neither read nor write; but she had an instinctive esthetic taste which surmounted those obstacles to good taste in dress which ignorance and fashion jointly create. Her prehistoric aspect was further heightened by her hair,—long, black, thick as a mane, and betraying by its tendency to frizzle the strong tinge of African blood in Dolly's veins. This she generally wore loose to the waist,—a mass so heavy and dense that a breeze could not wave it, and so deeply dark as to recall those irregular daubs of solid black paint whereby the painters of the pyramid-chambers represented the locks of weird court dames. Dolly was very careful of this strange hair; but she indulged, from time to time, in the savage luxury of greasing it with butter. Occasionally, too, she arranged it in a goblin sort of way, by combing it up perpendicularly, so that it flared above her head as though im-bued with an electric life of its own. Perhaps she inherited the tendency to these practices from her African blood.

In fact, Dolly was very much of a little savage, despite the evidences of her natural esthetic taste in dress. The very volup-tuousness and freedom of her movements had something sav-age about it, and she had a wild love for violent physical exercises. She could manage a pair of oars splendidly, and was so perfect a shot that knowing steamboatmen were continually fleecing newcomers by inducing them to bet heavily against Dolly's abilities in the Sausage Row shooting gallery. Turning her back to the mark, with a looking-glass hung before her, Dolly could fire away all day, and never miss making the drum rattle. Then she could swim like a Tahitian, and before daybreak on sultry summer mornings often stole down to the river to strike out in the moon-silvered current. "Ain't you ashamed to be seen that way?" reproachfully inquired an astonished police officer, one morning, upon encountering Dolly coming up the levee, with a single wet garment clinging about her, and wringing out the water from her frizzly hair.

"Only the pretty moon saw me," replied Dolly, turning her dark eyes gratefully to the rich light.

Dolly was a much better character, on the whole, than her sisters of the levee, chiefly because she seldom quarreled, never committed theft, and seldom got tipsy. Smoke she did, inces-santly; for tobacco is a necessity of life on the Row. It was an odd fact that she had no confidants, and never talked about herself. Her reticence, comparative sobriety, and immunity from arrest, together with the fact that she never lacked money enough for the necessities of life, occasioned a peculiar, unpleasant feeling toward her among the other women, which expressed itself in the common saying that Dolly was "putting on airs." Once it became suddenly fashionable on the Row to adorn windows with pots containing some sort of blossoming weed, which these dusky folks euphemistically termed "flowers." Dolly at once "put on airs" by refusing to conform to the growing custom.

"Why don't you have any flower-pots in your window?" cu-riously queried Patsy Brazil.

"Because," said Dolly, "I ain't a-going to be so d—d mean to the flowers. The Row ain't no place for flowers."

One of her greatest pleasures was to pet a little bandy-legged negro child, whose parents nobody knew, and whom old fat Maggie Sperlock had adopted. She would spend whole hours amusing the little fellow, romping and laughing with him, and twisting her extraordinary hair into all sorts of fantastic horns and goblin devices in order to amuse him. Then she taught him the names of all the great white boats, and the names of the far cities they sailed from, and the odd symbolism of the negro steamboat slang. When a long vessel swept by, plowing up the yellow current in curving furrows about her prow, and leaving in her rear a long line of low-hanging nimbus-clouds, Dolly would cry: "See, Tommy, how proud the old gal is to-day; she's got a fine *ruffle* on. Look at her *switch*, Tommy; see how the old gal's curling her hair out behind her." Dolly could not read the names of the boats, but she knew by heart their gleaming shapes, and the varying tones of their wild, deep voices. So she taught the child to know them, too, until to his infantile fancy they became, as it were, great aquatic things, which slept only at the levee, and moved upon the river through the white moonlight with an awfully pulsating life of their own. She likewise made out of a pine plank for Tommy, a funny little vessel, with a cunning stern-wheel to it, which flung up the water bravely as the child drew it along the shore with a cotton string. And Dolly had no end of terrible stories to tell Tommy, about Voodoos—she called them "hoodoos"—people who gathered heads of snakes, and spiders, and hideous creeping things to make venomous charms with, by steeping them in whisky until the foul liquor became "green as grass." Tommy would have become frightened out of his little life at these tales, but that Dolly gave him a dried rabbit's foot in a bag to hang round his neck; for Dolly, like all the colored folks of the levee, believed a rabbit's foot to be a sure charm against all evil.

Of course Dolly had "her man"—a rather good-looking yellow roustabout known along the levee as Aleck. In the summer time, when the river was "lively," as the steamboatmen say, she was rather faithful to Aleck; but when the watery highway was all bound in ice, and there was no money on the Row, and Aleck was away on the Lower Mississippi or perhaps out of work, Dolly was decidedly immoral in her mode of life. But

Aleck could scarcely expect her to be otherwise, for his money went almost as fast as it came. It was generally a feast or a famine with him. He did come home one spring with forty-odd dollars in his pocket—quite a fortune, he thought it, and a new silver watch for Dolly; but that was, perhaps, the great pecuniary event of his career. Somehow or other the watch did not keep perfect time, and poor Dolly, who knew far more about steamboats than she did about watches, opened the chronometer "to see what was the matter with it."

"Why, it's got a little hair wound around its guts," said Dolly; "of course it won't go right." Then she pulled out the mainspring. "Such a doggoned funny looking hair," further observed Dolly.

Unlike the other women of the levee, however, Dolly had a little respect for her own person, and did not sell her favors indiscriminately. On the contrary, she managed for a long time to maintain a certain comparative reputation for respectability. And when she did, at last, become utterly abandoned, perhaps the Great Father of each one of us, black and white, fully pardoned all her poor errors.

For it came to pass in this wise: Aleck, one summer evening, became viciously drunk at a Bucktown ball, and got into a free fight, wherein one roustabout, to use Dolly's somewhat hyperbolic expression, "was shot and cut all to pieces." Aleck was only charged at the Hammond Street Police Station with being drunk and disorderly, but inasmuch as it was not his first offense of the kind, he was sentenced to pay a fine of fifty dollars, and to be imprisoned in the Work-house for a period of thirty days. When the Black Maria had rolled away, and the gaping crowd of loafers had dispersed, after satisfying their unsympathetic curiosity, Dolly wandered into the City Park, and sitting down upon one of the little stone lions at the fountain, cried silently over the broken watch which Aleck had given her. She arose with the resolve to pay Aleck's fine as soon as the thirty days of his Work-house sentence had expired, and went slowly back to the Row.

Now when Dolly had fairly resolved upon doing a thing, it was generally done. We dare not say too much about how Dolly had resolved to earn that fifty dollars in thirty days—about the only way, indeed, that it was remotely possible for her to earn it on the Row. Those who know the social life of the Row will, however, understand the difficulties in Dolly's way. The sudden change in her habits, the recklessness of her life—compared with what it had been; the apparently absolute loss of all the little self-respect she once had, at once excited the surprise of her companions and of the police officers, who watch closely every habitant of the levee. She bought food only when she could not beg it, seldom paid for a cigar, and seemed to become a ubiquitous character in all the worst haunts of the Row, by night and day.

"If you keep on this way, Dolly," finally exclaimed Patsy Brazil, "I'll 'vag' you." It was then nearly thirty days since Aleck had been sentenced. Patsy, kindly but always firm, never threatened in vain, and Dolly knew it.

It is hardly necessary to say, however, that Dolly had not been able to earn the amount of Aleck's fine, nor is it necessary to state how much she had earned, when Patrolman Brazil was obliged to threaten her with the Work-house. She had one recourse left, however,—to sell her dresses and her furniture, consisting of a stove, a bed, and an ancient clock—for much less than their pitiful value. She did sell them, and returned from the second-hand store to her bare room, to fall into an exhausted sleep on the floor, hungry and supperless, but happy in the possession of enough money to pay "her man's fine." And Aleck again found himself a free man.

He felt grateful enough to Dolly not to get drunk for a week, which he naturally considered no small piece of self-abnegation in return for his freedom. A keener-eyed man in a blue uniform with brass buttons, who looked into Dolly's great hollow eyes and sunken face with a muttered "God help her!" better understood how dearly that freedom had been purchased. Hunger and sleeplessness had sapped the vitality of Dolly's nervous though vigorous organization. At last Aleck got work on a Maysville packet boat, and sailed away from the levee, and from the ghost of what was once Dolly, waving a red, ragged handkerchief from her window in defiance of Pickett's orders. Just before the regular starting time some one had "tolled" the boat's bell.

"Who's fooling with that bell," exclaimed Dolly, suddenly dropping her cigar. "It's bad luck to do that." She often thought of the bell again, when week after week the vessel regularly steamed up to the long wharfboat—without Aleck. Aleck had told her that he intended to "see God's people"—the roustabout term for visiting one's home; but she never thought he would have remained away from her so long.

At last one evening while sitting at Pickett's door, filing some little shirt-studs for Aleck out of a well-bleached beef bone, some one told her how Aleck had got married up at Maysville, and what "a tip-top weddin'" it was. Dolly said nothing, but picked up her beef bones and her little file and went up stairs.

"They never die round here," said Patsy Brazil, "until their will's gone. The will dies first." And Dolly's will was dead.

Some women of the levee picked her thin body up from the floor of the empty room and carried her to a bed. Then they sent for old Judge Fox, the gray-haired negro preacher, who keeps a barber-shop on Sausage Row. The old negro's notions of theology were probably peculiar to himself, yet he had comforted more than one dying woman. He closed his shop at once, and came to pray and sing for Dolly, but she heeded neither the prayers nor the strange slave-hymns that he sang. The evening gray deepened to night purple; the moon looked in through the open window at Dolly's thin face; the river reflected its shining ripple on the whitewashed walls within, and through all the sound of the praying and singing there boomed up from below the furious thrumming of banjos and bass-viols, and the wild thunder of the dancers' feet. Down stairs the musicians were playing the tune, "Big Ball Up Town;" up-stairs the women were chanting to a weirdly sweet air, "My Jesus Arose."

Oh, ain't I mighty glad my Jesus arose,
Oh, ain't I mighty glad my Jesus arose,
Oh, ain't I mighty glad my Jesus arose
   To send me up on high.

Here comes my pilgrim Jesus,
A-riding a milk-white horse;
He's rode him to the east and he's rode him to the west,
And to every other quarter of the world.
   Oh, ain't I mighty glad, &c.

Here comes my master Jesus,
With heaven in his view,
He's goin' home to glory,
And bids this world adieu.
　　Oh, ain't I mighty glad, &c.

He'll blow out the sun and burn up the world,
And turn that moon to blood,
And sinners in ——

"Hush," said Dolly, rising with a desperate effort. "Ain't that the old gal talking?"

A sound deeper and sweeter and wilder than the hymned melody or the half-savage music below, filled all the moon lit levee—the steam-song of the Maysville packet coming in.

"Help me up!" gasped Dolly—"It's the old gal blowing off steam; it's Aleck; it's my man—my man."

Then she sunk back suddenly, and lay very still—in the stillness of the Dreamless Sleep.

When they went to lay her out, they found something tightly clutched in one little bony hand—so tightly that it required no inconsiderable exertion to force the fingers open.

It was an old silver watch, with the main-spring pulled out.

Cincinnati Commercial, August 27, 1876

FROST FANCIES

DURING the intense cold of the past forty-eight hours, the great panes of large plate-glass windows throughout the city presented scenes of such beauty as the artistic Spirit of the Frost seldom favors us with. The crystallizations were frequently on a gigantic scale—in likeness of such arabesque vegetation, although colorless, as somehow awakened fancies of strange fretwork about the moresque arches of the crystal palaces described in the Arabian Nights. Sometimes they presented such a combination of variedly intricate patterns, as to suggest a possible source for the fantastic scroll-work designs employed by the monkish masters of mediæval illumination in the decoration of their famous missals and manuscripts. There were double volutes of sharp-edged leaf design, such as occasionally formed a design for elegant vase handles with the antique proficients in the ceramic art; damascene patterns, broken by irregular markings like Cufic characters on a scimitar-blade; feathery interweavings of inimitable delicacy, such as might form elfin plumage for the wings of a frost-spirit; spectral mosses, surpassing in their ephemeral beauty the most velvety growths of our vegetable world; ghost ferns, whose loveliness attracts the eye, but fades into airy nothingness under the breath of the admirer; evanescent shrubs of some fairy species, undreamt of in our botanical science; and snowy plumes, fit to grace the helmet of a phantom-knight, shaming the richest art of devisers in rare heraldic emblems. At moments the December sun intensified the brilliancy of these coruscations of frost-fire: lance-rays of solar flame, shivered into myriad sparkles against the glittering mail of interwoven crystals, tinged all the scintillating work with a fairy-faint reflection of such iridescence as flames upon a humming bird's bosom. The splendor of the frost-work was yesterday everywhere a matter of curious comment, and such a variety of pattern—often of a peculiarly "large-leaved" design—has not been seen for years in the city. On Walnut street, near Seventh, was a very beautiful and peculiar specimen of crystallization in a shop window. It presented the aspect of narrow-bladed wild grasses, thickly growing, and luxuriant; stems shot up bare to a certain height, when leaves sprouted from them on either side, bending suddenly downward at a sharp angle shortly after leaving the stem, in exquisite rivalry of nature. But at a certain height the pattern lost distinctness, and blended into a sharply bristling wilderness of grass-blades, so that the general effect, like that of a rough etching, was best observable at a short distance. The unearthly artist who created the scene, however, was not content with rivaling nature, for his wild grasses terminated beautifully but weirdly in a wild fantasy of leaf scrolls, which resembled nothing in the world of green things growing.

Cincinnati Commercial, December 10, 1876

AT THE GATE OF THE TROPICS

The New Orleans Levee—First Impression of the City—The French Market—A Monster Cotton Press—"Pere Antoine's Date Palm."

NEW ORLEANS, November 19.

EIGHTEEN miles of levee! London, with all the gloomy vastness of her docks, and her "river of the ten thousand masts," can offer no spectacle of traffic so picturesquely attractive and so varied in its attraction.

In the center of this enormous crescent line of wharves and piers lie the great Sugar and Cotton Landings, with their millions of tons of freight newly unshipped, their swarms of swarthy stevedores, their innumerable wagons and beasts of burden. Above the line of depot and storehouse roofs, stretching southward, rises the rolling smoke of the cotton-press furnaces. Facing the Sugar Landing, stretching northward, extend a line of immense sugar sheds, with roofs picturesquely-peaked, Sierrawise. Below, along the wooden levee, a hundred river boats have landed without jostling, and the smoky breath of innumerable chimneys floats, upward eddying, into the overarching blue. Here one sees a comely steamer from the Ohio lying at the landing, still panting, after its long run of a thousand miles; there a vast Mississippi boat lies groaning, with her cargo of seven thousand bales, awaiting relief by a legion of 'longshoremen. At intervals other vessels arrive, some, like mountains of floating cotton, their white sides hidden by brown ramparts of bales built up to the smokestacks; some deeply freighted with the sweet produce of the cane-fields. Black tugs rush noisily hither and thither, like ugly water-goblins seeking strong work to do; and brightly-painted luggers, from the lower coasts,—from the oyster beds and the fruit tree groves— skim over the wrinkled water, some bearing fragrant freight of golden oranges, and pomegranates, and bananas richly ripe; some bringing fishy dainties from the sea. Ocean steamers are

669

resting their leviathan sides at the Southern piers, and either way, along the far-curving lines of wharves, deep-sea ships lie silently marshaled, their pale wings folded in motionless rest. There are barks and brigs, schooners and brigantines, frigates and merchantmen, of all tonnages—ships of light and graceful build, from the Spanish Main; deep-bellied steamers, with East Indian names, that have been to Calcutta and Bombay; strong-bodied vessels from Norway and all the Scandinavian ports; tight-looking packets from English ports; traders under German, Dutch, Italian, French and Spanish flags; barks from the Mediterranean; shapely craft from West Indian harbors. They seem envoys of the world's commerce in sunny session at the Gate of the Tropics! Look either way along the river with a strong glass!—the fringe of masts and yards appears infinitely extended; the distant spars become blended together in a darkly outlined thicket of sharply-pointed strokes and thread, cutting the blue at all angles; further and further yet, the fringe seems but a fringe of needle points and fine cobweb lines; and, at last, only the points remain visible, the lines having wholly vanished.

—It is not an easy thing to describe one's first impression of New Orleans; for while it actually resembles no other city upon the face of the earth, yet it recalls vague memories of a hundred cities. It owns suggestions of towns in Italy, and in Spain, of cities in England and in Germany, of seaports in the Mediterranean, and of seaports in the tropics. Canal street, with its grand breadth and imposing facades, gives one recollections of London and Oxford street and Regent street; there are memories of Havre and Marseilles to be obtained from the Old French Quarter; there are buildings in Jackson Square which remind one of Spanish-American travel. I fancy that the power of fascination which New Orleans exercises upon foreigners is due no less to this peculiar characteristic than to the tropical beauty of the city itself. Whencesoever the traveler may have come, he may find in the Crescent City some memory of his home—some recollection of his Fatherland—some remembrance of something he loves.

New Orleans is especially a city of verandas, piazzas, porches and balconies; and the stranger is liable to be impressed with this fact immediately upon leaving the levee. All the streets in the business portion of the city are shaded with broad piazzas of wood and iron, which cover the whole sidewalk; and on the main streets, such as Canal, side awnings of canvas are also used, so that during the hottest portion of the day the sun can not cause discomfort to pedestrians from any possible direction. The front and also the back windows of most private houses have balconies at every story up to the roof; and in the old French quarter these are often multiplied and superimposed in the most picturesque way;—you see them right under the angle of gable ends, jutting out from queer corners, in a fashion half medieval. They are often hung with large pieces of cloth or carpet, or stuffs brightly dyed, especially above the French dry goods stores; and thus draped the effect is quite odd and pleasing. I find much to gratify an artist's eye in this quaint, curious, crooked French quarter, with its narrow streets and its houses painted in light tints of yellow, green, and sometimes even blue. Neutral tints are common; but there are a great many buildings that can not have been painted for years, and which look neglected and dilapidated as well as antiquated. Solid wooden shutters, painted a bright grass-green, and relieved by walls painted chocolate color, or tinted yellow, have a pretty effect, and suggest many memories of old France. Few houses in the quarter are without them.

A stranger can not avoid being also impressed with the solid character of the streets here throughout the business portion of the city. They are raised like causeways, and are usually either level with the sidewalks or above them, being separated from the curb by gutters of great depth and breadth. The street pavement consists mostly of square blocks of stone set diamond-wise; and this pavement is almost everlasting. It is very handsome and clean looking, and I am told that no other pavement can resist the wear and tear of the cotton traffic or the undermining effect of the rains which loosen bowlders and roll them from their beds.

Most of the finer public buildings must have been erected at a time when expense was the least consideration in the construction of an edifice. They are generously and beautifully built; yet it is sad to see that many of them are falling into decay. Especially is this the case in regard to the old St. Louis Hotel—now the State House—with its splendid dome, frescoed

by Casanova, and its grand halls. To repair it would now require an outlay of hundreds of thousands. It has been outraged
in a manner worthy of Vandals; soldiers have been barracked in
it; mold and damp have written prophecies of ruin within it.
Hither it was that the great planters of the South dwelt in the
old days when they visited New Orleans, and under their rich
patronage the hotel prospered well, till the wars swept away their
wealth, and, for a time at least, ruined New Orleans. I doubt if
any of the great hotels here are now doing well.

The St. Charles, with its noble Greek façade, is the handsomest of these. From the entrance of the rotunda looking outward and upward at the vast Corinthian columns, with their
snowy fluted shafts and rich capitals, their antique lines of
beauty, their harmonious relation to each other, the sight is
magnificent. I find a number of noble Greek facades in the city;
the City Hall, the Methodist Church, on Carondelet street,
and other structures I might name, are beautiful, and seem to
illumine the streets with their white splendor. This elegant,
gracious architecture appears adapted to this sky and this
sunny clime; and, indeed it was under almost such a sky and
such a sun that the Greek architecture was born.

But, after all, the glory of the city is in her Southern homes
and gardens. I can not do justice to their beauty. The streets
broaden there; the side-paths are bordered with verdant sod as
soft and thick as velvet, and overshadowed with magnolias; the
houses, mostly built in Renaissance style, are embowered in
fruit-bearing trees and evergreen gardens, where statues and
fountains gleam through thick shrubbery, cunningly trimmed
into fantastic forms. Orange and fig trees; bananas and palms;
magnolias and myrtles; cypresses and cedars; broad leaved,
monstrous-flowering plants in antique urns; herbs with leaves
shaped like ancient Greek sword-blades, and edged with yellow; shrubs exotically luxuriant, bearing blossoms of curious
form and equatorial brilliancy of color; and flowers so rich of
hue, so sweet, so fragrant, that they vary the varied green with
a thousand tints, and make the tepid air odorous with drowsy
perfume. And you can walk through this paradise hour after
hour, mile after mile; and the air only becomes yet more fragrant and the orange trees more heavily freighted with golden

fruit, and the gardens more and more beautiful, as you proceed southwardly.

Color and light and bright contrasts,—those warmly picturesque effects which artists seek to study in tropical climes, may be studied in perfection at the French Market. The markets of London are less brightly clean and neatly arranged; the markets of Paris are less picturesque. It consists of a succession of huge buildings, extending for nearly a quarter of a mile, and covering an area of about four squares. Oh, the contrasts of color, the tropical picturesqueness of a morning market-scene here; the seductiveness of the succulent fruits; the brilliancy of the brightly dyed stuffs in the hosiery and notion booths; the truly French taste exhibited in the arrangements of vegetables, and fowls and fruits and fish; the costumes of the quadroon girls; the Indian squaws selling droll trinkets; the blue jackets from the ships of all Nations; the red-shirted fishermen from the luggers; the Spaniards, Mexicans, Italians, Englishmen, Portuguese, Greeks, Frenchmen, Acadians, Creoles! One may see almost everything, and buy almost anything in the French market; and he must have a hard heart or an empty pocket who can always withstand the softly syllabled request of some bright-eyed Creole girl to buy something that he does not want.

You never smell an unpleasant odor in the French market; there is nothing to offend the nostrils, nothing to displease the eye. You inhale the fragrance of fruits and flowers—such fruit, such flowers!—you breathe the odor of delicious coffee from the lunch booths. What coffee it is, too—Oriental in strength and fragrance, but clear as wine. Oranges are selling at ten cents a dozen; bananas "five for a picayune;" and mountains of them are coming in from the Picayune landing, where all the luggers lie. Here are huge fruits that resemble oranges, but are nearly eight inches in diameter; pomegranates piled up in blushing pyramids; red bananas from Spanish America arranged in towers; figs, ripe and green; fresh dates; pale green grapes in giant clusters; apples rosy enough to have tempted rosy Eve; citrons and lemons; cocoanuts and pecans and pine-apples; and strange-looking fruits peculiar to the tropics. Here are flowers of a hundred kinds, in pots, in boxes, in nosegays, in bouquets, in bunches for the button-hole. Here are boots and shoes, silks and muslins, handkerchiefs and hosiery, cutlery and delf-ware, porcelain and crockery, tin-ware and plated-ware, dry goods of all varieties, and shirts of all dyes. I can not attempt to give any idea of the vegetable market, with its green and brown and purplish and ruddy mountains of fresh stock; or the admirably clean meat market, with the polite French butchers in white caps and aprons; or the bread stalls, where are piled up rolls as white as milk and sweet as cream; or the poultry market, with its questionable luxuries. The fish market has a glass roof, and all the rainbow tints of the fresh fish come out well on a bright day. Here are hills of shrimps and pyramids of oysters, and enormous baskets of live crabs, wherein hideous claw-battles are incessant. But one can not see, much less describe, all the sights of the French market in a month. It is a perpetual exhibition of industry—a museum of the Curiosities of Marketing.

NOVEMBER 20.

I have just witnessed a terrible exhibition of the power of machinery. Friends had advised me to visit the huge cotton press at the Cotton Landing, and I spent several hours in watching its operation. Excepting, perhaps, some of the monster cotton presses of India, it is said to be the most powerful in the world; but the East Indian presses box the cotton instead of baling it, with enormous loss of time. This "Champion" press at the New Orleans Levee weighs, with all its attachments, upwards of three thousand tons, and exerts the enormous pressure of four million pounds upon the bales placed in it. When I first arrived at the gate of the building where the machinery is placed, they were loading the newly pressed bales upon drays—bales much smaller than the ordinary plantation bales. I was considerably surprised to see three or four negroes straining with all their might to roll one of these bales; but I was not then aware that each of the packages of cotton before me weighed upward of *one thousand pounds.* They were really double—two bales pressed into one, and bound with twelve ties instead of six, and were being packed thus for shipment upon the vessel Western Empire for foreign parts. One of the gentlemen connected with the office kindly measured a double bale for me, with an ingenious instrument especially made for such measurements. It proved to be less than two feet through its thickest diameter—considerably less than most ordinary single bales.

The spectacle of this colossal press in motion is really terrific. It is like a nightmare of iron and brass. It does not press downward, but upward. It is not a press as we understand the term generally, but an enormous mouth of metal which seizes the bale and crushes it in its teeth. The machine did not give me the idea of a machine, it seemed rather some vast, black genie, buried up to his neck in the earth by the will of Soliman, the pre-Adamite Sultan.

Fancy a monstrous head of living iron and brass, fifty feet high from its junction with the ground, having pointed gaps in its face like gothic eyes, a mouth five feet wide, opening six feet from the mastodon teeth in the lower jaw to the mastodon in the upper jaw. The lower jaw alone moves, as in living beings, and it is worked by two vast iron tendons, long and thick and solid as church pillars. The surface of this lower jaw is equivalent to six square feet.

The more I looked at the thing, the more I felt as though its prodigious anatomy had been studied after the anatomy of some extinct animal,—the way those jaws worked, the manner in which those muscles moved.

Men rolled a cotton bale to the mouth of the monster. The jaws opened with a low roar, and so remained. The lower jaw had descended to a level with the platform on which the bale was lying. It was an immense plantation bale. Two black men rolled it into the yawning mouth. The titan muscles contracted, and the jaw closed, silently, steadily, swiftly. The bale flattened, flattened, flattened—down to sixteen inches, twelve inches, eight inches, five inches. Positively less than five inches! I thought it was going to disappear altogether. But after crushing it beyond five inches the jaws remained stationary and the monster growled like rumbling thunder. I thought the machine began to look as hideous as one of those horrible, yawning heads which formed the gates of the *teocallis* at Palenque, and through whose awful jaws the sacrificial victims passed.

I noticed that the iron tie-bands which had been passed through the teeth were not fastened by hand. No hand could pull them tight enough to resist the internal pressure of the captive bale. They were fastened by very powerful steel levers, called "pullers," which slid along a bar, and by which the bands were pulled so tight that all the "slack" (or at least nearly all) is taken out of the bale, and the bands cut deeply into the cotton. With the "pullers" the strain upon the bands becomes two thousand pounds to each band, a peculiar tie-grip being invented to insure against breaking. The levers pull both ends of the band at the same time with the same tension.

It seemed to me evidently less than a minute from the time of feeding the machine until the bale was rolled out, flat as a pillow, and hard as the hardest wood. It still remained only five inches thick at the sides, but the internal pressure bent out the bands ovally so that the bale became about a foot thick in the center. Yet the reduction seemed magical. I am told this machine presses upwards of six hundred bales a day. Afterwards I saw in the yard near by about a thousand bales thus pressed, standing balanced on end, and at a distance they looked rather like mattresses than bales, with their edges turned toward the spectator. I saw "floats" arrive at the gate with plantation bales piled upon them, one tier above another, fifteen bales being the legal load for a float; and I saw them drive off to the levee with their freight repressed, neatly packed in one tier with room to spare. Perhaps I could not give you a better idea of the power of this machine than by stating the fact that not long ago, during a test exhibition, it compressed a bale of good cotton to a density of *eighty pounds per cubic foot!* Considerable discussion has been held on the question whether such tremendous pressure does not injure the cotton fiber; and experiments have been made both at Liverpool and New Orleans with a view to ascertaining the actual result to the cotton. I am informed that as yet microscopical investigation has shown no injury whatever to the fiber.

—Do you remember that charming little story, "Pere Antoine's Date-Palm," written by Thomas Bailey Aldrich, and published in the same volume with "Marjorie Daw" and other tales?

Pere Antoine was a good old French priest, who lived and died in New Orleans. As a boy he had conceived a strong friendship for a fellow student of about his own age, who, in after years, sailed to some tropical island in the Southern Seas, and wedded some darkly beautiful woman, graceful and shapely and tall as a feathery palm. Pere Antoine wrote often to his friend, and their friendship strengthened with the years, until death dissolved it. The young colonist died, and his beautiful wife also passed from the world; but they left a little daughter for some one to take care of.

The good priest, of course, took care of her, and brought her up at New Orleans. And she grew up graceful and comely as her mother, with all the wild beauty of the South. But the child could not forget the glory of the tropics, the bright lagoon, the white-crested sea roaring over the coral reef, the royal green of the waving palms, and the beauty of the golden-feathered birds that chattered among them.

So she pined for the tall palms and the bright sea and the wild reef, until there came upon her that strange home-sickness which is death; and still dreaming of the beautiful palms, she gradually passed into that great sleep which is dreamless. And she was buried by Pere Antoine near his own home.

By and by, above the little mound there suddenly came a gleam of green; and mysteriously, slowly, beautifully, there grew up towering in tropical grace above the grave, a princely palm. And the old priest knew that it had grown from the heart of the dead child.

So the years passed by, and the roaring city grew up about the priest's home and the palm tree, trying to push Pere Antoine off his land. But he would not be moved. They piled up gold upon his door-steps and he laughed at them; they went to law with him and he beat them all; and, at last, dying, he passed away true to his trust; for the man who cuts down that palm tree loses the land that it grows upon.

"And there it stands," says the Poet, "in the narrow, dingy street, a beautiful dreamy stranger, an exquisite foreign lady, whose grace is a joy to the eye, the incense of whose breath makes the air enamored. May the hand wither that touches her ungently!"

Now I was desirous above all things to visit the palm made famous by this charming legend, and I spent several days in seeking it. I visited the neighborhood of the old Place d'Armes —now Jackson Square—and could find no trace of it; then I visited the southern quarter of the city, with its numberless gardens, and I sought for the palm among the groves of orange-trees overloaded with their golden fruit, amid broad-leaved bananas, and dark cypresses, and fragrant magnolias and tropical trees of which I did not know the names. Then I found many date palms. Some were quite young, with their splendid crest of leafy plumes scarcely two feet above the ground; others stood up to a height of thirty or forty feet. Whenever I saw a tall palm, I rang the doorbell and asked if that was Pere Antoine's date-palm. Alas! nobody had ever heard of the Pere Antoine.

Then I visited the ancient cathedral, founded by the pious Don Andre Almonaster, Regidor of New Orleans, one hundred and fifty years ago; and I asked the old French priest whether they had ever heard of the Pere Antoine. And they answered me that they knew him not, after having searched the ancient archives of the ancient Spanish cathedral.

Once I found a magnificent palm, loaded with dates, in a garden on St. Charles street, so graceful that I felt the full beauty of Solomon's simile as I had never felt it before: "Thy stature is like to a palm-tree." I rang the bell and made inquiry concerning the age of the tree. It was but twenty years old; and I went forth discouraged.

At last, to my exceeding joy, I found an informant in the person of a good-natured old gentleman, who keeps a quaint bookstore in Commercial Place. The tree was indeed growing, he said, in New Orleans street, near the French Cathedral, and not far from Congo Square; but there were many legends concerning it. Some said it had been planted over the grave of some Turk or Moor,—perhaps a fierce corsair from Algiers or Tunis —who died while sailing up the Mississippi, and was buried on its moist shores. But it was not at all like the other palm trees in the city, nor did it seem to him to be a date palm. It was a real Oriental palm: yea, in sooth, such a palm as Solomon spake of in his Love-song of Love songs.

"I said, I will go up to the palm tree; I will take hold of the boughs thereof."

I found it standing in beautiful loneliness in the center of a dingy wood-shed, on the north side of Orleans street, towering about forty feet above the rickety plank fence of the yard. The gateway was open, and a sign swung above it bearing the name

"M. Michel." I walked in and went up to the palm tree. A laborer was sawing wood in the back shed, and I saw through the windows of the little cottage by the gate a family at dinner. I knocked at the cottage door, and a beautiful Creole woman opened it.

"May I ask, Madame, whether this palm tree was truly planted by the Pere Antoine?"

"Ah, Monsieur, there are many droll stories which they relate of that tree. There are folks who say that a young girl was interred there, and it is also said that a Sultan was buried under that tree—or the son of a Sultan. And there are also some who say that a priest planted it."

"Was it the Pere Antoine, Madame?"

"I do not know, Monsieur. There are people also who say that it was planted here by Indians from Florida. But I do not know whether such trees grow in Florida. I have never seen any other palm tree like it. It is not a date-palm. It flowers every year, with beautiful yellow blossoms the color of straw, and the blossoms hang down in pretty curves. Oh, it is very graceful! Sometimes it bears fruit,—a kind of oily fruit, but not dates. I am told they make oil from the fruit of such palms."

I though it looked so sad, that beautiful tree, in the dusty wood-yard with no living green thing near it. As its bright verdant leaves waved against the blue above, one could not but pity it as one would pity some being, fair and feminine and friendless in a strange land. "*Oh, c'est bien gracieux,*" murmured the handsome Creole lady.

"Is it true, Madame, that the owner of the land loses it if he cuts down the tree?"

"*Mais oui!* But the proprietors of the ground have always respected the tree, because it is so old, so very old!"

Then I found the proprietor of the land, and he told me that when the French troops first arrived in this part of the country they noticed that tree. "Why," I exclaimed, "that must have been in the reign of Louis XIV!" "It was in 1679, I believe," he answered. As for the Pere Antoine, he had never heard of him. Neither had he heard of Thomas Bailey Aldrich. So that I departed, mourning for my dead faith in a romance which was beautiful.

Cincinnati Commercial, November 26, 1877

NEW ORLEANS IN WET WEATHER

Dampness—Graveyards—Alligators and Art Notes—Mementoes of "Picayune" Butler—Beggars and Bootblacks—Greek Sailors in the French Market.

The dampness of New Orleans upon a wet day impresses one as something phenomenal. You do not know in the North what such dampness is. It descends from the clouds and arises from the soil simultaneously; it exudes from wood-work; it perspires from stone. It is spectral, mysterious, inexplicable. Strong walls and stout doors can not keep it from entering; windows and doors can not exclude it. You might as well try to lock out a ghost. Bolts of steel and barriers of stone are equally unavailing, and the stone moulders, and this steel is smitten with red leprosy. The chill sweat pouring down from the walls, soaks into plank floors, and the cunning of the paper-hanger is useless here. Carpets become so thoroughly wet with the invisible rain that they utter soughy, marshy sounds under the foot. Consequently few houses are carpeted within, and those good folks who insist upon carpets soon learn the folly of putting them down on more than one or two of the upper rooms. Matting is the substitute even in aristocratic houses—dry, crisp, neat matting. Paper-hangers and carpet-layers would starve to death here. If you even lay a few sheets of writing paper upon your table at nightfall you will find them quite limp and rebellious of ink by morning. Articles of steel must be carefully laid away in tight drawers. The garments hung upon the wall, the coverings of beds, the well-starched shirts in the bureau seem as if they had been rained upon; the stair carpets become like wet turf; and a moldy, musty smell pervades the atmosphere.

Fire is the only remedy possible against this invasion of moisture and mildew, and fires are absolutely necessary in all bedrooms almost all through the winter. During the daytime in winter months doors and windows are generally left open, except upon exceptionally cold or rainy days; the fires are allowed to go out, and the winds are invited to come in and keep things dry. But when night falls, chill mists invade the city, and exhalations of dampness rise from the moist earth. This is the case even in clear weather, and Louisianians would not think of sleeping without a fire in their bedrooms to dry the air and banish the specter of dampness. Even in the heat of summer the night-dews are often heavy like heavy rain.

In the North you place open vessels of water upon your heating stoves that the warm air may be kept moist. Here all possible efforts are made to heat the air so that it may hold in suspension as little moisture as possible. For the city sits upon a marsh, and swamps lie about her crescent boundary.

Carpets become an affliction here. Save in the houses of the wealthier, where continual fires keep them dry, they absorb the unhealthiness of dampness in the wet season. They fill the house with an odor of mustiness that makes one think of bacteria and vibriones, and divers other horrors of the microscope. I say "houses of the wealthier," because here there are few families who can afford to maintain a good fire to fight all the year round with the swamp dampness.

Here, after a certain hour of night, the streets are as silent and deserted as the graveled walks of a grave-yard. Occasionally, indeed, one may hear a company of volunteer firemen returning from a midnight fire, all singing some jolly refrain to some saucy air borrowed from "La Fille de Madame Angot;" but even the ubiquitous reporter and the all-enduring telegraph messenger yield to the despotism of dampness ere the dead waste and middle of the night.

On the finest days in the winter months there are early fogs, that seem visible exhalations from the damp soil below the pavements. The gutters smoke whitely in the heavy air, and the face of the morning sun beyond the spectral mists assumes the sickly yellow of an unripe orange. When the long, burning summer comes, these sheeted fogs do not wholly cease to haunt the streets by night, and often long after daybreak; but their ghostly rule is unstable, for at intervals there comes a mighty sea breath from the Spanish Main, blowing over the cane fields and the fruit groves, driving the shadowy haze from the river banks, and filling the streets with bright air and a faint odor of orange flowers. Even in summer, however, fires are kept up in many houses through the night, partly to preserve the furniture against the mouldering damp, and partly owing to a wide-spread belief that Yellow Jack will not enter the room made cheery by a warm hearth.

I suspect that these fogs and night-damps account for the peculiar habits of late rising prevalent here. In the North at 8 o'clock business is brisk; here, at 8 o'clock, the city has but just given its awakening yawn, rubbed its eyes and lazily stretched itself in bed.

Strange it is to observe the approach of one of these eerie fogs, on some fair night. The blue deeps above glow tenderly beyond the sharp crescent of the moon; the heavens seem transformed to an infinite ocean of liquid turquoise, made living with the palpitating life of the throbbing stars. In this limpid clearness, this mellow, tropical moonlight, objects are plainly visible at a distance of miles; far sounds come to the ear with marvelous distinctness—the clarion calls of the boats, the long, loud panting of the cotton presses, exhaling steamy breath from their tireless lungs of steel. Suddenly sounds become fainter and fainter, as though the atmosphere were made feeble by some unaccountable enchantment; distant objects lose distinctness; the heaven is cloudless, but her lights, low burning and dim, no longer make the night transparent, and a chill falls upon the city, such as augurs the coming of a ghost. Then the ghost appears; the invisible makes itself visible; a vast form of thin white mist seems to clasp the whole night in its deathly embrace; the face of the moon is hidden as with a gray veil, and the spectral fog extinguishes with its chill breath the trembling flames of the stars.

—The subject of dampness seems to me inseparably connected in New Orleans with the ghastlier subject of graveyards. Here at the depth of a foot or two feet one strikes water in digging, so that the labor of digging a grave is even as the labor of digging a well, and the end result the same. Consequently the practice of burying the dead in the ground has been almost abandoned. They are simply placed in dry tombs built above the ground, but nevertheless termed burial vaults. In some of the cemeteries here these buildings have evidently been designed after the beautiful sepulchers of antiquity, such as still line the Street of the Tombs at Pompeii, or as are scattered along the Appian Way without the city of Rome. They are mostly built of brick, cased with white marble, and entered by two small but ponderous doors of black iron. Over the double entrance way is carved the name of the proprietor, in this wise: "Family Tomb of John A——," or "Family Tomb of Richard B——." But, notwithstanding the beautiful designs of various tombs, the glare of the white stone and the gloom of the iron doors form a most dismal and unpleasant contrast.

What impresses one as most peculiar about some of these New Orleans cemeteries is the character of their inclosure—a wall of white stone, honeycombed with tombs. At a short distance the wall suggests the idea of an enormous system of pigeon-holes, the entrance of each pigeon-hole being apparently about two feet square, but really large enough to admit the insertion of the largest coffin. Here and there you see a row of twenty or thirty "pigeon-holes" closed up with lids of white marble and hermetically sealed. These contain coffins and corpses. Most of these horrid holes are, happily, tenantless, and spiders of incredible size and unspeakable audacity sit within and weave their dusty tapestries of clammy silk across the yawning aperture. Irreverent people term these sepulchers "*bake-ovens.*" Fancy being asked by a sexton whether you wished to have the remains of your wife or child deposited in "one of them bake-ovens."

I wonder whether something of the old pagan faith of the elder civilizations does not yet linger in our midst despite eighteen centuries of Christianity—something of a vague idea that the manes of the dead must be appeased by offerings at the sepulcher? The aspect of some of the cemeteries here is certainly apt to awaken such a fancy. Everywhere one observes, hanging to the walls of the dismal vaults or suspended from the sealed lids of those dreadful catacombs, wreaths of faded leaves, garlands of withered flowers, crumbling to colorless dust, curious decorations wrought from paper in imitation of lace or crotchet-work, images, pictures, and many other innocent trifles and foolish ornaments. I do not believe it possible that any rational mind could believe such gifts as the pictures I have here seen, to be in themselves pleasing to the eye; they are such terrible things that I dare not venture to describe them. Nor can I suppose that the good folks, who decorated their family tomb with wreaths of parti-colored paper, did so in the belief that such articles are intrinsically graceful. Perhaps it will be more charitable to suppose that these baubles and flimsy decorations were hung upon the tombs because of an ancient faith that the dead sleep a deeper sleep in their sepulcher when offerings are there placed; that the ghosts of departed friends accept such offerings as a token that they are not wholly forgotten, however pitiful the poor trifles may be.

—The French love of the beautiful, the Italian spirit of art, have made this city beautiful; something of Southern Europe lives in the Garden District, with its singing fountains, its box-trees cut into distaffs, its statues and fantastically-trimmed shrubs, its palms and fig trees, and the yellow riches of its banana and orange orchards. In all quarters of New Orleans one likewise encounters some pleasing evidences of esthetic taste. For instance, it is visible in the iron work of railings and verandas, partly, perhaps, because the immense demand for iron-work for verandas and balconies has developed the natural taste of French designers in this direction. Vine leaves and bunches of grapes enter largely into iron tracery for balconies; oak leaves and acorns form an equally pleasing design. But the prettiest thing I have ever seen in this phase of art applied to industry is a railing for private gardens, fashioned in the form of growing corn, the long ears forming the points above the upper rail. This design is really exquisite; one could not have believed it possible to imitate the grace of growing corn, the plumy wave of its half crispy leaves, the elegant poise of the ears upon their stalks, so perfectly. And to imitate it in iron, of all things. These railings, however, do not look well from within, as they are cast hollow; but their shadows produces some charming silhouettes when cast upon a white stretch of pavement. The corn railing looks well when painted a yellowish green—about the color of an unripe orange—or even a clear green; but some people here have had the shocking bad taste to paint them chocolate color! I wonder, too, why it has not occurred to some people to have nature imitated in the painting of these railings, observing the differing tints of stalk, leaf, and pale golden ear.

Then, again, I have seen some glorious stairways here, broad, massive, antiquated; with bronze Amazons bearing brazen lamps at each landing, and perhaps a bronze Caryatid upholding a ponderous candelabrum standing sentinel at the lower step of the flight.

But it is in the very heart of the city, in the center of the business blocks, and hard by the Cotton Exchange, that one encounters the most charming surprise of this sort. Entering a paved archway from Common street, you suddenly find yourself in a double court; and through the second archway beyond gleams a musical fountain, whose marble basin is made verdant with water plants and flowers. Above Hebe stands ever youthful in bronze, pouring nectar into her shapely cup; swan-birds curve stony necks at her feet, and about the lower basin four sinewy Tritons, whose nervous thighs end gracefully in dolphin tails, blow mightily through marble horns. It is delightful to meet these fragmentary dreams of antique art,—these fancies of that older world which is yet ever young with the youth of immortality,—thus hidden like treasures in the city's bosom. The windows of this central court all look down upon the fountain; and quaint balconies, worthy of Seville or Cordova, jut out overhead at all possible angles. This is Gallia Court, devoted, alas! to office purposes, by lawyers and by doctors.

—The matter of art reminds me that shortly after my arrival in the city I paid a visit to the venerable statue of Henry Clay, on Canal street. It stands in the center of the grand thoroughfare, and is inclosed by a railing. On the eastern face of the quadrangular pedestal I observed the following inscription, deeply cut into the stone and blacked. At least two-thirds of the inscription had been well nigh erased by the removal of the black pigment of the letters, but the phrase "deepest stain" was wonderfully distinct, and the word "SLAVERY" as black as the changeless skin of the Ethiopian:

"IF I COULD BE INSTRUMENTAL IN ERADICATING THIS DEEPEST STAIN, SLAVERY, FROM THE CHARACTER OF OUR COUNTRY, I WOULD NOT EXCHANGE THE PROUD SATISFACTION WHICH I SHOULD ENJOY FOR THE HONORS OF ALL THE TRIUMPHS EVER DECREED TO THE MOST SUCCESSFUL CONQUERORS. — HENRY CLAY."

Surely, I said to myself, no Southern man could have aided in the erection of a statue with such an inscription as that.

Crossing Canal street, I wandered through the French quarter into Jackson Square, and proceeded to examine the great equestrian statue of Andrew Jackson, erect upon a rampant steed. Upon the eastern face of the stone I beheld characters deeply graven, and I discovered that the characters were even these:

"THE UNION MUST AND SHALL BE PRESERVED."

Then I inquired what might be the history of these extraordinary inscriptions, and received this pithy, trisyllabic and all-satisfying reply:

"Beast Butler!"

It is certainly difficult to imagine what could be the object of thus chiseling the monuments of a conquered people, except that of inflicting petty annoyance, or perhaps, indeed, that of leaving a historical memento of the conqueror's visitation. It was this ingenuity in discovering acrid blisters for the sorest spots of Southern character that still makes the name of Butler a synonym for abomination in New Orleans. A history of his government of the city is still circulated here, under the title of "Beauty and Booty," having for a frontispiece a savage caricature of Butler surrounded by silver candlesticks and silver spoons. The book is wretchedly written and poorly arranged; but as it contains a large number of Butler's military orders, and records of interesting events republished *verbatim* from the papers of the day, it is not without some value.

—It has become customary with Northern jokers visiting New Orleans to send to their friends in the boreal regions a young alligator; and even I have had some difficulty in conquering the temptation to do likewise. Alligators are here for sale cheap. Certainly they ought to be cheap. I asked an acquaintance the other day what were the boundaries of the city on the west. "Swamps," he replied; "if you walk right to the end of Canal street beyond the graveyard, and into the swamp, why, you'll get up to your neck in alligators." I never attempted to learn by actual experience whether his statements were literally correct; but from the fact that young alligators are sometimes found swimming in the street gutters upon rainy days I suspect that he was not far from the truth. Mr. M——, a friend of mine, picked one up quite recently in the gutter opposite Lafayette

Square. It was unpleasantly lively, and about six inches long. He took the hideous little monster home, carelessly flung it into a bureau-drawer, and threw it a piece of bread. It seized the bread ferociously and forthwith choked itself to death, amid the lamentations of the family.

—I must say a word concerning a certain trade and a certain profession which are profitable in this poverty-stricken city. The trade is that of the bootblack. The profession is that of the beggar. There are a few bootblacks only; but there are beggars in number even as a swarm of flies. This is because certain social restrictions have been placed upon the exercise of the trade of bootblack; while no social restriction whatever, save that of the general impecuniousness of New Orleans, limits the ambition of the profession of beggar.

When I left Cincinnati the bootblacking business was in a bad way. There were many bootblacks, and they were being forced into a reduction of prices. Nobody cared to pay more than a nickel for the most perfect possible "shine." But here prices keep up well. The New Orleans bootblack would reject a nickel with scorn. It takes capital to go into the business here. You must be able to buy a wooden platform, a soft-bottomed chair, a stationary blacking-box with raised foot-supports, five or six brushes, the best description of blacking, and a piece of carpet to kneel upon. Then you must pay a rent of eight or ten dollars a month for permission to exercise your calling upon any sidewalk in any busy part of town. The trade is wholly in the hands of men here, mostly colored, and is said to be profitable in the winter season. Nobody here would think of having his boots blacked unless the bootblack could furnish him with a comfortable chair to sit down upon during the operation.

As for the beggars, I can only say that they seem to be regarded here as a necessary evil, and have become a nuisance in numbers, and an affliction by reason of their persistent impertinence. They follow you along the street, often two at a time, thrusting hats or hands under your nose in the ferocious determination to wring some mark of attention from you. Several have been locked up since I came here,—not, indeed, for begging, but for violently abusing the unfortunate people who dared refuse them alms.

—"Oranges fifty cents a hundred!—twelve for a nickel!" is a

daily cry nowadays in the French Market, and they are good, large, ripe, sweet oranges, too,—fresh from the deep-green trees, with fragments of stalk and bright leaf still attached. They are piled up in huge wooden bins, like potatoes, and these hills of fruit glow like gold under the morning sun. I bought twelve fine ones the other morning, and the swarthy orange-dealer furnished me a strong paper bag to put them in. While wondering within myself how large the fruit-vender's profit could possibly be, I was insensibly attracted by something unusual in his face—a shadow of the beauty of the antique world seemed to rest upon it. "Are you not a Greek?" I asked, for there was no mistaking the metoposcopy of that head. Yes; he was from Zante—first a sailor, now a fruit-vendor; some day, perhaps, he would be a merchant.

It is among those who sell, not among those who buy, that the most curious studies of human nature and of the human face are to be made in the French Market. These dealers are by no means usually French, but they are mostly from the Mediterranean coasts and the Levant—from Sicily and Cyprus, Corsica and Malta, the Ionian Archipelago, and a hundred cities fringing the coasts of Southern Europe. They are wanderers, who have wandered all over the face of the earth, to find rest at last in this City of the South; they are sailors who have sailed all seas, and sunned themselves at a hundred tropical ports, and finally anchored their lives by the levee of New Orleans. The Neapolitan Italian, the Spaniard, the Corsican, the Levantine Greek seek rest from storm here, in a clime akin to their own and under a sky as divinely blue, and at a port not far distant from their beloved sea. For these Levantine sailors hate dusty inland cities and the dry air of the Great West.

If you, O reader, chance to be a child of the sea;—if, in earliest childhood, you listened each morning and evening to that most ancient and mystic hymn-chant of the waves, which none can hear without awe, and which no musician can learn;—if you have ever watched wonderingly the far sails of the fishing vessels turn rosy in the blush of sunset, or silver under the moon, or golden in the glow of sunrise;—if you once breathed as your native air the divine breath of the ocean, and learned the swimmer's art from the hoary breakers, and received the Ocean-god's christening, the glorious baptism of salt,—then, perhaps, you know only too well why these sailors of the Levant can not seek homes within the heart of the land. Twenty years may have passed since your ears last caught the thunder of that mighty ode of hexameters which the sea has always sung and will sing forever,—since your eyes sought the far line where the vaulted blue of heaven touches the level immensity of rolling waters,— since you breathed the breath of the ocean, and felt its clear ozone living in your veins like an elixir. Have you forgotten the mighty measure of that mighty song?—have you forgotten the divine saltiness of that unfettered wind? Is not the spell of the sea strong upon you still?

So that when the long, burning summer comes, and the city roars dustily around you, and your ears are filled with the droning hum of machinery, and your heart full of the bitterness of the struggle for life, then comes to you at long intervals in the dingy office or the crowded streets some memory of white breakers and vast stretches of wrinkled sand and far-fluttering breezes that seem to whisper "Come!"

So that when the silent night comes, you find yourself revisiting in dreams those ocean shores thousands of miles away. The wrinkled sand, ever shifting yet ever the same, has the same patches of vari-colored weeds and shining rocks along its level expanse; and the thunder-chant of the sea which echoes round the world, eternal yet ever new, is rolling up to heaven. The glad waves leap up to embrace you; the free winds shout welcome in your ears; white sails are shining in the west, while sea birds are flying over the gleaming swells. And from the infinite expanse of eternal sky and everlasting sea, then comes to you, with the heavenly ocean breeze, a thrilling sense of unbounded freedom, a delicious feeling as of life renewed, an ecstasy as of youth restored. And so you start into wakefulness with the thunder of that sea-dream in your ears and tears of regret in your eyes to find about you only heat and dust and toil; the awakening rumble of traffic, and "the city sickening of its own breath."

And I think that the Levantine sailors dare not dwell in the midst of the land, for fear lest dreams of a shadowy sea might come upon them in the night, and phantom winds call wildly to them in their sleep, and they might wake to find themselves a thousand miles beyond the voice of breakers.

Somtimes, I doubt not, these swarthy sellers of fruit, whose black eyes sparkle with the sparkle of the sea, and whose voices own the tones of ocean winds, sicken when a glorious breeze from the Gulf enters the city, shaking the blossoms from the magnolia trees and the orange groves. Sometimes, I doubt not, they forsake their Southern home when the dream comes upon them, and take ship for the Spanish Main. Yet I think most men may wake here from dreams of the sea, and rest again. It is true that you can not hear the voice of the hoary breakers in the moonlight,—only the long panting of the cotton-presses, the shouting of the boats calling upon each other through the tropical night, and the ceaseless song of the night birds and crickets. But the sea ships, with their white wings folded, are slumbering at the wharves; the sea-winds are blowing through the moon-lit streets, and from the South arises that wondrous, pale glow, like the far reflection of the emerald green of the ocean. So that the Greek sailor, awaking from the vision of winds and waves, may join three fingers of his right hand, after the manner of the Eastern Church, and cross himself, and sleep again in peace.

Cincinnati Commercial, December 22, 1877

NEW ORLEANS

Ruffians in New Orleans—The Sicilian Vendetta—Some Curiosities of Creole Grammar—A Weird Creole Love-song—Voudooism—The Grace of the Serpent.

NEW ORLEANS, December 21.
AMONG the dark-eyed sailors from the Mediterranean who have anchored their fortunes at the port of New Orleans, there are swarthy hundreds in whose veins throbs the mingled blood of Roman, Carthaginian, Moor and Norman; and perhaps, too, of those antique colonists who brought into the volcanic lands of Sicily the civilization of Athens. This strange blending of Nations seems always productive of strange results. One would suppose, from comparing those results in various lands,

that the more good blood is mixed, the more savage it becomes. From whom are the Greek brigands? From whom are the Italian and Sicilian banditti descended? What blood flows in the veins of the Spanish *matador* or the Spanish *contrabandista*?

I do not think that these Sicilians of New Orleans—these descendants of those who gave to history the terrible memory of the "Sicilian Vespers," and who live here side by side with descendants, no doubt, of French citizens slaughtered in Palermo —are readily distinguishable from Neapolitans, or other Italians, by any outward characteristics. They are, indeed, volcanic-hearted, like the land whence they came, but the eruption of a Sicilian's hatred always bursts forth without premonition. It is the Sicilian of all men who may naturally smile and smile and be a villain still. He masters his passion only for the more complete gratification of it at some judicious moment. But the satisfaction of a wrong by the use of the knife can not be indulged under ordinary circumstances in such a community as this. The spirit of healthier laws than the laws of Sicily prevails against the natural instinct of vengeance for a personal injury. There are, however, circumstances that are extraordinary and injuries that are not strictly personal, under which circumstances and for which injuries the Sicilian seeks vengeance as best he may, without regard to any law save the law of *vendetta*.

Under the code of the vendetta, the civil code is ignored. The avenger never seeks the aid of the state or the municipal law. He is a law unto himself. He feels assured of the sympathy and silence of his compatriots; and he is never betrayed. Even the dying victim will never utter the name of his assassin,— except to his *compadre* or to his nearest male relative as natural avenger. Even the priest who bears the *viaticum* and hears the last confession may seek in vain, as "ghostly father" of the victim, to learn that name. The shrewdest detective may follow the surest clues only to a certain point where all is deafness and blindness,—shrugging of shoulders and multiplied gestures of ignorance. "*Eet ees vendetta*; I know nothing!" The assassin may even be arrested and imprisoned; none will appear against him; the relatives of the murdered man refuse to testify in the case or accuse the prisoner; the very man whose duty it has become to murder the murderer in *vendetta* will feign utter ignorance of all circumstances connected with the case.

The son avenges his father, the brother his brother, the cousin his cousin, the friend his friend; and the vendetta only dies when the last victim is friendless. The Sicilian who has killed a Sicilian feels safe only when he feels assured that the family of the dead died with him, and that the slain had no *compadre*. But it is rarely indeed that he can feel thus assured.

It is only the Spaniard or the Italian who really knows how to use the knife, and the Italian uses it as naturally as a wild beast uses its claws and teeth, or the serpent its fangs. The knife is the fittest weapon for the vendetta. The pistol speaks, the knife is silent. The pistol leaves a leaden record of circumstantial evidence; the knife leaves none. Consequently the victim of the vendetta is usually a victim of the knife; but sometimes the pistol has been used with equally mysterious secrecy even in the vicinity of the French Market.

West of the Market many of the squares contain huge courts, entered by narrow passages which end on opening into the square, and which are faced by no corresponding passages on the other side. These courts swarm with Sicilians, and these narrow archways have shadowed the perpetration of more than one vendetta. It was in such a narrow passage bearing the rather ghastly-sounding name of Oudade Alley, that one of the most memorable and mysterious acts of vengeance was perpetrated. At either corner of the alley, at its opening on Front Levee street, were stores, and at the time of the assassination the proprietors of these stores were seated at their doors, watching the passersby. They saw a man enter the alley shortly after dark, and suddenly rush out again, staggering as though drunk. He reeled into the middle of the street and fell dead as stone. There were three poinard wounds in his breast and back, all evidently delivered by a strong and dextrous hand, for they had reached the heart, and the man died without a cry. It had been all the work of an instant, silent and invisible, save to the victim. No one had heard anything; no person, except the dead man, had seen anything. But the assassin who had shadowed this victim of vendetta, and whose hand must have been red with fresh blood, had not followed the dying Sicilian into the light. He had gone back into the darkness, and beyond the darkness into the great court, where hundreds of his compatriots must have seen him, for it was then quite early in the evening. Yet all the efforts of the police were fruitless, the cunning of the detectives availed nothing, and the murder still remains, as it will probably continue to remain, a mystery. The perpetrator of a vendetta is never brought to justice.

Nevertheless, there is something viperine in this sultry Sicilian blood. The dangerous quality in the character of the strong hater who shadows his intended victim year after year awaiting a certain chance for unwitnessed vengeance, is the dangerous quality of the ophidian, which never misses its victim, but gladly glides away from the face of its enemy, if permitted to do so, unharmed. The Sicilian is utterly incapable of comprehending that icy courage of Northern character that enables a strong man to grin back into the grinning face of death. The Sicilian is dangerous only as the snake is dangerous. Those who incur his hate must watch him, not for a day or a week, but for years.

Let me relate an incident illustrative of Sicilian nature. The Sicilians have their clubs here—clubs strong enough to wield considerable influence in local politics. They are a people to whom leaders are a necessity, and will follow their leaders as sheep follow the shepherds. It is of importance, therefore, for either political party to win over the leaders of the Sicilian clubs. On one occasion it was supposed that Warmoth had succeeded in gaining their support, and the White League determined to interfere. At that time the Sicilian Clubs were having great torch-light parades, and had already exhibited some symptoms of ferocity. A drunken negro had fired into one of their processions, and not satisfied with the almost instant death of the negro, they had killed (by way of vendetta, perhaps,) thirty or more other negroes, who unfortunately happened to be watching the parade. However, only about forty or fifty White Leaguers undertook one evening to break up a large out-door meeting of these clubs. They formed beside the speaker's stand in a solid body, and hooted off the scene the first speaker who attempted to address the meeting. Then the Sicilians procession wheeled and marched four deep along the side-walk in order to clear it. The White Leaguers made no demonstration until the foremost torches arrived within fifteen yards of them, when somebody called out: "Let them have it, boys," and every man "went for his hip-pocket." The procession instantly broke up; and the meeting scattered in all directions. Yet the Sicilians were all well-armed.

—I think it is very strange that so little has been written in regard to the curiosities of Creole grammar, and the peculiar poetical adaptation of the dialect. English antiquarians have produced elaborate treatises on the dialects of Devonshire, Lancashire, and Cornwall. French scholars have even established periodicals exclusively devoted to the study of their various *provincial patois*, and the collation of popular legends, traditions, superstitions, and curious customs preserved in dialect songs. Indeed, it is doubtful whether there be any provincial dialect of Europe which has not received considerable attention from philologists. Yet there is certainly no European patois owning greater curiosities of construction, greater beauties of melody and rhythm than this Creole speech; there is no provincial dialect of the mother country wealthier in romantic tradition and ballad legends than this almost unwritten tongue of Louisiana.

I will venture a few remarks in this letter upon certain peculiarities of Creole grammar which I doubt not may prove interesting to some of your readers. Any one who has studied the French grammar conscientiously knows that it is not over easy to thoroughly memorize all that code of minute rules whereby the French verb is governed throughout the ramifications of its conjugations and moods and variously terminating tenses. These rules have almost been abolished from Creole grammar, and the protean character of the verb changed after a fashion to make a school-boy howl with joy. The languid speaker of the patois simply declines to change the termination of his verb according to tense at all, and refuses to endure the tyranny of subjunctive or potential moods. He acknowledges only the primary tenses—past, present and future—and adapts these to all his wants, not perceiving the usefulness of the secondary tenses. He commences, as a general rule, by changing the entire form of the verb, as *aimin* for *aimer*, *connin* for *connaitre*, *gagnin* for *gagner*, or as *courri* for *courrir*, *reste* for *rester*, *souffri* for *souffrir*—according to conjugation; the Creole dialect possessing regular conjugations of its own adapted from the French. This done, the tense is never indicated by any change in the termination of the verb, but by the additional use of the monosyllables *te* and *sre*,—*te* taking the place of the past tenses of the auxiliary verb *etre*, and *sre* being a convenient substitute for the future tenses of the same. I give an example of this method of conjugating,—the Creole verb *courri* in its various forms. I translate it by the verb "run" only as derived from the French *courrir*; for it is most generally used in the sense of "go," and corresponds more closely to the verb *aller*. The Creole speaker does not say, "I will go to see him:" he says, "Me *run* see him." This is the thought of the child, who naturally *runs* to satisfy a desire, and can not, like the adult, walk calmly to the accomplishment of his wishes.

PRESENT.

Mo courri.	I run.
To courri.	Thou runnest.
Li courri.	He, she, or it runs.
No courri.	We run.
Yo courri.	You run.
Ye courri.	They run.

PAST.

Mo te courri.	I ran.
To te courri.	Thou rannest.
Li te courri.	He ran.
No te courri.	We ran.
Yo te courri.	You ran.
Ye te courri.	They ran.

FUTURE.

Mo sre courri.	I will run.
To sre courri.	Thou wilt run.
Li sre courri.	He will run.
No sre courri.	We will run.
Yo sre courri.	You will run.
Ye sre courri.	They will run.

The more I investigate the curiosities of this dialect, the more I find that it differs very considerably according to locality; in some parishes it resembles the French far less than in others. Here is a specimen closely akin to the Creole of the Antilles. It is said to be an old negro love song, and I think there is a peculiar weird beauty in several of its stanzas. I feel much inclined to doubt whether it was composed by a negro, but the question of its authorship can not affect its value as a curiosity, and, in any case, its spirit is thoroughly African. Unfortunately, without accented letters it is impossible to convey any idea of the melody, the liquid softness, the languor of some of the couplets. My translation is a little free in parts.

I.

"Dipi me vouer toue, Adele,
    Ape danse calinda.
Mo reste pour toue fidele,
    Liberte a moin caba.
Mo pas soussi d'autt negresses,
    Mo pas gagnin cœur pour yo;
Yo gagnin beaucoup finesses;
    Yo semble serpent Congo.

II.

"Mo aime toue trop, ma belle,
    Mo pas capab resiste;
Cœur a moin tout comme sauterelle,
    Li fait ne qu'appe saute.
Mo jamin contre gnoun femme
    Qui gagnin belle taille comme toue;
Jie a toue jete la flame;
    Corps a toue enchene moue.

III.

"To tant comme serpent sonnette
    Qui connin charme zozo,—
Qui gagnin bouche a li prette
    Pour servi comme gnoun tombe.
Mo jamin voue gnoun negresse
    Qui connin marche comme toue,—
Qui gagnin gnoun si belle gesse;
    Corps a toue ce gnoun poupe.

IV.

"Quand mo pas vouer toue, Adele,
    Mo senti m'ape mourri,—
Mo vini com' gnoun chandelle
    Qui ape alle fini:

Mo pas vouer rien sur la terre
  Qui capab moin fait plaisi;—
Mo capab dans la riviere
  Jete min pour pas souffri.

V.

"Dis moin si to gagnin n'homme;—
  Mo va fais ouanga pour li;
Mo fais li tourne fantome,
  Si to vie moin pour mari.
Mo pas le in jour toue boudeuse;
  L'autt femme, pour moin ce fatras;
Mo va rende toue bien heureuse;
  Mo va baill' tous bell' madras."

TRANSLATION.

I.

Since first I beheld you, Adele,
While dancing the *calinda*,
I have remained faithful to the thought of you;
My freedom has departed from us.
I care no longer for all the other negresses,
I have no heart left for them;—
You have such grace and cunning;—
You are like the Congo serpent.

II.

I love you too much, my beautiful one,—
I am not able to help it.
My heart has become just like a grasshopper,—
It does nothing but leap.
I have never met any woman
Who has so beautiful a form as yours.
Your eyes flash flame;
Your body has enchained me captive.

III.

Ah, you are so like the serpent-of-the-rattles
Who knows how to charm the little bird,
And who has a mouth ever ready for it
To serve it for a tomb!

I have never known any negress
Who could walk with such grace as you can.
Or who could make such beautiful gestures;
Your body is a beautiful doll.

IV.

When I can not see you, Adele,
I feel myself ready to die;
My life becomes like a candle
Which has almost burned itself out.
I can not, then, find anything in the world
Which is able to give me pleasure;—
I could well go down to the river
And throw myself in it that I might cease to suffer.

V.

Tell me if you have a man;
And I will make an *ouanga* charm for him:
I will make him turn into a phantom,
If you will only take me for your husband.
I will not go to see you when you are cross;
Other women are mere trash to me;
I will make you very happy,
And I will give you a beautiful Madras handkerchief.

I think there is some true poetry in these allusions to the snake. Is not the serpent a symbol of grace? Is not the so-called "line of beauty" serpentine? And is there not something of the serpent in the beauty of all graceful women?—something of undulating shapeliness, something of silent fascination?—something of Lilith and Lamia? The French have a beautiful verb expressive of this idea, *serpenter*, "to serpent"—to curve in changing undulations like a lithe snake. The French artist speaks of the outlines of a beautiful human body as "serpenting," curving and winding like a serpent. Do you not like the word? I think it is so expressive of flowing lines of elegance—so full of that mystery of grace which puzzled Solomon: "The way of a serpent upon a rock."

The allusion to Voudooism in the last stanza especially interested me, and I questioned the gentleman who furnished me with the song as to the significance of the words: "I will make him turn into a phantom." I had fancied that the term *fantome* might be interpreted by "ghost," and that the whole line simply constituted a threat to make some one "give up the ghost."

"It is not exactly that," replied my friend; "it is an allusion, I believe, to the withering and wasting power of Voudoo poisons. There are such poisons actually in use among the negro obi-men—poisons which defy analysis, and, mysterious as the poison of the Borgias, slowly consume the victims like a taper. He wastes away as though being dried up; he becomes almost mummified; he wanes like a shadow; he turns into a phantom in the same sense that a phantom is an unreal mockery of something real."

Thus I found an intelligent Louisianan zealous to confirm an opinion to which I was permitted to give expression in the Commercial nearly three years ago—that a knowledge of secret septic poisons (probably of an animal character), which leave no trace discoverable by the most skillful chemists, is actually possessed by certain beings who are reverenced as sorcerers by the negroes of the West Indies and the Southern States, but more especially of the West Indies, where much of African fetichism has been transplanted.

Cincinnati Commercial, December 27, 1877

NEW ORLEANS

The Curious Nomenclature of New Orleans Streets.

SOME LITTLE CREOLE SONGS.

NEW ORLEANS, January.

I HAVE somewhere read a fantastic story about an artist who once wandered into a curious-looking village in some unfamiliar part of Germany, where he found quaint people who spoke a forgotten dialect and wore the costumes of by-gone centuries and lived in houses of a style built hundreds of years before his generation saw the light. The plan of the story was not unlike that of Irving's "Adelantado of the Seven Cities"—with the exquisite difference that the artist actually made water-color drawings of the scenes which he was fortunate, or perhaps unfortunate enough to behold. Like the Adelantado of the Spanish legend, our artist was received with a strangely fervent welcome, and finally found himself over head and ears in love with a ghostly beauty who deserted him precisely as the bell in the spire of the antequated church struck midnight. He fell asleep, and awoke in the midst of a frightful swamp. Afterward he learned that he had unwittingly visited a spectral village, which had been anciently accursed for its sins and sunk into the bowels of the earth, where it was permitted to arise but once in a hundred years.

When, on the first day of my arrival in New Orleans, I left the American portion of the city, and, crossing Canal street, plunged into the narrow thoroughfares of the old French quarter, I felt the impression of this fantastic legend revived. The antiquated houses, with their countless balconies and odd architecture, seemed of another age; I could have fancied myself in a phantom city, like that of the German tale—for the sun had but just arisen, and the streets being deserted the charm was not broken by the sight of human figures in modern attire. As I became more familiar with the quaint streets, the romantic impression produced by their old look is rather enhanced than lessened by the knowledge of their names. Each name suggests some local tradition or some historic fact, and the nomenclature of the streets of New Orleans is, beyond all question, the most extraordinary of all nomenclatures of this sort in the history of all modern cities of Europe or America.

The limits of the ancient city, as it existed under the early French and Spanish dominations, are still well defined by the huge breadth of Canal, Rampart and Esplanade streets, which mark three sides of the quadrilateral formerly inclosed by strong walls and deep lines of fortification. On the eastern side, in the old days, the walls fronted upon the Mississippi River. The earliest bastions had priest-caps at the four angles of the quadrilateral, and an additional priest-cap on the western side. These five priest-caps were enlarged subsequently into forts—Forts Burgundy, St. Ferdinand, San Carlos, St. Louis, and another of which I forget the name. Fort St. Louis occupied the present site of the Custom-house, and Fort San Carlos stood where now stands the United States Mint. The latter work of defense still existed at the time of the battle of New Orleans, and General Jackson, it is known, stationed his reserves in this fort previous to the engagement. The city remained thus fortified up to the beginning of the present century, when the American authorities leveled the works for good sanitary reasons. Pestilential miasma had been engendered in the stagnant moats; newts and unhealthy forms of vegetation had propagated extensively in the old ditches. It became necessary to drain and fill up these moats, and they were filled with the *debris* of the fortifications. Where the old walls once stood we have now therefore the broadest and finest streets in the city.

Much of the early history of New Orleans might be traced alone in the names of the old streets inclosed within the quadrilateral I have spoken of. The first French settlers and Creoles were loyal monarchists, and they delighted to name their streets with the names of the Princes and nobility of the mother country. Thus we find Burgundy street, named in honor of the Duke of Burgundy; Dauphine street, in honor of the Dauphin of France, afterward Louis XV.; Bourbon and Royal streets, in honor of royalty; Chartres street, after the Duc De Chartres. Orleans, Du Maine, Toulouse, Condé and Conti streets were, I need scarcely observe, christened after French noblemen and statesmen; St. Louis street after that pious crusader and severe Judge, St. Louis, King of France; and Phillip street was so named in honor, not of a Spanish, but a French monarch. The old Louisiana Frenchmen always sandwiched their religion and their loyalty together after a fashion peculiar to themselves, so that at certain regular intervals we find their streets bearing the names of saints, such as St. Peter's street, St. Ann's street, &c. In other parts of the city we find mixed traces of French and Spanish piety in such names as St. Armand's street, St. Bartholomy's (now Erato) street, St. John the Baptist's street, St. Charles street, Annunciation street (named thus by Spanish piety in honor of the Virgin), St. Claude's street, St. Anthony's street, and others. I need hardly say, however, that these names are only translations of Rue de St. Claude or the like, and that the possessive case is no longer used in their application.

Of the other great streets in the old district, it is almost superfluous to observe that Bienville was named in honor of Roger de Bienville, the founder of New Orleans, and the Father of Louisiana. He was thrice Governor of the colony—first in 1701, and lastly in 1744. Other Governors subsequently gave their names to streets. We have still Périer street, Carondelet street, Galvez street, Salcedo street, Unzaga street, Casa Calvo street, and Miro street. Of these, Bienville and Périer were French Governors; Unzaga, Galvez, Miro, Carondelet, Casa Calvo and Salcedo were Spanish; the last named, Salcedo, being in power in 1803, just before the close of the Spanish régime. Then the American Governors have had many streets named in honor of them. We have Claiborne street, from W. C. C. Claiborne; Villere street, from James Villere; Robertson street, from Thomas B. Robertson; Johnson street, probably from either Henry Johnson, who held office in 1824–29, or Isaac Johnson, who was Governor from 1846–50; Derbigny street, from Peter Derbigny; Roman street, from A. B. Roman, and White street, from Edward D. White.

Without the old boundary of the walls the newer districts were formerly traversed by streets in whose nomenclature the spirit of rivalry between the French and Spanish colonists shone forth. There are still of these French street and Spain street. Within the elder district Custom-house street has kept its name for a hundred years; and it runs by the United States Custom-house to-day, as it did by that of the Spanish Colonial Government in another century. Arsenal street was formerly so called because it led to the arsenal; it has since been changed to Ursulines street, because of its proximity to the old Convent of the Ursuline Nuns; but even this change is an old one. I suppose Nun street must have obtained its appellation in an almost similar way. Before leaving the boundaries of the fortification lines, drawn by the Spaniards, I must not omit to mention that the old city had three gates—one at the head and one at the foot of Royal street, and also one through which the old Bayou road led out to the bayou.

The gallantry (often, I fear, wicked gallantry) of the French Creoles is commemorated upon old city maps by a number of streets christened with the sweetest and prettiest feminine names imaginable. I am told some of these streets were thus named after the favorite children of rich parents, for the plantations were extended up to the shadow of the walls; but I am also told, and I can not help believing, that they were just as often named after favorite concubines. There used to be such a list of names as these on the old maps: Adèle, Celeste, Suzette, Estelle, Annette, Félicite, Louise, Constance, Julia, Josephine, Elizabeth, Belle and Azilie streets. But who shall now be able to revive the dead history of these names?

At about the same period of New Orleans history which gave girls' names to some streets, a fervor of classicism seized upon some other great landowners, and compelled them to seek names for their thoroughfares in the domains of pagan mythology. Thus we have got the streets of the Nine Muses—Calliope street, Clio street, Erato street, Polymnia street, Thalia street, Urania street, Terpsichore street, Euterpe street, Melpomene street, and Euphrosyne street. There used also to be the Street of the Naiads, and the old name Rue des Dryades still lives in the modern Dryades street, with the French termination *es*. Upper Rampart street used to be the Street of Hercules; and the more modernly named Carondelet and Baronne streets—so called in honor of Baron Louis Hector de Carondelet and his fair lady *la Baronne*—were of yore, I think, known as the streets of Apollo and of Bacchus. Triton Walk, in Tivoli Circle, formerly the Promenade *des Tritons*, was so called in irony when the land mapped out was so swampy that only Tritons or alligators could have wandered over it without danger of drowning or getting quagmired. I think Palmyra street and Coliseum street owe their names to this classic era.

Good Children street (*Rue des Bons Enfants*), Piety street, Victory street, Greatmen street, Love street, Music street are names that sound oddly enough in English. But what do you think of such names as *Desire* street, *Misery* street, *Despair* street, *Insanity* street? These streets only exist, indeed, on the map; for the alligators still own the land surveyed, but the names have not been changed. I suppose they were named in regular psychical order—desire begetting misery, and misery despair, and despair insanity. Perhaps the nomenclator was making a grim joke upon the possibilities of extending the city in that direction when he thus named these streets.

Many of the early French planters have bequeathed their

names to streets, without the old town lines. We have Montegut street (the old Montegut family is not yet extinct); Marigny and Mandeville streets, from old Bernard de Marigny de Mandeville, who spent an enormous fortune in entertaining Louis Philippe during his exile and his residence in New Orleans among the loyal Creoles; Gravier street, named after John Gravier, partner with Edward Livingstone in the famous "Batture suits;" Girod street, after old Mayor Girod. Bernard Marigny it was who named Kraps street (they will persist in pronouncing it *Crab* street) after the German game of chance —*Kraps*, at which he had lost a fortune; and I suspect he also christened Bagatelle street.

There is still a descendant of Bernard's family living in New Orleans. And speaking of old John Gravier, I must not forget to tell you that what is now Lafayette Square used to be called "Mr. Gravier's Square," and was bequeathed by John Gravier to the city as a playground for children and a sojourn for nurse-maids. Mayor Girod was a very, very little man in stature, but his dignity was gigantic and his manners worthy of a Marquis of the old school. He filled the office of Mayor in the most exemplary and decorous manner.

Then we have Poydras street and Poydras market.

Julien Poydras, who bequeathed his name to this street, and of whom a quaint portrait may still be seen in the reception-room of the Charity Hospital, was quite a peculiar character. Judging from this portrait he must have been in his old age tall, lank, and bony with snow-white hair, and a complexion made florid by many bumpers of Burgundy and Bordeaux. One hundred years ago Poydras was a great man in Louisiana. He had a fine residence in New Orleans, but lived generally on his plantation in the Parish of Point Coupé, where he has left a monument to his memory in the shape of a fund for the dowries of all marriageable girls in the said parish. Any young woman who gets married there can claim and receive fifty dollars—(I think that is the sum allowed)—of old Poydras' money; and I am told that the claim is often made. And yet withal Poydras lived and died a bachelor.

—When I read for the first time Alphonse Daudet's wonderful novel, "*Fromont jeune et Risler aîné,*" which has been excellently translated under the title of "Sidonie," I was particularly charmed with the refrain of the pretty Creole song, which Sidonie sings at various dramatic passages of the story:

> "Pauvre p'tit Mamzel Zizi!
> C'est l'amou', l'amou' qui tourne la tête."

I determined on coming to New Orleans, that should opportunity offer, I would make some efforts to procure the entire song, made famous by this refrain. As yet I have not wholly succeeded; but here is something which makes it appear as if I was not far from success. I have only been able to procure one stanza with the refrain:

> Z'autres qu'a di moin, ça yon bonheur;
> Et moin va di, ça yon peine:—
> D'amour quand porté la chaine,
> Adieu, courri tout bonheur!
>> Pauvre piti' Mamzel Zizi!
>> Pauvre piti' Mamzel Zizi!
>> Pauvre piti' Mamzel Zizi!
> Li gagnin doulor, doulor, doulor—
> Li gagnin doulor dans cœur à li!

> Others say, it is your happiness;
> I say, it is your sorrow:
> When we are enchanted by love,
> Farewell to all happiness!
>> Poor little Miss Zizi!
>> Poor little Miss Zizi!
>> Poor little Miss Zizi!
> She has sorrow, sorrow, sorrow;—
> She has sorrow in her heart.

This appears to be an old fragment from either the beginning or from the end of an entire song. I can not venture to aver, however, that it is a part of the same song whose refrian I found preserved in the leaves of *Fromont jeune et Risler aîné*, for a great number of Creole songs, having various airs and differing greatly in their metrical construction, have similarly worded refrains. A very common burthen in these songs is—

> "Mo l'aimin vous
> Comme cochon aimin la boue!"

"*I love you just as a little pig loves the mud!*" This refrain I have found attached, in various forms, to at least half a dozen various ditties. Here is one specimen:

> Si to té 'tit zozo
> Et moi-même mo té fusil
> Mo sré tchoné toi,—*Boum!*
>   Ah, cher bijou
>   D'acajou,
>   Mo l'aimin vous
> Comme cochon aimin la boue!

> If thou wert a little bird,
> And I were a little gun,
> I would shoot thee—*bang!*
>   Ah, dear little
>   Mahogany jewel,
> I love thee as a little pig loves the mud.

In another stanza of the same love song, the lover expresses a wish that his little "mahogany jewel" were a little pig and that he were a little knife, so that he might cut her little throat,—*zip!* The sound of the knife is well imitated.

While on this subject allow me to give you several odd little Creole songs which I have just collected. Some of these are very old. I am told that Bernard Marigny de Mandeville, of famous memory, used to have them sung in his house for the amusement of guests—among whom, perhaps, was Louis Philippe himself. The airs are very lively and very pretty:

> 'Delaide, mo la reine,
> Chimin-là trop tongue pour aller,—
> Chimin-là monté dans les hauts;
> Tout piti qui mo yé
> M'allé monté là haut dans courant
>   C'est moin, Liron, qui rivé
>   M'allé di yé,
>   Bon soir, mo la reine,
>   C'est moin, Liron, qui rivé.

['Delaide, my queen, the way is too long for me to travel;—that way leads far up yonder. But, little as I am, I am going to stem the stream up there. "I, Liron, am come," is what I shall say to them. My queen, good night; 'tis I, Liron, who has come.]

> Tous les jours de l'an,
> Tous les jours de l'an,
> Tous les jours de l'an,
> Vous pas vini 'oir moin:
> Mo té couché malade dans lit;
> Mo voyé nouvelles auprés mo la reine;
> Vous pas seulement vini 'oir moin:
> A prèsent qui mo bien gaillard,
> Cher ami, mo pas besoin 'oir vous.

[Every New Year's day you neglected to visit me. I was lying sick in bed. I sent word to my queen. But you did not even once come to see me. Now that I am quite well, dear friend, I do not want to see you.]

> L'autre jour, mo couché dèyors;
> C'est toi qui courri di Madame:
> Ah, c'est 'jordi, c'est 'jordi, c'est 'jordi!—
> Ah, c'est 'jordi moin qu'allé connin toi;
> Aie!—moin qu'allé connin toi,
> Aie!—moin qu'allé connin toi,
> Mo té prend toi pour zami moin
> Pendant to té toujours trahi moin,
> Ah, c'est 'jordi, c'est 'jordi, c'est 'jordi!—
> Aie!—moin qu'allé connin toi!

[The other night I slept out-of-doors; 'Tis you who went to tell Madame. Ah, 'tis to-day, 'tis to-day, 'tis to-day! Ah, 'tis to-day I am going to know you! Ay!—I am going to know you! Ay!—I am going to know you! I had taken you to be my friend All the while you were betraying me. Ah, 'tis to-day, &c.]

The French exclamation, "*Aie!*" indicates pain or distress. The gentleman who furnished me with the above song, how-ever, translates the Creole "*Aie!*" by the English term of asseveration, "Ay!" This translation is at least harmonious, if not correct.

[*La chanson qui suit a été faite pour ridiculiser une malâtresse nommée Toucouton qui voulait se faire passer pour blanche.*]

[Refrain.]
Ah! Toucouton!
Mo connin toi:
To semblé Morico:
Y'a pas savon
Qui assez blanc
Pour laver to la peau.

Quand blancs la yo donné yo bal,
    To pas capable aller:
Comment t'a vaillant-giabal,
    Toi qui l'aimé briller!
        Ah! Toucouton!
        Mo connin toi, &c.

Longtemps to contume prend' loge
Avec gens comme il faut:
    Asteur faut to
Prend' Jacques—déloge!
    Y'a pas passé tantot.
        Ah! Toucouton!
        Mo connin toi, &c.

[The following song was composed to ridicule a mulatto girl named Toucouton, who tried to make herself pass for a white one:]

Ah, Toucouton!
I know you well;
You are like a blackamoor:
There is no soap
Which is white enough
To wash your skin.

When the white folks give a ball,
You are not able to go there;
Ah, how will you be able to play the flirt?

You who so love to shine.
  Ah, Toucouton, &c.

Once you used to take a seat
Among the fashionable people;
Now you must take leave, decamp,
Without any delay whatever.
  Ah, Toucouton, &c.

     Cincinnati Commercial, February 18, 1878

THE GLAMOUR OF NEW ORLEANS

THE season has come at last, when strangers may visit us without fear, and experience with unalloyed pleasure the first delicious impression of the most beautiful and picturesque old city in North America. For in this season is the glamour of New Orleans strongest upon those whom she attracts to her from less hospitable climates, and fascinates by her nights of magical moonlight, and her days of dreamy languors and perfumes. There are few who can visit her for the first time without delight; and few who ever leave her without regret; and none who can forget her strange charm when they have once felt it influence. To a native of the bleaker Northern clime,—if he have any poetical sense of the beautiful in nature, any love of bright verdure and luxuriance of landscape—the approach to the city by river, must be in itself something indescribably pleasant. The white steamer gliding through an unfamiliar world of blue and green,—blue above and blue below, with a long strip of low green land alone to break the ethereal azure; —the waving cane; the evergreen fringe of groves weird with moss; the tepid breezes and golden sunlight—all deepening in their charm as the city is neared, make the voyage seem beautiful as though one were sailing to some far off glimmering Eden, into the garden of Paradise itself. And then, the first impression of the old Creole city slumbering under the glorious sun; of its quaint houses; its shaded streets; its suggestions of a hundred years ago; its contrasts of agreeable color; its streets re-echoing the tongues of many nations; its general look of somnolent contentment; its verdant antiquity; its venerable memorials and monuments; its eccentricities of architecture; its tropical gardens; its picturesque surprises; its warm atmosphere, drowsy perhaps with the perfume of orange flowers, and thrilled with the fantastic music of mocking-birds—can not ever be wholly forgotten. For a hundred years and more has New Orleans been drawing hither wandering souls from all the ends of the earth. The natives of India and of Japan have walked upon her pavements; Chinese and swarthy natives of Manilla; children of the Antilles and of South America; subjects of the Sultan and sailors of the Ionian sea have sought homes here. All civilized nations have sent wandering children hither. All cities of the North, East, and West have yielded up some restless souls to the far-off Southern city, whose spell is so mystic, so sweet, so universal. And to those wondering and wandering ones, this sleepy, beautiful, quaint old city murmurs: "Rest with me. I am old; but thou hast never met with a younger more beautiful than I. I dwell in eternal summer; I dream in perennial sunshine; I sleep in magical moonlight. My streets are flecked with strange sharp shadows; and sometimes also the Shadow of Death falleth upon them; but if thou will not fear, thou are safe. My charms are not the charms of much gold and great riches; but thou mayst feel with me such hope and content as thou hast never felt before. I offer thee eternal summer, and a sky divinely blue; sweet breezes and sweet perfumes, bright fruits, and flowers fairer than the rainbow. Rest with me. For if thou leavest me, thou must forever remember me with regret." And, assuredly those who wander from her may never cease to behold her in their dreams—quaint, beautiful, and sunny as of old—and to feel at long intervals the return of the first charm —the first delicious fascination of the fairest city of the South.

Daily City Item, November 26, 1878

THE CITY OF DREAMS

LATTERLY it has been said that if New Orleans has any special mania which distinguishes it from other cities, it is the mania of "talking to one's self." It were useless to deny so widely recognized a fact as the propensity of people in New Orleans to perambulate their native streets conversing only with themselves. And strangers visiting us have said: "The people of New Orleans are inclined to madness; they converse continually with themselves, which is a sign of insanity." Is it that the people are being driven mad by stupid legislation and business losses and outrageous taxes? God only knows! But they do talk either to themselves or to viewless beings or to the sleepy shadows that fling jagged bits of darkness across the streets on sunny days.

They are comparatively many, these lovers of solitary musing; and usually seek the quiet of the most deserted streets—those streets to which the Secret Police of the East give the ominous name of *dead streets*. Perhaps one might say as well, *streets of the dead*.

At one time we took a special interest in watching those wandering and murmuring spirits. They are of various ages; but most generally advanced in years. The action of the younger men or women is usually quick and nervous; that of the older, slow and meditative. The former often speak angrily as if brooding over some wrong; the latter, rather in sorrow than in anger. All of which is quite natural and to be expected from those who talk to themelves.

What do they talk about?

That is a matter not always easy to find out. The hard echo of a brisk footstep on the pavement, even the sudden fluttering of a leafy shadow, seems often sufficient to break the reverie; the speaker looks about him like one awakened from a dream, gazes with a half-timid kind of suspicion at those who pass by, as if fearing to have been overheard; and walks off at a quicker gait. To study the character of these people perfectly, one must wear rubber shoes.

It would be cruel to wear india-rubber shoes for such a purpose; it would also be despicable. Therefore we cannot fully answer the question—

What are they talking about?

But occasionally the most innocent passer-by cannot fail to catch a word or two—sometimes strangely full of meaning, sometimes meaningless. We have heard such words. Occasionally vast sums of money were mentioned—billions, quintillions! —a sure sign that the speaker was financially stripped, and had little hope of favors from the goddess Fortuna. Sometimes we heard odd curses—men cursing themselves, and others, nameless places and nameless people, unknown memories and unknown misfortunes. Sometimes they spoke cheerfully, and laughed to themselves softly;—but this was seldom, very, very seldom.

Before the epidemic we fancied that the majority of these conversations with airy nothings were upon the subject of money. Indeed, most of the fragmentary mutterings which reached us seemed related to dreams of wealth—wild, vague, and fantastic —such dreams as are dreamed by those who have lost all and hope for nothing, but who seek consolation in the splendor of dreams of the Impossible.

Then came the burning summer with its burning scourges of fever;—under the raw, merciless, dizzy sunlight, and the pitilessly clear infinite of warm blue above, the mutterers still wandered the silent streets seeking out the bits of shadow, as Arabs oases in a world of yellow sand;—and they talked more than ever to themselves and to the shadows, to the vast void above and to the whispering trees that drooped in the mighty heat.

So the months rolled dryly and fiercely by; the sun rose each day with the same glory of angry heat; and the sky glowed each evening with the glare of molten brass. And the talkers became fewer; but they seemed to talk much more than they ever had before done. They talked to the black streamers that fluttered weirdly at the handles of muffled bells, and to ghostly white things hung to cottage doors and to the long processions that rumbled ominously toward the Places of Tombs.

Sometimes it seemed that one heard a sound of sobbing— stifled sobbing; as if a man were swallowing a bitter grief with bitter determination—but this was perhaps imaginary; for there were so many strange sounds in that strange summer that no one could well trust his ears.

The summer waned; and yet it seemed at last as though the number of those who talked to invisible things became greater. They *did* become greater in number. There was no doubt of it remaining before the first cold wind came from the far North, boisterous and wild as though suddenly freed from some Arctic enchanter. And the numbers of the mysterious ones waxed greater.

Then at intervals their words fell upon our ears; and it seemed that the character of them had undergone a change—no longer expressing ideas of wealth. They had ceased to speak in our hearing of money. They spoke of the dead—and muttered remembered words uttered by other tongues—and asked information from waving shadows and white walls regarding people that God only knows anything about.

Perhaps they remembered that the only witnesses of some last interview were the same white walls and waving shadows. And the shadows lay there at just the same angle—well, perhaps, the angle was a little sharper—and they were waving just as dreamily as then. And perhaps a time might come in which all Shadows that have been must answer all questions put to them.

Seeing and hearing these things, we somehow ceased to marvel that some people dwelling in the city of New Orleans should speak mysteriously and hold audible converse with their own thoughts; forasmuch as we, also, dreaming among the shadows, spoke aloud to our own hearts, until awakened by an echo of unanswered words.

Daily City Item, March 9, 1879

"WHY CRABS ARE BOILED ALIVE"

AND for why you not have of crab? Because one must dem boil live! It is all vat is of most beast to tell so. How you make for dem kill so you not dem boil? You can not cut dem de head off, for dat dey have not of head. You not can break to dem de back for dat dey not be only all back. You not can dem bleed until de die, for dat dey not have blood. You not can stick to dem troo de brain, for dat dey be same like you—dey not have of brain.

Daily City Item, October 5, 1879

GOTTSCHALK

THERE comes to us from the ancient Spanish town of Havana, a beautifully printed Life of Gottschalk, the famous pianist, whom New Orleans has the honor of claiming for a son. The book is published by the Propaganda Literaria of that city, and its author is Louis Ricardo Fors, an intimate friend of the great composer.

It is not our purpose, however, to make any review at this moment of a work, whose beauties a brilliant cotemporary has already shown to the public. Only, after glancing over these pages, when we gaze on the dark, sad Jewish face which forms its frontispiece, we can not avoid expressing our opinion of the very painful and curious impression caused by this most curious book.

The whole strange life of this most strange man seems to have been a long and bitter conflict between passion and art. Almost superhuman in his power as a musician,—capable, almost without an effort, of moving an audience to tears,—unrivaled perhaps in the history of music by any modern player who made harmony the medium of passionate expression,—when one reads this biography one can not help fancying that Gottschalk forever heard in his ears a soft sweet voice, the voice of his beloved Art calling to him,—"I am thy life, thy genius, thy future, thy all-in-all;—as thy wedded bride, I claim thy whole life, thy whole being,—all the love thou hast to give,—all the devotion of which thou art capable. I am jealous though I love. Love is strong as death; jealousy is cruel as the grave. Betray me; and I shall be avenged."

Have you ever read Balzac's "Peau de Chagrin," that weird tale of one who curtailed the thread of his life each time he gratified a desire? Gottschalk's career recalls that wild story. Each time that Passion usurped the place of Art, the life of the musician seems to have contracted a little like the fatal parchment of the romancer. If not his life on all occasions, his musical career certainly suffered. Almost worshipped at his advent in a hundred cities, how many was he obliged to leave secretly, as a fugitive from the wrath of husbands or fathers? He was literally a wanderer upon the face of the earth—a bubble madly tossed hither and thither on that sea of life whose waves are moved only by winds of passion. Nor was the artist all to blame. With his extraordinary powers of fascination as a wizard of art, a magician of music, a necromancer of harmony—is it strange that he should have yielded where stronger wills have not been able to hold their own. He might have become, no doubt, one of the richest of artists, could he have pursued the even tenor others have followed; but a strange fate seemed to hang over him, rendering his story one of the most painful narratives, perhaps, ever written. And it is deeply written in lines of grief on the handsome face which looks up at us from the pages of Fors' biography as we write these lines.

But if Art be the most jealous of brides, surely she is also the most forgiving. How often did this wandering spirit turn to her for consolation and pardon in his wanderings,—from European palaces to the cities of the South Pacific, from the busy North-American metropolis to the quaint places of the Spanish Main. And these most beautiful and pathetic fragments of passionate harmony, reprinted in this volume, and still bearing in their facsimiles the faint trembling of a hand shaken by heart-tempests and soul-tortures;—these strange fragments that are but pages of brief and bitter tragedies through which he passed,—do they not sound also like the caressing voice of the pardoning love of that Art which remained faithful to him even until the first shadowy moments of the last dreamless sleep?

Daily City Item, September 22, 1880

THE TALE OF A FAN

PAH! it is too devilishly hot to write anything about anything practical and serious—let us dream dreams.

We picked up a little fan in a street-car the other day,—a Japanese fabric, with bursts of blue sky upon it, and grotesque foliage sharply cut against a horizon of white paper; and wonderful clouds as pink as Love, and birds of form as unfamiliar as the extinct wonders of ornithology resurrected by Cuvieresque art. Where did those Japanese get their exquisite taste for color and tint-contrasts?—is their sky so divinely blue?—are their sunsets so virginally carnation?—are the breasts of their maidens and the milky peaks of their mountains so white?

But the fairy colors were less strongly suggestive than something impalpable, invisible, indescribable, yet voluptuously enchanting which clung to the fan spirit-wise—a tender little scent,—a mischievous perfume,—a titillating, tantalizing aroma,—an odor inspirational as of the sacred gums whose incense intoxicated the priests of oracles. Did you ever lay your head upon a pillow covered with the living supple silk of a woman's hair? Well, the intoxicating odor of that hair is something not to be forgotten: if we might try to imagine what the ambrosial odors of paradise are, we dare not compare them to anything else;—the odor of youth in its pliancy, flexibility, rounded softness, delicious coolness, dove-daintiness, delightful plasticity,—all that suggests slenderness graceful as a Venetian wine glass, and suppleness as downy-soft as the necks of swans.

Naturally that little aroma itself provoked fancies;—as we looked at the fan we could almost evoke the spirit of a hand and arm, of phantom ivory, the glimmer of a ghostly ring, the shimmer of spectral lace about the wrist;—but nothing more. Yet it seemed to us that even odors might be analyzed; that perhaps in some future age men might describe persons they had never seen by such individual aromas, just as in the Arabian tale one describes minutely a maimed camel and its burthen which he had never beheld.

There are blond and brunette odors;—the white rose is

sweet but the ruddy is sweeter; the perfumes of pallid flowers may be potent, as that of the tube-rose whose intensity sickens with surfeit of pleasure, but the odors of deeply tinted flowers are passionate and satiate not, quenching desire only to rekindle it. There are human blossoms more delicious than any rose's heart nestling in pink. There is a sharp, tart, invigorating, penetrating, tropical sweetness in brunette perfumes; blonde odors are either faint as those of a Chinese yellow-rose, or fiercely ravishing as that of the white jessamine—so bewitching for the moment, but which few can endure all night in the sleeping room, making the heart of the sleeper faint.

Now the odor of the fan was not a blonde odor:—it was sharply sweet as new mown hay in autumn, keenly pleasant as a clear breeze blowing over sea-foam;—what were frankincense, and spikenard and cinnamon, and all the odors of the merchant compared with it?—what could have been compared with it, indeed, save the smell of the garments of the young Sulamitess or the whispering robes of the Queen of Sheba? And these were brunettes.

The strength of living perfumes evidences the comparative intensity of the life exhaling them. Strong sweet odors bespeak the vigor of youth in blossom. Intensity of life in the brunette is usually coincident with nervous activity and slender elegance. Young, slenderly graceful, with dark eyes and hair, skin probably a Spanish olive!—did such an one lose a little Japanese fan in car No. — of the C. C. R. R. during the slumberous heat of Wednesday morning?

Daily City Item, July 1, 1881

THE DEATH OF MARIE LAVEAU

NOT far from Rampart, on St. Ann street, there is a queer old house, with walls mostly constructed of moss and plaster, and trees all about it,—said to have been constructed by some Spanish builder at a remote epoch in the history of New

Orleans. This house was for many years the residence of one of the most famous characters of New Orleans—one who is whispered to have inspired George Cable's remarkable figure of "Palmyre," in "Old Creole Days," and one whose name inspired much superstitious and foolish fear even in recent years, —Marie Laveau, vulgarly styled the "Queen of the Voudous," although her connection with voudouism was very mythical. Marie Laveau died yesterday at the advanced aged of ninety-seven years.

Marie was certainly a very wonderful old woman with a very kind heart. Whatever superstitious stories were whispered about her, it is at least certain that she enjoyed the respect and affection of thousands who knew her, of numbers whom she befriended in times of dire distress, of sick folks snatched from the shadow of death and nursed by her to health and strength again with that old Creole skill and knowledge of natural medicines which is now almost a lost art. In her youth she was a very beautiful woman,—one of the most beautiful perhaps, of those famous free women of color, who have almost wholly disappeared within the last twenty years. She was married in the St. Louis Cathedral by Pere Antoine to Jacques Paris, a carpenter, nearly seventy years ago. Paris strangely disappeared a year after the marriage and was never heard of again. Marie was subsequently married to one Capt. Christophe Glapion, who served under Jackson, in the war of 1815, in the San Domingo battalion. By this marriage Marie became the mother of fifteen children, only one of whom now lives,—a very estimable widow.

It is pretty certain that the strange stories in circulation about Marie Laveau were wholly due to her marvellous skill in the use of native herb medicines, and her ready wit also in aiding those who came to her for advice or relief. Her medicines were almost infallible; her tisanes were elixirs; and her kind heart inspired her to undertake any trouble with the view of alleviating misery or securing the happiness of those in whom she became interested. In the great epidemic of 1853, a committee of citizens was appointed to wait upon her, and beg her to lend her aid to the fever-smitten, numbers of whom she saved. It is also said that whenever Marie could be induced to exercise her influence to save the life of a condemned prisoner she rarely failed; nor were the fruits of her interference ever regretted. No shrewder judge of character could have been found, and when Marie interceded there was generally good ground for mercy.

Of late years numbers of persons, including very prominent citizens, called upon Marie Laveau frequently, in the hope of obtaining certain information from her that would have been invaluable to historians and others. But unfortunately the old woman's memory was failing; and those who had neglected her when she most needed and wanted their kindness, found ample cause for regret. There were problems in the history of New Orleans she could have elucidated; there were traditions of extinct families she might have told; there were incidents in the lives of some of the greatest men of the United States she could have related. But it was too late. Her knowledge of all the events of New Orleans for nearly a century died with her; and thousands of strange secrets also which she always kept locked up in her own heart and never could have been induced to reveal under any circumstances. She had seen Aaron Burr, had been kissed by Lafayette, knew Gen. Humburt, and the Louisiana Governors of a hundred years, besides every prominent personage in New Orleans history since Claiborne.

The funeral ceremony was performed by Father Mignot, and the attendance was very large.

Marie Laveau was one of the kindest women who ever lived, and one who probably did more good to a greater number of people here than any other who lived to her great age. What good she did was done unselfishly and what she did not do was not done only because she was not able to do it.

Daily City Item, July 17, 1881

VOICES OF DAWN

"A dreadful sound is in his ears"—Job xv, 21.

THERE have never been so many fruit peddlers and viand peddlers of all sorts as at the present time—an encouraging sign of prosperity and the active circulation of money.

With the first glow of sunlight the street resounds with their cries; and, really, the famous Book of London Cries contains nothing more curious than some of these vocal advertisements, —these musical announcements, sung by Italians, negroes, Frenchmen and Spaniards. The vendor of fowls pokes in his head at every open window with cries of "Chick-EN, Ma-damma, Chick-EN," and the seller of "Lem-ONS—fine Lem-ONS!" follows in his footsteps. The peddlers of "Ap-PULLS," of "Straw-BARE-eries" and "Black-Breezes,"—all own sonorous voices. There is a handsome Italian with a some-what ferocious pair of black eyes, who sells various oddities, and has adopted the word "lagniappe" for his war cry,—pro-nouncing it Italian wise. He advances noiselessly to open windows and doors, plunges his blazing black glance into the interior, and suddenly queries in a deep bass, like a clap of thunder, "LAGNIAPPA-Madam-a!—lagniapPA!" Then there is the Cantelope Man, whose cry is being imitated by all the children:

> Cantel-lope-ah!
> Fresh and fine,
> Jus from the vine,
> Only a dime!

There are also two peddlers, the precise meaning of whose cries we have never been able to determine. One shouts, or seems to shout, "A-a-a-a-ah! SHE got." Just what "she got" we have not yet been able to determine; but we fancy it must be disagreeable, as the crier's rival always shouts,—"I-I-I!—I want nothing!" with a tremendous emphasis on the eye. There is another fellow who seems to shout out something which is not exactly proper for modest ears to hear; but he is really only announcing that he has fine potatoes for sale. Then there is the Clothes-pole Man, whose musical, quavering cry is heard at the distance of miles on a clear day, "Clo-ho-ho-ho-ho-ho-ho-ho-se-poles!" As a trilling tenor he is simply marvelous. The "Coaly-coally" Man, a merry little Gascon, is too well known as a singer to need any criticism; but he is almost ubiquitous. There is also the fig-seller, who crieth in such a manner that his "fresh figs" seems to be "Ice crags!" And the fan-sellers who intend to call, "cheap fans," but who really seem to yell "Jap-ans!" and

"Chapped hands!" Then there is the seller of "Tow-wells!" and the sellers of "Ochre-A," who appear to deal in but one first-class quality of paint, if we dare believe the mendacious sounds which reach our ears; neither must we forget the vendors of "Tom-ate-toes!" Whose toes we should like to know.

These are new cries, with perhaps three exceptions;—with the old cries added to the list,—the "calas" and the "plaisir" and other Creole calls, we might "spread out" over another column. If any one has a little leisure and a little turn for amusement, he can certainly have plenty of fun while listening to the voices of the peddlers entering his room together with the first liquid gold of sunrise.

Daily City Item, July 22, 1881

A RIVER REVERIE

An old Western river port, lying in a wrinkle of the hills,—a sharp slope down to the yellow water, glowing under the sun like molten bronze,—a broken hollow square of buildings framing it in, whose basements had been made green by the lipping of water during inundations periodical as the rising of the Nile,—a cannonade-rumble of drays over the boulders, and muffled-drum thumping of cotton bales,—white signs black-lettered with names of steamboat companies, and the green latticework of saloon doors flanked by empty kegs,—above, church spires cutting the blue,—below, on the slope, hogs-heads, bales, casks, drays, cases, boxes, barrels, kegs, mules, wagons, policemen, loungers, and roustabouts, whose apparel is at once as picturesque, as ragged, and as colorless as the fronts of their favorite haunts on the water-front. Westward the purple of softly-rolling hills beyond the flood, through a diaphanous veil of golden haze,—a marshaled array of white boats with arabesque lightness of painted woodwork, and a long and irregular line of smoking chimneys. The scene never varied save with the varying tints of weather and season. Sometimes the hills were grey through an atmosphere of rain,—sometimes they vanished altogether in an autumn fog; but the port never changed. And in summer or spring, at the foot of the iron-stairway leading up to a steamboat agency in the great middle building facing the river, there was a folding stool—which no one ever tried to steal—which even the most hardened wharf thieves respected,—and on that stool, at the same hour every day, a pleasant-faced old man with a very long white beard used to sit. If you asked anybody who it was, the invariable reply was: "Oh! that's Old Capt. ——; used to be in the New Orleans trade;—had to give up the river on account of rheumatism;—comes down every day to look at things."

Wonder whether the old captain still sits there of bright afternoons, to watch the returning steamers panting with their nightly run from the far South,—or whether he has sailed away upon that other river, silent and colorless as winter's fog, to that vast and shadowy port where much ghostly freight is discharged from vessels that never return? He haunts us sometimes,—even as he must have been haunted by the ghosts of dead years.

When some great white boat came in, uttering its long, wild cry of joy after its giant race of eighteen hundred miles, to be re-echoed by the hundred voices of the rolling hills,—surely the old man must have dreamed upon his folding stool of marvelous nights upon the Mississippi,—nights filled with the perfume of orange blossoms under a milky palpitation of stars in amethystine sky, and witchery of tropical moonlight.

The romance of river-life is not like the romance of the sea —that romance memory evokes for us in the midst of the city by the simple exhalations of an asphalt pavement under the sun,—divine saltiness, celestial freshness, the wild joy of wind-kissed waves, the hum of rigging and crackling of cordage, the rocking as of a mighty cradle. But it is perhaps sweeter. There is no perceptible motion of the river vessel; it is like the move-ment of a balloon, so steady, that not we, but the world only, seems to move. Under the stars there seems to unroll its end-lessness like an immeasurable ribbon of silver-purple. There is a noiseless ripple in it, as of watered silk. There is a heavy, sweet smell of nature, of luxuriant verdure; the feminine out-lines of the hills, dotted with the chrome-yellow of window-lights, are blue-black; the vast arch of stars blossoms overhead; there is no sound but the colossal breathing of the laboring

engines; the stream widens; the banks lessen; the heavens seem
to grow deeper, the stars whiter, the blue bluer. Under the
night it is all a blue world, as in a planet illuminated by a
colored sun. The calls of the passing boats, sonorous as the
music of vast silver trumpets, ring out clear but echoless;—
there are no hills to give ghostly answer. Days are born in gold
and die in rose color; and the stream widens, widens, broadens
toward the eternity of the sea under the eternity of the sky. We
sail out of Northern frosts into Southern lukewarmness, into
the luxuriant and somnolent smell of magnolias and lemon
blossoms;—the sugar-country exhales its incense of welcome.
And the giant crescent of lights, the steam-song of joyous
boats, the world of chimneys, the forests of spars, the burst of
morning glory over New Orleans, viewed from the deck of a
pilot-house. . . .

These may never be wholly forgotten; after the lapse of fifty
years in some dusty and dreary inland city, an odor, an echo, a
printed name may resurrect their recollection, fresh as one of
those Gulf winds that leave sweet odors after them, like coquettish women, like Talmudic angels.

So that we beheld all these things yesterday and heard all
these dead voices once more; saw the old Western port with its
water-beslimed warehouses, and the Kentucky hills beyond the
river, and the old captain on his folding stool, gazing wistfully
at the boats; so that we heard once more the steam whistles of
vessels that have long ceased to be, or that, changed into floating
wharves, rise and fall with the flood, like corpses.

And all because there came an illustrious visitor to us, who
reminded us of all these things; having once himself turned the
pilot's wheel, through weird starlight or magical moonshine,
grey rain or ghostly fog, golden sun or purple light,—down
the great river from northern frosts to tepid southern winds—
and up the mighty stream into the misty North again.

To-day his name is a household word in the English-speaking
world; his thoughts have been translated into other tongues;
his written wit creates mirth at once in Paris salons or New
Zealand homes. Fortune has also extended to him her stairway
of gold; and he has hobnobbed much with the great ones of
the world. But there is still something of the Pilot's cheery
manner in his greeting; and the keenness of the Pilot's glance

in his eyes, and a looking-out and afar-off, as of the man who of old was wont to peer into the darkness of starless nights, with the care of a hundred lives on his hands.

He has seen many strange cities since that day,—sailed upon many seas,—studied many peoples,—written many wonderful books.

Yet, now that he is in New Orleans again, one cannot help wondering whether his heart does not sometimes prompt him to go to the river, like that old captain of the far northwestern port, to watch the white boats panting at the wharves, and listen to their cries of welcome or farewell, and dream of nights beautiful, silver-blue, and silent,—and the great Southern moon peering into a pilot-house.

Times-Democrat (New Orleans), May 2, 1882

NEW ORLEANS IN CARNIVAL GARB

THE artistic and financial objects of the New Orleans Carnival are now too well known to demand any detailed history or explanation, and even the aspect of that singular metropolis during its celebrated holiday has become familiar to a degree that provokes some reflection upon the peculiar loss of individuality which the city always appears to undergo at the epoch in question. A very considerable number of those who visit New Orleans at Carnival-time do so quite as much for the sake of seeing the city itself as of witnessing the great pageant. But during Mardi Gras the place is disguised by its holiday garb— almost as much so, indeed, as the King of the Carnival: the native picturesqueness of the quainter districts is overlaid and concealed by the artificial picturesqueness of the occasion. One finds the streets themselves masked, so much are their salient features concealed by those innumerable wooden frame-works temporarily erected to provide against the falling of galleries under an unaccustomed burden of spectators. The romantic charm of the old city is not readily obtained at such a time; the curious cosmopolitan characteristics that offer themselves to artistic eyes in other seasons are lost in the afflux of American visitors, and true local color is fairly drowned out by the colors of Rex. There really exist for the artist and the poet many rich sources of inspiration in quaint New Orleans, but these sources gush more freely at other times. They are difficult to discover during the pushing and squeezing of Carnival excitement. To see the Queen of the South in her most natural and pleasing mood one should visit her during that dreamy season called St. Martin's summer, when the orange blossoms exhale their fragrance, and the winds are still lukewarm, and the autumn glow bronzes those faint tints which the old-fashioned edifices wear. Then the curious confusion of gables and balconies gracefully jutting against the blue above, the Doresque oddity of the shadows wrought below, give the more antiquated streets a peculiarly impressive aspect—a foreign look not of this hemisphere nor even of this century. There also linger the Latin tongues of Southern Europe with softer syllabification, tempered by those mysterious climatic forces which make themselves manifest even in the transplantation of language; and together with these Mediterranean dialects one hears that remarkable creole *patois* which in the mouth of a woman or a child has a fantastic sweetness rivalling the many-vowelled Polynesian speech. Deep surprises of green refresh the eye that peeps through the half-opened gates of drowsy old creole courts—the broad watered silk of banana leaves, tropical creepers clawing their upward way over trellis-work, vines curling and clinging, lizard-footed ivy, the sinister "Spanish-bayonet," perhaps a young palm also, plumed like a cacique. In those quaint interiors the colonial life still endures together with many rococo things bearing as little relation to modern ideas and fashions as the New Orleans of *Manon Lescaut* to the Crescent City of to-day. In that season the nights are tepid, vast, wine-colored, like the Homeric ocean, and vibrant with an infinite variety of insect music. From the bayous and the low lands arise sounds as of ghostly violins, phantom flutes, elfish bells; mocking-birds utter their weird and wonderful pipings, immense beetles fizz by, stridulous crickets work their invisible buzz-saws, frogs hold tintinnabulary converse—every surface inch of land or water seems to possess a voice of its own; the water-lilies speak one unto the other, the shadows cry out.

THE BALL.

NEW ORLEANS FROM THE RIVER BY NIGHT.

CROWD AWAITING THE ARRIVAL OF KING REX, AT THE LEVEE.

FORMING THE PROCESSION.

THRONE AND PRESENTATION SCENE

KREWE PROTEUS

CARNIVAL NIGHT. THE PROCESSION

And through the Egyptian uniformity of the landscape the Mississippi serpentines its way with Nilotic solemnity, so coiling that to dwellers upon it eastern bank the sun appears, as in the Moslem prophecy, to rise in the west.

Few of the real attractions of New Orleans are likely to be observed by Carnival visitors, bewildered as they are by the great eddying of people, the confusion of preparation, the general inappropriateness of the moment to curious research and romantic investigation. But a Carnival night in New Orleans, during the coming and going of the great display, offers in itself much remarkable material for study—at least to one who can look about him undisturbed by the surging of the enormous crowd. Canal Street presents its long deep vista of illumination—monograms of fire, eagles of flame, ladders of light, blaze along the way; and the uncommon breadth of the great thoroughfare, with its starry lines of electric lamps threading the middle, appears to be increased by the luminosity. For eight miles to right and left the city begins to empty its population into the great central highway, through all the tributary streets and alleys, and the force of that human circulation is resistless—to strive against the current is out of the question. The physician or telegraph messenger whom duty summons in an opposite direction at such a time must take the middle of the street if he hopes to reach his destination. Rising one above another through the glow of illumination, the broad galleries packed with spectators seem like the tiers of an enormous hippodrome. When the human spring-tide has reached its fullest the pageant issues from its hiding-place, and sails by like a grotesque Armada, while the ocean of witnesses ebbs away in its wake. That Canal Street offers, in a large sense, the best view of the procession is beyond dispute; but the strictly *local* picturesqueness of the exhibition may be studied to advantage in the antiquated French by-ways. The Canal Street spectacle is imposing, but not unique. Under similar conditions a street of equal breadth in any other great modern city would offer a spectacle of magnificence scarcely inferior. The grotesque silhouettes of the moving panorama are partially lost in such a street—the shadows can not reach the sides of the buildings. But through the queer old streets of the French quarter the Carnival procession must almost squeeze its way, casting eccentric shapes of darkness upon the walls, and lighting its path with torch-light that flings upward the shadows of projecting galleries, and lends much Rembrandtesqueness to the faces peering down from balconies or dormer-windows. The artist whose very impressive sketch accompanies this brief article has effected a happy compromise between the broad glory of the Canal Street view and the still odder aspects above described. The effect has been seized at the moment the living panorama is passing the corner of the old Rue Royale, so that we have a suggestion of the side-street view and of the central thoroughfare at once.

After the pageant has gone glimmering, and the whirl of the midnight ball is over, day dawns upon a scene of merry wreck. Streets are strewn with fragments of brightly colored paper, tatters of tinsel, remnants of torn decorations; perhaps some gorgeous wagon, or "float," disabled during the great review, may be seen lying abandoned at some point of the route, like a gold-freighted galleon astrand. Last year did not the eyes of early risers behold, glittering upon Canal Street, North, the ruined gates of the New Jerusalem? But the city soon rids itself of all these souvenirs—the wrecks and waifs mysteriously vanish, the pictured Carnival journals are devoured by the post-office, the King's standards cease to fill the streets with shadowy flutterings, the intricate paraphernalia of illumination are removed, and the nervous system of New Orleans returns to its normal condition. Only the unsightly skeleton woodwork still shoulders up the galleries to provide against accident upon the 4th of March, which is "Fireman's Day." Already the Carnival societies are secretly preparing for the display of 1884. Ere long the moist and odorous spring will blow in the streets, and the city will gradually settle down into its long and dreamy summer languor; the pulses of its commercial life will beat more slowly with the lengthening of the days, the forest of masts along its eighteen miles of wharves will dwindle as the sultriness thickens, the wilderness of smoking chimneys at its sugar and cotton landings will diminish, and the somnolent and burning season will come, with warm winds and lightnings from the Gulf, with clouds splendid and ponderous as those of geologic eras, when the heavens were heavy with vaporized iron and gold.

Harper's Weekly, February 24, 1883

SAINT MALO

A LACUSTRINE VILLAGE IN LOUISIANA

Region of Saint Malo.

FOR nearly fifty years there has existed in the southeastern swamp lands of Louisiana a certain strange settlement of Malay fishermen—Tagalas from the Philippine Islands. The place of their lacustrine village is not precisely mentioned upon maps, and the world in general ignored until a few days ago the bare fact of their amphibious existence. Even the United States mail service has never found its way thither, and even in the great city of New Orleans, less than a hundred miles distant, the people were far better informed about the Carboniferous Era than concerning the swampy affairs of this Manila village. Occasionally vague echoes of its mysterious life were borne to the civilized centre, but these were scarcely of a character to tempt investigation or encourage belief. Some voluble Italian lugger-men once came to town with a short cargo of oysters, and a long story regarding a ghastly "Chinese" colony in the reedy swamps south of Lake Borgne. For many years the inhabitants of the Oriental settlement had lived in peace and harmony without the presence of a single woman, but finally had managed to import an oblique-eyed beauty from beyond the Yellow Sea. Thereupon arose the first dissensions, provoking much shedding of blood. And at last the elders of the people had restored calm and fraternal feeling by sentencing the woman to be hewn in pieces and flung to the alligators of the bayou.

Possible the story is; probable it is not. Partly for the purpose of investigating it, but principally in order to offer HARPER's artist a totally novel subject of artistic study, the *Times-Democrat* of New Orleans chartered and fitted out an Italian lugger for a trip to the unexplored region in question—to the fishing station of Saint Malo. And a strange voyage it was. Even the Italian sailors knew not whither they were going, none of them had ever beheld the Manila village, or were aware of its location.

Starting from Spanish Fort northeastwardly across Lake Pontchartrain, after the first few miles sailed one already observes a change in the vegetation of the receding banks. The shore itself sinks, the lowland bristles with rushes and marsh grasses waving in the wind. A little further on and the water becomes deeply clouded with sap green—the myriad floating seeds of swamp vegetation. Banks dwindle away into thin lines; the greenish-yellow of the reeds changes into misty blue. Then it is all water and sky, motionless blue and heaving lazulite, until the reedy waste of Point-aux-Herbes thrusts its picturesque light-house far out into the lake. Above the wilderness of swamp grass and bulrushes this graceful building rises upon an open-work of wooden piles. Seven miles of absolute desolation separate the light-house keeper from his nearest neighbor.

Nevertheless, there is a good piano there for the girls to play upon, comfortably furnished rooms, a good library. The pet cat has lost an eye in fighting with a moccasin, and it is prudent before descending from the balcony into the swamp about the house to reconnoitre for snakes. Still northeast. The sun is sinking above the rushy bank line; the west is crimsoning like iron losing its white heat. Against the ruddy light a cross is visible. There is a cemetery in the swamp. Those are the forgotten graves of light-house keepers. Our boat is spreading her pinions for flight through the Rigolets, that sinuous waterway leading to Lake Borgne. We pass by the defenseless walls of Fort Pike, a stronghold without a history, picturesque enough, but almost worthless against modern artillery. There is a solitary sergeant in charge, and a dog. Perhaps the taciturnity of the man is due to his long solitude, the vast silence of the land weighing down upon him. At last appears the twinkling light of the United States custom-house, and the enormous skeleton of the Rigolets bridge. The custom-house rises on stilts out of the sedge-grass. The pretty daughter of the inspector can manage a skiff as well as most expert oarsmen. Here let us listen awhile in the moonless night. From the south a deep sound is steadily rolling up like the surging of a thousand waves, like the long roaring of breakers. But the huge blind lake is scarcely agitated; the distant glare of a prairie fire illuminates no spurring of "white horses." What, then, is that roar, as of thunder muffled by distance, as of the moaning that seamen hear far inland while dreaming at home of phantom seas? It is only a mighty chorus of frogs, innumerable millions of frogs, chanting in the darkness over unnumbered leagues of swamp and lagoon.

On the eastern side of the Rigolets Lake Borgne has scalloped out its grass-fringed bed in the form of a gigantic clover leaf—a shallow and treacherous sea, from which all fishing-vessels scurry in wild terror when a storm begins to darken. No lugger can live in those short chopping waves when Gulf winds are mad. To reach the Manila settlement one must steer due south until the waving bulrushes again appear, this time behind muddy shoals of immense breadth. The chart announces depths varying from six inches to three and a half feet. For a while we grope about blindly along to the banks.

The Lacustrine Village of St. Malo.

Drawn by Charles Graham from Sketches by J. O. Davidson.

Suddenly the mouth of a bayou appears—"Saint Malo Pass." With the aid of poles the vessel manages to shamble over a mud-bar, and forthwith rocks in forty feet of green water. We reached Saint Malo upon a leaden-colored day, and the scenery in its gray ghastliness recalled to us the weird landscape painted with words by EDGAR POE—"Silence: a Fragment."

Out of the shuddering reeds and banneretted grass on either side rise the fantastic houses of the Malay fishermen, poised upon slender supports above the marsh, like cranes or bitterns watching for scaly prey. Hard by the slimy mouth of the bayou extends a strange wharf, as ruined and rotted and unearthly as the timbers of the spectral ship in the "Rime of the Ancient Mariner." Odd craft huddle together beside it, fishing-nets make cobwebby drapery about the skeleton timber-work. Green are the banks, green the water is, green also with fungi every beam and plank and board and shingle of the houses upon stilts. All are built in true Manila style, with immense hat-shaped eaves and balconies, but in wood; for it had been found that palmetto and woven cane could not withstand the violence of the climate. Nevertheless, all this wood had to be shipped to the bayou from a considerable distance, for large trees do not grow in the salty swamp. The highest point of land as far as the "Devil's Elbow," three or four miles away, and even beyond it, is only six inches above low-water mark, and the men who built those houses were compelled to stand upon ladders, or other wood frame-work, while driving down the piles, lest the quagmire should swallow them up.

Below the houses are patches of grass and pools of water and stretches of gray mud, pitted with the hoof-prints of hogs. Sometimes these hoof-prints are crossed with the tracks of the alligator, and a pig is missing. Chickens there are too—sorry-looking creatures; many have but one leg, others have but one foot: the crabs have bitten them off. All these domestic creatures of the place live upon fish.

Here is the home of the mosquito, and every window throughout all the marsh country must be closed with wire netting. At sundown the insects rise like a thick fog over the lowland; in the darkness their presence is signaled by a sound like the boiling of innumerable caldrons. Worse than these are the great green-headed *tappanoes*, dreaded by the fishermen.

Sand-flies attack the colonists in warm weather; fleas are insolent at all hours; spiders of immense growth rival the net-
weavers of Saint Malo, and hang their webs from the timbers
side by side with the seines and fishing-tackle. Wood-worms
are busy undermining the supports of the dwellings, and
wood-ticks attack the beam and joistings. A marvellous variety
of creatures haunt the surrounding swamp—reptiles, insects,
and birds. The *prie-dieu*—"pray-god"—utters its soprano
note; water-hens and plovers call across the marsh. Numberless snakes hide among the reeds, having little to fear save from
the wild-cats, which attack them with savage recklessness.
Rarely a bear or a deer finds its way near the bayou. There are
many otters and musk-rats, minks and raccoons and rabbits.
Buzzards float in the sky, and occasionally a bald-eagle sails
before the sun.

Such is the land: its human inhabitants are not less strange,
wild, picturesque. Most of them are cinnamon-colored men; a
few are glossily yellow, like that bronze into which a small proportion of gold is worked by the moulder. Their features are
irregular without being actually repulsive; some have the
cheek-bones very prominent, and the eyes of several are set
slightly aslant. The hair is generally intensely black and straight,
but with some individuals it is curly and browner. In Manila
there are several varieties of the Malay race, and these
Louisiana settlers represent more than one type. None of them
appeared tall; the greater number were under-sized, but all well
knit, and supple as fresh-water eels. Their hands and feet were
small; their movements quick and easy, but sailorly likewise, as
of men accustomed to walk upon rocking decks in rough
weather. They speak the Spanish language; and a Malay dialect
is also used among them. There is only one white man in the
settlement—the ship-carpenter, whom all the Malays address
as "Maestro." He has learned to speak their Oriental dialect,
and has conferred upon several the sacrament of baptism according to the Catholic rite; for some of these men were not
Christians at the time of their advent into Louisiana. There is
but one black man in this lake village—a Portuguese negro,
perhaps a Brazilian maroon. The Maestro told us that communication is still kept up with Manila, and money often sent
there to aid friends in emigrating. Such emigrants usually ship

as seamen on board some Spanish vessel bound for American ports, and desert at the first opportunity. It is said that the colony was founded by deserters—perhaps also by desperate refugees from Spanish justice.

Justice within the colony itself, however, is of a curiously primitive kind; for there are neither magistrates nor sheriffs, neither prisons nor police. Although the region is included within the parish of St. Bernard, no Louisiana official has ever visited it; never has the tax-gatherer attempted to wend thither his unwelcome way. In the busy season a hundred fierce men are gathered together in this waste and watery place, and these must be a law unto themselves. If a really grave quarrel arises, the trouble is submitted to the arbitration of the oldest Malay in the colony, Padre CARPIO, and his decisions are usually accepted without a murmur. Should a man, on the other hand, needlessly seek to provoke a difficulty, he is liable to be imprisoned within a fish-car, and left there until cold and hunger have tamed his rage, or the rising tide forces him to terms. Naturally all these men are Catholics; but a priest rarely visits them, for it costs a considerable sum to bring the ghostly father into the heart of the swamp that he may celebrate mass under the smoky rafters of HILARIO's house—under the strings of dry fish.

There is no woman in the settlement, nor has the treble of a female voice been heard along the bayou for many a long year. Men who have families keep them at New Orleans, or at Proctorville, or at La Chinche; it would seem cruel to ask any woman to dwell in such a desolation, without comfort and without protection, during the long absence of the fishing-boats. Only two instances of a woman dwelling there are preserved, like beloved traditions, in the memory of the inhabitants. The first of these departed upon her husband's death; the second left the village after a desperate attempt had been made to murder her spouse. In the dead of night the man was unexpectedly assailed; his wife and little boy helped to defend him. The assailant was overcome, tied hand and foot with fish-lines, and fastened to a stake deep driven into the swamp. Next morning they found him dead: the mosquitoes and tappanoes had filled the office of executioner. No excitement was manifested; the Maestro dug a grave deep in the soft gray mud, and fixed above it a rude wooden cross, which still shows its silhouette against the sky just above the reeds.

Such was the narrative which El Maestro related to us with a strange mixture of religious compassion for the unabsolved soul, and marvelous profanity expressed in four different languages. "Only mosquitoes live there now," he added, indicating the decaying edifice where the dead man had dwelt.

But for the possession of modern fire-arms and one most ancient clock, the lake-dwellers of Saint Malo would seem to have as little in common with the civilization of the nineteenth century as had the inhabitants of the Swiss lacustrine settlements of the Bronze Epoch. Here time is measured rather by the number of alligator-skins sent to market, or the most striking incidents of successive fishing seasons, than by ordinary reckoning; and did not the Maestro keep a chalk record of the days of the week, none might know Sunday from Monday. There is absolutely no furniture in the place; not a chair, a table, or a bed can be found in all the dwellings of this aquatic village. Mattresses there are, filled with dry "Spanish beard"; but these are laid upon tiers of enormous shelves braced against the walls, where the weary fishermen slumber at night among barrels of flour and folded sails and smoked fish. Even the clothes (purchased at New Orleans or Proctorville) became as quaint and curiously tinted in that moist atmosphere as the houses of the village, and the broad hats take a greenish and grotesque aspect in odd harmony with the appearance of the ancient roofs. All the art treasures of the colony consist of a circus poster immemorially old, which is preserved with much reverence, and two photographs jealously guarded in the Maestro's sea-chest. These represent a sturdy young woman with creole eyes, and a grim-looking Frenchman with wintry beard—the wife and father of the ship-carpenter. He pointed to them with a display of feeling made strongly pathetic by contrast with the wild character of the man, and his eyes, keen and hard as those of an eagle, softened a little as he kissed the old man's portrait, and murmured, "Mon cher vieux père."

And nevertheless this life in the wilderness of reeds is connected mysteriously with New Orleans, where the headquarters of the Manila men's benevolent society are—*La Union Philipina*. A fisherman dies; he is buried under the rustling reeds, and a pine cross planted above his grave; but when the flesh has rotted from the bone, these are taken up and carried by some lugger to the metropolis, where they are shelved away in those curious niche tombs which recall the Roman *columbaria*.

How, then, comes it that in spite of this connection with civilized life the Malay settlement of Lake Borgne has been so long unknown? Perhaps because of the natural reticence of the people. There is still in the oldest portion of the oldest quarter of New Orleans a certain Manila restaurant hidden away in a court, and supported almost wholly by the patronage of Spanish West Indian sailors. Few people belonging to the business circles of New Orleans know of its existence. The *menu* is printed in Spanish and English; the fare is cheap and good. Now it is kept by Chinese, for the Manila man and his oblique-eyed wife, comely as any figure upon a Japanese vase, have gone away. Doubtless his ears, like sea-shells, were haunted by the moaning of the sea, and the Gulf winds called to him by night, so that he could not remain.

The most intelligent person in Saint Malo is a Malay half-breed, VALENTINE. He is an attractive figure, a supple dwarfish lad almost as broad as tall, brown as old copper, with a singularly bright eye. He was educated in the great city, but actually abandoned a fine situation in the office of a judge to return to his swarthy father in the weird swamps. The old man is still there —THOMAS DE LOS SANTOS. He married a white woman, by whom he had two children, this boy and a daughter, WINNIE, who is dead. VALENTINE is the best pirogue oarsman in the settlement, and a boat bears his name. But opposite the house of THOMAS DE LOS SANTOS rides another graceful boat, rarely used, and whitely christened with the name of the dead WINNIE. Latin names still prevail in the nomenclature of boats and men; Marcellino, Francesco, Serafino, Florenzo, Victorio, Paosto, Hilario, Marcetto, are common baptismal names. The solitary creole appellation Aristide offers an anomaly. There are luggers and sloops bearing equally romantic names: *Manrico de Aragon, Maravilla, Joven Imperatriz*. Spanish piety has baptized several others with sacred words and names of martyrs.

Of the thirteen or fourteen large edifices on piles, the most picturesque is perhaps that of CARPIO—old CARPIO, who

Gambling at Saint Malo.

Drawn by T. de Thulstrup from a Sketch by J. O. Davidson.

deserts the place once a year to play monte in Mexico. His home consists of three wooden edifices so arranged that the outer two advance like wings, and the wharf is placed in front of the central structure. Smoked fish black with age hang from the roof, chickens squeak upon the floor, pigs grunt under the planking. Small, squat, swart, dry, and grimy as his smoked fish is old CARPIO, but his eye is bright and quick as a lizard's.

It is at HILARIO's great *casa* that the Manila men pass stormy evenings, playing monte or a species of Spanish keno. When the *cantador*, (the caller) sings out the numbers, he always accompanies the annunciation with some rude poetry characteristic of fisher life or Catholic faith:

Pareja de uno;
Dos piquetes de rivero—

a pair of one (11); the *two stakes* to which the fish-car is fastened.

Número cuatro;
La casa del gato—

number 4; the cat's house.

Seis con su nuéve;
Arriba y abajo—

six with its nine (69); *up and down.*

De dos pareja;
Dos paticos en laguna—

pair of two (22); two *ducklings* in the lagoon or marsh—the Arabic numerals conveying by their shape this idea to the minds of fishermen. Picturesque? The numbers 77 suggest an almost similar idea—*dos gansos en laguna* (two geese in the lagoon):

Tres y parejo;
Edad de Cristo—

thirty-three; the age of Christ.

Dos con su cinco;
Buena noche pasado—

twenty-five (Christmas-eve); the "Good-night" past.

Nuéve y parejo;
El mas viejo—

ninety, "the oldest one." Fifty-five is called the "two boats moored" together, as the figures placed thus turn ⌀ convey that idea to the mind—*dos galíbos amarrados.* Very musical is the voice of the *cantador* as he continues, shaking up the numbers in a calabash:

Bits of Saint Malo Scenery.

Drawn by Charles Graham from Sketches by J. O. Davidson.

Dos y nuéve:
Viente y nuéve—29.
Seis con su cuatro:
Sesenta y cuatro—64.
Ocho y seis:
Borrachenta y seis—86 (*drunken* eighty-six).
Nina de quince (a girl of fifteen):
Uno y cinco—15.

Polite, too, these sinister-eyed men: there was not a single person in the room who did not greet us with a hearty *buenas noches*. The artist made his sketch of that grotesque scene upon the rude plank-work which served as a gambling table by the yellow flickering of lamps fed with fish-oil.

There is no liquor in the settlement, and these hardy fishers and alligator-hunters seem none the worse therefor. Their flesh is as hard as oarwood, and sickness rarely affects them, although they know little of comfort, and live largely upon raw fish, seasoned with vinegar and oil. There is but one chimney—a wooden structure—in the village, fires are hardly ever lighted, and in the winter the cold and damp would soon undermine feeble constitutions.

A sunset viewed from the balcony of the Maestro's house seemed to us enchantment. The steel blue of the western horizon heated into furnace yellow, then cooled off into red splendors of astounding warmth and transparency. The bayou blushed crimson, the green of the marsh pools, of the shivering reeds, of the decaying timber-work, took fairy bronze tints, and then, immense with marsh mist, the orange-vermillion face of the sun peered luridly for the last time through the tall grasses upon the bank. Night came with marvellous choruses of frogs; the whole lowland throbbed and laughed with the wild music—a swamp-hymn deeper and mightier than even the surge sounds heard from the Rigolets bank: the world seemed to shake with it!

We sailed away just as the east began to flame again, and saw the sun arise with reeds sharply outlined against the vivid vermilion of his face. Long fish-formed clouds sailed above him through the blue, green-backed and iridescent-bellied, like the denizens of the green water below. VALENTINE hailed us from the opposite bank, holding up a struggling *poule-d'eau* which he had just rescued from a wild-cat. A few pirogues were already flashing over the bayou, ribbing the water with wavelets half emerald, half orange gold. Brighter and brighter the eastern fires grew; oranges and vermilions faded out into fierce yellow, and against the blaze all the ragged ribs of HILARIO's elfish wharf stood out in black. Somebody fired a farewell shot as we reached the mouth of the bayou; there was a waving of picturesque hand and hats; and far in our wake an alligator plashed his scaly body, making for the whispering line of reeds upon the opposite bank.

Harper's Weekly, March 31, 1883

THE ROAR OF A GREAT CITY

WHEN Hogarth painted his story of "The Enraged Musician," whose music was drowned in the thousand cries and noises that surrounded him; when Chambers described "The Roar of a Great City," the blending of a thousand noises, it was of the city of the past they told. Since then this roar has been growing louder and louder, until now, miles away, even before you see the smoky coronet that surrounds the modern city, you can hear a wild growl like that of some enraged beast. Neither Hogarth nor Chambers dreamed of the fierce whistle of the steamboat and locomotive, of the rattle of engine and machinery, or the cannonade as a cotton float flies over the granite pavement, or the stunning noise of the New York Elevated Railroad. All these have come of late years.

The electric light, the telephone and telegraph wires have added new music to our city. When the winds blow at night one can hear a sombre, melancholy music high up in the air—as mysterious as that of Ariel himself or the undiscovered music of the Pascagoula. If you want to hear it in perfection go some of these windy nights we have lately enjoyed to Delord or Dryades, or some of the streets in the neighborhood of the electric light works, where the wires are numerous and the houses low, and where there is a clean sweep for the wind from the New Basin to the river. There the music becomes wild and grand indeed. The storm whistling and shrieking around some sharp corner never equalled it. Above, around, in every direction can be heard this music, sighing, mourning like the tree tops, with a buzzing metallic sound that almost drowns your conversation. There is something in it weird and melancholy—it is like the last wail of a dying man, or the shriek of the angel of death as he clasps his victim to him.

If such it is to-day, what have we to hope for in the future? If the city is already a monstrous spider web, a great Æolian harp, what is its destiny with several new telegraph and telephone companies, and thousands of new poles, and millions of new wires promised us. If this aerial music increases, this shrieking and wailing and moaning will reach such a pitch that we will greet the rattle of the floats and tinkle of the street cars as tending to drown this new noise, and welcome the roar of the city as likely to muffle its moaning.

Times-Democrat (New Orleans), November 30, 1884

THE CREOLE PATOIS

ALTHOUGH the pure Creole element is disappearing from the *Vié faubon*, as creole children call the antiquated part of New Orleans, it is there nevertheless that the patois survives as a current idiom; it is there one must dwell to hear it spoken in its purity, and to study its peculiarities of intonation and construction. The patois-speaking inhabitants—dwelling mostly in those portions of the quadrilateral furthest from the river and from the broad American boundary of Canal Street, which many of them never cross when they can help it—are not less *bizarre* than the architectural background of their picturesque existence. The visitor is surrounded by a life motley-colored as those fantastic populations described in the *Story of the Young King of the Black Isles*; the African ebon is least visible, but of bronze-browns, banana-yellows, orange-golds, there are endless varieties, paling off into faint lemon tints, and even dead-silver

whites. The paler the shade, the more strongly do Latin characteristics show themselves; and the oval faces, with slender
cheeks and low broad brows, prevail. Sometimes in the yellower types a curious Sphinx visage appears, dreamy as Egypt.
Occasionally, also, one may encounter figures so lithe, so animal,
as to recall the savage grace of Prion's "Satyress." For the true
colorist the contrast of a light saffron skin with dead-black hair
and eyes of liquid jet has a novel charm, as of those descriptions in the Malay poem "Bidasari," of "women like statues of
gold." It is hard to persuade one's self that such types do not
belong to one distinct race, the remnant of some ancient
island tribe, and the sound of their richly vowelled creole
speech might prolong the pleasant illusion.

It must be not be supposed, however, that the creole dialect
is the only one used by these people; there are few who do not
converse fluently in the French and English languages, and
to these acquirements many add a knowledge of the sibilant
Mexican-Spanish. But creole is the maternal speech; it is the
tongue in which the baby first learns to utter its thoughts; it is
the language of family and of home. The white creole child
learns it from the lips of his swarthy nurse; and creole adults
still use it in speaking to servants or to their own little ones. At
a certain age the white boys or girls are trained to converse in
French; judicious petting, or even mild punishment, is given
to enforce the use of the less facile but more polite medium of
expression. But the young creole who remains in Louisiana
seldom forgets the sweet patois, the foster-mother tongue, the
household words which are lingual caresses.

Now the colored inhabitants of the *carré* regulate the use of
the creole after the manners of their former masters, upon whose
time-honored customs they base their little code of urbanity.
Let us suppose you are dwelling in one of the curious and
crumbling houses of the old quarter of the town, and that some
evening while dreaming over a pipe as you rock your chair
upon the gallery, the large-eyed children of the habitation
gather about you, cooing one unto the other in creole like so
many yellow doves. Invariably you will then hear the severe
maternal admonition, "Allons, Marie! Eugène! faut pas parler
créole devant monsieur; parlez Français, donc!" Creole must
not be spoken in the presence of "monsieur"; he must be

addressed in good French, the colonial French of Louisiana that has been so much softened by tropicalization.

The general purpose of these little sketches will not admit of any extended linquistic dissertation, otherwise it would be a pleasant task to follow the foot-prints of many philological harvesters, and glean something in fields where French, English, and American scholars have reaped so well. It would be interesting to trace back the origin of the creole to the earlier ages of Latin-American slave colonies, showing how the African serf softened and simplified the more difficult language of his masters, and made to himself that marvellous system of grammar in which philologists have found material for comparison with the tongue of Homer and the speech of Beowulf. But the writer's purpose is to reflect the spirit of existing things rather than to analyze the past, to sketch local peculiarities and reflect local color without treating broadly of causes. It will be sufficient, therefore, to state that the creole patois is the offspring of linguistic miscegenation, an offspring which exhibits but a very faint shade of African color, and nevertheless possesses a strangely supple comeliness by virtue of the very intercrossing which created it, like a beautiful octoroon.

That word reminds one of a celebrated and vanished type—never mirrored upon canvas, yet not less physically worthy of artistic preservation than those amber-tinted beauties glorified in the Oriental studies of Ingres, of Richter, of Gérôme! Uncommonly tall were those famous beauties—citrine-hued, elegant of stature as palmettos, lithe as serpents; never again will such types re-appear upon American soil. Daughters of luxury, artificial human growths, never organized to enter the iron struggle for life unassisted and unprotected, they vanished forever with the social system which made them a place apart as for splendid plants reared within a conservatory. With the fall of American feudalism the dainty glass house was dashed to pieces; the species it contained have perished utterly; and whatever morality may have gained, one can not help thinking that art has lost something by their extinction. What figures for designs in bronze! what tints for canvas!

It is for similar reasons that the creole tongue must die in Louisiana; the great social change will eventually render it extinct. But there is yet time for the philologist to rescue some of its dying legends and curious lyrics, to collect and preserve them, like pressed blossoms, between the leaves of enduring books.

The creoles of the Antilles seem to have felt more pride in the linguistic curiosities of their native isles than the creoles of Louisiana have manifested regarding their own antiquities. In Trinidad fine collections of creole legends and proverbs have been made, and an excellent grammar of the dialect published; in Martinique, hymn-books, *paroissiens*, and other works are printed in creole; the fables of La Fontaine and many popular French fairy tales have found creole translators in the West Indies, while several remarkable pamphlets upon the history and construction of the West Indian dialects are cited in Parisian catalogues of linguistic publications. But it was not until the French publishers of *Mélusine* showed themselves anxious to cull the flora of Louisiana creole that the creoles themselves made any attempt to collect them. Happily the romantic interest excited throughout the country by George Cable's works stimulated research to further exertion, and even provoked the creation of a Franco-Louisianian novel, written by a creole, and having a considerable portion of its text in patois. Nevertheless nothing has yet been attempted in Louisiana comparable with the labors of MM. Luzel and Sébillot in Bretagne; no systematic efforts have been made to collect and preserve the rich oral literature of the creole parishes.

The inedited creole literature comprises songs, satires in rhyme, proverbs, fairy tales—almost everything commonly included under the term *folk-lore*. The lyrical portion of it is opulent in oddities, in melancholy beauties; Alphonse Daudet has frequently borrowed therefrom, using creole refrains in his novels with admirable effect.

Some of the popular songs possess a unique and almost weird pathos; there is a strange naïve sorrow in their burdens, as of children sobbing for lonesomeness in the night. Others, on the contrary, are inimitably comical. There are many ditties or ballads devoted to episodes of old plantation life, to surreptitious frolic, to description of singular industries and callings, to commemoration of events which had strongly impressed the vivid imagination of negroes—a circus show, an unexpected holiday, the visit of a beautiful stranger to the planter's home, or even some one of those incidents indelibly marked with a crimson spatter upon the fierce history of Louisiana politics. Of these lyrics I shall speak in another paper.

Harper's Weekly, January 10–17, 1885

THE NEW ORLEANS EXPOSITION

THE attention of the visitor to the Main Building is apt to be especially attracted at the present time by the Japanese exhibit, which is already much more nearly complete than any other Oriental and than most European displays. The entrance is through a screen-work, decorated with various odd designs above—red balls on a white ground, alternated with circular ornaments suggesting the outspread tops of painted paper umbrellas; beneath these, to the right and left of the doorway, are maps fastened upon a ground of gilt wall-paper curiously stamped with complicated designs. One map represents the western provinces of Japan, the other the whole of Nippon, that island which the Emperor ZIN-MU TEN-ô thought to resemble the form of a Dragon-fly, and to which he gave the name of the insect. The presence of a Greek border might seem an anachronism in this curious screen-work to many persons unfamiliar with the archaic art of Japan, where the same simply beautiful design has been in vogue from time immemorial—a striking instance of the fact that certain general laws which operate in the evolution of art ideas may have many times produced similar results in the development of widely different civilizations. Not only may the visitor be surprised to find the same border design upon many antique bronzes and ceramics in the Japanese department (especially on one beautiful iron box inlaid with silver and gold), but he may almost feel tempted to doubt the origin of certain tripods, pateræ vases, perfuming pans, etc., whose forms bear a strange similarity to the gracious conceptions of old Greek or Etruscan industry, or to certain relics of Pompeii preserved in the Museum of Naples.

The display of bronzes and ceramics—in which the antique

art of Nippon is largely represented—dazzles and deceives the inexperienced eye. Great incense-burners, with double-headed and triple-clawed dragons interlinked about them in monstrous contortion, seem to be wrought in fine bronze; but they are only faience-ware dexterously metal-tinted. Delicate vases of porcelain aspect, covered with grotesque paintings, and surmounted by a cover on which a frog, a tiger, or a gargoyle-shaped creature is sitting, turn out to be made of the finest and hardest statue metal. But these and many other industrial specimens are modern; and it requires little artistic training to discern the superiority of the antique work. One figure standing upon the cover of a perfume-burner haunts me still—some vigorous little deity on tiptoe, lifting a prayer-scroll to heaven. The smoke of the aromatics, like the very incense of prayer, rises by a simple and pretty contrivance up through the scroll itself. The tiny god seems to move his lips of bronze; the muscles of his limbs appear to live and quiver. Palpitant with life also is a species of Japanese Cerberus, from whose open jaws should pass the smoke of another perfume-burner; even the artistic conversion of the tail into a fantastic leaf scroll does not wholly destroy his illusive animation. The antiquated porcelains have none of that conventional frankness of composition in design nor the flaring color which distinguishes many of the best new pieces; they are sober-tinted; they affect no accepted pattern; their figures are strangely puzzling to the eye at first glance, but when the puzzle is read, what marvellous movement! Compared with some of these quaintly painted groups, all muffled and intermuffled in party-colored vesture, the most animated modern vase-figures seem stiff and clumsy. Perhaps the best of the latter is that of a furious Japanese swordsman, whose long blade reaches half-way around the flank of a gigantic porcelain vessel near the entry, to encounter the sabre of a painted antagonist who seems to have retreated to the other side of the vase.

What Japanese art of the best era is unrivalled in—that characteristic in which, according even to the confession of the best French art connoisseurs, it excels all other art—is *movement*, the rhythm, the poetry, of visible motion. Great masters of the antique Japanese schools have been known to devote a whole lifetime to the depiction of one kind of bird, one variety of insect or reptile, alone. This specialization of art, as ARY RENAN admirably showed us in a recent essay, produced results that no European master has ever been able to approach. A flight of gulls sweeping through the gold light of a summer morning; a long line of cranes sailing against a vermilion sky; a swallow twirling its kite shape against the disk of the sun; the heavy, eccentric, velvety flight of bats under the moon; the fairy hoverings of moths or splendid butterflies—these are subjects the Japanese brush has rendered with a sublimity of realism which might be imitated, perhaps, but never surpassed. Except in the statues of gods or goddesses (Buddhas which almost compel the Christian to share the religious awe of their worshippers, or those charming virgins of the Japanese heaven, "slenderly supple as a beautiful lily"), the Japanese have been far less successful in delineations of the human figure. But their sculpture or painting of animal forms amazes by its grace: their bronze tortoises, crab, storks, frogs, are not mere copies of nature; they are exquisite idealizations of it. I scarcely think the Japanese display here sufficiently illustrates this particular branch of the art in all respects; but examples are not wanting, particularly in regard to birds. Two storks seven feet high are to be shortly placed at the entrance, and, like all such bronzes, they will stand on their own claws without any pedestal support. Bronze is but one of countless materials, however, wherein these bird forms have been imitated. Cranes of all sizes and of innumerable colors hold up their graceful necks in every direction among the show-cases; they stand in every position possible to the living creature; they describe K angles with their legs, and curve their necks into an S line, and poke their heads under their wings; they fight, fly, fish, watch, hatch.

Perhaps it is bad taste on the writer's part, but the bugs and reptiles in cotton attracted his attention even more than the cranes. You see a Japanese tray covered with what appear to be dead and living bugs and beetles—some apparently about to fly away; others with upturned abdomen, legs shrunk up, antennæ inert. They are so life-like that you may actually weigh one in your hand a moment before you find that it is made of cotton. Everything, even to the joints of legs or abdomen, is exquisitely imitated: the metallic lustre of the beetle's armor is reproduced by a bronze varnish. There are cotton crickets with the lustre of lacquer, and cotton grasshoppers of many colors; the korogi, whose singing is like to the "sound of a weaver weaving rapidly" ("Ko-ro-ru, ko-ro-ru"), and the kirigisi, whose name is an imitation of its own note. Tree-frogs are delightfully mocked with the same materials.

Of course there are fans of all values and varieties, *papeterie*, oddities in ivory, mantel-piece figurines, bric-à-brac dainties, exquisite porcelain sets decorated with scenes of Japanese life, or with stanzas inscribed in those long, straggling black characters which Japanese poets compare to a flight of birds winging their way against the light, and which recall to me memories of LÉON DE ROSNY's "Si-Ka-Zen-Yo." Perhaps some of those little cups are inscribed with verses from the same poets whom he translated—simple, touching, beautiful, in their naturalness:

"Wert thou a jewel, I would wear thee in my bracelet;
  Wert thou a garment, never would I find time to undress me."

One misses the rice-paper drawings, but these are promised at a later day; meanwhile photographs of Japanese life and scenery partly supply the deficiency. There is a sort of tableau on exhibition, representing two celebrated historical personages, which affords one a very fair idea of the elegance of the old national costumes now passing away. I observed also with interest some fine swords—but not of the famous work which outrivalled in beauty and temper the blades of Toledo or Damascus, and was inlaid with dragon designs in gold. Splendid silks are hanging up everywhere; some exquisitely embroidered with attractive compositions, figures, landscapes, and especially views of Fusiyama, the matchless mountain, whose crater edges are shaped like the eight petals of the Sacred Lotos; Fusiyama, of which the great artist HOUKOUSAÏ alone drew one hundred different views; Fusiyama, whose snows may only be compared for pearly beauty to "the white teeth of a young girl," and whose summit magically changes its tints through numberless variations of light. Everywhere it appears, the wonderful mountain—on fans, behind rains of gold, or athwart a furnace light of sunset, or against an immaculate blue, or gold-burnished by some wizard dawn; in bronze, exhaling from its mimic crater a pillar of incense smoke; on porcelain, towering above stretches of vineyard and city speckled plains, or, perchance, begirdled by a rich cloud sash of silky shifting tints, like some beauty of Yosiwara.

Harper's Weekly, January 31, 1885

THE LAST OF THE VOUDOOS

In the death of Jean Montanet, at the age of nearly a hundred years, New Orleans lost, at the end of August, the most extraordinary African character that ever obtained celebrity within her limits. Jean Montanet, or Jean La Ficelle, or Jean Latanié, or Jean Racine, or Jean Grisgris, or Jean Macaque, or Jean Bayou, or "Voodoo John," or "Bayou John," or "Doctor John," might well have been termed "The Last of the Voudoos"; not that the strange association with which he was affiliated has ceased to exist with his death, but that he was the last really important figure of a long line of wizards or witches whose African titles were recognized, and who exercised an influence over the colored population. Swarthy occultists will doubtless continue to elect their "queens" and high-priests through years to come, but the influence of the public school is gradually dissipating all faith in witchcraft, and no black hierophant now remains capable of manifesting such mystic knowledge or of inspiring such respect as Voudoo John exhibited and compelled. There will never be another "Rose," another "Marie," much less another Jean Bayou.

It may reasonably be doubted whether any other negro of African birth who lived in the South had a more extraordinary career than that of Jean Montanet. He was a native of Senegal, and claimed to have been a prince's son, in proof of which he was wont to call attention to a number of parallel scars on his cheek, extending in curves from the edge of either temple to the corner of the lips. This fact seems to me partly confirmatory of his statement, as Berenger-Feraud dwells at some length on the fact that the Bambaras, who are probably the finest negro race in Senegal, all wear such disfigurations. The scars are made by gashing the cheeks during infancy, and are considered a sign of race. Three parallel scars mark the freemen of the tribe; four distinguish their captives or slaves. Now Jean's face had, I am told, three scars, which would prove him a free-born Bambara, or at least a member of some free tribe allied to the Bambaras, and living upon their territory. At all events, Jean possessed physical characteristics answering to those by which the French ethnologists in Senegal distinguish the Bambaras. He was of middle height, very strongly built, with broad shoulders, well-developed muscles, an inky black skin, retreating forehead, small bright eyes, a very flat nose, and a woolly beard, gray only during the last few years of his long life. He had a resonant voice and a very authoritative manner.

At an early age he was kidnapped by Spanish slavers, who sold him at some Spanish port, whence he was ultimately shipped to Cuba. His West-Indian master taught him to be an excellent cook, ultimately became attached to him, and made him a present of his freedom. Jean soon afterward engaged on some Spanish vessel as ship's cook, and in the exercise of this calling voyaged considerably in both hemispheres. Finally tiring of the sea, he left his ship at New Orleans, and began life on shore as a cotton-roller. His physical strength gave him considerable advantage above his fellow-blacks; and his employers also discovered that he wielded some peculiar occult influence over the negroes, which made him valuable as an overseer or gang leader. Jean, in short, possessed the mysterious obi power, the existence of which has been recognized in most slave-holding communities, and with which many a West-Indian planter has been compelled by force of circumstances to effect a compromise. Accordingly Jean was permitted many liberties which other blacks, although free, would never have presumed to take. Soon it became rumored that he was a seer of no small powers, and that he could tell the future by the marks upon bales of cotton. I have never been able to learn the details of this queer method of telling fortunes; but Jean became so successful in the exercise of it that thousands of colored people flocked to him for predictions and counsel, and even white people, moved by curiosity or by doubt, paid him to prophesy for them. Finally he became wealthy enough to abandon the levee and purchase a large tract of property on the Bayou Road, where he built a house. His land extended from Prieur Street on the Bayou Road as far as Roman, covering the greater portion of an extensive square, now well built up. In those days it was a marshy green plain, with a few scattered habitations.

At his new home Jean continued the practice of fortune-telling, but combined it with the profession of creole medicine, and of arts still more mysterious. By-and-by his reputation became so great that he was able to demand and obtain immense fees. People of both races and both sexes thronged to see him—many coming even from far-away creole towns in the parishes, and well-dressed women, closely veiled, often knocked at his door. Parties paid from ten to twenty dollars for advice, for herb medicines, for recipes to make the hair grow, for cataplasms supposed to possess mysterious virtues, but really made with scraps of shoe-leather triturated into paste, for advice what ticket to buy in the Havana Lottery, for aid to recover stolen goods, for love powders, for counsel in family troubles, for charms by which to obtain revenge upon an enemy. Once Jean received a fee of fifty dollars for a potion. "It was water," he said to a creole confidant, "with some common herbs boiled in it. I hurt nobody; but if folks want to give me fifty dollars, I take the fifty dollars every time!" His office furniture consisted of a table, a chair, a picture of the Virgin Mary, an elephant's tusk, some shells which he said were African shells and enabled him to read the future, and a pack of cards in each of which a small hole had been burned. About his person he always carried two small bones wrapped around with a black string, which bones he really appeared to revere as fetiches. Wax candles were burned during his performances; and as he bought a whole box of them every few days during "flush times," one can imagine how large the number of his clients must have been. They poured money into his hands so generously that he became worth at least $50,000!

Then, indeed, did this possible son of a Bambara prince begin to live more grandly than any black potentate of Senegal. He had his carriage and pair, worthy of a planter, and his blooded saddle-horse, which he rode well, attired in a gaudy Spanish costume, and seated upon an elaborately decorated Mexican saddle. At home, where he ate and drank only the best—scorning claret worth less than a dollar the *litre*—he continued to find his simple furniture good enough for him; but he had at least fifteen wives—a harem worthy of Boubakar-Segou. White folks might have called them by a less honorific name, but Jean declared them his legitimate spouses according to African ritual. One of the curious features in modern slavery was the ownership of blacks by freedmen of their own color, and these negro slave-holders were usually savage and merciless masters. Jean was not; but it was by right of slave purchase that he obtained most of his wives, who bore him children in great multitude. Finally he managed to woo and win a white woman of the lowest class, who might have been, after a fashion, the Sultana-Validé of this Seraglio. On grand occasions Jean used to distribute largess among the colored population of his neighborhood in the shape of food—bowls of *gombo* or dishes of *jimbalaya*. He did it for popularity's sake in those days, perhaps; but in after-years, during the great epidemics, he did it for charity, even when so much reduced in circumstances that he was himself obliged to cook the food to be given away.

But Jean's greatness did not fail to entail certain cares. He did not know what to do with his money. He had no faith in banks, and had seen too much of the darker side of life to have much faith in human nature. For many years he kept his money under-ground, burying or taking it up at night only, occasionally concealing large sums so well that he could never find them again himself; and now, after many years, people still believe there are treasures entombed somewhere in the neighborhood of Prieur Street and Bayou Road. All business negotiations of a serious character caused him much worry, and as he found many willing to take advantage of his ignorance, he probably felt small remorse for certain questionable actions of his own. He was notoriously bad pay, and part of his property was seized at last to cover a debt. Then, in an evil hour, he asked a man without scruples to teach him how to write, believing that financial misfortunes were mostly due to ignorance of the alphabet. After he had learned to write his name, he was innocent enough one day to place his signature by request at the bottom of a blank sheet of paper, and, lo! his real estate passed from his possession in some horribly mysterious way. Still he had some money left, and made heroic efforts to retrieve his fortunes. He bought other property, and he invested desperately in lottery tickets. The lottery craze finally came upon him, and had far more to do with his ultimate ruin than his losses in the grocery, the shoemaker's shop, and other establishments into which he had put several thousand dollars as the silent partner of people who cheated him. He might certainly have continued to make a good living, since people still sent for him to cure them with his herbs, or went to see him to have their fortunes told; but all his earnings were wasted in tempting fortune. After a score of seizures and a long succession of evictions, he was at last obliged to seek hospitality from some of his numerous children; and of all he had once owned nothing remained to him but his African shells, his elephant's tusk, and the sewing-machine table that had served him to tell fortunes and to burn wax candles upon. Even these, I think, were attached a day or two before his death, which occurred at the house of his daughter by the white wife, an intelligent mulatto with many children of her own.

Jean's ideas of religion were primitive in the extreme. The conversion of the chief tribes of Senegal to Islam occurred in recent years, and it is probable that at the time he was captured by slavers his people were still in a condition little above gross fetichism. If during his years of servitude in a Catholic colony he had imbibed some notions of Romish Christianity, it is certain at least that the Christian ideas were always subordinated to the African—just as the image of the Virgin Mary was used by him merely as an auxiliary fetich in his witchcraft, and was considered as possessing much less power than the "elephant's toof." He was in many respects a humbug; but he may have sincerely believed in the efficacy of certain superstitious rites of his own. He stated that he had a Master whom he was bound to obey; that he could read the will of this Master in the twinkling of the stars; and often of clear nights the neighbors used to watch him standing alone at some street corner staring at the welkin, pulling his woolly beard, and talking in an unknown language to some imaginary being. Whenever Jean indulged in this freak, people knew that he needed money badly, and would probably try to borrow a dollar or two from some one in the vicinity next day.

Testimony to his remarkable skill in the use of herbs could be gathered from nearly every one now living who became well acquainted with him. During the epidemic of 1878, which uprooted the old belief in the total immunity of negroes and colored people from yellow fever, two of Jean's children were "taken down." "I have no money," he said, "but I can cure my children," which he proceeded to do with the aid of some weeds plucked from the edge of the Prieur Street gutters. One of the herbs, I am told, was what our creoles call the "parasol." "The children were playing on the *banquette* next day," said my informant.

Montanet, even in the most unlucky part of his career, retained the superstitious reverence of colored people in all parts of the city. When he made his appearance even on the American side of Canal Street to doctor some sick person, there was always much subdued excitement among the colored folks, who whispered and stared a great deal, but were careful not to raise their voices when they said, "Dar's Hoodoo John!" That an unlettered African slave should have been able to achieve what Jean Bayou achieved in a civilized city, and to earn the wealth and the reputation that he enjoyed during many years of his life, might be cited as a singular evidence of modern popular credulity, but it is also proof that Jean was not an ordinary man in point of natural intelligence.

Harper's Weekly, November 7, 1885

THE LAST OF THE

NEW ORLEANS FENCING-MASTERS

I.

PERHAPS there is no class of citizens of New Orleans—the Marseilles of the western world—about whom so little is generally known as our Spanish element. I do not refer to those numerous West Indian and foreign residents who speak Spanish—Cubans, Manilla-men, Mexicans, Venezuelans, natives of Honduras, etc.—or even to our original Spanish Creoles, descendants of those colonists who have left us few traces of the ancient Spanish domination besides a few solid specimens of

Latin architecture and a few sonorous names by which certain streets and districts are still known. The old Spanish Creole families exist, indeed, but they have become indistinguishable from the French Creoles, whose language, manners and customs they have adopted. The true Spanish element of modern New Orleans is represented by a community of European immigrants, who preserve among them the various customs and dialects of the mother country, and form an association of about three hundred families. They are more numerous than the Greeks, mostly heavy cotton-buyers and wholesale merchants, who have their own church; more numerous than the Portuguese, who have a large benevolent association; but much fewer than the Italians and Sicilians, who control the whole fruit and fish trade, and own fleets of sailing craft and lines of steamers. Yet, for various reasons, the Spaniards are less publicly visible than the other Latins; they live in the less-frequented parts of the city, they pursue special callings, and form special industrial organizations; they have their own trades-unions, their own benevolent associations, their own priests, physicians, and lawyers, and before 1853 they formed an excellent militia corps, the *Cazadores.* This fine body voluntarily disbanded because of the refusal of the governor to permit them to suppress a great anti-Spanish riot, incited by Cuban refugees. The governor wisely preferred to trust the work of suppression to the cooler-blooded and disinterested American militia, justly fearing the consequences of giving rein to the rage of the Spanish soldiery, mostly Asturians, Catalonians, and Biscayans. Since the disbandment of its military organization the Spanish community, though numerically as strong as ever, has almost disappeared from public view.

Whether Catalonians, Biscayans, Gallegos, Asturians, or men from the Balearic Islands, nearly all of these Spaniards are inter-associated as brothers of one order, and Catalan is the prevalent dialect. At their meetings, indeed, Castilian is supposed to be the official tongue; but should any discussion of an exciting nature arise, the speakers involuntarily abandon the precise speech of the *Academia* for the rougher and readier argumentative weapon of dialect.

A great number of these men are in business on their own account; those who are not independent are, for the most part, fresh immigrants or elder sons beginning life; and the trade generally followed is tobacco manufacturing. Many Spaniards own factories. So soon as a young man lays by a certain sum, he marries—usually either a Creole of the poorer class or a European woman, Irish, English, or German—and thus it happens that almost every one of our Spaniards above thirty is the head of a large family.

The New Orleans Spaniard has all the self-reliance, the shrewdness, the economy, and the sobriety of the Italian; he has less patience, perhaps, and is more dangerous to provoke; but strangely enough, crimes of violence are almost unheard of among the Spaniards, while they are fearfully common among our Sicilians, who practice vendetta. Moreover, the Spaniard is rarely found among the criminal classes; if he happens, by some extraordinary chance, to get into trouble, it is because he has used his knife or other weapon, not as a skulking assassin but as an open enemy. Colonel J. A. Fremaux, for many years in command of the second police district, and for many years also captain of the prison, tells me that in all his experience he did not remember a single case of crime among the Spanish immigrants, with the exception of a few assaults made under extreme provocation. In one instance, which appeared at first to form an anomaly, the arrested party proved to be not a Spaniard but a gypsy. Here, as well as elsewhere, the Spaniard is reserved, grave, pacific; but if aroused beyond endurance he becomes a very terrible antagonist. As a rule, he fraternizes with the Creole, but has more or less antipathy for the Cubans and Mexicans, who do not share his patriotism.

There are few Spanish houses in the antiquated portions of the city where a visitor will not observe a certain portrait or photograph—the likeness of a vigorous, keen-eyed man, with a slightly curved nose, long firm lips, facial muscles singularly developed, and a fair beard having that peculiar curl in it which is said to indicate a powerful constitution. The face is a very positive one, though not harsh, and the more you observe it the more its expression pleases. If you should happen to visit a Spanish home in which the photograph is not visible, it is more than probable that it is treasured away in the *armoire* or somewhere else; it has become one of the Spanish *penates*. But a few years ago it was an even more familiar object in Havana, perhaps also in far Madrid; and the Havanese soldiery, the *voluntarios*, the loyalists, the Spanish ladies, were eagerly purchasing copies at the rate of two *pesos* per copy. Thousands upon thousands were placed in Cuban parlors. Still, the original of that picture, photograph, or engraving (for the likeness of the man has been reproduced in many ways) is not a prince, a diplomat, or a soldier, but a private citizen of New Orleans, a member of our Spanish community. His face is now seldom seen on Canal Street, but he is still a very active and vigorous man, despite his three-score and ten years. He is a hero, and a titled hero who won his fame by sole virtue of those qualities named in enamel upon the golden cross he is privileged to wear: *Virtus et Honor*—"*Virtus*," of course, with the good old Roman signification of the word, which is valor.

II.

SEÑOR Don José Llulla, or Pepe Llulla, as he is more affectionately styled by his admirers, is a person whose name has become legendary even in his life-time. While comparatively few are intimate with him, for he is a reserved man, there is scarcely a citizen who does not know him by name, and hardly a New Orleans urchin who could not tell you that "Pepe Llulla is a great duelist who has a cemetery of his own." Although strictly true, this information is apt to create a false impression of some connection between Pepe's duels and Pepe's necropolis; the fact being that none of his enemies repose in the Louisa-street Cemetery, which he owns, and that he has never killed enough men to fill a solitary vault. There is, in short, no relationship between the present and the past occupations of the cemetery proprietor; but before speaking of the former, I may attempt to give a brief outline of the career of this really extraordinary character who won his way to fortune and to fame by rare energy and intrepidity.

Pepe was born near Port Mahon, capital of Minorca, one of those Balearic Islands whose inhabitants were celebrated in antiquity for their skill in the use of missile-weapons, and have passed under so many dominations—Carthaginian, Roman, Vandal, Moorish, Spanish, French, and English. His own uncommon dexterity in the use of arms, however, does not appear due to any physical inheritance from ancient Balearic fore-fathers, as he traces back his family to a Moorish origin. This assertion, in view of Pepe's chestnut hair and bluish-grey eyes, would seem untenable unless we reflect that those desert horse-men who first invaded Spain in the cause of Islam were mostly Berbers, kindred of the strange nomads who still preserve their fair skins and blue eyes under the sun of the Sahara—the "Veiled People," who are known afar off by their walk, "long and measured, like the stride of the ostrich." I can not say that Pepe is really a Berber; but he possesses physical characteristics which harmonize well with the descriptions in Henri Du-veyrier's "*Les Touareg du Nord*;" and Southern Louisiana is full of surprises for the ethnographer. The photograph, which obtained so much celebrity, was taken more than fifteen years ago, and Pepe has but slightly changed since then. He is only a little grayer and remains very erect, agile, and elastic in his movements; a man about the average height, rather vigorously than powerfully built. He attributes his excellent physical pre-servation to his life-long abstinence. No liquor ever passed his lips, and his nerves still retain the steadiness of youth.

Pepe's imagination was greatly impressed during early boy-hood by the recitals of sailors who used to visit his father's home at Port Mahon; and his passion for the sea became so strong as he grew older that it required constant vigilance to keep him from joining some ship's crew by stealth. Finally, when an American captain—John Conkling, of Baltimore, I believe—made known in Port Mahon that he wanted an intelligent Spanish lad on his vessel, Pepe's parents deemed it best to allow their son to ship as cabin-boy. He remained several years with the Captain, who became attached to him, and attempted to send him to a school to study navigation, in the hope of making a fine sailor of him. But the boy found himself unable to endure the constraints of study, ran away and shipped as a common seaman. He went with whalers to the antarctic zone, and with slavers to the West African coast, and, after voyaging in all parts of the world, entered the service of some merchant company whose vessels plied between New Orleans and Havana. At last he resolved to abandon the sea, and to settle in New Orleans in the employ of a Spaniard named Biosca, proprietor of a ball-room and *café*. Being a very sinewy, determined youth, Pepe was intrusted with the hazardous duty of maintaining order; and, after a few unpleasant little experiences, the disorderly element of the time recognized they had found a master, and the peace of Biosca's establishment ceased to be disturbed.

Pepe soon began to visit the popular fencing-schools of New Orleans. He was already a consummate master in the use of the knife (what thorough Spaniard is not?) but he soon astonished the best *tireurs* by his skill with the foils.

At that time fencing was a fashionable amusement. It was the pride of a Creole gentleman to be known as a fine swordsman. Most of the Creole youths educated in Paris had learned the art under great masters; but even these desired to maintain their skill by frequent visits to the *salles d'armes* at home. Indeed, fencing was something more than a mere amusement; it was almost a necessity. In New Orleans, as in Paris, the passions of society were regulated if not restrained by the duel; and the sword was considered the proper weapon with which gentlemen should settle certain disputes. But the custom of dueling prevailed in New Orleans to an extent unparalleled in France since the period of the Revolution. Creole society in Louisiana was an aristocratic and feudal organization based upon slavery. Planters and merchants lived and reigned like princes; the habit of command and the pride of power developed characters of singular inflexibility; passions, tropicalized under this strong sun of ours, assumed a violence unknown in calmer France, and the influences of combined wealth and leisure aided to ferment them. Three or four duels a day were common; this number was often exceeded; and young men seemed anxious to fight for the mere ferocious pleasure of fighting. A friend tells me this queer reminiscence of the old *régime*: "A party of young Creoles, slightly flushed with wine, are returning from an evening entertainment. The night is luminous and warm; the air perfumed with breath of magnolias; the sward is smooth, level, springy as an English turf. Suddenly one of the party stops, feels the sod with his foot, and, leaping nearly to his own height, vociferates, '*Quel lieu pour se battre!*' (What a place for a fight!) His enthusiasm proves contagious; a comrade proposes that the party shall take all possible advantage of the situation. Sword-play begins, at first jestingly; then some fencer loses his temper, and the contest all at once becomes terribly earnest, to end only with the death of several participants."

The demand for fencing-masters was amply supplied by foreigners and also by some local experts, *maîtres d'armes* whose names are now remembered only by a very few venerable citizens. The most celebrated were L'Alouette, an Alsatian; Montiasse, also an Alsatian and Napoleonic veteran; Cazères, of Bordeaux; Baudoin, of Paris; the two brothers Rosière, of Marseilles; Dauphin, a famous expert (killed at last in a shot-gun duel which he had recklessly provoked). Behind these fading figures of the past, three darker ghosts appear: Black Austin, a free negro, who taught the small-sword; Robert Séverin, a fine mulatto, afterward killed in Mexico, and Basile Croquère (I am not sure that I spell the name correctly), also a mulatto, and the most remarkable colored swordsman of Louisiana. Those of my readers who have not seen Vigeant's beautiful little book, "*Un Maître d'Armes sous la Restauration*," may perhaps be surprised to learn that the founder of the modern French school of swordsmanship, and the greatest swordsman of his century, was a mulatto of San Domingo, that famous Jean Louis, who in one terrible succession of duels, occupying only forty minutes, killed or disabled thirteen master-fencers of that Italian army pressed into service by Napoleon for his Peninsular campaign.

III.

IT was under L'Alouette that Pepe principally studied; and the fencing-master, finding after a time that his pupil excelled him, appointed him his *prevôt* or assistant. In a succession of subsequent encounters the young man proved that, though he might have one or two rivals with the foils, he had no real superior among the *maîtres d'armes.* Then he began to study the use of other varieties of weapons; the saber, with which he became the most expert perhaps in the South; the broad-sword, with which he afterward worsted more than one accomplished English teacher. With the foil, which is only a training weapon and allows of a closer play, fine fencers have been able to make some good points with him; but with the rapier or small sword he was almost invulnerable. With fire-arms his skill was not less remarkable. Pepe's friends were accustomed to hold a dollar in their fingers or a pipe between their teeth for him to shoot at. Twenty years ago he would often balance an egg on the head of his little son, and invariably break the shell with a Colt-ball at the distance of thirty paces; with a rifle he seldom failed to hit any small object tossed in the air, such as a ball, a cork, or a coin.

L'Alouette and his pupil became very warm friends; their intimacy was only once chilled by an unfortunate incident. At a time when the bowie-knife was still a novel arm in New Orleans, L'Alouette insisted upon a public contest with Llulla, the weapons to be wooden bowies with hickory blades. Pepe had no equal, however, in the use of a knife of any sort; and L'Alouette, finding himself repeatedly touched and never able to make a point, lost his temper and made a violent assault on the young Spaniard, who, parrying the thrust, countered so heavily that the fencing-master was flung senseless to the floor with two ribs fractured. But the friendship of the two men was renewed before long, and continued until L'Alouette's death several years later. Llulla, in whose arms he died, succeeded him as a teacher, not only of fencing, but also of the use of fire-arms. He did not, indeed, teach the knife, but he has often given surprising proofs of his skill with it. A gentleman who is quite expert with most weapons, told me that after having succeeded in persuading Pepe to have a sham contest with him only a few years ago, he received the point of Pepe's mock weapon directly in the hollow of his throat almost at the very first pass, and was repeatedly struck in the same place during five or six vain efforts to make a point. None of the serious contests in which Pepe has engaged lasted more than a few moments; he generally disabled his adversary at the very outset of the encounter.

Although remunerative in those days, the profession of fencing-master did not suit Llulla's energetic character. He kept his *salle d'armes*, but hired assistants, and only devoted so much of his own time to teaching as could be spared from more practical duties. He had already laid down the foundation of his fortune, had brought out from Minorca his mother and brother, had married, and commenced to do business on his own account. Few men have attempted as many different things as he has with equal success. He built slaughter-houses and speculated in cattle; he bought up whole fleets of flatboats and sold the material for building purposes (working all day up to his waist in water, and never getting sick in consequence); he bought land on the other side of the river and built cottages upon it; he built a regular Spanish bull-ring and introduced bull-fights; he bought a saw-mill and made it pay, and finally purchased the Louisa-street cemeteries, after accumulating a capital of probably several hundred thousand dollars. During the war he remained faithful to the Union, declaring that he could not violate his oath of allegiance to the *United* States. After the war he bought the island of Grande Terre, in the Gulf (excepting, of course, the government reservation on which Fort Livingston and the Barataria Light-house are situated) a wild, wind-swept place, to which cattle from neighboring islands sometimes swim in spite of the sharks. In summer it is a fine pleasure resort for sea-bathers, and Pepe could never wholly separate himself from the sea.

During all those years Pepe kept his fencing-school, but rather as a recreation than as a money-making establishment. He is now the last of the old fencing-masters, and although he has practically retired from public life will not refuse to instruct (*gratis*) pupils introduced to him by personal friends. For nearly half a century he was the confidant and trainer of New Orleans duellists, and figured as second in more than a hundred encounters. The duello is now almost obsolete in the South; and Creole New Orleans is yielding in this respect to the influences of Americanization. It is fully three years since Pepe's services were last called into requisition.

While his formidable reputation as an expert often secured him against difficulties and dangers to which another in his position would have been exposed, it did not save him from the necessity of having some twenty or more affairs of his own. In half a score of these affairs his antagonists weakened at the last moment, either apologizing on the field or failing to appear at all, and that only after having attempted to take every advantage attached to their privilege of the choice of weapons. One individual proposed to fight with poniards in a dark room; another with knives inside a sugar hogshead; another wanted a duel with Colt revolvers, each of the principals to hold one end of the same pocket-handkerchief; another proposed that lots should be drawn for two pistols—one empty, the other loaded;

and a Cuban, believing no such weapons procurable in New Orleans, proposed to fight with *machétes*; but, to the horror of the man, Pepe forthwith produced two *machétes*, and proposed to settle the difficulty then and there, a proposal which resulted in the Cuban's sudden disappearance. Only once was Pepe partly thwarted by a proposition of this sort, when some Havanese filibuster proposed that both principals and witnesses should "fight with poisoned pills," lots to be drawn for the pills. Pepe was willing, but the seconds declared they would not take the pills or permit them to be taken. Several of Llulla's duels were undertaken in behalf of friends, while he was actually acting in the *rôle* of second only, and when one of the principals could not fulfill the duties of the moment. On a certain occasion the second of the opposite side, who was a German fencing-master, declared his principal in no condition to fight, and volunteered to take his place. "We accept," replied Llulla instantly, "but in that case you shall deal, not with my principal but with me!" Ten seconds later the German lay on the ground with a severely gashed arm and both lungs transpierced. It was seldom, however, that Pepe cared to wound an antagonist so severely; and although he has had duels or difficulties with men of most European nationalities, only two men died at his hands, after having placed him under the necessity of killing or of being killed. In none of his duels, even at the time when the duel regulated society, was he actuated by other motives than friendship or pride; and the only gift he would ever accept from the man whose part he assumed, was a weapon of some sort. But his admirers have treated him so well in this respect that he now possesses a perfect arsenal, including all kinds, not only of swords but of rifles, pistols, revolvers, poniards, cutlasses, etc., which forms quite a curiosity in itself. Since the war Pepe has had no personal difficulties, except those assumed in the cause of Spanish patriotism; but these affairs first made him really famous, and form the most interesting incidents of his singular career.

IV.

AFTER having long been the headquarters of the Cuban filibusters, New Orleans was violently convulsed, in 1853, by the fate of the Lopez expedition, and serious outbreaks occurred, for the results of which the Spanish government subsequently demanded and obtained satisfaction from the United States. It was Pepe Llulla who at that time saved the Spanish Consul's life, by getting him out of the city safely to the plantation of a compatriot. Pepe's own life was then menaced; and though none ventured to attack him in broad daylight, his determination and courage alone saved him from several night-attempts at assassination. After the Lopez riots the anti-Spanish fury died down to be revived again in 1869 by another Cuban tragedy. But in 1869 the United States garrison was strong, and there was no serious rioting. The rage of the Cuban revolutionaries vented itself only in placards, in sanguinary speeches, in cries of *Death to Spain!* and in a few very petty outrages upon defenseless Spaniards. Pepe Llulla challenged one of the authors of the outrages, who, failing to accept, was placarded publicly as a coward.

Then he resolved to take up the cause of Spain in his own person, and covered the city with posters in English, in French, and in Spanish, challenging all Cuban revolutionaries, either in the West Indies or the United States. This challenge was at first accepted by a number, but seemingly by men who did not know the character of Llulla, for these Cuban champions failed to come to time, a few declaring they respected Pepe too much to fight him; yet at the same time a number of efforts were made to assassinate him—some by men who seemed to cross the Gulf for no other purpose. Fortunately for himself Pepe has always proved an uncommonly hard man to kill; moreover, he had become so accustomed to this sort of danger that it was almost impossible to catch him off his guard. Even gangs bold enough to enter his house or place of business had been terribly handled; and a party of seven drunken soldiers who once attempted to wreck his establishment left five of their number *hors de combat*, felled by an iron bar. Again, a Mexican, who had hidden behind a door to attack Llulla with a knife, had his weapon wrested from him and was severely beaten for his pains. The Cuban emissaries and others fared no better in 1869. Two men, who concealed themselves in the cemetery at dusk, were unexpectedly confronted with Pepe's pistols, and ordered to run for their lives, which they proceeded to do most expeditiously, leaping over tombs and climbing over walls in their panic. Another party of ruffians met the Spaniard at his own door in the middle of the night, and were ingloriously routed. Once more, hearing that a crowd of rowdies were collecting in the neighborhood after dark with the intention of proceeding to his house, Llulla went out and attacked them single-handed, scattering them in all directions.

At last the Cubans found a champion to oppose to the redoubtable Pepe, an Austrian ex-officer who had entered the Cuban revolutionary service, a soldier of fortune, but a decidedly brave and resolute man. He was a good swordsman, but considering the formidable reputation of his antagonist, chose the pistol as a weapon more likely to equalize the disparity between the two men. The conditions were thirty paces, to advance and fire at will. When the word of command was given, the Spaniard remained motionless as a statue, his face turned away from his antagonist; while the Austrian, reserving his fire, advanced upon him with measured strides. When within a short distance of Llulla he raised his arm to fire, and at that instant the Spaniard, wheeling suddenly, shot him through both lungs. The Austrian was picked up, still breathing, and lingered some months before he died. His fate probably deterred others from following his example, as the Cubans found no second champion.

The spectacle of a solitary man thus defying the whole Cuban revolution, bidding all enemies of Spain to fight or hold their peace, evoked ardent enthusiasm both among the loyalists of Cuba and the Spaniards of New Orleans. Pepe soon found himself surrounded by strong sympathizers, ready to champion the same cause; and telegrams began to pour in from Spaniards in Cuba and elsewhere, letters of congratulation also, and salutations from grandees. There is something particularly graceful and sympathetic in Spanish praise; and in reading those now faded missives, hung up in pretty frames upon the walls of Pepe's dwelling, I could not help feeling myself some of the generous enthusiasm that breathed in them: *"Felicitamos cordialmente y afectuosamente al pundonoroso y valiente Señor Llulla; ofriciendole, si necessario fuere, nuestras vidas"* (*Voluntarios de Artilleria*). . . . *"Los Voluntarios de Cardenas admiran y abrazan al valiente Señor Llulla"* (*El Comandante La*

Casa). . . . "Felicitamos al Señor Llulla por su noble, generosa, y patriotica conducta, ofriciendole nuestra coöperacion en todos tiempos y lugares."

Such telegrams came fluttering in daily like Havanese butterflies, and solicitations for Pepe's photograph were made and acceeded to, and pictures of him were sold by thousands in the streets of the great West Indian City. Meanwhile the Cubans held their peace, as bidden. And then came from Madrid a letter of affectionate praise, sealed with the royal seal, and signed with the regent's name, Don Francisco Serrano y Dominguez, el Regente del Reino, and with this letter the Golden Cross of the Order of Charles III (*Carlos Tercero*), and a document conferring knighthood, *libre de gastos*, upon the valiant son who had fought so well for Spain in far-away Louisiana.

But I have yet to mention the most exquisite honor of all. Trust a Spanish heart to devise a worthy reward for what it loves and admires! From Havana came one day a dainty portrait of Pepe Llulla worked seemingly in silk, and surrounded by what appeared to be a wreath of laurels in the same black silk, and underneath, in black letters upon a gold ground, the following honorific inscription: "A Don Jose Llulla, Decidido Sostenedor de la Honra Nacional entre los Traidores de New Orleans." But that woven black silk was the silk of woman's hair, the lustrous hair of Spanish ladies who had cut off their tresses to wreathe his portrait with! It hangs in the old man's parlor near the portrait of his dead son, the handsome boy who graduated at West Point with honors, and when I beheld it and understood it, the delicious grace of that gift touched me like the discovery of some new and unsuspected beauty in human nature.

Southern Bivouac, November 1886

LETTERS

To Henry Edward Krehbiel

NEW ORLEANS, 1877

"O-me-taw-Boodh!"

Have I not indeed been much bewitched by thine exotic comedy, which hath the mild perfume and yellow beauty of a Chinese rose? Assuredly I have been enchanted by the Eastern fragrance of thy many-colored brochure; for mine head "is not as yellow as mud." In thy next epistle, however, please to enlighten my soul in regard to the mystic title-phrase,— "Remodeled from the original English;" for I have been wearing out the iron shoes of patience in my vain endeavor to comprehend it. What I most desired, while perusing the play, was that I might have been able to hear the musical interludes,—the barbaric beauty of the melodies,—and the plaintive sadness of thy serpent-skinned instruments. I shall soon return the MSS. to thy hands.

By the by, did you ever hear a *real* Chinese gong? I don't mean a d——d hotel gong; but one of those great moon-disks of yellow metal which have so terrible a power of utterance. A gentleman in Bangor, North Wales, who had a private museum of South Pacific and Chinese curiosities exhibited one to me. It was hanging amidst Fiji spears, beautifully barbed with sharks' teeth, which, together with grotesque New Zealand clubs of green stone and Sandwich Is.d paddles wrought with the baroque visages of the Shark-God, were depending from the walls. Also there were Indian elephants in ivory, carrying balls in their carven bellies, each ball containing many other balls inside it. The gong glimmered pale and huge and yellow, like the moon rising over a Southern swamp. My friend tapped its ancient face with a muffled drumstick, and it commenced to sob, like waves upon a low beach. He tapped it again, and it moaned like the wind in a mighty forest of pines. Again; and it commenced to roar; and with each tap the roar grew deeper and deeper, till it seemed like thunder rolling over an abyss in the Cordilleras, or the crashing of Thor's chariot wheels. It was awful, and astonishing as awful. I assure you I did not laugh at it at all. It impressed me as something terrible and mysterious. I vainly sought to understand how that thin, thin disk of trembling metal could produce so frightful a vibration. He informed me that it was very expensive, being chiefly made of the most precious metals,—silver and gold.

Let me give you a description of my new residence. I never knew what the beauty of an old Creole palace was until now. I do not believe one could find anything more picturesque outside of Venice or Florence. For six months I had been trying to get a room in one of these curious buildings; but the rents seemed to me maliciously enormous. However I at last obtained one for $3 per week. Yet it is on the third floor, rear building;—these old princes of the South built always double-edifices, covering an enormous space of ground, with broad wings, court yards, and slave quarters.

The building is on St. Louis Street, a street several hundred years old. I enter by a huge Roman archway, about a hundred feet long,—full of rolling echoes, and commencing to become verdant with a thin growth of bright moss. At the end, the archway opens into a vast court. There are a few graceful bananas here with their giant leaves splitting in ribbons in the summer sun, so that they look like young palms. Lord! how the carriages must have thundered under that archway and through the broad paved court in the old days. The stables are here still; but the blooded horses are gone, and the family carriage, with its French coat-of-arms, has disappeared. There is only a huge wagon left to crumble to pieces. A hoary dog, sleeps like a stone sphinx, at a corner of the broad stairway; and I fancy that in his still slumbers he might be dreaming of a Creole master who went out with Beauregard or Lee, and never came back again. Wonder if the great grey hound is waiting for him.

The dog never notices me. I am not of his generation, and I creep quietly by lest I might disturb his dreams of the dead South. I go up the huge stairway. At every landing, a vista of broad archways reechoes my steps—archways that once led to rooms worthy of a prince. But the rooms are now cold and cheerless and vast with emptiness. Tinted in pale green or yellow, with a ceiling moulded with Renaissance figures in plaster, the ghost of luxury and wealth seems trying to linger in them. I pass them by, and taking my way through an archway on the right, find myself in a broad piazza, at the end of which is my room.

It is vast enough for a Carnival ball. Five windows and glass doors open flush with the floor and rise to the ceiling. They open on two sides upon the piazza, whence I have a far view of tropical gardens and towering masses of building, half-ruined and ivy eaten, but still magnificent. The walls are tinted pale orange color; green curtains drape the doors and windows; and the mantel piece, surmounted by a long oval mirror of Venetian pattern, is of white marble, veined like the bosom of a Naiad. In the center of the huge apartment, rises a bed as massive as a fortress, with tremendous columns of carved mahogany, supporting a curtained canopy at the height of sixteen feet. It seems to touch the ceiling, yet it does not. There is no carpet on the floor, no pictures on the wall,—a sense of something dead and lost fills the place with a gentle melancholy;— the breezes play fantastically with the pallid curtains, and the breath of flowers ascends into the chamber from the verdant gardens below. O, the silence of this house, the perfume, and the romance of it. A beautiful young Frenchwoman appears once a day in my neighborhood to arrange the room;—but she comes like a ghost and disappears too soon in the vast recesses of the awful house. I would like to speak with her;—for her lips drop honey, and her voice is richly sweet like the cooing of a dove. "O my dove, that art in the clefts of the rock, in the secret hiding places of the stairs, let me see thy face, let me hear thy voice; for thy voice is sweet and thy countenance is comely!"

Let me tell thee, O Bard of the Harp of a Thousand Strings, concerning a Romance of Georgia. I heard of it among the flickering shadow of steamboat smoke, and the flapping of sluggish sails. It has a hero, greater, I think, than Bludso; but his name is lost. At least it is lost in Southern history; yet perhaps it may be recorded on the pages of a great book, whose leaves never turn yellow with Time, and whose letters are eternal as the stars. But the reason his name is not known is because he was a "d—d nigger."

The war was just over, and the Confederacy writhing its life out under the crushing heel of the North. Fugitives from the South, were seeking the sea-coast, and negroes the far North as a haven of freedom and indolent rest. "Freedom" meant to their childish mind, an infinite plantation, where it was never too hot, where nobody had any work to do, where everybody had plenty to eat and to drink like the king-planters of the South, and where the Government watched over her black children like God the Father "leaning over his Eternity."

So it happened that the General Throop was steaming up the Savannah River one burning day like a white palace, with her cabin full of Confederate fugitives and her hold full of cotton, and negroes going to that vague and phantom thing called "freedom in the North," to seek new houses, and to kiss the hand of President Lincoln,—not knowing that Lincoln was lying in awful state, with a whole nation mourning for him at that very moment.

Well they never saw "Massr' Abe Linkum" even in the solemnity of his last sleep; for the Throop burst into a sheet of flame long before nearing her destination. The cotton took fire, and the white timber withered and vanished like dry leaves in the fierce heat.

Some leaped in the river; some rushed out to the guards of the boat. These were whites. The poor black creatures below never went to "freedom in the North;" but perhaps they did find freedom on a fairer plantation than the Southern sun ever shone upon, where there were no overseers, and no cotton-picking under the blistering noon-day, and a Government which takes better care of them than even the dead President could ever have done.

The Captain and engineers deserted the vessel: there was a panic of selfish and furious men. One man kept to his post. He was not a white man; but a d—d nigger,—a "yaller feller" from Georgy. He was a free mulatto. He was the Pilot.

The Pilot stuck to his post, and to his wheel. The smoke rolled up like the night, and the flames flickered through it like lightning; but he held on bravely. The wood roof of the pilot house caught the flame, the glass shivered and the frames of the windows burned, the blazing embers rained in upon him; but he said nothing and kept his position.

He was heading her into the bank, where the land was low and the groves bowed down under their ragged garments of moss. His eyes were on the Georgia shore. A few more strokes of the engines would bring her in to the landing. Below men shouted madly to him to leap for his life; but he never heard them.

Suddenly the engines ceased to pant; their iron hearts were broken in the great heat. The cords of the tiller vanished; and the wheel turned helplessly in the Pilot's hands. But he had brought her in to the bank, and three-score souls were saved.

"And as for the Pilot," said my friend, one of the saved, "I think I was the last to see him. I watched him in the very embrace of the flames, as it seemed to me, holding on to the wheel. Against the bright glare, he seemed like a Statue of Bronze. I saw him at last fold his arms and wait. The Pilot-house rocked and trembled and fell with a crash into the hell below. When I looked up again, the Statue was gone."

L. Hearn

To Henry Edward Krehbiel

NEW ORLEANS, 1878

My dear Musician:

I wrote you such a shabby disjointed letter last week that I feel I ought to make up for it,—especially after your newsy, fresh pleasant letter to me, which came like a cool Northern breeze speaking of life, energy, success, and strong hopes.

I am very much ashamed that I have not yet been able to keep all my promises to you. There is that Creole music I had hoped to get copied by Saturday & could not succeed in obtaining. But it is only delayed, I assure you; and New Orleans is going to produce a treat for you soon. George Cabell, a charming writer, some of whose dainty N. Orleans stories you may have read in Scribner's monthly, is writing a work containing a study of Creole music, in which the songs are given, with the musical text in footnotes. I have helped Cabell a little in collecting the songs; but he has the advantage of me in being able to write music by ear. Scribner will publish the volume. This is not, of course, for publicity.

My new journalistic life may interest you,—it is so different from anything in the North. I have at last succeeded in getting right into the fantastic heart of the French quarter, where I hear the antiquated dialect all day long. Early in the morning I visit a restaurant, where I devour a plate of figs, a cup of black coffee, a dish of cream-cheese—not the northern stuff, but a delightful cake of pressed milk floating in cream,—a couple of corn muffins, and an egg. This is a heavy breakfast here; but costs only about twenty five cents. Then I slip down to the office, and rattle off a couple of leaders on literary or European matters, and a few paragraphs based on telegraphic news. This occupies about an hour. Then the country papers,—half French, half-English,—altogether barbarous, come in from all the wild, untamed parishes of Louisiana. Madly I seize the scissors and the paste-pot, and construct a column of crop-notes. This occupies about half an hour. Then the New York dailies make their appearance. I devour their substance, and take notes for the ensuing day's expression of opinion. And then the work is o'er; and the long golden afternoon welcomes me forth to enjoy its perfume and its laziness. It would be a delightful existence for one without ambition or hope of better things. On Saturday the brackish Lake Pontchartrain, offers the attraction of a long swim; and I like to avail myself of it. Swimming in the Mississippi is dangerous on account of great fierce fish, the alligator-gars, which attack a swimmer with ferocity. An English swimmer was bitten by one only the other day in the river, and losing his presence of mind, was swept under a barge and drowned.

Folks here tell me now that I have been sick, I have nothing more to fear, and will soon be acclimatized. If acclimatization signifies becoming a bundle of sharp bones and saddle-colored parchment, I have no doubt of it at all. It is considered dangerous here to drink much water in summer. For 5 cents, one can get half-a-bottle of strong claret, and this you mix with your drinking water, squeezing a lemon into it. Limes are better, but harder to get,—you can only buy them when schooners come in from the Gulf-islands. But no one knows how delicious lemonade can be made, until he has tasted lemonade made of limes.

I saw a really pleasing study for an artist this morning. A friend accompanied me to the French market, and we bought an enormous quantity of figs for about 15¢. We could not half-finish them; and we sought rest under the cool waving shadow of a eunuch banana tree in the Square. As I munched and munched a half-naked boy ran by,—a fellow that would have charmed Murillo, with a skin like a new cent in color, and heavy masses of hair, massed as tastefully as if sculptured in ebony. I threw a fig at him and hit him in the back. He ate it; and coolly walked toward us with his little bronze hands turned upward and opened to their fullest capacity, and a pair of great black eyes flashed a request for more. You never saw such a pair of eyes,—deep and dark, a night without a moon. Spoke to him in English,—no answer; in French,—no response. My friend bounced him with *Spak-ne Italiano*, or something of that kind, but it was no good. We asked him by signs where he came from; and he pointed to a rakish lugger rocking at the Picayune tier. I filled his little brown hands with figs; but he did not smile. He gravely thanked us with a flash of the eye like the gleam of a black opal, and murmured "Ah, mille gratias, Señor." Why that boy *was* Murillo's boy after all, in propria persona. He departed to the rakish lugger and we dreamed of Moors and gipsies under the emasculated banana.

L Hearn.

To Henry Edward Krehbiel

NEW ORLEANS, 1878

My dear Krehbiel:

That I should have been able even by a suggestion to have been of any use to us is a great pleasure. Your information in regard to Père Rouquette interested me. The Father—the last of the Blackrobe Fathers—is at present with his beloved Indians at Ravine-les-Cannes; but I will see him on his return, and read your letter to the good old soul. If the columns of a good periodical were open to me, I should write the romance of his life—such a wild strange life—inspired by the magical writings of Chateaubriand in the commencement; and latterly devoted to a strangely beautiful religion of his own—not only the poetic religion of *Atala* and *Les Natchez*; but that Religion of the Wilderness which flies to solitude, and hath no other temple than the vault of Heaven itself, painted with the frescoes of the clouds, and illumined by the trembling tapers of God's everlasting altar, the stars of the firmament.

I have received circular and organ-talk. You are right, I am convinced in your quotation of St. Jerome. Today I send you the book—an old copy I had considerable difficulty in coaxing from the owner. It will be of use to you chiefly by reason of the curious list of writers on mediæval and antique music quoted at the end of the volume.

If you do not make a successful volume of your instructive Talks, something dreadful ought to happen to you,—*especially as Cincinnati has now a musical school in which children will have to learn something about music.* You are the Professor of Musical History at that College. Your work is a work of instruction for the young. As the Professor of that College, you should be able to make it a success. This is a suggestion. I know you are not a wire-puller—couldn't be if you tried; but I want to see those talks put to good use, and made profitable to the writer, and you have friends who should be able to do that I think.

Your friend is right, no doubt, about the
>"Tig, tig, malaboin
>　　La chelema che tango,
>　　　Redjoum!"

I asked my black nurse what it meant. She only laughed and shook her head,—"Mais c'est Voudoo, ça; je n'en sais rien!" "Well," said I, "don't you know anything about Voudoo songs?" "*Yes*," she answered, "*I know Voudoo songs; but I can't tell you what they mean.*" And she broke out into the wildest, weirdest ditty I ever heard. I tried to write down the words; but as I did not know what they meant I had to write by sound alone, spelling the words according to the French pronunciation:

>Yo so dan godo
>　Héru mandé
>Yo so dan godo
>　Héru mandé
>　Héru mandé.
>Tig à la papa
>　Ha Tinguoaiée

> Tig à la papa
>   Ha Tinguoaiée
>   Ha Tinguoaiée
>   Ha Tinguoaiée

I have undertaken a project which I hardly hope to succeed in, but which I feel some zeal regarding,—viz: to collect the Creole legends, traditions, and songs of Louisiana. Unfortunately I shall never be able to do this thoroughly without money,—plenty of money—but I can do a good deed, perhaps.

I must also tell you that I find Spanish remarkably easy to acquire; and believe that at the end of another year I shall be able to master it,—write it and speak it well. To do the latter, however, I shall be obliged to spend some time in some part of the Spanish American colonies,—whither my thoughts have been turned for some time. With a good knowledge of three languages, I can prosecute my wanderings over the face of the earth without timidity,—without fear of starving to death after each migration.

After all, it has been lucky for me that I was obliged to quit hard newspaper work; for it has afforded me opportunities for self-improvement which I could not otherwise have acquired. I should like indeed, to make more money; but one must sacrifice something in order to study, and I must not grumble, as long as I can live while learning.

I have really given up all hope of creating anything while I remain here, or, indeed until my conditions shall have altered and my occupation changed.

What material I can glean here, from this beautiful and legendary land,—this land of perfume and of dreams—must be chiseled into shape elsewhere.

One cannot write of these beautiful things while surrounded by them; and by an atmosphere, heavy and drowsy as that of a conservatory. It must be afterward, in times to come, when I shall find myself in some cold, bleak land, where I shall dream regretfully of the graceful palms; the swamp groves, weird in their ragged robes of moss; the golden ripples of the cane-fields under the summer wind, and this divine sky—deep and vast and cloudless as Eternity, with its far-off horizon tint of tender green.

I do not wonder the South has produced nothing of literary art. Its beautiful realities fill the imagination to repletion. It is regret and desire and the Spirit of Unrest that provoketh poetry and romance. It is the North, with its mists and fogs, and its gloomy sky haunted by a fantastic and ever-changing panorama of clouds, which is the Land of Imagination and Poetry.

———

The fever is dying. A mighty wind, boisterous and cool lifted the poisonous air from the city at last.

I cannot describe to you the peculiar effect of the summer upon one unacclimated. You feel as though you were breathing a drugged atmosphere. You find the very whites of your eyes turning yellow with biliousness. The least overindulgence in eating or drinking prostrates you. My feeling all through the time of the epidemic was about this: I have the fever-principle in my blood,—it shows its presence in a hundred ways,—if the machinery of the body gets the least out of order, the fever will get me down. I was not afraid of serious consequences, but I felt conscious that nothing but strict attention to the laws of health would pull me through. The experience has been valuable. I believe I could now live in Havana or Vera Cruz without fear of the terrible fevers which prevail there. Do you know that even here we have no less than eleven different kinds of fever,—most of which know the power of killing?

———

I am very glad winter is coming, to lift the languors of the air and restore some energy to us. The summer is not like that north. At the north you have a clear, dry, burning air; here it is clear also, but dense, heavy and so moist that it is never so hot as you have it. But no one dares expose himself to the vertical sun. I have noticed that even the chickens and the domestic animals, dogs, cats, etc., always seek shady places. They fear the sun. People with valuable horses will not work them much in summer. They die very rapidly of sunstroke.

In winter, too, one feels content. There is no nostalgia. But the summer always brings with it to me,—always has, and I suppose always will,—a curious and vague species of home-sickness, as if I had friends in some country far off—where I had not been for so long that I have forgotten even their names and the appellations of the places where they live. I hope it will be so next summer, that I can go whither the humor leads me,—the propensity which the author of the Howadji in Syria calleth the Spirit of the Camel.

But this is a land where one can really enjoy the Inner Life; —every one has an inner life of his own,—which no other eye can see, and the great secrets of which are never revealed;— although occasionally when we create something beautiful, we betray a faint glimpse of it—sudden and brief, as of a door opening and shutting in the night. I suppose you have such a life, too,—a double existence—a dual entity. Are we not all doppelgangers?—and is not the invisible the only life we really enjoy?

————

You may remember I described this house to you as haunted-looking. It is delicious therefore to find out that it is actually a haunted house. But the ghosts do not trouble me; I have become so much like one of themselves in my habits. There is one room, however, where no one likes to be alone; for phantom hands clap, and phantom feet stamp behind them. "And what does that signify?" I asked a servant. "Ça veut dire, *Foutez-moi le camp*"—a vulgar Creole expression for "Git!"

————

There is to be a *literary* (God save the mark!) newspaper here. I have been asked to help edit it. As I find that I can easily attend to both papers I shall scribble and scrawl and sell 'em translations which I could not otherwise dispose of. Thus I shall soon be making, instead of $40 about $100 per month. This will enable me to accumulate the means of flying from American civilization to other horrors which I know not of— some place where one has to be a good Catholic (in outward appearance) for fear of having a *navaja* stuck into you; and where the whole population is so mixed up that no human being can tell what nation anybody belongs to. So in the meantime I must study such phrases as:—

¿Tiene U. un leoncito?—	Have you a small lion?
No señor, pero tengo un fero perro—	No: but I've an ugly dog.
¿Tiene U. un muchachona?	Have you a big strapping girl?
No: pero tengo un hombrecillo.	No: but I've got a miserable little man.

May the Gods of the faiths living and dead, watch over thee, and thy dreams be made resonant with the sound of mystic and ancient music, which on awaking, thou shalt vainly endeavor to recall, and forever regret with a vague and yet pleasant sorrow; knowing that the gods permit not mortals to learn their sacred hymns.

L Hearn

By the way, let me send you a short translation from Baudelaire. It is so mystic and sad and beautiful.

—

From Petits Poèmes en Prose: "*Les Bienfaits de la Lune.*"

"While thou wert dreaming in thy cradle, the Moon looked through the window, whispered to herself, 'The child pleases me.' And she softly descended her stairway of clouds, and noiselessly passed through the window panes.

* * * She filled all the chamber like a phosphoric atmosphere—like a luminous poison; and all that living light thought and said:

" 'Thou shalt forever remain under the influence of my kiss. Thou shalt be beautiful after my fashion. Thou shalt love all that I love, and all that loves me: the waters, the clouds; Silence and Night; the vast green sea; the waters which are formless and yet multiform; *the place where thou shalt never be;* the lover thou shalt never know; the flowers which are monstrous; the perfumes which are maddening; and the cats which swoon upon pianos and sigh like women, with a sweet vibrant voice.

"And thou shalt be beloved, by my lovers, courted by my courtesans.* * Thou shall be the queen of all those who love the sea, the vast, green, and tumultuous sea;—the waters, formless and yet multiform,—*the places where they shall never be;—the women they shall never know;*—the sinister flowers which seem the causes of a religion without a name;—and the perfumes which destroy the human will" * *

To Henry Edward Krehbiel

NEW ORLEANS, 1880

39 Constance St.
New Orleans

Friend Krehbiel:

I was so glad to hear from you.

Hereafter you had better address me in care of Major Wm M. Robinson 308 Baronne, as I have moved into the rear portion of a dilapidated French house in a dilapidated part of the city, and do not know whether my letters would come there safely or not.

I would not on any account have put you to so much trouble about the clipping, had I known the difficulty you had in finding it. But I will put myself to a little trouble for you sometime or other.

Your letter gave me much amusement. I wish I could have been present at that Chinese concert. It must have been the funniest thing of the kind ever heard of in Cincinnati.

Do not fail to remember me kindly to the Gazette boys,— especially Feldwisch & Tunison. I have heard nothing of newspaper life in Cincinnati for a long time; and when you have time please tell me what changes, accidents, etc. have transpired since my departure.

It gives me malicious pleasure to inform you that my vile and improper book will probably be published in a few months. Also that the wickedest story of the lot,—"King Candaules"— is being published as a serial in one of the New Orleans papers, with delightful results of shocking people. I will send you copies of them when complete.

I am interested in your study of Assyrian archæology. It is a pity there are so few good works on the subject. Layard's *unabridged* works are very extensive; but I do not remember seeing them in the Cincinnati Library. Rawlinson, I think, is more interesting in style and more thorough in research. The French are making fine explorations in this direction.

I find frequent reference made to Overbeck's Pompeji, a German work as containing valuable information on antique music, drawn from discoveries at Herculaneum & Pompeii;

also to Mazois, a great French writer upon the same subject. I have not seen them; but I fancy you would find some valuable information in them regarding musical instruments. I suppose you have read Sir William Gell's Pompeiiana,—at least the abridged form of it.—You know the double flutes &c of the ancients are preserved in the museum of Naples. In the Cincinnati Library is a splendid copy of the work on Egyptian antiquities prepared under Napoleon I, wherein you will find colored prints—from photographs—of the musical instruments found in the catacombs and hypogea. But I do not think there are many good books on the subject of Assyrian antiquities there. Vickers could put you in the way of getting better works on the subject than are in the library, I believe.

You will master these things much more thoroughly than ever I shall—although I love them. I have only attempted, however, to photograph the *rapports* of the antiquities in my mind, like memories of a panoramic procession; while to you, the procession will not be one of shadows, but of splendid facts, with the sound of strangely ancient music and the harmonious tread of sacrificial bands,—all preserved for you through the night of ages. And the life of vanished cities and the pageantry of dead faiths will have a far more charming reality for you,— the Musician,—than ever for me,—the Dreamer.

I can't see well enough yet to do much work. I have written an essay upon luxury and art in the time of Elagabalus; but now that I read it over again, I am not satisfied with it, and fear it will not be published. And by the way—I request, and beg, and entreat, and supplicate, and petition, and pray that you will not forget about Mephistopheles. Here—in the sweet perfume laden air, and summer of undying flowers,—I feel myself moved to write the musical romance whereof I spake unto you in the days that were.

I can't say that things look very bright here otherwise. The prospect is dark as that of stormy summer night, with feverish pulses of lightning in the far sky-border,—the lightning signifying hopes and fantasies. But I shall stick to my pedestal of faith in literary possibilities like an Egyptian colossus with a broken nose, seated solemnly in the gloom of its own originality.

Times are not good here. The city is crumbling into ashes. It has been buried under a lava-flood of taxes and frauds and maladministrations so that it has become only a study for archaeologists. Its condition is so bad, that when I write about it as I intend to do soon, nobody will believe I am telling the truth. But it is better to live here in sackcloth and ashes, than to own the whole state of Ohio.

I have not seen anybody from Cincinnati as yet. I am highly moral and virtuous here. I am as chaste as a monk of the Thebaid desert. The climate is voluptuous and the women are simply perfection and heaven and houris, but like the sailing Ulysses, I close my eyes and stuff up my ears, and pay no attention to them. It is delightful to make a virtue of necessity. I am getting so accustomed to saintliness from compulsion, that I shall certainly ere long become a saint in fact.

Once in a while I feel the spirit of restlessness upon me, when the Spanish ships come in from Costa Rica and the islands of the West Indies. I fancy that some day, I shall wander down to the Levee, and creep on board, and sail away to God knows where. I am so hungry to see those quaint cities of the Conquistadores and to hear the sandalled sentinels crying through the night—*Sereno alerto!—sereno alerto!*—just as they did two hundred years ago.

I send you a little bit of prettiness I cut out of a paper. Ah!—*that* is style, is it not?—and fancy and strength and height and depth. It is just in the style of Richter's "Titan."

Major sends his compliments. I must go to see the Carnival nuisance. Remember me to anybody who cares about it, and believe me always

faithfully yours
L Hearn

To Henry Edward Krehbiel

NEW ORLEANS, 1880

My dear Krehbiel:

Your letter delighted me. I always felt sure that you would unshackle yourself sooner or later; but I hardly expected it would come so soon.

The great advantage of your new position, I think, will be the leisure it will afford you to study, and that too while you are still in the flush of youth and ambition, and before your energies are impaired by excess of newspaper drudgery. I think your future is secure now beyond any doubt;—for any man with such talent and knowledge, such real love for art, and such a total absence of vices should find the road before an easy one. It is true that you have a prodigious work to achieve; but the path is well oiled, like those level highways along which the Egyptians moved their colossi of granite. I congratulate you; I rejoice with you; and I envy you with the purest envy possible. Still more, however, I envy your youth, your strength, and that something which is partly hope and partly force and love for the beautiful which I have lost, and which having passed away with the summer of life, can never be recalled. When a man commences to feel what it is to be young, he is beginning to grow old. You have not felt that yet. I hope you will not for many years. But I do; and my hair is turning grey at thirty!

I liked your letter very much also in regard to our discussion. It is just and pleasant to read. I thought your first reproaches much too violent. But I am still sure you are not correct in speaking of the Greeks as chaste. You will not learn what the Greeks were in the time of the glory of their republics either from Homer or Plato or Gladstone or Mahaffy. Perhaps the best English writer I could refer you to,—without mentioning historians proper,—is John Addington Symonds, author of "Studies of the Greek Poets," and "Studies and Sketches of Southern Europe." His works would charm you. The Greeks were brave, intelligent, men of genius, men who wrote miracles—*un peuple de demi-dieux* as a French poet terms them; but the character of their thought as reflected in their mythology, their literature, their art, and their history certainly does not indicate the least conception of chastity in the modern signification of the word. No: you will not go down to your grave with the conception you have made of them,—unless you should be determined not to investigate the contrary.

I would like to discuss the other affairs, also; but I have so little time that I must forego the pleasure.

As to the Fantastics you greatly overestimate me, if you think me capable of doing something much more "worthy of my talents" as you express it. I am conscious they are only trivial; but I am condemned to move around in a sphere of triviality until the end. I am no longer able to study as I used to; and being able to work only a few hours a day, cannot do anything outside of my regular occupation. My hope is to perfect myself in Spanish and French, and if possible to study Italian next summer. With a knowledge of the Latin tongues, I may have a better chance hereafter. But I fancy the idea of the Fantastics is artistic. They are my impressions of the strange life of New Orleans. They are dreams of a tropical city. There is one twin-idea running through them all—Love and Death. And these figures embody the story of life here, as it impresses me. I hope to be able to take a trip to Mexico in the summer just to obtain literary material,—sun-paint, tropical color &c. There are tropical lilies which are venomous, but they are more beautiful than the frail and icy-white lilies of the North. Tell me, if you received a fantastic founded upon the Story of Ponce de Leon: I think I sent it since my last letter. I have not written any Fantastics since except one,—inspired by Tennyson's fancy,—

> My heart would hear her and beat
> Had it lain for a century dead
> —Would start into life under her feet
> And blossom—

Jerry, Krehbiel, Ed Miller, Feldwisch! All gone! It is a little strange. But it will always be so. Looking around the table at home at which are gathered wanderers from all nations and all skies, the certainty of separation from all societies and coteries is very impressive. We are all friends. In six months probably there will not be one left. Dissolution of little societies in this city is more rapid than with you. In the tropics, all things decay more speedily, or mummify. And I think that in such cities there is no real friendship. There is no time for it. Only passion for women, a brief acquaintance for men. And it is only when I meet some fair-haired Northern stranger here, rough and open like a wind from the great lakes, that I begin to realize I once lived in a city whose heart was not a cemetery two centuries old, and where people who hated did not kiss each other, and where men did not mock at all that youth and faith hold to be sacred—

Your sincere friend,

L Hearn.

Read Bergerat's article on Offenbach—the long one. I think you will like it.

To Henry Edward Krehbiel

NEW ORLEANS, FEBRUARY 1881

My dear Krehbiel:

Your letter rises before me as I write like a tablet of white stone bearing a dead name. I see you standing beside me. I look into your eyes and press your hand and say nothing.

- - - - - - - - - - -

Remember me kindly to Mrs. Krehbiel. I am sure you will soon have made a cosy little home in the metropolis. In my last letter I forgot to acknowledge the receipt of the musical articles, which do you the greatest credit, and which interested me much although I know nothing about music further than a narrow theatrical experience and a natural sensibility to its simpler forms of beauty enables me to do. I see your name also in the programme of The Studio, and hope to see the first number of that periodical containing your opening article. I should like one of these days to talk with you about the possibility of contributing a romantic—not musical—series of little sketches upon the creole songs and colored creoles of New Orleans, to some New York periodical. Until the summer comes, however, it will be difficult for me to undertake such a thing: the days here are much shorter than they are in your northern latitudes, the weather has been gloomy as Tartarus, and my poor imagination cannot rise on dampened wings in this heavy and murky atmosphere. This has been a hideous winter,—incessant rain, sickening weight of foul air, and a sky gray as the face of Melancholy. The city is half under water. The lake and the bayous have burst their bounds, and the streets are Venetian canals. Boats are moving over the sidewalks; and mocassin snakes swarm in the old stonework of the gutters. Several children have been bitten.

I am very weary of New Orleans. The first delightful impression it produced has vanished. The city of my dreams bathed in the gold of eternal summer, and perfumed with the amorous odors of orange flowers, has vanished like some of those phantom cities of Spanish America, swallowed up centuries ago by earthquakes, but reappearing at long intervals to deluded travellers. What remains is something horrible like the tombs here,—material and moral rottenness which no pen can do justice to. You must have read some of those medieval legends in which an amorous youth finds the beautiful witch he has embraced all through the night crumble into a mass of calcined bones and ashes in the morning. Well, I feel like such a one, and almost regret that unlike the victims of these diabolical illusions I do not find my hair whitened and my limbs withered by sudden age; for I enjoy exuberant vitality, and still seem to myself like one buried alive or left alone in some city cursed with desolation like those described by Sinbad the sailor. No literary circle here;—no jovial coterie of journalists;—no association save those vampire ones of which the less said the better. And the thought, When must all this end? may be laughed off in the daytime; but always returns to haunt me like a ghost in the night.

Your friend
L Hearn

To Henry Edward Krehbiel

NEW ORLEANS, 1881

My Dear Krehbiel:

To what could I now devote myself? To nothing! To study art in any one of its branches with any hope of success requires years of patient study, vast reading, and a very considerable outlay of money. This I know. I also know that I could not write one little story of antique life really worthy of the subject without such hard study as I am no longer able to undertake and a purchase of many costly works above my means. The world of Imagination is alone left open to me. It allows of a vagueness of expression which hides the absence of real knowledge, and dispenses with the necessity of technical precision of detail. Again, let me tell you that to produce a really artistic work, after all the years of study required for a such a task, one cannot possibly obtain any appreciation of the work for years after its publication. Such works as Flaubert's "Salammbo" or Gautier's "Roman de la Momie" were literary failures until recently. They were too learned to be appreciated. Yet to write on a really noble subject, how learned one must be! There is no purpose, as you justly observe, in my fantastics,—beyond that gratification of expressing a Thought which cries out within one's heart for utterance, and the pleasant fancy that a few kindred minds will dream over them, as upon pellets of green hascheesch,—at least should they ever assume the shape I hope for. And do not talk to me of work, dear fellow, in this voluptuous climate. It is impossible! The people here are so languidly lazy that they do not even dream of chasing away the bats which haunt these crumbling buildings.

—

Is it possible you like Dr. Ebers? I hope not! He has no artistic sentiment whatever,—no feeling, no color. He is dry and dusty as a mummy preserved with bitumen. He gropes in the hypogea like some Yankee speculator looking for antiquities to sell. You must be Egyptian to write of Egypt;—you must feel all the weird solemnity and mighty ponderosity of the antique life;—you must comprehend the whole force of those ideas which expressed themselves in miracles of granite and mysteries of black marble. Ebers knows nothing of this. Turning from the French writers to his lifeless pages, is like leaving the warm and perfumed bed of a beloved mistress for the slimy coldness of a sepulchre.

—

The Venus of Milo!—the Venus who is not a Venus. Perhaps you have read Victor Rydberg's beautiful essay about that glorious figure! If not, read it; it is worth while. And let me say, my dear friend, no one dare write the whole truth about Greek sculpture. None would publish it. Few would understand it. Winklemann, although impressed by it, hardly realized it. Symonds, in his exquisite studies, acknowledges that the spirit of the antique life remains and will always remain to the greater number, an inexplicable although enchanting mystery. But if one dared! . . . .

———

And you speak of the Song of Solomon. I love it more than ever. But Michelet, the passionate freethinker, the divine prose-poet, the bravest lover of the beautiful, has written a terrible chapter upon it. No lesser mind dare touch the subject now with sacrilegious hand.

———

I doubt if you are quite just to Gautier: I had hoped his fancy might please you. But Gautier did not write those lines I sent you. They are found in the report of conversations held with him by Emile Bergerat;—they are mere memories of a dead voice. Probably had he ever known that these romantic opinions would one day be published to the world, he would never have uttered them.

———

I think you are incorrect in speaking of the use of the birch among the antique Greeks. Impotence was very uncommon among them,—and most common among the class of athletes, who destroyed their virility by excessive training. Under the Roman Empire, however degeneration commenced.

———

Your Hindoo legends charmed me; but I do not like them as I love the Greek legends. The fantasies created in India are superhumanly vast, wild and terrible;—they are typhoons of the tropical imagination;—they seem pictures painted by madness; —they terrify and impress, but do not charm. I love better the sweet human story of Orpheus. It is a dream of human love,— the love that is not only strong, but stronger than death,—the love that breaks down the dim gates of the world of Shadows and bursts open the marble heart of the tomb to return at the outcry of passion. Yet I hold that the Greek mind was infantine in comparison to the Indian thought of the same era; nor could any Greek imagination have created the visions of the visionary East. The Greek was a pure naturalist, a lover of "the bloom of young flesh;"—the Hindoo had fathomed the deepest deeps of human thought before the Greek was born.

—

Zola is capable of some beautiful things. His "Le Bain" is pure romanticism, delicate, sweet, coquettish. His contribution to *Les Soirées de Medan* is magnificent. His "faute de l'Abbé Mouret" does not lack real touches of poetry. But as the copy of Nature is not true art according to the Greek law of beauty, so I believe that the school of naturalism belongs to a low order of literary creation. It is a sharp photograph colored by hand with the minute lines of veins and shading of dawn. Zola's pupils, however,—those who wrote the Soirées de Medan have improved upon his style; and have mingled Naturalism with Romanticism in a very charming way.

—

I was a little disappointed, although I was also much delighted, with parts of Cable's "Grandissimes." He did not follow out his first plan,—as he told me he was going to do: viz., to scatter about 50 Creole songs through the work, with the music in the shape of notes at the end. There are only a few ditties published; and as the Creole music deals in fractions of tones, Mr. Cable failed to write it properly. He is not enough of a musician, I fancy, for that.

—

By the time you have read this I think you will also have read my articles on Gottschalk and translations. I sent for his life to Havana; and received it with a quaint Spanish letter from one Enrique Barrera, begging me to find an agent for him. I found him one here. This West Indian volume is one of the most extraordinary books I have ever seen—it is the wildest of possible romances.

—

I have a curious work in my possession by Huysmans, the most promising of Zola's pupils. He has written a terrible essay on the odors which emanate from a woman's armpits, the differences of the emanation being studied from the standpoint of character and passionate possibility. It is not surprising, however; since the London Academy acknowledges that the most beautiful poem in the French language is on the curls of the mons veneris,—

> "O douce barbe féminine
>   que l'Art a toujours voulu raser,
>   Sur ta soie annelée et fine
>   Reçois mes vers comme un baiser!"

Some of these days I shall send you a translation of the whole poem.

—

What else can I gossip about! Not much that could interest you. Except perhaps that I have suffered the tortures of a thousand damned souls. I went too near the flame and got cruelly burned. I approached my lips too often to lips that set my blood on fire. I was foolish enough to say,—"I am too strong by experience to be entrapped;" and I got caught in a terrible net. If you knew all, I am sure you would pity me. I became passionately in love before I knew it; and then!—It required all the reason and all the strength I could summon to save myself; but it took me months to do it. I went out almost nightly to visit different places and pass each evening with a different woman; but even while sleeping with living arms around me, the other came to me in dreams and made me feel her shadowy caresses. Don't think I am exaggerating! You have no idea of the strange fascination possessed by some of these serpent-women. And at last the dreams became vaguer and have finally vanished. Yet as I write, I do not dare to state that I am cured. I know that another kiss, even another look, would plunge me into a depth of ruin which no earthly power could save me from. And the temptation is always before me. You do not understand me, perhaps! You think I am writing folly and madness. But you could never understand me further unless you had lived in this accursed city. Still I love it so much. I love New Orleans.

Your friend

To Page Baker
GRAND ISLE, 1884

Gentleman's
bathing-houses

DEAR PAGE,—I wish you were here; for I am sure that the enjoyment would do you a great deal of good. I had not been in sea-water for fifteen years, and you can scarcely imagine how I rejoice in it,—in fact I don't like to get out of it at all. I suppose you have not been at Grande Isle—or at least not been here for so long that you have forgotten what it looks like. It makes a curious impression on me: the old plantation cabins, standing in rows like village-streets, and neatly remodelled for more cultivated inhabitants, have a delightfully rural aspect under their shadowing trees; and there is a veritable country calm by day and night. Grande Isle has suggestions in it of several old country fishing villages I remember, but it is even still more charmingly provincial. The hotel proper, where the tables are laid,—formerly, I fancy, a sugar-house or something of that sort,—reminds one of nothing so much as one of those big English or Western barn-buildings prepared for a holiday festival or a wedding-party feast. The only distinctively American feature is the inevitable Southern gallery with white wooden pillars. An absolutely ancient purity of morals appears to prevail here:—no one thinks of bolts or locks or keys, everything is left open and nothing is ever touched. Nobody has ever been robbed on the island. There is no iniquity. It is like a resurrection of the days of good King Alfred, when, if a man were to drop his purse on the highway, he might return six months later to find it untouched. At least that is what I am told. Still I would not *like* to leave one thousand golden dinars on the beach or in the middle of the village. I am still a little suspicious —having been so long a dweller in wicked cities.

I was in hopes that I had made a very important discovery; viz.—a flock of really tame and innocuous cows; but the innocent appearance of the beasts is, I have just learned, a disguise for the most fearful ferocity. So far I have escaped unharmed; and Marion has offered to lend me his large stick, which will, I have no doubt, considerably aid me in preserving my life.

Could n't you manage to let me stay down here until after the Exposition is over, doing no work and nevertheless drawing my salary regularly? . . . By the way, one could save money by a residence at Grande Isle. There are no temptations —except the perpetual and delicious temptation of the sea.

The insects here are many; but I have seen no frogs,—they have probably found that the sea can outroar them and have gone away jealous. But in Marion's room there is a beam, and against that beam there is the nest of a "mud-dauber." Did you ever see a mud-dauber? It is something like this when  flying;—but when it is n't flying I can't tell you what it looks like, and it has the peculiar power of flying without noise. I think it is of the wasp-kind, and plasters its mud nest in all sorts of places. It is afraid of nothing—likes to look at itself in the glass, and leaves its young in our charge. There is another sociable creature—hope it is n't a wasp—which has built two nests under the edge of this table on which I write to you. There are no specimens here of the *cimex lectularius*, and the mosquitoes are not at all annoying. They buzz a little, but seldom give evidence of hunger. Creatures also abound which have the capacity of making noises of the most singular sort. Up in the tree on my right there is a thing which keeps saying all day long, quite plainly, "*Kiss, Kiss, Kiss!*"—referring perhaps to the good young married folks across the way; and on

the road to the bath-house, which we travelled late last
evening in order to gaze at the phosphorescent sea, there
dwells something which exactly imitates the pleasant sound of
ice jingling in a cut-glass tumbler.

As for the grub, it is superb—solid, nutritious, and without
stint. When I first tasted the butter I was enthusiastic, imagining
that those mild-eyed cows had been instrumental in its production; but I have since discovered they were not—and the
fact astonishes me not at all now that I have learned more concerning the character of those cows.

At some unearthly hour in the morning the camp-meeting
quiet of the place is broken by the tolling of a bell. This means
"Jump up, lazy-bones; and take a swim
before the sun rises." Then the railroad-car
comes for the bathers, passing
up the whole line of white cottages.
The distance is short to the
beach; Marion and I prefer to
walk; but the car is a great convenience for
the women and children and invalids. It is
drawn by a single mule, and always accompa-
nied by a dog which appears to be the intimate friend of the
said mule, and who jumps up and barks all the grass-grown
way. The ladies' bathing-house is about five minutes' plank-

walking from the men's,—where I am glad to say drawers and
bathing-suits are unnecessary, so that one has the full benefit
of sun-bathing as well as salt-water bathing. There is a man
here called Margot or Margeaux—perhaps some distant relative of Château-Margeaux—who always goes bathing accom-

panied by a pet goose. The goose follows him just like a dog; but is a little afraid of getting into deep water. It remains in the surf presenting its stern-end to the breakers:—

The only trouble about the bathing is the ferocious sun. Few people bathe in the heat of the day, but yesterday we went in four times; and the sun nearly flayed us. This morning we held a council of war  and decided upon greater moderation. There are three bars, between which the water is deep. The third bar is, I fear, too "risky" to reach, as it is nearly a mile from the other, and lies beyond a hundred-foot depth of water in which sharks are said to disport themselves. I am almost as afraid of sharks as I am of cows. . . . Marion made a dash for a drowning man yesterday, in answer to the cry, "Here, you fellows, help! help!"

and I followed. We had instantaneous visions of a gold-medal from the Life-Saving Service, and glorious dreams of newspaper fame under the title "Journalistic Heroism,"—for my part, I must acknowledge I had also an unpleasant fancy that the drowning man might twine himself about me, and pull me to the bottom,—so I looked out carefully to see which way he was heading. But the beatific Gold-Medal fancies were brutally dissipated by the drowning man's success in saving himself before we could reach him, and we remain as obscure as before.

Interlude

Miss B. B. through our lorgnette

Miss Bisland's A No 1. Chaperone

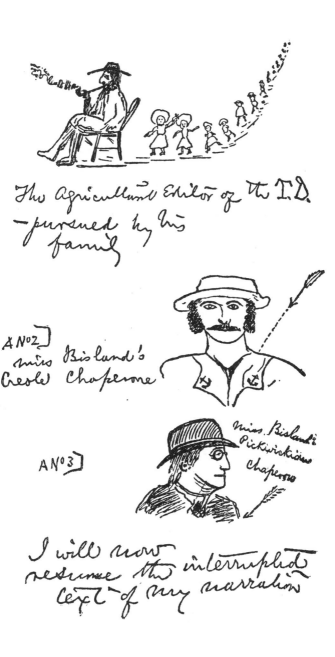

The Agricultural Editor of the T.D.
—pursued by his
family

A N°2]
miss Bisland's
Creole Chaperone

miss Bisland's
Pickwickian
Chaperone

A N°3]

I will now
resume the interrupted
text of my narration

The proprietor has found what I have vainly been ransacking the world for—a civilized hat, showing the highest evolutional development of the hat as a practically useful article. I am going to make him an offer for it.

Alas! the time flies too fast. Soon all this will be a dream:— the white cottages shadowed with leafy green,—the languid

rocking-chairs upon the old-fashioned gallery,—the cows that look into one's window with the rising sun,—the dog and the mule trotting down the flower-edged road,—the goose of the ancient Margot,—the muttering surf upon the bar beyond which the sharks are,— the bath-bell and the bathing belles,—the air that makes one feel like a boy,—the pleasure of sleeping with doors and windows open to the sea and its everlasting song,—the exhilaration of rising with the rim of the sun. . . . And then we must return to the dust and the roar of New Orleans, to hear the rumble of wagons instead of the rumble of breakers, and to smell the smell of ancient gutters instead of the sharp sweet scent of pure sea wind. I believe I would rather be old Margot's goose if I could. Blessed goose! thou knowest nothing about the literary side of the New Orleans *Times-Democrat*; but thou dost  know that thou canst

 have a good tumble in the sea every day. If I could live down here I should certainly live to be a hundred years old. One *lives* here. In New Orleans one only exists. . . . And the boat comes—I must post this incongruous epistle.

Good-bye,—wish you were here, sincerely.

Very truly,
LAFCADIO HEARN.

To Henry Edward Krehbiel

SAINT-PIERRE, MARTINIQUE, 1887

281 Rue Victor Hugo, St. Pierre
Martinique
French W.I.

Dear Krehbiel:

I was delighted to get your letter, the first which reached me from America during my trip. My own correspondence has been irregular, though I have written a good many short letters; but the amount of work on my hands has been something enormous,—and I have only had five idle days, caused by a fever due to imprudence. I got into a marshy town, got wet, and came home with a burning headache. The result was not serious, except that I had to stop all writing for a while.

You ask me to send you a hint about my work; but I think it were best to say nothing about it. I have a very large mass of mss prepared & don't yet know what I am going to do with it: it is not polished as I should wish, but I hope to work it into proper shape in a few days more. It consists simply of a detailed account of impressions, sensations, colors &c. I have tried to put the whole *feeling* of the trip on paper. Then I have about $60 worth of photos to illustrate it. My photo set is very complete;—I have also a rich collection of Coolie and half-breed types, including many nude studies.

Strange as you might think it, this trip knocks the poetry out of me! The imagination is not stimulated, but paralyzed by the satiation of all its aspirations and the realization of its wildest dreams. The artistic sense is numbed by the display of colors which no artist could paint; and the philosophical sense is lulled to inactivity by the perpetual current of novel impressions, by the continual stream of unfamiliar sensory experiences. Concentration of mind is impossible.

It pleases me, however, to have procured material for stories, which I can write up at home; and for romantic material the West Indies offer an unparalleled field of research. I shall return to them again at my earliest opportunity;—the ground is absolutely untilled, and it is not in the least likely that any body in the shape of a Creole is ever going to till it.

By this time you will have seen the doll. I want to remind that this is more than a doll: it is really an artistic model of the dress worn by the women of Martinique,—big earrings and all. The real earrings and necklaces are pure gold; the former worth 175 francs a pair; the latter often running as high as 500, 600, even 900 francs.

I was very glad to hear of your success with the Century; I only trust you will charge high: as a specialist you ought to receive more than the ordinary writer.

In case this reaches you before leaving N.Y., I hope you will be able to make some arrangement with Joe or somebody, so that I can put my things in a place of safety for a day or two, until I can try to arrange matters with the Harpers. I will be obliged to stay a short while in New York,—and shall want a room badly, until my ms. & photos have been disposed of, and my proof-reading has been done on "Chita."

Very truly yours
with affectionate regards to all
Lafcadio Hearn

P.S.—I return with the Barracouta.

My enquiries about the marimba and other instruments have produced no result, except the discovery that our negroes play the guitar, the flute, the flageolet, the cornet-à-piston! Some play very well; all the orchestras and bands are colored. But the civilized instrument has killed the native manufacture of aboriginalities. The only hope would be in the small islands, or where slavery still exists, as in Cuba. There are one or two African songs still current, but they are sung to the tamtam—

> Welleli, welleli,
>   hm, hm!
> Papa mon ca papa mon
>   hm, hm!
> Welleli, welleli,
>   hm, hm!
> Maman mon ca maman mon
>   hm, hm!
> Welleli, etc.

To George M. Gould

GRAND ANSE, MARTINIQUE, JUNE 1888

DEAR DR. GOULD,—I am writing you from an obscure, pretty West Indian village, seldom visited by travellers. Tall palms, and a grand roaring sea, blue as lapis lazuli in spite of its motion.

I was certainly even more pleased to hear from you than you could have been at the receipt of my letter;—for in addition to the intellectual and sympathetic pleasure of such a correspondence, the comparative rarity of friendly missives, enhancing their value, lends them certain magnetism difficult to describe, —the sensation, perhaps, of that North, and that Northern vigour of mind which has made the world what it is, and that pure keen air full of the Unknowable Something which has made the Northern Thought.

I seldom have a chance now to read or speak English; and English phrases that used to seem absolutely natural already begin to look somewhat odd to me. Were I to continue to live here for some years more, I am almost sure that I should find it difficult to write English. The resources of the intellectual life are all lacking here,—no libraries, no books in any language;— a mind accustomed to discipline becomes like a garden long uncultivated, in which the rare flowers return to their primitive savage forms, or are smothered by rank, tough growths which ought to be pulled up and thrown away. Nature does not allow you to think here, or to study seriously, or to work earnestly: revolt against her, and with one subtle touch of fever she leaves you helpless and thoughtless for months.

But she is so beautiful, nevertheless, that you love her more and more daily,—that you gradually cease to wish to do aught contrary to her local laws and customs. Slowly, you begin to lose all affection for the great Northern nurse that taught you to think, to work, to aspire. Then, after a while, this nude, warm, savage, amorous Southern Nature succeeds in persuading you that labour and effort and purpose are foolish things,—that life is very sweet without them;—and you actually find yourself ready to confess that the aspirations and inspirations born of the struggle for life in the North are all madness,—that they wasted years which might have been delightfully dozed away in land where the air is always warm, the sea always the colour of sapphire, the woods perpetually green as the plumage of a green parrot.

I must confess I have had some such experiences. It appears to me impossible to resign myself to living again in a great city and in a cold climate. Of course I shall have to return to the States for a while,—a short while, probably;—but I do not think I will ever settle there. I am apt to become tired of places,—or at least of the disagreeable facts attaching more or less to all places and becoming more and more marked and unendurable the longer one stays. So that ultimately I am sure to wander off somewhere else. You can comprehend how one becomes tired of the very stones of a place,—the odours, the colours, the shapes of Shadows, and tint of its sky;—and how small irritations become colossal and crushing by years of repetition;—yet perhaps you will not comprehend that one can actually become weary of a whole system of life, of civilization, even with very limited experience. Such is exactly my present feeling,—an unutterable weariness of the aggressive characteristics of existence in a highly organized society. The higher the social development, the sharper the struggle. One feels this especially in America,—in the nervous centres of the world's activity. One feels at least, I imagine, in the tropics, where it is such an effort just to live, that one has no force left for the effort to expand one's own individuality at the cost of another's. I clearly perceive that a man enamoured of the tropics has but two things to do:—To abandon intellectual work, or to conquer the fascination of Nature. Which I will do will depend upon necessity. I would remain in this zone if I could maintain a certain position here;—to keep it requires means. I can earn only by writing, and yet if I remain a few years more, I will have become (perhaps?) unable to write. So if I am to live in the tropics, as I would like to do, I must earn the means for it in very short order.

I gave up journalism altogether after leaving N. O. I went to Demerara and visited the lesser West Indies in July and August of last year,—returned to New York after three months with some MS.,—sold it,—felt very unhappy at the idea of staying in New York, where I had good offers,—suddenly made up my mind to go back to the tropics by the very same steamer that had brought me. I had no commission, resolved to trust to magazine-work. So far I have just been able to scrape along;— the climate numbs mental life, and the inspirations I hoped for won't come. The real—surpassing imagination—whelms the ideal out of sight and hearing. The world is young here,—not old and wise and grey as in the North; and one must not seek the Holy Ghost in it. I suspect that the material furnished by the tropics can only be utilized in a Northern atmosphere. We will talk about it together; for I will certainly call on you in Philadelphia some day.

I would not hesitate, if I were you, to begin the *magnum opus*,—the only time to hesitate would be when it is all complete, before giving to the printer. Then one may perhaps commune with one's self to advantage upon the question of what might be gained or lost by waiting for more knowledge through fresh expansions of science. But the true way to attempt an enduring work is to begin it as a duty, without considering one's self in the matter at all, but the subject only,—which you love more and more the longer you caress it, and find it taking form and colour and beauty with the patient years.

I am horribly ignorant about scientific matters; but sometimes the encouragement of a layman makes the success of the prelate.

Now, replying to your question about "Chita." "Chita" was founded on the fact of a child saved from the Lost Island disaster by some Louisiana fisher-folk, and brought up by them. Years after a Creole hunter recognized her, and reported her whereabouts to relatives. These, who were rich, determined to bring her up as young ladies are brought up in the South, and had her sent to a convent. But she had lived the free healthy life of the coast, and could not bear the convent;—she ran away from it, married a fisherman, and lives somewhere down there now,—the mother of multitudinous children.

And about my work, I can only tell you this:—I will have two illustrated articles on a West Indian trip in the *Harper's Monthly* soon,—within four or five months. These will be followed by brief West Indian sketches. Other sketches, not suited for the magazine, will go to form a volume to be published later on. I do not correspond or write for any newspaper, and I would always let you know in advance where anything would be published written by me.

You know what the nervous cost of certain imaginative work means; and this sort of work I do not think I shall be able to do here. One has no vital energy to spare in such a climate. I cannot read Spencer here,—gave up the "Biology" (vol. II) in despair. But I did not miss the wonderful page about the evolution of the eye—hair—snail-horn—etc., etc. . . . I want to see anything you write that I can understand, with my limited knowledge of scientific terms and facts. And when you write again, tell me what you said of Loti in the letter I never received. Did you read his "Roman d'un Spahi"? I thought you would like it. If you do not, let me know why,—because Loti has had much literary influence upon me, and I want to know his faults as well as his merits. With love to you,

LAFCADIO HEARN.

To George M. Gould

DEAR GOULD,—Many thanks for the *quid*!—the surprising *quid*. I have been waiting to send you the *quo*, which I do not like so well as one taken in New Orleans, of which I have no copy within reach. But before I tell you anything about the *quo*, I ought to scold you for your startling deception. I pictured you as a much younger man than myself—although quite conscious of meeting an intelligence much more virile and penetrating than my own, and with an experience of life larger: this did not, however, astonish me; for whatever qualities I have lie only in that one direction which pleased you and won your friendship,—moreover, I had met several *much* younger men than myself, my mental superiors in every respect. But, all of a sudden you come upon me with such a revelation of your personality as makes me half afraid of you. I perceive that your *envergure* is much larger than I imagined:— I mean, of course, the mental spread-of-wing; and then your advice and suggestions while manifesting your ability to teach me much in my own line, resemble only those proffered by old experienced masters in literary guidance. It is exactly the advice of Alden, among one or two others.

Now about the *quo*. I am about five feet three inches high, and weigh about 137 pounds in good health;—fever has had me down to 126. Nothing phthisical,—36¾ inches round the chest, stripped. Was born in June (27th), 1850, in Santa Maura (the antique Leucadia), of a Greek mother. My father, Dr. Charles Bush Hearn, who spent most of his life in India, was surgeon-major of the 76th British regiment (now merged in West Riding Battalion). Do not know anything about my mother, whether alive or dead;—was last heard of (remarried) in Smyrna, about 1858–9. My father died on his return from India. There was a queer romance in the history of my father's marriage. It is not, however, of the sort to interest you in a letter. I am very near-sighted, have lost one eye, which disfigures me considerably; and my near-sightedness always prevented the gratification of a natural *penchant* for physical exercise. I am a good swimmer; that is all.

Your advice about story-writing is capital; I am not so sure about your suggestion of plot. I cannot believe—in view of the extraordinary changes (changes involving even the whole osseous structure) wrought in the offspring of Europeans or foreigners within a single generation by the tropical climate—that anything of the parental moral character on the *father's* side would survive with force sufficient to produce the psychical phenomena you speak of. In temperate climates these do survive astonishingly, even through generations; in the tropics, Nature moulds every new being *at once* into perfect accord with environment, or else destroys it. The idea you speak of occurred to me also; it was abandoned after a careful study of tropical conditions. It could only be used on an *inverse* plot,— transporting the tropical child to the North. At least, I think so, with my present knowledge on the subject,—which might be vastly improved, no doubt. . . .

About story-writing, dear friend, you ought to know I would like to be able to do nothing else. But even in these countries, where life is so cheap, I could not make the pot—or as they call it here, the *canari*—boil by story-writing until I gain more literary success, and can obtain high prices. A story takes at least ten or twelve months to write, that is, a story of the length of "Chita." Suppose it brings only $500,—half as much as you will soon be able to obtain for a single operation! It is pretty hard to live even in the tropics on that sum. I must write sketches too. They do me other good also, involve research I might otherwise neglect. I have prepared some twelve sketches in all, which obligated investigation that will prove invaluable for a forthcoming novelette.

I like your firm, strong, sonorous letter, better than anything of the sort I ever received. The only thing I did not relish in it was the suggestion that I should prepare a lecture, or make an appearance before a private club. I would not do it for anything! I shrink from real life, however, not at all because I am pessimistic. It is a very beautiful world:—the ugliness of some humanity only exists as the shadowing that outlines the view; the nobility of man and the goodness of woman can only be felt by those who know the possibilities of degradation and corruption. Philosophically I am simply a follower of Spencer, whose mind gives me the greatest conception of Divinity I can yet expand to receive. The faultiness is not with the world, but with myself. I inherit certain susceptibilities, weaknesses, sensitivenesses, which render it impossible to adapt myself to the ordinary *milieu*; I have to make one of my own, wherever I go, and never mingle with that already made. True, I lose much knowledge, but I escape pains which, in spite of all your own knowledge, you could not wholly comprehend, for the simple reason that you *can* mingle with men. By the way, it is no small disadvantage in life to be 5 ft. 3 in. high. I remember observing, at a great gathering of American merchant princes, that the small or insignificant looking men present might have been counted on the fingers of one hand. Success in life still largely depends upon the power to impose respect, the reserve of mere physical force; since the expansion of everybody's individuality—at the expense of everybody else's individuality—is still the law of existence.

I am not yet sure what I am going to do. One thing certain is that I am to go to South or to Central America—for monetary reasons. I may linger here long enough to finish a novelette. If not able to do so, I will perhaps be in New York before December. I left it October 2, 1887, after a stay of only three weeks, to return to the tropics. It was then impossible to visit Philadelphia. Should I go to the Continent from here, you will know at least six weeks in advance.

Thanks for the superb paper on Loti. I cannot imagine anything much finer in the way of literary analysis. But what does James want?—evolution to leap a thousand years? What he classes as sensual perceptions must be sensitized and refined supernally,—fully evolved and built up *before* the moral ones, of which they are the physiological foundations, pedestals. Granting the doubt as to the ultimate nature of Mind, it is still tolerably positive that its development—so far as man is concerned—follows the development of the nervous system; and that very sensuousness which at once delights and scandalizes James, rather seems to me a splendid augury of the higher sensitiveness to come, in some future age of writers and poets, — the finer "*sensibility of soul*," whose creative work will caress the nobler emotions more delicately than Loti's genius ever caressed the senses of colour and form and odour.

You ask about my idea of Whitman? I have not patience for him,—not as for Emerson. Enormous *suggestiveness* in both, rather than clear utterance. I used to like John Weiss better than Emerson. Then there is a shagginess, an uncouthness, a Calibanishness about Whitman that repels. He makes me think of some gigantic dumb being that sees things, and wants to make others see them, and cannot for want of a finer means of expression than Nature gives him. But there is manifest the rude nobility of the man,—the primitive and patriarchal soul-feeling to men and the world. Whitman lays a Cyclopean foundation on which, I fancy, some wonderful architect will yet build up some marvellous thing. . . . Yes, there is nonsense in Swinburne, but he is merely a melodist and colourist. He enlarges the English tongue,—shows its richness, unsuspected flexibility, admirable sponge-power of beauty-absorption. He is not to be despised by the student.

Let me pray you not to make mention of anything written to you thus, even incidentally, to newspaper folk—or to any literary folk who would not be *intimate* friends. There are reasons, more than personal, for this suggestion, acceptance of which would remove any check on frankness.

Best love to you, from
LAFCADIO HEARN.

Speaking of Whitman, I must add that my idea of him is not consciously stable. It has changed within some years. What I like, however, was not Whitman exactly,—rather the perception of something Whitman feels, and disappoints by his attempted expression of.

After closing letter I remember you wanted to know about illustrations in magazine. They are after photos. I am sorry to say incorrect use has been made of several: the types published as *Sacratra* were not *Sacratra*, but in two cases half-breed Coolie,—one seemingly of Southern India, showing a touch of Malay. There were other errors. It is horrible not to be able to correct one's *own* work,—on account of irregularities in mail involved by quarantine. In the December number you will see a study of a peculiar class of young girls here. If you want, yourself, to have some particular photo of some particular thing, send word, and I will try to get it for you.

I can only work here of mornings. Nobody dreams of eating before noon: all rise with the sun. After 2 P.M., the heat and weight of the air make thinking impossible. Your head gets heavy, as if there was lead in it, and you sleep.

CHRONOLOGY

NOTE ON THE TEXTS

NOTES

Chronology

1850   Born Patrick Lafcadio Tessima Carlos Hearn on June 27 on Lefkada (the ancient Leucadia, also known as Lefkas or Santa Maura), one of the Ionian Islands, to Rosa Antonia Cassimati, a native of Kythira (Cerigo or Cythera), and Surgeon-Major Charles Bush Hearn, of King's County, Ireland. Father had served with the occupying British Army throughout the Ionian Islands. Mother eloped with him from Kythira to Lefkada in June 1849; they had a son, George Rambert, in July, and married in November. Father was transferred to the British West Indies three months later; the infant George died two months after Hearn was born. Father's family included many military officers and claimed gypsy ancestry; his brother Richard was a member of the Barbizon circle of artists in France, and his grandmother was great-niece of Dr. John Arbuthnot, of Pope's *Epistle to Dr. Arbuthnot.*

1852   Father arranges to have Rosa and Lafcadio sent to Dublin.

1853   Father returns to Dublin. "I can remember seeing father only four times—no, five," Hearn later writes. "He never caressed me; I always felt afraid of him."

1854   Father leaves Dublin in March to join regiment in the Crimean War. Homesick, pregnant, and distraught, mother returns to Kythira, where she gives birth to Daniel James Hearn. (Lafcadio never meets this younger brother, but later writes to him: "do you not remember that dark and beautiful face—with large, brown eyes like a wild deer's—that used to bend above your cradle?")

1856   Charles Hearn has marriage to Rosa annulled on technicality (illiterate, she had not signed the contract), and marries Alicia Goslin Crawford the following year. (Mother later remarries and has four children.) Hearn is informally adopted by Sarah Brenane, his widowed great-aunt, and lives in her house in the prosperous Dublin suburb of Rathmines.

1862   On the advice of Sarah Brenane's friend and financial ad-
            viser Henry Molyneux, Hearn is sent to the Institution
            Ecclésiastique at Yvetot, France, a Catholic boarding
            school near Rouen. Guy de Maupassant, who attended
            the school just after Hearn left, wrote that it "smelled of
            prayers the way a fish market smells of fish."

1863–67   Attends St. Cuthbert's, a Roman Catholic preparatory
            school, at Ushaw, near Durham, England. Injured in
            playground incident, either accidentally by a knotted rope
            or intentionally by a classmate's fist, and loses vision in
            left eye, later calling himself "the Raven" in honor of Poe.
            Sarah Brenane's affections and financial affairs are increas-
            ingly transferred to Molyneux, who suffers business set-
            back in 1867, and Hearn is removed from St. Cuthbert's.

1868   Declared Brenane's heir upon her death, Molyneux
            arranges to have Hearn sent to the home of a former
            maid of Mrs. Brenane's in London, where he is miserable
            and poor. Reads Swinburne.

1869–71   Molyneux, determined to end his relations with Hearn,
            arranges to have him sent to the United States, where he
            is to seek assistance from Molyneux's brother-in-law in
            Cincinnati. Adopts the name "Lafcadio," and finds inter-
            mittent work in New York before traveling on to Cincin-
            nati, where Molyneux's relatives refuse to help him. Lives
            in crushing poverty. "I was dropped moneyless on the
            pavement of an American city to begin life," he later
            writes. Often slept in the street, etc." Befriended by En-
            glish printer Henry Watkin, who gives him work. Begins
            writing for Cincinnati newspapers in 1871.

1872–73   Becomes a regular visitor to the Cincinnati Public Li-
            brary; reads Gautier, Gérard de Nerval, Flaubert. Works
            on small newspaper, the *Trade List*, and as a proofreader
            for a small publisher. Begins romantic relationship with
            Alethea ("Mattie") Foley, a former slave who works in the
            kitchen of the boardinghouse where he lives. Contributes
            first articles to *Cincinnati Daily Enquirer*, eventually be-
            coming a daily reporter and writing on a wide range of
            subjects from Henry James to the occult; develops circle
            of friends among local newspapermen including Henry
            Edward Krehbiel, a police reporter and music critic for
            the Cincinnati *Gazette*.

1874   Marries Alethea, probably on June 14, in spite of anti-miscegenation laws which make the marriage illegal in Ohio, and against the counsel of friends. Along with Mattie's child from a previous relationship, they take up residence together. Collaborates with French-born artist Henry Farny on *Ye Giglampz: A Weekly Illustrated Journal Devoted to Art, Literature, and Satire*, which runs for nine issues.

1875–76 Fired from *Daily Enquirer* in August for "deplorable moral habits" after revelation of marriage. Threatens to commit suicide by jumping off Vine Street Bridge into Miami Canal. Hired by the *Cincinnati Commercial*, writes "Levee Life," "Gibbeted," and many other reports on city life.

1877   Separates from Alethea, never seeing her again. (She makes an unsuccessful claim on his estate after his death; her role in Hearn's life is silently omitted or pointedly denied by early biographers.) In October leaves Cincinnati for New Orleans. Takes train to Memphis and learns riverboat is delayed. Depressed and short of money, finally arrives in New Orleans on the *Thompson Dean* in November. First lives at boarding house on Baronne Street. Writes 13 articles, mainly about New Orleans, for the *Cincinnati Commercial* under the pen-name "Ozias Midwinter" (a character in Wilkie Collins' 1866 novel *Armadale*).

1878   Lives in dire poverty. Hired as assistant editor for New Orleans *Daily City Item*, a paper committed to political reform. Befriends New Orleans writer and civil rights activist George Washington Cable, whose story "Jean-ah Poquelin" he had read. Accompanies Cable in collecting Creole songs of French-speaking African-Americans in New Orleans: "but he has the advantage of me in being able to write music by ear."

1879   Invests earnings from work on *Item* in a small eatery variously called "The 5 Cent Restaurant" or "The Hard Times Restaurant"; business partner leaves town with Hearn's capital.

1880   Publishes in *Item* approximately 180 short unsigned satirical texts illustrated with his own woodblock prints, while also publishing series of "fantastics," literary sketches inspired by French literature and based loosely on factual material. "Times are not good here," he writes Krehbiel. "But it is better to live here in sackcloth and ashes, than to own the whole State of Ohio."

1881   Hired as literary editor and translator for newly formed New Orleans *Times-Democrat*. Works closely with brothers Page Baker, editor of the paper, and Marion Baker, literary editor. (Elizabeth Bisland, Marion Baker's assistant, later serves as Hearn's biographer and compiler of his correspondence.) Tells Krehbiel that his "fantastics" have no purpose "beyond the gratification of expressing a Thought which cries out within one's heart for utterance, and the pleasant fancy that a few kindred minds will dream over them, as upon pellets of green hascheesch."

1882   Meets Mark Twain in New Orleans, presumably through George Washington Cable, who later joins Twain on a lecture tour. Hearn's mother, who had remarried and had four more children, dies on December 12 at the National Mental Asylum at Corfu, where she had lived for ten years. Hearn's translation of six stories by Théophile Gautier published as *One of Cleopatra's Nights*.

1883   At Cable's instigation, writes "The Scenes of Cable's Romances" for *Century Magazine*. Encouraged by Cable, accompanies illustrator J. O. Davidson to island settlement in Lake Borgne, east of New Orleans, aboard *Susy B*, a boat owned by the *Times-Democrat*. Submits report on unknown village of Filipino fishermen and alligator hunters to *Harper's Weekly*, published as "Saint Malo" in March 31 issue. Late spring, travels among Cajun settlements on Bayou Teche west of New Orleans. Collaboration with Cable in collecting Creole songs comes to an end. Complains of Cable's Christian faith: "Don't try to conceive how I could sympathize with Cable! Because I never sympathized with him at all. His awful faith—which to me represents an undeveloped mental structure—gives a neutral tint to his whole life among us. . . . But Cable is more liberal-minded than his creed; he has also rare analytical powers on a small scale."

1884   August, vacations for the first time in Grand Isle (which he describes the following year as "an old-fashioned, drowsy, free-and-easy Creole watering-place"), in the

Gulf of Mexico southwest of New Orleans. Around this time, Cable tells Hearn the story of the storm in 1856 that destroyed L'Ile Dernière, or Last Island, west of Grand Isle, the inspiration for *Chita*. "I was very nearly in love," he tells Krehbiel of his encounter with a young woman of Basque descent, "not quite sure whether I am not a little in love still,—but I never told her so. It is so strange to find one's self face to face with a beauty that existed in the Tertiary epoch,—300,000 years ago." Inspired by exotic writings of Pierre Loti, considers publishing "a tiny book of purely original sketches"; publishes one of these, "Torn Letters," a first attempt at the style of *Chita*, in *Times-Democrat* of September 14. *Stray Leaves from Strange Literature* published, a collection of folk tales and legends adapted from various traditions including Egyptian, Arabic, Polynesian, and Finnish.

1885   January to April, covers the New Orleans World's Fair (the World's Industrial and Cotton Centennial Exposition) for *Harper's Weekly* and *Harper's Bazar*, including several articles on the Japanese exhibit. With Cable, helps compile *Historical Sketch Book and Guide to New Orleans*, which includes "Scenes of Cable's Romances," for visitors to the fair. *Times-Democrat* leads attacks on Cable after publication of his "The Freedman's Case in Equity," which calls for end to discrimination against African-American citizens. Travels to Florida, collecting material for articles. Writes W. D. O'Connor in July: "Fiction seems to be the only certain road to the publishers' hearts"; considers basing fiction on "ethnographic and anthropologic readings." *Ghombo Zhèbes: A Little Dictionary of Creole Proverbs, Selected from Six Creole Dialects* published, along with *La Cuisine Creole*, a collection of recipes with commentary.

1886   Works on *Chita*, and sends first section to *Harper's Magazine* in October. Reads works of Herbert Spencer and discusses Spencer's ideas with young physician Rudolph Matas. Spencer "has completely converted me away from all 'isms, or sympathies with 'isms."

1887   Resigns from *Times-Democrat* in May. Visits Henry Watkin in Cincinnati on way to New York to meet with editors. Stays with Krehbiel, now music critic for New York *Tribune*, in New York and spends time "polishing

and repolishing phrase after phrase" of *Chita*. Looks up
Elizabeth Bisland, who has moved from New Orleans to
New York to become editor of *Cosmopolitan Magazine*.
Writes Matas: "I met Miss Bisland again. She has expanded
mentally and physically into one of the most superb
women you could wish to converse with." In July, travels
to West Indies aboard the *Barracouta*, a "long, narrow,
graceful steel steamer," and visits St. Croix, St. Kitts, Mon-
serrat, Dominica, and Martinique. Stays in Martinique
until his return to New York in September, when Henry
Alden at *Harper's* buys his essay "A Midsummer Trip to
the Tropics." Guest of Alden's in Metuchen, New Jersey.
On September 28, writes Matas: "I am going back to the
Tropics, probably for many years . . . I find myself able
to abandon journalism, with all its pettiness, cowardices,
selfishnesses, forever." Buys a camera and new clothes; in
October, returns to Martinique aboard the *Barracouta*.
Takes rooms first in city of St. Pierre, then, after outbreak
of smallpox, rents cottage in small mountain town of
Morne Rouge, overlooking "wild surges of purple and
green mountains, all fissured and jagged, and stormy-
looking: a volcanic sea of peaks and craters." Tells Bisland
he loves Martinique "as if it were a human being." *Some
Chinese Ghosts*, dedicated to Krehbiel, published. Hearn
later describes it as the "early work of a man who tried to
understand the Far East from books—and couldn't."

1888   Returning to St. Pierre in late January, learns that Alden
             has rejected his novella "Lys," written during the pre-
             vious two months, about the shock of New York on a
             Creole girl from the tropics. Comments on difficulty of
             finding inexpensive rooms during Carnival: "I have been
             happy to secure one even in a rather retired street—so
             steep that it is really dangerous to sneeze while descending
             it, lest one lose one's balance and tumble right across the
             town." Begins collecting voodoo tales from neighbors.
             Tells Alden in April that he has been "seriously ill," prob-
             ably with typhoid. Begins sending nonfiction sketches to
             Alden of what will become *Two Years in the French West
             Indies*. Makes summer trips into the interior of Martini-
             que. At Grande Anse (now Lorrain), visits a plantation
             and hears a story, supposedly based on fact, of a slave girl
             entrusted with a white child during the 1848 slave rebel-
             lion, which becomes the basis for his short novel *Youma*.

1889 With lifting of quarantine imposed during smallpox epidemic, decides to leave Martinique. Short novel *Chita: A Memory of Last Island* published, after first appearing in *Harper's New Monthly Magazine* (April 1888). On May 8, arrives in New York. Writes Matas: "It seemed like tearing my heart out to leave Martinique." Travels to Philadelphia by train and stays at the home of Dr. George M. Gould, an ophthalmologist and admirer of *Some Chinese Ghosts*, with whom he had corresponded from Martinique. Gould examines Hearn's damaged eye. Completes *Youma* in Philadelphia and writes "Karma," a short story. Returns to New York in October. Attends dinner at the Union League Club; is introduced to William Dean Howells. Relationship with Elizabeth Bisland intensifies; tells Gould in November, "When I see Miss Bisland I feel out of the world for a while." Becomes friendly with Ellwood Hendrick, a young chemical engineer; later corresponds with him extensively.

1890 Receives letter from Daniel James Hearn, the younger brother he has never met, now a farmer in Ohio; they exchange recollections of their parents. Inspired by Percival Lowell's *Soul of the Far East*, which he describes to Gould as "an astounding book,—a godlike book," makes arrangements to travel to Japan, with commission from Harper and Brothers for books and magazine articles. With *Harper's* illustrator C. D. Weldon, takes Canadian Pacific Railway via Montreal to Vancouver, where they board Canadian Pacific steamer *Abyssinia*. Arrives in Yokohama on April 12. Tours the city and its surroundings; writes "A Winter Journey to Japan" to pay for his trip, but soon quarrels with *Harper's*, giving up much needed potential earnings. Works briefly as a private tutor. Through efforts of Basil Hall Chamberlain, professor of Japanese literature at Tokyo Imperial University, hired as teacher at Shimane Prefectural Common Middle School and Normal School in Matsue, on coast of the Japan Sea in western Japan. *Youma: The Story of a West Indian Slave*, *Two Years in the French West Indies*, and translation of Anatole France's *The Crime of Sylvestre Bonnard* published.

1891 Falls ill during the winter. Consents to a marriage suggested and arranged by Nishida Sentaro, a senior colleague, with Koizumi Setsu, 22-year-old daughter of a local samurai family. The newlyweds rent a traditional

Japanese house. Accepts invitation, unprecedented for a European, to visit Izumo Taisha, a major Shinto shrine. Late in the year, accepts teaching position in Kumamoto, on the southern island of Kyushu, at the Fifth Higher Middle School, where he remains three years as the only foreign teacher. Complains to Chamberlain that Kumamoto, in contrast to Matsue, has "no poetry—no courtesy —no myths—no traditions—no superstitions." Through Chamberlain, hires translators, including Okakura Yoshisaburo, to provide him with literal versions of Japanese poems and folktales.

1892   Travels with wife during the summer to little-visited Oki Islands, spending a month there. Writes while in transit, on August 6: "But with what hideous rapidity Japan is modernizing, after all!—not in costume, or architecture, or habit, but in heart and manner. The emotional nature of the race is changing. Will it ever become beautiful again?"

1893   Finishes *Glimpses of Unfamiliar Japan*, his first book on Japanese subjects. Reports considerable savings. Birth of son on November 17, named Leopold Kazuo Koizumi (known as Kazuo), in Kumamoto.

1894   Writes Chamberlain on September 11: "We are all tired of Kumamoto." In October, resigns from teaching post and moves with family to Kobe, where he works as an editorial writer for the *Kobe Chronicle*, an English-language newspaper (contributions include "The Labour Problem in America" and "The Race-Problem in America"). Suffers from eyestrain. *Glimpses of Unfamiliar Japan* published.

1895   Becomes Japanese citizen, taking the name Koizumi Yakumo: "'Eight clouds' is the meaning of 'Yakumo,' and is the first part of the most ancient poem extant in the Japanese language," he writes. Koizumi is wife's family name. In December, at Chamberlain's instigation, is offered Chair of English Language and Literature at Tokyo Imperial University. Describes Tokyo as "the most horrible place in Japan." *Out of the East: Reveries and Studies in New Japan* published.

1896   In September, begins teaching English literature at Tokyo Imperial University. *Kokoro: Hints and Echoes of Japanese Inner Life* published, which includes the stories "At a Railway Station" and "A Conservative." Second son, Iwao, born.

1897   Spends summer with family in Yaizu, a modest fishing vil-
        lage, beginning an intermittent annual tradition; they also
        climb Mt. Fuji. Leaves Houghton Mifflin, his American
        publisher, alleging it invaded his privacy by publishing,
        without his consent, a biographical sketch as an advertise-
        ment. *Gleanings in Buddha-Fields: Studies of Hand and
        Soul in the Far East* published.

1898   On April 1, meets the Harvard-educated scholar of Japa-
        nese art Ernest Fenollosa, formerly of Tokyo Imperial
        University, and his wife, the writer Mary McNeil Fenol-
        losa, who gives him germ of story of the "Mountain of
        Skulls," published as "Fragment" in *In Ghostly Japan*.
        Writes Fenollosa: "I have been meditating, and after the
        meditation I came to the conclusion not to visit your
        charming new home again—not at least before the year
        1900." Takes family on summer vacation to seaside near
        Enoshima. A visitor writes, "Lafcadio, a good swimmer,
        makes somersaults in the water to show us his skill." *Ex-
        otics and Retrospectives* published.

1899   *In Ghostly Japan* published.

1900   Dr. Toyama Shoichi, Hearn's friend and patron at Tokyo
        Imperial University, and a supporter of foreign teachers,
        dies. Attends Toyama's funeral. *Shadowings* published.

1901   Giant cedars destroyed at temple complex of Kobudera,
        behind Hearn's house in Ushigome, where he liked to take
        walks. New abbot at Kobudera accelerates tree-cutting for
        profit. Manacled inmates from nearby prison parade past
        Hearn's house. *A Japanese Miscellany* published.

1902   In a letter, Hearn refers to changes in modern Japan as
        "ugly and sad." Disgusted with modernizing tendencies in
        Tokyo, Hearns have a Japanese-style house built for them
        in partly rural neighborhood of Nishi-Okubo, known as
        the Gardeners' Quarter. Wife, Setsu, manages all building
        arrangements. "My home," Hearn writes, "will always
        have its atmosphere of thousands of years ago." Hearn
        avoids company and writes intensely, sometimes through
        the night, rarely leaving the house. Finishes stories col-
        lected posthumously in *Kwaidan: Stories and Studies of
        Strange Things* (1904) and *Romance of the Milky Way*
        (1905). Learns of the destruction of St. Pierre, in Mar-
        tinique, by eruption of Mt. Pelée on May 8: "Never again

will sun or moon shine upon the streets of that city;—
never again will its ways be trodden;—never again will its
gardens bloom—except in dreams." In July, anxious
about his situation in Japan and hoping to see his son educated in the West, asks Elizabeth Bisland (now Wetmore) to see if any positions might be available for him in
the United States. In November, receives offer from Cornell University, apparently arranged by Wetmore, to deliver lecture series on Japanese civilization. At end of year,
suffers bronchitis and hemorrhage from burst blood vessel in throat. Writes Henry Watkin, "I'm getting down
the shady side of the hill,—and the horizon before me is
already darkening, and the winds blowing out of it, cold."
Kotto; Being Japanese Curios, with Sundry Cobwebs, published by Macmillan.

1903   Informed in March that as a Japanese citizen he is no
longer entitled to "foreigner's salary" and his pay will be
sharply reduced. Asks for sabbatical year due him, in
order to accept Cornell invitation, but is refused. Resigns
from Tokyo Imperial University. Students agitate for his
reinstatement. Writes in August, "After having worked
thirteen years for Japan, I have been only driven out of
the service, and practically banished from the country."
In fall, a daughter, Suzuko, born. Plans short trip to
America to lecture at Cornell, but Cornell withdraws invitation after typhoid outbreak on campus. Completes
manuscript of proposed Cornell lectures, published posthumously as *Japan: An Attempt at Interpretation* (1904).

1904   Russo-Japanese War begins on February 10. Hearn lectures at Waseda University. Receives invitation from University of London to give ten lectures on Japanese
civilization. On August 1, writes "A Letter from Japan,"
about home-front during Russo-Japanese War: "This
contest, between the mightiest of Western powers and a
people that began to study Western science only within
the recollection of many persons still in vigorous life, is,
on one side at least, a struggle for national existence."
Dies of heart failure in Tokyo on September 26, at age 54.
Buried in Zoshigaya Public Cemetery in Tokyo.

Note on the Texts

This volume contains four of Lafcadio Hearn's published books—
Some Chinese Ghosts (1887), *Chita: A Memory of Last Island* (1889),
Two Years in the French West Indies (1890), and *Youma* (1890)—along
with a selection of 25 newspaper and magazine articles published
between 1875 and 1886, and 11 letters written between 1877 and 1888.
The texts of the books have been taken from the first editions. Articles have been reprinted from their original appearances in periodicals. The texts of the letters have been prepared, where possible,
from Hearn's manuscripts. In three instances, where manuscript
sources are not known to be extant, letter texts have been reprinted
from *The Life and Letters of Lafcadio Hearn* (1906), edited by Elizabeth Bisland.

Some Chinese Ghosts, a collection of tales based on Chinese legends, was first published by Roberts Brothers in Boston on February
24, 1887. "[T]here are only six little stories," Hearn wrote Henry
Edward Krehbiel, to whom he dedicated the book, "but each of them
cost months of hard work and study." He had published one of the
six, "The Legend of Tchi-Niu," in the October 31, 1885, issue of
Harper's Bazar, having begun work on the collection, according to
his biographer Elizabeth Stevenson, around December 1884. At some
point prior to October 1886, Hearn's manuscript was rejected by
Ticknor & Fields. Accepting it later in the year, Roberts Brothers
asked Hearn "to cut out a multitude of Japanese, Sanscrit, Chinese,
and Buddhist terms." Hearn responded with what he described for
Krehbiel as "a colossal document of supplication and prayer,—citing
Southey, Moore, Flaubert, Edwin Arnold, Gautier, 'Hiawatha,' and
multitudinous singers and multitudinous songs, and the rights of
prose poetry and the supremacy of Form." Roberts Brothers apparently yielded on questions of vocabulary, but poor sales and a dispute over royalties clouded his relations with the firm, and *Some
Chinese Ghosts* was not reprinted during his lifetime. The present volume prints the text of the 1887 Roberts Brothers edition.

The writing of *Chita: A Memory of Last Island* was already under
way when *Some Chinese Ghosts* appeared in print. "I am trying to find
the Orient at home—to apply the same methods of poetical-prose
treatment to modern local and living themes," Hearn explained to
his friend Elizabeth Bisland. The book's principal incidents—the

devastation of L'Île Dernière by hurricane on August 10, 1856, and the rescue of a young survivor by fishermen—were reportedly recounted by George Washington Cable in conversation at an 1883 dinner Hearn attended in New Orleans. In the summer of 1884, Hearn made the first of several trips to Grand Isle, a popular summer resort to the east of L'Île Dernière in the Gulf; he published "Torn Letters," a collection of fragmentary prose evocations of Gulf scenes, in the New Orleans *Times-Democrat* on September 19, 1884. He began *Chita* on Grand Isle during the summer of 1886, sending the book's first section, "The Legend of L'Île Dernière," to *Harper's* editor Henry M. Alden in October 1886 and the finished manuscript in April 1887. *Chita* was published in its entirety in the April 1888 issue of *Harper's New Monthly Magazine*. Hearn revised *Chita* for book publication during the summer of 1889, while a guest of Dr. George Gould in Philadelphia. Harper & Brothers published the book on September 27, 1889. The text printed here is that of the first edition.

Hearn sailed to Martinique in July 1887 and on his return in September presented Henry Alden with "A Midsummer Trip to the Tropics." Alden bought the article for *Harper's*—it appeared in three parts, in July, August, and September 1888, and eventually formed the opening of *Two Years in the French West Indies*—and he encouraged Hearn to continue submitting to the magazine. With Alden's encouragement and the $700 he received for "A Midsummer Trip," Hearn decided to return to the Caribbean. He spent $400 of his earnings on a camera he planned to use to provide illustrations for his articles, and he sailed again in October 1887. From Martinique, Alden received "La Vérette" (published in *Harper's* in October 1888), "Les Porteuses" (July 1889), and "At Grand Anse" (November 1889); in December 1887 he rejected a longer work, "Lys," which Hearn then destroyed in its initial form (he included a much truncated version in *Two Years in the French West Indies*). Hearn's plans for his new camera appear to have gone largely unfulfilled—he is reported to have found it unwieldy and instead enlisted the aid of local photographers, including William Lawless, the British consul at St. Pierre, and a professional, Léon Sully. He complained at length and at times bitterly to Alden that he was not afforded the opportunity while in Martinique to read proofs of his sketches, but on his return to the United States in May 1889 he was able to devote his full attention to polishing and proofreading his Caribbean writings for book publication. Harper & Brothers published *Two Years in the French West Indies* on March 11, 1890; the text printed here and the accompanying illustrations have been taken from the first edition.

Hearn's short novel *Youma*, like much of *Two Years in the French West Indies*, was written in Martinique, published first in *Harper's*

New Monthly Magazine (in January and February 1890), and then considerably revised before it appeared in book form. Hearn had finished the book—which "made itself out of an incident related to me," he wrote Bisland, "about a case of heroism during the great negro revolt" of 1848—by February 1889. This volume prints the text of the first edition, published on May 12, 1890 by Harper & Brothers.

The penultimate section of this volume, "Selected Journalism," contains 25 newspaper and magazine articles written by Hearn between 1875 and 1886, first in Cincinnati and then in New Orleans. These articles have been reprinted from the original periodicals; none was collected by Hearn in book form during his lifetime. All of Hearn's newspaper journalism included here was published anonymously, with the exception of four reports on New Orleans for the *Cincinnati Commercial,* which appeared under the pseudonym "Ozias Midwinter," after a character in Wilkie Collins' novel *Armadale.* Hearn's magazine articles appeared with his byline. One article, "The Death of Marie Laveau," was originally published without a title; the present title was first used by S. Frederick Starr, editor of *Inventing New Orleans: Writings of Lafcadio Hearn* (Jackson: University Press of Mississippi, 2001). The source of each article included in the present volume is listed below:

"Some Strange Experience: The Reminiscences of a Ghost-Seer," *Cincinnati Commercial,* September 26, 1875.

"Levee Life: Haunts and Pastimes of the Roustabouts," *Cincinnati Commercial,* March 17, 1876.

"Black Varieties: The Minstrels of the Row," *Cincinnati Commercial,* April 9, 1876.

"Gibbeted: Execution of a Youthful Murderer," *Cincinnati Commercial,* August 26, 1876.

"Dolly: An Idyl of the Levee," *Cincinnati Commercial,* August 27, 1876.

"Frost Fancies," *Cincinnati Commercial,* December 10, 1876.

"At the Gate of the Tropics," *Cincinnati Commercial,* November 26, 1877.

"New Orleans in Wet Weather," *Cincinnati Commercial,* December 22, 1877.

"New Orleans (Ruffians in New Orleans—The Sicilian Vendetta— Some Curiosities of Creole Grammar—A Weird Creole Lovesong—Voudooism—The Grace of the Serpent)," *Cincinnati Commercial,* December 27, 1877.

"New Orleans (The Curious Nomenclature of New Orleans Streets —Some Little Creole Love Songs)," *Cincinnati Commercial,* February 18, 1878.

"The Glamour of New Orleans," *Daily City Item*, November 26, 1878.

"The City of Dreams," *Daily City Item*, March 9, 1879.

"Why Crabs Are Boiled Alive," *Daily City Item*, October 5, 1879.

"Gottschalk," *Daily City Item*, September 22, 1880.

"The Tale of a Fan," *Daily City Item*, July 1, 1881.

"The Death of Marie Laveau," *City Item*, July 17, 1881.

"Voices of Dawn," *Daily City Item*, July 22, 1881.

"A River Reverie," *Times-Democrat* (New Orleans), May 2, 1882.

"New Orleans in Carnival Garb," *Harper's Weekly* 27 (February 24, 1883): 122.

"Saint Maló, A Lacustrine Village in Louisiana," *Harper's Weekly* 27 (March 31, 1883): 198–99.

"The Roar of a Great City," *Times-Democrat* (New Orleans), November 30, 1884.

"The Creole Patois," *Harper's Weekly* 29 (January 10 and 17, 1885): 27; 43.

"The New Orleans Exposition," *Harper's Weekly* 29 (January 31, 1885): 155.

"The Last of the Voudoos," *Harper's Weekly* 29 (November 7, 1885): 726–27.

"The Last of the New Orleans Fencing-Masters," *Southern Bivouac* N.S. 2 (November 1886): 349–54.

The final section of this volume contains a selection of 11 letters written by Hearn between 1877 and 1888. All of these letters have been published previously, in *The Life and Letters of Lafcadio Hearn* (Boston: Houghton Mifflin, 1906) and elsewhere, but sometimes with extensive omissions, revisions, and mistranscriptions. The texts of eight of the letters included in this volume have been newly prepared from Hearn's manuscripts (Ms Am 2243, Lafcadio Hearn papers, Houghton Library, Harvard College Library, Harvard University); these letters are published by permission of the Houghton Library, Harvard University. The remaining three letters—of which the original manuscripts are not known to be extant—have been reprinted from *The Life and Letters of Lafcadio Hearn*. The following is a list of recipients and sources:

To Henry Edward Krehbiel (New Orleans, 1877): ms. Houghton.
To Henry Edward Krehbiel (New Orleans, 1878): ms. Houghton.
To Henry Edward Krehbiel (New Orleans, 1878): ms. Houghton.
To Henry Edward Krehbiel (New Orleans, 1880): ms. Houghton.
To Henry Edward Krehbiel (New Orleans, 1880): ms. Houghton.
To Henry Edward Krehbiel (New Orleans, February 1881): ms. Houghton.

To Henry Edward Krehbiel (New Orleans, 1881): ms. Houghton.
To Page Baker (Grand Isle, 1884): *Life and Letters*, vol. 1, pp. 87–95.
To Henry Edward Krehbiel (Martinique, 1887): ms. Houghton.
To George M. Gould (Martinique, June 1888): *Life and Letters*, vol. 1, pp. 422–27.
To George M. Gould (Martinique, August 1888): *Life and Letters*, vol. 1, pp. 428–34.

This volume presents the texts of the original printings and manuscripts chosen for inclusion here, but it does not attempt to reproduce features of their typographic design, such as the display capitalization of chapter openings, or holographic features, such as variation in the length of dashes. The texts are presented without change, except for the correction of typographical errors. Spelling, punctuation, and capitalization are often expressive features, and they are not altered, even when inconsistent or irregular. The following is a list of typographical errors and slips of the pen corrected, cited by page and line number: 71.18, Porlain-God; 93.4, swing!"; 143.15, She; 266.30, *Toutt*; 328.28, yche moin; 345.9, face; 367.33, *alle*; 370.6, hen!"); 417.9, bed of-Jesus; 428.34, *atouèelement*; 429.3, Perè; 436.10, church holds; 438.40, Grammar. [no closing bracket]; 452.29, slavery,; 459.27, Every body; 461.29, plantations,; 489.39, *larue.*"; 504.12, founderies; 519.1, little; 564.1, no mamma!; 567.37, . . . *Quim*; 580.12, happy! . . . ; 611.35, ruining; 617.37, "old man,"; 619.19, doorstep,; 621.27, a is; 622.19, you? Well; 633.26, could'nt; 634.27, troublle; 634.31, in her; 638.31, Picket's; 638.34, Picket; 638.37, betweet; 639.6, Picket; 639.15, Picket; 640.19, row; 641.7, Rows; 645.22, or light; 647.14, was; 657.17, guilty."; 669.24–25, 'longshoresmen; 678.15, anchient; 678.32, to to him; 679.13, Antonie; 681.17, fire fight; 683.40, wreath; 691.30, *viatecum*; 693.10, it; 694.1, the; 694.37, *courir*; 695.7, *courir*; 704.39, *Froment*; 705.32, *Froment*; 705.32, Rilser; 706.9, Mol 'aimin; 708.4, *nommé. Toucouton*; 715.20, Fors; 719.25, Laveau,; 745.17, sibillant; 768.40, *Lulla*; 774.28, Beaugard; 776.12, saw Massr'; 778.20, Mississipi; 780.18, what; 784.20, me."; 784.28, which formless; 787.25, Carnaval; 788.16, a a; 788.31, *des*; 790.18, than the a; 794.6, Soirees; 794.6, Abbe; 794.12, *Soirees*; 804.15, unparalled.

Notes

In the notes below, the reference numbers refer to page and line of this volume (the line count includes titles and headings). No note is made for material found in standard desk-reference books such as the *American Heritage Dictionary* or *Webster's Biographical Dictionary*. Foreign phrases with which Hearn assumes a reader's familiarity, or where the meaning is clear from context, are generally left untranslated. Arlin Turner provides a useful and informative introduction to *Chita: A Memory of Last Island* in the edition of the work in the Southern Literary Classics Series (Chapel Hill: University of North Carolina Press, 1969). For more detailed notes, references to other studies, and further biographical background than is contained in the Chronology, see: Elizabeth Bisland, *The Life and Letters of Lafcadio Hearn* (Boston and New York: Houghton Mifflin, 1906); Simon J. Bronner, ed., *Lafcadio Hearn's America: Ethnographic Sketches and Editorials* (Lexington: University Press of Kentucky, 2002); Jonathan Cott, *Wandering Ghost: The Odyssey of Lafcadio Hearn* (New York: Alfred A. Knopf, 1991); Delia LaBarre, ed., *The New Orleans of Lafcadio Hearn: Illustrated Sketches from the Daily City Item* (Baton Rouge: Louisiana State University Press, 2007); P. D. & Ione Perkins, *Lafcadio Hearn: A Bibliography of His Writings* (Boston: Houghton Mifflin, 1934); S. Frederick Starr, ed., *Inventing New Orleans: Writings of Lafcadio Hearn* (Jackson: University Press of Mississippi, 2001); Elizabeth Stevenson, *Lafcadio Hearn* (New York: Macmillan, 1961; reprinted as *The Grass Lark: A Study of Lafcadio Hearn*).

SOME CHINESE GHOSTS

1.1   SOME CHINESE GHOSTS]   Hearn knew no Chinese. His reliance on French, German, and British Sinologists (some of whom are mentioned in his "Preface" and "Notes") is evident in the variant names he uses: both "Pe-King" and "Pekin" for the city now known as Beijing, for example, and both "Confucius" and "Kong-fu-tze." The meanings he assigns to most of his Chinese words and phrases are clear from context.

3.2   HENRY EDWARD KREHBEIL]   Prominent music critic and musicologist (1854–1923). From 1874 to 1880, he served as music critic for the *Cincinnati Gazette*, where he befriended Hearn; later he became music editor of the *New York Tribune*. He wrote articles for various journals, translated opera libretti, and published several books, including a pioneering study of African-American music, *Afro-American Folksongs: A Study in Racial and National Music* (1914). He championed the music of Wagner, Brahms, and Tchaikovsky.

10.16   the Son of Heaven]   The emperor.

53.17   the City of King-te-chin]   The city now known as Jingdezhen in Jiangxi Province is often called the "Porcelain Capital" because of its long history of porcelain production.

65.37   the Tai-Ping rebellion]   An extensive revolt against the Chinese government (1850–1864) led by a heterodox Christian convert.

CHITA

73.3–4   *"But Nature . . . way."*]   Complete text of an untitled notebook poem by Ralph Waldo Emerson.

76.1–6   *Je suise . . . Et poursuivant.*]   From the "Océan" section of Victor Hugo's long poem *La Légende des siècles.* (1883). "I am the vast fray—reptilian since I'm a wave, winged since I'm the wind—power and flight, hate and life, immense swell, pursued and pursuing."

83.18   Πνεύμα]   "Pneuma," Greek for "breath" or "spirit."

85.21   the *grande-écaille*]   Tarpon.

87.26   the dreamy Têche]   The Bayou Têche, a major waterway in south central Louisiana.

91.33   *"Il n'y a rien de mieux . . . de s'amuser!"*]   "There's nothing better to do than to have a good time!"

92.12–13   the night of . . . and fifty-six]   Date on which a strong Atlantic hurricane made landfall and destroyed Last Island.

100.23   Virgin with an Indian face]   The Virgin of Guadalupe, who reportedly appeared to an indigenous Mexican farmer in 1531.

115.29–116.4   *Aussi . . . Priez pour eux!*]   "Also to the memory of her husband, JULIEN RAYMOND LA BRIERRE, born in St. Landry parish the 29th of May 1828, and to their daughter, EULALIE, age four years and five months, all of whom perished in the great storm that swept away Last Island on the 10th of August 1856. Pray for them!"

116.37   *crête-de-coq*]   The flowering plant known as cockscomb.

121.13   Hermes]   Presumably a reference to the "Hermetic" writings attributed to an Egyptian priest known as Hermes Trismegistus, which were influential during the Renaissance.

136.20   Mont-de-Piété]   A municipal pawnshop.

139.14–17   "*M'ama ancor, . . . tuo cor.*"]   Love me again, fiery beauty, as you loved me then,—don't listen to anyone, only ask your own heart.

139.22–25   "*M'ama pur . . . sol è.*"]   Love me yet with eternal love, let it not seem a crime to you; I assure you that hell is only a fable.

142.32   *tutoiement*]   The use of informal French pronouns (*tu* and *toi*) as a form of intimacy.

144.10–11   Chancellorsville]   The Civil War battle at Chancellorsville, Virginia, took place during the spring of 1863. It was a significant victory for the Confederacy.

TWO YEARS IN THE FRENCH WEST INDIES

149.1–2   TWO YEARS IN THE FRENCH WEST INDIES]   Hearn includes a great deal of French Creole dialect in this book and in *Youma*, which follows. He provides his own translations or paraphrases for much of it, apparently expects his readers to understand many untranslated phrases according to context, and deliberately leaves others obscure.

151.1–7   A MON CHERI AMI . . . *Revanants*.]   "To my dear friend, Leopold Arnoux, notary at Saint Pierre, Martinique. A souvenir of our walks, our voyages, our conversations, of fellow-feelings exchanged, of all the charm of an unchangeable and unforgettable friendship, and of everything that speaks to the soul in the sweet Country of Revenants."

152.1–5   "*La façon . . . LE PÈRE DUTERTE (1667)*]   "The way of life in the country is so pleasant, the temperature so good, and one lives there in such a state of straightforward freedom, that I have never met one single man, nor one single woman, of all those who came back therefrom, in whom I have not remarked a most passionate desire to return thereunto." The author of the passage is the French missionary and historian Jean-Baptiste du Tertre (1610–1687), author of *Histoire générale des Antilles habitées par les Français* (Paris 1667).

170.34   Danish soldiers]   The Virgin Islands were part of the Danish West Indies until Denmark sold the islands to the United States in 1917.

176.15   the Montagne Pelée . . . green]   The French word "pelé" can mean "bald," "peeled," or "naked."

188.25   Dr. J. J. J. Cornilliac]   Hearn mentions Cornilliac's "Recherches chronologiques et historiques sur l'Origine et la Propagation de la Fièvre Jaune aux Antilles" ("Chronological and historical studies of the origin and propagation of yellow fever in the Antilles"), a "curious compilation," in a letter to George M. Gould sent from Martinique in February 1889: "It contains a great deal of valuable matter regarding the climate of the West Indies, and formative influences of that climate on races and temperament." Cornilliac also wrote a general history of the Antilles. According to Edward Larocque Tinker, in *Lafcadio Hearn's American Days* (1924), Hearn met Cornilliac in Martinique and was given free run of his library, "easily the richest on the island."

190.1   *mouillage . . . morne*] Mooring; a place where boats are anchored. For Hearn's explanation of *morne*, see 385.25 in this volume.

190.20–21   Coomans . . . Pompeiian studies] The Belgian artist Pierre Oliver Joseph Coomans (1816–1889) was known for academic renditions of classical sites.

192.20   *bourdon*] Great bell.

196.26   "'Arboribus suus horror inest.'"] "In those trees resides a natural rustling" (Lucan, *Pharsalia*, book 3, line 411). The Latin "horror" can also mean "dread" or "fright," which is how Hearn seems to construe it.

202.34   Josephine] Joséphine de Beauharnais (1763–1814), Napoleon Bonaparte's first wife and empress of France, was born and raised in Martinique.

204.6   *Allée des duels*] The local dueling grounds.

208.10   *sabliers*] Tropical trees with spines on the trunk and branches.

212.17–18   Nelson's monument] Horatio Nelson (1758–1805), Vice-Admiral in the British Navy, is best known for his participation in the Napoleonic Wars, especially the British victory at Trafalgar in October 1805, in which he was killed; earlier in the same year, Nelson had unsuccessfully pursued the French fleet across the Atlantic to Martinique and back again to Europe.

226.23   Charles Kingsley's "At Last"] *At Last: A Christmas in the West Indies* (1871), travel book by Kingsley (1819–1875), best known for his novels including *Westward Ho!* (1855).

232.12   babagee] *Babaji*, Hindu priest or teacher.

239.24   *baragouin*] Gibberish.

243.1   the Island of the Seven Cities] In his *Life and Voyages of Christopher Columbus* (1828), Washington Irving mentions "the Island of Seven Cities, so called from an ancient legend of seven bishops, who, with a multitude of followers, fled from Spain at the time of its conquest by the Moors, and, guided by Heaven to some unknown island in the ocean, founded on it seven splendid cities."

288.37–38   "Le plus court . . . très-gros bambou."] "The shortest of these drums is called *Bamboula* because it is sometimes made of a very thick piece of bamboo."

298.30   ajoupas] Small huts.

301.24   Dr. Rufz] In a letter to George M. Gould, February 1889, Hearn writes: "Martinique has had several physicians of colonial celebrity,—how great I cannot estimate, being ignorant of their comparative value; but some of them have a decided charm as writers and historians. Such was Rufz de Lavison, author of a delightful history of the colony." See Bisland, *Life and Letters of Lafcadio Hearn*, volume one, pages 441–42.

307.22   M. Adrien Dessalles] Author of *Histoire générale des Antilles* (1671).

309.34   Père du Tertre] See note 152.1–5.

324.24   trigonocephalus] A pit viper named for its triangular head.

341.36   Hagar] See Genesis 16 and 21.

342.19   *degringolade*] Falling down; going from bad to worse.

355.6   *sang-mêlée*] A woman of mixed blood.

368.3–4   comparison . . . Nausicaa] In the sixth book of the *Odyssey*, Odysseus tells the Phaeacian princess Nausicaa that she resembles a young palm tree he once saw growing by the altar of Apollo in Delos.

385.6–7   Olive and Duplessis] Charles Liénard, Sieur d'Olive, and Jean Duplessis, Sieur d'Ossonville, were early French explorers and colonizers in the West Indies.

387.12–13   Japanese painter . . . Fusiyama] Hokusai Katsushika (1760–1849) was the Japanese master whose *One Hundred Views of Mt. Fuji*, a three-volume series of woodblock prints, began appearing in 1834.

388.15   Moreau de Jonnés] Alexandre Moreau De Jonnes's *Adventures in Wars of the Republic and Consulate* was published in 1858. Moreau de Jonnes was known for his later work in social statistics; his memoirs included his experiences in the Caribbean during the Carib-English War of 1795.

394.10   The pilot was a poor mulatto] See Hearn's story "The Pilot," appended to his letter to Krehbiel on page 775 of this volume.

399.11–12   the next transit of Venus] Following the much anticipated transits of Venus in 1874 and 1882, the next transit would not occur until 2004.

400.7–11   *Saison fraîche . . . Saison chaude et sèche . . . Saison chaude et pluvieuse.*]   Cool season; hot and dry season; hot and rainy season.

403.36   "De la piqûre . . . Martinique,"]   "On snakebite in Martinique."

419.4–5   Pelion upon Ossa]   In Greek mythology, the giants Otus and Ephialtes tried to reach heaven to overthrow the gods by piling Mount Ossa on Mount Olympus and Mount Pelion on Mount Ossa.

420.1–2   a *canot*, waiting for the *embellie*]   A dinghy, waiting for fair weather.

420.22–23   tremendous . . . Job]   See Job 15:7: "Art thou the first man that was born? or wast thou made before the hills?"

425.36   chabin]   In Martinique, a person of mixed race, with light skin color and often light hair color.

426.40   *requin*]   Shark.

435.26   *belles affranchies*]   Refers to the Creole practice of keeping mistresses who were formerly slaves but had been freed (*affranchies*) by their masters.

442.10   author of that "Voyage aux Antilles"]   Jean-Baptiste Labat (1663–1738), a French missionary, scientist, and explorer also known as Père Labat (1693–1705), author of *Voyages aux isles de l'Amérique (Antilles)*. Chateaubriand mentions Labat in his *Mémoires d'outre-tombe* (1848).

442.31   "*De la naissance . . . mulastres*"]   "On the shameful origin of mulattos."

444.37   "Leur sueur . . . de la Guinée,"]   "Their sweat is not fetid like that of the Negroes of Guinea."

451.36–39   *La race . . . aux Antilles Françaises.*"]   "The mixed race, issuing from whites and blacks, is eminently civilizable. As physical types, it produces in many individuals, and in women in general, the most beautiful specimens of the human race."—*Racial Prejudice in the French Antilles.*

454.1–2   *Née de l'amour . . . d'oublis.*]   "Born of love . . . the woman of color lives on love, laughter, and forgettings."

454.35–40   L'Amour . . . yeux.]   Love took care to make her tender, naïve, and caressing, made to please, even more to love, bearing all the precious character traits of a lover, pleasure in her mouth and love in her eyes.

456.22   *pour services . . . maîtres*]   For services (or favors) rendered to their masters.

456.34–35   *pour service . . . milice*]   For service performed in the militia.

458.11   *"C'est un pays perdu!"*]   It's a lost country!

463.32   *lepismæ*]   Genus of primitive insects including the silverfish.

481.32   *"pouloss . . . cassé-y."*]   She asks him to remove the heart-shaped peel without breaking it.

502.34–35   idyl of Bernardin de Saint-Pierre]   Jacques-Henri Bernardin de Saint-Pierre (1737–1814) was the author of *Paul et Virginie* (1787). In the short novel, two children from the unspoiled island of Mauritius fall in love with each other, but encroaching civilization brings their love to a tragic end.

503.24   political tragedies of 1848]   Exiles from political unrest in France, Italy, and elsewhere during the revolutionary year of 1848 found refuge in Louisiana.

509.26   torrefaction]   Heat or dryness.

511.11   *berceuse*]   Rocking-chair.

512.30   *cabritt-bois*]   Thomas Bailey Aldrich, in his essay "On Early Rising" in *Ponkapog Papers* (1904), identifies the insect as "a species of colossal cricket called the wood-kid; in the creole tongue, *cabritt-bois.* This ingenious pest works a soothing, sleep-compelling chant from sundown until precisely half past four in the morning, when it suddenly stops and by its silence awakens everybody it has lulled into slumber with its insidious croon."

518.12   *zicaques*]   Creole for "les icaques," tropical fruits resembling plums.

524.8   *pouémiè communion*]   First communion.

YOUMA

544.2   JOSEPH S. TUNISON]   A former colleague of Hearn's at the *Cincinnati Gazette.* See page 785 of his volume.

547.24–26   *"Si elle . . . valet!"*]   "If she's nothing but a servant . . . then you're nothing but a valet!"

550.17   the Queen of Sheba]   See 1 Kings 10.

558.20   *quimboiseurs*]   Sorcerers.

559.20   *vesou*]   Sugar syrup or juice.

568.16   *panseur*]   Wound-dresser.

573.11   *griffone*]   Woman of mixed race.

576.33   *manicou*]   Opossum.

579.8   *rafale*]   Squall.

579.35   *tonnelle*]   Bower or arbor.

581.20   *falaises*]   Cliffs.

593.14–15   The Republic had been proclaimed]   The French Second Republic, established in 1848.

593.28   Rochambeau]   During the 1790s, Donatien-Marie-Joseph de Vimeur, vicomte de Rochambeau (1755–1813), sought to re-establish French authority in Martinique and Saint-Domingue (later Haiti).

596.23   insulting *tutoiement*]   See note 142.32.

599.4   memory of Hayti]   The Haitian Revolution of 1791–1804, a slave revolt, resulted in the independent republic of Haiti.

603.10   "*Tas de charognes!*"]   "Pile of carrion!"

607.10   *rez-de-chaussée*]   Ground floor.

SELECTED JOURNALISM

615.3   A GHOST-SEER]   A portrait of Alethea ("Mattie") Foley, a former slave, whom Hearn married in 1874.

634.26   fodder-shock]   Harvested corn heaped in a field for winter feed for cattle.

638.11   men patted juba]   African-American musical practice of slapping arms, legs, and cheeks in percussive rhythm.

639.36   policy shop]   Illegal lottery operation for "playing the numbers." The term "policy" came to denote an African-American clientele.

644.15   Gretchen-faced]   Innocent-looking, like Margarete (Gretchen) in Goethe's *Faust*.

647.12   "Damon and Pythias"]   Legendary Greek figures exemplifying loyal friendship. When Pythias was condemned to death, Damon took his place as hostage while Pythias returned home to settle his affairs. Both were freed in recognition of their loyalty.

649.39   the "Iron Shroud"]   "The Iron Shroud," a gothic tale by William Mudford, was published in *Blackwood's Edinburgh Magazine* in August 1830.

665.12   "I'll 'vag' you."]   A threat to put her out of the house, making her a vagrant.

668.6   Cufic characters]   Or Kufic: older, highly ornamental Arabic script.

672.1   Casanova]   Hearn means Domenico Canova, a relative of the neo-classical sculptor Antonio Canova, who arrived in New Orleans in 1838.

675.9–10   Soliman, the pre-Adamite Sultan]   In the gothic novel *Vathek* (1786) by William Beckford (1760–1844), Caliph Vathek, a cruel tyrant, sets out to find the city of Istakhar and the treasures of the pre-adamite sultans, who governed rational beings before the creation of Adam. The sultans include "Soliman Raad, Soliman Daki, and Soliman Di Gian Ben Gian, who, after having chained up the Dives in the dark caverns of Kaf, became so presumptuous as to doubt of the Supreme Power."

675.35   the *teocallis* at Palenque]   Mayan temple complex in the Yucatan in Mexico.

676.33–36   "Pere Antoine's . . . Thomas Bailey Aldrich]   Aldrich (1836–1907) included the story in *Marjorie Daw and Other People* (1873).

678.19–20   "Thy stature is like to a palm-tree."]   Song of Solomon 7:7.

678.35–36   "I said, I will go up to the palm tree . . . "]   Song of Solomon 7:8.

681.15   vibriones]   A genus of microorganisms, some of which carry diseases.

681.23   "La Fille de Madame Angot,"]   *Madame Angot's Daughter*, comic opera in three acts by Charles Lecocq, first performed in 1872.

682.2   Yellow Jack]   Yellow fever.

686.11   "Beast Butler!"]   General Benjamin Butler (1818–1893) led the Union occupation of New Orleans in April 1862. His harsh treatment of the locale populace, including his notorious "Woman's Order" of May 15 (". . . when any female shall, by word, gesture, or movement, insult or show contempt for any officer or soldier of the United States, she shall be regarded and held liable to be treated as a woman of the town plying her avocation"), earned him the nickname "Beast Butler." He later served as a congressman and governor of Massachusetts.

688.12   metoposcopy]   Practice of divination developed in the sixteenth century by Jerome Cardan (1501–1576) for discerning character and destiny based on the pattern of lines on the subject's forehead.

691.7   "Sicilian Vespers,"]   Insurrection against French rule that began in Sicily at the start of vespers on Easter Monday in 1282 and resulted in the massacre of thousands of French inhabitants.

693.23   Warmoth]   Henry Clay Warmoth (1842–1931), a Republican from

Illinois, was governor of Louisiana from 1868 until his impeachment and removal from office in December 1872.

693.24   the White League] Paramilitary force that promoted white supremacy in Louisiana during the period of Reconstruction. The White League staged a military coup in New Orleans (known as the "Battle of Liberty Place") on September 14, 1874, and briefly took control of the state government before President Ulysses S. Grant sent in federal troops to restore order.

698.24–25   the so-called "line of beauty"] The English artist William Hogarth (1697–1764) argued in his treatise *The Analysis of Beauty* (1753) that an S-shaped or serpentine line, which he called the "line of beauty," best conveys the liveliness and movement of nature.

698.28   Lilith and Lamia] Legendary female demons associated with snakes. In John Keats's "Lamia" (1819), the heroine is initially trapped in the body of a snake.

698.34–35   "The way of a serpent upon a rock."]   Proverbs 30:19.

699.7   obi-men] Or *obeah* men: Practitioners of a form of sorcery or witchcraft of African origin involving fetishes. In his article on "Creole Slave Songs" (*Century Magazine*, April 1886), George Washington Cable writes, "Voodoo . . . is the name of an imaginary being of vast supernatural powers residing in the form of a harmless snake. This spiritual influence or potentate is the recognized antagonist and opposite of Obi, the great African Manitou or deity."

699.33   Irving's "Adelantado of the Seven Cities"]   The story by Washington Irving (1783–1859) appeared posthumously in 1866.

700.35   priest-caps at the four angles]   In military parlance, protruding salients or angles that, when viewed from above, looked like the caps worn by Catholic priests.

704.4–5   Louis Philippe . . . residence in New Orleans]   Louis Philippe, Duc d'Orléans, spent four years in exile in the United States after the French Revolution. He and his two brothers lived briefly in New Orleans in early 1798 as they prepared for their return voyage to France. Louis Philippe was king of France, 1830–48.

704.7–8   Batture suits]   A series of lawsuits involving jurisdiction over conflicting claims to riverbank alluvial property (or "batture"). In 1811, Justice John Marshall ruled for the federal government against the property owner Edward Livingston, a prominent Louisiana attorney and statesman.

704.38–39   Alphonse Daudet's wonderful novel]   Daudet's *Young Fromont and Old Risler* (1874) appeared in Mary Neal Sherwood's translation as *Sidonie* (Boston, 1877).

712.13   the epidemic] New Orleans suffered a major outbreak of yellow fever in 1878. See Hearn's remarks on the epidemic in a letter on page 782 of this volume.

714.5   GOTTSCHALK] Louis Moreau Gottschalk (1829–1869), composer and widely traveled piano virtuoso. Born in New Orleans, the son of a Jewish businessman and a white Haitian woman, he drew from many cultural sources, including African-American music, for popular pieces such as the "Bamboula: Danse de Nègres."

714.7   Life of Gottschalk] Luís Ricardo Fors, *Gottschalk* (Havana, 1880).

714.33   Balzac's "Peau de Chagrin,"] In Balzac's philosophical novel *The Wild Ass's Skin* (1831), a young man acquires a magic piece of shagreen that shrinks with each wish granted.

717.18–19   the young Sulamitess or . . . the Queen of Sheba] The Sulamitess (or Shulamite) is Solomon's lover in Song of Solomon. The Queen of Sheba visited Solomon (1 Kings 10); passages in Song of Solomon have sometimes been interpreted as alluding to the Queen of Sheba.

717.27   the C.C.R.R.] The Crescent City Railroad.

718.3–4   George Cable's . . . Days"] Palmyre actually appears in Cable's novel *The Grandissimes: A Story of Creole Life* (1880), which Hearn reviewed in the *City Item* on September 27, 1880.

720.2   the famous Book of London Cries] Many illustrated books and broadsides devoted to merchants' cries in London appeared from 1590 to 1861. Perhaps the most famous is Edward Ryland's *Cries of London* (c. 1760).

720.12   "lagniappe"] In his "New Orleans Letter" (*Cincinnati Commercial*, January 7, 1878), Hearn wrote that lagniappe might be translated "the give-away": "If you buy a ten-cent loaf of the delicious, cream-white bread for which New Orleans is famous, the baker presents you with a handful of ginger-cakes or a few doughnuts for *la gniape*."

723.28   an illustrious visitor] Mark Twain visited New Orleans in 1882.

725.2–3   the colors of Rex] Founded in 1872, Rex is among the principal organizations or "krewes" of Mardi Gras celebrations in New Orleans. The colors are purple, green, and gold.

725.13–14   Doresque oddity of the shadows] A reference to the atmospheric illustrations of the French artist Gustave Doré (1832–1883), such as his popular images for Dante's *Inferno* (1861).

725.31   *Manon Lescaut*] Short novel by the French writer Antoine François Prévost. The novel, first published in Paris in 1731, is a tragic love story set in France and Lousiana during the early eighteenth century.

734.6   "Silence: a Fragment"]   "Silence—A Fable" (1845).

738.4   the Roman *columbaria*]   Roman tombs with niches for urns.

742.40   *poule-d'eau*]   Aquatic bird also known as the coot.

743.13   "The Enraged Musician,"]   Print by William Hogarth (1697–1764), published in 1741.

743.26   The electric light]   Electric lighting was first installed along New Orleans streets in 1882.

743.30   the Pascagoula]   A small Indian tribe that lived along the Pascagoula River in southern Mississippi. According to legend, the Pascagoula committed mass suicide rather than fight with another tribe. Singing tribal songs, they walked into the river, which their ghostly voices turned into a "singing river."

744.31–32   *Story of . . . Isles*]   The story, contained in *The Thousand and One Nights*, recounts how an enchantress transforms the diverse races of a royal capital into fish of different colors.

745.6   Prion's "Satyress"]   Louis Prion's painting "A Family of Satyrs" was first exhibited in Paris in 1879.

745.9   the Malay poem "Bidasari,"]   A Malay folktale in verse, of uncertain authorship, with a plot resembling "Snow White."

746.25   Oriental studies . . . Gérôme!]   The painters Jean Auguste Dominique Ingres (1780–1867), Edouard Richter (1844–1913), and Jean-Léon Gérôme (1824–1904) were known for their depictions of native women of the Middle East in exotic surroundings.

747.9   *paroissiens*]   Prayer-books.

747.15   *Mélusine*]   *Mélusine: Recueil de mythologie, litterature opulaire, traditions et usages,* by H. Galdoz and E. Rolland, published in Paris, 1878–1887.

747.18   George Cable's works]   George Washington Cable (1844–1925) published *Old Creole Days* (1879), a volume of stories, and the novel *The Grandissimes* (1880), both of which stimulated national interest in the creole culture and racial strife of Louisiana.

747.20   a Franco-Louisianian novel]   *L'Habitation Saint-Ybars* (1881) by Alfred Mercier.

747.23   M.M. Luzel and Sébillot in Bretagne]   François-Marie Luzel and Paul Sébillot were nineteenth-century collectors of folktales in Lower and Upper Brittany respectively.

747.29   Alphonse Daudet]   See note 704.38–39.

748.3   another paper] Hearn did not publish such an article though his sometime collaborator in researching creole music, George Washington Cable, published an article on "Creole Slave Songs" in the *Century Magazine* in April 1886, including a "genuine Voodoo song, given me by Lafcadio Hearn." Hearn's *Gombo Zhèbes: A Little Dictionary of Creole Proverbs* was published in 1885.

748.5   THE NEW ORLEANS EXPOSITION] The World's Industrial and Cotton Centennial Exposition, held in New Orleans 1885–86.

748.17   the Emperor ZIN-MU TEN-ô] Emperor Jimmu (Jimmu Tennô), first emperor of Japan and mythical founder of the nation.

750.1–2   ARY RENAN] French art critic (1858–1900) associated with the Symbolist movement; he published articles on the depiction of animals in Japanese art.

751.12   LÉON DE ROSNY's "Si-Ka-Zen-Yo."] Anthology of Japanese poetry in original Japanese with French translations, published in Paris in 1870.

751.27–29   views of Fusiyama . . . the great artist HOUKOUSAÏ] See note 387.12–13. Hearn adopts the French spelling of Hokusai.

752.2   Yosiwara] Japanese woodblock artists depicted the celebrated beauties of the pleasure quarters of Yoshiwara, on the outskirts of Edo (Tokyo).

752.22   another "Rose," another "Marie,"] Presumably Marie Laveau and her rival, Rosalie, celebrated practitioners of voodoo.

752.31   Berenger-Feraud] Laurent J. Bérénger-Féraud, *Les Peuplades de la Sénégambie* (Paris, 1879).

753.25   the mysterious obi power] See note 699.7.

755.1—2   Boubakar-Segou] Senegalese leader in Pierre Loti's *Le Roman d'un spahi* (1881).

755.11   Sultana-Validé] An allusion to the story of Aimée du Buc de Rivéry (1776–1817), from a wealthy French family. Returning home to Martinique after her schooling in Nantes, she was supposedly captured by pirates, sold into slavery, then given as a present to the Sultan of Constantinople. Aimée became Sultana Validé, mother of Sultan Mahmoud II.

757.7   *banquette*] Sidewalk.

757.31   Spanish Creoles] The original meaning of "creole" was a native-born inhabitant of New Orleans.

758.36–37   precise speech of the *Academia*] Correct Spanish speech as defined by the Real Academia (Royal Academy).

761.11–12   Henry Duveyrier's "*Les Touareg du Nord*,"] Henri Duveyrier (1840–1892), French explorer of the Sahara, author of *Exploration du Sahara: les Touareg du nord* (1864).

762.13   *salles d'armes*] Fencing club or school.

763.16–17   Vigeant's beautiful little book] Arsène Vigeant, *Un Maître d'armes sous la Restauration* (Paris, 1883), a biography of the mulatto fencing master Jean-Louis Michel (1785–1865).

767.1   fate of the Lopez expedition] Narciso López (1797–1851) was a Venezuelan-born general who served in the Spanish Army before leading several filibustering expeditions to liberate Cuba from Spanish rule. After a failed attempt in 1851, López was executed in Havana, but supporters in New Orleans took up the cause.

767.10   another Cuban tragedy . . . in 1869] The first Cuban war of independence began in 1868.

LETTERS

773.1   *Henry Edward Krehbiel*] See note 3.2.

775.29   a hero, greater . . . than Bludso] John Hay's popular poem "Jim Bludso of the Prairie Belle" (1871) was about the African-American engineer of a Mississippi steamboat who died saving his passengers.

777.24   George Cabell] See note 747.18.

779.2   Murillo] The Spanish painter Bartolomé Esteban Murillo (c. 1617–1682) was known for his genre scenes of beggar children.

779.25   Père Rouquette] Adrien Rouquette (1813–1887), New Orleans–born missionary priest and poet among the Choctaw Indians and a scholar of creole dialects.

779.30–31   magical writing of Chateaubriand . . . *Les Natchez*] *Atala* (1801) and *Les Natchez* (1826) were popular romances of American Indian life by the French writer and statesman François-René de Chateaubriand (1768–1848). He traveled in the United States for five months in 1791.

782.8   The fever is dying.] The yellow fever epidemic of 1878.

783.5   the author of the Howadji in Syria] George William Curtis, *The Howadji in Syria* (1852). Curtis writes of "the spirit, which, like the camel, on the first morning, will raise its head and scent the wild fascination of the desert."

783.25   a *literary* . . . newspaper]   The New Orleans *Times-Democrat.*

783.33   *navaja*]   A Spanish knife.

784.17   "*Les Bienfaits de la Lune.*"]   From Baudelaire's book of prose poems *Le Spleen de Paris* ["Petits poèmes en prose"]   (1869). Hearn's "Selections from Baudelaire, the Edgar Poe of France," appeared in the New Orleans *Times-Democrat* (Dec. 31, 1882).

785.24–25   my vile and improper book]   *One of Cleopatra's Nights, and Other Fantastic Romances,* Hearn's translation of six tales by the French writer Théophile Gautier (1811–1872), was published in 1882.

785.26   "King Candaules"]   In his *Histories,* Herodotus tells the story of King Candaules, who offered to show off the beauty of his wife to his concealed bodyguard Gyges. Hearn's translation of Gautier's version of the tale was included in *One of Cleopatra's Nights.*

785.31–32   Layard's *unabridged* works]   The British archeologist Austen Henry Layard (1817–1894) published many works on his excavations in the Middle East, including *Discoveries in the Ruins of Nineveh and Babylon* (1853) and a companion volume, *A Second Series of the Monuments of Nineveh* (1853).

785.33   Rawlinson]   The many published works of Sir Henry Rawlinson (1810–1895) include *Outline of the History of Assyria* (1852).

785.36   Overbeck's Pompeji]   Johannes Adolph Overbeck (1826–1895), German archeologist and art historian known for his works on Pompeii, including *Pompeii,* first published in 1856, and, with August Mau, *Pompeji in seinen Gebäuden, Alterthümern und Kunstwerken* (*Pompeii in its Buildings, Antiquities, and Works of Art*) (1884).

786.1   Mazois]   Charles François Mazois (1783–1826), author of *Les ruines de Pompéi,* published in four volumes between 1809 and 1838.

786.4   Sir William Gell's Pompeiiana]   Gell (1777–1836), with the architect John P. Gandy, published *Pompeiiana,* his work on the excavations at Pompeii, between 1817 and 1819.

786.7–8   work on Egyptian antiquities . . . Napoleon I]   *Description de l'Egypte,* published in multiple volumes from 1809 to 1826.

787.24   Richter's "Titan."]   The German romantic writer Johann Paul Friedrich Richter (1763–1825) published, under the name Jean Paul, the eccentric bildungsroman *The Titan* (1800–3).

788.25   Gladstone or Mahaffy]   The British statesman and scholar William Ewart Gladstone (1809–1898) published various works on Greece including *Studies on Homer and the Homeric Age* (1858); John Pentland Mahaffy (1839–1919) was an Irish classicist and scholar.

788.27   John Addington Symonds] English poet and literary critic (1840–1893), author of *Studies of the Greek Poets* (1873–76) and *Sketches and Studies in Southern Europe* (1880).

788.31   *un peuple de demi-dieux*] Victor Hugo, in his poem "Les Feuilles d'automne," referred to the Greeks as "a people of demigods."

789.1   the Fantastics] In 1880, Hearn began publishing his "fantastics," literary sketches inspired by contemporary French literature and based loosely on factual materials.

792.10–11   Flaubert's "Salammbo" . . . Gautier's "Roman de la Momie"] Gustave Flaubert (1821–1880) heavily researched the background for his novel *Salammbô* (1862), set in ancient Carthage. Théophile Gautier's "Novel of the Mummy" was published in 1857.

792.23   Dr. Ebers] Georg Moritz Ebers (1837–1898), German novelist and Egyptologist known for his discovery and publication of the Ebers Egyptian Medical Papyrus.

792.36   Victor Rydberg's beautiful essay] Abraham Viktor Rydberg (1828–1895) was a Swedish writer whose *Romerska Dagar* (*Roman Days*) (1877) includes an essay on the Venus de Milo.

793.2   Winklemann] Johann Joachim Winckelmann (1717–1768), German art historian and archeologist who argued for the superiority of Greek art.

793.8–10   Michelet . . . terrible chapter] Hearn refers to the sixth chapter of *La Bible de l'humanité* (1864) by the historian Jules Michelet (1798–1874).

793.12–15   Gautier . . . Emile Bergerat] Hearn refers to Bergerat's volume *Théophile Gautier: entretiens, souvenirs et correspondence* (Paris, 1879).

794.29–30   Huysmans . . . a terrible essay] Joris-Karl Huysmans was the pen-name of the novelist and art critic Charles-Marie-Georges Huysmans (1848–1907). His *Croquis parisiens* (*Parisian Sketches*) of 1880 contained a prose poem titled "Le Gousset" ("The Armpit").

795.1–4   "O douce . . . un baiser!"] Hearn quotes, presumably from memory, a passage from Théophile Gautier's erotic poem "Musée secret": "Sur ta laine annelée et fine / Que l'art toujours voulut raser, Ô douce barbe féminine, / Reçois mon vers comme un baiser." ("O sweet feminine beard, which art has always wanted to shave, receive my verse like a kiss, on your fine and ringed wool.") Hearn rearranges the lines and substitutes "soie" (silk) for "laine" (wool), along with other small changes.

796.1   *Page Baker*] Editor of the New Orleans *Times-Democrat*.

797.11   Marion]   Marion Baker, Page Baker's brother, was literary editor of the *Times-Democrat*.

797.14   the Exposition]   See note 748.5.

797.34   *cimex lectularius*]   Bedbug.

800.9   Miss Bisland]   Elizabeth Bisland, Marion Baker's assistant and Hearn's friend and colleague at the *Times Democrat*, later published *The Life and Letters of Lafcadio Hearn* (1906) in two volumes.

805.1   cornet-à-piston]   Brass wind instrument resembling a trumpet, with valves moved by small pistons.

805.16   *George M. Gould*]   A physician in Philadelphia who had written to Hearn.

808.25   Spencer]   Hearn was a fervent admirer of Herbert Spencer (1820–1903), English philosopher and popularizer of Darwinian ideas.

808.30–31   Loti . . . his "Roman d'un Spahi"]   Pierre Loti was the pen-name of Louis Marie-Julien Viaud (1850–1923), a popular French writer of exotic romances such as *Le Roman d'un spahi* (1881), set in Africa, and *Madame Chrysanthème* (1887), set in Japan. His plots often revolved around a romance between a European man and a native woman.

809.22   Alden]   Henry M. Alden, Hearn's editor at *Harper's*.

811.27   superb paper on Loti]   Henry James's essay on Loti appeared in the *Fortnightly Review* in May 1888.

812.5   John Weiss]   American writer and Unitarian minister (1818–1879) of the Transcendentalist group, author of *The Immortal Life* (1880) and translator of Schiller and Goethe.

812.14–15   Swinburne]   The English poet Algernon Charles Swinburne (1837–1909).

THE LIBRARY OF AMERICA SERIES

The Library of America fosters appreciation and pride in America's literary heritage by publishing, and keeping permanently in print, authoritative editions of America's best and most significant writing. An independent nonprofit organization, it was founded in 1979 with seed money from the National Endowment for the Humanities and the Ford Foundation.

To subscribe to the series or to order individual copies,
please visit www.loa.org or call (800) 964.5778.

This book is set in 10 point Linotron Galliard,
a face designed for photocomposition by Matthew Carter
and based on the sixteenth-century face Granjon. The paper
is acid-free lightweight opaque and meets the requirements
for permanence of the American National Standards Institute.
The binding material is Brillianta, a woven rayon cloth made
by Van Heek-Scholco Textielfabrieken, Holland. Composition by Dedicated Business Services. Printing by
Malloy Incorporated. Binding by Dekker Book-
binding. Designed by Bruce Campbell.

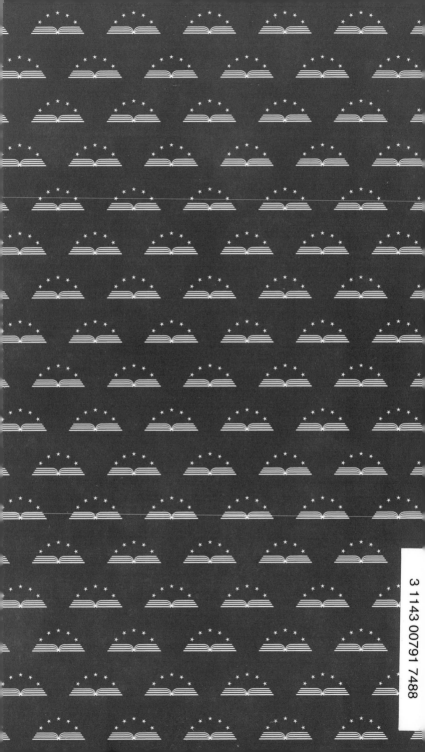